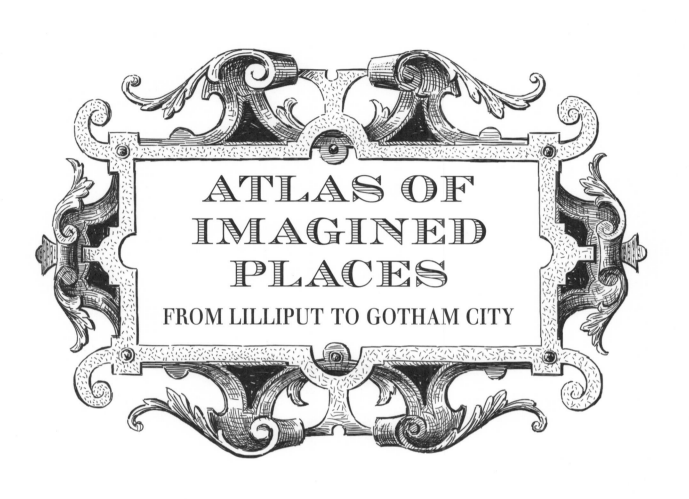

ATLAS OF IMAGINED PLACES

FROM LILLIPUT TO GOTHAM CITY

First published in the United Kingdom in 2021 by
B.T. Batsford
43 Great Ormond Street
London WC1N 3HZ

Copyright © B.T. Batsford Ltd, 2021
Text © Matt Brown and Rhys B. Davies, 2021
Maps and colour illustrations by Mike Hall

ISBN: 9781849946414

A CIP catalogue record for this book is available from the British Library.

30 29 28 27 26 25 24 23 22
10 9 8 7 6 5 4 3 2

Reproduction by Rival Colour Ltd, UK
Printed by Vivar Printing Sdn. Bhd., Malaysia

This book can be ordered direct from the publisher at the website
www.batsford.com, or try your local bookshop.

ATLAS OF IMAGINED PLACES

FROM LILLIPUT TO GOTHAM CITY

Matt Brown and Rhys B. Davies

BATSFORD

CONTENTS

06 INTRODUCTION

10 THE USA
ALTERED STATES

24 CANADA AND THE ARCTIC
GREEN GABLES AND GOLD NUGGETS

30 CENTRAL AMERICA AND THE CARIBBEAN
THE OLD NEW WORLD

36 SOUTH AMERICA
CITIES OF GOLD AND BANANA REPUBLICS

42 WESTERN EUROPE
THE OLD COUNTRIES

48 EASTERN EUROPE
SCIENCE AND SORCERY, SHTETLS AND SOVIETS

54 THE NORDIC COUNTRIES
HERE BE DRAGONS (AND TROLLS)

60 UK AND IRELAND
FAKE BRITAIN AND SHAM ROCK

70 THE MIDDLE EAST AND CENTRAL ASIA
BEYOND THE SILK ROAD

76 SOUTH ASIA
FROM PESHAWAR TO THE PENINSULA

82 AFRICA
THINGS COME TOGETHER

88 SOUTHEAST ASIA
WILDS, WAVES, WORLDS AND WARS

94 JAPAN
THE LAND OF THE RISING GUNDAM

100 CHINA AND NORTH-EAST ASIA
JOURNEY TO THE EAST

106 AUSTRALIA AND NEW ZEALAND
THE ORIGINAL LAND OF OZ

112 ANTARCTICA
THE NIGHTMARE CONTINENT

118 THE PACIFIC OCEAN
ISLAND HOPPING

124 THE ATLANTIC OCEAN
LOST WORLDS OF THE WESTERN SEA

130 LOCATION INDEX
151 SOURCE INDEX
168 ACKNOWLEDGEMENTS
168 ABOUT THE AUTHORS

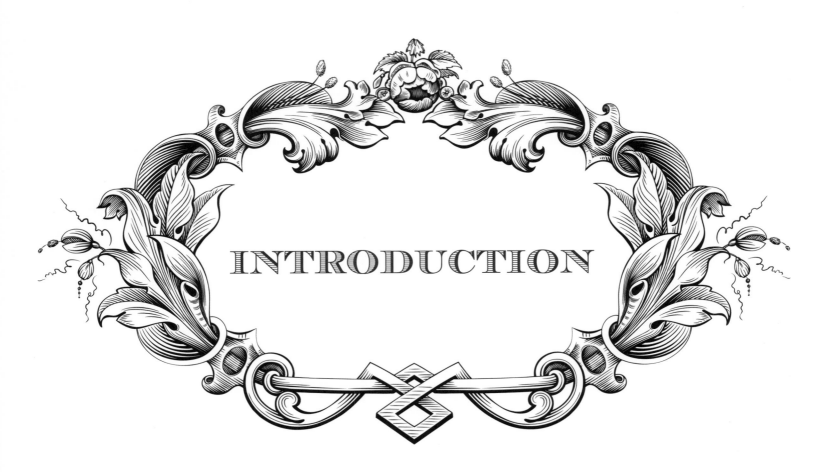

INTRODUCTION

elcome to the atlas of places that do not exist. Across these pages, you'll find around 5,000 fictional locations, including towns, cities, countries, seas, buildings, deserts, mountains, forests, underwater tunnels, space elevators and at least one giant, time-manipulating baby buried in an Antarctic glacier. None are found in a conventional atlas, but all exist in works of the imagination.

This atlas began life in 2018, when we published our map 'Fake Britain' on the website Londonist.com, followed by its companion 'Unreal London'. We got so much positive feedback that the 'Fake Britain' project escalated into a full-blown world atlas of fictional locations, which you now hold in your hands.

The maps feature age-old legends like El Dorado, Atlantis, Utopia, Camelot, the Mountains of Kong and lost continent of Lemuria. We've woven in inventions from classic literature, such as Charles Dickens' Coketown, Mary Anne Evan's Middlemarch, Proust's Combray or García Márquez's Macondo. Hundreds of locales from popular culture are baked into the mix, including Gotham City, Metropolis, Hogwarts, Twin Peaks, Erinsborough, Vice City, Schitt's Creek, Arendelle, King Solomon's Mines, a heap of *Pokémon* gym-cities, and – hardest to map of all – Springfield from *The Simpsons*. We've also peppered the maps with fictional locations from more surprising sources, including military training scenarios, theme-park rides, a Frank Zappa song, TV commercials and even a few unfortunate slips of the tongue that led to the birth of entire fictional nations (see Central America and Africa maps on pages 16–17 and 84–85).

Dozens of genres and subgenres emerge from the pages. Look out for the many Ruritanian romances of central Europe, the international Utopias inspired by Thomas More's original and their dystopian cousins, Brazilian telenovelas, Australian soaps, Robinsonades, high-school manga, Scandi noirs, polar weirdness, the 'lost world' tales of Africa and South America, and many more.

We hope that the atlas helps you to better understand the geography of your favourite works of fiction. But it also serves as a springboard for finding stories you might not already know. Look at the area around your hometown; do you recognize all the nearby creations? Or perhaps check out our entry for a country you're planning on visiting, and track down the local fiction. Then there's the joy of looking for unusual juxtapositions. The village of Asterix the Gaul is right next door to the climactic battleground of *Saving Private Ryan*; while the stranded hero of *Cast Away* might have been within rescue range of Captain Nemo's *Nautilus* (and those are just the Tom Hanks connections).

It's a whole new world!

WHAT DO WE MEAN BY A FICTIONAL PLACE?

It might seem like a question with an easy answer. A fictional place is any location that has no existence in reality, a creation of pure imagination. Yet, in compiling this atlas, we've found that not all fictional places are created equal. We've identified four different classes listed in order below, from the most heavily fantastical, down to those grounded closest to reality:

1. An entirely made-up place, but which exists somewhere other than our familiar Earth (e.g. Narnia, Westeros). Such places are not shown in this atlas.

2. An entirely made-up place, set somewhere on Earth (e.g. Liberty City, Genovia, the Island of Sodor). These places make up the majority of locations in the atlas.

3. A location whose name is fictional, but which is heavily based on somewhere real (e.g. Thomas Hardy's 'Wessex' towns, or Charlotte Brontë's Villette, heavily modelled on Brussels). These too are shown in the atlas.

4. A location whose name is real, but whose characteristics have been fictionalized (e.g. the Oxford of *His Dark Materials*). We have not mapped such locations.

Thus, to qualify for inclusion a place has to have at least a fictional name and to exist upon our Earth.

For visual media, we've generally mapped locations to where they're 'meant to be', rather than where they were filmed. It frequently has to be that way. For example, had we matched Sokovia (from Marvel's *Avengers: Age of Ultron*) to its filming location, then this Central European country would lie within the north London suburb of Hendon, the 'Battle of Sokovia' being filmed here at the Metropolitan Police's former training college. Elsewhere, however, we have used filming locations as secondary canon in the absence of other clues.

DECISIONS, DECISIONS ...

Read the introduction to almost any cartographic book and you'll spot a health warning: 'Maps are not 100 per cent faithful reproductions of the terrain they seek to cover, but reflect the biases of their compilers' (or something to that effect). This observation has become something of a cliché, though it is grounded in truth. All mapmakers are faced with choices about what to include and what to exclude. The decisions they reach may be influenced by political or cultural biases, or to suit the needs of a particular audience. A *factual* atlas of the world published in China will look very different to one published in India, the UK or Mozambique. The print language will vary, of course, but so too might accepted political boundaries and the locations given most prominence.

A *fictional* atlas, as we have discovered, is even more prone to partisanship. For starters, it cannot hope to be comprehensive. While nobody knows just how many novels have ever been published in human history, they must run into the tens of millions; as of December 2020, IMDb.com – the world's largest database of film, television and video games – listed 7.5 million titles, up from 6.5 million at the start of the year. And then there are radio plays, podcasts, folklore, comics, board games and other media to consider. The fruits of human creativity are essentially infinite, and while not all of these works will include fictional locations, a fraction of infinity is itself still infinite.

In compiling this atlas, we've thus had to make dizzying, whimsical, utterly biased decisions at every turn. We find that mapping the fictional is more of an art than a science. While you'd expect a conventional atlas to at least show every major city, we'll leave one out with blithe abandon if we find it too obscure, boring, or difficult to ascribe a location to. Sometimes, we'll include individual buildings, such as the Bates Motel from *Psycho*, or Dorothy's farm from *The Wizard of Oz*, because one *expects* to see them, and at other times leave equally noteworthy buildings unaccounted for due to pressures of space.

Furthermore, the constraints of language mean that the vast majority of entries are from English-language sources (or at least works translated into English). That's a huge bias right there, but a necessary one if we were to keep the material manageable in book form.

That said, we tried to stick to an equitable set of rules where possible:

* To qualify for inclusion, fictional places must play a *major* role in the source material. This excludes locations that (say), only merit a passing mention in one episode of a TV show.

* A location should be reasonably well-anchored in real geography. A fictional town described as being 'somewhere in the American Midwest' probably wouldn't cut it – the area is too vast – but one located 'somewhere in northern Wisconsin' probably would.

* That 'real geography' must also be somewhere on our Earth, or a closely parallel Earth. Sadly, that means realms such as Earthsea or Middle Earth are not eligible for this atlas. (Tolkien's legendarium supposedly takes place on our Earth, but in a

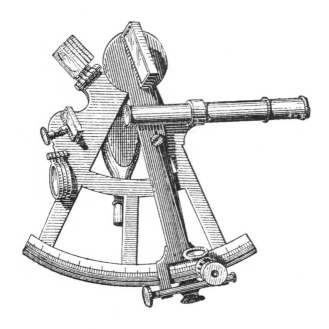

different geological age, and so can't be mapped in any meaningful way onto the present arrangement of continents.)

* Some sources, such as Greek mythology, the universes of Marvel and DC – or even *Pokémon* (!) – offer hundreds of potential locations. In these cases, we've tried to strike a balance, including locations considered important or interesting or geographically diverse. This also prevented the maps being overloaded by any one source.

* Locations that are inherently offensive are generally not included. For example, the 1980s *Transformers* cartoon had several episodes featuring the fictional North African nation of Carbombya, a parody Arab state named and portrayed in such poor taste as to prompt voice actor Casey Kasem (who was of Lebanese descent) to leave the show.

And, most importantly ...

* *Any* of the above rules can be broken if a location is so famous that it simply has to be included ... or if we found it fun to do so.

THE ONES THAT GOT AWAY ...

In compiling these maps, we had to make some tough decisions. Perhaps the hardest was 'What to do with Oz?' Though most famously associated with MGM's 1939 classic *The Wizard of Oz*, author L. Frank Baum's imagined world is far wider than Munchkinland, the Yellow Brick Road and the Emerald City. Over the course of 14 novels, Baum sketched out a whole continent, with such evocative place names as Winkie Country, the Nonestic Ocean, Rinkitink and the Kingdom of Ix. It would be a joy to include.

At first blush, Oz would seem to be another realm like Narnia – a parallel dimension, somewhere over the rainbow, ineligible for inclusion within this atlas. But Baum had somewhere a bit more tangible in mind. His literary Oz has always been depicted as a part of our world, and some entries in the canon even hint as to its location. In one story, Dorothy returns to Oz after being swept overboard during a voyage from California to Australia, indicating a location in the northern Pacific. A sighting of the North Star further confirms Oz to lie within the boreal hemisphere. Even so, these realms feel too hallucinatory or otherworldly to fit the real Earth. Most famously, Dorothy's adventures in the 1938 movie end with her awakening in her own bed, as though Oz were all a dream. And so we have left it (for now, at least), as an eternal realm of the imagination, rather than terra firma upon this good Earth.

Other near misses should be noted. George Orwell's *1984* is very much set on our planet; within an horrifically totalitarian vision of the (then) near-future.

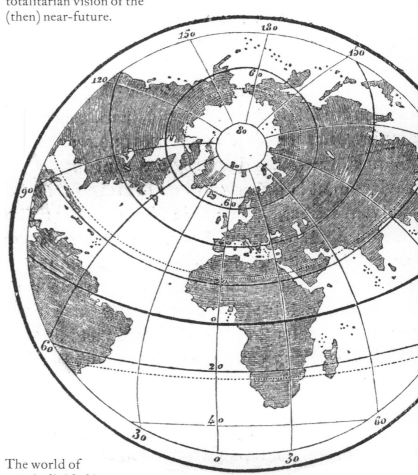

The world of *1984* is divided into three superstates – Eurasia, Eastasia and Oceania, the latter including Airstrip One (formerly Great Britain), where protagonist Winston Smith lives under the menacing gaze of Big Brother. Each superstate stretches over such vast territories that it would be cumbersome to record across our maps, thus they have been omitted. Other empires or polities larger than the scope of our maps have been similarly left off. Gilead (a reworked USA) from *The Handmaid's Tale*, and the World State of *Brave New World* are further examples. The vast future continent of Zothique, dreamed up by Clark Ashton Smith, is another.

Finally, the atlas *almost* contained a further thousand or so locations drawn from a wide variety of sources, yet which sadly proved too sketchily located to pin on a map. The most frustrating of all must be the 55 fictitious metropoli from Italo Calvino's *Invisible Cities*, all of which have some remarkable and exotic quality. Their locations are never described, so they can't be charted, while the 'solution' of considering all 55 as reflections of Venice is an equally unmappable proposition.

A NOTE ON SOURCES

We've been asked many times: 'How do you find fictional locations in the first place?' There is no quick answer. Our starting point was our own intuition. What films, books and games had we enjoyed with fictional settings? We then scoured the internet, beginning with Wikipedia. Whatever your opinion on the accuracy of the site, its innumerable lists make excellent starting points for research. These range from broadly helpful topics like 'List of Fictional Countries' and 'List of Fictional Islands' right through to more specific pages, such as 'Places in the Works of Madeleine L'Engle' and 'List of Fictional Prisons'. Another key source has been fan sites and wikis. Any major work of fiction these days has at least one. These have been invaluable for mining locations and helping to narrow down where they should be placed on the map.

We've consulted numerous books during this project, from the original source materials through to other atlases and compilatory works. Chief among them is *The Dictionary of Imaginary Places*, by Alberto Manguel and Gianni Guadalupi. First published in 1980, this remarkable tome is a gazetteer of fictional places from literature (including places we couldn't map, such as the aforementioned Middle Earth and Earthsea). We'd highly recommend it to anyone who enjoys this atlas. Other works we commend include *The Writer's Map* (2018, edited by Huw Lewis-Jones), *The Phantom Atlas* (2016, Edward Brooke-Hitching) and the *Marvel Atlas* (2007, Stuart Vandal *et al*).

A NOTE ON ACCURACY

As you'd imagine, some locations are easier to map than others. The Wessex towns of Thomas Hardy, for example, are a doddle to position, because they're simply alternative names for real towns. Others are much more sketchy. We might easily discover the country a town belongs to, but not its region. In such instances (and there are many), we've used clues such as the terrain (mountainous, coastal, flat ...), hints in the place name, natural resources in the area, tip-offs in the dialogue (such as the mention of nearby real towns), and even the flora and fauna. In other words, educated guesswork. We'd like to emphasize that the ultimate authority is the author(s) of the work in question; our placements should be regarded as our own personal interpretation, and by no means definitive.

HOW TO USE THIS BOOK

The world has been divided up into 18 territories, with some overlap around the edges. We've written a brief introduction to each territory, which pulls together some of the major themes and genres seen upon that map. We've further picked out 20 locations or more on each map for specific annotations. These are places that may have interesting tales to tell, or which require a bit of explanation. Every location in the atlas is given in the index at the end, complete with its source.

THE USA

ALTERED STATES

pringfield, Bedford Falls, Gotham City, Smallville ... the Land of the Free is apparently the Land of Make Believe, for the USA provides the stage for hundreds of A-list locations that only exist in the imagination.

Within these pages we've charted everything from prehistoric cities (*The Flintstones*) to dystopias (*The Hunger Games, The Walking Dead*). But America's dramatic ballast lies in the small town. You find them all over the map, offering a blank canvas for adventure and misadventure. Here is the gossipy backwater of Sherwood Anderson's *Winesburg, Ohio*; there is the St Petersburg, Missouri, of *Tom Sawyer* and *Huckleberry Finn*, and cartoonish burgs like Frostbite Falls, the Minnesota home of *Rocky & Bullwinkle*. Horror and tragedy abound, too, from the sickly miasma of Dickens's Eden (*Martin Chuzzlewit*) to the shark-infested waters of Amity, Massachusetts (*Jaws*), the small town is, as Americans say, where it's at.

Let us not ignore the metropolis, though. That's with a big 'M' in the case of Superman, whose adopted city lies on the coast of Delaware. Batman's Gotham City is just next door in New Jersey. Though both began as reflections of New York, Metropolis and Gotham have developed unique identities that mirror their favourite sons: the Man of Tomorrow and the Dark Knight. We've mapped several dozen analogues of Los Angeles or its suburbs, encompassing

every genre and medium. There's *Knots Landing* of the eponymous 1980s soap opera, Cuesta Verde from *Poltergeist*, Los Santos from the *Grand Theft Auto* games, and even *Beaverly* Hills – an alternate reality populated by anthropomorphic animals, courtesy of DC Comics.

Likewise, echoes of New York City dominate the East Coast. Readers of *The Great Gatsby* will quickly recognize East and West Egg on Long Island, while gamers will clock *Grand Theft Auto's* Liberty City. Even the animators of Japan have made their mark here, contributing post-apocalyptic Paradigm City (*The Big O*). And who can resist the charms of sophisticated Empire City (*Steven Universe*) or bemaned Gnu York, another animal metropolis? New New York and Long Long Island meanwhile hail from Matt Groening's *Futurama*.

Some states are tepid. Hawaii, Michigan, Oklahoma, Utah and much of the south-east are minnows of fictional geography. Yet even here we find some remarkable creations. Take Stones Hill (elevation 550m/1,800ft), the Floridan mountain from which Jules Verne chose to launch his voyage *From the Earth to the Moon*. Standing five times higher than any 'real' hill in the Sunshine State, it may even be visible from nearby Xanadu, the palatial hermitage of *Citizen Kane*. Spurious the mountain may be, yet Verne's use of Florida as a springboard to the lunar surface foreshadowed actual history.

Further writers have contributed to the fictive weft, sometimes providing entire regions. H.P. Lovecraft wove sinister settlements so convincingly into the landscape of his native New England that Massachusetts is often referred to as *Lovecraft Country*, quite literally in the case of Matt Ruff's recent novel of the same name. Neighbouring Maine is the playground of Stephen King, whose eerie pen has conjured such disagreeable locations as Jerusalem's Lot, Shawshank Prison, and the ubiquitous Castle Rock and Derry. Further afield, while Vladimir Nabokov's *Lolita* is infamous for its portrayal of the relationship between a middle-aged man and a 12-year-old girl, it is also notable for its fictional topography, which stretches from New England to the Midwest.

Sinclair Lewis meanwhile fills his fictitious state of Winnemac – an amalgamation of Wisconsin, Minnesota, and Michigan – with imagined cities. Other fictive states, with evocative names such as Keystone, Euphoria, and New Temperance, come to us from every medium.

Of all the maps in this atlas, the fictional US is likely to have the most omissions. The source material is simply too vast. Like prospectors of the Old West, we sift for slivers of gold, knowing that the widest pan cannot catch every grain. But with nearly 1,200 fictional nuggets on the map, these are no slim pickings.

WHERE IS SPRINGFIELD?

'1796; a fiercely determined band of pioneers leaves Maryland after misinterpreting a passage in the Bible. Their destination: New Sodom. This is their story.'

- *The Simpsons,'Lisa the Iconoclast'.*

So begins the saga of Springfield, fiction's most cromulent burg. After 30 seasons and over 600 episodes, the hometown of *The Simpsons* has become the unquestionable capital of sitcom cities. Bedrock of *The Flintstones* might proudly proclaim itself 'First With Fire' but no location has made quite as much impact on pop culture as Springfield.

Part of this longevity must be grounded in the town's endless versatility. Springfield can twist itself to represent any part of the USA, allowing stories to remain unconstrained by a fixed geographic location. *Family Guy* resolutely sets its Quahog in Rhode Island, thus constraining itself to a cultural heritage of puritanism, clam-fishing, and snooty rich types from Newport. Springfield meanwhile is ever-adaptive to the topographic and demographic needs of the script, as evidenced by its exceptionally diverse range of cultural enclaves; this one town sports Italian, Jewish, Russian and New Jersey communities – there's even a tiny Tibet Town in a gated alley beside Chinatown.

Of course, this makes Springfield an *utter nuisance* to map! The show itself is notoriously gleeful in how it reinterprets history and topography on a whim. In some episodes, the town was founded by settlers led west by Jebediah Springfield, while other times it's Jebediah's *birthplace*. Something's fishy here, and it has nothing to do with the nuclear plant's mutagenic discharge. Perhaps we can point the finger at Jebediah's secret past as silver-tongued pirate Hans Sprungfeld, his falsified identity and doctoring of history helping to explain some of the inconsistencies in the town's backstory.

Truthfully, the subject of Springfield's geographic location has become a much-loved joke within the show. The name of its state might be drowned out by a sound-effect when spoken, or Bart might step into foreground just as Lisa points to a map. Infamously, *The Simpsons Movie* saw Ned Flanders lead Bart Simpson to a peak from where all four states that border Springfield may be viewed: Ohio, Nevada, Maine and Kentucky ... *Doh!*

The best explanation is that Springfield is Anytown, USA; like Schrodinger's Cat, it can exist in multiple states (both quantum and federal) simultaneously, collapsing back into a nether-realm of impossibilities once attempts are made to study it closer.

But for the purposes of this map, Springfield had to be charted. Our most satisfactory solution was to embrace the oft-cited notion that it occupies a fictional state (official motto: Not Just Another State). Frequent *Simpsons* director David Silverman has even named Springfield's state as North Tacoma, which squares with the 'NT' or 'TA' postal abbreviations sometimes seen in the show.

At last, things fall into place. 'Tacoma' is the Salish name for Mount Rainier, the highest peak in the Pacific Cascades, and Springfield's frontier-times founding, temperate climate and proximity to mountains, deserts, forests and the ocean all align with the Pacific Northwest. Meanwhile, creator Matt Groening was born in Oregon and educated in Washington state.

And so we proudly present to you the city of Springfield, an iconic settlement that brings both pride and shame to the great Pacific Northwest state of North Tacoma. Never mind that Springfield's founding predates the Lewis and Clarke expedition – we'll blame that discrepancy on Jebediah.

Stick that in your pipe and smoke it, Flanders!

INPUT! INPUT!

Loveable robot Johnny 5 might have affirmed his life in 1986's *Short Circuit*, but it took a sequel to see his personhood recognized by the world at large. *Short Circuit 2* (1988) thus saw Johnny up sticks to a major American metropolis, one that sits within a geological location at once specific and vague. Something about the place suggests New York, but Johnny is presented with a guidebook emblazoned with an image of the St Louis Arch, and a climactic dockside fight is identified as taking place off a street named 'Lakeshore'...

... and the cars all carry Ontario license plates. Oh Canada!

Yup, it's a classic case of budget-crunch in action. Although the scriptwriters had hoped to take Johnny to NYC, the film was actually shot entirely on location in Toronto, with most direct references to New York being scrubbed from the script. But based on all the above clues, a Midwest location suggests itself, somewhere on the Great Lakes, close enough to St Louis to explain that travel guide, and proximate to the Canadian border, justifying all those Ontario-registered cars.

There's just one problem preventing us from including this fascinating city on the map – it's never given a name! Johnny, buddy, if you're reading this, we need your input!

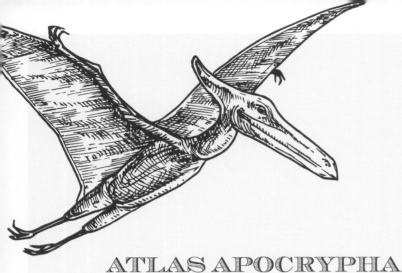

ATLAS APOCRYPHA

Bedrock, home of *The Flintstones'* modern Stone Age family, proved surprisingly easy to map. Following the franchise's grand tradition of dinosaurs doing service as domestic appliances and heavy machinery, the 1994 live-action movie opens on a passenger-carrying pterodactyl descending into Bedrock, complete with a flight attendant informing passengers that to the left they'll be able to see the Grand Canyon ... in about 15 million years! This not only gave us license to map the town to Arizona, but to also chart the fictional Bedrock River as a prehistoric forebear of the mighty Colorado.

Everyone knows of *Thomas the Tank Engine*, but not many people are aware of his sibling franchise, *TUGS*. Set during the Roaring Twenties, this short-lived television series followed the exploits of two rival tugboat fleets competing for business within the fictional Bigg City Port. Although a British production, the visual aesthetic of *TUGS* was entirely American; based on the prominence of upriver logging camps and the classically-transatlantic profiles of the ocean liners that make frequent calls at the port, we confidently chose to place Bigg City on the coast of Maine.

A less-fortunate vessel is the *Antonia Graza*, titular setting of the 2002 horror flick *Ghost Ship*. Inspired by the ill-fated SS *Andrea Doria*, this sumptuous Italian liner vanished in the mid-Atlantic in 1962, only to be discovered derelict off the Alaskan coast decades later, drifting dangerously close to an island chain named Bowers Bank.

Twin Peaks, *Gravity Falls*, *Wayward Pines*, *The Goonies*: The Pacific Northwest holds a special attraction for writers of the strange, though the adventures that take place here are typically less sinister than those found in the countries of King and Lovecraft. Maybe that has something to do with the many generations who've spent happy (or at least tolerable) childhood summers in locations such as Camp Campbell and Kamp Krusty, amidst wooded backhills where Bigfoot is said to roam.

The *Hunger Games'* dystopian nation of Panem is ideally named, invoking both the Latin *panem et circenses* (bread and circuses) and a corruption of 'Pan-American'. Appropriately, Panem's 12 districts and dictatorial Capital are situated within a North America rendered almost unrecognizable by war and climatological disasters. The Capitol itself is located within the fortress-like ramparts of the Rockies, while heroine Katniss Everdeen's home in District 12 is matched to the deep coal seams of the Appalachians.

SIGHT-SEEING HORROR SHOW

For your consideration, a budget tour through America's premier horror destinations – storied locations just dying to make you feel welcome ...

Our first stop is Black Lake, Maine, a rural idyll celebrated for its wildlife. The aspiring angler is heartily advised to get out on the lake's placid waters and see what surprises might rise to his bait! Just a few hours' drive away, the questing holidaymaker discovers Derry, boasting a civic spirit guaranteed to put a smile on anyone's face. You'll feel free as a floating balloon. And as for your friends, why they'll float too!

Just a hop across the border brings us to Friar, New Hampshire. The trailhead for countless adventurous hikers, Friar is a charming town with a deep and abiding love for classic cinema. Why not check out a screening of *The Wizard of Oz* and then find your own Yellow Brick Road up there in the hills?

Following our own road we continue towards secluded Innsmouth, Massachusetts, not far from where the darkly muttering waters of the Miskatonic reach the grey Atlantic. Situated in close proximity to historic Arkham, fishy Innsmouth is fiercely proud of its native culture and traditions, and would love nothing more than to share its blessings with you.

If your tastes run more towards sun and surf, then continue a short way south and take a great big bite out of Amity Island. Possessing pristine beaches and some of the most exciting swimming along the whole eastern seaboard, Amity is a patch of water you'll safely find yourself going back into again and again.

Continuing into Connecticut, we arrive at the picture-perfect idyll of Stepford, a town that seems frozen in plastic. Smiling faces await you at every turn. Stepford is a particular must for married couples; husbands are welcomed to embrace the empowering fraternity of the sterling Men's Association, and wives are encouraged to take up the town's promise to make a new woman out of any newcomer.

In the backcountry of New Jersey, children can experience mystery and adventure at Camp Crystal Lake – voted America's most infamous summer camp 13 years straight! Alternatively, those seeking to get back to nature and tell witchy stories around the campfire are advised to head for old Blair Township in Maryland, surrounded by woodlands you just have to get lost in!

Staying in Maryland, why not head down to Chesapeake Bay to sample the delights of Claridge, which throws an Independence Day second to none. Come for the party, stay for the fun, amidst celebrations so wild you'd swear there was something in the water!

A short jaunt north from Maryland brings us to McKinley, Pennsylvania, home of bone-shaking thrills and a final destination for adrenaline junkies out to cheat death one day at a time. Dare you ride the Devil's Flight, pride of McKinley Park and easily the world's most breakneck rollercoaster?

To experience nature at its most extreme we recommend heading inland towards the Appalachians, descending into the world-famous Boreham Caverns of North Carolina's Chatooga National Park. If you desire physical thrills without claustrophobia, then try the fast-flowing watercourses of Georgia. We especially recommend the white-water delights of the Cahulawassee River, which promises any city slicker a guaranteed deliverance from the tedium of the urban jungle. Alternatively, if you're down Texas way, why not take a dip in the shining waters of Lost River Lake? Recently redeveloped as a water park, the only thing you'll have to worry about is an occasional nibble from the fish.

Continuing into the American west, the budget-minded tourist is directed to Perfection, Nevada. Located in the heart of a protected wildlife zone, Perfection is the native habitat of many rare and wonderful species. You might even get a face-to-face encounter with the amazing El Blanco, great white whale of the desert. Look for the tremors as he approaches.

Let's push on to California, where affordable hostelries can be found on any highway. We highly recommend the Bates Motel, a family-run business just outside of Fairvale with year-round vacancies and a standard of customer service that is frankly insane. Down on the coast, Santa Clara may not possess the student spirit of Sunnydale, but has a teen culture second to none. The local nightlife is known to party it up with such vigour that you'd think the dead were rising! Lost boys (and girls) of all ages will be chomping at the bit to join this Never-Never Land where youth never dies. Nearby Antonio Bay presents a quieter getaway, an escape in time to misty shores and tall ships. As the evening fog unfurls across the town, breathe deep and embrace a peace you've never known.

Nothing beats the getaway idyll of a cabin in the woods, and up in Washington you'll find plenty available at the Shelter Mountain Inn, complete with a media library that is sure to keep guests locked in an endless ring of entertainment. Alternatively, just a short ferry-ride out into the Puget Sound you'll discover picturesque Moesko Island, whose haunting beauty has been captured on the tapes of countless home movies.

We're well into the high mountains now as we enter Colorado, at last arriving at the triumphant summit of our tour, the Overlook Hotel. With over ~~217~~ 237 rooms and a history that has seeped into the very foundation of the building, this shining destination is never short of bookings, yet always has a room available for the hopeful traveller.

Pleasant dreams ...

OPEN-WORLD ROCKSTARS

When it comes to fictional locations, nothing can beat the open-world video game in bringing imagined settings to visceral life. The undisputed masters of this medium are Rockstar Games, who have gifted the world such blockbuster franchises as *Grand Theft Auto* and *Red Dead Redemption*. As art holds a mirror up to life, these games show us the USA through a mirror darkly, re-sequencing the nation's DNA into twistedly familiar chimeras. Thus a real metropolis such as New York might become *Grand Theft Auto's* Liberty City, a cracked reflection that magnifies every blemish and vice present in the original source, quite literally in the case of Vice City, a neon-swirled analogue of Miami.

Within these games, the player is not just a passive viewer, but an active participant. Mount up on a stallion or strap in behind the wheel of a mustang. Run wild and rampant across the wilds of New Austin (Texas) and the highways of San Andreas (California). Chase dreams of fortune and freedom down the barrel of a gun, while chasing a bounty down the streets of St Denis (New Orleans). The allure is as real and vivid as the virtual worlds themselves ... and the deeper the temptation, the more vivid the social commentary strikes home. Because within these warped geometries, where everything becomes so much *easier* if we set aside society's laws and mores, we might just perceive our own shadowed demons ...

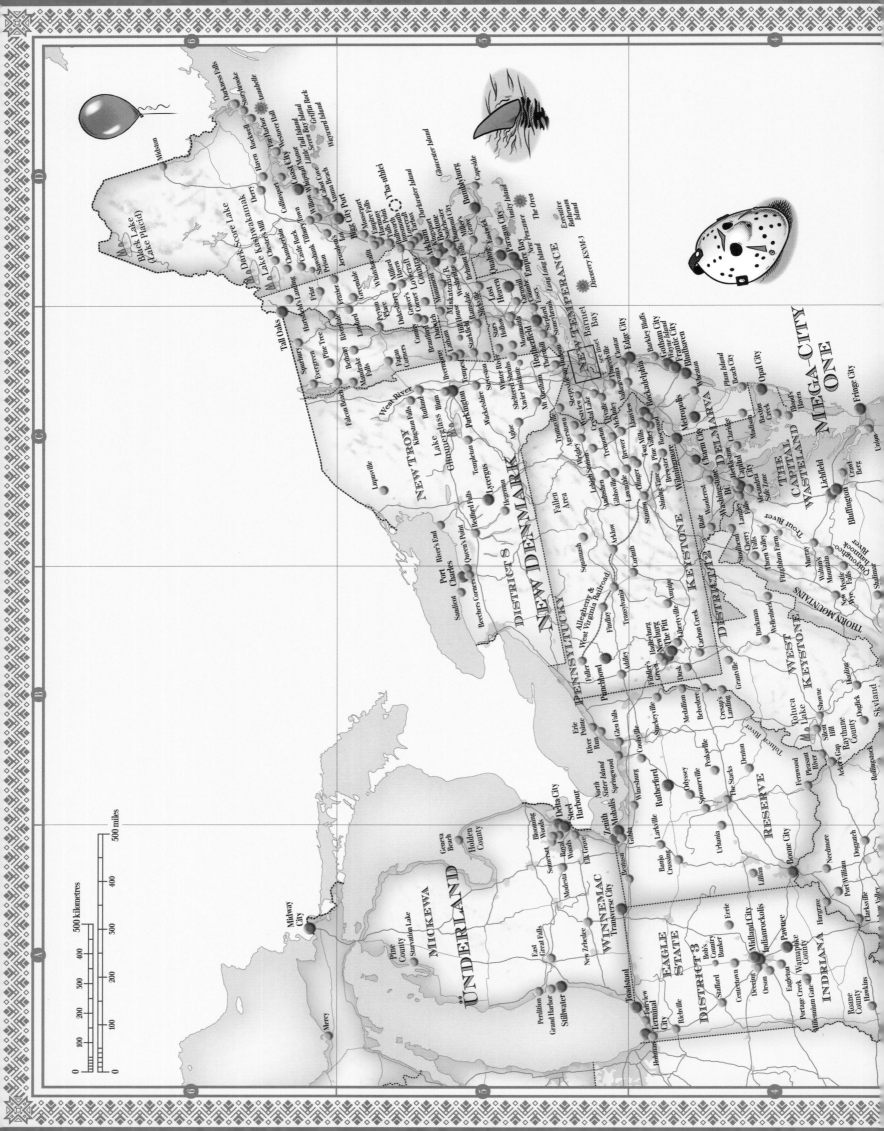

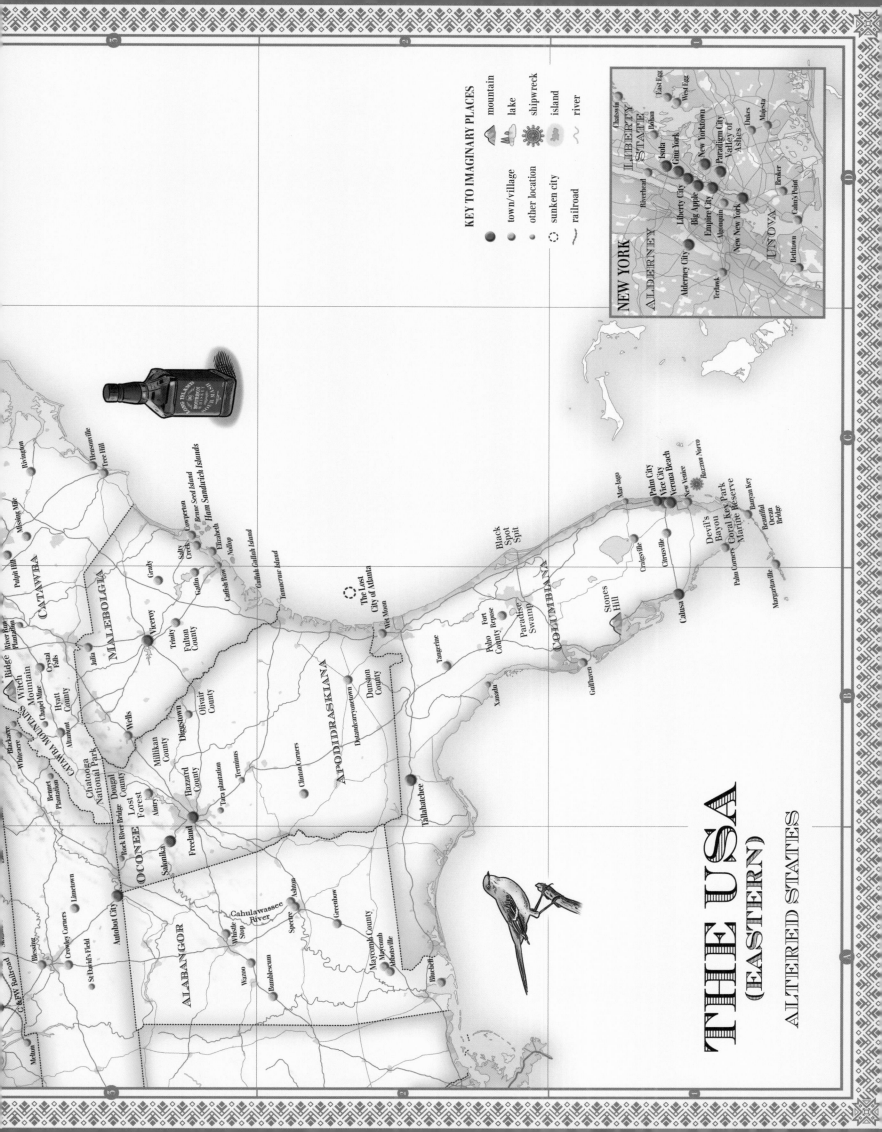

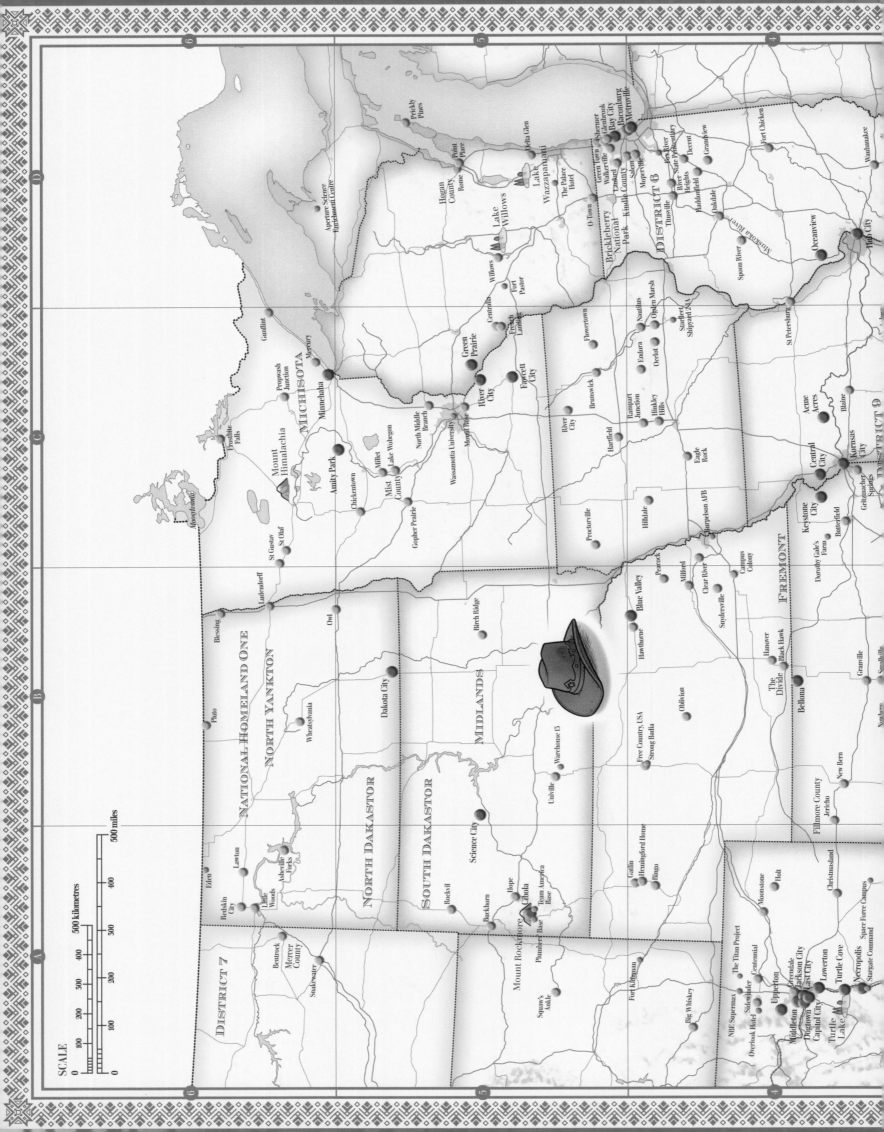

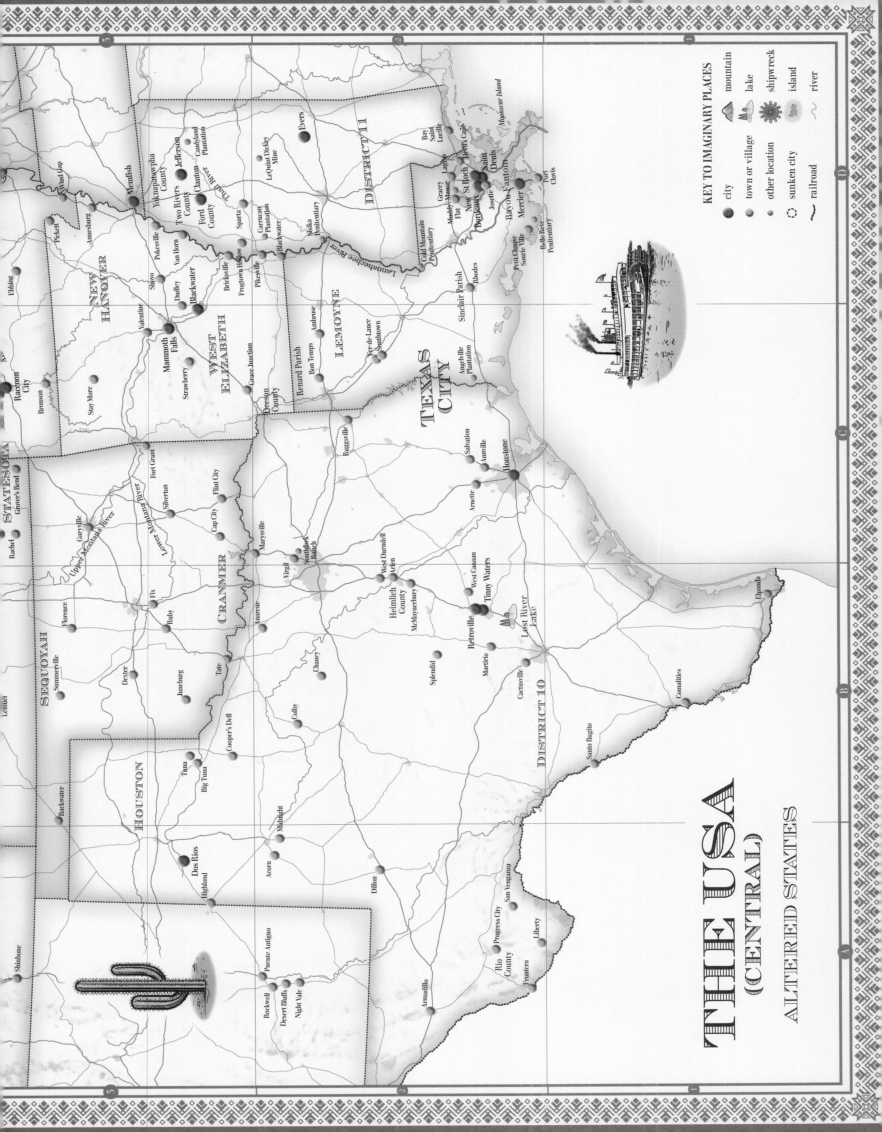

THE USA
(CENTRAL)
ALTERED STATES

KEY TO IMAGINARY PLACES

- ● city
- ● town or village
- · other location
- ◌ sunken city
- ⌂ mountain
- ≋ lake
- ✻ shipwreck
- ⬤ island
- ∿ river
- ⌐ railroad

STATESOMA

SEQUOYAH

NEW HANOVER

HOUSTON

WEST ELIZABETH

CRANMER

LEMOYNE

TEXAS CITY

DISTRICT 11

DISTRICT 10

Shinbone
Rachel
Lemuel
Racoon City
Grover's Bend
Bronson
Ebbing
Pickett
Wind Gap
Annesburg
Memfish
Yoknapatawpha County
Jefferson
Candyland Plantation
Clanton
Ford
Two Rivers County
Sparta
Evers
LeQuint Dickey Mine
Carrucan Plantation
Siska Penitentiary
Blackwater
Cold Mountain Penitentiary
Bay Saint Lucille
Lagras
New Bordeaux
Saint Denis
Gracey
Manley Manor
Flat
Josette
Fort Clovis
Bayou Fantom
Mercier
Belle Reve Penitentiary
Petit Chaye
Sourie Ville
Rhodes
Sinclair Parish
Monsear Island
Backwater
Summerville
Florence
Fix
Ruby
Garyville
Upper Montana River
Lower Montana River
Fort Grant
Silverton
Flint City
Cap City
Marsville
Virgil
Southfork Ranch
Arlen
West Durnfield
Heimlich County
McMayneberry
Tinny Waters
West Canaan
Retroville
Martirio
Lost River Lake
Cactusville
Splendid
Elpanda
Conalities
Santo Bugito
Dexter
Juneburg
Tate
Anarene
Chaney
Colby
Cooper's Dell
Tuna
Big Tuna
Dos Rios
Highland
Acorn
Midnight
Dillon
Liberty
Frontera
San Venganza
Progress City
Rio County
Armadillo
Rockwell
Desert Bluffs
Night Vale
Puente Antiguo
Valentine
Pokesville
Van Horn
Dudley
Shoyo
Mammoth Falls
Strawberry
Brickville
Frogtown Hollow
Pikesville
Grace Junction
Deeson County
Renard Parish
Bon Temps
Ambrose
Fer-de-Lance
Southtown
Ruggsville
Angelville Plantation
Salvation
Annville
Houstone
Arnette
Mouse Hole
Stay More

Laurathechee River

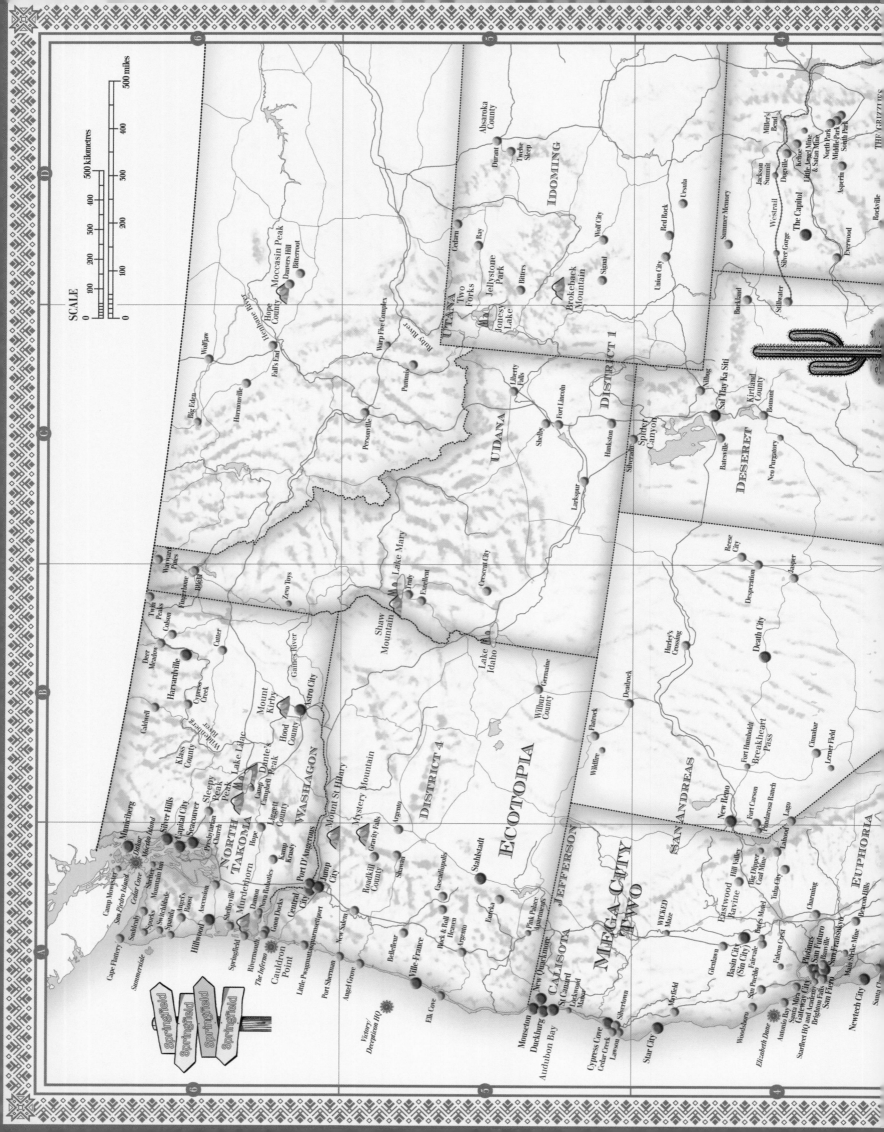

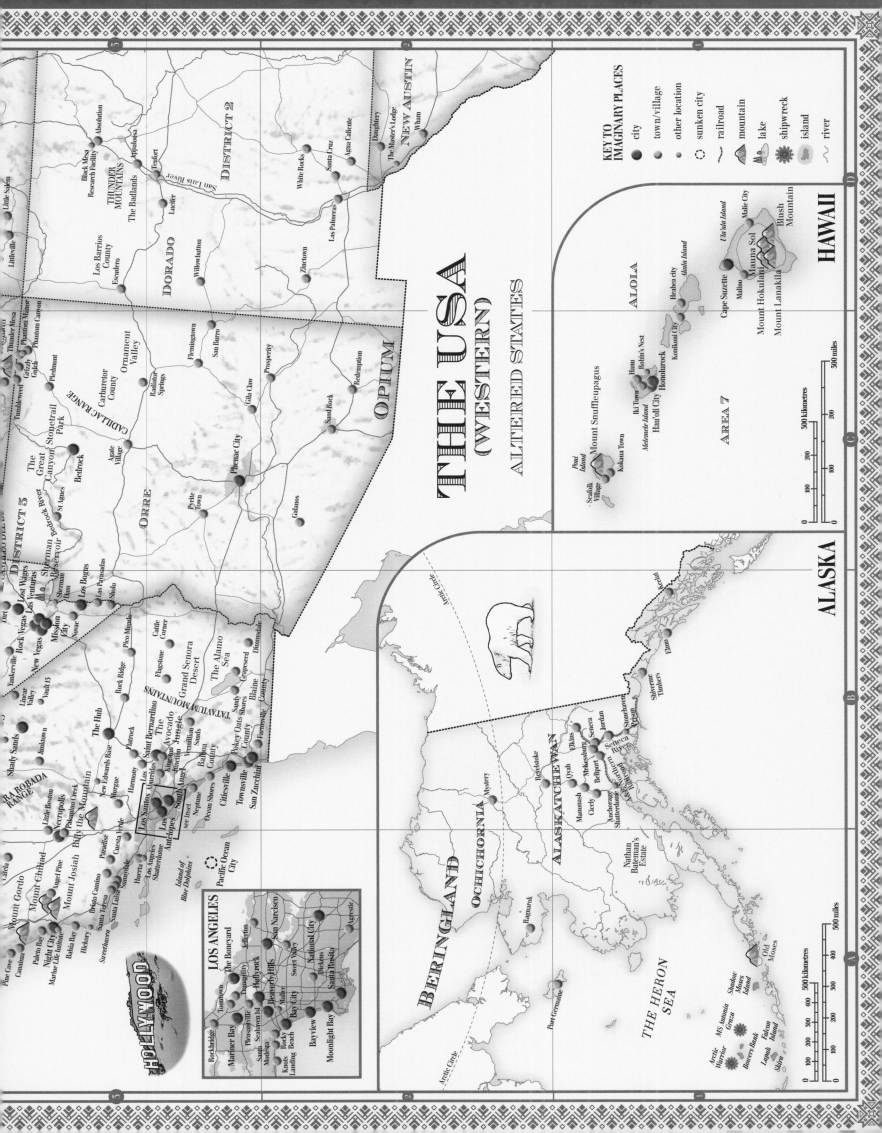

THE USA

KEY LOCATIONS

For a full list of locations, see the location index on pages 130–150.

ALEXANDRIA SAFE ZONE *The Walking Dead*
VIRGINIA | TV/COMIC
Post-apocalyptic commune, built outside the real Alexandria. The refuges of Hilltop, Oceanside and the Kingdom (not shown) are all within a half-day's travel. **MAP pp.14–15, C4**

AMITY ISLAND
Jaws **BY PETER BENCHLEY | MASSACHUSETTS | NOVEL/FILM**
Amity Island presents the perfect example of why authors and film-makers often create fictional locations rather than use a real setting. Imagine what might have happened to the tourist industry in, say, Cape Cod had the vicious shark attacks been placed there. The fictional town of Amity was sited on Long Island by novelist Peter Benchley. However, Spielberg's film adaptation is now much better known, and here the setting is heavily based on (and filmed in) Martha's Vineyard. **MAP pp.14–15, D5**

AUTOBOT CITY
Transformers: The Movie
TENNESSEE | FILM
Autobot HQ on Earth in the 1986 animated movie. According to DVD special features, this fortress-city is located near Chattanooga, adjacent to the (real) Lookout Mountain, which is mentioned by name in the film. Presumably the Autobots thus needed death certificates from the state of Tennessee to officiate the passing of Optimus Prime, Wheeljack, Windcharger, and all the other characters killed off in the movie to make way for new toys! **MAP pp.14–15, A3**

BARKLEY DAM
The Fugitive **ILLINOIS | FILM**
Where Richard Kimble makes his famous dive. Lies on the (real) Route 13 just north of the fictional town of Doverville, which we have mapped to real-world Murphysboro. A southern Illinois location is supported by references in the film to the I-57 and I-24 interstates, and the fact that Kimble was being transported to the (also real) Menard Correctional Centre in nearby Randolph County. However, Illinois does not possess the mountainous scenery shown in this sequence, which was actually shot at the Cheoah Dam in North Carolina. **MAP pp.16–17, D4**

BEACH CITY
Steven Universe **DELMARVA | TV**
Coastal community situated on the Eastern Seaboard's Delmarva peninsula, which in the show's universe is a state in its own right. Not mapped is Beach City's next-door neighbour Ocean Town, which can proudly boast to be 'No Longer On Fire!' **MAP pp.14–15, C4**

BEDROCK
The Flintstones
ARIZONA | VARIOUS
At first blush, this classic cartoon's Bedrock might seem unmappably vague. But in both the 1994 movie and the original series, Bedrock is within a short drive of the Grand Canyon (then a small trickle). Appropriately, a *Flintstones* Bedrock-themed theme park was for many years located just south of the Grand Canyon at the intersection of Routes 180 and 64. **MAP pp.18–19, C3**

BENNE SEED ISLAND
WORKS OF MADELEINE L'ENGLE | SOUTH CAROLINA | NOVELS
One of several locations from the works of L'Engle, we were amused to find it in close proximity to the Ham Sandwich Islands from *Pirates!*. A benne seed is another name for a sesame seed, which might feature on such a sandwich. **MAP pp.14–15, C3**

BIG THUNDER MOUNTAIN
BIG THUNDER MOUNTAIN RAILROAD | UTAH | ROLLERCOASTER
The original incarnation of this iconic Disney attraction took inspiration from the rock formations of Utah's Bryce Canyon National Park, while subsequent versions reference Monument Valley, which extends into neighbouring Arizona. Our solution maps Big Thunder Mountain just north of the Utah/Arizona border, allowing us to encircle it with the various old-western towns paired with the ride in the various Disney parks: Rainbow Ridge, Grizzly Gulch, Phantom Canyon, Thunder Mesa and Tumbleweed. **MAP pp.18–19, C3**

BILLY THE MOUNTAIN
'Billy the Mountain'
BY FRANK ZAPPA | CALIFORNIA | SONG
A mountain found between Rosamund and Gorman, with his lady love, a tree called Ethel. **MAP pp.18–19, A3/B3**

BROKEBACK MOUNTAIN
Brokeback Mountain
WYOMING | SHORT STORY/FILM
Brokeback Mountain is in sheep-farming country some distance north of the nearest town, the equally-fictional Signal. Both are located in northern or central Wyoming. **MAP pp.18–19, D5**

CACTUSVILLE
The Dandy **TEXAS | COMICS**
Home of Desperate Dan, the world's strongest cowboy and lover of cow pies! Beyond being situated in Texas, official canon gives us little to work with. However, since Dan's adventures are based on classic Wild West conventions, we've mapped Cactusville to Bandera, TX, a town that proclaims itself 'the Cowboy Capital of the World'
MAP pp.16–17, B2

CAMP CAMPBELL
CAMP CAMP | WASHINGTON | WEB ANIMATION
This run-down summer camp lies in a forested, mountainous area adjacent to fictional Lake Lilac and the dormant volcano Sleepy Peak Peak (formerly 'Wide Awake Peak'). The volcanism and evergreen forests suggested a Pacific Northwest location, and the nearest city's resemblance to Seattle (complete with rotating-restaurant atop a Space Needle analogue) led to us mapping Camp Campbell in Washington, next-door to Dante's Peak. Campe Diem! **MAP pp.18–19, B6**

CARRUCAN PLANTATION
Django Unchained
MISSISSIPPI | FILM
Django's 'home' plantation where he and his wife Broomhilda were both branded as runaway slaves and subsequently sold separately at a slave auction in the real town of Greenville. This might be a rough guide as to the planation's location. It also means Django and his fellow chain-ganged slaves were forced to walk almost 1,500km (900 miles) by the time a chance encounter frees them in the vicinity of El Paso. **MAP pp.16–17, D2**

DENTON
The Rocky Horror Picture Show **OHIO | FILM**
Although named after Denton in Texas, clues in the film suggest an Ohio setting. A book based on the film includes a rough map, which appears to place Denton in south-eastern Ohio. **MAP pp.14–15, B4**

DOROTHY GALE'S FARM *The Wizard of Oz*
KANSAS | NOVEL/FILM
Everybody knows that Dorothy came from Kansas, but precisely where is difficult to pinpoint. L. Frank Baum is said to have been inspired by a tornado incident that happened in Irving, killing a girl called Dorothy Gale, so we've located the farm close to that town. **MAP pp.16–17, C4**

DUCKBURG
Uncle Scrooge / Ducktales
CALISOTA | COMICS/TV
Where life is like a hurricane! The hometown of the various Disney Ducks lies on the Pacific coast in the fictional state of Calisota, occupying what would in reality be northern California. In recent years Duckburg has been codified as lying on the opposite side of fictional Audubon Bay to the metropolis of St. Canard, residence of the heroic Darkwing Duck. **MAP pp.18–19, A5**

EAGLE STATE
Desperate Housewives
EASTERN USA | TV
Location undefined. Fictional Eagle State was founded in the same year as Colorado, but also lies adjacent to a large body of water, which that state lacks. The best fit may be Indiana, as the show references Purdue University, the Indianapolis Colts and Chicago O'Hare airport. **MAP pp.14–15, A4**

FLAGSTONE
Once Upon a Time in the West
CALIFORNIA | FILM
Small western town named in reference to Flagstaff, Arizona. However, railroad tickets within the film display the following stations between Sante Fe and Flagstone: Albuquerque, Valencia, Prescott, Aztec Pass and Aubrey City. All are real places in New Mexico and Arizona, and Aubrey City (a ghost town now drowned under Lake Havasu) sat on the border with California. Since the railroad continues west to Flagstone, the town has to lie within California proper, and so we have mapped it midway between Lake Havasu and Los Angeles, the most likely destination for the railroad. **MAP pp.18–19, B3**

GOBLU
OHIO | MAP
Two non-existent towns (see also Beatosu) inserted into an official map as a pun and a copyright trap, at least one of which was then adopted into the lore of GI Joe! **MAP pp.14–15, A5**

GOTHAM CITY
DC COMICS | NEW JERSEY | COMIC
Batman's home city is built on a cluster of fictional islands just off the coast of New Jersey. **MAP pp.14–15, C4**

GRAVITY FALLS
Gravity Falls **OREGON | TV**
Located in Oregon's fictional Roadkill County. Although in-universe maps place Gravity Falls in arid eastern Oregon, the show itself displays the verdant pine forests and temperate climate that characterise the state's geography west of the Cascade Mountains, so for this atlas we've mapped the town to the vicinity of real-world Marion Forks. **MAP pp.18–19, A5**

HAWKINS
Stranger Things **INDIANA | TV**
Set in fictional Roane County, Indiana, the location of Hawkins is never defined but the terrain is hilly, so we've gone for the south of the state. **MAP pp.14–15, A4**

HEGEMAN
MARVEL COMICS | NEW YORK | COMICS
Town that is home to the prestigious (and fictional) State University, Alma Mater to Reed Richards and Doctor Doom! State is most likely an analogue to Cornell University, which would make Hegeman a parallel to Ithaca. **MAP pp.14–15, C5**

HILL VALLEY
Back to the Future
CALIFORNIA | FILMS
In Northern California, 19km (12 miles) east of Grass Valley – A Nice Place to Live! The only other fictional location from the franchise is Eastwood Ravine, located about 6 or 8km (4 or 5 miles) WSW of Hill Valley. Originally Shonash Ravine and then Clayton Ravine, the consequences of time travel ultimately see it renamed 'Eastwood Ravine' in honour of Marty McFly's 1885 alias, 'Clint Eastwood'. **MAP pp.18–19, A4**

HILLWOOD
Hey Arnold! **WASHINGTON | TV**
Hillwood amalgamates features of several cities in the Pacific Northwest, where show creator Craig Barlett grew up. It straddles the estuary of a fictionalized version of the real Skookumchuck River, which would

place Hillwood where the real city of Aberdeen, Washington stands, though Hillwood is a metropolis on the scale of Seattle or Portland, with aspects of New York thrown in. **MAP pp.18–19, A6**

INNSMOUTH
Cthulhu Mythos **BY H.P. LOVECRAFT | MASSACHUSETTS | VARIOUS**
One of many Lovecraft locations on the map. It plays a prominent role in the short story 'The Shadow Over Innsmouth'. In the video game *The Sinking City*, the coastal town of Oakmont (not mapped) is located nearby, and has recently become an island after an inundation. *The Simpsons* has also parodied Innsmouth, with their own Fogburyport (a fictional version of a fictional town). **MAP pp.14–15, D5**

KINGSTON FALLS
Gremlins **NEW YORK | FILM**
Although filmed in California (using the same outdoor sets as 'Hill Valley' from *Back to the Future*), Kingston Falls is firmly in New York. We have few other clues to its location, other than a backdrop of low mountains. The town is subtly referenced in *Explorers* (also directed by Joe Dante), when it is mentioned in a newspaper headline. **MAP pp.14–15, C5**

LAKE EDNA
KENTUCKY FRIED CHICKEN | KENTUCKY | ADVERTISING
An all-American small-town idyll created for a long-running KFC advertising campaign. We've mapped it to real-world Corbin, where the chain's first restaurant opened. **MAP pp.14–15, A3**

MAR-IAGO
Mac Trump **BY IAN DOESCHER AND JACOPO DELLA QUERCIA | FLORIDA | BOOK**
This Shakesperian tragicomedy of the Trump Administration has peppered our atlas with many wonderful locations from the world of its imagined United Fiefdoms of America, some of which – such as Pennsylvanus and Connecticutia – had to be eliminated for lack of space. Lord MacTrump's estate of Mar-Iago, however, must be among the most perfectly-recast among these, blending reality's Mar-a-Lago with 'honest' Iago, trusted lieutenant of Othello and most duplicitous of all the Bard's villains. **MAP pp.14–15, C1**

MERCY *Song of Solomon*
BY TONI MORRISON | MICHIGAN | NOVEL
The opening paragraphs establish that the fictional town of Mercy is on the shore of Lake Superior. We also learn that the

town is at the junction of Routes 2 and 6 – not possible in real life as the two never intersect. We later learn that it has a train station, a suburb called Fairfield Heights, and is close to a lakeside retreat called Honoré. The name has also been used as a fictional western town in *Doctor Who* ('A Town Called Mercy'), not mapped. **MAP pp.14–15, A6**

METROPOLIS
DC COMICS | DELAWARE | COMICS
The chief city from *Superman* is well established at the north end of the Delaware Peninsula. **MAP pp.14–15, C4**

MIDLANDS
MIDWEST | COLLEGE MOCK TRIAL COMPETITIONS
This fictional Midwestern state is where all American Mock Trial Association cases take place. **MAP pp.16–17, B5**

MINNEHAHA
D2: The Mighty Ducks
MINNESOTA | FILM
In-between films, coach Gordon Bombay briefly played professional hockey for the Minnehaha Waves, a fictional minor league team based in and named for this fictional city. The film's novelisation instead depicts Bombay playing for a team in Duluth, MN, so we chose to consider Minnehaha an analogue for Duluth. **MAP pp.16–17, C6**

MOUNT SNUFFLEUPAGUS
Sesame Street **HAWAII | TV**
On a trip to Hawaii, Big Bird and Aloysious 'Snuffy' Snuffleupagus search for and eventually find Mount Snuffleupagus (aka Mount Ihu Papa'a Lo'ihi Nui). The feature used as Mount Snuffleupagus is actually the Sleeping Giant on the island of Kauai. **MAP pp.18–19, C1**

MOUSETON
Mickey Mouse **CALISOTA | VARIOUS**
Mickey's hometown, which, since the 1990s, has been placed close to, and within the same fictional state (Calisota) as Duckburg. It is a coastal city with a harbour. **MAP pp.18–19, A5**

NIGHT VALE
Welcome to Night Vale
NEW MEXICO | PODCAST
Night Vale and its neighbour Desert Bluffs are located somewhere in the deserts of the American Southwest, 'Where the sun is hot, the moon is beautiful, and mysterious lights pass overhead while everyone pretends to

sleep'. Based on these clues, we decided to match it to Roswell, New Mexico, a town which needs no introduction in matters of the strange. **MAP pp.16–17, A2**

PONDAROSA RANCH
Bonanza **NEVADA | TV**
The main setting of this iconic show has a well-established location between Lake Tahoe and Carson City. It stands within the 'Pondarosa land' which was said to be 1,000 sq. miles (2,600 sq. km). **MAP pp.18–19, A4**

PROGRESS CITY
TEXAS | SCAM
Nonexistent town that featured in a 1910 land scam, where people were conned into buying lots in said town. Progress City was putatively sited in Brewster County, about 40 miles (64km) south of the town of Alpine, amidst the Santiago Mountains. **MAP pp.16–17, A2**

RADIATOR SPRINGS
Cars **ARIZONA | FILM**
Town situated on Route 66 in fictional Carburetor County. Production materials place it between Gallup (New Mexico) and Kingman (Arizona), hence eastern Arizona. An on-screen map shows that it's just north of Interstate 40 (a bypass that sucked away all traffic from the town). **MAP pp.18–19, C3**

RAGNAROK
New Captain Scarlet **ALASKA | TV**
Small town (population 52) and abandoned coal mine situated in a remote Alaskan valley. In-universe it is situated within two-hours drive of a fictional bridge across the Bering Strait, so on the Seward Peninsula seemed the most likely location, in the York or Kigluaik Mountains. **MAP pp.18–19, A2**

RICHVILLE
Richie Rich **INDIANA | COMICS**
Hometown of Richie Rich. In the Macaulay Culkin movie, Rich Industries was based in Chicago, and the Forbes Fictional 15 appropriately shows the Rich family as living nearby in Indiana. Thus we mapped Richville to the northwest corner of Indiana, within commuting distance of Chicago while still remaining in the countryside. **MAP pp.14–15, A4**

ROCKWELL
The Iron Giant **BY TED HUGHES | MAINE | NOVEL/FILM**
Many of the locations in this atlas are speculative, but here we can nail things down precisely. The town's coordinates are given in the film as 67.71972 degrees

west, 44.50177 degrees north, which maps to a spot on the coast of Maine. **MAP pp.14–15, D6**

SAN FRANSOKYO
Big Hero 6 CALIFORNIA | FILM/TV
Alternate history version of San Francisco that was heavily settled by Japanese immigrants who helped rebuild after the 1906 earthquake, resulting in the city evolving a unique east/west fusion aesthetic that eventually led to it being officially renamed to reflect this. The Muirahara Woods National Monument is located just north, a fictional version of Muir Woods. **MAP pp.18–19, A4**

SHERMER
FILMS OF JOHN HUGHES | ILLINOIS | FILMS
Based on Northbrook, Chicago, this fictional town featured in many films including *The Breakfast Club, Planes, Trains & Automobiles, Weird Science, Ferris Bueller's Day Off, Sixteen Candles, Pretty in Pink, Uncle Buck,* the *Home Alone* films, and the *National Lampoon's Vacation* films. **MAP pp.16–17, D5**

SHINING TIME
Thomas and the Magic Railroad SHINING TIME STATION, PENNSYLVANIA | TV/FILM
Town set on the fictional Indian Valley Railroad. A location is never specified, but railroad scenes for the feature-length Thomas the Tank Engine movie were shot on the historic Strasburg Railroad in Pennsylvania. Mapping Shining Time to Strasburg also allowed us to place it along the route of the equally-fictional Allegheny & West Virginia Railroad, setting of runaway-train action-movie *Unstoppable*. Now there's a crossover waiting to happen! **MAP pp.14–15, C4**

SOUTH PARK
South Park COLORADO | TV/FILM
Fictional town located in and named for the real geographic feature called South Park, a grassland flat in the Rocky Mountains, and partly based on Fairplay. Middle Park and North Park lie nearby. **MAP pp.18–19, D4**

SOUTHFORK RANCH
Dallas TEXAS | TV
The super-famous Southfork does actually exist in real life. It was originally built in the 1970s as Duncan Acres, but changed its name to Southfork Ranch on the back of the fame it got from the TV series. So it's a slightly awkward inclusion, but one we feel is important, given the prominence of the show. **MAP pp.16–17, C2**

SPRINGWOOD
A Nightmare on Elm Street
OHIO | FILMS
Director Wes Craven is from Cleveland and conceived of Freddy Kruger (name and all) growing up in that area. Our best guess is to position Springwood in that area and imagine it to be a fictional suburb of Cleveland. **MAP pp.14–15, B5**

SUMMERVILLE
Ghostbusters: Afterlife
OKLAHOMA | FILM
We're really on the ball with this one, as this book will be going to the presses before the film's release. However, we can get a definite location thanks to the trailer, which includes a map placing Sumerville where the real town of Woodward, OK is located. **MAP pp.16–17, B3**

SUNNYDALE
Buffy the Vampire Slayer
CALIFORNIA | TV
Located 'near to Santa Barbara' according to creator Joss Whedon. In-universe maps show Sunnydale to be at the 'bend' in the Californian coast with the Pacific to the south and west. Maps of the fictional 'Sunnydale County' actually show Santa Barbara County with the fictional name superimposed. **MAP pp.18–19, A3**

TARA PLANTATION
Gone With the Wind
BY MARGARET MITCHELL | GEORGIA | NOVEL/FILM
The central plantation of this Hollywood classic is located near Jonesboro, south of Atlanta. Neighbouring fictional plantations, not shown, include Fairhill, MacIntosh, Mimosa, Pine Bloom, Slattery Farm, Twelve Oaks and Green Acres. **MAP pp.14–15, B3**

THNEEDVILLE
The Lorax NEW JERSEY | VARIOUS
In the original Doctor Suess book and animated special, directions to where Thneedville will be built in the 2012 film mention a notable clue: 'Take the road to North Nitch. Turn left at Weehawken. Sharp right at South Stitch'. Weehawken is a real location in Hudson County, New Jersey, just opposite NYC, thus suggesting somewhere in north-central New Jersey. This is reinforced by the original edition of the book, which describes conditions for wildlife as being worse 'up in Lake Erie'. **MAP pp.14–15, C5**

TULLS POINT
Dad's Army MAINE | TV
Tulls Point might have been the American Walmington-on-Sea. The writers of

British comedy *Dad's Army* pitched a US version, to be set in the fictional coastal town of Tulls Point, Maine, with the characters reworked accordingly. Mainwairing would have become Cornelius Bishop, the pompous president of Tulls Bank, who believes town founder Thomas Tull was the real hero who warned that 'the British are coming' during the American Revolution and that Paul Revere unduly got all the publicity 'because he had a fancy name'. Since Revere lived in Boston, this probably suggests a location in southern Maine. The town was not named in a filmed pilot, but it would be nice to finally do justice to the original script and put Tulls Point on the map. **MAP pp.14–15, D5**

WESTVIEW
Wandavision NEW JERSEY | TV
A town surrounded by a forcefield, and under the control of the Avenger Wanda Maximoff, whose residents are held captive as though characters in an ever-changing TV sitcom. It is located in New Jersey, probably to the north of the state to match up with the character's home of Leonia (non-fictional) in the comics. Westview appears to be rural in character, so we've placed it outside the metropolitan areas. Note, this was the very last location to be added to this Atlas, while the show's first series was still airing, so our placement will not reflect any revelations in the second half of that series. **MAP pp.14–15, C5**

WILLOWS *Barbie*
WISCONSIN | FASHION DOLL/TV/FILM
Home town of Barbie before she moved to Malibu. Pure speculation on this one, but clues can be found in the cartoon. Willows is on a river that runs north–south. There's an extensive cave system under the town. We're guessing that Willows is somewhere in the Western Upland region of Wisconsin, an area characterized by hills and caves in a state that is mostly glacial plains. The general area west of the town of Wisconsin Dells is a good match. **MAP pp.16–17, D5**

XANADU
Citizen Kane FLORIDA | FILM
Charles Foster Kane's sumptuous mansion and estate of Xanadu is said to be the world's largest private estate at 76 sq. miles (nearly 200 sq. km). It is situated on Florida's Gulf Coast. **MAP pp.14–15, B2**

CANADA AND THE ARCTIC

GREEN GABLES AND GOLD NUGGETS

n the media, Canada is often stereotyped as 'America's Hat' (conversely making the USA 'Canada's shorts'). It is the friendly, polite, ice-hockey-obsessed counterpart to its more rambunctious neighbour. Unsurprising then that America and Canada, as depicted in fiction, both show commonalities.

Both share a romantic love for rural life and community, as embodied in *Sunshine Sketches of a Little Town*. The little town in question is Mariposa, a loving parody of author Stephen Leacock's Ontario home of Orillia. But romanticism must also adjust to pragmatism, and nothing demonstrates this like Canada's most famous

contribution to children's literature, Lucy Maud Montgomery's *Anne of Green Gables*. This coming-of-age saga about a young orphan on Prince Edward Island, learning to balance her dreams with down-to-Earth reality, in many ways reflects Canada's own developing maturity, with Anne growing into adulthood and motherhood at the same time as her homeland grows to become a world power. Indeed, Anne's stories are so beloved, and her world so well-realized, that we've had to split off Prince Edward Island into its own map to ensure the key places fit in (and, even then, we haven't mapped everything)!

Like the USA, Canada also features a wide variety of landscapes in which to tell stories – mountains,

coastlines, prairies, towns and cities. The difference here lies in population. Much of this region is sparsely inhabited, and we make no apology for the large chunks of blank space on this particular map. Among the more unusual inclusions are the Evergreen Forest, home of the anthropomorphic cast of *The Racoons*, another piece of Canadian children's entertainment that is enjoyed worldwide. And then there's Brobdingnag, situated off British Columbia, which Johnathan Swift's ever-travelling Gulliver discovers to be inhabited by giants.

Perhaps that, then, is the best analogue of Canada as portrayed in this map, as a giant whose potential is yet to be fully seen. Let's discover it together!

THE ULTIMATE REALMS OF THE BOREAL POLE

Ask any child where Santa lives and most will answer 'the North Pole!' Be it the cosy cottage industry depicted in *Rudolph the Red-Nosed Reindeer*, or the immense manufactory metropolis of *The Polar Express*, let all good children rest assured there is something up there – at least so far as your authors are concerned. In fact, the far north is so populated that Santa appears to have neighbours.

First, let's resolve a matter of terrain. Reality is clear: there is no land at the pole. Santa must reside in a network of caves burrowed into the floating ice cap. But solid footing can be found in the fictive north, courtesy of Jules Verne's *The Adventures of Captain Hatteras*. Its titular explorer discovered Queen's Island, a volcanic islet situated right at the summit of the world, in the summer of 1861. Although Verne's captain only described one mountain on the island, a volcano now named Mount Hatteras in his honour, the *Arabian Nights* suggests at least another peak, Mount Qaf (said to lie at the farthest point of the Earth, which is often equated with the North Pole). Elsewhere in this strangely crowded region we find another volcano, sulphurous Mount Yaanek, a peak of groaning lavas attributed to Edgar Allan Poe. Beneath lies the tunnel to the Blazing World, titular setting of Margaret Cavendish's peculiar 1666 'sci-fi' novel. Perhaps the same passage system leads to the ultimate stygian realm of Atvatabar – a subterranean landmass identical to North America, also reached via the North Pole.

All this tunnelling and geological activity must generate plenty of thermal energy, suggesting a source of heat and power, not just for Santa and his workshops, but for the other civilizations situated in these parts. We have accounts of *The Island at the Top of the World's* Astragard, where the old Norse ways still reign. Meanwhile, the animators of Rankin/Bass presented us with the Island of Misfit Toys, ruled over by the leonine King Moonracer. Perhaps the king gave shelter to another misfit, Frankenstein's monster, who was last seen drifting on the ice in these parts.

There is also the subterranean city of Glacia, guarded by Canada's home-grown heroine, *Nelvana of the Northern Lights*. One of media history's first-ever superheroines, Nelvana is noticeable for also being Inuit, a remarkable distinction for a character who made her debut in 1940. And she finds herself in good company, for a little way south lies the Fortress of Solitude, Arctic retreat of fiction's most iconic hero, Superman!

GOLDEN DREAMS AT WHITE AGONY CREEK

In August of 1896, gold was discovered along Rabbit Creek, an event that transformed the face of this sleepy corner of the Yukon. Previously just a minor tributary of the mighty Klondike River, Rabbit Creek was quickly renamed Bonanza Creek, and over the following three years thousands of people would migrate into the region, stirred up by fantastic newspaper reports of gold! Gold! Gold! Gold!

Most who set out to strike it rich never completed the journey. The vast majority returned penniless. But enough met with success to inspire new waves of pilgrims. Boom towns such as Dawson City emerged overnight to serve the needs of the many dreamers. The Gold Rush ended as suddenly as it started, but this brief, madcap blaze for glory had established itself in the cultural landscape.

Author Jack London experienced it first-hand, and made Dawson City and the Yukon the central setting of classic novels such as *White Fang* and *Call of the Wild*. Jules Verne touched on the ultimate futility of the Gold Rush in *The Golden Volcano*, where the discovery of a literal volcano of gold leaves its discoverers poorer than when they set out. Charlie Chaplin played up this commingled folly and fortune in early silent films, paving a way for future media to follow. The Irish television drama *An Klondike* followed the exploits of three brothers in the fictional boom town of Dominion Creek, while the vegetarian vampire *Count Duckula* encountered the withered boom-to-bust town of Goldville.

Yet at least one hopeful succeeded: a young Scotsman, an immigrant of humble origins, who made his fortune when he discovered the Goose Egg Nugget at fictional White Agony Creek in the bitter winter of 1897. Like Count Duckula we speak of an anthropomorphic waterfowl, none other than Scrooge McDuck!

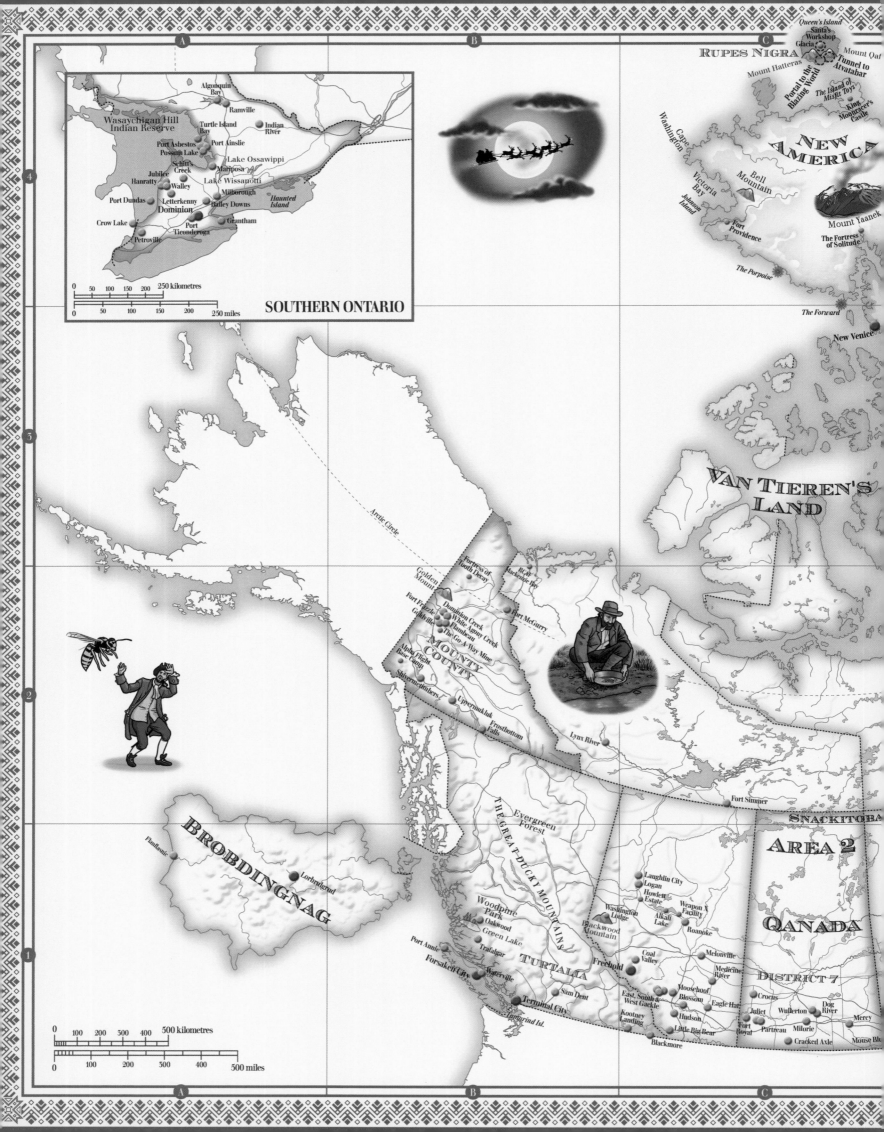

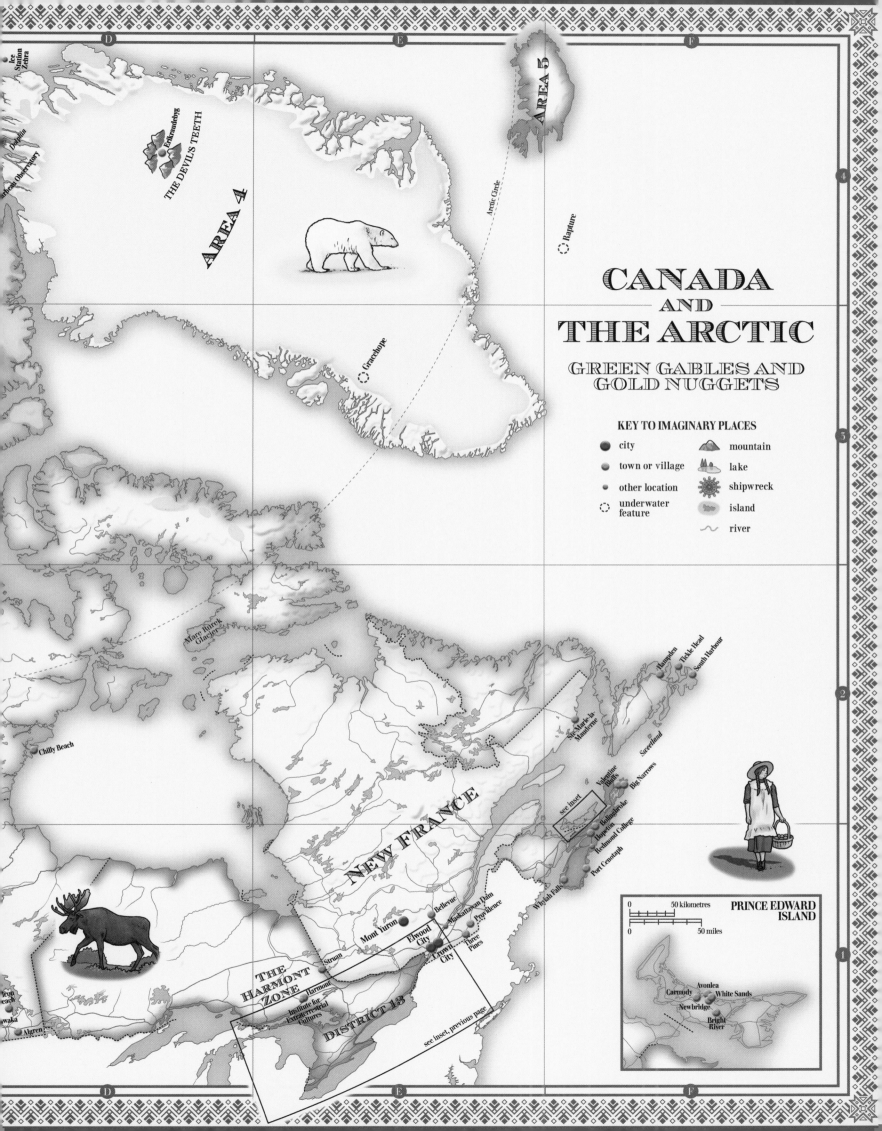

CANADA AND THE ARCTIC

KEY LOCATIONS

For a full list of locations, see the location index on pages 130–150.

AREA 2 *Code Geass*
NORTHERN NORTH AMERICA | ANIME
Area 2 equates to real-world Canada. The colonial territory of the Holy Britannian Empire was established in a world where the American Revolution failed and Napoleon invaded Great Britain, leading to surviving nobles fleeing to found a new Empire in Britain's North American colonies. Britannia itself (Area 1) encompasses the real-world USA. Numerically, Canada being Area 2 would thus make it the first region Britannia invaded and conquered in their quest to dominate the world. **MAP pp.26–27, C1**

AVONLEA
Anne of Green Gables
BY LUCY MAUD MONTGOMERY | PRINCE EDWARD ISLAND | NOVEL
The main setting of the novel is based on Cavendish, Prince Edward Island. Curiously, the farm of Green Gables is not fictional, and Montgomery chose not to change the name. **MAP pp.26–27, F1**

BAILEY DOWNS
Ginger Snaps FILMS
AND *Orphan Black*
ONTARIO | FILMS/TV
The *Ginger Snaps* films and TV show *Orphan Black* share several cast and crew, and though no direct references are made, each is set in the town of Bailey Downs. This is a fictional Ontario suburb, possibly in Toronto, where filming took place. **MAP pp.26–27, A4**

BOLINGBROKE
Anne of Green Gables
BY LUCY MAUD MONTGOMERY | NOVA SCOTIA | NOVEL
Birthplace of Anne, which was based on New London (PEI), but set somewhere in Nova Scotia. The location is never given, but we've placed it reasonably close to Prince Edward Island. **MAP pp.26–27, F1/F2**

BROBDINGNAG
Gulliver's Travels BY JONATHAN
SWIFT | PACIFIC OCEAN | NOVEL
The land of giants, which Gulliver explores following his voyage to Lilliput. As with Lilliput, Swift describes the journey in detail and even provides a map, yet neither is geographically convincing (supposedly, this was Swift taking a deliberate swipe at the embellished travelogues of his day). What we do know is that Brobdingnag is a large landmass off the north-west coast of North America. Swift's map shows that it must be some distance north of Oregon (Cape Blanco is labelled), though not so far north as Alaska. The scale is also mischievous. Gulliver describes a continent-sized landmass, some 9,650km (6,000 miles) long, yet the map shows something an order of magnitude smaller. We've gone for somewhere in between, tracing the same outline that Swift penned. The eastern end is blocked by a peninsula of volcanoes – which explains why the inhabitants of Canada have never strayed across their giant neighbours (or vice versa). We've pinned Brobdingnag to Moresby Island for added isolation from the rest of the world. **MAP pp.26–27, A1**

DISTRICT 13
The Hunger Games
BY SUZANNE COLLINS | ONTARIO/QUEBEC | NOVELS/FILMS
Officially, the chief industry of the supposedly destroyed District 13 was graphite mining. The largest reserves in North America are in eastern Canada. **MAP pp.26–27, E1**

DOMINION
George Sprott BY SETH ONTARIO |
GRAPHIC NOVEL/CARDBOARD MODEL
Specified as Southern Ontario; the location is unknown, but Seth has likened it in size to Hamilton. He lives in nearby Guelph. A location near these two seems plausible. The author has spent years making a cardboard model of Dominion. **MAP pp.26–27, A4**

ELWOOD CITY,
CROWN CITY
Arthur QUEBEC | TV
Twin cities. Evidence in the show suggests equally a US or Canadian setting, but the clincher for us is the in-show map of the cities, which are unmistakably laid out like Montreal. **MAP pp.26–27, E1**

ERIKRAUDEBYG
La Citadelle des Glaces
BY PAUL ALPERINE | GREENLAND | NOVEL
Last remaining Viking colony, hidden by the mountain range the Devil's Teeth, 17 days' journey from the coast. **MAP pp.26–27, D4**

THE EVERGREEN FOREST *The Raccoons*
BRITISH COLUMBIA/ALBERTA | TV
Primary setting for this animated show, a bucolic forest community of grand mountains and clear lakes. Originally a bit of a vague fantasy land, but later redefined as an entire alternate Earth of anthropomorphic animals that live and work as humans do. With this in mind, the mountains and evergreen foliage suggest somewhere in (possibly northern) British Columbia or Alberta, as the climate appears to be too temperate to be much further north in the Yukon. **MAP pp.26–27, B1/B2**

FALCON BEACH *Falcon Beach* **MANITOBA | TV**
Resort town filmed in real-world Winnipeg Beach, Manitoba. Interestingly, two versions of each episode of the show were produced, one filmed for Canadian audiences, and another for American audiences, changing Falcon Beach's location to New England (see USA map). **MAP pp.26–27, D1**

THE FORTRESS OF SOLITUDE
DC COMICS | NUNAVUT | VARIOUS
Superman's home away from home. Its location not usually specified aside from being in a remote region of ice, snow and tundra, but in the movie *Man of Steel* it was placed on the real Ellesmere Island, in Nunavut. **MAP pp.26–27, C4**

FORTRESS OF TOOTH DECAY *South Park* **YUKON | TV**
From the episode 'Royal Pudding', this is somewhere in the tundra of Yukon. Tooth Decay, a monstrous incarnation of the dental ailment, resides there. **MAP pp.26–27, B2**

THE GO-A-WAY MINE *Count Duckula* **YUKON | TV**
Full name, 'The Go-A-Way This Mine Is Mine, Mine' – shown on a crude map to be roughly south-east of the fictional ghost town of Goldville, which we have mapped to Dawson City. **MAP pp.26–27, B2**

HARMONT *Roadside Picnic* **BY ARKADY AND BORIS STRUGATSKY | ONTARIO | NOVEL**
In this iconic Soviet sci-fi story, Harmont is a mining town within the Harmont Zone, one of six areas across the world 'littered' with strange artefacts and phenomena as a result of an alien visitation. Harmont's exact location is unknown, but the book *Canadian Literary Landmarks* suggests it is inspired by Greater Sudbury in Ontario, which is situated in a region (the Sudbury Basin) created as the result of a meteor strike. The minerals deposited by the meteor formed the basis for Sudbury's mining and smelting economy, much as the Zone influences life in Harmont. **MAP pp.26–27, E1**

HOPETON *Anne of Green Gables* **BY LUCY MAUD MONTGOMERY | NOVA SCOTIA | NOVEL**
Location of Anne's asylum. Written as Hopetown in some versions. Its location is never specified, but it is likely to be close to Anne's (also fictional) birthplace of Bolingbroke. **MAP pp.26–27, F1**

HOWLETT ESTATE
MARVEL COMICS | ALBERTA | COMICS
In the 2000 movie *X-Men*, we first meet Hugh Jackman's incarnation of Logan (aka. Wolverine) during a cage fight in the fictional town of Laughlin City, Alberta (also mapped). His birthplace in the films is later revealed as his family's palatial mansion, the mountainous Howlett Estate. This is where the young cub first discovered his concealed claws and regenerative healing powers. Nearby, you'll also find the Alkali Lake Weapons X facility (where Logan becomes Wolverine). **MAP pp.26–27, C1**

MOUNTY COUNTY *Droopy: Northwest Hounded Police* **YUKON | TV**
The most sensible place to locate this county on the map is the Dawson City region, as this is where the Yukon mounted police were headquartered during the era being portrayed. Note that Yukon does not have counties in real life. **MAP pp.26–27, B2**

PORT TICONDEROGA *The Blind Assassin* **BY MARGARET ATWOOD | ONTARIO | NOVEL**
A blend of Ontario towns, including Stratford, St Mary's, Elora and Paris. We've placed it near the latter, as it needs to be a port. **MAP pp.26–27, A4**

PORTAL TO THE BLAZING WORLD *The Blazing World* **BY MARGARET CAVENDISH | NORTH POLE | NOVEL**
A 17th-century novel about a young woman who reaches a fantastic realm via a portal at the North Pole. It is remarkable both as a very early example of science fiction, and as a novel by a woman in a century when this was rare. **MAP pp.26–27, C4**

RAPTURE *Bioshock* **NORTH ATLANTIC | VIDEO GAME**
Undersea city and free-enterprise paradise turned dystopian nightmare. Accessed by a mid-ocean lighthouse and located at 63° 2' N, 29° 55' W, about halfway between Greenland and Iceland. **MAP pp.26–27, F4**

RUPES NIGRA
TRADITION | ARCTIC | VARIOUS
A phantom island at the magnetic North Pole made of black rock and measuring 53km (33 miles) wide. It appeared on genuine maps in the 16th and 17th centuries, and has featured in subsequent works of fiction. It was the inspiration, for example, for Verne's Queen's Island, also shown. **MAP pp.26–27, C4**

SANTA'S WORKSHOP
TRADITION | NORTH POLE | VARIOUS
Santa Claus is said to live at either the North Pole or in Lapland. The polar location has perhaps more evidence on film. The North Pole is Mr Claus's abode in such films as *The Polar Express*, *Santa Claus the Movie*, *The Snowman* and *Elf*, to name but a few. **MAP pp.26–27, C4**

SCHITT'S CREEK *Shitt's Creek* **CANADA | TV**
Rural town. Location intentionally left vague aside from probably being in Canada, but filmed around the Ontario Peninsula and Greater Toronto. Highway 10 is mentioned in one episode. **MAP pp.26–27, A4**

UPYERMUKLUK *Yvon of the Yukon* **TV**
'The hottest cold town in the Arctic', fictional Upyermukluk is home to the titular Yvon, a hapless French explorer who became accidentally frozen in an iceberg for three centuries. The town lies midway between two other communities, Shivermetimbers and Frostbottom Falls (which have also been charted within this atlas), and an episode where the townsfolk are dismayed to learn their community has been left off of maps of Canada suggests a location somewhere in the vicinity of Whitehorse. **MAP pp.26–27, B2**

CENTRAL AMERICA AND THE CARIBBEAN

THE OLD NEW WORLD

The history of the USA has become so predominant in popular culture that it is easy to forget that the first Europeans to permanently settle in the Americas were not the Pilgrims of Massachusetts but the conquistadors and missionaries of the Spanish Empire, come to the New World to preach Christianity to the natives and pick their pockets. It was Spain's early successes in the New World that led to a boom climate of expedition, exploration and exploitation by the French, Dutch, Portuguese and English, cultures whose descendant nations now comprise the majority of the Americas.

The Spanish, of course, left their own mark, branding this region with their genetics, language, faith and culture. Present-day Mexico and the nations of the Caribbean and Central America comprise a vibrant region that has mingled European and American influences into a syncretic society. Where else might one experience something like the Day of the Dead, a celebration merging Roman Catholicism with pre-Columbian tradition? It is unsurprising then that the stories and legends associated with this region should also reflect such a dynamic mix of cultures. If we had to pick just one entry to exemplify this, it would be Robert Rodriguez's *From Dusk till Dawn*, which begins as a fairly conventional armed-robbers-take-hostages romp, turns into a vampiric horror, and ends with an Aztec twist.

Seek La Tetilla del Diablo, a little way south of the border.

The Caribbean offers a saltier take on this rich mix of cultures. This is a maritime space, and the fictional world's hotspot for shipwrecks, buried treasure, castaways and comedy pirates. We've added over 100 islands to the familiar West Indies, and even a pastiche of the Bermuda Triangle – one of many additions from the *Pirates of the Caribbean* franchise.

Taken as a whole, this most diverse of maps contains bandits, Aztecs, drug cartels, space elevators, dinosaurs, adventurers, shipwrecked heroes and pirates. Lots, and lots, and lots of pirates.

AN ISLAND THAT NOBODY CAN FIND ...

During the Spanish conquests of the 16th century, the Aztecs placed 882 pieces of gold in a stone chest and presented it to conquistador Hernán Cortés, as payment to stop his slaughter of their people. When the gold only fuelled Cortés's greed, a terrible curse fell upon the treasure. Within a day of leaving port, doom overtook the ship carrying the chest and its golden cargo back to Spain, and it was subsequently wrecked on an uncharted island. In the centuries since, the curse of the gold seeped into the very rock and stone of the place, transforming it into a bleak and desolate haunt; an island of death, the dreaded Isla de Muerta.

So goes the backstory to the swashbuckling hit *Pirates of the Caribbean, Curse of the Black Pearl*, and how could we resist the chance to include Isla de Muerta on our map? Of course, the problem is that the island itself cannot be found, unless you're lucky enough to have a magic compass to hand, but we can use the evidence of the films as a guide.

Wherever it may lie, the Isla de Muerta still falls within the Caribbean (it's in the title after all), and many of the surrounding locations are real. Heading to the island in pursuit of the cursed *Black Pearl*, Captain Jack Sparrow and blacksmith Will Turner leave from historic Port Royal, Jamaica, and sail to pick up a crew from Tortuga, off the north coast of Haiti. Turning east from here would put the Isla de Muerta somewhere in the northern end of the Lesser Antilles, which is where we've chosen to chart the *Black Pearl*'s fearsome home port. As it happens, this also places it as a neighbour of that other piratical island of death: Treasure Island.

THE ISLANDS OF ADVENTURE

Robert Louis Stevenson may not have invented pop culture's vision of the Golden Age of Sail, but he certainly codified it. His classic adventure *Treasure Island* bequeathed to the world a romantic paradigm best encapsulated in Long John Silver, the ruthless sea cook complete with peg leg and parrot.

Although never stated outright, it is commonly assumed that Treasure Island itself lay somewhere in the Caribbean, forever associating the region with buccaneers and buried gold. There is, of course, truth behind the stories. Central America was once the Spanish Main, and these waters saw whole fleets of treasure ships carrying plundered wealth back to Europe – a tempting prize for any pirate worth his salt.

Hence, in this map we see more wrecks, pirate lairs and desert islands than anywhere else in this atlas. There's booty to be found everywhere, be it hidden in the caves fof Monkey Island, or secluded in the offshore accounts of the Payment Islands. And, of course, somewhere in these parts lies the dreaded Isla de Muerta, just described.

But beyond the exploits of figures like Robinson Crusoe (located with more certainty near Tobago), Horatio Pugwash, Guybrush Threepwood and Jack Sparrow (apologies, *Captain Jack Sparrow*), at a glance it becomes obvious that this corner of the world continues to be colonized by writers and adventurers into the present day. Here we find countless holiday getaways, snuggled alongside the island lairs of fiends such as Cobra Commander and Black Hat, forever plotting their diabolic schemes.

And on the far side of Costa Rica, we discover Isla Nublar, and the nearby island cluster known as Las Cinco Muertes – the Five Deaths – well named indeed, for here are the lost worlds of *Jurassic Park*, where genetically re-created dinosaurs once again rule the Earth!

WHERE IN THE WORLD IS SAN ESCOBAR?

In this atlas we've encountered fictional nations with all sorts of origins, but there can be none stranger or funnier than the Central American nation of San Escobar, a country that originated as a gaffe and then grew as a meme.

In a 2017 speech, Poland's Minister of Foreign Affairs cited San Escobar among a number of nations with which Poland was establishing new diplomatic ties. The problem was that the proud nation of San Escobar did not exist! In truth this was simply a slip of the tongue, but if we accepted that explanation, then where would be the fun? Clearly, Poland had sent envoys to a nation unknown to the rest of the world.

Nature abhors a vacuum and so too does the internet. Bloggers and pranksters began to document the geography and history of San Escobar, which as it turns out is a nation rich in beauty, culture and humour. Among its features are great metropolises, such as Al Pacino, Gargamele and Guacamole, and the delightfully-named rivers Mojito, Tequila and Pina Colada, all of which sound like the ideal spot for a swim and a drink on a balmy summer's day.

A4 · B4 · C4
A3 · B3 · C3
A2 · B2 · C2
A1 · B1 · C1

Pendragon · Los Robles
San Simon
Santa Teresa

EL ESTADO DORADO

DISTRICT 10

El Lugar
Vacio

Tomatán

Atahalpa

THE ISLAND
OF CALIFORNIA

Las Rémoras

Aqua
Mexico

Escalera
Santa Rosa · Albores
Chuparosa
Placedes

San Luis River

Mesa
de la
Luna · Mesa
del Sol

Pencas Mudas
San Miguel

NUEVO
PARAISO

Carrizales
Carrizalejo

Rio Gordo

Cobra Island

EL GOLFO NOSTRUM

MEXITLÁN

CAPILA
San Chema
Remadrín
Brinquillo

Salimiento

AREA 3

San Francisco
el Alto

Dorado
Castillo

Sierra Vieja

Titty Twister
(La Tetilla del Diablo)

Mina Escondida

Paracuán

Arepa

Obeah

Pueblo Nuevo

Isla de Tiburon

Comala

San Pedro
de las Peñas

Ciudad Trinidad

Ciudad Santiago
San Pedro del Oro
Saint Lucia

San Gaspar
Nuevo Toledo

Ciudad Polaca

San Gaspar

Isla Dorada

Angagua · Santa Cecilia

Los Reyes

San Rafael
Senderos

Playa Escondida
Agua Azul
San Lazaro

Port de la Senoritas

Apaco

El Gran Centro-Capital
Quaunahuac
San Cristóbal Tlaxico

San Angel

ALDAMA

Rio Tequila

Isla Pixol

La Matosa
Santo Subito

Vilena

Beyhualé

Zacatillo
Gargamele

Rio Molito
Dos Ríos

Al Pacino

SANTO
RICO

Wallaceville

Guacamole

Santo
Domestos

Puerto
Grande

MEX-CITY

Rio Pina
Colada

Audiovideo

Nemesis
(wreck)

Neverland

SAN ESCOBAR

LAND OF THE
STINKAS

Puerto Clara

TERRA VERDE
COSTA VERDE
COSTA PERDITA

Quetzalacatenango

Hotta-Watta-
Bottle

Jeronimo

Isla de Mara

Buenaventura

SAN LORENZO

BOCA GRANDE

EL CORONADO

TECA...

Isla Mora...

KEY TO IMAGINARY PLACES

- ● city
- ● town or village
- ● other location
- ⛏ space elevator
- ⬭ stone circle
- ⛰ mountain
- ✶ shipwreck
- 🝢 island
- 〜 river
- 🌀 unmappable location

Molasses Park
Isla Nubl...

LAS CINCO
MUERTES

SCALE

0 · 100 · 200 · 300 · 400 · 500 kilometres

0 · 100 · 200 · 300 · 400 · 500 miles

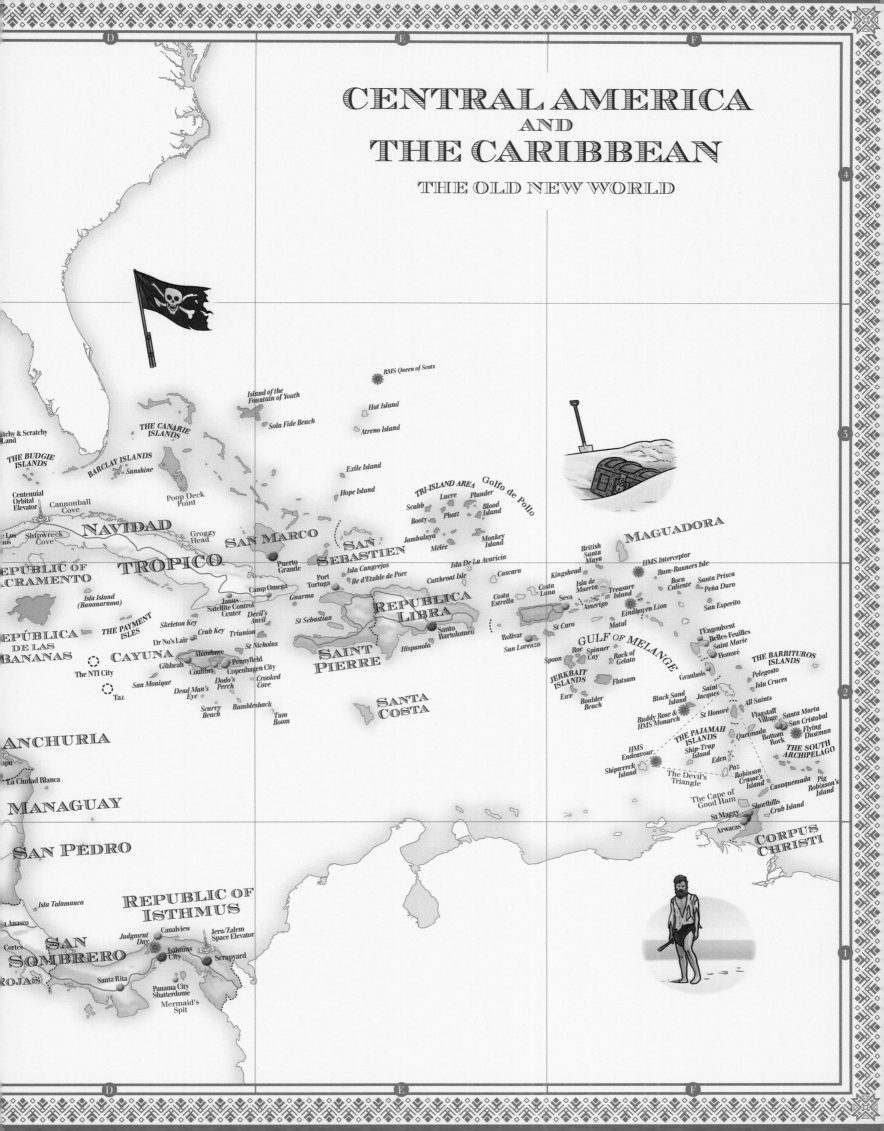

CENTRAL AMERICA AND THE CARIBBEAN

KEY LOCATIONS

For a full list of locations, see the location index on pages 130–150.

AREPA *Maten al león*
BY JORGE IBARGÜENGOITIA | MEXICO | NOVEL
An island in the Gulf of Mexico whose towns include Puerto Alegre. It is a perfect circle, 35km (21¾ miles) in diameter. **MAP pp.32–33, C3**

ARWACAS
A House for Mr Biswas
BY V.S. NAIPAUL | TRINIDAD | NOVEL
A fictionalized version of Chaguanas. Naipaul uses a curious mixture of real place names and fictional alternatives, which we don't have space to map. For example, Tunapuna is renamed Pagotes. **MAP pp.32–33, F1/F2**

BARCLAY ISLANDS
The Deceiver BY FREDERICK FORSYTH | CARIBBEAN | NOVEL
A British-dependent archipelago of eight islands with a beef against Cuba. The Barclay Islands are described by Forsyth as 'situated at the western edge of the Great Bahama Bank, west of the Bahamas' Andros Island, northeast of Cuba, and due south of the Florida Keys.' **MAP pp.32–33, D3**

BLOOD ISLAND
Monkey Island SERIES/
Pirates! Band of Misfits
CARIBBEAN | VIDEO GAMES/FILM
Part of the Tri-Island area, 'Blood Island' also appears in the Aardman animated film *The Pirates!* (where it holds claim as 'Winner of Caribbean in Bloom 1824',

and is twinned with Weston-Super-Mare). We've conflated the two. In *Monkey Island*, a small islet called Skull Island lies to the west. **MAP pp.32–33, E3**

CAPE OF GOOD HAM
The Pirates! Band of Misfits
CARIBBEAN | FILM
Many of the locations from *The Pirates!* are only ever shown on maps within the film, and play no part in the story. We've included them simply because they amused us. **MAP pp.32–33, F2**

COBRA ISLAND
G.I. Joe GULF OF MEXICO | VARIOUS
Cobra Island is somewhere in the Gulf of Mexico, created after a series of bombs triggered a fault line causing an upthrust of land. There are no major faults in the gulf, but we've placed the island in a shallower area of sea. **MAP pp.32–33, B3/C3**

COSTA PERDITA
MARVEL COMICS /*Air America*
SOUTH-WEST CENTRAL AMERICA | COMICS/UNRELATED TV SERIES
Small Central American nation located on the Pacific coast. A Central American country of the same name also appeared in the TV series *Air America*, so we've combined the two. The Marvel version is home to the Citadel of Science of the secret organization known as the Enclave. **MAP pp.32–33, C2**

CRAB ISLAND
Peter Duck (Swallows and Amazons SERIES*)* BY ARTHUR RANSOME | CARIBBEAN | NOVELS
Elderly seaman Peter Duck tells the

children of his voyage to Crab Island in the Caribbean, where he witnessed the burial of a treasure chest. The island is near Trinidad. A fictional island of the same name appears in the *La Patrouille des Castors* comics. **MAP pp.32–33, F2**

DEVIL'S TRIANGLE
Pirates of the Caribbean
CARIBBEAN | VARIOUS
Not the Bermuda Triangle, but another location of similar power, west of the Windward Isles, demarked by points of land at each of its corners to form an equilateral triangle. **MAP pp.32–33, F2**

DISTRICT 10
The Hunger Games BY SUZANNE COLLINS | MEXICO | BOOKS/FILMS
Most of the *Hunger Games* Districts are in the former USA, but District 10 covers Mexico and Texas. **MAP pp.32–33, A4/B4**

ISLA NUBLAR
Jurassic Park BY MICHAEL CRICHTON | COSTA RICA | VARIOUS
The main setting for *Jurassic Park* and *Jurassic World* is described in both book and films as 120 miles (193km) off the west coast of Costa Rica. **MAP pp.32–33, C1**

THE ISLAND OF CALIFORNIA
Las sergas de Esplandián
BY GARCI RODRÍGUEZ DE MONTALVO | MEXICO | NOVEL
The Baja peninsula appeared on countless European maps as 'the Island of California' between the 16th and 18th centuries, despite plenty of evidence that it was not, in fact, an island. The

misconception – and the name 'California' – have their roots in a work of fiction, published in 1510. When the peninsula was discovered in 1535, it gained the name California, and a phoney status as an island, in honour of the novel. **MAP pp.32–33, A3**

JUDGMENT DAY
The Three-Body Problem
BY LIU CIXIN | PANAMA | NOVEL
A converted oil tanker that is sliced into strips by a nanomaterial 'zither' in the Panama Canal. By coincidence, the nanomaterial was under development for a space elevator, an example of which appears on our map nearby from another source (see Jeru/Zalem space elevator, D1). **MAP pp.32–33, D1**

LAS CINCO MUERTES (THE FIVE DEATHS)
The Lost World **BY MICHAEL CRICHTON | COSTA RICA | VARIOUS**
Five islands – Isla Pena, Isla Tacaño, Isla Sorna, Isla Muerta, Isla Matanceros. In the novel of *The Lost World*, described as an island chain about 16km (10 miles) off the bay of Puerto Cortés. Never shown on a map – the films move these islands over 320km (200 miles) offshore (Isla Sorna is stated to be 207 miles/333km west of Costa Rica in *Jurassic Park 3*) and depicts them as such on a map. **MAP pp.32–33, C1**

MAGUADORA
Whoops! Apocalypse
CARIBBEAN | FILM
Although a thinly-veiled caricature of Galtieri-ruled Argentina, this is explicitly an island nation in the Caribbean, whose shape can be determined by its inclusion on the Maguadorian flag. Maguadora invades the neighbouring, equally fictional British Overseas Territory of British Santa Maya. It seems reasonable to assume that British Santa Maya would be close to the real-life Caribbean territories, with Maguadora relatively nearby. **MAP pp.32–33, F3**

MONKEY ISLAND
Monkey Island **SERIES | CARIBBEAN | VIDEO GAMES**
Easternmost of the Tri-Island chain, after which the game series is named. Its location is not specified, but we've placed it close to British territories to reflect the character of the games. The tiny Dinky Island (unmarked) lies to the north-east, while LeChuck's Island Getaway and Spa is also nearby. **MAP pp.32–33, E3**

NEVERLAND *Peter Pan*
BY J.M. BARRIE | BELIZE | NOVELS/FILMS
Barrie's magical realm is never geographically pinpointed in the books or films. However, YouTube channel The Film Theorists has put together a convincing case that equates Turneffe Atoll in Belize with the land of eternal youth. **MAP pp.32–33, C2**

NUEVO PARAISO
Red Dead Redemption **SERIES | MEXICO | VIDEO GAMES**
Fictional Mexican state, lying to the south of the border with the in-game analogue of Texas. In-game maps give a good idea of where its towns and villages lie, of which we've mapped a handful. **MAP pp.32–33, B3**

PIG ROBINSON'S ISLAND *The Tale of Little Pig Robinson* **BY BEATRIX POTTER | CARIBBEAN | SHORT STORY**
A slightly vague entry, as the island Pig Robinson finishes up on is never named or located. However, it is described as very similar to Crusoe's island, so we've placed it nearby. The real reason for its inclusion is that it connects together several fictional universes. According to Beatrix Potter, Pig Robinson's island was also visited by the Owl and the Pussycat from Edward Lear's pen. Meanwhile, Lear's owl was said by A.A. Milne to be a relative of Owl from *Winnie the Pooh*. Ultimately, that means Winnie the Pooh and Peter Rabbit (a friend of Pig Robinson) occupy the same fictional universe! You heard it here first. **MAP pp.32–33, F2**

ROBINSON CRUSOE'S ISLAND
Robinson Crusoe **BY DANIEL DEFOE | CARIBBEAN | NOVEL**
Literature's most famous shipwreck occurs around 9 degrees, 22 minutes north, and north-west of the Orinoco. Tobago is an obvious candidate, and often claims inspiration. An actual Robinson Crusoe Island exists in the Pacific Ocean, this being the island where Alexander Selkirk, who inspired the novel, was marooned. However, the novel is explicitly set in the Caribbean. *Foe*, by J.M. Coetzee, takes place on the same island. **MAP pp.32–33, F2**

SAN ANGEL
Book of Life **MEXICO | FILM**
Built on a lake, this is an analogue of Mexico City, as shown in a map towards the end of the film. **MAP pp.32–33, B2**

SAN LORENZO
Hey Arnold!
SOUTHERN CENTRAL AMERICA | TV
Fictional nation located between Guatemala and Belize. Major rivers (not shown) include the Rio Clara and Rio de Oscuridad. The Volcán Terrible volcano lies somewhere to the west, along with the San Lorenzo Rainforest Preserve. **MAP pp.32–33, C2**

SAN MIGUEL
A Fistful of Dollars **MEXICO | FILM**
Fictional town located close to the Rio Grande and the border with Texas – Chihuahua or Coahuila most likely. An unusual clue comes from a prologue filmed exclusively for a US TV broadcast of the film in 1977 (starring Harry Dean Stanton). Stanton's character mentions that the gangs in San Miguel are trading guns and whiskey with the Apache across the border. Two Apache cultures had lands close to the Rio Grande, the Mescalero and the Lipan. The Mescalero territory seems too close to El Paso to be the sort of lawless environment seen, which would suggest San Miguel lies in that part of Coahuila facing the lands of the Lipan people. **MAP pp.32–33, B3**

SKELETON KEY
Skeleton Key **BY ANTHONY HOROWITZ | CUBA | NOVEL**
Cayo Esqueleto (Skeleton Key) is a few miles south of Cuba. A good companion for Crab Key from *Dr No* – especially as Horowitz is also known for penning James Bond novels. **MAP pp.32–33, D2**

TITTY TWISTER (LA TETILLA DEL DIABLO)
From Dusk till Dawn
MEXICO | FILM
This vampire bar is somewhere over the Mexican border from Texas, in sight of a mountain range and (spoilers) built on the site of an Aztec pyramid. We've placed it at the northern extreme of the Aztec empire, within sight of the Sierra Madre. **MAP pp.32–33, B3**

TREASURE ISLAND
Treasure Island
BY ROBERT LOUIS STEVENSON | BRITISH VIRGIN ISLANDS | NOVEL
Stevenson was coy about the location of his most famous creation, though it is surely in the Caribbean (the final chapter has the survivors head for Spanish America). Among a dozen contenders, Norman Island in the British Virgin Islands is most tempting, as a noted island for pirate booty. **MAP pp.32–33, F2**

SOUTH AMERICA

CITIES OF GOLD AND BANANA REPUBLICS

outh America offers many unfamiliar countries to explore. The prospective tourist might consider the silvery coast of Costaguana, wine-growing Olifa, or tropical San Theodoros. All of these nations sound beguiling, and all of them are entirely imaginary.

Take Costaguana. It hails from Joseph Conrad's *Nostromo*, a novel so highly praised that F. Scott Fitzgerald expressed the wish that he had written it himself. Loosely based on the geography of Columbia and Conrad's own experiences and travels as a sailor, Costaguana has a life, geography and a soul all its own, troubled though it may be by political instability. The port city of Sulaco may also sound familiar to film aficionados, along with Nostromo itself, for both are the names of starships that feature in the *Alien* horror franchise.

By contrast we have Olifa, setting of *The Courts of the Morning*, a ripping adventure penned by John Buchan of *The Thirty-Nine Steps* fame. Buchan provided a wealth of Scottish material for this atlas, and we were happy to also include his slightly-Peruvian nation of Olifa, gripped by tension and corruption and headed towards revolution. Although Buchan never visited South America, he had a clear vision of his setting, laying out towns, mountains, rivers and railways in so much detail that no fewer than three maps were printed within the novel to ensure readers did not get lost!

Though far removed in scope, reception and legacy, both of these narratives depict vivid countries, but also nations either torn apart or sundering. Seemingly, one of the prime uses authors in the wider world have for South America is to plant within it a corrupt regime, thus creating tension

within which their protagonists become enmeshed. San Theodoros might be considered a prime example. Created by Hergé as a setting for several of the adventures of Tintin, boy reporter, it is a nation ruled over by a series of ineffectual or corrupt military juntas, and preyed upon by foreign powers and industries, either for its natural resources or as a pawn in various proxy conflicts.

This is fiction, but sadly based on real-world history. The so-called 'banana republic' has been the template for many of popular culture's depictions of this region, all conflict-stricken, ruled over by tinpot dictators and drug barons. The fact that so much of this region's political ills are a result of foreign intervention in domestic affairs is not quite as frequently commented upon.

But there are exceptions, as we shall see ...

CHARTING THE RIVER SEA

The Amazon is easily the world's largest river, by volume at least, and perhaps no other watercourse can evoke such a sense of adventure. In myth and imagination, this is a realm of lost treasures, forgotten cities and secret tribes. Even the name 'Amazon' evokes a sense of wonder and mystery, originating as it does from a mythic race of warrior women (see the Middle East map for the location of Amazonia). Perhaps that is why we find so few fictional analogues of the Amazon River. No make-believe setting is needed when the prototype can serve just as well. Ultimately, however, we did discover several analogues, not at the expense of the Amazon itself, but of billionaire Jeff Bezos.

Bezos is the controversial founder of the internet-based retail giant Amazon. As a globally-recognized brand, parody versions exist in multiple forms of media, especially in the world of anime. Given that Bezos named his fledgling empire after the Amazon River, we thus felt justified in appending the names of parody brands such as Omozan, Mamadon and Zonama to different parts of the real-world Amazon.

UTOPIA AMONG THE SOAPS

When Thomas More first published *Utopia* in 1516, he not only created the Utopian genre, but bequeathed to the world one of the first imagined lands to be described in detail. Though written as satire – perhaps explaining why although pronounced 'Eutopia' (happy place) the name is rendered as 'Utopia' (no place) – More laid out his fictional realm with the same confidence and authority that Plato bestowed upon mythic Atlantis. But rather than evoke a realm long-drowned beneath the sea, More placed Utopia firmly in a contemporary setting. His narrator Raphael Hythlodaeus (his last name meaning 'dispenser of nonsense'), is associated with the real-life explorer Amerigo Vespucci, whose accounts of the New World ultimately led to these lands being named the 'Americas' in his honour. Thus it is that we present Utopia off the coast of Uruguay, perhaps the first great fictional locale to emerge from South America – the second, obviously, being El Dorado, city of gold!

Others followed in More's footsteps. Francis Bacon veered even closer to Plato with the title of his own vision of a future society, *New Atlantis*, which explores the island nation of Bensalem, situated west of Peru. Then political reformer Thomas Spence placed his own idealized land (humbly named *Spensonia*) as the middle island in a chain containing both Utopia and Oceana, itself a satire of England, complete with analogues for Scotland and Ireland. We'd like to suggest that this is history's first 'crossover universe', with fictions by different authors blending into one shared 'reality'.

None of these men ever experienced the New World for themselves, though we may imagine they explored their fictional additions greatly in their imaginations. Since then, however, creators both native and foreign have populated South America with all manner of fictive locales, and among the most prolific are those who write soap operas, or to give them their proper name, telenovelas. Novelas are especially popular in Brazil, and their imagined settings have become iconic enough that the shows sometimes reference one another.

A shining example must be the novella *Agora É Que São Elas*, which introduces its setting of Santana de Bocaiúvas by panning along a row of signposts denoting distances to other popular telenovela settings, such as Greenville (*A Indomada*), Porto dos Milagres (*Porto dos Milagres*), São Tomás de Trás (*Meu Bem Querer*) and Tubiacanga (*Fera Ferida*). You'll find all of these on this map, along with other delightful destinations such as the Vale do Café ('Valley of Coffee'), setting of *Orgulho e Paixão* (Pride and Passion), a high-concept narrative that transposed the canon of Jane Austen to the interior of Rio de Janeiro. Thus, in importing and transforming classic English stories to suit a New World setting, the pattern started by Thomas More with *Utopia* comes full circle.

THE CITY OF GOLD

El Dorado is, by far, South America's – if not the world's – most famous fictional city. The fabled city of gold crops up time and again across media, ranging from the adventures of Voltaire's *Candide* to a turn-of-the-millennium film from DreamWorks.

It started out as term for a person rather than city. El Dorado, meaning 'the golden one' was first applied to the king of the Muisca people (indigenous to what is now Colombia). As an offering to the gods, the ruler would cover himself in gold dust before bathing in a lake. Over the years, the king became a whole city, or kingdom, bedecked in gold – a lustrous lure for adventurers at a time when much of the continent was still uncharted.

El Dorado was never discovered, of course. It is now considered fictional. However, El Dorado has been found countless times in the pages of books and on frames of celluloid. Where should we place it on our map? The obvious, historical location would be somewhere in central Colombia, in the heartlands of the Muisca people. But popular consensus goes for somewhere farther east. El Dorado appeared on several 17th-century maps within the densely forested terrain between the Amazon and Orinoco basins. The 1656 map by French cartographer Nicolas Sanson gives us a precise location. El Dorado is due south of Trinidad, and due west of the Amazon's mouth – in the region of the town of Boa Vista. This roughly accords with a sketchy map seen in the 2000 film *The Road to El Dorado*. The lost city is found.

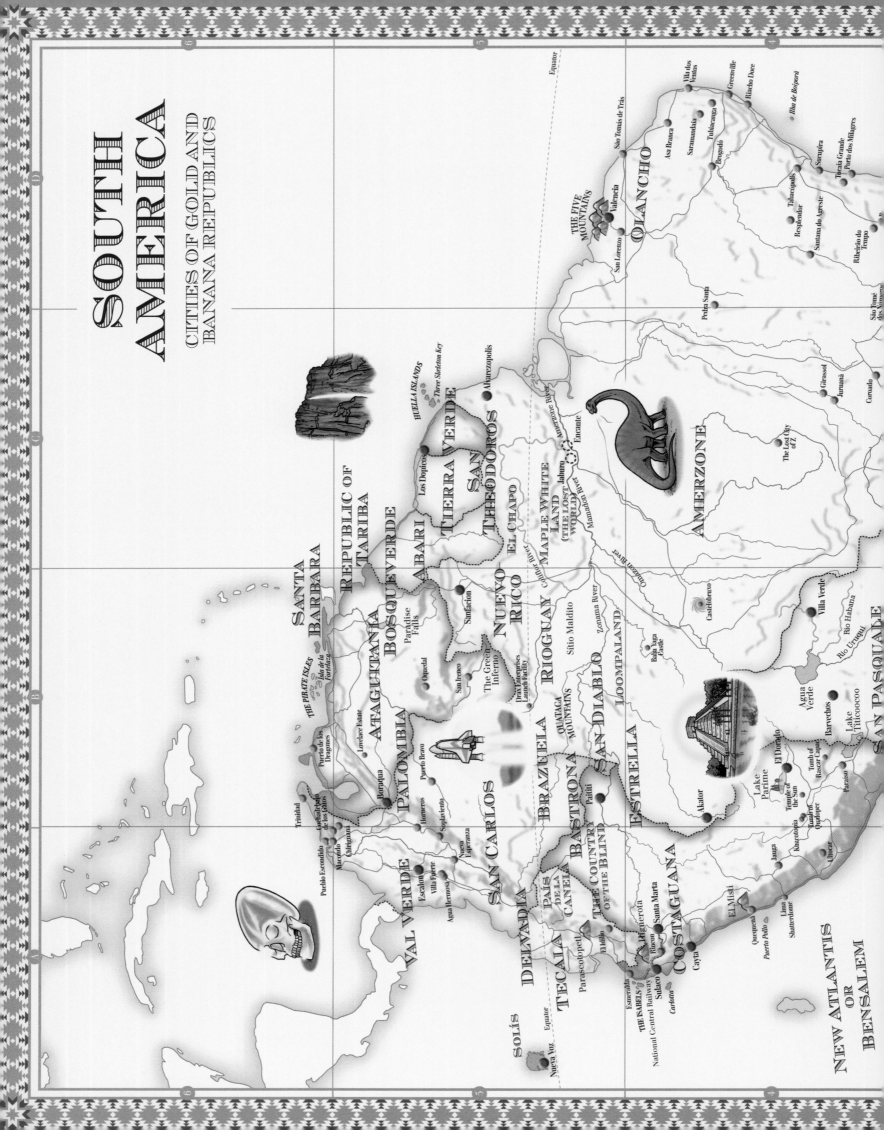

SOUTH AMERICA

CITIES OF GOLD AND BANANA REPUBLICS

SOLÍS

Nueva Voz

Equator

THE PIRATE ISLES

Isla de la Fortaleza

Puerto de los Dragones

Trinidad

Leche/Cabello de los Gatos

Macondo

Chiringuana

Pueblo Escondito

VAL VERDE

Escalon

Villa Fuerte

Agua Hermosa

Borâqua

PALOMBIA

Puerto Bravo

Horneros

Suplavienito

Nueva
Esperanza

ATAGUITANIA

Lovelace Estate

**SANTA
BARBARA**

**REPUBLIC OF
TARIBA**

BOSQUE VERDE

Paradise
Falls

Oquedal

San Ireneo

The Green
Inferno

ABARI

Sanfarion

Los Dopicos

HUELA ISLANDS

Three Skeleton Key

Alvarezopolis

TIERRA VERDE

**SAN
THEODOROS**

El Chapo

**NUEVO
RICO**

Drax Enterprises
Launch Facility

DELVADIA

TECALA

Parascolopetl

El Infilio

**PAÍS
DE LA
CANELA**

SAN CARLOS

BASTRONA

Paititi

BRAZELA

OUATACA
MOUNTAINS

RIOGUAY

Cotitur River

Jahuro

Sitio Maldito

Zonama River

SAN DIABLO

LOOMPALAND

Baia Taga
Castle

Castelobravo

AMERZONE

Amerzone River

Encante

The Lost City
of Z

Calder River

Mamadon River

Oroazon River

**THE COUNTRY
OF THE BLIND**

Esmeralda

THE ISABELS
National Central Railway

Sulaco

Carlotta

COSTAGUANA

La Higuerota

Santa Marta

Rincon

Cayta

ESTRELLA

Akator

Lake
Parime

Temple of
the Sun

El Dorado

Tomb of
Rascar Capac

Paraiso

Khazaratola

Kandrof

Oudolpec

Jauga

Litocar

El Misti

Quequerá

Puerto Pollo

Lima

Shattertiorne

Villa Verde

Rio Habana

Rio Uruqui

Agua
Verde

Barrechos

Lake
Titicoocoo

SAN PASQUALE

**NEW ATLANTIS
OR
BENSALEM**

OLANCHO

San Lorenzo

Valencia

THE FIVE
MOUNTAINS

São Tomás de Trás

Vila dos
Ventos

Greenville

Riacho Doce

Ilha de Boiporá

Asa Branca

Saramandaia

Tubiacanga

Brogodó

Tabacopolis

Sucupira

Resplendor

Santana do Agreste

Teraja Grande

Porto dos Milagres

Ribeirão do
Tempo

São Tomé
dos Alzados

Pedra Santa

Corrado

Girassol

Juruanã

Equator

SOUTH AMERICA

KEY LOCATIONS

For a full list of locations, see the location index on pages 130–150.

AKATOR
Indiana Jones and the Kingdom of the Crystal Skull BRAZIL | FILM
A legendary city located close to the Peruvian border, on a tributary of the Amazon River. The city actually conceals a massive alien spacecraft that lifts off at the climax of the film, destroying Akator. The name derives from a hoax perpetuated by German journalist Karl Brugger, who described an ancient underground city of this name somewhere in the region of Brazil/Bolivia/Peru. Akator has parallels with the equally fabled El Dorado. MAP pp.38–39, B4

ATAGUITANIA
If on a Winter's Night a Traveller BY ITALO CALVINO | NORTHERN SOUTH AMERICA | NOVEL
Fictional South American country where everyone is a revolutionary or counter-revolutionary. Location unspecified, though it has been compared to Venezuela. MAP pp.38–39, B5

BARVECHOS
GHOST RECON WILDLANDS | BOLIVIA | VIDEO GAME
Barvechos is a major city in this Ghost Recon game, and scene of a dirty bomb attack. It is one of dozens of fictional locations taken from this Tom Clancy-inspired game, all of which are vaguely located within the interior of Bolivia. We've only mapped a handful. The

Bolivian government took umbrage at the portrayal of their country in the game, so we'd like to reiterate that our map pins reflect an alternative reality Bolivia and not real cities and villages! MAP pp.38–39, B4

BORAQUA
Parks and Recreation VENEZUELA | TV
The Venezuelan sister city of Pawnee. Its location is pointed out on a globe in the episode 'Sister City', close to the real city of San Cristobal. MAP pp.38–39, B5

CARLOTTA
The Bribe / Dead Men Don't Wear Plaid PACIFIC OCEAN | FILMS
This fictitious island features in two films: in *The Bribe*, it is part of Central America, whereas in *DMDWP* it is off the coast of Peru. We've gone for a spot at the northern extremity of Peru. MAP pp.38–39, A4

CITY OF THE CAESARS
CHILE/ARGENTINA | MYTHOLOGY
An enchanted city said to lie in the mountainous border between Argentina and Chile (43 or 44 degrees south). Stories about the city take many forms, but it is often said to be only visible under certain circumstances or at certain times. MAP pp.38–39, B2

DRAX ENTERPRISES LAUNCH FACILITY
Moonraker BRAZIL | FILM
This shuttle launch facility appeared in *Moonraker*, the eleventh film in the James

Bond series. It was described as being in the upper Amazon Basin, concealed in a set of ancient ruins, and likely on or close to the Equator to maximize launch availability. MAP pp.38–39, B5

ENCANTE
BRAZIL | MYTHOLOGY
In legends this was said to be an underworld Atlantis-like paradise within or below the Amazon, inhabited by shapeshifting river dolphins that take human form to lure men and women into the river and to Encante. MAP pp.38–39, C5

ISLE ESME
Twilight: Breaking Dawn BY STEPHENIE MEYER | BRAZIL | NOVEL/FILM
A private island a short boat ride from Rio, owned by the Cullen family. It is the scene of Edward and Bella's honeymoon. MAP pp.38–39, D3

JABURO
Mobile Suit Gundam/Hellsing BRAZIL | TV/ANIME/MANGA
Jaburo first appeared in *Mobile Suit Gundam* as an underground military facility located in the heart of the Amazon Basin – a megacity serving as production facility and HQ for the Earth Federation's military. The name was homaged in the manga/anime *Hellsing* where Nazi vampire organization Millennium operates out of an underground fortress in the Brazilian rainforest identified as 'Jaburo, the Panther's Den'. We've placed it close to the similarly subterranean Encante. MAP pp.38–39, C5

KUZCOTOPIA
The Emperor's New Groove
PERU | FILM
Retreat built by Emperor Kuzco following the events of *The Emperor's New Groove*. He sites it on a hilltop near to the home of Pancha, a llama herder. A map in the film indicates Pancha lives west by south of Kuzco's main palace home, with jungle and hill between. Since a real-life Sapa Inca would have lived in Cusco, and based on aforementioned details, we estimate that Kuzco would have built Kuzcotopia somewhere in the area around real-life hamlet Kiuñalla. **MAP pp.38–39, B4**

LOVELACE ESTATE
Black Lagoon VENEZUELA | MANGA
Plantation and home of the Lovelace family, described as one of the 'thirteen great houses of South America'. Likely located somewhere near the city of Barinas: the former patriarch of the family was assassinated during a political rally in Barinas (which is also the state capital). Suspects for the killing went to ground in Calabozo, and someone from the estate was able to reach Calabozo and torture/kill five of them (individually) for information within a day, then moved on to the next suspect in Caracas, suggesting a west-east path from Barinas to Caracas via Calabozo. This general location is also supported by the fact that a former Columbian soldier and family friend took shelter at the Lovelace Estate after an escape through 'the mountains' – the Cordillera de Merida Mountains do indeed extend from the Colombian border up past Barinas. **MAP pp.38–39, B5**

LOOMPALAND
Charlie and the Chocolate Factory BY ROALD DAHL |
BRAZIL | NOVEL/FILMS
Home of the Oompa Loompas. A few hints on the location of Loompaland are given. It is full of thick, dangerous jungles where cocoa beans grow. This suggests a Mesoamerican location, possibly in the Amazon Basin. Dahl mentions that the Oompa Loompas use eucalyptus leaves to flavour food. Although Australian, eucalypts were introduced to Brazil in 1910 for timber purposes and thrived, further reinforcing a location in the Amazon. **MAP pp.38–39, B5**

MACONDO
One Hundred Years of Solitude
BY GABRIEL GARCÍA MÁRQUEZ |
COLOMBIA | NOVEL
Macondo is most famous from *One Hundred Years*, but appears in several of Márquez's stories (and, indeed, stories by others). It is based on his childhood town of Aracataca. In 2006, the town held an unsuccessful referendum to change its name to Macondo. **MAP pp.38–39, A5/A6**

MAPLE WHITE LAND *The Lost World*
BY ARTHUR CONAN DOYLE |
BRAZIL | NOVEL
This dinosaur-boasting setting is thought to be inspired by Huanchaca Plateau in Bolivia (which contains zero dinosaurs). However, readily available fan maps online suggest a location north of the main flow of the Amazon. **MAP pp.38–39, C5**

PAITITI
Tad: The Lost Explorer
PERU | FILM
Paititi was a fabled lost city of the Incas, not dissimilar to the more famous El Dorado. Some evidence suggests that it may have genuinely existed but remains hidden in some overlooked region of the Amazon. It may be considered slightly less 'fictional' than most of the other entries in this atlas. We've included it because a version appears in at least two works of fiction: the first *Tad* film, and the 2018 video game *Shadow of the Tomb Raider*. Various locations have been proposed for the lost city, but the most common theory is that it was somewhere in the Peruvian Amazon. **MAP pp.38–39, B5**

QUEQUENÂ
Ripping Yarns PERU | TV
Sleepy Peruvean town whose local population are more interested in the 1927 FA Cup Final (Arsenal v. Cardiff City) than explorer Walter Snetterton's doomed efforts to prove frogs capable of crossing high mountain ranges – apparently Cup Night is 'the biggest celebration of the year' in this part of the world. Although a slightly-nonsensical map within the episode puts Quequenâ to the east of the Andes, Snetteron's efforts to cross the mountains and push onwards to Brazil confirms a westerly location. Overlooking the town is the equally-fictional (and also-mapped) volcano of El Misti. Oh, and by the way, Cardiff won one-nil. **MAP pp.38–39, A4**

SAN CARLOS
Delta Force 2: The Colombian Connection NORTH-EASTERN
SOUTH AMERICA | FILM
A fictional country in which the film takes place, San Carlos is presumably an analogue of Colombia because, despite having the name Colombia in the title, not a single mention of that country is made in the whole film. **MAP pp.38–39, A5/B5**

TEMPLE OF THE SUN *The Adventures of Tintin* BY HERGÉ | PERU | COMIC
Surviving enclave of the Inca civilization. Reached by a trail starting in (real-world) Jauga which over the course of several days crosses a high mountain range before descending into a belt of jungle. A further three days' travel brings Tintin, Captain Haddock and guide Zorrino to a second mountain range, among whose peaks the Temple is secreted. This implies an east-southeast journey across the Cordillera Occidental Mountains and a southward projection of the Amazon basin. If we're right, the Temple would lie just south of the border between Peru's Madre de Dios and Cusco Departments, within an outlying spur of the Cordillera Occidentals. **MAP pp.38–39, B4**

UTOPIA
Utopia BY THOMAS MORE |
ATLANTIC OCEAN | NOVEL/PARABLE
More's Utopia is one of the earliest fictional lands to be conceived in detail. Its location is never revealed, other than that it lies in the New World, beyond 'New Castille' – a region of South America that extended south to areas like Rio. Maps of Utopia traditionally place the island south of a mainland that runs east–west, cut off by a small channel of water. We've chosen a stretch of coast to the south of Uruguay in the south-west of South America. The unusual shape of the island is a modern interpretation, deduced by Andrew Simoson, a mathematician at King University in Bristol, Tennessee, who decoded mathematical clues in More's text. In truth, we're on something of a fool's errand mapping Utopia. The name means 'no place' in Greek while, as mentioned on page 37, the surname of the protagonist, Hythlodaeus, means 'dispenser of nonsense'. Even More's derived name of Morus is similar to the Greek word for fool. **MAP pp.38–39, C2**

VAL VERDE
NORTH-EASTERN SOUTH AMERICA | FILMS
Fictional state that for a time was used in Hollywood movies in place of real countries around the border between Central and South America. It first appeared in *Commando* where creator Steven de Souza likened it to Guyana. It has since moved around a bit. We've placed it where South and Central America meet. This suits the name 'Val Verde' (Green Valley) since the geography of the border region of Columbia is dominated by the Rio Atrato. **MAP pp.38–39, A5**

WESTERN EUROPE

THE OLD COUNTRIES

sk someone to name a place in Europe and they may cite romantic Paris, or historic Rome, or the sun-kissed beaches of the Mediterranean. Ask that same person to name an *imagined* place in Europe, and a very different landscape might spring to mind: the dark forests of *Grimm's Fairy Tales*, sinister schlosses such as the castles Wolfenstein or Frankenstein, and the mountainous kingdom of Vulgaria, home of the dreaded Child Catcher!

Yes, the densest grouping of fictional locations we found in Western Europe is a cluster around the Alps, many of which come from stories with a macabre twist. This shadowy side to the Europe of imagination contrasts with the region's more celebrated heritage as a centre of sophisticated culture.

Yet there is joy, delight and innocence here too. In Belgium we might discover Tintin and Captain Haddock in residence at charming Moulinsart (not to be confused with Marlinspike, its Anglicized counterpart), or join the animated Parisian adventures of *Miraculous Ladybug* and *Code Lyok*o. And somewhere in Armorica (what is today called Brittany) we still find that last redoubt against the Roman Empire, the village of Asterix the Gaul.

Even the Alps, redolent of Teutonic gloom and solemnity, can raise a smile or two. Consider the delightful Spaghetti Harvests of Switzerland (an old British TV joke), the antics of the tiny wine-producing Duchy of Grand Fenwick (*The Mouse That Roared*), and the delicious wordplay of locales such as Switzerloan or Thermostadt. But the sinister twist is never far away. Witness Pinocchio's adventures in the Land of Toys – a Tuscan utopia that turns out to be a trap for children. Or even the whimsical village of Asterix which, it turns out, is but a menhir's throw away from Ramelle, the tragic town from the climax of *Saving Private Ryan*.

Perhaps the biggest surprise in Europe, home of so many Old Countries, is how modern its fictional topography reads. When we set out to catalogue its geography, we expected the map to be crowded with villages from classical fiction. Not so. Literary titans such as Alexandre Dumas and Victor Hugo seemed determined to keep it real, with very few make-believe locations gracing their tales – perhaps it was considered gauche to add fictional varnish to a landscape already so rich with inspiration. That said, the greats did lend us some aid, thus Charlotte Brontë's Villette, Flaubert's Yonville-l'Abbaye and Voltaire's unforgettable (and unpronounceable) Waldberghoff-trarbk-dikdorff are all mapped here, alongside locations from the likes of Cervantes, Proust and even Winston Churchill.

We found far more locations from modern film, TV and video games. Europe, it seems, has become something of a playground. Fictional Brits flock to make-believe resorts on the Med. All-American heroines marry into the royal houses of Monaco-like principalities, such as Genovia and Cordinia. France is over-run with Pokémon, while Paris has been colonized by fantasy theme parks.

But the old Europe lurks in the background. The original fairy-tale castles still flourish in the German foothills. Homeric heroes patrol the Mediterranean. Even Jurassic Europe makes an appearance in the shape of George the Volcano. This is a continent that forever reinvents itself.

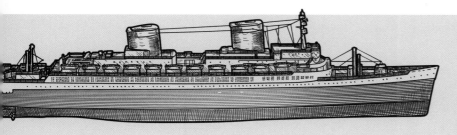

MAYDAY! MAYDAY! THIS IS SS POSEIDON

Of all the versions of *The Poseidon Adventure*, the most famous must surely be the 1972 film, having eclipsed Paul Gallico's original 1969 novel. That film saw the ill-fated vessel en route to the breaker's yard in Greece, only to be capsized by a tidal wave triggered by an undersea earthquake near Crete. This would suggest that *Poseidon* sank in the Aegean Sea, but a closer viewing of the film says otherwise. The ship's troupe of singers are described as providing music in exchange for free passage from Gibraltar to Sicily, and survivors are ultimately rescued by the French Coastguard. With this evidence in mind, we've placed the wreck of the *Poseidon* in the western Mediterranean, and reasoned that although far distant from Crete, the old liner was unlucky enough to meet the submarine shockwave in shallow waters, where it piled up into the freak wave that doomed her.

COSTA WHATTA?

Ever since Beelzebub invented the package holiday, holidaymakers worldwide have braved airport security to enjoy the summer sunshine (and booze) of the Spanish Riviera, be their destination the Costa Brava, the Costa del Sol, or the Costa Plonka ... yes, you read that right.

The region has inevitably become the subject of affectionate parody, especially in Britain. Among the first to poke fun at the package holiday phenomenon were the *Carry On* gang, who brought their raunchy humour to the inglorious Costa Bomm in 1972's *Carry On Abroad*. Sadly for the disappointed cast, the fictional island resort of Elsbels would not be shot in sunny Spain, but a car park at the back of Pinewood Studios. Similar budget-saving methods also occurred when the cast of classic television series *Are You Being Served?* took to the big screen in 1977, the premises of Elstree Studios doubling for the delightfully-named Costa Plonka.

Of course, the only thing cheaper than shooting on a backlot is to shoot nothing at all, as perfected by the classic Australian video game *Terrormolinos*. A text adventure from the days of the Commodore 64, *Terrormolinos* sent players on a package holiday whose beautiful vistas existed solely as words on a screen.

Appropriately enough, it was the Australian template of sun-soaked ensemble dramas that inspired what might be the most genuine attempt to bring Spain into Britain's homes, an effort that also proved the biggest flop. In the early 1990s the BBC bankrolled a short-lived series named *Eldorado*, a television soap revolving around the lives of various European expatriates living on the fictional Costa Eldorado. At massive cost a complete town was built on location in the Costa del Sol to portray the community of Los Barcos, and though *Eldorado* itself was cancelled after a single series, the massive set still stands. Britain's affection for the Spanish coast has added a permanent fictional landmark to the genuine article.

DISNEY DINING

Where does one go for the finest in fictional cuisine? Well, in the Paris of Disney-Pixar's *Ratatouille*, you might avail yourself of Gusteau's, the 3- (formerly 5-) star restaurant of the late chef Auguste Gusteau. But where is it?

An envelope in a crucial scene reveals the restaurant's full address as '3 Place Augustine, Paris, 75005'. The Place Augustine is fictional, but the real area code narrows it down to the 5th arrondissement. And here, on the left bank of the River Seine we may find the Tour D'Argent, a world-famous restaurant whose exterior bears a remarkable similarity to that of Gusteau's.

If your budget runs a little more modest, you might instead choose to sample the delights of 'La Ratatouille', the bistro ultimately opened by the film's protagonists. The final shot places this thriving establishment on a hillside looking westwards towards the Eiffel Tower and the setting sun. Guided by these clues, we suggest searching among the streets of Montagne Saint-Geneviève, also located within the 5th arrondissement, and well-known for both a lively culture and many excellent bistros ... as the French might say, 'Le voilà!'

A COPYRIGHT NIGHTMARE IN WISBORG

Bram Stoker might have defined pop-culture vampirism in his classic *Dracula*, but many of the tropes now associated with these undead icons have a slightly more convoluted origin. In 1922, auteur German filmmaker F.W. Murnau released his celebrated classic *Nosferatu*, an unlicensed adaptation of Stoker's text that starred Max Shreck as the inhuman Count Orlok. Among Murnau's adaptive embellishments was the concept that sunlight is fatal to vampires, with Orlok meeting his destruction by daylight. Alas, film is also vulnerable to sunlight. Upon *Nosferatu's* release, Stoker's estate successfully took Murnau to court for his infringement of copyright, with the ultimate ruling that all copies of the film should be destroyed. Thankfully some prints survived, allowing Murnau's film to cement its legacy as a classic – and viewers to continue to be chilled and thrilled as Max Shreck's monstrous Orlok plagues the streets of Wisborg, a fictional German port which we've equated with Hamburg.

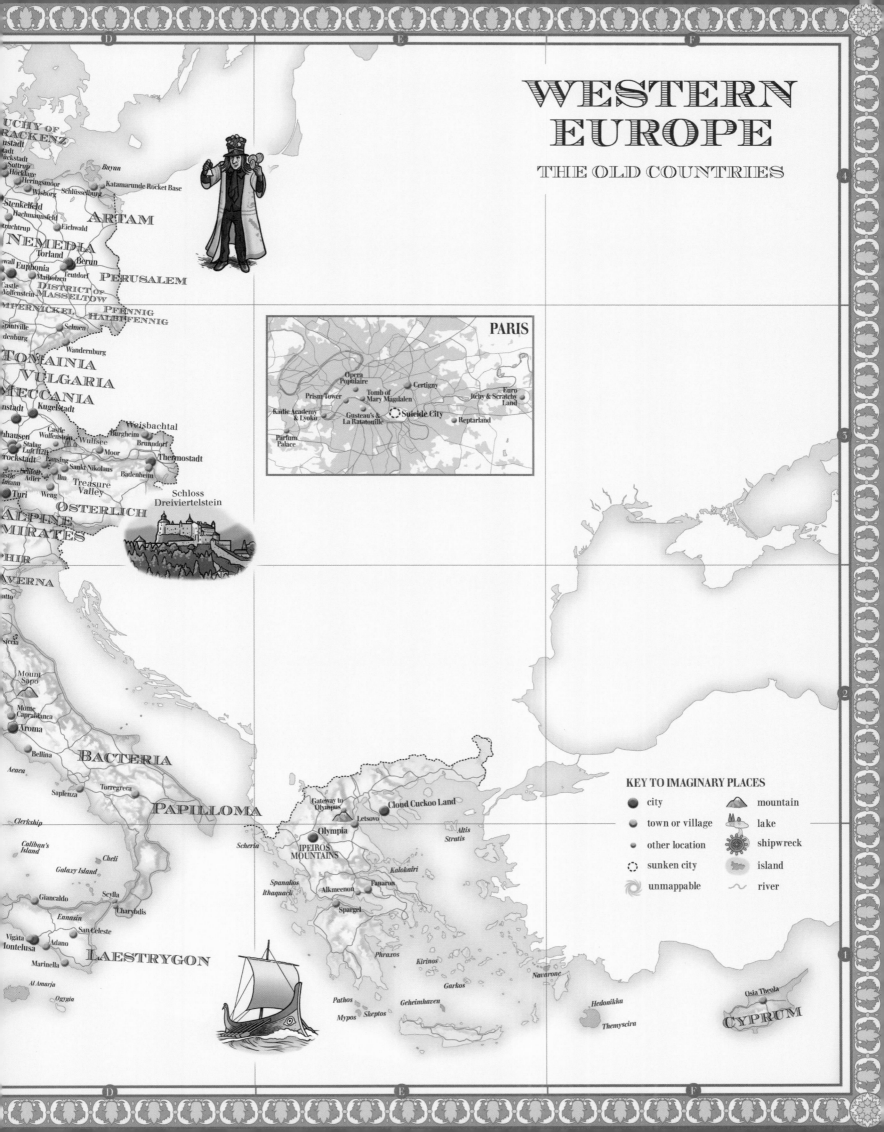

WESTERN EUROPE
THE OLD COUNTRIES

PARIS

- Opera Populaire
- Prism Tower
- Kadic Academy & Lyoko
- Parfum Palace
- Tomb of Mary Magdalen
- Gusteau's & La Ratatouille
- Certigny
- Suicide City
- Itchy & Scratchy Land
- Euro Reptarland

DUCHY OF BRACKENZ
ustadt
rückstadt
Sottrup
Höcklage
Heringsmoor
Wisborg
Schlüsselburg
Buyan
Katamarunde Rocket Base
Stenkelfeld
Hachmannsfeld
bruchtrup
Eichwald
ARTAM
NEMEDIA
Torland
Berun
wall Euphonia
Maihölzen
Mailbolzen
Teutdorf
PERUSALEM
Castle
Wollenstein
DISTRICT OF MASSELTOW
MITTERNICKEL
PFENNIG
HALBPFENNIG
grantville
denburg
Selmen
Wandernburg
TONAINIA
VULGARIA
MECCANIA
nstadt
Kugelstadt
Weisbachtal
Castle
Wolfenstein
Burgheim
Wulfsee
Moor
Bruandorf
thhausen
Stalag
Luft Izit
Fansing
Sankt Nikolaus
Thermostadt
Badenheim
rockstadt
hloss
Adler
Ilm
Erann
Turi
Weng
Treasure Valley
ÖSTERLICH
Schloss Dreiviertelstein
ALPINE MIRATES
THIR
AVERNA
atto
siccia
Mount Sapo
Mome Caprabianca
Aroma
Bellina
BACTERIA
Acaea
Sapienza
Torregreca
PAPILLOMA
Clerkship
Caliban's Island
Cheli
Galaxy Island
Giancaldo
Scylla
Charybdis
Ennasin
San Celeste
Vigàta
Montelusa
Adano
LAESTRYGON
Marinella
Al Amarja
Ogygia
Scheria
Spanakos
Ithaquack
Alkmeenon
Spargel
Gateway to Olympus
Olympia
IPEIROS MOUNTAINS
Letsovo
Cloud Cuckoo Land
Altis Stratis
Kalokairi
Fanaron
Pathos
Mypos
Skeptos
Phraxos
Kirinos
Garkos
Geheimhaven
Navarone
Hedonikka
Themyscira
Osia Theola
CYPRUM

KEY TO IMAGINARY PLACES

- city
- town or village
- other location
- sunken city
- unmappable
- mountain
- lake
- shipwreck
- island
- river

WESTERN EUROPE

KEY LOCATIONS

For a full list of locations, see the location index on pages 130–150.

ALTIS *ARMA 3*
GREECE | VIDEO GAME
Inspired by the island of Lemnos. Indeed, staff working for the developer were arrested for spying while on a fact-finding mission to the island. **MAP pp.44–45, E1**

ASTERIX'S VILLAGE
Asterix the Gaul **BY RENÉ GOSCINNY AND ALBERT UDERZO | FRANCE | COMICS, TV, FILMS**
Asterix's village is never named, but is such an important fictional location, we had to include it. Official maps place it near what is now Cherbourg. It is surrounded by the four fictional Roman camps of Aquarium, Totorum, Laudanum and Compendium (not shown). **MAP pp.44–45, B3**

BALBEC *In Search of Lost Time* **BY MARCEL PROUST | FRANCE | NOVEL**
Normandy resort town, inspired by and set in the same location as real-world Cabourg. The fictional Forest of Chantepie (not shown) is nearby. **MAP pp.44–45, C3**

BARATARIA
Don Quixote **BY CERVANTES | MEDITERRANEAN SEA | NOVEL**
This 'island' is the only one in the world surrounded by land rather than water, which is a puzzling one to map. However,
a kingdom of the same name is also a setting for *The Gondoliers* by Gilbert and Sullivan. Its inhabitants have Italian-sounding names, so a location between Spain and Italy seemed appropriate. **MAP pp.44–45, C2**

BEAUXBATONS ACADEMY *Harry Potter stories* **BY J.K. ROWLING | FRANCE | NOVELS/FILMS**
An academy for witches, thought to be in the Pyrenees. Like the better-known Hogwarts, it is protected by spells, making its true location unmappable. **MAP pp.44–45, B2**

BUYAN *Russian folklore*
GERMANY | FOLKLORE
A mysterious island with the ability to appear and disappear, which occurs in numerous Russian texts. As with many lands from folklore, its location is nebulous, but some scholars have equated it to the real island of Rügen. **MAP pp.44–45, D4**

CALIBAN'S ISLAND
The Tempest
BY WILLIAM SHAKESPEARE | MEDITERRANEAN SEA | PLAY
Perhaps the most famous fictional location from the pen of William Shakespeare, the island of *The Tempest* is unnamed, so could equally be listed as Prospero's Island. Its location is uncertain, though presumably somewhere between Tunis and Naples. **MAP pp.44–45, D1**

CASTLE FRANKENSTEIN
Frankenstein **BY MARY SHELLEY | SWITZERLAND | VARIOUS**
There is a real Castle Frankenstein in Germany, but the protagonist of Shelley's novel is Swiss. The original text makes no mention of an ancestral castle ('We possessed a house in Geneva, and a campagne on Belrive, the eastern shore of the lake, at the distance of rather more than a league from the city'). Later iterations of the tale, however, introduced the stormy castle of pop-culture, with various locations. The 1931 film cites the Bavarian Alps, whereas *Young Frankenstein* places events in Transylvania. However, Marvel Comics attributed their version of Castle Frankenstein to the original novel's native Geneva. We think a similar location would be the happiest marriage of this diverse range of sources. **MAP pp.44–45, C3**

CASTLE WOLFENSTEIN
Castle Wolfenstein **SERIES | GERMANY | VIDEO GAMES**
Originally said to be located in the northern German Harz mountains, but in later iterations of the franchise reimagined to the Bavarian Alps. **MAP pp.44–45, D4**

CHATEAU PICARD
Star Trek: The Next Generation **FRANCE | TV**
Jean-Luc Picard's family vineyard.

Located near the village of La Barre, in the department of Haute-Saône. **MAP pp.44–45, C3**

CLOUD CUCKOO LAND *The Birds* BY

ARISTOPHANES | GREECE | MYTH/LEGEND
One of the oldest fictions in the book, Aristophanes invented Cloud Cuckoo Land in 414 BCE. It's built above the plain of Phlegra in Greece. **MAP pp.44–45, E2**

COMBRAY *In Search of Lost Time* BY MARCEL PROUST |

FRANCE | NOVEL
Heavily inspired by the village of Illiers, where Proust spent his childhood. It has since been renamed Illiers-Combray in tribute – a rare example of a location being renamed to match a fictional counterpart. **MAP pp.44–45, C3**

EUPHONIA
Les Soirées de l'Orchestre
BY HECTOR BERLIOZ | GERMANY | SATIRE
A fictional city in the Harz mountains invented by Romantic composer Berlioz. It is populated entirely with musicians, and set in the far future. **MAP pp.44–45, D4**

GEHEIMHAVEN
Raiders of the Lost Ark
AEGEAN SEA | FILM
Secret Nazi island base from the climax of the film, located in the Aegean Sea north of Crete. **MAP pp.44–45, E1**

GENOVIA *The Princess Diaries* BY MEG CABOT | FRENCH/

ITALIAN BORDER | NOVEL/FILM
In the novel this fictional principality is clearly inspired by Monaco and set on the border between France and Italy. The film version instead opts for the France-Spain border in analogue with Andorra. We've mapped it there. **MAP pp.44–45, C2**

GEORGE THE VOLCANO

VOLVIC MINERAL WATER | FRANCE | ADVERTISING
The living volcano from the Volvic adverts in the 2000s is presumably a fictionalized version of Puy de Dôme, the volcano adjacent to the spring from which Volvic is sourced. Since the campaign also features a tyrannosaurus, strictly speaking it's set several million years before Puy de Dôme formed, but the pterodactyls in one of the ads do have French accents, so the extreme anachronism can probably be chalked up to artistic licence. **MAP pp.44–45, C3**

GIBRALTAR BRIDGE
SPAIN | VARIOUS
A vast bridge spanning the Strait of Gibraltar has long been a dream of engineers in real life, but it has also featured in many works of fiction. Examples include a suspension bridge in *Wolfenstein* (video game), built in 1957 as a military project, and in the novel *The Fountains of Paradise* by Arthur C. Clarke. **MAP pp.44–45, A1**

(DUCHY OF) GRAND FENWICK *The Mouse that Roared* BY LEONARD WIBBERLEY |

NORTHERN ALPS | NOVEL
A tiny duchy in the Northern Alps, bordering Switzerland and France. Internal evidence points to a location in the Franche-Comté region of eastern France, near (or on top of) Les Gras. **MAP pp.44–45, C3**

LAND OF TOYS
Pinocchio **ITALY | NOVEL/FILMS**
Seemingly a magical haven for children, the Land of Toys turns out to be a trap, where boys and girls are turned into donkeys. The original novel (one of the best-selling children's stories of all time, beating most of the *Harry Potter* novels) suggests it is in Tuscany. Most adaptations, including the Disney film, place it on an island. It is also known as Pleasure Island and The Land Where Dreams Come True. **MAP pp.44–45, C2**

LANSQUENET-SOUS-TANNES *Chocolat* BY JOANNE

HARRIS | FRANCE | NOVEL/FILM
The village is in the Gers region and described as 'a blip on the fast road between Toulouse and Bordeaux'. It is on the River Tannes, a fictional tributary of the Garonne. **MAP pp.44–45, B2/B3**

MARINELLA *Inspector Montalbano novels* BY ANDREA

CAMILLERI | ITALY | NOVELS/TV
The Sicilian seaside village where Inspector Montalbano lives is actually Punta Secca. **MAP pp.44–45, D1**

METROPOLIS
Metropolis **GERMANY | FILM**
Though inspired by New York in the early skyscraper years, Fritz Lang's *Metropolis* is presumably set in Germany, given the character names. The industrial Ruhr valley makes as good a setting as any for the future 'machine city' of Metropolis. **MAP pp.44–45, C4**

MOUNT SAPO
ITALY | MYTH/LEGEND
A mountain near Rome. Supposed location of the invention of soap. **MAP pp.44–45, D2**

PANORAMA SPAGHETTI FARM
Panorama **SWITZERLAND | TV**
From the infamous 1957 April Fool's episode of BBC documentary series *Panorama*, which documented the annual 'Spaghetti Harvest' at a farming community overlooking Lake Lugano in the canton of Ticino, on the borders of Switzerland and Italy. **MAP pp.44–45, C3**

POICTESME *Novels of James Branch Cavell*

MEDITERRANEAN REGION | NOVELS
Maps of this fictional country have been made, but bear no resemblance to real geography. It is said to be a small country bordering Provence, yet has a west coast. The name is reminiscent of Poitiers and Angoulesme (the medieval spelling of Angoulême), and so we have placed it in this region. The fantasy kingdom contains many towns and castles, which are not mapped here. **MAP pp.44–45, B3**

SCYLLA AND CHARYBDIS
HOMER'S *The Odyssey*
ITALY | MYTH/LEGEND
We haven't included everything from Homer's *Odyssey* – many locations are of uncertain location, or difficult to pin as real or fictional. Not so Scylla and Charybdis, the first a six-headed sea monster, the second a whirlpool (though regarded as a monster). The twin shipping hazards are located in the Strait of Messina. To this day, people choosing between two difficult courses are described as 'between Scylla and Charybdis'. **MAP pp.44–45, D1**

THEMYSCIRA
Wonder Woman **AEGEAN OR EASTERN MEDITERRANEAN |**
COMICS/FILM/TV
Island home of DC Comics' Amazons. In the live-action *Wonder Woman* film, Steve Trevor crashes (in a short-ranged biplane) on the island after escaping a military base situated somewhere in Turkey, suggesting a location either in the waters of the Aegean or Eastern Mediterranean. Themyscira was also the capital city of Amazonia, a fictional province in Asia Minor in Greek Mythology (see page 74) and a source of inspiration for *Wonder Woman*'s homeland. **MAP pp.44–45, F1**

EASTERN EUROPE

SCIENCE AND SORCERY, SHTETLS AND SOVIETS

The impression I had was that we were leaving the West and entering the East ...', writes Bram Stoker's Jonathan Harker upon his departure from Budapest for Transylvania, there to meet with the region's most notorious denizen, the immortal Count Dracula. Viewed from a Westerner's perspective, this is Europe's hinterland, a liminal region where peoples have mingled and clashed for centuries, producing a wealth of tradition and culture, but also violence and persecution. This strategic border territory has a long history of assimilation into entities such as the Austro-Hungarian Empire or the Soviet Union, subdividing back into smaller polities once the centre of power can no longer hold on. The same refrains repeat throughout fiction as well; we've found dozens of make-believe countries carved out between the cracks, and they dominate the map.

Depictions of Eastern Europe also tend towards extremes. At one end there is the quaint, almost fairy-tale view presented in the *Ruritania* novels of Anthony Hope, a land of peasantry and pageantry, of medieval fortresses, damsels in distress and political reverses triggered by mistaken identity. Not many people read Hope nowadays, but the Ruritanian adventure is more popular than ever. How many Hollywood films have seen an all-American girl swept off her feet by a mysterious prince from an obscure European nation? Many, is the answer, and they're all on this map. But every light casts a shade, and the other fictional extreme fills these steppes, mountains and forests with shadows both mundane and supernatural.

A MOST SINISTER ZONE

Dracula's not the only fiend to have made his home in the Carpathian Mountains. There's something about this patch of land that makes it particularly appealing to the psychotic and strange. As Jonathan Harker notes in his journal, 'Every known superstition in the world is gathered into the Carpathians, as if it were the centre of some sort of imaginative whirlpool.' Fitting then that Hungarian author Ádám Bodor dubbed this land *The Sinistra Zone*.

Indeed, in the world of *Ghostbusters*, the entire Carpathian region was once ruled by despotic magician Vigo Von Homburg Deutschendorf – until his subjects rebelled and subjected him to a fittingly unholy death: poisoned, shot, stabbed, hung, stretched, disembowelled, drawn and quartered (ouch!).

It's not all bad though, and some of the locals are downright welcoming. Count Duckula of Castle Duckula is himself an avowed vegetarian, and if the word-of-mouth is to be believed, even old Drac' himself has gone into the hospitality business, throwing open the doors of *Hotel Transylvania* to men and monsters alike.

UNTANGLED THREADS

Before *Frozen* and *Moana*, there was *Tangled*. This 2010 take on *Rapunzel* paved the way for modern fables starring not-so-distressed damsels. Rather than passively awaiting rescue from her tower, Disney's Rapunzel is an empowered young woman who ultimately leaves to discover her own destiny. But unlike *Frozen*, whose Arendelle is firmly set in Norway, the geography of Rapunzel's homeland is less clear.

A major clue lies in the onion-domed turrets of the kingdom's castle. A classical flourish of Eastern European architecture, these were intentionally chosen by the filmmakers to distinguish *Tangled's* setting from the more 'Western' fairy-tale castles of past Disney princesses. With that clarified, a close viewing of the film quickly suggests a location: the capital is a port, and a map in the end credits shows it facing northward out to sea, with hilly woodlands behind. We can also assume a location fairly close to Scandinavia, since Rapunzel and her beau, Eugene cameo in *Frozen* as guests at Elsa's coronation.

Thus, we've placed Rapunzel's homeland on Poland's Baltic coast. Oh, and its name? Prophetically for this ultimate tale of self-isolation, the film-makers chose to dub it the Kingdom of Corona.

AMONG THE LANTZMEN

The Yiddish word 'lantzman' denotes a very specific kind of Jewish individual, sometimes a countryman or a man respected for his knowledge of the Torah, but usually a native of the speaker's own community or *shtetl*.

It is also the name of the SS *Lantzman*, a steamship which, in 1886, brought one of pop culture's most famous immigrants (almost) all the way to the shores of the New World. That immigrant was *An American Tail's* Fievel Mousekewitz, a young mouse who no doubt knew many lantzmen growing up in his native Shostka, Ukraine. He's one of many Jews (real or imagined) who trace roots back to this region. Fiction has peppered Poland, Lithuania and the Ukraine with imagined shtetls, be they comic communities such as Sholem Aleichem's beloved Anatevka (*Fiddler on the Roof*) and Kasrilevke, or the slightly fairy-tale town of Helmsburgville, setting of *Hershel and the Hanukkah Goblins*.

But Jewish history is frequently tragic, and fiction does not pull its punches. Just as Fievel and his family fled Europe to escape the Cossacks (and their cats), many of these fictional towns reflect a brutal history. Gurówka, setting of the Polish-language film *Aftermath* is one such example. Inspired by real events, this town conceals a dark secret, the population having conspired to murder their Jewish neighbours during the German occupation. Likewise, it was personal experience of the Holocaust that inspired writer Elie Wiesel to pen *The Trial of God*, where the surviving Jews of the 17th-century town of Shamgorod place the Creator on trial for allowing His chosen people to be slaughtered in a recent pogrom.

Seventies disaster-flick *The Cassandra Crossing* presents us with Janov, a former concentration camp repurposed as a quarantine centre for the victims of a plague spread aboard a transcontinental express. Except Janov is never reached. The titular Cassandra Crossing (a long-disused railway bridge) collapses under the weight of the diverted train, sending half of its complement to a ghastly death. The film does not shy away from the grim historical parallel, depicting frightened passengers held under armed guard aboard a sealed train, bound for their own destruction.

And yet, for all this historical pain, many Jewish writers and their creations experience a deep yearning for Eastern Europe. Lisa Pearl Rosenbaum's *A Day of Small Beginnings* and its fictional town of Zokof were inspired by a lost sense of history after her family emigrated to America. Likewise, the protagonist of Boris Zaidman's *Hemingway and the Dead-Bird Rain*, although a naturalized Israeli, feels a deep nostalgia for his childhood home in Soviet Ukraine. While flying from Tel Aviv to Zaidman's imagined city of Dnestrograd, he notes his fellow passengers reverting to speaking Russian during the flight, as if symbolically going home ... Perhaps you can take the lantzman out of the shtetl, but never the shtetl out of the lantzman.

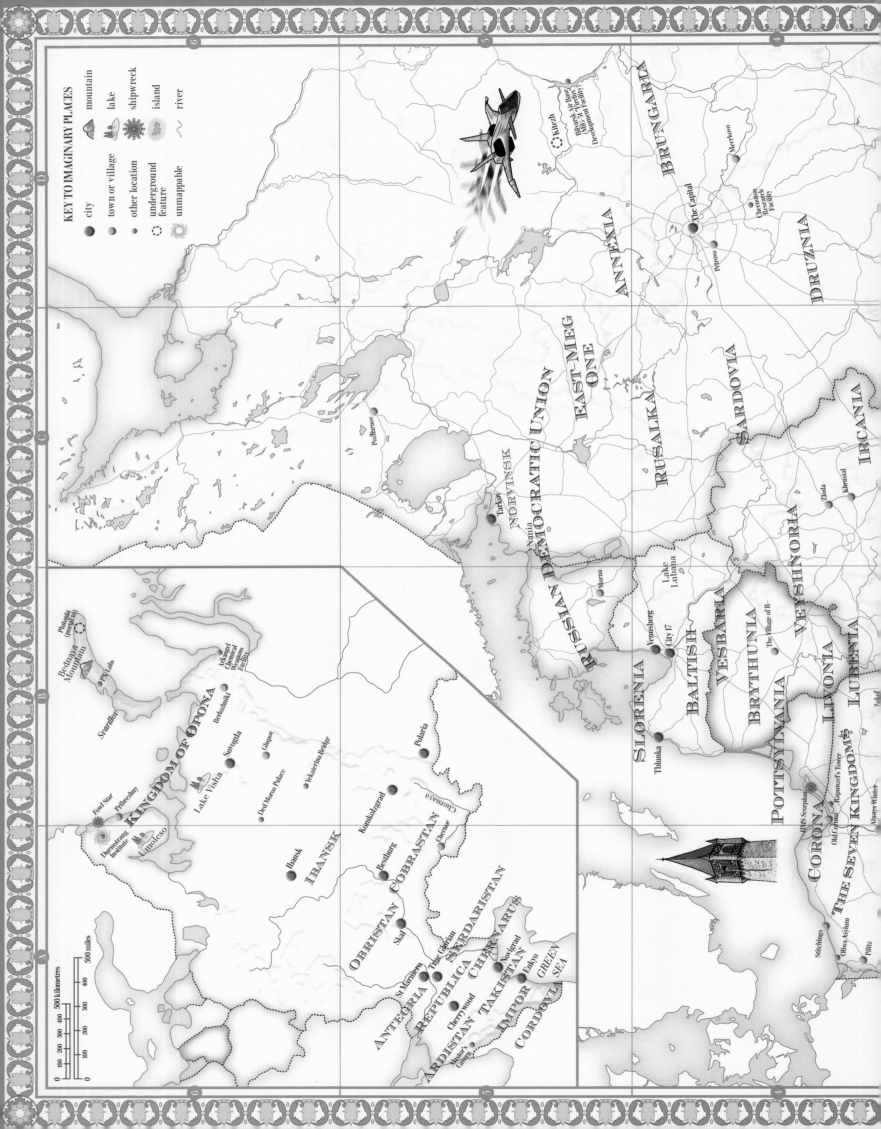

KEY TO IMAGINARY PLACES

- ● city
- ● town or village
- · other location
- ⌾ underground feature
- ◠ mountain
- ⩙ lake
- ✺ shipwreck
- ▨ island
- ～ river
- 🌀 unmappable

Phantja (portal to)

Bezinga Mountain

Svardlov

PV Labs

Fowl Star

Pribrezhny

Durmstrang Institute

Limoleso

KINGDOM OF OPONA

Arkanged Chemical Weapons Facility

Berlozhniki

Lake Vishta

Sovogda

Ghupet

Ded Moroz Palace

Icekaterina Bridge

Pularia

Komkolzgrad

Chernaya

Chernoe

Ibansk

IBANSK

Bestburg

COBRASTAN

OBRISTAN

Skal

SERDARISTAN

St Marmero

Tigu Glevian

ANTEGRIA

REPUBLICA

Cherrywood

Nestor's Canopy

ARDISTAN

TAKISTAN

CHERNARUS

Novigrad

Enkyo

IMPOR

CORDOVIA

GREEN SEA

PuzHarnov

Tarkov

NORVINSK

Vania

RUSSIAN DEMOCRATIC UNION

EAST-MEG ONE

ANNEXIA

Kitezh

Bisark Air Base (MiG-31 "Firefox" Development Facility)

BRUNGARIA

Meerkovo

The Capital

Petrovo

Chernobog Research Facility

DRUZNIA

RUSALKA

SARDOVIA

IRCANIA

Narnia

Lake Lubana

Venisberg

City 17

Tllunka

SLORENIA

BALTISH

VESBARIA

BRYTHUNIA

The Village of B—

VEYSHNORIA

Zloda

Khrestal

LIVONIA

POTTSYLVANIA

LUBENIA

Zdal

CORONA

Old Cafrad

Rapunzel's Tower

Altears Winter

HMS Scorpion

THE SEVEN KINGDOMS

Stitchings

Oliwa Asylum

Plitz

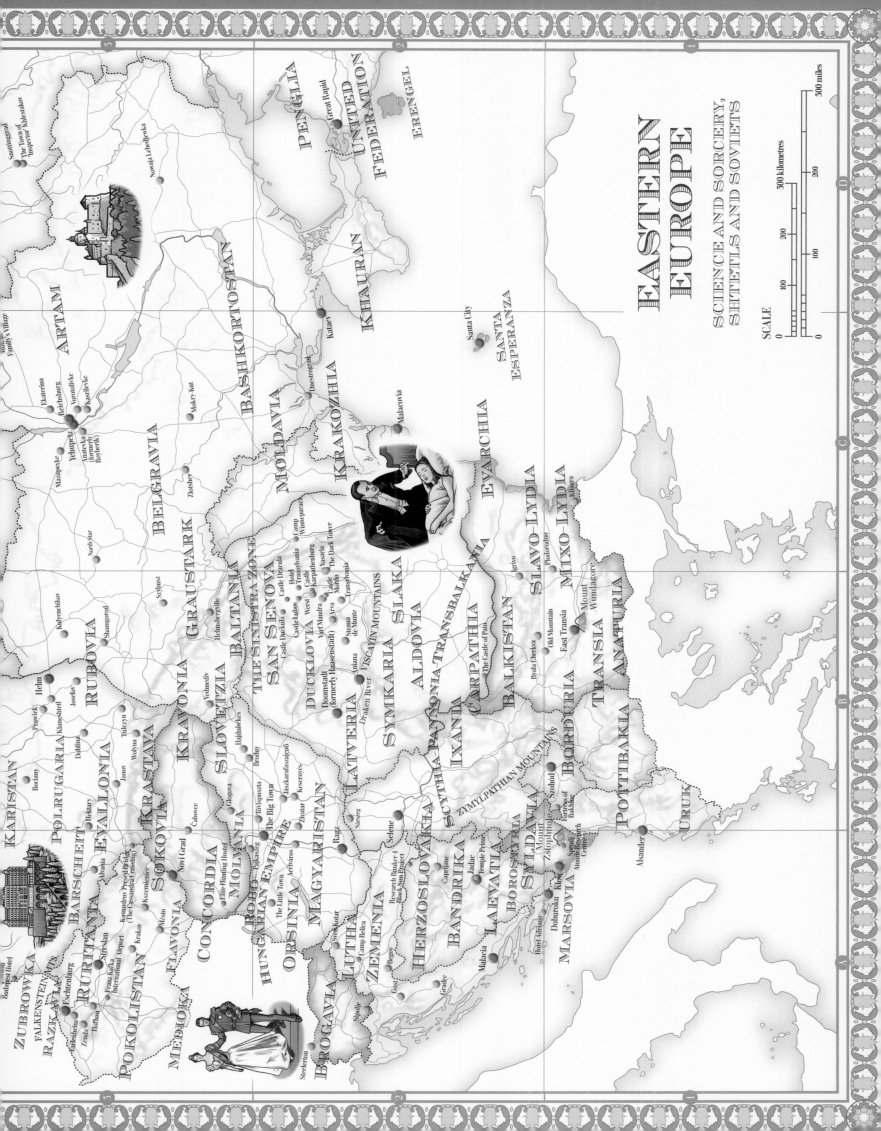

EASTERN EUROPE

SCIENCE AND SORCERY, SHTETLS AND SOVIETS

SCALE

0   100   200   300 kilometres

0   100   200   300 miles

ARTAM
Snottingrad
The Town of Inspector Khlestakov
Stolice Family's Village

PENGLIA
Great Rapid
UNITED FEDERATION
ERENGEL

KHAURAN
Katatev

BASHKORTOSTAN
Mokry Aut

BELGRAVIA
Ekaterina
Reichsburg
Vurotolbke
Kestrelsk
Yehupetz
Anatevka (formerly Boyberik)
Mazepake
Zlotshev
North Star

KRAKOZHIA
Malacovia
Dnestrovград

EVARCHIA
Santa City
SANTA ESPERANZA

MOLDAVIA

RUBOVIA
Kalyvechkov
Shangurod
Soltjusz

GRAUSTARK
Helmsbergville
Helmsdeviv

THE SINISTRA ZONE
Vednediv

SAN SENOVA
Camp Winneparacac
Hotel Transylvania
Castle Dracula
Castle Karpathenburg
Vaseria
Castle The Dark Tower
Castle Morbo
Transylvania
Castle Labos
Werst
Yarf Mandra
Arva
Duumstadt (formerly Haasenstädt)

SLAVO-LYDIA
grivo
MIXO-LYDIA
Pladorolmo
Old Mountain
Mount Wundagore
East Transia

BALTANIA
Hajduk Acs

KRAVONIA
SLOVETZIA

DUCKLOVIA
Azinma
Draken River

LATVERIA
VISCAIN MOUNTAINS

SYMKARIA
Stenna de Mute

SLAKA

ALDOVIA

CARPATHIA
The Castle of Pain

BALKISTAN
Byala Cherkva

TRANSBALKANIA
PAYNONIA-
SCYTHIA-

ZYMLPATHIAN MOUNTAINS

TRANSIA
ANATPURIA

POTTIBAKIA
Alsander

URUK

KARISTAN
Boclany
POLRUGARIA
Prawicki
Kamystniel
Josefov
Dobitnol
RUBOVIA
Helm

EYALLONIA
Streslau
Janow
Tulczyn
Wolyna

KRASTAVA
Kszemienaz
Alesto
Alvania

SOKOVIA
Novi Grad

FLAVONIA
Cabovce

MOLVANIA
Glugnva

CONCORDIA

BOBO
Talkaszeg
Panovce
Blue Big Town
The Little Town

HUNGARIAN EMPIRE
Archvams

ORSINIA
SvekKotar

MAGYARISTAN
Jhatar
Rug
Sarszeg
Jaszkarafaszajenő
Keszernyés
Tővispuszta
Brodny

LUTHA
Camp Beltra

ZEMENIA
Sipolje

Selene
Research Bunker 4
Black Aqua Project

HERZOSLOVAKIA
Caprifane
Temple Prime

BANDRIKA
Jadaz

LAEVATIA
Malacia
Spradj
Atomic Research Centre

BOROSEYVIA
Szobol
Szoboz
Fortress of Bakhine

SVLIDAVIA
Mount Zstoplmoje

MARSOVIA
Doburoku
Klon
Hotel Adriatica

KARISTAN
ZUBROWKA
Grand Budapest Hotel
FALKENSTEIN
RAZKAVIA
Habelheim
Zenda
Halhau
Eschtenburg
RURITANIA
Franz Kafka International Airport
Krakov
Kosandrov Present Bridge (The Cassandra Crossing)

POKOLISTAN
MEBOKA
Steuberton

BROGAVIA
Gost
Begin
Gradec
Sipolje
Malacia

EASTERN EUROPE

KEY LOCATIONS

For a full list of locations, see the location index on pages 130–150.

ALDOVIA
A Christmas Prince SERIES |
SOUTHERN AND CENTRAL EUROPE | FILM
Constitutional monarchy ruled by Prince Richard's dynasty; a soapy, nonsensical mishmash of monarchical clichés.
A Christmas Prince 3 reveals that Aldovia is a huge monarchy, encompassing all of Romania, the Balkans and chunks of Austria and Hungary. **MAP pp.50–51, B2**

ARKANGEL CHEMICAL-WEAPONS FACILITY
GoldenEye
RUSSIA | FILM
This Soviet-era chemical-weapons facility located in Northern Russia featured in Pierce Brosnan's debut as James Bond. It could be assumed to be located in the real Arkhangelsk Oblast, but the mountainous terrain feels more in line with the Urals. **MAP pp.50–51, B6**

ARTAM
Artam: One Reich, One Race, a Tenth Leader BY VOLKMAR WEISS |
EASTERN EUROPE | NOVEL
In this alternate history evolution of Nazi Germany, Hitler dies in 1941 and Germany never declares war on the USA. Artam is a dystopian eugenics-driven state located in the East and centred on its capital of Reichsburg (formerly Kiev). **MAP pp.50–51, C3/D3**

BILYARSK AIR BASE
Firefox BY CRAIG THOMAS |
RUSSIA | NOVEL/FILM
Bilyarsk is a real town, the air base is not. The base is the development and testing facility for the MiG-31 Firefox, a fictional Soviet super-fighter featured in the novel and Clint Eastwood film. **MAP pp.50–51, D5**

CASTLE DRACULA
Dracula **ROMANIA | VARIOUS**
Often assumed to be located at the real Borgo Pass/Tihuta Pass – so much so that a Hotel Castle Dracula was built there in real life. In the book, however, Borgo Pass is just where Dracula's carriage picks up Jonathan Harker from the scheduled mail coach. Bram Stoker's great-nephew, based on a close reading of Stoker's notes, believes Castle Dracula was imagined to lie about 24km (15 miles) to the south-east, atop the dormant real-world volcano Izvorul Calimanului. **MAP pp.50–51, B2**

THE CASTLE OF PAIN *Ghostbusters II*
CARPARTHIA | FILM
Home of Prince Vigo, Scourge of Carpathia and Sorrow of Moldavia: 'on a mountain of skulls, in the castle of pain, I sat on a throne of blood' – perhaps a name not meant to be taken literally, but simply too fun not to map! **MAP pp.50–51, B2**

CHERNARUS *ARMA 2*
SOUTH-EASTERN EUROPE | VIDEO GAME
The landscape for this tactical shooter is decidedly based on lands in the northern Czech Republic. However, maps of the game clearly show the country to share a northern border with Russia, as well as a lengthy coastline along a major body of water (the 'Green Sea') – two properties that make no sense for the Czech Republic. Further clues suggest it is in the Caucasus region. We've thus placed Chernarus on the west coast of the Caspian Sea. The name of another ARMA 2 location, Ardistan, was also used by Karl Friedrich May in a pulp fiction novel of the same name. That Ardistan was somewhere in the Middle East. **MAP pp.50–51, A5**

COBRASTAN
Papers, Please
EASTERN EUROPE | VIDEO GAME
Doubly fake in that this is a made-up country IN UNIVERSE! However the fake Cobrastan passport has the same colour-scheme as those of Obristan, which is also the nation that the character who tries to blag his way through customs on the Cobrastan passport eventually produces a passport for. See page 74 for more on *Papers, Please*. **MAP pp.50–51, A5/B5**

CONCORDIA
Romanoff and Juliet
BY PETER USTINOV |
CENTRAL EUROPE | PLAY/FILM
The tiniest of European states, which has won independence so many times that it celebrates independence day every day. The location is non-specific, but it is

contested by both the US and USSR, so likely on the border of the Iron Curtain. It has also been threatened by both Albania and Lithuania. **MAP pp.50–51, A3**

DED MOROZ PALACE
RUSSIA | FOLKLORE
This is the residence of Ded Moroz (usually translated to Father Frost in English), the Slavic analogue of Santa Claus. In Russian tradition, he lives in a so-called palace in the town of Veliki Ustyug, a convention that the local tourist bureau have taken full advantage of. **MAP pp.50–51, B6**

DURMSTRANG INSTITUTE
Harry Potter/Wizarding World
BY J.K. ROWLING | RUSSIA | VARIOUS
A secretive school of magic known to be located in a mountainous region in the far north of Europe. An official map suggests somewhere in the vicinity of Finland or western Russia. The mountains near Murmansk make this a possible fit. **MAP pp.50–51, A6**

FRANZ KAFKA INTERNATIONAL AIRPORT
The Onion
CZECH REPUBLIC | WEB SERIES
International airport serving Prague, named 'most alienating' by *Business Week*. **MAP pp.50–51, A3**

KINGDOM OF OPONA
RUSSIA | FOLKLORE
A fabled utopian kingdom, lying somewhere beyond the bounds of charted Russia. There are accounts of explorers setting off to the far north of Russia in search of this realm, which is also known as the Golden Land, Land of Chud and Belovodye. **MAP pp.50–51, B6**

LATVERIA
MARVEL COMICS | CENTRAL EUROPE | COMICS
Ruled by autocratic supervillain Doctor Doom. Latveria is bordered by the fictional Symkaria and Puternicstan (not shown). Their locations have been retconned over the years. The region where Hungary, Romania and Serbia meet appears to be the current canon, and a similar arrangement is shown on a seperate map on Wikipedia. Its capital of Doomstadt (formerly Haasenstadt) is also shown. **MAP pp.50–51, B2**

MEERKOVO
COMPARE THE MARKET | RUSSIA | ADVERTISING
A small, meerkat-inhabited village 'just outside' Moscow. Parodies the common Russian settlement name 'Markovo' – one such village is indeed found some two hours' drive south-east of Moscow. **MAP pp.50–51, D4**

MOLDAVIA
Dynasty **EASTERN EUROPE | TV**
Scene of a notorious series cliff-hanger in which half the cast appeared to have been killed in a terror attack. Moldavia is an historic region and former country within modern Moldova, but here a fictional country is implied. **MAP pp.50–51, C2/C3**

PLUTONIA (PORTAL TO)
Plutonia **BY VLADIMIR OBRUCHEV | ARCTIC | NOVEL**
One of many 'hollow Earth' novels, which imagines a subterranean world populated by dinosaurs. The entrance is said to lie in the Fridtjof Nansen Land, around 81 degrees north. **MAP pp.50–51, B6**

POTTSYLVANIA
Rocky and Bullwinkle
POTTSYLVANIA | TV
A nation so committed to espionage that its newspaper is printed in invisible ink. Although a pastiche of the Eastern Bloc in general, the homeland of Rocky and Bullwinkle's arch-enemies also has a Germanic flair. This is best evidenced by its ruler, Fearless Leader, who embodies all the stereotypes associated with a militant Prussian aristocrat, right down to the monocle and duelling-scar. An argument may thus be made that Pottsylvania specifically parodies East Germany, but a map within the show clarifies it to be an Eastern European state on the Baltic coast, and so we have mapped it as such. Plus, there's nothing Teutonic about the names of Fearless Leader's lackeys, Boris Badenov and Natasha Fatale. **MAP pp.50–51, B4**

RAZKAVIA
The Tin Princess
BY PHILIP PULLMAN | CENTRAL EUROPE | NOVEL
Pullman's *His Dark Materials* novels have contributed many locations to this atlas, but his lesser-known work *The Tin Princess* is also set in a fictional country. Razkavia is 'between Bohemia and ... wherever was next to Bohemia: Prussia, possibly'. A detailed map of the realm can be found in *The Writer's Map*, edited by Huw Lewis-Jones. **MAP pp.50–51, A3**

SOKOVIA
MARVEL CINEMATIC UNIVERSE | CENTRAL EUROPE | FILM
Location of the climactic scenes of *Avengers: Age of Ultron*. Sokovia's rough location is shown on a map during the film as between the Czech Republic and Slovakia. The Battle of Sokovia, in which the capital Novi Grad is lifted miles into the air, was actually filmed in Hendon, North London. **MAP pp.50–51, A3**

SYLDAVIA
The Adventures of Tintin
BY HERGÉ | SOUTH-CENTRAL EUROPE | VARIOUS
The location of this idyllic kingdom is never confirmed, but stated population sizes suggests a country about the size of Montenegro, which Hergé confirms as being the primary inspiration for Syldavia. The architecture is Turko-Slavic, which also reflects the nation's fictional history, where power oscillated between Slavs and Turks for a time. The country has also been mistaken for Greece, notably when Thompson and Thomson acquired Greek national dress for a mission inside Syldavia. The name of the coastal town of Dbrnouk may also be a reference to real-world Dubrovnik, Croatia. **MAP pp.50–51, A2/B2**

THE TOWN OF 'INSPECTOR' KHLESTAKOV
The Government Inspector
BY NIKOLAI GOGOL | RUSSIA | PLAY
The town is not named in the original play, but this story is such a cultural touchstone in Russia, that we decided to include it (in part of Russia adjacent to Ukraine, since Gogol was born in east-central Ukraine). The adjacent town of Snottinggrad was used for the inspector's town in a production by Nottingham Youth Theatre, and is surely the among the most obscure entries in the entire atlas. See also Brodny (B3), for the film version set in Hungary. **MAP pp.50–51, D3**

VEYSHNORIA
NORTH-EAST EUROPE | MILITARY EXERCISE
A country supposedly in north-west Belarus created for a Russo–Belarusian military training exercise. The neighbouring fictional regions of Lubenia and Vesbaria were also part of the game. The internet was quick to react to the wargaming, with parody Twitter and Facebook accounts for the fictional states. **MAP pp.50–51, B4/C4**

THE NORDIC COUNTRIES

HERE BE DRAGONS (AND TROLLS)

 he Nordic realm is a land of contrasts. This region birthed both the ferocious Vikings and the egalitarian ethos of modern Scandinavia. Never forget that Swedish chemist Alfred Nobel was not just the inventor of dynamite but also the founder of the Nobel Peace Prize.

Contrasts and guilty consciences make for a potent combination; small wonder then that Nordic noir has become a key mainstay of European television over the past decade, with its dark crime sagas exported to over 100 different countries. We expected that our map would be peppered with fictional locations from these shows, but it seems that part of their chill factor lies in adherence to reality. *The Killing* is centered on Copenhagen, *The Bridge* namechecks the Øresund Bridge between Copenhagen and Malmö, while their illustrious predecessor *Wallander* is set in the Swedish town of Ystad.

One major exception to the rule is the *Millennium* series of novels (and later films) by Stig Larsson. The most famous, *The Girl With the Dragon Tattoo*, is largely set in real locales, but the fictional town of Hedestad and nearby Hedeby Island are entirely imagined. The films used locations south of Stockholm, but the original novel sets Hedestad just north of Gävle, which is where we've placed it.

The fjords, glaciers, mountains and icy wastes of central and northern Scandinavia, meanwhile, lend themselves to works of high fantasy. Somewhere in the Finnish wastes, we may discover Bolvangar, the creepy concentration camp of *His Dark Materials*. Armoured bears patrol still-higher latitudes. Disney, meanwhile, has spun many fairy tales from the Danish repertoire of Hans Christen Andersen. The villainous Ice Queen, for example, is reformed in the guise of *Frozen's* Queen Elsa, who reigns supreme from her palace in Arendelle.

Heading out to sea, through waters reportedly home to little mermaids, one enters the Barbaric Archipelago. Here be dragons, at least according to Cressida Cowell's *How to Train Your Dragon* books and their DreamWorks movie adaptations. And then, of course, we have the *Moomins*. Creator Tove Jansson was heavily influenced by Finnish landscapes when she created the valley home of her hippo-faced trolls.

Indeed, trolls of one stripe or another are everywhere when you start looking. Grieg's towering composition 'In the Hall of the Mountain King', as originally written for the play *Peer Gynt*, is played within the court of troll king Dovregubbens, who rules from somewhere within Norway's Dovrefjell mountains. Grieg's legendary theme has since been celebrated throughout pop culture, and eventually returned to its roots with a prominent appearance in children's film *Trolls*, itself derived from a Danish toy line. And while trolls may not appear within *His Dark Materials*, you can certainly feel their influence in the naming of Trollesund, the icy harbour town where protagonist Lyra first encounters her companions Lee Scoresby and Iorek Byrnison.

A SANCTIFIED KINGDOM

In the world of the anime *Gundam Wing*, humans have broken free of Earth's bonds to establish new lives in orbital space colonies. Earth itself has, however, come under the tyrannical rule of a military junta, the United Earth Sphere Alliance. One of the final nations to be assimilated was the Sanc Kingdom, which under the monarchical rule of the Peacecraft dynasty had so thoroughly rejected war as to embrace a policy of Total Pacifism, not even offering resistance when invaded. Thus the kingdom fell in a single day.

But where did the Sanc Kingdom lie? Well, appropriately enough for a nation depicted as scenically beautiful and civically enlightened, supplementary materials point to it lying within Scandinavia, most likely corresponding to parts of Denmark and Sweden. For this atlas we've chosen to map it accordingly, and opted to chart the kingdom's capital, Newport City, as an analogue of Copenhagen.

DO YOU WANT TO BUILD A KINGDOM? THE WHEREABOUTS OF ARENDELLE

Frozen is the Disney tale of two princesses – one enchanted with ice, the other disenchanted with love. But where does their homeland of Arendelle lie?

The evidence screams Norway. Arendelle's majestic fjords and civilized society are a perfect match, and the short film *Olaf's Frozen Adventure* depicts one citizen preparing a giant cake in the shape of that country. There's also the slightly risqué joke hidden within the name of 'Wandering Oaken's' trading-post and sauna – it's an anagram of 'naked Norwegians'! The kingdom's name even evokes the real Norwegian town of Arendal, though the filmmakers have confirmed their primary influence was the city of Bergen.

But this atlas charts Arendelle to neither Arendal nor Bergen, thanks to a map featured in *Frozen II*. This helpfully gives us the kingdom's latitude and longitude – 62 degrees north of the equator, 27 degrees east of the prime meridian ... coordinates which would place it slap-bang in the middle of Finland, miles from the sea. *Whoops*!

But is this a mistake, or a very subtle joke? The map from *Frozen II* is dated 1840. History tells us that the nations of the world only agreed upon a standard prime meridian in 1884. Working backwards, this suggests icebound Arendellians use *Ice*land as their prime meridian. Elsa would approve! Latitude is less mutable, however, and from the map we can see that Arendelle lies far, *far* to the north, almost up in the Arctic Circle. We chose to set it in the vicinity of real-world Trondheim, whose geography broadly matched that of the map.

Frozen II and the various specials provide further locations. Hans, Anna's dastard of a love interest, is styled as a prince of 'the Southern Isles', and the *Frozen Fever* short provides its own blink-and-you'd-miss-it map, clarifying the isles' shape and geographic relation to Arendelle (naturally, they're located to the south). *Frozen II* meanwhile takes the cast (and ourselves) into the unknown, to the enchanted lands of the Northuldra people and the mystic glacier of Ahtohallen, 'where the north wind meets the sea'. Although fictional, the Northuldra are heavily inspired by the Saami people of northern Scandinavia, so we've mapped their lands to match, and set Ahothallen's island off their coast, amidst the waters of what the film names 'the Dark Sea'.

We had also hoped to include the home province of the bombastic Duke of Weselton on this map, but its location remains elusive. Guess we'll just have to *let it go* ...

MOOMINS, FROM MOOMINVALLEY

Anna and Elsa might be the current pop-culture stars of the Nordic countries but, over to the east, an altogether quieter phenomenon has spent the better part of a century establishing itself as perhaps Finland's most celebrated cultural creation. We speak (of course) of the Moomins, those roly-poly hippo-like creatures that sprang from the imagination of author-illustrator Tove Jansson. Over 20 adaptations of the books have been produced for film and television, Moomin shops and cafes can be found on at least three continents, and Moomin theme parks enrich both Finland and Japan.

But where is the elusive Moominvalley whence all of this sprang? The tales often come accompanied by a map of the region, but one that offers little information as to the setting, besides establishing that Moominvalley is bordered by sea to the west, lying on a rocky stretch of coast that runs from south-west to north-east.

The natural temptation is to place it in Sweden. After all, Jansson was a Swedish-speaking Finn who spent much of her childhood on the island of Blidö, north-east of Stockholm. Her tales surely drew inspiration from the rugged, windswept scenery. Yet the books are so firmly part of Finnish lore that it would feel wrong to place Moominvalley in any other nation. One option would be to site this hallowed land in the same spot as the real-world Moomin theme park, which can be found on an island north-west of Helsinki. The scenery isn't a bad match, though the location has no deep connection to the author or her stories.

Instead, we've opted for the Pellinge islands off Finland's south coast. Jansson made several childhood trips to these islands, and settled here in later life, so it seems a fitting location. That's our decision, but like any other judgement in this atlas, you may agree with Muskrat's words from *Finn Family Moomintroll*: 'I have every respect for your deductions, but you are wrong, completely and absolutely, and without any doubt.'

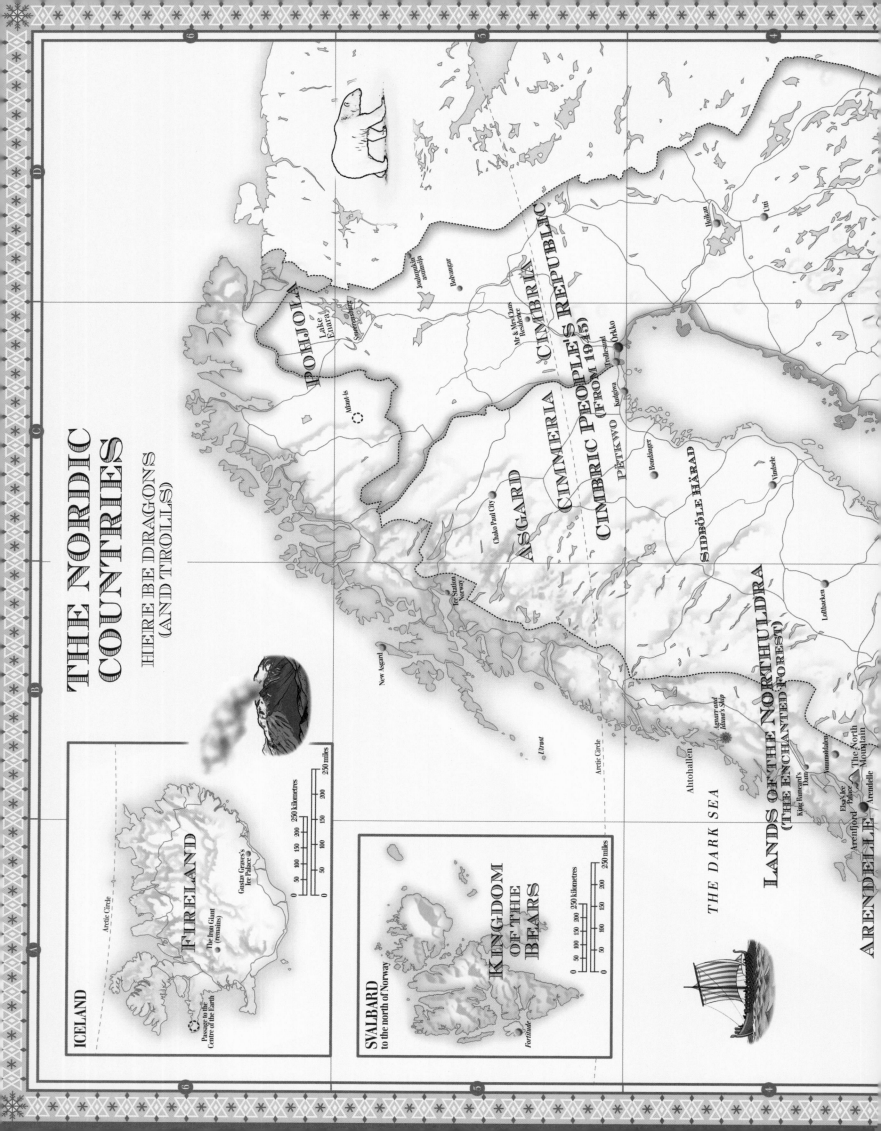

THE NORDIC COUNTRIES

HERE BE DRAGONS (AND TROLLS)

ICELAND

Arctic Circle

Passage to the Centre of the Earth

FIRELAND

The Iron Giant (remains)

Gustav Graves's Ice Palace

250 miles
250 kilometres
0 50 100 150 200

SVALBARD
to the north of Norway

KINGDOM OF THE BEARS

Fortitude

250 miles
250 kilometres
0 50 100 150 200

New Asgard

Utrost

Ice Station Norway

Chako Paul City

ASGARD

POHJOLA

Lake Enara

Superstorbyen

Atlant-is

Joulupukki asuinsija

Bolvangar

Mr & Mrs Claus Residence

Trolle-tunf

Orkko

Kudeljna

PETKWO

Bondanger

CIMBRIA

CIMMERIA

CIMBRIC PEOPLE'S REPUBLIC
(FROM 1945)

Rolkan

Utti

Vindsele

SIDBÖLE HÄRAD

Loftbacken

Arctic Circle

THE DARK SEA

Ahtohallen

Aguar and Iduna's Ship

LANDS OF THE NORTHULDRA
(THE ENCHANTED FOREST)

King Runeard's Dam

Jommdalen

Elsa's Ice Palace

The North Mountain

Arenfjord

Arendelle

ARENDELLE

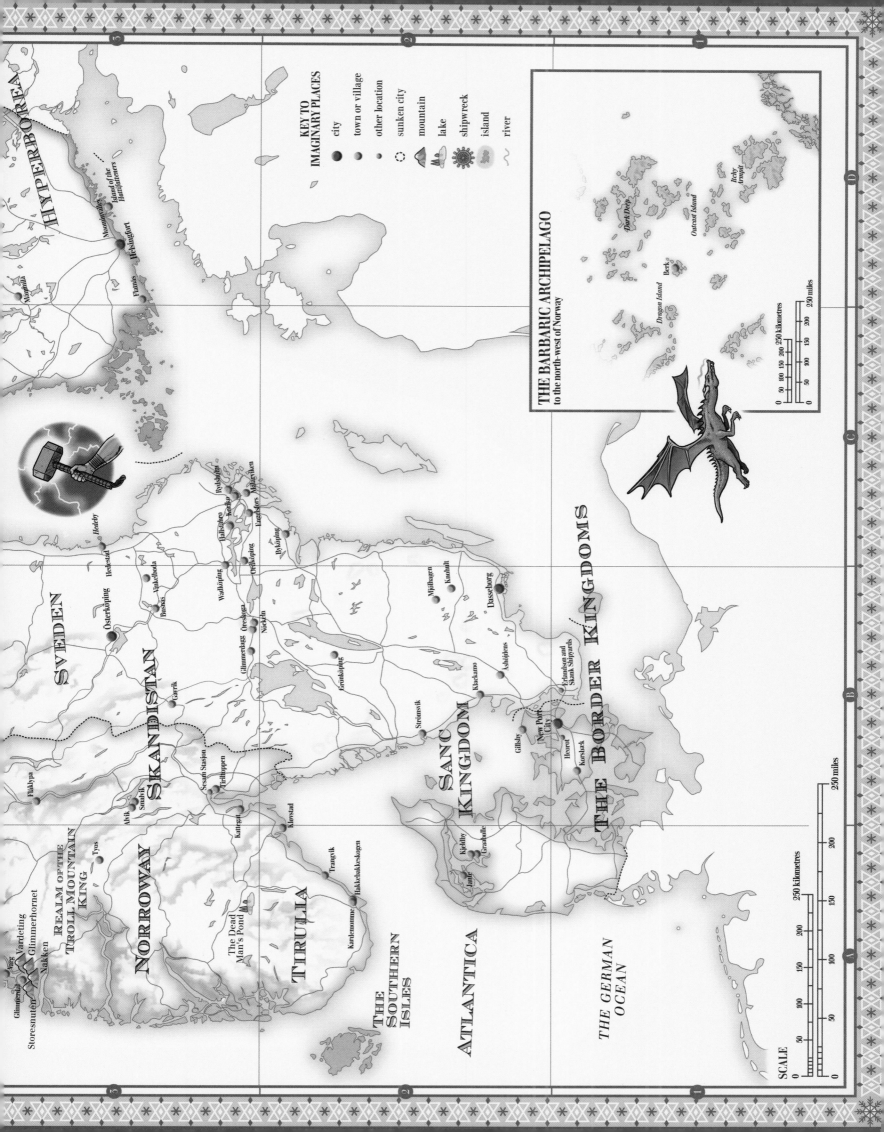

KEY TO IMAGINARY PLACES

- ● city
- ◑ town or village
- • other location
- ◌ sunken city
- ⛰ mountain
- 🏞 lake
- ✳ shipwreck
- 🏝 island
- 〰 river

THE BARBARIC ARCHIPELAGO
to the north-west of Norway

Dark Deep

Outcast Island

Berk

Dragon Island

Itchy
Armpit

0 50 100 150 200 250 kilometres
0   50   100 150 200 250 miles

HYPERBOREA

Mariehilla

Moominvalley

Island of the
Hattifatteners

Platnäs

Helsingfort

SVEDEN

Hedeby

Fläkhypa

Glimmersal
Storesnuten
Nokken
Vardeting
Glimmerhornet

REALM OF THE
TROLL MOUNTAIN
KING

NORROWAY

Tyes

SKANDISTAN

Österköping

Hedestad

Ankelbodta

Busnäs

Gävrik

Afvik

Smalvik

Trangvik

TIRULIA

Hakkebakkeskogen

Karlemomme

The Dead
Man's Pond

THE
SOUTHERN
ISLES

ATLANTICA

THE GERMAN
OCEAN

Rydsholm

Korsko
Mälariken
Engelsfors

Hallstabro

Bykoping

Örilöping

Wadköping

Glimmerdagg
Överskoga
Nückeln

Grönköping

Straimsvik

Mjalhagen
Knohult

Dassehorg

Klackamo

Ashojtens

SANC
KINGDOM

Kjelloy
Jante

Granbolle

Gillsby

New Port
City

Heorot
Korslæk

Erlandson and
Skank Shipyards

THE BORDER KINGDOMS

Sesam Stasion
Tirilltoppen

Klovstad

Kattegat

SCALE
0   50   100 150 200 250 kilometres
0   250 miles

THE NORDIC COUNTRIES

KEY LOCATIONS

For a full list of locations, see the location index on pages 130–150.

ASGARD
Conan NOVELS OF ROBERT E. HOWARD
NORTHERN SCANDINAVIA | NOVELS
Asgard was the home of the Norse gods in mythology, and may be most familiar these days as the home of Marvel's Thor and his compatriots. As neither of these Asgards are of this Earth, they do not qualify for the Atlas (though, see New Asgard). However, the name is also used in the Conan universe to describe lands corresponding to northern Scandinavia.
MAP pp.56–57, C5

ATLANT-IS
The Brothers Dal
NORWAY | TV
'Atlant-Ice' in English translations. Lost Saami city which is eventually discovered beneath the Finnmarksvidda plateau.
MAP pp.56–57, C5

ATLANTICA
The Little Mermaid
NORTH SEA | FILM
It may appear tropical, but there are good reasons for mapping this Disney classic to the Scandinavian coast. Most of the human characters have a North European bearing; the tale is from the pen of Danish Hans Christian Andersen; a famous statue of the Little Mermaid can be found in Copenhagen, and the name of Disney's mermaid kingdom of Atlantica supports a sea with access to the Atlantic. Plus, this also places it near the kingdoms shown in

Frozen and *Tangled*. Those palm trees? A cold-resistant variety imported from Asia (this is true!). MAP pp.56–57, A2

THE BARBARIC ARCHIPELAGO
How to Train Your Dragon
BY CRESSIDA COWELL | NORWEGIAN SEA | NOVELS/FILMS
The various islands of the Barbaric Archipelago are well documented across multiple novels, films and numerous TV spin-offs, while online maps suggest a location off the northern coast of Norway. We have only highlighted a fraction of the named locations. MAP pp.56–57, C1/D1

BOLVANGAR
His Dark Materials
BY PHILIP PULLMAN | FINLAND | VARIOUS
Concentration camp for children, described as four day's travel (by foot) north-east of the coastal town of Trollesund. We know it is located in the Witch Lands, but it doesn't seem to fall in the specific territory of any of the witch clans. MAP pp.56–57, D5

CHAKO PAUL CITY
SWEDEN | HOAX
Hoax city reported in the Chinese press. It was reputedly inhabited solely by man-hating lesbians, which prompted millions of Chinese men to approach Swedish travel agencies for more information. A commentator from the tourist office in Umea said that the story reminded him of the town of Pajala, also in northern Sweden, which in the 1990s

brought in large numbers of women because there 'weren't enough of them' in the town. We placed it nearby, so as not to offend with a direct comparison!
MAP pp.56–57, C5

CIMMERIA
If on a Winter's Night a Traveller BY ITALO CALVINO | NORTHERN SCANDINAVIA | NOVEL
Calvino is deliberately playful about the location of his fictional country. It is clearly somewhere in or close to Scandinavia. Mention of the Bothno-Ugaric languages suggests a location on the Gulf of Bothnia. After the Second World War it was subsumed into the Cimbric People's Republic, with (it is assumed) Cimbria. The name is also used in the Conan stories to indicate the southern regions of Norway and Sweden and extended across to Scotland and England in a hypothetical time of lower seas. MAP pp.56–57, C5

GLIMMERDAL
Tonje Glimmerdal
BY MARIA PARR | NORWAY | NOVEL
'Glimmer Valley' is a hamlet that appears to have been based on the author's home in Vanylven, Sunnmøre. The book's map places it inland, at the foot of the mountains. MAP pp.56–57, A3

GRÖNKÖPING
Grönköpings Veckoblad
SWEDEN | NEWSPAPER
The *Grönköpings Veckoblad* ('Greenville Weekly') is a satirical newspaper that

claims to report from the fictional town of Grönköpings, which is characterized as 'Sweden in miniature' – at least one source suggests it to lie between Hjo and Skövde. MAP pp.56–57, B2

HAKKEBAKKESKO-GEN *Climbing Mouse and the Other Animals in the Hunchback Wood*
NORWAY | TV
A community of talking animals with no identifiable inspiration, but we thought it would be fun to map it to Kristiansand Zoo, where there is a Hakkebakkeskogen attraction. MAP pp.56–57, A2

HEDEBY
The Millennium SERIES
BY STIG LARSSON | SWEDEN | NOVELS/FILMS
Island community located just off the east coast of Sweden, connected to it by a bridge and 'about an hour north' of Gävle. MAP pp.56–57, C3

HEOROT
Beowulf DENMARK | POEM
Semi-mythical great hall, which scholars sometimes equate with archaeological remains at Lejre on the island of Zealand. MAP pp.56–57, B1

JOULUPUKIN ASUINSIJA
FINLAND | TRADITION
Literally 'Joulupukki's home', residence of the Finnish analogue of Santa Claus, on Korvatunturi. As is typical of Santa Claus mythology, sources vary on the nature of his home (and of Joulupukki himself), with some also placing it as the site of his workshop. MAP pp.56–57, D5

KATTEGAT
Vikings NORWAY | TV
The Kattegat is the name of the real sea between Denmark and Sweden. The village of Kattegat is confirmed in the show to be in Norway, distant from its namesake sea, and within a spectacular fjord. The best fit is probably the Oslofjord in southern Norway (though not a true fjord). MAP pp.56–57, B3

KORIKO
Kiki's Delivery Service
SWEDEN | ANIME
Inspired by the old town in Stockholm, with aspects of Gotland thrown in – the setting of the film is not necessarily Sweden but a fantasy analogue, but we think it still works. MAP pp.56–57, C3

MR AND MRS CLAUS'S RESIDENCE
FINLAND | TRADITION
We've placed Santa's Workshop near the North Pole, which seems to be the leading location for the bearded one's main residence – certainly in the most popular films. But we can't entirely ignore Lapland, a common contender among European believers. The Lapland residence of Mr and Mrs Claus is here located close to the real-world Santa Claus holiday village in Rovaniemi. MAP pp.56–57, C5

NEW ASGARD
Avengers Endgame
NORWAY | FILM
Formerly known as Tønsberg, Thor's adopted home is said to be the oldest village in Norway, so we've equated it with Bleik, which holds that title in real life. Scenes in the film were shot in Scotland. MAP Nordic, B5

ÖRESKOGA
Bert Diaries BY ANDERS JACOBSSON AND SOREN OLSSEN | SWEDEN | NOVELS
Öreskoga is located somewhere between Karlskoga and Örebro, the authors' home towns. MAP pp.56–57, B3

PASSAGE TO THE CENTRE OF THE EARTH
Journey to the Centre of the Earth BY JULES VERNE | ICELAND | NOVEL
The way to the centre of the Earth lies inside the real volcano of Snæfellsjökull, should you ever be passing by. MAP pp.56–57, A6

SIDBÖLE HÄRAD
'Sidböle Härad' BY TED STRÖM | SWEDEN | SONG
This fictional region comes from the song of the same name by Ted Ström, located somewhere within one of the Glesbygd, Sweden's remotely populated regions, probably intended to be Norrland (northern Sweden). MAP pp.56–57, C4

SKANDISTAN
The Years of Rice and Salt
BY KIM STANLEY ROBINSON | SCANDINAVIA | NOVEL
Islamic state comprising most of Scandinavia. MAP pp.56–57, B3

SMEERENSBURG
Klaus FINLAND | FILM
Island community north of the Arctic Circle and 'the unhappiest place on Earth'. Since this is a Santa origin story, we've placed it on a lake island in Lapland. MAP pp.56–57, C5

TROLLESUND
His Dark Materials
BY PHILIP PULLMAN | FINLAND | VARIOUS
The coastal town where Lyra meets Lee Scoresby and Iorek Byrnison is within Lapland. If this corresponds to the Lapland of our world, then we can place it in the Gulf of Bothnia – the one sea coast in the region. MAP pp.56–57, C5

UK AND IRELAND

FAKE BRITAIN AND SHAM ROCK

f the viands of world literature were assembled at a picnic, then Britain and Ireland would surely provide the largest and most sumptuous hamper. The people of these islands have always supplied the literary crowd-pleasers. How many keen readers have partaken of Lady Macbeth, Robinson Crusoe, Long John Silver, Ebenezer Scrooge, Sherlock Holmes, Peter Pan, Winnie the Pooh, Miss Marple, James Bond, Mary Poppins and Harry Potter, to name but a few? All these characters need places to live, work, scheme, sleuth, fly or play Pooh sticks. This map collects almost 800 such settings, from the world-famous to the delightfully obscure.

Greater London alone could include hundreds of locations. Here we have room only for a few, such as the Borough of Walford from the long-running soap opera *EastEnders*, or the post-apocalyptic island of Ham (formerly Hampstead) from Will Self's *Book of Dave*.

The Home Counties around London, meanwhile, are replete with stately homes, such as Bleak House, Gosford Park, Howards End, Toad Hall and even Croft Manor, where Lady Lara rests her head between strenuous bouts of tomb raiding. Moving west, we encounter the many fictional locations of Anthony Trollope's Barsetshire and Thomas Hardy's Wessex (or at least the ones we could fit in), while Devon and

Cornwall are the homelands of such unlikely compatriots as Lorna Doone, Doctor Dolittle, the Hound of the Baskervilles, Poldark and Basil Fawlty.

Wales holds its own treasures. A rich vein of fictional mining towns can be hewn from literature and television alike, along with old children's' favourites such as Pontypandy (*Fireman Sam*) and the railway communities of *Ivor the Engine*. Look out too for Llareggub, from Dylan Thomas's *Under Milk Wood* – just don't say it backwards in polite company.

The Cotswolds and West Midlands are perhaps more populated than might be expected, thanks to writers such as Jane Austin, P.G. Wodehouse and George Eliot. This is the agricultural homeland of long-running radio drama *The Archers*, principally set in the Borsetshire village of Ambridge. This region was also the cradle of the Industrial Revolution. Arnold Bennett, chronicler of the Potteries, lends us his famous Five Towns, while the mills and foundries of L.T.C. Rolt's Winterstoke and Hawley Bank mirror historic Ironbridge and Coalbrookdale, birthplace of the steam locomotive. By contrast, the East Midlands and East Anglia are relatively spartan.

The gradient gets denser and the hills steeper as we press farther north. Industrial cities like Coketown (*Hard Times*) intermingle with isolated hamlets and farms like *Emmerdale* and *Wuthering Heights*. Understandably, the

Lake District has inspired many a creative mind, from Arthur Ransome (*Swallows and Amazons*) to the writers of the evergreen *Postman Pat*, beloved of children's television.

The rich and often tragic history of Scotland is reflected in the fictional realms, where the works of Sir Walter Scott and John Buchan, and dramas such as *Outlander*, make full use of the landscape and historiography to weave spells upon the imagination. This is indeed a land of magic and mystery, home to Brigadoon, Kennaquahair and Hogwarts. At least a dozen fictional islands nestle among the Hebrides, their rugged and remote charms only adding to the romance (though perhaps not on Summerisle, overlooked by *The Wicker Man*).

Ireland and Northern Ireland are less densely populated than Great Britain, and this is perhaps reflected in their fictional topography. Aside from a dense cluster around Dublin (including Roddy Doyle's *Barrytown* and locations from the *Artemis Fowl* books), our Irish selection is spread pretty evenly across the Emerald Isle. Many of the locations here are remote, rural communities, such as Ballykissangel on the east coast, or the Craggy Island of *Father Ted*, but there's true grit here, too. Witness the many border towns where fictionalized accounts of the Troubles have played out, or Kevin Barry's remarkable *City of Bohane*, a setting that incorporates gang warfare into everyday life.

MISCHIEF MANAGED: HOGWARTS DISCOVERED

Hogwarts School of Witchcraft and Wizardry – the primary setting for J.K. Rowling's *Harry Potter* novels – has a reputation for safety and security. The castle is guarded by powerful spells to ward off assault from the Wizarding World ... and to deflect the attention of meddling muggles like ourselves. Hogwarts, you see, is unplottable. By enchantment, it is rendered impossible to chart on a map.

Which is not to say that educated guesses can't be made. We know for a fact that Hogwarts and the neighbouring village of Hogsmeade are situated among the lochs and peaks of Scotland, both from the original text and from the films, which digitally inserted the castle into the spectacular landscapes of the Western Highlands. The first film placed the school squarely in the lee of Ben Nevis. It has since drifted around, most usually perching itself on the shores of Loch Shiel (near Glenfinnan) and Loch Morar (near Mallaig). Crucially, all of these locations lie near the Mallaig Extension of the West Highland Railway, along which the Hogwarts Express is most frequently seen journeying to and from the school.

However, herein lies a problem. Pottermore lore (and the deeper magics of railway history) tells us that Hogwarts received its rail connection in the mid-1800s. Yet the Mallaig Extension was among the later blooms of Britain's Victorian railway network, only breaking ground in 1897, an engineering feat so well-documented that no magic could fudge the details of its construction. It seems not even the Ministry of Magic can compete with the bureaucratic minutiae of the Ministry of Transport!

So what else do we know? Well, in both the original books and the films, escaped (and wrongfully accused) convict Sirius Black is spotted passing through the real community of Dufftown en route to Hogwarts. This turns our attention to eastern Scotland and the mountains of the Cairngorms. Only 48km (30 miles) from Dufftown we find the skiing resort of Aviemore, and it is at Aviemore's railway station (opened in 1863) that second-generation Potter-protagonists Albus and Scorpius arrive after an overnight walk from Hogwarts, during the events of the *Harry Potter and the Cursed Child* stage production. Keeping all this in mind, we're pretty confident in saying that both Hogwarts and Hogsmeade lie within a short walk of Aviemore, and have charted it as such within these pages. So much for being unplottable!

Of course, Hogwarts is not the only school of magic in these isles. In Wales we find Cackle's Academy, an independent educator of witches, from Jill Murphy's *The Worst Witch* series. The mountain-top school is disguised to non-magical folk, who perceive instead the ruined Castle Overblow. Just like Hogwarts, it is a thousand years old and heavily steeped in romantic (and frequently violent) lore. Just a few mountaintops away there is a rival school operated by Miss Pentangle, and it is only a short broomstick ride to the island of Cairnholme, seat of the preternatural Miss Peregrine's Home for Peculiar Children. Meanwhile, from the imagination of Anthony Horowitz comes Groosham Grange, a school that specializes in evil magic, located on bleak Skrull Island off the coast of Norfolk. Many other institutions, such as *Little Witch Academia*'s Luna Nova Magical Academy (located near Glastonbury), and the Casterbrook magic school in Buckinghamshire (from the *Lost Rivers* novels of Ben Aaronovitch) have disapparated from the map through lack of space. There may be others lurking across these enchanted isles.

MAPPING SODOR: THE ISLAND OF ENGINES

The Island of Sodor, home of Thomas the Tank Engine and the Fat Controller's other famous locomotives, is perhaps one of the world's best-realized fictional landmasses, standing apart by the sheer thoroughness with which its fictional topography and history have been woven into reality.

J.R.R. Tolkien might have charted the history of Middle Earth through four ages, and made the coasts, rivers and mountain plains of Gondor, Rohan and the Shire as instantly recognizable (to some) on a map as the outline of Europe, but comparatively tiny Sodor achieved this without the same degree of geographic freedom. Indeed, in the mind of creator the Reverend Wilbert Awdry, Sodor was a constituent part of the United Kingdom (politically attached to the Duchy of Lancaster) and its culture and history should reflect that truth.

The really fascinating thing, though, is that this mapping of Sodor, and indeed its very naming and 'discovery', were not pursued as a fancy but as a practical necessity. The process was managed with the methodical care that a modern franchise might devote to ensuring its canon all interlocks nicely.

The Railway Series, to properly name Awdry's stories, began as a series of tales told to his bedridden son Christopher during the Second World War. When these little stories saw mass publication, very quickly Wilbert found himself managing a roster of characters on a fictional railway network, one that was growing both in size and following among children. Here we come to the

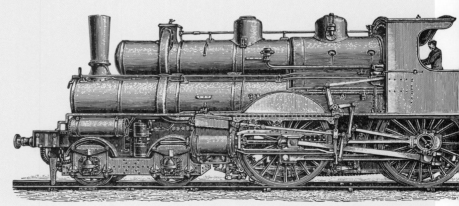

crux: *children can be awful nitpickers*, and Wilbert quickly found himself besieged by correspondence from readers who had spotted inconsistencies between stories, and even within the same story.

Many of these critiques rested in the illustrations, and Wilbert's answer was to carefully map out the various locations from his stories and the rail routes that connected them, so as to create a standardized geography. The problem was, where to put it? Having already established the Fat Controller's Railway as part of the nationalized British Rail system, Wilbert discovered there was no suitable space left within Britain into which he could squeeze this imaginary new network, thanks to the Railway Mania of the Industrial Revolution.

Then, in 1950, Wilbert was asked to speak as a guest preacher on the Isle of Man, situated in the Irish Sea halfway between England and Ireland. During this brief visit, he developed a liking for the character of the island, and discovered that the diocese to which Man was attached was named the Bishopric of Sodor and Man. 'Sodor' was an old Norse term, referring to the southern islands of Scotland, which had fallen out of common use. Awdry realized that if he reclaimed it for his books, he could not only create a location for his fictional railways, but restore the missing part of the Bishopric. Thus the Island of Sodor was born. It is over five times the size of Man and slots neatly in between the existing island and the Cumbrian town of Barrow-in-Furness, which gained the unusual boast of becoming the mainland junction for the Fat Controller's empire – now officially titled the North Western Railway.

In Sodor, Wilbert found not only all the space he needed for his fictional lines, but room into which to expand with further stories. The island gained towns, mountains, valleys, a history dating back centuries, and even its own language – a variant of Manx named Sudric. All of this creativity became a fulfilling exercise for Wilbert and brother George (very much an amateur historian), and even a minor money-maker in its own right, when in 1958 a map of Sodor was published for public consumption for the first time. Colourful and slightly fanciful, Wilbert nevertheless posted a copy to the then-Bishop of Sodor and Man, attached to a letter declaring that he was happy to at last present the poor Bishop back with the 'other half' of his diocese.

The rest is pseudo-history.

THE WIDER ISLES

If Sodor remains the most famous fictional isle in these waters, it is not the only one. Mythical islands have a history within Britain stretching back millennia. Avalon is one such name to echo down the ages, being the island upon which King Arthur's sword Excalibur was forged and where, in some tellings, the great king was buried. This sacred place is usually identified with Glastonbury Tor in Somerset, a rocky prominence which although nowadays landlocked, once towered over half-submerged fenland. As sea levels rise, it may one day feel the lap of

the tides again; a once-and-future island for the Once and Future King.

The 'lost land' of Lyonesse off the tip of Cornwall is another Arthurian remnant. The home of Tristan, and site of the final battle between Arthur and Mordred (if you believe Tennyson), the ancient story of Lyonesse has inspired many modern works of fiction, including the *Lyonesse Trilogy* by Jack Vance. The Welsh equivalent is Cantre'r Gwaelod, a supposedly sunken landmass in Cardigan Bay which has been part of Welsh folklore since time immemorial. Scotland, meanwhile, possesses the island of Rocabarraigh which, according to myth, shall only appear three times. On its third outing, 'the world will likely come to be destroyed'. Our apologies if placing it in this atlas has unforeseen consequences: *No apocalyptic liability accepted.*

And people keep inventing new islands to add to these fabled peers. Perhaps the most enviable are the Scottish twins of Great and Little Todday, where a freighter carrying some 50,000 cases of Scotch is wrecked in Compton Mackenzie's novel *Whisky Galore*, and the two films it inspired. Coming during the dry years of wartime rationing, the villagers naturally scurry to salvage this precious cargo before it is reclaimed by HM Revenue and Customs!

Woe betide any authority figures who stray a few islands north to Summerisle, though. Here, the pagan inhabitants have the tendency to immolate prying policemen, as documented in *The Wicker Man*. Nearby Muir Island has been used for mutant research (Marvel Comics' X-Men stories), while the North Sea island-prison of Azkaban is so infamous as to warrant no description. But Scottish islands can be charming, too. Witness the hugs and smiles and woolly jumpers prevalent on the Isle of Struay, setting for the beloved *Katy Morag* stories of Mairi Hedderwick (now a television show), or the community spirit of Ronansay from *Two Thousand Acres of Sky*.

Perhaps the most memorable of fictional islands are also the strangest. We've already encountered Skrull Island (*Groosham Grange*), the Island of Cairnholme (*Miss Peregrine's Home for Peculiar Children*) and Sodor (home of

sentient steam engines). We might add to the register Ireland's Craggy Island (and its near-identical neighbour Rugged Island), windswept homes for the bewilderingly unsuitable priests of *Father Ted*. To find them, we're told, just head out from Galway until you sight the English ships dumping radioactive waste, at which point you know you're in the right waters.

We might also visit the vowel-shy islands of Qwghlm (pronounced 'Taghum'), a recurring background location in the works of Neal Stephenson. And we must certainly mention the travelling island of Penguina, whose natives were once great auks, prior to being baptized and transformed into humans (*Penguin Island*, by Anatole France). You'll find it down amongst the Channel Islands, along with Forau Island (*The Devil's Rock*) where rituals of a decidedly more diabolic nature have been known to take place. Speaking of matters infernal, despite having no location from which to work, we simply had to include *Daily Mail Island*, a satirical creation of Charlie Brooker, wherein seemingly normal people are left stranded on an island with nothing to read but right-wing newspaper the *Daily Mail*.

Finally, as we were putting this atlas to bed, we heard tell of a new fictional island that had appeared off the north-east coast of Ireland. This is the crescent shaped Isle of Eroda, which may be inspired in its backwards-read name by Samuel Butler's Erewhon (see Australia/New Zealand map). Eroda is the only fictional island we know of that was created to promote a new LP – specifically, *Fine Line* by Harry Styles – but it takes all sorts to make a fictional atlas.

THE NAMES HAVE BEEN CHANGED TO PROTECT THE INNOCENT

Thomas Hardy began building his own fictional gazetteer a full century before the creators of this atlas were even born. His major novels are famously set in the counties of Wessex, named after a long-defunct kingdom from the time of Alfred the Great. We're clearly in the south and south-west of England here; indeed, most editions of Hardy's novels include a map of Wessex, which is shaped exactly like this part of Britain. But look closely at the place names. They're different. Downstaple, Exonbury, Emminster, Budmouth – all sound plausibly native to this region, yet are not. Hardy took reality's map and rebadged it.

Even if you've never read a Hardy novel, you'll probably recognize the alias for his home town of Dorchester. It appears in the title of one of his most famous works, *The Mayor of Casterbridge*. His towns and cities often carry names suggestive of the place he is renaming, from Christminster (Oxford) to Sandbourne (Bournemouth). All-in-all, around 60 towns, cities and villages were relabelled in this way.

Why did Hardy do this? In truth it seems he had no strong reason, other than artistic licence. Using fictional names lent an air of romanticism, and allowed the author to be playful with his settings rather than sticking rigidly to real geography and street plans. Whatever his motivations, it certainly struck a chord with readers. The Anglo-Saxon 'Wessex' was all but forgotten outside academic circles by Hardy's time, but his reclamation of the name brought it back into popular imagination, enough to be used later in the 1998 film *Shakespeare in Love*. Reportedly, this inspired the very real Prince Edward to adopt the title of Earl of Wessex a year later.

Hardy might have been the most prodigious of the rebadgers, but he was not the first. Mary Anne Evans (George Eliot) chronicled provincial life in *Middlemarch*, a town easily identified as Coventry. Charlotte Brontë's third novel is called *Villette*, and not 'Brussels'. Even Charles Dickens, noted for his minute exploration of London, chose to rename Preston as Coketown in *Hard Times*, while Rochester became Cloisterham in *The Mystery of Edwin Drood*.

Nor would Hardy be the last to build a fictional geography within England. Arnold Bennett swiftly followed on with his *Five Towns* novels, set in what is recognizably the Staffordshire Potteries, albeit with Hardy-esque altered names such as Knype (Stoke), Burslem (Bursley) and Tunstall (Turnhull). Meanwhile, Winifred Holtby's *South Riding* of 1936 plays with the geographic oddity that Yorkshire contains East, West and North Ridings but not one to the south. Her novel reclaimed the South Riding for Yorkshire, with fictional Kingsport replacing Hull, Flintonbridge standing for Beverley, and even the mighty Humber rechristened as the Leame Estuary. Come the 1980s, Russell Hoban's sci-fi novel *Riddley Walker* not only renamed the towns of Kent, but also layered them with mild innuendo; Faversham and Sandwich becoming Father's Ham and Sam's Itch, while Herne Bay is Horny Boy.

These and many other examples can be found across the map. Some have been renamed to protect the innocent; others to sound more guilty.

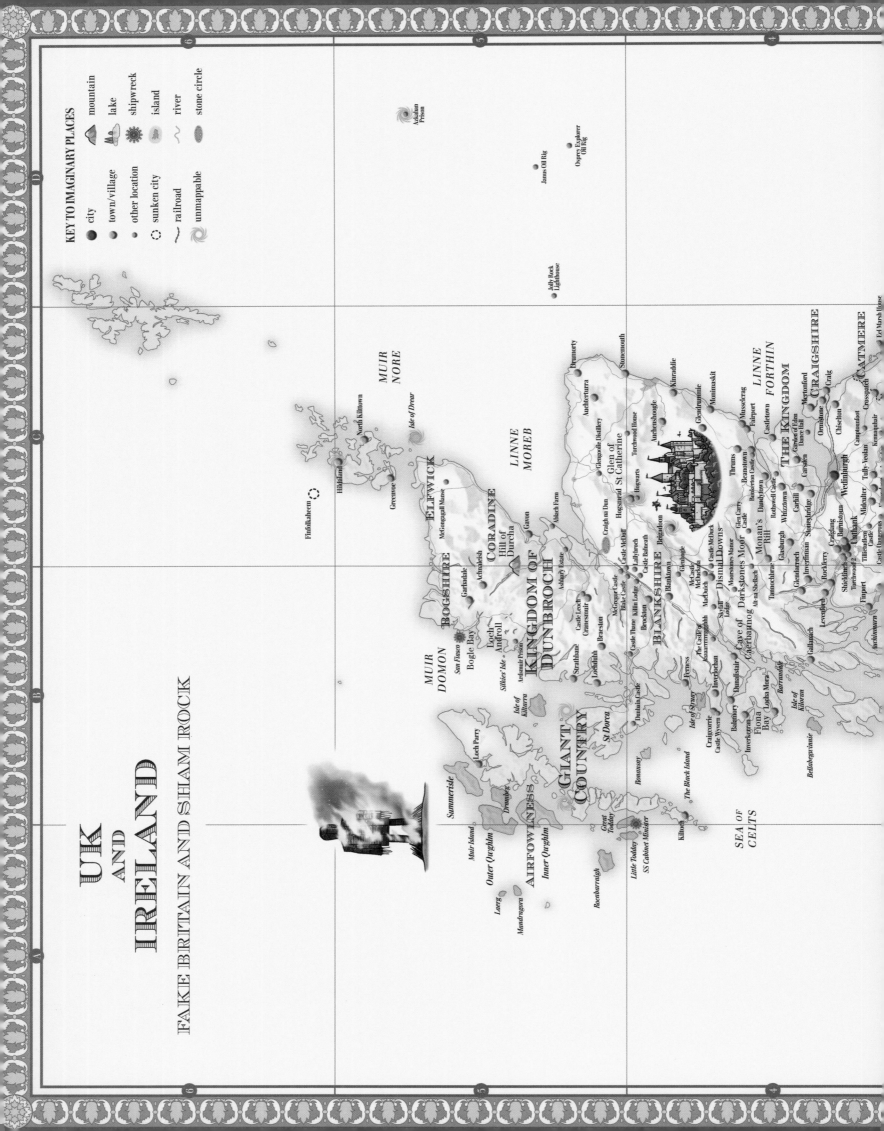

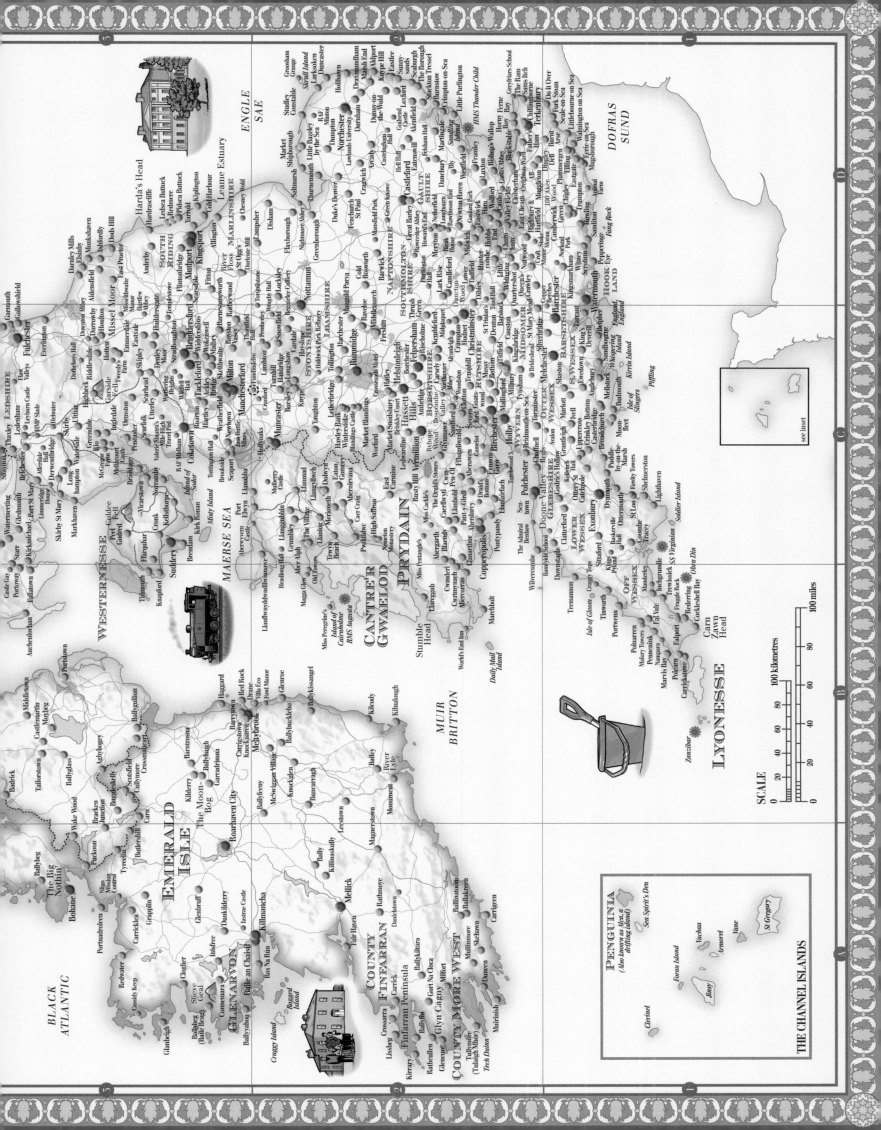

UK AND IRELAND

KEY LOCATIONS

For a full list of locations, see the location index on pages 130–150.

ABERGARTH
Island of Apples BY GLYN JONES | WALES | NOVEL
This idyllic West Wales market town is based almost entirely on real-life Carmarthen, to the extent that studying the text in secondary school felt like a walking-tour to one of your authors, who was raised in that area. Not depicted on our map is Abergarth's industrial counterpart Ystrad, an analogue for Merthyr Tydfil. MAP pp.64–65, C2

ANIMAL FARM
Animal Farm BY GEORGE ORWELL | ENGLAND | NOVELLA
Although Orwell's farm full of politically aware animals might seem to be a fable of anywhere, it does namecheck the East Sussex village of Willingdon – an area Orwell is known to have explored. MAP pp.64–65, D1

BALLAKREEN
Brass Eye IRELAND | TV
Village where sightings of a statue of the Virgin Mary driving a car have been reported. A parody of real-life Ballinspittle in County Cork, where several residents claimed to witness a statue of the Virgin Mary move in 1985. MAP pp.64–65, A2

BARSETSHIRE
NOVELS OF ANTONY TROLLOP | ENGLAND | NOVELS
Trollope's fictional county is loosely based on Somerset, although its main city of Barchester is an analogue of Winchester in Hampshire. Barsetshire contains numerous fictional locations, only some of which we have space for here. Other towns include Hogglestock, Greshamsbury, Uffley and Puddingdale. MAP pp.64–65, C1

BASKERVILLE HALL
Sherlock Holmes: The Hound of the Baskervilles BY ARTHUR CONAN DOYLE | ENGLAND | NOVEL
We've included a fair selection of Holmesian locations, though a comprehensive mapping is beyond the resolution of this map. Baskerville Hall is one of the most famous locations from the canon and is readily identified as Dartmoor. MAP pp.64–65, C1

BEANOTOWN
The Beano SCOTLAND | COMICS
Location unknown, but hints are dropped that it's near the publisher's HQ in Dundee. MAP pp.64–65, C4

BLAENDY
The Proud Valley WALES | FILM
Central location from this wartime film starring African-American actor and singer Paul Robeson as a shiphand whose physical strength and amazing bass baritone voice see him welcomed into a Welsh mining community. Blaendy appears to be located on the far western fringes of the South Wales coalfields, as signposts prominently depict it as being 49 miles (79km) from Cardiff and 208 miles (335km) from London (via the old Gloucester road). We've thus chosen to map it to the vicinity of Ammanford, and in the next valley over we find another fictional mining town, 'Caerflwyti' from Jules Verne's *Rocket to the Moon*, which was actually filmed in County Wicklow, Ireland. MAP pp.64–65, C2

BLANDINGS CASTLE
NOVELS OF P.G. WODEHOUSE | ENGLAND | NOVELS
Home to Lord Emsworth and a primary setting of many of Wodehouse's novels. We've included many other Wodehousian names on this map, but could not find room for all of them. MAP pp.64–65, C2

BOHANE *City of Bohane*
BY KEVIN BARRY | IRELAND | NOVEL
The City of Bohane is never precisely located. We know it is somewhere in western Ireland, on a peninsula. It is said to exist 'in the high fifties of latitude', which points to Donegal. The presence of limestone in the surrounding Big Nothin' further narrows down the region. MAP pp.64–65, A3

BRIGADOON
Brigadoon SCOTLAND | FILM
Lerner and Loewe's magical village appears only once every 100 years. We've given it an 'unmappable' symbol in sympathy with its scarce existence and lack of appearance on other maps. Although it takes its name from the real Brig o' Doon bridge in Ayrshire, the time-sensitive village materializes in the highlands. MAP pp.64–65, C4

BUGGLESKELLY
Oh, Mr Porter!
NORTHERN IRELAND | FILM
This classic comedy stars veteran actor (and amateur astronomer) Will Hay alongside supporting stars Moore Marriott and Graham Moffatt as the wily (yet often witless) staff of Buggleskelly, an extremely rural (and allegedly haunted) railway station located on the fictional Southern Railway of Northern Ireland. Riffing on the phenomenally successful *The Ghost Train* (see Fal Vale, below), Buggleskelly itself lies just north of the border with what was then the Irish Free State, and the local ghost-stories a cover exploited by gun-runners moving arms across the frontier via a derelict bit of line. A map within the film places the station where the real community of Lisnaskea lies. MAP pp.64–65, B3

CASTERBRIDGE
NOVELS OF THOMAS HARDY | ENGLAND | NOVELS
See the main text for a discussion of Hardy's Wessex towns. MAP pp.64–65, C1

COPPEROPOLIS
Copperopolis WALES | COMIC
This is both a nickname for real-life Swansea and also an alternate reality version of the city from an indy comic of the same name. MAP pp.64–65, C2

CRAGGY ISLAND
Father Ted IRELAND | TV
Off the west coast of Ireland. 'The best way to find it is generally to head out from Galway and go slightly north until you see the English boats with the Nuclear symbol on the side. They come very close to the island when they're dumping the old glow-in-the-dark.' MAP pp.64–65, A2

DOFRAS SUND *Total War: Thrones of Britannia*
ENGLAND | VIDEO GAME
Total War provides an exhausting list of fictional villages from the Dark Ages. We've restricted ourselves to plotting only the fictional sea names from that game. MAP pp.64–65, D1

DOONE VALLEY *Lorna Doone* BY RICHARD DODDRIDGE BLACKMORE | ENGLAND | NOVEL
There really is a Doone Valley in Devon, but in an usual reversal this geographic feature was named for the fictional locale of Richard Doddridge Blackmore's celebrated novel, and not the other way around. Thus, we feel justified in including it. MAP pp.64–65, C2

DOWNTON ABBEY
Downton Abbey ENGLAND | TV
As any Downton fan will tell you, the series exteriors were filmed at Highclere Castle in Hampshire. However, that's not where Downton is meant to be: almost all local towns mentioned are real towns in North Yorkshire. MAP pp.64–65, C3

EMMERDALE
Emmerdale ENGLAND | TV
This famous fictional farm of Emmerdale was located in the equally fictitious village of Beckindale until the mid-1990s. The village then changed its name to match the farm. MAP pp.56–57, C3

ENGLAND, ENGLAND *England, England* BY JULIAN BARNES | ENGLAND | NOVEL
Not a typo, but a name given to the Isle of Wight by Julian Barnes, who turned the island into a giant theme park of Anglophilia. MAP pp.64–65, C1

FAIR HAVEN
Star Trek: Voyager
IRELAND | TV
Somewhat-stereotypical Irish village programmed into the holodeck of the *USS Voyager*. A signpost within the simulation provides directions to other nearby (real) towns, placing Fair Haven within County Clare. A later episode reveals it to be a coastal town (as implied by the name). MAP pp.64–65, A2

FAL VALE
The Ghost Train BY ARNOLD RIDLEY | ENGLAND | PLAY/FILM
Writer-actor Arnold Ridley created this particular location decades before he played much-loved Private Godfrey in Dad's Army. After spending a lonely night at Mangotsfield junction (having missed a connection), he was inspired to write a play wherein several passengers become similarly-stranded at remote Fal Vale station, reputed to be haunted by a phantom train – in truth a ruse devised by gangsters to conceal their illicit dealings. With this twist, Ridley inspired a range of imitation narratives where 'supernatural' activity disguises criminal enterprise (see Buggleskelly, above, for one such example). The play itself was a runaway hit with multiple film adaptations, but Ridley did not profit much from this success, as he had already sold the rights to his plays during a period of financial hardship. Fal Vale itself is described as lying near Truro in Cornwall. MAP pp.64–65, B1

FAWLTY TOWERS
Fawlty Towers ENGLAND | TV
England's worst hotel is stated several times to be in the resort town of Torquay. MAP pp.64–65, C1

FOWL MANOR
Artemis Fowl STORIES
BY EOIN COLFER | IRELAND | NOVELS
A mansion/estate in the outskirts of Dublin, about an hour from the city centre. In the 2020 film it is shown to have a coastal location. MAP pp.64–65, B2

FRAGGLE ROCK LIGHTHOUSE
Fraggle Rock ENGLAND | TV
One of those occasions where we can't pinpoint a location but we felt it had to be included. The lighthouse scenes were filmed in Falmouth, so that's where we've placed it. MAP pp.64–65, B1

FULCHESTER
Viz ENGLAND | COMICS
Location unknown, but has the hallmarks of Newcastle. MAP pp.64–65, C3

GARSIDE FELL
The Garside Fell Disaster
BY LTC ROLT | ENGLAND | SHORT STORY
Sinister mountain from the ghost stories of writer and engineer LTC Rolt, whose fictional locales usually drew inspiration from real-world environs. Garside Fell was among the first locations to be mapped for this atlas, and is inspired by the landscapes along the border of Yorkshire and Cumbria. The mountain's name is derived from real world Garsdale, while the railway tunnel that bores beneath it, within which two trains are consumed by fire in the titular disaster, is inspired by Blea Moor Tunnel on the Settle and Carlisle railway. MAP pp.64–65, C3

GIANT COUNTRY
The BFG BY ROALD DAHL | SCOTLAND | NOVEL
Giant Country is an unmappable location. The BFG tells Her Majesty the Queen that she 'is not be finding it a second time'. Judging from shots in the film, it appears to be a long way north of London, through mountainous terrain reminiscent of the Highlands. MAP pp.64–65, B5

GREENDALE
Postman Pat ENGLAND | TV
Technically, Greendale is the name of the valley rather than the village, though Royal Mail would still deliver to that address! MAP pp.64–65, C3

HAYSLOPE *Adam Bede*
BY GEORGE ELIOT | ENGLAND | NOVEL
The main setting of the novel is based on the Shropshire village of Ellastone, which the author knew well. **MAP pp.64–65, C2**

HOGWARTS
Harry Potter NOVELS BY J.K. ROWLING | SCOTLAND | NOVELS/FILMS
See page 61 for discussion.
MAP pp.64–65, C4

HOLDWICK PARK REFINERY
Look Around You ENGLAND | TV
Fictional producer of 'Industrial Strength Calcium' located in the (non-existent) 'Staffordshire Downs. According to this parody of educational television programming, 'If you've ever written with a calcium nib, or peered through a calcium lens, they've probably come from Holdwick'. **MAP pp.64–65, C2**

INVERFINNAN
The Hurricanes SCOTLAND | TV
Rural town on a sea loch, visited in an episode of this short-lived series about a globe-trotting football team. We've mapped the town near(ish) to Glasgow, since the local football team, Inverfinnan Celtics, are based upon Celtics FC of Glasgow. The Hurricane's team coach Jock Stone, was himself based upon Jock Stein, a legendary manager of Celtic FC. **MAP pp.64–65, B4**

ISLAND OF SODOR
Thomas the Tank Engine
BY REV. W. AUDREY | IRISH SEA | BOOKS/TV
See page 61 for discussion.
MAP pp.64–65, C3

ISLE OF KILTARRA
The Maggie SCOTLAND | FILM
Remote Scottish island and destination of the titular *Maggie*, a worn-down old coastal steamer. Her wily captain manages to con his way into transporting a valuable cargo of furniture for an American tycoon building a holiday home on the island, leading to a cat-and-mouse game of wits up the Scottish coast. Locations seen in the film are real until after the *Maggie* transits the Crinan canal, after which they become fictional, including such delightfully named communities as Bellabegwinnie, Loch Mora and Inverkerran. A close viewing of the film and charts seen in the opening credits suggests much of the action takes place in the vicinity of the Isle of Mull, with Kiltarra itself being located further north in the Outer Hebrides. **MAP pp.64–65, B5**

LAMPSHER
Night and Day BY VIRGINIA WOOLF | ENGLAND | NOVEL
Fans of Virginia Woolf are directed to the author's map of every location from every one of her novels, to be found on Londonist.com. **MAP pp.64–65, D2**

LOCH PARRY
An Appointment with the Wicker Man BY GREG HEMPHILL | SCOTLAND | PLAY
Remote Scottish settlement where a local amateur theatre group are trying to put on a stage musical version of *The Wicker Man*. The plot deliberately parallels that of *The Wicker Man* itself, so we placed Loch Parry on the isle of Lewis, opposite where we mapped the film's fictional Summerisle. **MAP pp.64–65, B5**

LLAREGGUB
Under Milk Wood BY DYLAN THOMAS | WALES | RADIO
Read it backwards. **MAP pp.64–65, B2**

MARLINSHIRE
Tintin BY HERGE | ENGLAND | COMICS
County of residence for Captain Haddock in English translations of *The Adventures of Tintin*. The description is a good fit for Lincolnshire, though the captain's family home at Marlinspike Hall is not mapped. For its Belgian prototype, see 'Moulinsart' in Western Europe. **MAP pp.64–65, D3**

LYONESSE
ENGLAND | FOLK TRADITION
Britain may terminate at Land's End, but the Fake Britain of our atlas extends a further 48km (30 miles) west to the lost island of Lyonesse, risen from the depths of Arthurian legend. **MAP pp.64–65, B1**

MCGREGOR FARM
Peter Rabbit BY BEATRIX POTTER ENGLAND | BOOKS/FILMS/TV
Clearly identified as Windemere in the underrated film version. **MAP pp.64–65, C3**

MCSWIGGAN VILLAGE
Family Guy IRELAND | TV
Peter's ancestral home. He takes a taxi there from the airport, implying it is within reasonable driving distance of Dublin. **MAP pp.64–65, B2**

MILFORT MILFORT
A FICTIONAL IRISH TOWN | IRELAND | COMEDY CLUB
Name of a comedy club/act based in Kenmare, Australia. We've mapped it to the real Irish town of Kenmare, County Kerry in a reverse homage. **MAP pp.64–65, A2**

NEMETON MONASTERY
Koudelka | WALES | VIDEO GAME
9th-century structure and primary location for this 1999 video-game. The game's Japanese production team wanted a setting across the sea from Ireland, and so chose Aberystwyth as the monastery's location, though the environment is inspired more by the landscapes of Pembrokeshire. **MAP pp.64–65, C2**

NEWTON HAVEN
The World's End ENGLAND | FILM
Inspired by, and filmed in, Welwyn Garden City, where we've spotted plaques marking some of the pubs from the film. **MAP pp.64–65, D2**

NORTH KILTTOWN
The Simpsons SCOTLAND | TV
Orkney hometown of Groundskeeper Willie. **MAP pp.64–65, C5**

PEMBERLEY
Pride and Prejudice BY JANE AUSTEN | ENGLAND | NOVEL
The grand mansion is often equated with Chatsworth in Derbyshire. **MAP pp.64–65, C2**

PONTYPANDY
Fireman Sam WALES | TV
Wales's greatest emergency services export lives in a town whose name is a portmanteau of two real towns, Pontypridd and Tonypandy. We've placed him in the general area, though on the coast, as per on-screen evidence. **MAP pp.64–65, C2**

PUCKOON
Puckoon BY SPIKE MILLIGAN | IRELAND/NORTHERN IRELAND | NOVEL
Fictional village torn in two during the partition of Ireland, thus most of Puckoon lies in the Irish Free State, but a fair portion is assigned to Northern Ireland. It is sited in the text as 'several and a half metric miles northeast of Sligo', which would suggest a location somewhere around Lough Melvin. However, it is also described as being a coastal village facing the Atlantic, an impossible contradiction given the border swings north before it reaches the coast. Given that this is all a Spike Milligan comedy, by the end of which nobody knows quite where the border is anyway, we've got some leeway. A further contribution from Spike can be spotted nearby in the form of 'Sligo Mission

Control', courtesy of his infamous 'Irish Astronauts' skit – or should that be Astr O'Naughts? **MAP pp.64–65, A3**

ROYSTON VASEY
The League of Gentlemen
ENGLAND | TV
This frighteningly 'local' community inhabited by nightmare grotesques was inspired by a village in Cumbria, but actually filmed in Derbyshire. After much feedback (including from one of the creators) we opted for the Derbyshire location, as that felt more 'right'. **MAP pp.64–65, C3**

SKYFALL LODGE
Skyfall **SCOTLAND | FILM**
James Bond's family estate is at some undisclosed location in the Highlands. We've mapped it to the film location of Glen Etive. **MAP pp.64–65, B4**

SS VIRGINIAN
The Legend of 1900
ENGLAND | FILM
Grand old ocean-liner that the titular 'Danny Boodman T. D. Lemon 1900' lives his entire life aboard without ever setting foot ashore, dying with the ship when she is scuttled after WW2. The *Virginian* caused us some confusion during mapping; we knew from descriptions of the narrative that she was scuttled off the coast of Plymouth, and mistakenly assumed this to be Plymouth, Massachusetts. It was only after a comparatively late-in-the-day viewing of the film that we realised this actually referenced Plymouth in Devon, leading to a scramble to adjust our maps accordingly. **MAP pp.64–65, C1**

ST MARY MEAD
NOVELS OF AGATHA CHRISTIE | ENGLAND | NOVELS
We've mapped a handful of the fictional creations from Christie's output, of which St Mary Mead is perhaps the best known. It's also her most fickle village, having appeared in at least four counties (including the fictional Downshire, Radfordshire and Middleshire, as well as Kent). It's later established to be relatively close to London, and served by trains from Paddington. We've placed it near Basingstoke on the evidence that it is said to lie close to the fictional village of Market Basing (not shown). **MAP pp.64–65, C2**

TECH DUINN
IRELAND | MYTHOLOGY
Despite the name, this has nothing to do with technology! Another otherworldly

island, this time hailing from Irish folklore, Tech Duinn is the abode of Donn, a god of the dead, and the place where souls of the dead muster. It is often identified with the real Bull Rock to the southwest of Ireland. **MAP pp.64–65, A2**

TILLIETUDLEM CASTLE *Old Mortality*
BY SIR WALTER SCOTT | SCOTLAND | NOVEL
Though fictional, Scott's castle has since inspired the name of a real railway station and housing estate. **MAP pp.64–65, C4**

TITFIELD-MALLINGFORD RAILWAY
The Titfield Thunderbolt
ENGLAND | FILM
Rural branchline which is purchased and operated by local volunteers (with a cash injection from the village soak!) after British Railways announces imminent closure. As the first of the celebrated Ealing Comedies to be shot in colour, *The Titfield Thunderbolt* was filmed on a recently-closed line near Bath during the glorious summer of 1952, and we've plumped for a similar location on our map. **MAP pp.64–65, C2**

TOTTINGTON HALL
Wallace and Gromit: The Curse of the Were-rabbit
ENGLAND | FILM
The *Wallace and Gromit* films are set in Wigan, but Tottington Hall is fictional. **MAP pp.64–65, C3**

TWEEDY'S FARM
Chicken Run **ENGLAND | FILM**
'No chicken escapes from Tweedy's farm!' We're pretty confident where said chickens would be trying to escape from, as paperwork seen during this feature-length Aardman animation confirms a location within the North Riding of Yorkshire. For further refinement, the plane built by the chickens to ultimately fly the coop incorporates a signpost for its propellor, showing the farm to be situated midway between Lancaster, Halifax and Sunderland. Not included on our map is the nearby town of Dulldale. **MAP pp.64–65, C3**

VALERIE SINATRA'S MILE-HIGH TRAVEL POD
The Day Today **ENGLAND | TV**
A mile-high structure from where Valerie Sinatra broadcasts her travel reports. Stated to be in the geographical centre of Great Britain, which would be 6.4km

(4 miles) north-west of Dunsop Bridge. **MAP pp.64–65, C3**

THE VILLAGE
The Prisoner **WALES | TV**
A slightly dubious one, as internal evidence points to a location closer to London. However, the film location of Portmeirion is so intimately associated with *The Prisoner* that we would be castigated for choosing a less established placement. **MAP pp.64–65, C2**

WALFORD
EastEnders **ENGLAND | TV**
Britain's most famous soap opera is self-evidently set in London's East End. On-screen clues, including a tube map, indicate a location near Bromley-by-Bow. The series is actually filmed in Borehamwood, Hertfordshire. Your author lives nearby, and can see the set from his rooftop! **MAP pp.64–65, D2**

WALMINGTON-ON-SEA
Dad's Army **ENGLAND | TV**
What should have been among the easiest of locations to map turned out to perhaps the most fiddly. Walmington is, after all, obviously located on the south coast of England, facing across to France. The question is, where specifically should we place the home of Britain's most beloved Home Guard platoon? No two maps seen within the franchise agree, and dialogue has suggested locations everywhere from the vicinity of Eastbourne in East Sussex to Dover in Kent. Ultimately we chose a location just on the Kent side of the border between the two counties, since Home Guard units usually adopted the insignia of their local regiments, and the proud defenders of Walmington wear the rearing horse of the now-defunct Queen's Own Royal West Kent Regiment on their forage caps. **MAP pp.64–65, D1**

WENTWORTH PRISON
Outlander **NOVELS BY DIANA GABALDON | SCOTLAND | NOVELS/TV**
Nothing to do with the one in *Prisoner Cell Block H*! **MAP pp.64–65, C4**

WUTHERING HEIGHTS *Wuthering Heights* **BY EMILY BRONTË**
ENGLAND | NOVEL
Probably inspired by real landscapes near the Brontë family home in Haworth. **MAP pp.64–65, C3**

THE MIDDLE EAST AND CENTRAL ASIA

BEYOND THE SILK ROAD

The first thing that will surely strike you when looking at this map is the sheer number of fictional countries staring back. The Middle East has a long history of 'being fiddled with', both in reality and in fiction. Many of the international borders in this region were drawn arbitrarily by Western powers in the first half of the 20th century, during the process of dismantling the former Ottoman Empire, setting up tensions that remain raw to this day. Likewise, the collapse of the Soviet Union in the second half of the century led to the formation of new, independent and frequently fractious states and 'stans' (a suffix derived from the Persian word for 'land of').

The same nation building continues within these pages. Together we've collected about 70 fake polities on this map, spanning the entire alphabet from Aldastan to Zekistan (which happen to be neighbours). Indeed,

some of these names seem to have spilled from a random name generator, while others such as Urzikstan, Azmenistan, Tyrgyzstan and Turgistan are all so plausible that we've had a hard time typing them without a spelling autocorrect. Meanwhile, the less-convincingly-named Derkaderkastan (courtesy of *Team America: World Police*) was conceived at a time the USA was invading Afghanistan and painting Iran as part of an 'axis of evil'. We've mapped it between the two, though it is, of course, neither.

Why is this such a popular region for make-believe countries? It would be nice to say that it is solely due to the region's rich culture, born from centuries of trade along the fabled Silk Road. However, the sad truth is that recent fiction has drawn more inspiration from the decades of unrest and foreign intervention that have blighted these lands, rather than their cultural treasures. The notional War on Terror and subsequent conflicts in Iraq,

Afghanistan and Syria have sparked countless fictional works, analyzing, sensationalizing and satirizing current events. Political shows like *The West Wing*, *Designated Survivor* and *24* routinely feature such places. It is far less risky to make up a country than to set harrowing events in a real territory.

In some cases, even parody proved too cruel for us to chart without risk of offence. Hence, you won't find *The Onion's* Ethniklashistan on the map, nor nations such as Trashcanistan or Absurdistan. Neither have we plotted El Ohtar from the 1980s film *Protocol*, whose insult may be more apparent to those who read right-to-left. Less ribald parodies have a long and honourable history, however. In 1516, Thomas More, in an aside from his magnum opus *Utopia* (see South America), dreamed up a region of Persia he named Polylerit, meaning 'people of much nonsense'. One modern translation has rebadged it as Tallstoria, and both are mapped here.

GENIES AND MAGIC CARPETS

If you've never read *The Arabian Nights* – also known as *One Thousand and One Nights* – you would probably assume from the title that its action is confined to present-day Saudi Arabia or perhaps Iran, the region once known as Persia. But this trove of tales has a far wider geography. You'll find locations from the stories scattered throughout this atlas, including on the maps of India, Africa and even the Canadian Arctic! Many of these locations are 'best guesses', based on sketchy and sometimes contradictory information, but such is the importance of this epic work that we would be remiss to leave them out.

The Arabian Nights is a collection of folk stories that have coalesced over many centuries, perhaps millennia, into the book we know today. By turn humorous, heroic and (truly) horrific, these tales are also prodigious in number. Some versions of the book essay the full 1,001 narratives, though most only print a selection, and variations emerge across numerous translations. The more famous tales have, in turn, been adapted and reimagined across other media, further evolving these stories in unexpected ways. Pick up any two versions of *The Arabian Nights* and you'll encounter entirely different experiences. It's a beast as slippery and multi-headed as any monster of mythology.

We've had to limit ourselves, therefore, to mapping the better-known tales. Chief among these has to be *Aladdin*, whose many iterations include a major Disney film, a stage musical and one of the most popular subjects for pantomime. In the original *Arabian Nights* tales, Aladdin's story is usually set somewhere in China, though the characters remain Arabian Muslims with Arabic names, thus we've had to polish our lamp of enquiry a little harder if we are to release this particular genie. As reimagined by the talents at Disney, Aladdin makes his home in the city of Agrabah, which is suggested to lie near to the River Jordan and the Dead Sea. Appropriately, the 2019 live-action version shot its desert scenes close to the Jordanian city of Aqaba, whose name is sufficiently similar to Agrabah that we decided to map the fictional city to this location.

The tale of *Julnar the Sea-born* is also mappable. The White City, abode and seat of King Shahriman is said to lie in the land of Khorassan, an ancient realm that is now a province in north-eastern Iran. Finding a place within ancient Khorassan that matches the White City's coastal locale led us to the extreme south-east corner of the Caspian Sea.

Other locations from the tales are more speculative. We can only guess at the coordinates of Great-Fish Island and Island of the Sea-Horses from Sinbad's first voyage, as well as the other islands shown on the Africa and India maps. And beyond the *Arabian Nights* themselves, the mythology of this region has lent us other locales, such as the mythical land of Paristan, home of a race of benevolent spirits.

Oh for a magic carpet to speed us across these exotic realms!

A TOUR OF THE (UNAUDITED) ARAB EMIRATES

As in real life, the Gulf region of our map contains numerous tiny emirates. We've marked them in a smaller font for practical reasons, though they are no lesser claimants to statehood than any other nation documented here. You certainly wouldn't want to argue with the authorities of Zahrain, whose despotic regime plotted the murder of a dissident in the 1962 film *Escape From Zahrain*. The same goes for Trucial Abysmia, where a team from *G.I. Joe* was captured, tortured and left for dead in the desert. The neighbouring Benzheen was also a source of strife for the Joes, many having died here during skirmishes with the forces of Cobra.

Across the Arabian Peninsula we encounter Khemed, which has appeared in two of Tintin's adventures, *The Land of Black Gold* and *The Red Sea Sharks*, names which say much about the location and character of the state. It is an absolute monarchy, on the coast of the Red Sea, whose main source of wealth (and Achilles' heel) is oil. Cities include the capital of Wadesdah and the punningly-named Khemikhal.

Oil is also a key resource to Salmaah and Hobeika, two neighbouring Arabian nations originating from the Tunisian film *Day of the Falcon* (also called *Black Gold*), who squabble over the Yellow Belt, a border desert rich in oil. Similar disputes are a hallmark of the Karrocan Emirate and its larger neighbour Qurac in the DC Comics universe, the two maintaining an uneasy peace following a border war in the early 21st century.

Kunami, featured in *Designated Survivor*, is another troubled nation. Located just south of Kuwait, it has been under Western sanctions for a decade, an attempt to thwart its nuclear ambitions. The wonderfully-named Unaudited Arab Emirates meanwhile, are so flush with money that parody travel guide *San Sombrèro* describes every hotel room coming with its own reception desk, and the local Bedouin market vendors selling plasma TVs and BMWs!

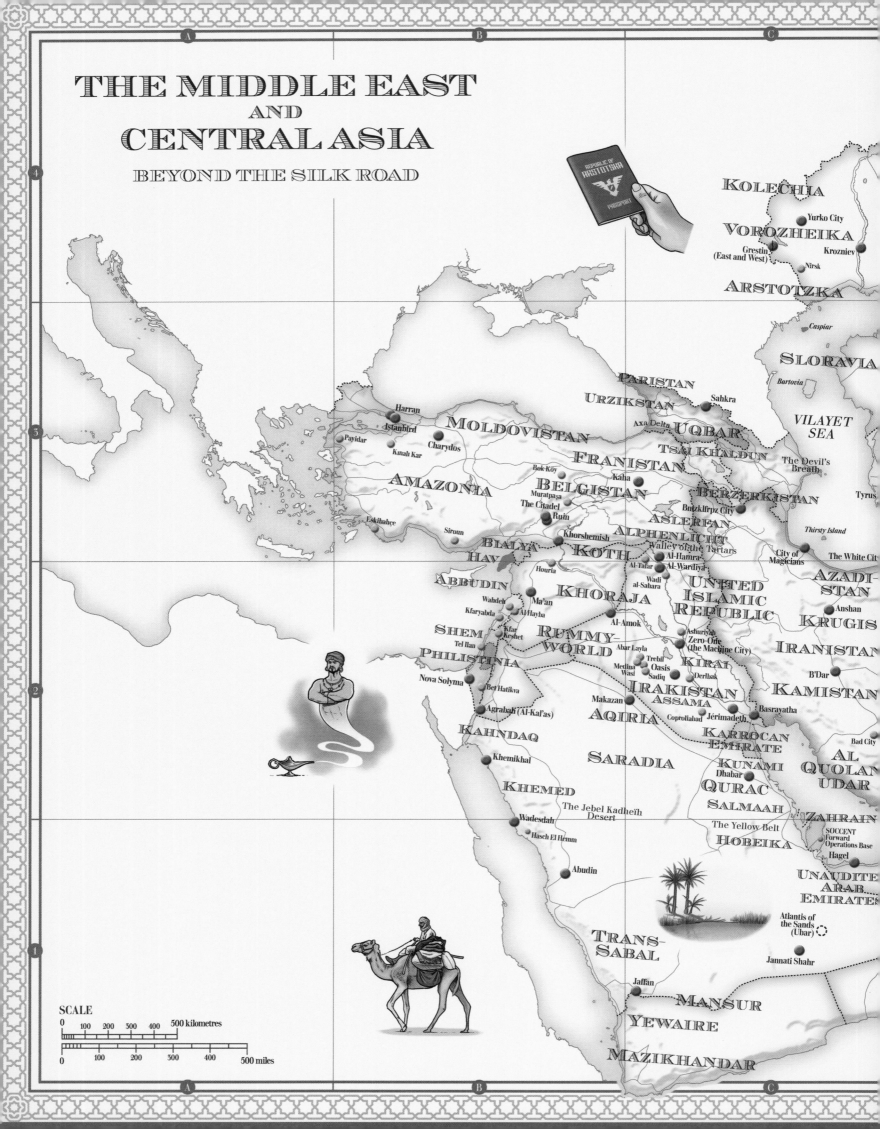

THE MIDDLE EAST
AND
CENTRAL ASIA
BEYOND THE SILK ROAD

KOLECHIA

Yurko City

VOROZHEIKA
Grestin
(East and West)
Krozniev
Nirsk

ARSTOTZKA

Caspiar

SLORAVIA
Bartovia

VILAYET
SEA

PARISTAN
URZIKSTAN

Harran
İstanbirl

Sahkra
Axa Delta

UQBAR

Payidar
Charydos
Kınalı Kar

MOLDOVISTAN

FRANISTAN

TSAI KHALDUN

The Devil's
Breath

Bok Köy

Kaha

Thirsty Island

Muratpaşa
The Citadel
Ruin

AMAZONIA

BELGISTAN

Brizklfrpz City

BERZERKISTAN

Tyrus

Eskibahçe

Siroun

Khorshemish

ASLERFAN

City of
Magicians

The White City

ALPHENLICHT
Valley of the Tartars

BIALYA

KOTH

Al-Hamra

AZADI-
STAN

HAV

Al-Tafar
Al-Wardiya

ABBUDIN

Houria

Wadi
al-Sahara

UNITED
ISLAMIC

Anshan

KRUGIS

KHORAJA

REPUBLIC

Wahdeh
Kfaryabda
Ma'an
Al-Hayba

IRANISTAN

Al-Amok

Ashuriyah
Zero-One
(the Machine City)

SHEM
Tel Ilan
Kfar
Keshet

RUMMY-
WORLD

Abar Layla

B'Dar

PHILISTINIA

Trebil
Medina
Wasi
Oasis
Sadiq

KIRAI

KAMISTAN

Nova Solyma

Bet Hatikva

IRAKISTAN
ASSAMA

Derlbak

Agrabah (Al-Kal'as)

AQIRIA

Makazan
Coproliabad
Jérimadeth

Basrayatha

KAHNDAQ

KARROCAN
EMIRATE

Bad City

AL
QUOLAN
UDAR

SARADIA

KUNAMI
Dhabar

Khemikhal

KHEMED

QURAC
SALMAAH

ZAHRAIN

The Jebel Kadheïh
Desert

The Yellow Belt

SOCCENT
Forward
Operations Base

Wadesdah
Hasch El Hemm

HOBEIKA

Hagel

Abudin

UNAUDITE
ARAB
EMIRATES

Atlantis of
the Sands
(Ubar)

TRANS-
SABAL

Jannati Shahr

Jaffan

MANSUR

YEWAIRE

MAZIKHANDAR

SCALE

0   100 200 300 400   500 kilometres

0   100 200 300 400   500 miles

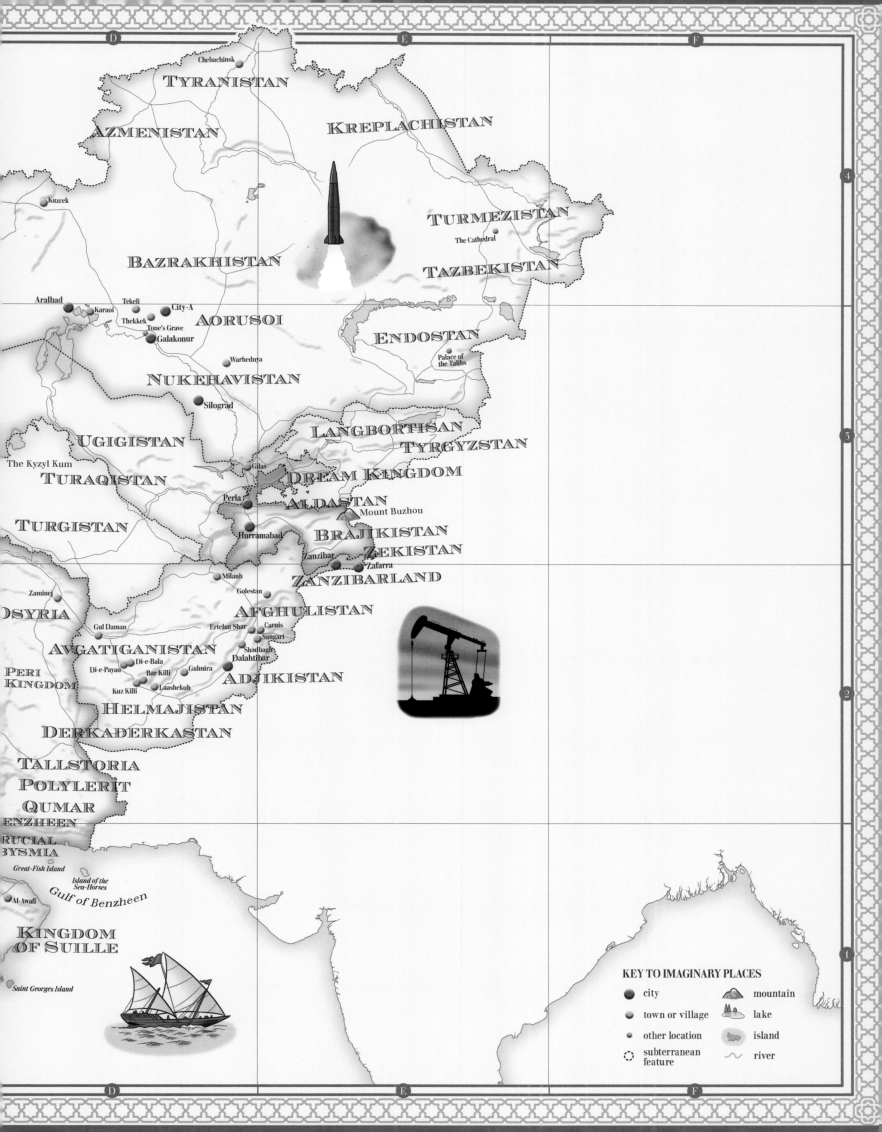

THE MIDDLE EAST AND CENTRAL ASIA

KEY LOCATIONS

For a full list of locations, see the location index on pages 130–150.

ABAR LAYLA
US MILITARY | IRAQ | TRAINING EXERCISE
The US military built several staged villages for training purposes during the Iraq and Afghanistan wars, all on US soil. This particular one was constructed in Fort Irwin, California, along with Medina Wasi (also mapped). **MAP pp.72–73, C2**

AMAZONIA
EASTERN TURKEY | MYTHOLOGY
The legendary home of the Amazons was traditionally somewhere between Albania and Chaldea. An Asia Minor location also places Amazonia close to our location for Thermyscira, the island home of the Amazons in *Wonder Woman* (see page 47). **MAP pp.72–73, B3**

ATLANTIS OF THE SANDS (UBAR)
SAUDI ARABIA | MYTHOLOGY
A Bedouin tradition speaks of a fabled 'lost city' somewhere in the deserts of the Arabian peninsula. Various archaeological expeditions, of varying repute, have claimed evidence of its existence, and multiple locations have been suggested. It has also gone by many names, though most commonly Ubar. **MAP pp.72–73, C1**

AZMENISTAN
The Expendables 3 AND
The Onion Movie | **FILMS**
Two very different films that both use the name Azmenistan. It is unclear where the

territory is supposed to lie, though in the *Onion* version, the inhabitants are Russian-speaking. **MAP pp.72–73, D4**

BAR KILLI
New Home, New Life
AFGHANISTAN | RADIO
This radio show, set in a pair of neighbouring villages, is basically what happened when the BBC transplanted *The Archers* to Afghanistan. It's remained popular since its first broadcast in 1994. Two versions are produced – one in Pashto, the other in Dari. We've mapped the village pairs along the Dari/Pashto-speaking border area. **MAP pp.72–73, D2**

BARTOVIA
The Simpsons **CASPIAN SEA | TV**
A fictional island nation (in the shape of Bart Simpson's head) that Sideshow Bob discovers on a globe when trying to find a place to make a new start in life. Based on the positioning of Bob's dagger, most likely located in the Caspian Sea. **MAP pp.72–73, C3**

CASPIAR
The mind of Andy Kaufman
CASPIAN SEA | PERFORMANCE ART
An island nation in the Caspian Sea (sometimes said to have sunk) and supposed home country of Kaufman's 'Foreign Man' character. Later referenced in *Taxi* as Latka Gravas's homeland. **MAP pp.72–73, C3**

GILAS
The Railway **BY HAMID ISMAILOV |**
UZBEKISTAN | NOVEL
This fictitious steppe town and cultural melting-pot is situated on the Silk Road nearby to Tashkent. **MAP pp.72–73, D3**

GRESTIN (EAST AND WEST)
Papers, Please
KAZAKHSTAN | VIDEO GAME
Papers, Please is a 2013 video game in which you play an immigration officer in the fictional country of Arstotzka who must check the paperwork of anyone trying to enter the country. Despite the unpromising premise, it is an addictive and much-loved game. It has also furnished this atlas with around a dozen fictional states (and cities) spread across this map and map of Eastern Europe (see pages 50–51). Grestin, where the immigration officer is based, has been divided into East Grestin and West Grestin, with a border wall and checkpoints, in the manner of Berlin during the Cold War. **MAP pp.72–73, C4**

GULMIRA
MARVEL CINEMATIC UNIVERSE |
AFGHANISTAN | FILM
A town in Afghanistan and home of Yinsen, the scientist and surgeon who saved the life of Tony Stark – located close to mountains, which probably puts it around the fringe of Afghanistan's central mountains. **MAP pp.72–73, D2**

HAV
Last Letters From Hav
BY JAN MORRIS
EASTERN MEDITERRANEAN | NOVEL
Though posing as a travelogue, *Last Letters from Hav* is an entirely fictitious account of a country that does not exist. Hav is described in great detail, though its location is left vague. We know, however, that it is a peninsula in the Eastern Mediterranean. **MAP pp.72–73, B2/B3**

JÉRIMADETH
So Boaz Slept
BY VICTOR HUGO | IRAQ | POEM
Hugo invented this fictional city because he couldn't find a real name that fit the rhyme of the piece. It is mentioned in the same line as the ancient city of Ur, and possibly lies in proximity to it. **MAP pp.72–73, C2**

KAMISTAN (ISLAMIC REPUBLIC OF)
24 IRAN | TV
A Middle-Eastern country bearing many similarities to Iran, including a nuclear arms programme, and an antagonistic relationship with the USA. **MAP pp.72–73, C2**

KIRAI
DC UNIVERSE | IRAQ | COMICS
An analogue of Iraq. Although Kirai only appears in one story, the 1999 graphic novel *JLA: Superpower*, its plot prophesised the results of America's interventionalism in the region. Kirai's breakaway province of Vudistan, and its southern neighbour Negraad are not shown. **MAP pp.72–73, C2**

KUZCEK
Borat FILMS | KAZAKHSTAN | FILM
Filmed in Romania. Few clues are given as to where in Kazakhstan this is meant to be, other than a mountainous, rural location. Despite the vagueness, we couldn't leave this one out. **MAP pp.72–73, D4**

LANGBORTISAN
Donald Duck (DANISH TRANSLATION) | KYRGISTAN | COMIC
For reasons not entirely clear, Donald Duck enjoys enormous popularity in Scandinavian countries. A Danish translation of one cartoon coined the term Langbortisan, meaning 'far-away-istan'. We've chosen the furthest 'stan' from Denmark, Kyrgistan, for the location. **MAP pp.72–73, E3**

NUKEHAVISTAN
The Onion KAZAKHSTAN/UZBEKISTAN | ONLINE SATIRE
A former Soviet republic shaped like a mushroom cloud (borders not shown here), which international observers suspect may be developing nuclear weapons. A map shows the location between Kazakhstan and Uzbekistan. **MAP pp.72–73, D3/E3**

PALACE OF THE TALIBS
Relic Hunter TV
Royal palace located in the fictional sultanate of Endostan. Although a location is never specified within this 66-episode Canadian TV series, a train shown approaching the Endostan frontier is clearly Chinese, not just in design, but in that the locomotive bears the emblem of China Railways. Thus we've chosen to map Endostan to eastern Kazakhstan, close to the Chinese border, all thanks to the editor's choice of stock footage. **MAP pp.72–73, E3**

PARISTAN
CAUCASUS MOUNTAINS | MYTHOLOGY
In Muslim folklore, Paristan is the fairyland-like home of benevolent jinn (genies); traditionally it is located in the Caucasus Mountains. **MAP pp.72–73, B3/C3**

QURAC
DC UNIVERSE | PERSIAN GULF | COMICS
Qurac appears in many DC comics stories, including *Batman*, *Wonder Woman* and *Young Justice*. Its location has varied, but we've gone for a common setting on the Persian Gulf. The DC Universe includes many other, rarely encountered countries in the region that we have not mapped, including Kyran and Negraab. **MAP pp.72–73, C2**

TAZBEKISTAN
The Ambassadors
KAZAKHSTAN | TV
This central Asian 'stan' is '3,500 miles to Whitehall'. Otherwise, the location is uncertain, but its national animal is the ibex, which narrows it down to the eastern, mountainous 'stans'. **MAP pp.72–73, E4/F4**

TONE'S GRAVE
Log Horizon
BY MAMARE TOUNO AND KAZUHIRO HARA | KAZAKHSTAN | NOVELS/ANIME
Ruins that correspond to Gagarin's Start in the real world (the pad at the Baikonur launch facility from where Yuri Gagarin was launched into space). **MAP pp.72–73, D3**

TURGISTAN
6 Underground
TURKMENISTAN | FILM
The location is not shown, though clues are given, such as an extensive desert and access to a large body of water. The name and the authoritarian dictator appear to be modelled on Turkmenistan, which also matches the geographic clues. Indeed, the film is reportedly outlawed in that nation. **MAP pp.72–73, D3**

TURMEZISTAN
Doctor Who
KAZAKHSTAN | TV
A central Asian country mentioned or seen in several outings of the Doctor. Its location is never revealed. However, one block of episodes sees Chinese, American and Russian military forces on the verge of clashing within the nation, which might suggest a location in real-world Kazakhstan, close to both Russia and China. **MAP pp.72–73, E4/F4**

UQBAR
Tlön, Uqbar, Orbis Tertius
BY JORGE LUIS BORGES | GEORGIA/ARMENIA | SHORT STORY
A doubly fictional place, since it turns out to be fake within this mind-bending story. The vague description of its location has led others to place it in a strip of land between Georgia and Armenia. **MAP pp.72–73, C3**

URZIKSTAN
Call of Duty: Modern Warfare
GEORGIAN-RUSSIAN BORDER | VIDEO GAME
The country was deliberately made fictional to avoid giving offence. The central plot of an incursion by Russian forces suggests that Urzikstan borders Russia. **MAP pp.72–73, B3/C3**

ZERO-ONE (THE MACHINE CITY)
The Matrix IRAQ | FILM
Nation/city established by the machines prior to their war with humanity. It is supposedly located in Mesopotamia, the 'cradle of human civilization'. The most likely location is therefore the Tigris/Euphrates region, somewhere south or south-east of Baghdad, the location of many important early human cultures such as Babylon, Kish and Ur. **MAP pp.72–73, C2**

SOUTH ASIA

FROM PESHAWAR TO THE PENINSULA

ndia and its not-so-long-ago partitioned neighbours are rightly characterized as cultural melting pots. More than 120 languages are spoken across this region, including five of the world's ten commonest tongues (English, Hindustani, Bengali, Punjabi and Marathi). This plurality has provided a vibrant springboard for storytellers. While our map reflects many well-known Western yarns (including *Indiana Jones*, *The Jungle Book*, *Around the World in Eighty Days* and *A Passage to India*), the homegrown fiction steals the show.

Bollywood, of course, has provided dozens of imagined towns and villages, such as Almore (*Ishaqzaade*), Lalgaon (*Article 15*) and Ramgarh (*Sholay*), but the region's deep and often turbulent history has also inspired countless novels and short stories. Vikram Seth's *A Suitable Boy* provides the Ganges town of Brahmpur, while Salman Rushdie's *Shame* and *Haroun and the Sea of Stories* describe the Pakistani town of Q (Quetta) and the notional country of Alifbay (likely situated in Kashmir). Many other well-known names such as R.K. Narayan, Mahasweta Devi and Anita Desai have established towns and villages throughout fiction's topography.

The varied geography of the subcontinent easily lends itself to other mediums. Consider the fictional kingdom of Kyrat, the video-game setting of *Far Cry 4*. This mountainous kingdom nestles in the Himalayas alongside such fellows as the remote country of Yogistan, where hapless mountaineers attempt their ascents of Rum Doodle. It is just one of numerous peaks and sacred sites dotting this landscape, including no less a holiest of holies than the central office of the Kwik-E-Mart!

BY TRAIN TO KHOLBY, KALAPUR, PAKISTAN AND BHOWANI

Although it was the British Empire who introduced railways to the subcontinent, India has taken the iron horse to her heart. Unsurprising then that the country's railways feature prominently in fiction, but their conflation with Imperial politics shines through.

One of the earliest examples may be Jules Verne's *Around the World in Eighty Days*. Both Phileas Fogg's epic adventure, and Verne's idea for it, were sparked by newspaper articles proclaiming that India could now be crossed coast-to-coast in three days, thanks to the completion of the Great Indian Peninsula Railway, furthermore making possible an 80-day circumnavigation of the globe. One wager later, and Fogg is on his way.

Verne did use his novel to take a jab or two at the British Empire's institutions. Halfway across India, Fogg discovers that *The Daily Telegraph* has reported incorrectly, when the railway abruptly terminates unfinished at the fictional town of Kholby. Passengers who have been sold through-tickets are expected to procure their own transport for the 50 miles (80km) to Allahabad! Still, Fogg has little reason for complaint, for during his subsequent journey by elephant he meets his bride-to-be, Aouda, at the imaginary pagoda of Pillaji.

In 1905 a more self-conscious examination of the Empire took place along the metals of the fictional North Indian Railway, primary setting for 1959's *North West Frontier*, a British-produced adventure film that finds room for introspection. Produced in the aftermath of the partition crisis, it depicts a motley international cast fleeing future-Pakistan amidst a Muslim uprising. Charged with delivering a young Hindu prince to safety, protagonist Captain Scott maintains that Britain's role in India is to keep order, but finds his convictions challenged throughout. Even the ramshackle escape train reflects a post-colonial awareness, being hauled by a battered old locomotive dubbed the 'Empress of India', or 'Victoria'. Finally, having reached safety in fictional Kalapur, young Prince Kishan asks if one day he will in turn have to fight Scott, so as to make the British 'go away' ...

In this atlas we've chosen to map Kalapur to Lahore, and nearby we find the border community of Mano Majra. Created by author Khushwant Singh for his historical novel *Train to Pakistan*, Mano Majra is presented as a mixed community of Sikhs and Muslims, whose mostly harmonious coexistence is suddenly torn apart by the partition crisis. Based on Singh's own experiences, the novel documents a rise in violence and tensions, but climaxes with a Sikh sacrificing his life to ensure a train of Muslim refugees safely crosses the border to Pakistan, inferring some small hope for the future.

Further south we encounter similar hope and yearning in Bhowani Junction, titular setting of the novel and film of the same name. While also exploring the tensions of the partition crisis through the lens of a railway town, this particular narrative features a protagonist of mixed ethnicities, torn between the worlds of Britain and India. And her name? Victoria.

GONE WITH GONDWANALAND: SUNKEN REALMS OF THE INDIAN OCEAN

In 1864, English zoologist Philip Sclater proposed that the Indian Ocean was once bridged by a now-sunken continent. How else to explain the fossils recently found in India that resembled the lemurs of far-off Madagascar? His lost land bridge was dubbed 'Lemuria' in their honour.

Though founded on little more than speculation, Lemuria proved influential. In 1870, German taxonomist Ernst Haeckel proposed it as the origin-point of the human species, a notion that appealed greatly to the Victorians' interest in theosophy and the occult. Consequently, Lemuria remains an established part of esoteric belief systems to this day, celebrated as a lost peak of human civilization akin to Atlantis.

Lemuria also won a subcontinental following, its 'discovery' coinciding with a renaissance in the Tamil culture of southern India and Sri Lanka. Supported by ancient Tamil legends of lost lands, mystic revivalists claimed that Lemuria, dubbed Kumari Kandam, was once the home of an advanced Tamil culture and birthplace of human civilization. Further parallels can be found within Ayyavazhi mythology, which speaks of the lost city of Thuvaraiyam Pathi, located somewhere to the south of present-day India.

In truth, Lemuria never existed, but Sclater was correct in a vague sense: India, Africa, Australia and even Antarctica were indeed once united, as part of the ancient supercontinent now known as Gondwanaland. His legacy lives on in Lemuria itself; the continent that Sclater named appears within literature, film, video games, comics and – inevitably – the works of both H.P. Lovecraft and Robert E. Howard.

Hence, for this atlas, we're happy to include Lemuria under both its Western and Tamil names, along with fabled Thuvaraiyam Pathi of the many-thousand streets. They stand in good company, lying in close proximity to the fictional island of Red Noah, which nineties anime *Nadia: The Secret of Blue Water* informs us to be a wrecked starship, a relic of ancient Atlantean spacefarers. Thus the myths of Lemuria and Atlantis once again align ...

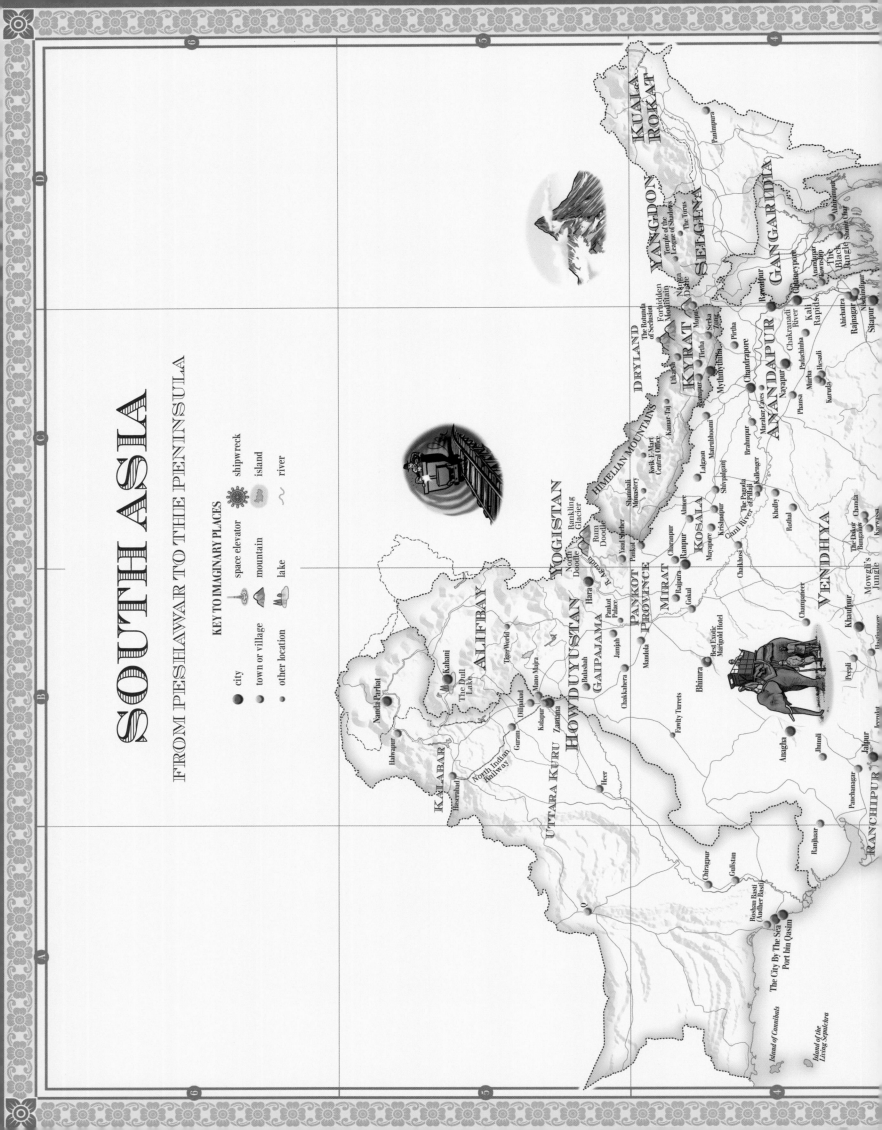

SOUTH ASIA

FROM PESHAWAR TO THE PENINSULA

KEY TO IMAGINARY PLACES

- ● city
- ● town or village
- • other location

- space elevator
- mountain
- lake

- shipwreck
- island
- river

KALABAR

Habrabad
Hiserabad

Nanda Parbat

Kahani
The Dull Lake

UTTARA KURU

North Indian Railway

Guran
Kalapur

Zamania
Mano Majra

Dilliphad

ALIFBAY

TigerWorld

Budlasah

Hara

HOWDUYUSTAN

GAIPAJAMA

Jamjah

Chakkahera

Mandola

Pankot Palace

PANKOT PROVINCE

YOGISTAN

Rankling Glacier

North Doodle

Rum Doodle

Aeonia

Vaatil Shreber

Pankot

Charanpur

Ranpur

MITRAT

Shivpalganj

Krishnapur

KOSALA

Mayapore

Gokul

Chakhbosi

Best Exotic Marigold Hotel

Bhimra

Fawlty Turrets

Champaneer

VENDHYA

Anagha

Jhumli

Peepli

Khattipur

Mowgli's Jungle

The Dâkor Bungalow

Chanda

Kurupya

RANCHIPUR

Jalpur

Panchanagar

Ranihaar

Gulistan

Chiragpur

Iheer

The City By The Sea
Port bin Qasim

Roshan Basti
Another Basti

Island of Cannibals

Island of the Living Sepulchra

HIMELIAN MOUNTAINS

DRYLAND

Shantholl Monastery

Kamar-Taj

Kwik-E-Mart Central Office

The Rotunda of Seclusion

Forbidden Mosifitah

Almore

Lalgaon

Matrubhoomi

ANANDAPUR

Brahmpur

Marabar Caves

Kalleenger

The Pagoda

Canal River of Pilhail

Rothal

Khulby

Nayapur

Phansa

Padatchinha

Murkha

Hesadi

Paikot

Chandrapore

Mythinithita

Tirtha

KYRAT

Serka

Banspur

Mogul

Pirtha

Utkarsh

YANGDON

Temple of the League of Shadows

Forbidden Mosifitah

Nanga Dale

SEHGENA

Rewadpur

Gnaneypure

Kali Rapids

The Black Jungle

Amitrampur

Shanti Char

Abichattra

Rajnagar

Nisindipur

Sitapur

GANGARIDIA

KUALA ROKAT

Panimpura

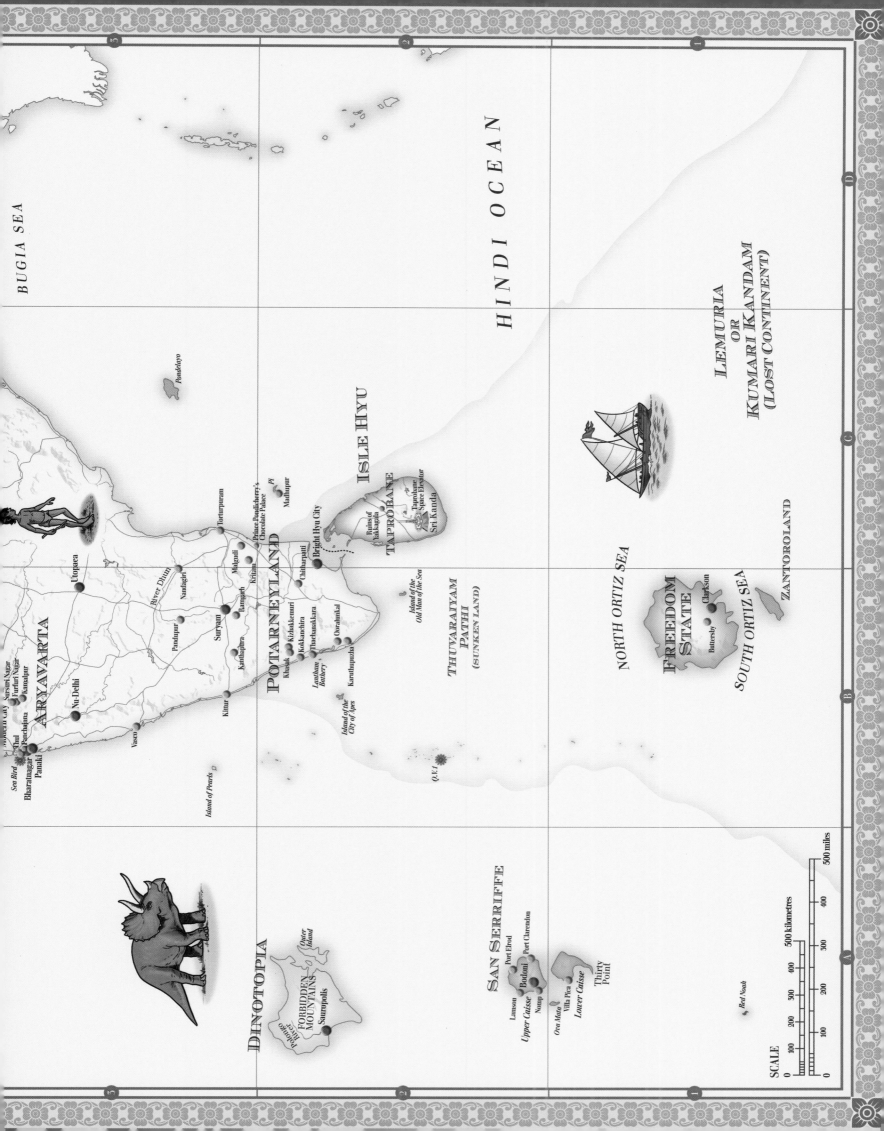

SOUTH ASIA

KEY LOCATIONS

For a full list of locations, see the location index on pages 130–150.

ALIFBAY
Haroun and the Sea of Stories BY SALMAN RUSHDIE | NORTH-WEST INDIA | NOVEL
Although the location is not specified, Alifbay contains a Dull Lake, which the novel's appendix associates with Dal Lake in Kashmir. **MAP pp.78–79, B5**

ANANDAPUR
DISNEY'S EXPEDITION EVEREST | INDIA | THEME PARK RIDE
We've explored railways built by the British within India (see page 77), so how about Indian trains built by Americans within Orlando? That's Disney's Animal Kingdom theme park, a portion of which is set within the fictional Indian Kingdom of Anandapur, depicted on maps as corresponding with real-world Bengal, Nepal and Bangladesh. Though the capital city of Nayapur exists only as a name on a map, park guests may freely explore the communities of Serka Zong and Anandapur Township. The latter is set on the country's Chakranadi River, offering rafting expeditions along its famous Kali Rapids, while Serka Zong is a former plantation town up in the Himilayan foothills. Here travellers may board the trains of the defunct Royal Anandapur Tea Company, now repurposed to ferry passengers to the foot of Mount Everest, via the ominous passes and chasms of the Forbidden Mountain, home of the fabled yeti! **MAP pp.78–79, C4**

DINOTOPIA
Dinotopia
INDIAN OCEAN | BOOKS/TV
Large island nation located in the Indian Ocean. It houses a hybridized civilization of shipwrecked humans and dinosaurs that survived the Cretaceous–Tertiary mass extinction event and eventually developed sentience. **MAP pp.78–79, A2**

FAWLTY TURRETS
Goodness Gracious Me
INDIA | TV
A parody of Fawlty Towers, this is the desert palace of a former Maharaja that has been converted into a hotel. With few clues to work with, we've mapped it to Lalgarh Palace, which is indeed the desert palace of a former Maharaja that has been converted into a hotel! **MAP pp.78–79, B4**

ISLAND OF THE OLD MAN OF THE SEA
Sinbad the Sailor
INDIAN OCEAN | SHORT STORY
On his fifth voyage, the unlucky Sinbad chances across the Old Man of the Sea, a legendary figure who delights in wrapping his legs around the shoulders of unfortunate sailors and never letting go. Little information is given about the location of the island, but Sinbad does later pass a place known for cinnamon and pepper, suggesting the Sri Lanka and Kerala region. On the same voyage, he encounters the City/Island of Apes and the Island of Pearls, both of which we've guessed locations for. **MAP pp.78–79, B2**

JALPUR
Mira, Royal Detective
JALPUR | TV
Slightly fantastic port city architecturally influenced by northwestern India, specifically parts of Rajasthan. However, as this state has no sea access, we've mapped Jalpur to the nearest piece of coastline, the Gulf of Khambhat. **MAP pp.78–79, B4**

KAMAR-TAJ
Doctor Strange NEPAL | FILM
Home of the Ancient one, and site of Doctor Strange's mystical training. It is located in the Himalayas, somewhere near Kathmandu. **MAP pp.78–79, C4**

KITTUR
Between the Assassinations
BY ARAVIND ADIGA | INDIA | NOVEL
Not the real town of this name in Northern Karnataka but a fictional place that began life as an analogue of author Aravind Adiga's hometown of Mangalore. **MAP pp.78–79, B3**

MADHUPUR
WORKS OF INDIRA GANESAN | INDIA | NOVELS
Madhupur is the primary town on the fictional island of Pi (no relation to *Life of Pi*), described as 'the tiniest crescent-shaped bindi above the eyebrows to Sri Lanka's tear, a small spit of an island floating in the Bay of Bengal, resembling Madras when Madras was Madras and not Chennai, but resembling Chennai as time went on.' **MAP pp.78–79, C2**

MALGUDI
WORKS OF R.K. NARAYAN |
INDIA | NOVELS
Malgudi lies in Southern India, on the
real-life railway connecting Trichinopoly
(now Trichy) and Madras (now Chennai),
though it lies closer to Madras than
Trichy. The town is bordered on one side
by the fictional Sarayu river and on the
other by the equally fictional Mempi
forest. **MAP pp.78–79, C3**

MARABAR CAVES
A Passage to India
BY E.M. FORSTER |
INDIA | NOVEL/FILM
A key location in the story, the caves are
based on the Barabar Caves in Bihar,
India. **MAP pp.78–79, C4**

MOWGLI'S JUNGLE
The Jungle Book
BY RUDYARD KIPLING |
INDIA | NOVEL
The world's most famous fictional jungle
doesn't have a specified name but we
can be confident of its rough location.
Kipling was inspired by the real jungles
around Seoni in Madhya Pradesh. Indeed,
'Seeonee' is mentioned several times in
the text as the home turf of the wolf pack.
MAP pp.78–79, B4/C4

PANKOT PALACE
Indiana Jones and the
Temple of Doom **INDIA | FILM**
Located in the fictional Province of
Pankot, which is in the remote northern
part of India, on the Yamuna River.
The name presumably comes from Paul
Scott's novel series, *The Raj Quartet*.
MAP pp.78–79, B5

PONDELAYO
Through Darkest Pondelayo
BY JOAN LINDSAY |
SRI LANKA | NOVEL
A fictional island some ten days' sailing
from Sri Lanka, possibly in the Bay
of Bengal. The island includes many
evocative place names, such as Dead
Mother-in-Law's Cove and Mount Blim
Blam (not shown). **MAP pp.78–79, C3**

PORT BIN QASIM
Noon **BY ASTISH TASEER |**
PAKISTAN | NOVEL
Fictional Pakistani port city whose
name is likely derived from the real Port
Muhammid Bin Qasim, located southeast
of Karachi. The real Port Qasim is just a
harbour, but the fictionalized one is a
full-blown city. **MAP pp.78–79, A4**

RAJNAGAR
RAJ COMICS | INDIA | COMICS
Home city of Dhruva Mehra, aka Super
Commando Dhruva. The character began
a personal quest against injustice after the
murder of his parents, an origin akin to
that of Bruce Wayne. However Dhruva's
primary-coloured costume and sleekly
optimistic native city, Rajnagar, are more
evocative of Superman and Metropolis
than Gotham City. Rajnagar can be
loosely translated as Raj City, so we've
conflated it with Kolkata (Calcutta),
one-time capital of the British Raj. We've
also placed the Gotham-esque port city
of Sitapur, from the Devi comics, nearby.
MAP pp.78–79, D4

ROSHAN BASTI
(ANDHER BASTI)
3 Bahadur **PAKISTAN | FILM**
This film, the first feature-length
animation to be produced in Pakistan,
details the exploits of three young heroes
to save their hometown of Roshan Basti
– the 'Town of Light' – which becomes
corrupted into Andher Basti, the 'Town of
Darkness'. Location-wise, we decided to
place it in proximity to Karachi, where the
film was produced. **MAP pp.78–79, A4**

THE ROTUNDA
OF SECLUSION
The Powerpuff Girls **TV**
Wonderfully-named headquarters of
AWSM (The Association of World
Super Men), itself a parody of alliances
such as the Justice League and Avengers.
It is located on the summit of Mount
Neverest, an obvious parallel of Everest
that also appears in the 2017 *Ducktales*
reboot. **MAP pp.78–79, C4**

SAN SERRIFFE
Guardian **NEWSPAPER |**
INDIAN OCEAN | NEWSPAPER
An April Fool's joke from 1977 featured
a story about this 'small archipelago,
its main islands grouped roughly in
the shape of a semicolon, in the Indian
Ocean'. The chain is populated with
location names inspired by typesetting
terms, many of which we've included; its
rough location is given on a map of the
Indian Ocean. **MAP pp.78–79, A1/A2**

SHAMBALI
MONASTERY
Overwatch **NEPAL | VIDEO GAME**
A temple located in the Nepalese
Himalayas, which is home to an order of
spiritually awakened mechanical monks
MAP pp.78–79, C4

TAPROBANE
The Fountains of Paradise
BY ARTHUR C. CLARKE
INDIAN OCEAN | NOVEL
Location of a proposed space elevator.
According to the author, Taprobane is
'about ninety percent congruent with the
island of Ceylon' (Sri Lanka). In reality,
it would need to be further south, on
the equator, as per the physics of space
elevators. Taprobana was the name used
by the Ancient Greeks for Sri Lanka.
MAP pp.78–79, C2

TEMPLE OF
THE LEAGUE
OF SHADOWS
Batman Begins
BHUTAN | FILM
Some sources put this temple in Tibet or
Ladakh. However, Bruce Wayne starts
the film in a Bhutan prison, and after
being dumped at the side of a road, travels
to the temple on foot. The temple is also
inspired by the real Bhutanese monastery
of Paro Taktsang (the Tiger's Nest).
MAP pp.78–79, D4

THE TORUS
Epoch **BHUTAN | FILM**
Not many western films have been set
in Bhutan. One exception is the science
fiction film *Epoch*. The film concerns
an extra-terrestrial object buried for
millennia in the mountains of that
country, and known as The Torus.
Scientists determine that this gigantic
artefact has played a shaping role in the
evolution of life on Earth, tying things
neatly in with Lemuria elsewhere on
this map. **MAP pp.78–79, D4**

AFRICA

THINGS COME TOGETHER

hile hosting a lunch of African leaders in September 2017, President Donald Trump paid tribute to his guests. 'I'm greatly honoured,' he said, ... to be joined by the leaders of Côte d'Ivoire, Ethiopia, Ghana, Guinea, Nambia ...' Unfortunately, the dignitary from Nambia was not in the room, as the country does not actually exist. This appears to have been a Trumpism for Namibia.

The hapless President is not the first to make up an African nation. As a quick glance at the map will show, the continent is swollen with fake states. We've mapped about 70, and the tally could have been much higher. Marvel Comics alone provide well over 30 candidates (including Wakanda, home of the Black Panther), of which we've only plotted a small number. Some of these make-believe territories are homegrown, such as the Kenya-inspired Aburiria from Ngũgĩ wa Thiong'o's *Wizard of the Crow*, or the Cameroon-like Ewawa from Alobwed'Epie's *The Death Certificate*. More often than not, though, Africa's bogus nations are Western inventions. Writers of the imperial age like Edgar Rice Burroughs (*Tarzan*), H. Rider Haggard (*King Solomon's Mines* and *She*), and Evelyn Waugh (*Scoop!* and *Black Mischief*) peppered the continent with fictional countries, towns and villages in which to stage their stories.

Their successors have continued this tradition into a post-colonial age. The real map of Africa changed radically in the decades following the Second World War, many nations winning their freedom from the dwindling Western empires. Sometimes the path to independence was smooth, though just as often it was not, a situation that proved potent inspiration for works of fiction. Thus dozens of entries on this map reflect the coups and corruption that have plagued many real African nations in the back half of the 20th century. Here we find Zangaro from Frederick Forsyth's *Dogs of War*, loosely based on Equatorial Guinea; the precarious Kinjaja, a parallel of Nigeria from William Boyd's *A Good Man in Africa*; and most overtly of all, the perpetually crisis-wracked state of Kush, from John Updike's *The Coup*.

Africa is also a continent of great natural beauty, whose abundant wildlife and stunning vistas have long fired the imagination of writers and film-makers. Although a human story, the *Tarzan* novels of Edgar Rice Burroughs are also an exploration of landscape. They transport us to a jungly realm as alien to most readers of the time as the lands of Barsoom (Mars), Burroughs's other famous contribution to pulp literature.

Animals make up the supporting cast of Tarzan but, a century later, they have become the stars of the show. *The Lion King*, set in the Serengeti of northern Tanzania, remains the highest grossing animated film of all time (the 2019 remake having regained the crown), and has also made the transition to a highly successful stage show. Meanwhile, DreamWorks Animation's *Madagascar*, which follows a bunch of New York zoo animals shipwrecked off that titular island, has spawned a bewildering succession of sequels and spin-offs. It seems the world still goes ape for the wild side of Africa.

THINGS FALL APART

Setting aside animated animal antics, let's take a closer look at a very different kind of blockbuster. Ask someone to name an African novel and they'll probably cite *Things Fall Apart* by Chinua Achebe. Published in 1958, this tale of Nigerian village life before and during the colonial era is thought to be the most widely read book in modern African literature. It's also very funny and very sad, in equal measure.

Achebe sets his scene in southern Nigeria, in a cluster of villages collectively known as Umuofia. The text is quite clear on the location, placing Umuofia on the east bank of the Niger River, near Achebe's own birthplace in the village of Ogidi. Most of the action takes place in one of these villages, a small settlement called Iguedo. While not mapped alongside Iguedo for reasons of space, we'd like to enter into the record the names of the 15 other villages mentioned in the novel: Abame, Aninta, Ezimili, Imo, Ire, Isike, Obodoani, Mbaino, Mbanta, Obodo, Uli, Umeru, Umuachi, Umuike and Umunso. The interested reader might enjoy sketching a map of their relative locations, using clues in the text.

As the title of the novel suggests, *Things Fall Apart* is the story of an unravelling. The protagonist, Okonkwo, is a self-made man who has overcome adversity to become the village leader of Iguedo. However, Okonkwo's flawed character eventually catches up with him, and a series of it-never-rains-but-it-pours events lead to his exile. At the same time, village life in Umuofia also begins to unravel with the coming of white people and Christianity. Neither thread leads to a happy place, with Okonkwo's own life ending in disgrace and suicide. One of the colonial overlords reflects that 'one could almost write a whole chapter on him. Perhaps not a whole chapter but a reasonable paragraph, at any rate'. We have done just that. But Okonkwo's eventful, if tragic, life has not ended in the obscurity predicted by the colonial officer. His tale has been read by millions, and his tiny village of Iguedo now appears in this atlas of the world.

Set in the 1890s, *Things Fall Apart* plays out amidst the Scramble for Africa, at the height of European meddling in Nigeria and surrounding nations. But Okwonko's village would have suffered in the post-colonial era too, located as it is in the region of Biafra, whose disastrous bid for independence in 1967 triggered the suffering and bloodshed of the Nigerian Civil War. This secessionist state serves as a template for the Democratic Republic of Dahum, which breaks away from the Nigeria-esque nation of Zanzarim in William Boyd's James Bond novel *Solo* (2013). Boyd has further contributed to the fictional topography of Nigeria with the country of Kinjanja, from his 1981 novel *A Good Man in Africa*.

Okwonko's homeland also finds itself beside another place of interest to colonial powers. If we head up what Boyd names the Zanza River (actually the Niger), the Victorian traveller might stumble into Borrioboola-Gha. This village, probably based on Lokoja, was the focus of the 'telescopic philanthropy' of Mrs Jellyby, in Charles Dickens's *Bleak House*. Matronly Mrs Jellyby wanted to send London's street vagrants over to Borrioboola-Gha to 'teach the natives to turn piano-forte legs and establish an export trade' – a satirical take by Dickens on some of the genuine 'African projects' of the day.

Continuing even further upriver we enter into Mali, and here we might find a haunting echo of slavery, half-buried amid the dunes. According to Clive Cussler's adventure novel *Sahara*, and its 2005 film adaptation, in 1865 the Confederate ironclad *Texas* escaped from Virginia in the final days of the American Civil War. Bearing the treasury needed to establish a government in exile, the ship crossed the Atlantic and sailed up a forgotten tributary of the Niger, becoming stranded when the watercourse sank underground. Like Ozymandias's broken statue, somewhere amidst the desert sands the *Texas* remains there still, a rusting relic of a war for a different kind of African emancipation.

THE BRONTËS IN AFRICA

The Brontë siblings might best be associated with Yorkshire, but their lively imaginations stretched much further, even from a young age. As children, sisters Charlotte, Anne and Emily and brother Branwell, invented whole fictional realms in which to play out their stories and games – an output of work that is today called the Brontë juvenilia. Though only fragments of the juvenilia survive, it remains an intriguing and surprisingly detailed corpus.

The first region of the juvenilia was known as the Glass Town Confederacy, a series of lands conjured into being by Branwell and Charlotte from 1827. Over time, the imaginary realm grew in detail, with a well-defined geography, historical backstory and a cast of (mostly martial) characters embodied by Branwell's toy soldiers. Glass Town eventually begat another land known as Angria, which became the focus of the later juvenilia.

Between them, the four siblings produced hundreds of poems, stories, plays and notes about their invented lands, all written in a tiny script as though composed by the toy soldiers. The role-playing often got competitive, and eventually Anne and Emily would turn to focus on their own creation of Gondal, an imaginary island in the North Pacific (see the South East Asia map on pages 90–91), and a contender for the first literary 'spin-off'.

We can be reasonably confident about the geography of the Glass Town Confederacy, because Branwell left a detailed map. Regions such as Wellington's Land, Parry's Land and Sneaky's Land cluster around the African coast, covering the region from Cote d'Ivoire to Cameroon. Well-defined islands such as Stump's Land, Monkey's Land and Frenchy Land complete the picture, and while the nation of Angria does not appear on Branwell's map (it was developed later), clues point to its location being somewhere in the region of Cameroon.

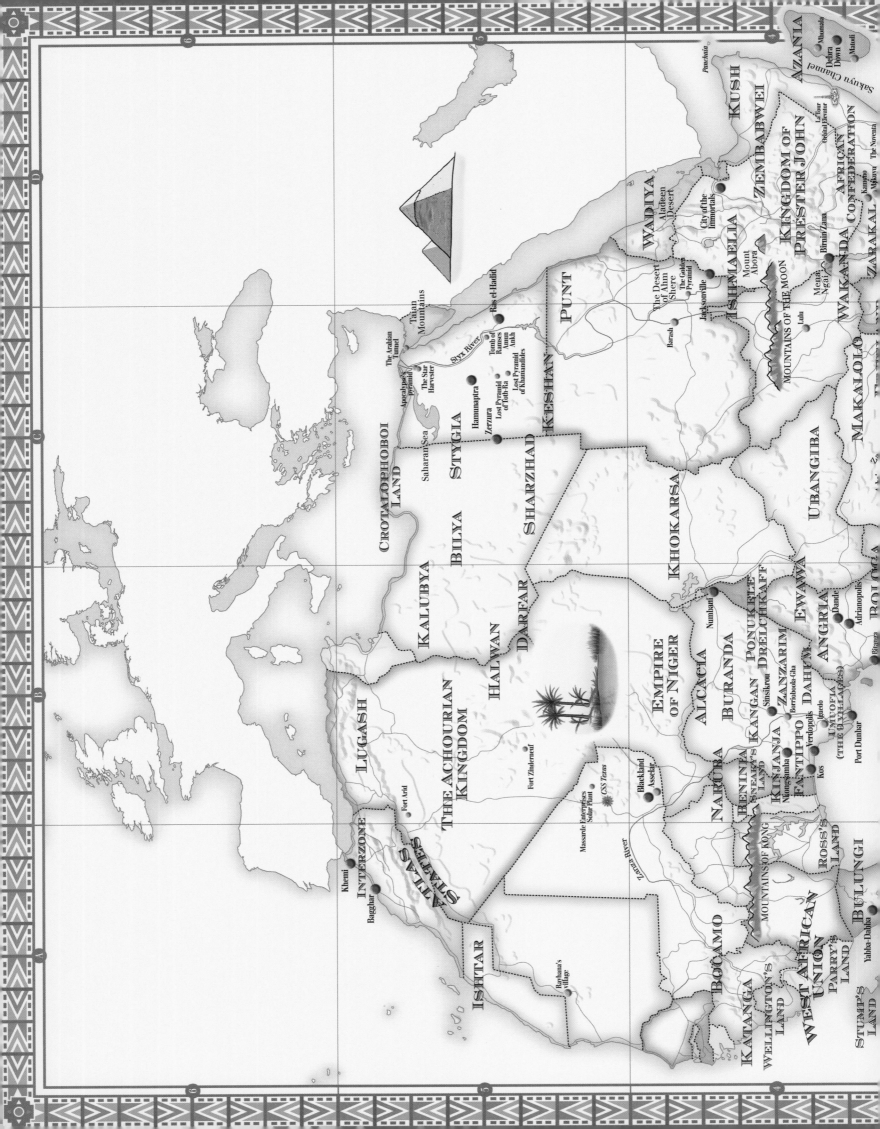

AFRICA
KEY LOCATIONS

For a full list of locations, see the location index on pages 130–150.

AFRICAN CONFEDERATION,
Star Trek: The Next Generation
BLOC | TV
A fictional confederation of nations including Somalia (birthplace of Geordi La Forge). Its extent is unknown, but we've gone for a collection of countries in eastern Africa. The United States of Africa is another bloc from Star Trek, and birthplace of Uhura. In the absence of any clues to location, however, we've left it off the map. **MAP pp.84–85, D4**

AZANIAN EMPIRE
Black Mischief BY EVELYN WAUGH |
INDIAN OCEAN | NOVEL
Waugh provided a detailed map of Azania, an island empire located off the coast of Somalia. The name is borrowed from the Romans who used 'Azania' for various parts of the African coast. The name has appeared in other works of fiction, including Kim Stanley Robinson's *Mars* novels, where Azania is a new name for South Africa. **MAP pp.84–85, D4**

BULUNGI
The Onion
WEST AFRICA | SATIRE
A fictional country lying south of the Ivory Coast and SE of Liberia in a satirical article, where the US's ambassador to the nation of Bulungi is accused of having made the country up. *The Onion* provides a handy map of this sizeable non-country. **MAP pp.84–85, A4**

EQUATORIAL KUNDU
The West Wing
WEST AFRICA | TV
When shown on maps, this fictional country occupies roughly the same space as Equatorial Guinea, although it is also sometimes described as being near the Ivory Coast, which is further west. The 'equatorial' part of the title reinforces the Guinea-analogue location. **MAP pp.84–85, B4**

GENOSHA
MARVEL COMICS | INDIAN OCEAN | COMICS/FILM
The Republic of Genosha is a fictional island nation located north-east of Madagascar, prominent in the X-Men series. The Ridgeback Mountains bisect the island. The smaller island of Krakoa is adjacent. **MAP pp.84–85, D3**

HAKUNA MATATA
The Lion King
TANZANIA | FILM
Not just a catchy song, but also Timon and Pumbaa's jungle oasis. It is divided from the Pride Lands by a swathe of desert. Simba travels into the sunset after his 'exile' and collapses near the oasis, so presumably it is some distance west of the Pride Lands (see below). **MAP pp.84–85, D3**

HAMUNAPTRA
The Mummy EGYPT | FILM
Fictional 'City of the Dead', lying in the remote deserts of Egypt; three days journey by boat upriver from Cairo, then two days by camel. O'Connell (Brendan Fraser) describes his former French Foreign Legion garrison as marching across Libya and into Egypt to reach Hamunaptra, so we've further refined its location as being west of the Nile. **MAP pp.84–85, C5**

ISHMAELIA
Scoop BY EVELYN WAUGH |
EAST AFRICA | NOVEL
Fictional country loosely based on Abyssinia/Ethiopia. Its capital is Jacksonville. **MAP pp.84–85, D4**

ISLAND OF THE ROC
Sinbad
INDIAN OCEAN | SHORT STORY
On his second voyage, Sinbad sails from Baghdad through many seas before being abandoned on an island somewhere in the Indian Ocean. The nearby mainland hosts rhinos and elephants, suggesting he is close to either Africa or India. He encounters a giant raptor called a *roc* or *rukh*, which carries him away to the Valley of Serpents. Rocs are mythical but traditionally associated with Madagascar. **MAP pp.84–85, D3**

JAKKALSDRIF
The Life and Times of Michael K BY J.M. COETZEE |
SOUTH AFRICA | NOVEL
Although Coetzee's masterpiece generally uses real geography, this relocation camp appears to be fictional. It is 8km (5 miles) from the real town of Prince Albert. A second camp, later in the story, is located in the real Cape Town suburb of Kenilworth, by the old racetrack. **MAP pp.84–85, C2**

JOLLIGINKI
The Story of Doctor Dolittle
BY HUGH LOFTING | EAST AFRICA | NOVEL
Home of the pushmi-pullyu, Jolliginki is on the east coast of Africa near Madagascar. MAP pp.84–85, D3

KAMENO
The River Between
BY NGŨGĨ WA THIONG'O |
KENYA | NOVEL
The two fictional villages of Kameno and Makuyu are somewhere in Thiong'o's native Kenya. The titular river that runs between them is also fictional, and named the Honia. MAP pp.84–85, D4

KARAIN *Islandia*
(AND SEQUELS) BY AUSTIN TAPPAN
WRIGHT | ATLANTIC OCEAN | NOVEL
A fictitious semi-continent whose history and topography Wright fleshed out over many years. Wright died tragically young in a car accident, but his papers were reworked and published as a novel after his death, with sequels written by Mark Saxton. Karain is near 'the unexplored wastes of Antarctica in the Southern Hemisphere', though there is debate over whether is should be in the Atlantic or the Pacific. Wright's unpublished notes favour the former, closer to Africa than South America; Saxton went for the Pacific. We're going with the fountainhead. MAP pp.84–85, A1/A2/B1/B2

KING SOLOMON'S MINES *King Solomon's Mines* BY H. RIDER HAGGARD | DEMOCRATIC REPUBLIC OF CONGO | NOVEL
Haggard's most famous novel provides a map, which gives the position of the mines, Sheba's Breasts (4,500m/15,000ft high mountains shaped like a bosom) and other locations relative to the non-fictional Lukanga River. We can conclude that the events take place in the modern Democratic Republic of Congo. MAP pp.84–85, C3

KINGDOM OF PRESTER JOHN
ETHIOPIA | FOLKLORE
Prester John was a mythical king who presided over a lost Christian kingdom of fabulous wealth. His lands were originally thought to lie in India or Central Asia, but over the centuries Africa became the favoured location, and specifically Ethiopia. MAP pp.84–85, D4

LIBERTATIA
MADAGASCAR | FOLKLORE
Mythical pirate colony, sometimes equated with Antongil Bay. It also appears in the video game *Uncharted 4* as Libertalia. MAP pp.84–85, D3

MOUNTAINS OF KONG
WEST AFRICA | FOLKLORE
A non-existent mountain range that was slavishly copied onto maps of the African interior for many decades, along with the Mountains of the Moon. Both have served as backdrops to numerous works of fiction. MAP pp.84–85, A4

NAMBIA
THE MYSTERIOUS BRAIN OF DONALD TRUMP | SOUTHERN AFRICA | GAFFE
President Trump's unique pronunciation of Namibia, in front of African leaders. The event has been mocked on social media to the point where Nambia has taken on a life of its own as a fictional country. MAP pp.84–85, B2/C2

NEW ZANZIBAR
The Simpsons EAST AFRICA | TV
In the episode *Simpson Safari*: during the Simpson's flight to Tanzania, they are informed that the country has been renamed 'New Zanzibar'. Seconds later it is renamed again to 'Pepsi Presents New Zanzibar'. We'll add the branding for the second print run if Pepsi agree to sponsor. MAP pp.84–85, C3/D3

THE NO. 1 LADIES' DETECTIVE AGENCY
The No.1 Ladies' Detective Agency BY ALEXANDER MCCALL SMITH | BOTSWANA | NOVEL
The book and its (many) sequels are set in the (real) south Botswanan town of Gaborone. MAP pp.84–85, C2

OPAR
Tarzan NOVELS OF EDGAR RICE BURROUGHS AND THE NOVELS OF PHILIP JOSÉ FARMER | CONGO/DRC | NOVELS
Opar, deep in the jungle, is a lost colony of Atlantis. While not the original source, the Disney animated series based on *Tarzan* (which featured Opar in several episodes) uses a map of Africa in the opening credits, with a rapid zoom/slash into the Congo basin region. The 2016 movie *The Legend of Tarzan* also specifically places Opar in the Belgian Congo. Opar was also used by Philip José Farmer, who expanded the 'Tarzan universe' created by Burroughs. MAP pp.84–85, C3

THE PRIDE LANDS
The Lion King
TANZANIA | FILM
This location is clearly inspired by the Serengeti, which is part of Tanzania. In the opening montage we see birds and elephants travelling past Kilimanjaro (which also lies in Tanzania, and is mentioned by name in the sequel) to attend Simba's presentation. The production team also visited Kenya for inspiration. We'd therefore suggest the Pride Lands are in the part of Tanzania that borders Kenya, in the vicinity of Kilimanjaro. Tanganyika (a former sovereign state that forms present-day mainland Tanzania) is also mentioned by name in the sequel. MAP pp.84–85, D3

SAHARAN SEA
Invasion of the Sea BY JULES VERNE | NORTH-EAST AFRICA | NOVEL
An earthquake causes waters from the Mediterranean to flood the low-lying regions of the Sahara Desert. The concept has been considered seriously as a desert-reclamation strategy by scientists and entrepreneurs, and also appears in the novel *The Secret People* by John Wyndham. We've mapped the sea to a particularly low-lying region known as the Qattara Depression. MAP pp.84–85, C5

WAKANDA
MARVEL COMICS | EAST AFRICA | VARIOUS
The home of Black Panther. The location is shown on maps in the films as a small area surrounding Lake Turkana. In reality this area is desert and does not possess the lush jungles seen in the film, but possibly that reflects Wakanda's intentional efforts to deflect attention from themselves. Numerous other settlements in Wakanda are mentioned in canon, though not mapped here. These include Birnin S'yan, Birnin Azzaria, Birnin T'Chaka, Birnin Bashenga, Birnin Djata, Birnin Benhazin and Birnin Tsauni. MAP pp.84–85, D4

SOUTHEAST ASIA

WILDS, WAVES, WORLDS AND WARS

The geography of Southeast Asia is truly unique. The mainland countries of Myanmar, Laos, Thailand and Vietnam all seem to stretch south as though striving to reach the equator, or to encircle Cambodia like a prized jewel. As we head south, the land breaks up into the innumerable isles of Indonesia, Malaysia, the Philippines and their neighbouring island groups. And while the winding rivers and dense jungles of the mainland have provided the setting for many works of fiction, it is to the islands we have found ourselves most drawn while compiling this atlas.

All life is here. Literally. Whether it's King Kong lurking on Skull Island (see below), Dave the Octopus's Secret Island from *The Penguins of Madagascar*, or the hostile wildlife of the Rook Islands of *Far Cry 3*, this is a region where the animals make as big an impact as humans. Humanoids both synthetic and undead feature too, represented by the rebellious robots of *Westworld* and the zombies of the Banoi Archipelago, courtesy of *Dead Island*.

Literary greats have populated these isles. Aldous Huxley gave us the lands of Pala and Rendang in his final novel, *Island*, while Johann David Wyss shipwrecked the Swiss Family Robinson nearby in his immortal novel of 1812. Both Biggles and Tintin have flown across these seas. We even find another set of fictional isles from the Brontë siblings; the island kingdom of Gondal and its surrounding territories were invented by Emily and Anne as a kind of spin-off from their childhood realms of Angria and the Glasstown Confederacy (see The Brontës in Africa, page 83). Fictional Southeast Asia may not be as densely populated as other regions in this atlas, but it's every bit as rich.

SURFING WITH CONRAD, BISON AND KURTZ

Every so often Hollywood bestows upon the world something wonderful and precious, a movie that is simultaneously so bad, and yet so utterly earnest, that it is destined to become a guilty pleasure. The 1990s were a goldmine for such offerings, and two spectacular examples arrived practically back-to-back: family comedy *Surf Ninjas* (1993) and video-game adaptation *Street Fighter* (1994). And both are set in Southeast Asia. *Surf Ninjas* is a schlocky comedy about two California youths who discover they are the deposed crown princes of an Asian island kingdom. The film apparently has higher cultural aspirations, because the fictional realm these 'surfer dudes' are destined to inherit is the island nation of Patusan, first invented by literary titan Joseph Conrad!

Surf Ninjas offers a map to Patusan, placing it off the coast of surf paradise Vietnam. This contradicts Conrad's 1900 novel *Lord Jim*, which not only codified Patusan, but implied a location somewhere in the vicinity of Sumatra. At first glance, Conrad's tale of English seaman 'Jim' winning the hearts and laurels of South Sea islanders has a smack of colonialism about it. But this adventure yarn is underpinned by the author's ever-present themes of doubt and self-deception. In that sense, *Surf Ninjas* could be interpreted as equally pseudo-colonialist – although the heroes are native-born Patusani, their successful return to their island home is enabled by their American friends and cultural upbringing. Though perhaps we're giving too much credit to a film whose entire plot revolves around surfing, ninjutsu and a magical Sega Game Gear …

… which offers us a neat segue into *Street Fighter*. While this video-game franchise's roster of heroes and villains is legendary, it is not exactly thick on plot. Filmmaker Steven E. de Souza thus had plenty of work to do when he wrote and directed his 1994 big-budget adaptation. His solution was to frame *Street Fighter* in the context of a situation familiar to the 1990s: an international crisis. Thus, the film introduces us to the war-torn Southeast Asian nation of Shadaloo, with the Street Fighters themselves representing various conflicting factions.

Further credit is due to the production department, because maps in the film consistently show Shadaloo and its environs to be geographically cohesive. The nation corresponds to parts of real-world Myanmar, and its capital is shown to lie on the Gulf of Martaban, at the mouth of the fictional Shadaloo River, which we have chosen to map to the real-world Salween River. And somewhere in this waterway's delta, we encounter (*of course!*) arch-antagonist Colonel Bison himself, operating out of a ruined temple which the would-be dictator envisions as his future world capital of Bisonopolis.

Another river on this map takes us back, both to the surf beaches of Vietnam and the work of Joseph Conrad, as interpreted through the lens of Francis Ford Coppola. 1979's *Apocalypse Now* is a loose adaptation of Conrad's *Heart of Darkness*, set among the mud and blood of the Vietnam War. Instead of following the original novel's journey up the Congo into the darkest depths of both the African jungle and the human heart, Coppola's narrative sends its cast up the fictional Nùng to locate and terminate rogue US officer Colonel Kurtz, with extreme prejudice. The resulting voyage into a hell of human making only magnifies the horrors of Conrad's novel. It is also a journey that can be easily traced in this atlas, thanks to a map produced by Dean Tavoularis, Coppola's production designer, that clearly shows the Nùng to be an analogue of the real-world Mekong River.

KONG'S KINGDOM

He lives on an island, somewhere out there in the furthest reaches of the Earth. It is a fractured isle, volcanic, ominous, forever shrouded in fog, as if nature had tried to secrete away an unfinished, blasphemous failure, one known only through whispered tales. Rumour speaks of ancient ruins, of a mighty civilization toppled by time's remorseless march, and of a great wall, as strong as the day its foundations were laid, holding back a dark jungle of primeval terrors. Beyond its ramparts, amidst shrouded peaks and tangled depths, reigns the monarch of this waking nightmare, a creature worshipped as a god, neither beast nor man. A primate king, for a primal kingdom. The lonely lord of Skull Island, mighty Kong!

For a character whose origins are rooted in pulp entertainment, King Kong has a staying power that few can deny. Ever since his 1930s debut, this great ape has captured the imaginations of cinemagoers and filmmakers alike, leading to an ongoing dynasty of reincarnation and reinterpretation. Kong embodies both brutal strength and tragic pathos, and has battled a bestiary of foes, including dinosaurs, monsters and Godzilla himself.

And if you should seek his kingdom, we're happy to point the way. With rare exceptions, Skull Island's location has consistently been painted in the Indian Ocean. The original 1933 film situated it about 2,000km (1,300 miles) south of India, while the 1976 remake gave a location far to the south of Java. One exception is the recent incarnation, *Kong: Skull Island*, which placed the King's demesne in the South Pacific, east of Kiribati according to the script.

For this atlas, however, we've taken Peter Jackson's 2005 blockbuster as our primary canon, since this incarnation not only invested the most energy into developing Skull Island, but also gave coordinates in supplementary materials: 6 degrees south and 93 minutes east. The same sources also reveal Skull Island to be gradually shrinking, crumbling in a series of death-throes, and that in 1948 a massive earthquake measuring 9.2 on the Richter Scale finally sunk the island beneath the waves, taking all its secrets and horrific marvels with it. But maybe, just maybe, something survives in that patch of trackless ocean, 1,000km west of Sumatra …

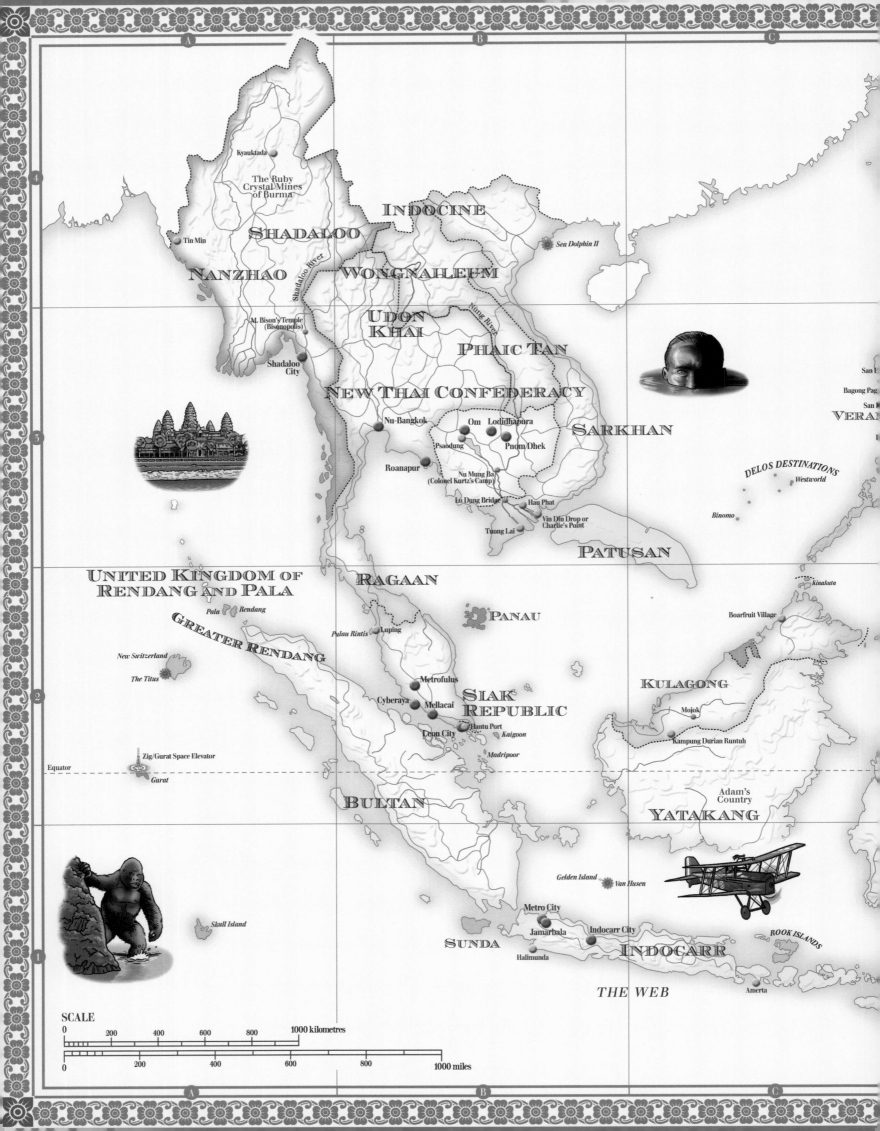

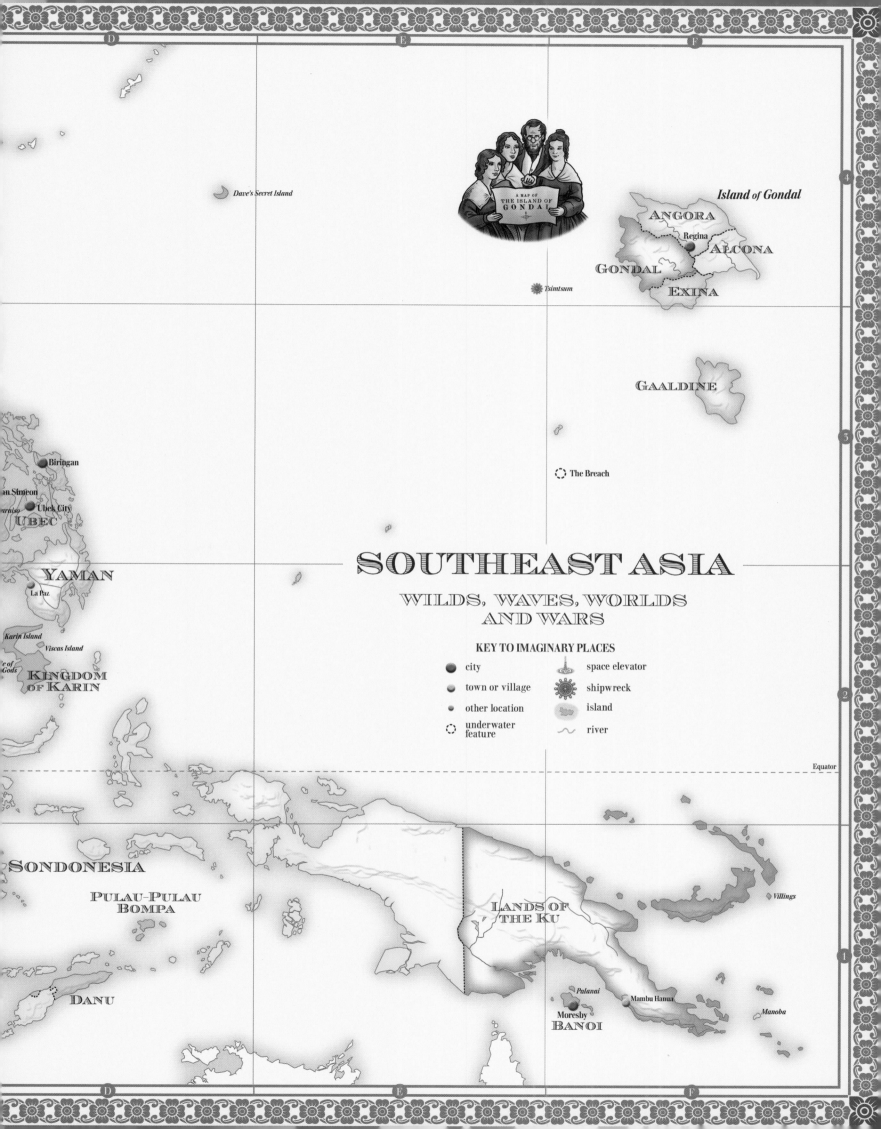

Island of Gondal

Dave's Secret Island

ANGORA
Regina
GONDAL   ALCONA
EXINA

✴ Tsimtsum

GAALDINE

⬡ The Breach

Biringan

n Simeon
arniso   Ubek City
UBEC

YAMAN

La Paz

Karin Island

Viscas Island

e of
Gods

KINGDOM
of KARIN

SOUTHEAST ASIA

WILDS, WAVES, WORLDS
AND WARS

KEY TO IMAGINARY PLACES

●	city	⟁	space elevator
●	town or village	✷	shipwreck
•	other location	▨	island
⬡	underwater feature	〰	river

- - - - - Equator - - - - -

SONDONESIA

PULAU-PULAU
BOMPA

LANDS OF
THE KU

◊ Villings

Palanai
Mambu Hanua

Moresby
DANU   BANOI   Manoba

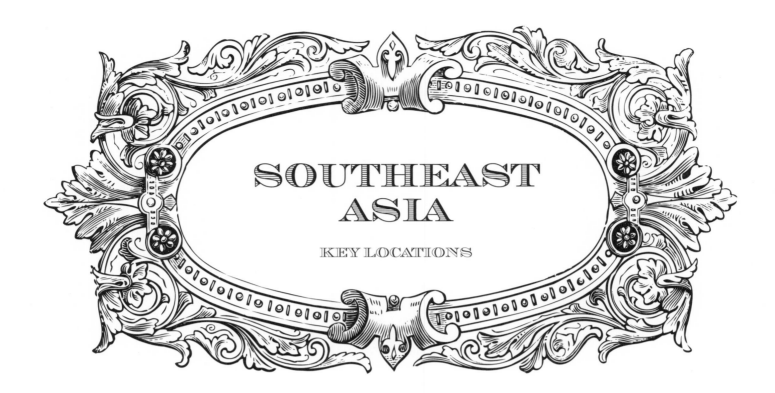

SOUTHEAST ASIA

KEY LOCATIONS

For a full list of locations, see the location index on pages 130–150.

BINOMO
VLADIMIR KUZNETSOV AND ALEXEI STOLYAROV | SOUTH CHINA SEA | PRANK
Fictional island nation in the South China Sea invented by two Russian comedians to prank the US Ambassador to the United Nations. **MAP pp.90–91, C3**

THE BREACH
Pacific Rim
PACIFIC OCEAN | FILM
Portal located on the floor of Challenger Deep, connecting Earth to the Anteverse. It is through the Breach that the monstrous Kaiju pass to attack humanity. **MAP pp.90–91, F3**

DAVE'S SECRET ISLAND
The Penguin's of Madagascar
PHILIPPINE SEA | FILM
Crescent-shaped island and the lair of Dave the Octopus. Its coordinates are shown as roughly 21.5N, 131.3E. **MAP pp.90–91, D4**

GONDAL
JUVENALIA OF THE BRONTË SISTERS | PACIFIC OCEAN | JUVENALIA
When they were young, the four Brontë children created a group of imaginary kingdoms based in Africa (see page 83) and the Pacific. Gondal and its neighbours were located on a northerly Pacific island, and were characterized by moorlands reminiscent of their home in Yorkshire. Much of their writing and maps have been lost, but enough information remains to partially piece together their imagined geography. Others have drawn detailed (if highly speculative) maps in an attempt to recreate the Brontës' worldbuilding. One of the best, found on the blog Man of Tin, imagined the main island as shaped like the county of Yorkshire, a conceit we've followed here. **MAP pp.90–91, F4**

LODIDHAPURA
Jungle Girl **BY EDGAR RICE BURROUGHS | CAMBODIA | NOVEL**
Burroughs is, of course, most famous for his African-set Tarzan novels, but he wrote many other stories of romance set in other parts of the world (and off-world in the case of his John Carter novels). *Jungle Girl* is a good example. Set among the Khmer ruins of Cambodia, hero Gordon King encounters the two warring cities of Lodidhapura and Pnom Dhek, as well as his titular love interest. **MAP pp.90–91, B3**

MADRIPOOR
MARVEL COMICS | SINGAPORE | COMICS
Principality of Madripoor (Madripura). Fictional island nation modelled on Singapore, lying in the Strait of Malacca between Singapore and Sumatra. The nation-state has appeared in dozens of Marvel comics, and is a particularly common setting in X-Men stories. Notably, Wolverine and Captain America's first canonical meeting was in Madripoor. **MAP pp.90–91, B2**

NEW SWITZERLAND
Swiss Family Robinson **BY JOHANN WYSS AND** *Second Fatherland* **BY JULES VERNE | INDIAN OCEAN | NOVEL/FILM**
Few details are given of the location of the island in the original novel. Its flora and fauna seem to come from all over the place and include penguins, bears and kangaroos. Verne's sequel offers more clues, placing it somewhere in the Indian Ocean. Its shape is provided in a map by the author. **MAP pp.90–91, A2**

PANAU
Just Cause 2
MALAYSIA | VIDEO GAME
The setting for the second installment of the *Just Cause* franchise is an archipelago in the Gulf of Thailand, known as Panau or the Panau Islands. Its size and shape are well defined by an in-game map. In fact, the country even has its own flag and national anthem. The game features various fictional island groups, towns and cities, including the capital of Panau City, which we have not shown. **MAP pp.90–91, B2**

PHAIC TẶN
INDOCHINA | BOOK
This parody of Indochina countries could be located anywhere in the region, so we've placed it spanning three nations so as not to pick on any one! Its capital is Bumpattabumpah (not mapped). **MAP pp.90–91, B3**

ROANAPUR
Black Lagoon BY REI HIROE |
THAILAND | MANGA/ANIME

Until 30 or 40 years ago, fictional Roanapur was a dying port. Deserters from the Vietnam War took refuge here and were soon followed by smugglers, mercenaries and killers of all stripes, prompting the city's rapid development as a centre of crime. What with the endless power-struggles between the cartels, triads, government actors and various mafia organisations that have dug themselves in here, it's certainly lively. A noose permanently hangs over the only bridge into the city, and the ocean approaches are dominated by a statue of the Buddha, which appropriately enough lies in ruins. According to an in-universe map, Roanapur is located in close proximity to the real Thai city of Trat. MAP pp.90–91, B3

ROOK ISLANDS
Far Cry 3
INDONESIA | VIDEO GAME

Said to lie somewhere in Indonesia, the location of these islands is uncertain, but online speculation about the diversity of wildlife has suggested a position between Bali and Lombok. MAP pp.90–91, C1

THE RUBY CRYSTAL MINES OF BURMA
The Transformers
MYANMAR | TV

Appears to be a stand-in for Myanmar's 'Valley of Rubies'. Appeared in the second-ever episode of the original cartoon, where the 'ruby crystals' were presented as a potent and potentially volatile energy source – the richest on the face of the Earth, to quote Megatron. MAP pp.90–91, A4

SAN SIMEON
The Sims 3
THE PHILIPPINES | VIDEO GAME

The subject of a highly popular fan-creation for *Sims 3*, this coastal city was modelled on the Spanish-era Philippines, and located within the fictional Nombre de Jesus province on Isla Paraiso island. Its architecture is based on several parts of the Philippines, including Silay and Taal. MAP pp.90–91, D3

SEA DOLPHIN II
Tomorrow Never Dies
VIETNAM | FILM

This stealth vessel was used by villain Elliot Carver in the 18th James Bond film as part of a scheme to provoke a war between Britain and China. Having been used to sink the British frigate HMS *Devonshire* (see China and North-East Asia, pag 104), it was discovered in the real Ha Long Bay (Vietnam) by Bond and his ally Wai Lin, who boarded the vessel and sunk it shortly after it sailed out of the bay to incite a clash between the fleets of the Royal Navy and the PLA Navy. It was only referred to as the 'Stealth Ship' in the film, but named *Sea Dolphin II* in the novelization. MAP pp.90–91, B4

TIN MIN
It Ain't Half Hot Mum
BURMA | TV

This beloved sitcom from the creators of Dad's Army was initially set in the real town of Deolali, India, and detailed the wartime exploits of a concert party made up of enlisted soldiers within the Royal Artillery. The second half of the series saw the company reassigned to the fictional Burmese village of Tin Min, located just across the Indian border. MAP pp.90–91, A4

TSIMTSUM
Life of Pi BY YANN MARTEL |
PACIFIC OCEAN | NOVEL/FILM

This is the Japanese-registered (and Swedish-built) cargo vessel that sinks while transporting protagonist Piscine Molitor 'Pi' Patel, his family and their zoo from India to Canada. The only human survivor is Pi himself, who ends up adrift in a lifeboat with Richard Parker, an adult Bengal Tiger. Slightly different accounts from the book and the film place the site of the sinking as four days out of Manilla and over the Mariana Trench, or as the novel rather nicely puts it, 'midway to Midway'. MAP pp.90–91, E4

UNITED KINGDOM OF RENDANG AND PALA
Island BY ALDOUS HUXLEY |
ANDAMAN SEA | NOVEL

Huxley's final novel concerns the fate of two island nations, Rendang and Pala. The pair are located between Sumatra and the Andamans, and eventually come together to form a United Kingdom. MAP pp.90–91, A2

THE WEB
2000 A.D. Comics
INDONESIA | COMICS

Mutated coral reefs that have overtaken the Indonesian islands. The fictional megacity of Djakarta is another creation of the *Judge Dredd* comics. It was built around old Jakarta, but is not shown as the name is too similar to reality. MAP pp.90–91, B1/C1

WESTWORLD
Westworld
SOUTH CHINA SEA | TV

In his 1973 sci-fi thriller *Westworld*, Michael Crichton introduced us to Delos, a high-concept theme park where guests could explore re-creations of medieval England, ancient Rome, or the Wild West. Staffed by robot hosts designed to look, act, talk (and bleed) like living humans, the Delos resort bears many similarities to Crichton's later *Jurassic Park*, including the way things go horribly wrong, very quickly. We are never told just where Delos is situated, though it appears to have been built in the harsh landscapes of the genuine American west. The recent TV adaptation, however, has not been so constrained, though it has played coy in handing out details. Eventually, a glimpse of a navigational chart makes everything clear: Westworld and its sister parks are located in the South China Sea (which real-world China has been steadily populating with artificial islands). More specifically, the park appears to lie in the non-fictional Spratly Islands, in the vicinity of aptly-named atoll Mischief Reef. MAP pp.90–91, C3

YAMAN
Recorded BY ARIZAL | WEB SERIES

Ancestral homeland of main character Arizal and her family. Canonically the character is Pinoy (Filipino), which suggests Yaman is what the Philippines have become in the show's far-future setting. MAP pp.90–91, D2

ZIG/GURAT SPACE ELEVATOR
Gunnm/Battle Angel Alita
INDIAN OCEAN | MANGA/ANIME/FILM

A Space Elevator connecting the space city of Zig (Binhar in some versions) to the ground anchor city of Gurat (Nezhar in some versions). MAP pp.90–91, A2

JAPAN

THE LAND OF THE RISING GUNDAM

This island nation has long fascinated the West, in part because of its cultural wealth and splendour. Even the name 'Japan' comes from an outside perspective (the actual Japanese name is 'Nihon' or 'Nippon'), from the Chinese 'Cipan', which Marco Polo's travel-writings introduced to the wider world as 'Zipangu'.

Another figure to travel this part of the world was Lemuel Gulliver, who we've encountered elsewhere in this atlas. Alas, Gulliver stops only briefly in Japan, spending the bulk of this particular voyage on the nearby (fictional) islands of Luggnagg and Balnibarbi. Both are included here, though we've had to grapple with Johnathan Swift's often contradictory descriptions and maps. Perhaps he was taking a satirical jab at the travelogues of his day, error-ridden imaginings produced by authors with no actual experience of the lands they described, to satisfy readers eager for accounts of exotic lands.

Japan continues to beguile the rest of the world to this day, thanks to its massive influence on popular culture through properties such as *Bleach*, *Your Name*, *Haruhi Suzumiya* and the many films of Studio Ghibli. The majority of our sources for this map came from such materials – manga, anime, video games and light novels. At times it was a struggle to fit everything in, but fans of *Pokemon* will be glad to see we managed to fit in (almost) all the 'home' locations of Nintendo's famous pocket-monsters.

Modern Japan is in some ways a dichotomy; a nation of stern and stoic tradition that has also produced some of the most charming and beloved fiction of recent generations; a land which gave birth to the samurai, and also the life-size *Gundam* mecha that now graces Yokohama's skyline. Fellow nerds, let's dive in together!

WARRING STATES AND SHOGUNATES

In 1467, Japan fractured into multiple states, sparking decades of civil warfare. Powerful *daimyo* houses fought one another to dominate the nation and claim for themselves the title of military dictator – Shogun. Central government was only re-established in the 17th century, when a victorious coalition of eastern *daimyo* unified the nation under a new and isolationist Shogunate.

The anime *Kabaneri of the Iron Fortress* imagines a history where it was the western *daimyo* that instead unified Japan. The nation (renamed Hinomoto) thus remained open, trading and industrializing alongside the western world while retaining a feudal caste system. Our map contains such locales as the railway workshops of Aragane Station, coal-mining Yashiro Station, and the fortress city of Kongoukaku, seat of the Shogun himself.

Oh, and this all takes place amidst a zombie apocalypse! It's bugnuts crazy, but even wilder is *Batman Ninja*, an animated film that displaces the Dark Knight and his rogues' gallery into Japan's period of warring states. Batman quickly allies with the fictional ninjas of the Bat Clan, while villains like Joker, Penguin and Poison Ivy establish themselves as warlords, ruling from fortresses named and tailored to their unique tastes.

Akira Kurosawa, Japan's greatest filmmaker, notably used history as a canvas on which to paint epic narratives such as *Throne of Blood*, which transformed Shakespeare's *Macbeth* into the tale of Washizu, an ambitious feudal general. Location-shooting took place on the volcanic slopes of Mount Fuji, which is where we've chosen to map Washizu's fictional Spider Web Castle. Sadly we could not include the village from *The Seven Samurai*, which doesn't even possess a name, let alone a hint as to its location!

Kamen Rider Build depicts a modern Japan suddenly (and literally) divided by a mysterious construct called the Sky Wall, splitting into three states (Hokuto, Seito and Touto) that rapidly diverge to the point of having their own heads of state, governing philosophies and units of currency.

Alternatively, anime series *Sora no Woto* (Sound of the Sky) presents future Japan as perhaps the last habitable place on a devastated Earth. Over many centuries, local customs and traditions have blended with those of refugees, resulting in a synergistic Euro-Asian culture that has largely forgotten its past. Even the name 'Japan' has faded away, replaced by Helvetia and Rome.

Log Horizon's Japan is also post-apocalyptic. Once a single entity, the nation splintered long ago into multiple polities, bound by loose alliances and old rivalries: there's the mercantile Ninetails Dominion, the Ezzo Empire, the Fourland Dukedom, the Holy Empire of Westelande, and Eastal, a coalition of city-states. Eastal's capital of Maihama is mapped to reality's Tokyo Disney Resort, and its landmarks (not all mapped) include the grass-grown ruins of Space Mountain, and the Venetian-themed waterfront of Tokyo DisneySea. Appropriately, Maihama's royal court exists at the heart of the former Disney resort – Castle Cinderella! And speaking of Tokyo ...

WELCOME TO (NEO) TOKYO!

Japan's capital has been destroyed more often in fiction than any other city, be it by giant monsters, robots, or regular-sized child psychics. Some call it the Matchstick City.

Notably, cyberpunk classic *Akira* opens with the city's mysterious destruction, before jumping us to the neon streets of its successor, Neo-Tokyo. *Neon Genesis Evangelion* takes things even further by introducing two replacements for Old Tokyo; there's Tokyo-2 in Nagano serving as a temporary capital pending completion of Tokyo-3. Sadly, none of these cities escape the fate of their prototype.

Sailor Moon, however, posits a utopian future where Crystal Tokyo is both the heart of Japan and the capital of Earth, ruled over by the titular sailor-suited heroine. Sailor Moon and her planetary pals presently reside in the real Tokyo district of Juban, renamed Crossroads for the belovedly bowdlerized American adaptation. These classic anime heroines appropriately live next door to Might Tower, centre of operations for All Might, the foremost Pro Hero of *My Hero Academia*'s superhuman society.

Schools and superheroes seem to go hand in hand within fictional Tokyo. The protagonists of *Ranma ¹/₂* reside in the fictional suburb of Furinkan, while the heroes of *Kamen Rider W* do battle nearby in ecologically-minded Futo City. *Yu-Gi-Oh!* meanwhile takes place in the imagined ward of Domino City, and it's fun to imagine what might happen if these card-game-playing protagonists were to wander west for a crossover game at *Kakegurui*'s Hyakkaou Private Academy, where the pecking order is determined by gambling skill! Along with the equally elite establishments of Shuchi'in and Ouran Academies, we've mapped Hyakkaou to the vicinity of the historic Gakushuin University, effectively Japan's Eton.

A more militaristic curriculum is enforced out in Tokyo Harbour at *Kill la Kill*'s Honnōji Academy, a school noted for its strict uniform code and the iron rule of its formidable Student Council President ('All Hail Lady Satsuki!'). Alternatively one might opt for *Code Geass*'s Ashford Academy, situated within the Britannian Concession, a part of Tokyo conceded to the Holy Britannian Empire after its brutal conquest of Area 11. Equally strange is the secret society of mages up at *Negima*'s Mahora Academy, the vampires living out on the artificial island known as the Bund, and Academy City's mutual indexing of magic and science.

Against these examples, *Cromartie High School* could almost be called normal, despite counting robots and Freddy Mercury among its students (yes, seriously). This rambunctious establishment bears the name of Warren Cromartie, an American baseball player who formerly played for the Tokyo Giants, thus we've mapped it to their stadium at the Tokyo Dome.

Similar guesswork was needed for the high-school setting of *Azumanga Daioh*, a gentle and much-loved slice-of-life comic. Ultimately we placed it within Shinjuku, the home ward of its original publisher. As for what to call this unnamed educational establishment, we followed the example of its fandom, dubbing it Azumanga High.

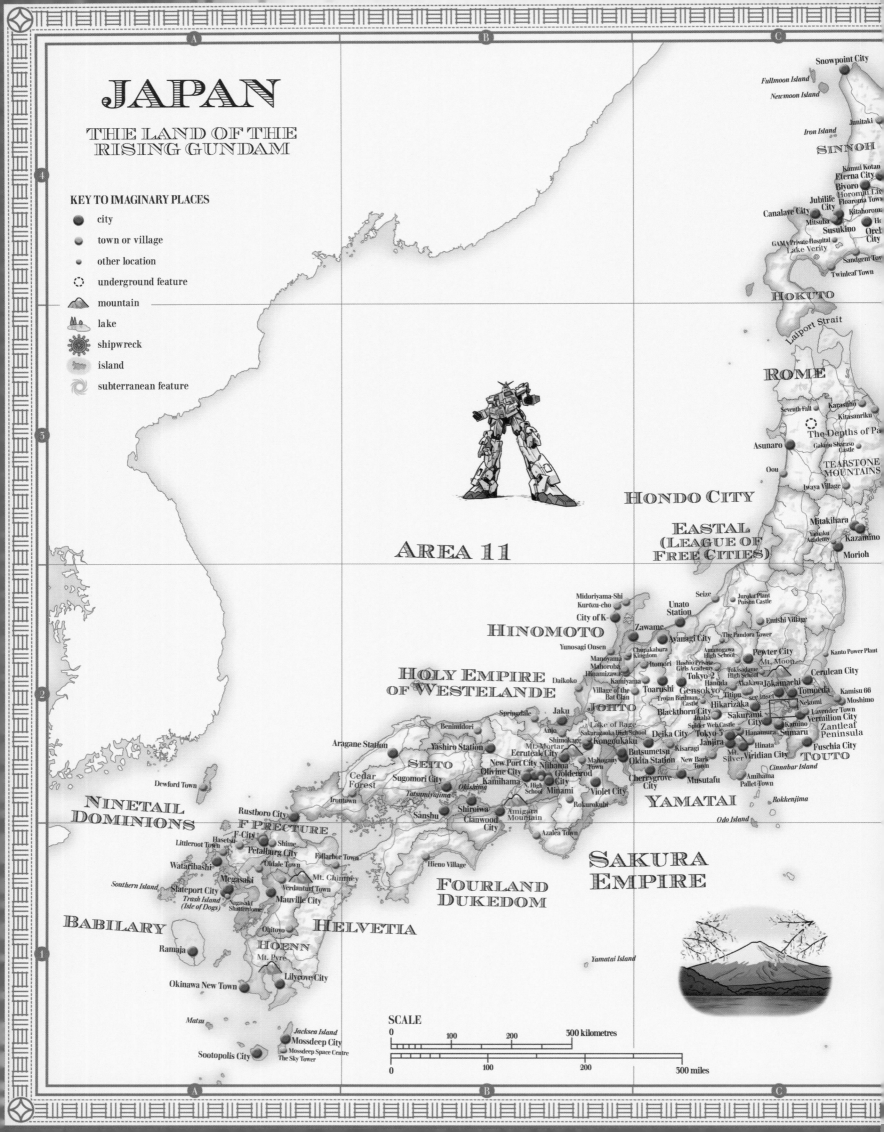

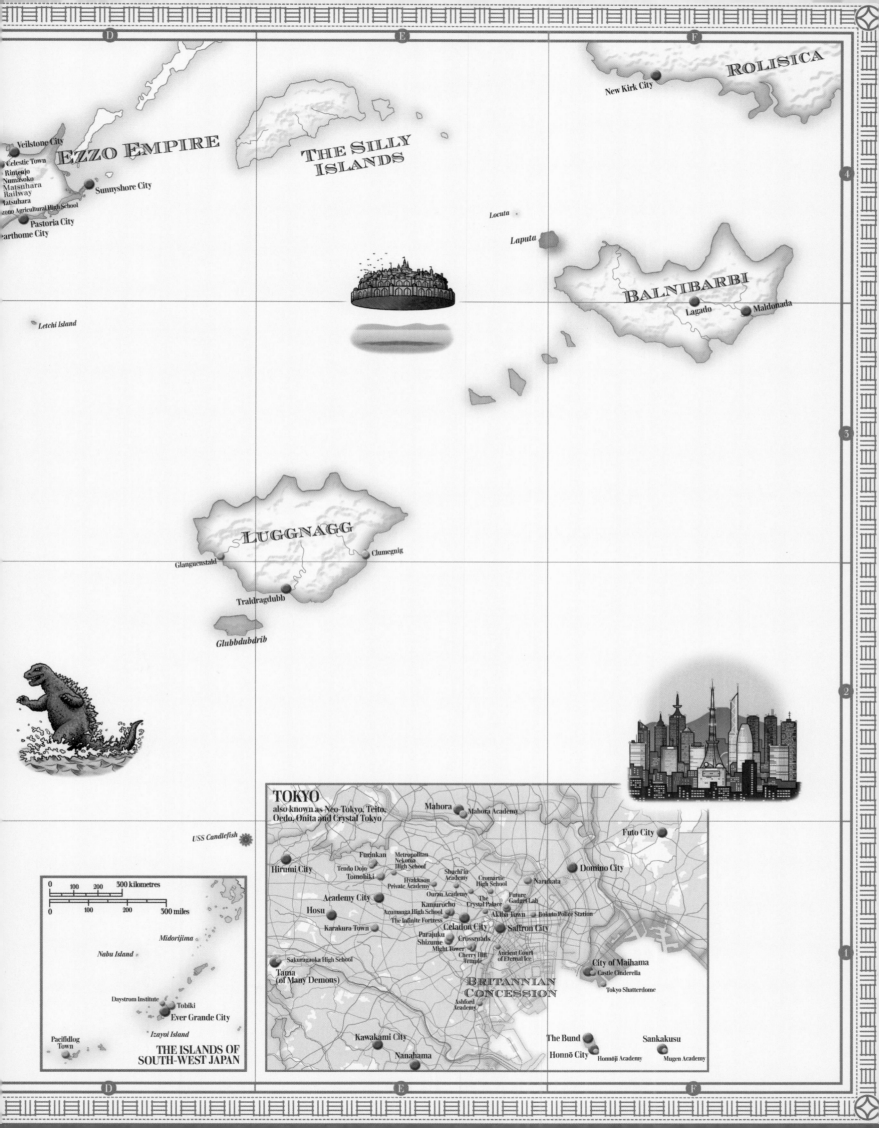

D · E · F

EZZO EMPIRE

Veilstone City
Celestic Town
Rintenjo
Numasoko
Matsuhara
Railway
Matsuhara
zono Agricultural High School
Pastoria City
arthome City

Sunnyshore City

THE SILLY ISLANDS

New Kirk City

ROLISICA

Locuta
Laputa

BALNIBARBI

Lagado
Maldonada

Letchi Island

LUGGNAGG

Glanguenstald
Clumegnig

Traldragdubb

Glubbdubdrib

USS Candlefish

TOKYO
also known as Neo-Tokyo, Teito,
Oedo, Onita and Crystal Tokyo

Mahora
Mahora Academy

Futo City

Furinkan
Metropolitan
Nekoma
High School

Hirumi City

Tendo Dojo
Tomohiki

Shuchi'in
Academy

Cromartie
High School

Domino City

Naruhata

Hyakkson
Private Academy

Ouran Academy

Academy City

Kamurocho

The
Crystal Palace

Future
Gadget Lab

Hosu

Azumanga High School

Akiba Town

Bokuto Police Station

Karakura Town

The Infinite Fortress

Celadon City

Saffron City

Parajuku
Shizume

Crossroads

Might Tower

Cherry Hill
Temple

Ancient Court
of Eternal Ice

City of Maihama

Castle Cinderella

Sakuragaoka High School

Tama
(of Many Demons)

**BRITANNIAN
CONCESSION**

Tokyo Shatterdome

Ashford
Academy

**THE ISLANDS OF
SOUTH-WEST JAPAN**

Midorijima

Nabu Island

Daystrom Institute
Tobiki
Ever Grande City

Izayoi Island

Pacifidlog
Town

0 100 200 500 kilometres
0 100 200 300 miles

Kawakami City

Nanahama

The Bund

Honnō City

Sankakusu

Honnōji Academy

Mugen Academy

D · E · F

4 · 3 · 2 · 1

JAPAN
KEY LOCATIONS

For a full list of locations, see the location index on pages 130–150.

THE BUND
Dance in the Vampire Bund
BY NOZOMU TAMAKI |
JAPAN | MANGA/ANIME
Artificial island built in Tokyo Harbour by the Queen of Vampires as a safe haven for her subjects, in return for paying off Japan's National Debt. It could happen. We've combined it with another artificial island, Honnō City, from *Kill la Kill.*
MAP pp.96–97, F1

DAIKOKO
Dennō Coil **JAPAN | ANIME**
A location for fictional Daikoko is never specified, but an argument could be made for matching it to real-world Sabae, a town on the coast of the Sea of Japan, which entered into a collaboration with the anime's production committee to promote augmented reality technology, a staple of the show. **MAP pp.96–97, B2**

DAYSTROM INSTITUTE
Star Trek
EAST CHINA SEA | VARIOUS
This technological institute is mentioned many times in the *Star Trek* canon, and is first shown on screen in the opening episode of *Star Trek: Picard.*
MAP pp.96–97, D1

EMISHI VILLAGE
Princess Mononoke
JAPAN | ANIME
Shown as a last redoubt of the tribal Emishi people, who were historically wiped out by the Japanese emperors 500 years before the setting of the film. The Emishi were historically concentrated in the Tohoku region, the north-east of Honshu. Based on the landlocked nature of the village (a valley surrounded by mountains), mention of the emperors having driven their peoples eastwards centuries ago, and the requirement for the main character to travel to lands 'far to the west' of the village, our best guess is that it would be located in the south-western part of the Fukushima Prefecture. **MAP pp.96–97, C2**

F CITY
Excel Saga **BY KŌSHI RIKUDŌ |**
JAPAN | MANGA/ANIME
An oddly-named metropolis, located in the equally-cryptic F Prefecture, F City is the target of would-be world-dictator Il Palazzo and his hapless subordinate, Excel – after all, they wouldn't want to push themselves too hard by attempting to conquer the whole planet in one go! As revealed by maps within the 'quack experimental anime' adaptation, F City is a parody of real-world Fukuoka, and is explicitly named as such in the original manga. **MAP pp.96–97, A1**

IRONTOWN
Princess Mononoke
JAPAN | TOWN | ANIME
Fortress town that smelts iron on the western fringes of the Cedar Forest, home of the Great Forest Spirit. The resulting conflict between industry and nature drives the story. Clues to the location are that it is remote, mountainous, and rich in ironsand (from which the Japanese extracted iron in the absence of ore deposits). This industry was traditionally centred on the westernmost part of Honshu, where the ironsand of the Shimane region was particularly prized. Based on these hints, we'd suggest the mountainous region where the Shimane, Hiroshima and Yamaguchi prefectures meet as the best location for both Irontown and the Cedar Forest.
MAP pp.96–97, B2

ITOMORI
Your Name **JAPAN | FILM**
A rural community extending around the borders of a vast crater-lake, Itomori is the hometown of one of this blockbuster animated film's two protagonists, who by a quirk of destiny end up switching bodies and living out one another's lives. Although both town and lake are fictional, Itomori is specifically located in Gifu Prefecture, near the town of Hida.
MAP pp.96–97, C2

KISARAGI

JAPAN | MYTH

This is an urban legend where a young woman riding a late-night northbound train on the Enshu Railway (out of Shin-Hamamatsu station in Hamamatsu) finds the train runs for much longer than expected without making any stops, eventually halting at a remote station called Kisaragi (Devil), a place surrounded by grasslands and mountains. Over the course of posts made on 2chan via her phone seeking help she backtracks along the line through a tunnel (called the Isanuki Tunnel) and, after a few unnerving encounters, is never heard from again. **MAP pp.96–97, C2**

LAPUTA

Gulliver's Travels

BY JONATHAN SWIFT | NORTH PACIFIC | NOVEL

The floating island from Gulliver, which spends much of its time above Balnibari. A deserted version of Laputa also features as the title location in Studio Ghibli's first animation, *The Castle in the Sky*. The island is also referenced in Charles Kingsley's most famous work, *The Water Babies*, where it has been rechristened the Isle of Tomtoddies. **MAP pp.96–97, E4/F4**

MATSU

You Only Live Twice

EAST CHINA SEA | FILM

Not the real Chinese-owned Matsu Islands, but a fictional Japanese island that appears in Sean Connery's fifth outing as James Bond. Despite dialogue mentioning the Sea of Japan region, Matsu is stated to lie directly on the shipping route between Kobe and Shanghai, which puts it either south or east of Japan. It seems to be fairly close to mainland Japan (close enough for Bond to visit and survey it in a small gyrocopter). We've placed it off Kagoshima, one of the filming locations. **MAP pp.96–97, A1**

NABU ISLAND

My Hero Academia

BY KŌHEI HORIKOSHI | EAST CHINA SEA | MANGA/ANIME

Primary setting for one of the franchise's films, situated SW of the Japanese Home Islands. *My Hero Academia*'s creator Horikoshi is an affirmed fan of *Star Wars*, and has peppered Japan with locations named for planets from that galaxy far, far away. Thus this map includes such entries as Nabu Island (Naboo), Mustafu (Mustafar), Hosu (Hoth) and Jaku (Jakku). **MAP pp.96–97, D1**

NEO TOKYO

JAPAN | VARIOUS

As noted in the introduction to this section, Tokyo has perhaps been destroyed in fiction more times than any other city. Understandably, then, many works have conjured a New Tokyo, or Neo Tokyo to take its place. A 1987 anime called *Neo Tokyo* is the most overt example, but the hypothetical metropolis is also named in *Akira* manga and anime, a mod of *Half Life 2*, and in David Mitchell's *Cloud Atlas*, among many others. **MAP pp.96–97, E1/F1**

NORTH HIGH SCHOOL

The Melancholy of Haruhi Suzumiya **BY NAGARU TANIGAWA AND NOIZI ITO | JAPAN | NOVELS/ANIME**

The unnamed town of this popular franchise is based almost entirely on Nishinomiya in Hyōgō Prefecture. North High, the central location of the series, is itself a one-to-one duplicate of the real Nishinomiya Kita High School, which has had to turn away fans on pilgrimage to the alma mater of the eccentric Haruhi and her SOS Brigade of aliens, psychics and time-travellers. **MAP pp.96–97, B2**

ODO ISLAND

Godzilla **NORTH PACIFIC | FILM**

Fictional island where Godzilla was first sighted, likely a made-up addition to the Izu Islands. **MAP pp.96–97, C1/C2**

OKISHIMA

Battle Royale **BY KOUSHUN TAKAMI | SETO INLAND SEA | NOVEL**

Apparently located in the Seto Inland Sea, between the real islands of Teshima and Ogijima. The name resembles a fabled island of Onigashima also said to exist in the same region. The novel's fictional city of Shiroiwa is located in Kagawa Prefecture in the original novel and manga adaptation, but shifted to Kanagawa Prefecture in the movie. **MAP pp.96–97, B2**

ROKUROKUBI VILLAGE

Churyō Manroku

JAPAN | LITERATURE/FOLKLORE

A village in the recesses of Mount Yoshino occupied by rokurokubi, apparitions that appear human but whose necks can extend to great lengths. **MAP pp.96–97, B2**

ROLISICA

Godzilla **FILMS | NORTH PACIFIC | FILMS**

A large island nation somewhere in East Asia combining elements of both USA and Russia, described as 'across the Pacific' from Japan. We've placed it to the extreme north-east of this map to put it somewhere between the two superpowers yet close to Japan. **MAP pp.96–97, F4**

SAKURAGAOKA HIGH SCHOOL

The Demon Girl Next Door

BY IZUMO ITŌ | JAPAN | TV

You'll find two unrelated Sakuragaoka High Schools on this map. One hails from the TV show *The Demon Girl Next Door*, and is located in a fictionalized version of Tokyo's City of Tama. The second is attended by the light musicians of the anime *K-ON!* That one's mapped to its real-life inspiration, Shiga Prefecture's Toyosato Elementary School (B2). **MAP pp.96–97, E1**

TAMA (OF MANY DEMONS)

The Demon Girl Next Door

BY IZUMO ITŌ | JAPAN | MANGA/ANIME

This is an odd one. Tama is a real part of Tokyo and this version occupies the same space. However, by changing one character in the Japanese name, the author altered its meaning to 'many demons' without changing the phonetic pronunciation or the English spelling! Hence its rendering here as Tama (of Many Demons). **MAP pp.96–97, E1**

TOKYO-3

Neon Genesis Evangelion

JAPAN | ANIME

Intended to become Japan's new capital once completed, Tokyo-3 is located at the north end of Lake Ashi in the mountainous Hakone region. Beneath the city lies the HQ of NERV, an enigmatic UN agency based in an immense subterranean cavern known as the Geofront, but which itself is just one part of the Black Moon, a 13.75km ($8\frac{1}{2}$ miles) wide alien vessel that crashed into the planet approximately 4 million years ago. **MAP pp.96–97, C2**

ZAWAME

Kamen Rider Gaim

JAPAN | TV

Batman Ninja is not the Dark Knight's only contribution to Japan. Kamen Rider Gaim used a map of Gotham City (turned sideways) to represent its fictional metropolis of Zawame: with sea to the north and land to the south and west, it seemed natural to locate it on Toyama Bay, at the base of the Noto Peninsula. **MAP pp.96–97, B2/C2**

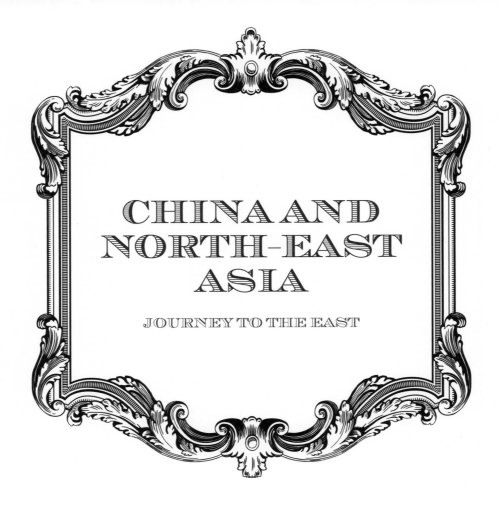

CHINA AND NORTH-EAST ASIA

JOURNEY TO THE EAST

his particular map covers more land than any other spread in the book. It has to, as this region encompasses Russia and China, two of the world's largest countries (plus Mongolia, itself no dwarf). But for all its expanse, much of this part of the world is sparsely inhabited. Take Siberia; 27 times the size of Germany, with less than half the population. China, too, is very spacious when you get away from the coastal plains. It's possible to divide the country into two roughly equal halves by drawing a line from south-west to north-east (known as the Heihe–Tengchong Line). Just 6 per cent of the billion-plus population lives in the agricultural regions west of that line.

These contrasts are mirrored in our map. Locations in Mongolia, Siberia and western China are spartan to say the least, save for the occasional mountain conjured from myth, novel or movie. The vast area is best epitomized by Hyperborea, an icy and uninhabited wilderness that crops up time and again in both ancient mythology and modern fiction. And even when we do find locations of note, they have otherworldly names that suggest we have journeyed to realms beyond the mundane. Look for the City of Lucid Shadows (with its lost colony of Neanderthals), or the Village of Moon

Rain, or the transformative Cursed Springs of Jusenkyo. And that's *before* we get to the mystic lands of Tibet ...

Thus the dragon's share of fictional Chinese locations match up to the established population centres of the east. The Hong Kong-Shenzhen region is particularly rich in source material. Cities and megacities cluster here like a rash, drawing from such wide genres as sci-fi (the city of Faxian from the TV show *Transformers: Rescue Bots*), poetry (Shangdu of Cathy Park Hong's *Engine Empire*), alternate realities (*Log Horizon*'s Yangdu), and even a set-up from a marble run (Hunluen, a city hailing from *Jelle's Marble Runs*). The region is so densely clustered, in fact, that we've had to leave out some fictional cities, like *2000 AD*'s Hong Tong and the Victoria of Dung Kai-cheung's *Atlas: The Archaeology of an Imaginary City*.

The Koreas have their fictional locales, too, from the corruption-ridden streets of Annam (*Asura: The City of Madness*) to the hamlet of Taean-gun. Lying just north of the DMZ, this particular village has won global recognition as the setting of TV phenomenon *Crash Landing on You*, the tale of an unlikely romance that develops between a North Korean army officer and a paragliding heiress accidently blown across the border from Seoul. Equally well-known is the titular community of *Welcome to Dongmakgol*, a

stage play that depicts North and South Korean soldiers uniting to protect an innocent village. Both of these fictions impart a hope for peaceful reunification, but equally often we see the Koreas' national identities edited in such a way as to play up their separation. Just as the US Army staged wargames against thinly veiled 'North Brownland' (one location we chose not to map here), the TV series *Designated Survivor* sees North and South Korea hiding behind the false beards of East and West Hun Chiu. Shakespearean political satire *MacTrump* meanwhile, parses the rivals as North and South Korasia. The two nations are, however, united in David Mitchell's *Cloud Atlas*, forming the nucleus of the Nea So Copros power-bloc (probably short for New East Asian Sphere of Cooperation), which is governed from the city of Neo Seoul.

To finish on a whimsical note, we were amused to find that the works of Peter Sellers unexpectedly sandwiched the map. High in the Arctic hides *Doctor Strangelove*'s Zokov Islands (and their Doomsday Machine), which we've conflated here with the real world's Zhokhov Island. Having taken that step, we couldn't resist including *Revenge of the Pink Panther*'s punnily-named Lee Kee Shipyards, one of the map's most southerly points. Now there's a bit of reasoning the great Inspector Clouseau would be proud of!

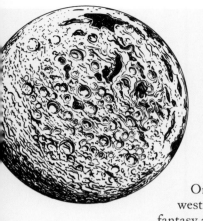

WHERE THE MOUNTAIN MEETS THE MOON

One exception to the sparsely-populated west of China comes from Grace Lin's fantasy adventure *Where the Mountain Meets the Moon*. This award-winning children's novel tells the story of a ten-year-old girl named Minli, who lives with her impoverished family in the shadow of the barren Fruitless Mountain. After pondering how she might improve her family's fortune, Minli goes on a quest for knowledge at the behest of a talking goldfish, a journey that takes her through such evocatively-named locations as the City of Bright Moonlight and the Village of Moon Rain, before she reaches her goal of the Never-Ending Mountain. Here, she meets a wise old man who indirectly grants her a wish. No spoilers, but let's just say that by the end of the novel her home of Fruitless Mountain has become Fruitful Mountain.

Where the Mountain Meets the Moon does not specify the exact locations of the story, though somewhere in western China is suggested. We can, however, make a guess from clues in the novel. The mythology of the book concerns the Jade dragon, bringer of rains, whose heart was broken when her four children (also dragons) left her for withholding rain from humanity. The children flew down to Earth to become China's four great rivers, while the Jade dragon became the Jade River (which Minli follows in the book) in hopes of finally re-uniting with her children. She fails.

The Jade River may be fictional, but this story is a wonderful match for the Tarim River of Xinjiang. As an endorheic river, it never reaches the sea – much as the Jade dragon cannot connect with her riverine offspring. As further evidence, the names of two of the Tarim's tributaries translate to the White Jade and Black Jade Rivers, thus it all seems to fit. Correspondingly, we've chosen to map Minli's destination of the Never-Ending Mountain to the extreme west, where it might 'touch' the setting Moon in fulfilment of the book's title. That's our interpretation anyway. Of course, it might all be moonshine.

IN SEARCH OF SHANGRI-LA

This map also brings us into contact with one of the true A-listers of fictional realms. Shangri-La is up there with Atlantis and El Dorado as one of those mythical, misplaced kingdoms that everybody has heard of. Though inspired by Buddhist traditions, it's a surprisingly recent fiction. While tales of Atlantis go back over 2,000 years, and the archetypal City of Gold was first rumoured in the 16th century, the name

'Shangri-La' originated from the pen of a British author as recently as 1933. Thus it shares a birth year with King Kong himself!

The source of this hidden realm is James Hilton's *Lost Horizon*, a novel rarely read today, and hardly an immediate success when first published. It was only after the author's *Goodbye, Mr Chips* struck a chord with readers the following year that attention fell upon his earlier book, and *Lost Horizon* went on to enjoy huge circulation in 1939 as the world's first mass-market paperback. FDR was a particular fan – Camp David was originally named Shangri-La under his administration, and a presidential quip about America having a secret airbase in Hilton's mythic paradise even led to the commissioning of the USS *Shangri-La*, an *Essex*-class aircraft carrier.

Shangri-La proper was the primary setting within *Lost Horizon*, providing refuge to the grateful survivors of a plane crash. Within its hidden valley the party discover a monastery (or lamasery) whose spiritually-minded inhabitants are in perfect health and enjoy extreme longevity. The novel is reasonably clear on the region – the plane's flight having taken it beyond the Western Himalayas into the Kunlun Mountains of northern Tibet – but the exact location is hotly contested. After all, any place that can assert itself as the 'real' Shangri-La is sure to rake in tourist dollars. That honour seems to have settled on Zhongdian County in north-western Yunnan, which is today officially named Shangri-La City. For this atlas we've gone for a location further to the west, however, in keeping with Hilton's description of the Kunluns. This would also place it close to regions of Pakistan and Kashmir visited by Hilton shortly before he wrote the novel.

Beyond *Lost Horizon*, Shangri-La has developed a repertoire as diverse as those of Atlantis and Lemuria, and while Hitlon's novel has diminished in popularity, the central location has become a household name. It has featured in films such as *Missing Link*, *Sky Captain and the World of Tomorrow* and video games like *Far Cry*, *Call of Duty* and the *Uncharted* series. Shangri-La's qualities have made it a shorthand – when we search for Shangri-La, we are seeking inner peace. Roosevelt was not the last to apply the name to a place of rest, relaxation and mindfulness; saunas, fitness centres and beauty salons all over the world have adopted the name, as has a large chain of luxury hotels. The chances are, if you search for Shangri-La today, you'll find it on your nearest high street.

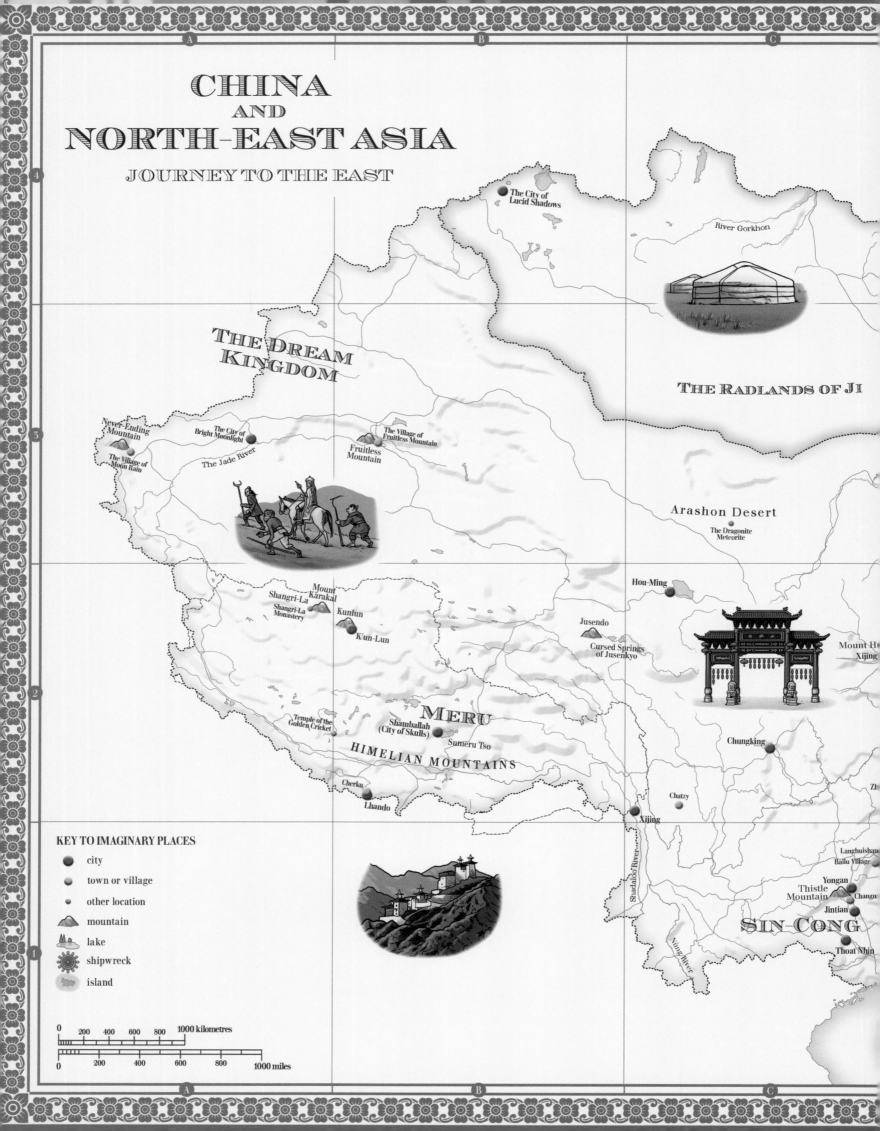

CHINA
AND
NORTH-EAST ASIA

JOURNEY TO THE EAST

The City of
Lucid Shadows

River Gorkhon

THE DREAM
KINGDOM

THE RADLANDS OF JI

Never-Ending
Mountain

The City of
Bright Moonlight

The Village of
Fruitless Mountain

The Village of
Moon Rain

The Jade River

Fruitless
Mountain

Arashon Desert

The Dragonite
Meteorite

Hou-Ming

Mount
Karakal

Shangri-La

Jusendo

Shangri-La
Monastery

Kunlun

K'un-Lun

Cursed Springs
of Jusenkyo

Mount H
Xijing

Chungking

MERU

Temple of the
Golden Cricket

Shamballah
(City of Skulls)

Sumeru Tso

HIMELIAN MOUNTAINS

Chatzy

Cherku

Lhando

Xijing

Zh

Langhuishan
Bailu Village

Yongan

Thistle
Mountain

Changn

Jintian

KEY TO IMAGINARY PLACES

- 🔴 city
- 🔴 town or village
- • other location
- ⛰ mountain
- 🌋 lake
- ✳ shipwreck
- 🏝 island

SIN-CONG

Thoat Nhin

Shadaloo River

Naung River

| 0 | 200 | 400 | 600 | 800 | 1000 kilometres |

| 0 | 200 | 400 | 600 | 800 | 1000 miles |

CHINA AND NORTH-EAST ASIA

KEY LOCATIONS

For a full list of locations, see the location index on pages 130–150.

ALPH
Kubla Khan BY SAMUEL TAYLOR
COLERIDGE | CHINA | POETRY
Described as the 'Sacred River' flowing from Kubla Khan's pleasure-dome at Xanadu (Shangdu) 'Through caverns measureless to man / Down to a sunless sea.' MAP pp.102–103, D3

ANNAM
Asura: The City of Madness
SOUTH KOREA | FILM
Grim and grittily-corrupt South Korean city, where pretty much everyone is on the take. Documents within the film show Annam to be located in Gyeonggi Province and satellite photos of the city are of the real (and similarly-named) Ansan, near Seoul. We've mapped it accordingly. MAP pp.102–103, E3

BINHAI
Angels Wear White
CHINA | FILM
Coastal town in the 'west' of China (presumably the western end of the coast). 'Binhai' is a name often used in Chinese fiction. MAP pp.102–103, D1

THE BALOU MOUNTAINS
WORKS OF YAN LIANKE | CHINA | NOVELS
Fictional mountain range that appears throughout the compendium of author Yan Lianke, populated with delightfully-named communities such as Liven and Explosion. The novels themselves place the Balou Mountains adjacent to the (real) River Yi in western Henan province, suggesting them to be analogues of the eastern ranges of the Qinling Mountains. This same region is also where Lianke lives in real-life, and after further analysis we have not only mapped the Balou Mountains here, but matched his hometown of Songxian to fictional Explosion City. MAP pp.102–103, D2

CHUNGKING
Adrift in the Middle Kingdom
BY JAN JACOB SLAUERHOFF |
CHINA | NOVEL
Not the actual Chungking/Chongqing, but one transposed to the north-west, and heavily inspired by Chengdu.
MAP pp.102–103, C2

THE CITY OF LUCID SHADOWS
Martin Mystère BY ALFREDO
CASTELLI AND GIANCARLO
ALESSANDRINI | MONGOLIA | COMIC
A lost city of Neanderthals in Mongolia. Our placement is a guess, but fossil evidence of this human species has been found as far east as Okladnikov Cave in Russia, just a few hundred kilometres from this location. MAP pp.102–103, B4

CURSED SPRINGS OF JUSENKYO
Ranma ½
CHINA | MANGA/ANIME
Legendary training ground consisting of multiple cursed springwater pools, each of which causes a specific transformation in those who fall into them. It is specifically located in the Bayan Har Mountains of Qinghai Province. The adjacent (fictional) mountain of Jusendo is the source of the springs. MAP pp.102–103, B2

THE DRAGONITE METEORITE
Outlaw Star CHINA | ANIME
Meteorite that crashes in the fictional Arashon Desert, composed of a crystalline substance (later named Dragonite) whose faster-than-light properties drives humanity's development as an interstellar civilisation.
MAP pp.102–103, C3

HMS DEVONSHIRE
Tomorrow Never Dies
SOUTH CHINA SEA | FILM
British frigate sunk by operatives of media baron Elilot Carver 11 miles (7.7km) off the south coast of the island of Hainan. Coordinates are shown in the film, but these point to the far north of China, well away from the actual scene of this thrilling act of terror and deception.
MAP pp.102–103, D1

HYPERBOREA
RUSSIA | MYTHOLOGY
A land of giants who lived beyond the North Wind. The myth of Hyperborea has shifted so many times over the millennia that we could map it almost anywhere north of Greece – much as Atlantis can be placed almost anywhere in the oceans. If we choose our clues selectively, though, a good case for placing Hyperborea in the Arctic, and specifically Siberia, can be made. Most notably, the land was said to enjoy never-ending sunshine, which is indicative of the Arctic in summer. **MAP pp.102–103, F1/F2**

JINGZHOU
In the Name of the People
CHINA | TV
A rare Chinese drama series exploring government corruption. Although genuine cities of this name exist in China, this one is intended to be fictional. The location is uncertain, but it is largely filmed in Nanjing. **MAP pp.102–103, D2**

KHITAI
Conan **NOVELS OF**
ROBERT E. HOWARD | CHINA | NOVELS
The name is derived from the nomadic Khitan people who inhabited north-east China and Mongolia from the 4th century. In Howard's mythology, Khitai is a shorthand for the whole China region. **MAP pp.102–103, D4**

KUNLUN
TIBET | MYTHOLOGY
One of the many mythological mountains of China. The Kunlun Mountains take their name from it. Various locations have been suggested, but we've placed it in the namesake Kunluns. **MAP pp.102–103, A2/B2**

LHANDO
Cursed Mountain
VIDEO GAME
Fictional city, described as the highest in the world and the gateway to the Himylayas. Lies at an elevation of over 16,000 feet on the real Tibetan mountain of Chomo Lonzo. *Cursed Mountain* also features the village of Cherku, situated further up the slopes of Chomo Lonzo. **MAP pp.102–103, B2**

LIAN YU
Arrow **CHINA | TV**
In the TV version of *Green Arrow*, the central character is marooned on an island in the 'North China Sea', whose name translates as 'purgatory'. There is no such sea, but the Yellow Sea seems a good fit. **MAP pp.102–103, D2/E2**

MOUNT HUAGUO
Journey to the West
BY WU CHENG'EN |
EASTERN CHINA | NOVEL
Mount Huaguo, or Flowers and Fruit Mountain, is one of the key locations in this famous 16th-century novel, and is the birthplace of the Monkey King. Various locations have been suggested, but it is now most closely associated with a site near Lianyungang City, in Jiangsu, which is now a popular tourist attraction. **MAP pp.102–103, D2**

MOUNT PENGLAI
CHINA | MYTHOLOGY
Another of China's many mythological mountains. Of the many suggested locations, an island in the Bohai Sea, near the real town of Penglai seems appropriate. **MAP pp.102–103, D3**

NISI
Bond **CHINA | PLAY**
This adaptation of *The Merchant of Venice* relocates Shakespeare's narrative to the Chinese Song Dynasty, and recasts Venice as the fictional city of Nisi, modelled on the then-capital, Kaifeng. **MAP pp.102–103, D2**

SEVERNAYA SATELLITE CONTROL CENTRE
Goldeneye
RUSSIA | FILM
Control centre for the Goldeneye weapons system, located in the fictional Severnaya region. At first glance, it might be assumed this relates to the real Severnaya Zemlya archipelago in Russia's first north. However, the film makes it clear that the dish is in central Siberia, while the much-cherished video game gives us actual coordinates. **MAP pp.102–103, E1**

SHAMBALLAH, CITY OF SKULLS
The City of Skulls
BY L. SPRAGUE DE CAMP AND LIN CARTER |
TIBET | NOVEL
The capital city of Meru, a country that is part of the Conan mythos, Shamballah is also a mythical city of much older tradition, and the possible inspiration for Shangri-La. The name has also been used by both Marvel Comics and the Cthulhu Mythos. It seems every universe has its own Shamballah. **MAP pp.102–103, B2**

SHAWEI
NOVELS OF RPRESTON SCHOYER |
CHINA | NOVELS
Modelled on the real city of Changsha, where Schoyer taught English in the early years of the Second World War. The author led a daring escape from the city during attack by the Japanese by sailing with a party of doctors, nurses and wounded along the Xiang River. That river is also fictionalised in his novels (and our Atlas) as the Lei Kiang. A fictional tributary, the Ginger River, corresponds to the real Xiao River, but is not shown for space reasons. **MAP pp.102–103, D1/D2**

SYBERIA
Syberia
RUSSIA | VIDEO GAME
Island where mammoths still live, inspired by the real-world Wrangel Island off the coast of Siberia, the last place on Earth where mammoths survived. **MAP pp.102–103, F2**

UST-CHILIM
RUSSIA | BAND
Setting of the songs of Russian band Buerak, described as a fictional city somewhere in Buryatia. **MAP pp.102–103, E1**

WOMAN LAKE
WORKS OF ELIZABETH MARSHALL
THOMAS | RUSSIA | NOVELS
Described by the author as a fictionalized (smaller) version of Lake Baikal. Thomas also describes three fictional rivers, the Char, Grass and Fire, which we've also mapped. We've conflated the Fire River with the real-world Angara River and the lower parts of the Yenisei, which the Angara drains into. If we merge realities with the universe of *Judge Dredd*, however, all the rivers would be obliterated underneath the sprawl of East-Meg Two, a Soviet Russian megacity wrapped around Lake Baikal. **MAP pp.102–103, E1**

XIJING
WESTERN CHINA | VARIOUS
Imaginary city created by a Japanese-Chinese-Korean trio of artists (the Xijing Men). The name literally translates as 'West Capital', and is meant to evoke a city balancing out Beijing, Nanking and Tokyo – historically the north, south and east capitals. Its geography is intentionally a bit 'floaty' but after a bit of experimentation we've equated it with Gongshan in Yunnan province, since this balances the axis formed by the other historic capitals. **MAP pp.102–103, C2**

AUSTRALIA AND NEW ZEALAND

THE ORIGINAL LAND OF OZ

o European or American eyes, Australia can seem like a magical, faraway land, home to strange and beloved creatures such as the kangaroo, wallaby and numbat. Even the name, often shortened to 'Oz', is redolent of the fantastic. Yet the same lands also include thousands of miles of deadly desert, and are home to some of the most poisonous animals on the planet. Such paradoxes abound in Australia, and the same is true of both her fiction and this map.

Just as in the real world, the scorching, illimitable acres of the fictional outback are sparsely populated, whereas coastal regions – notably in Victoria and New South Wales – are dense with locations. Many of these are the settings for sun-drenched soap operas. Shows such as *Neighbours*, set in the fictional Melbourne suburb of Erinsborough, and *Home and Away*, based in Summer Bay, north of Sydney, have come to symbolize Australia to an overseas audience (especially in the UK). Yet within walking distance of Erinsborough, we encounter a far less desirable destination in Wentworth Detention Centre (*Prisoner Cell Block H*), while a short drive inland from Summer Bay would bring one to the seemingly sleepy town of Paris, where strangers are mown down by spiked vehicles (according to *The Cars That Ate Paris*).

The throw-another-shrimp-on-the-barbie image of Australia is also challenged by the *Mad Max* franchise.

Set in a post-apocalyptic realm of dust, anger and scarcity, these films and their associated media imagine an Australia in which nobody sane would want to live, in stark contrast to the aspirational lifestyles and beach-filled days of the soap operas.

This blend of dystopia and utopia continues to this day. In the (underrated) 2015 animated movie *Home*, every person on the planet bar one is relocated to 'Happy Humans Town' in Australia by 'friendly' invading aliens. Despite the cheery name, this vast suburb is really the largest internment camp ever conceived.

Australia's history also reflects this disparity. The first settlers arrived here some 65,000 years ago – several dozen millennia before humans first arrived in the Americas. European colonization only began 300 years ago, with devastating consequences for indigenous peoples. While many films and novels have tackled the issues facing aboriginal communities, few have yielded fictional locations. Notable exceptions include the rural town of Corrigan from Craig Silvey's *Jasper Jones*, and the village of Wala Wala just west of Alice Springs from 1996 film *Dead Heart*.

The 1986 short film *BabaKiueria* meanwhile poses an intriguing 'what if'. It satirizes Anglo-Aboriginal relations by envisioning an alternate history where the roles are literally reversed: Australian Aborigines colonize a land already inhabited by white natives. The name 'BabaKiueria' is coined when a picnicking

'native' is asked what he calls this place: 'It's a BBQ area'. While BabaKiueria is meant to evoke the entire Australian continent, we've placed it near the barbecue capital of Sydney, where most of the film is set.

New Zealand's fictional landscape is, in the popular imagination, almost entirely dominated by the *Lord of the Rings* films, which were famously shot there. Much as we'd love to include the likes of Mount Doom and Hobbiton in this atlas, they are not supposed to be located on our Earth (or at least not in our geological era). Even so, we've snuck in 'Middle Zealand', a reference from *The Lego Movie*, and managed to tip the hat to director Peter Jackson with the inclusion of the village of Kaihoro, from his first feature film, 1987 horror-comedy *Bad Taste*.

That's not to say the islands of New Zealand are without any locales of their own. English-born author Samuel Butler's 1872 novel *Erewhon* satirizes Victorian society, and was set in a fictional land whose name, read backwards, almost spells 'Nowhere'. Erewhon is clearly inspired by New Zealand, where Butler spent some of his youth. An accompanying map shows his fictional settlements (some of which we've included) overlaid onto the topography of South Island. The many other locations we've featured in New Zealand may be familiar to Kiwis from TV shows, novels and comics, but perhaps less so to other readers.

Road gang known as the Buzzards also feature in the 2015 *Mad Max* video game, where they are based out of a long-abandoned international airport, which may be that of Sydney. With further sequels in the works, perhaps we'll one day find some answers.

LAND OF SOAP

At the time of writing, Wikipedia's page of Australian soap operas lists 50 separate shows. Many, like *Neighbours*, *Home and Away* and *The Young Doctors* have found success overseas, particularly in the UK, though this traffic is hardly one-way; in the 1960s, the British *Coronation Street* was more popular down under than in its home nation.

This vast outpouring of kitchen-sink drama is one of the chief sources of fictional locations from Australia. Many readers will be familiar with the Erinsborough of *Neighbours*, or the Summer Bay of *Home and Away*. But you'll also find the Wandin Valley from *A Country Practice*, Westside from *E-Street*, and the eponymous Richmond Hill – and those are just the ones from New South Wales!

CHARTING MAD MAX

The Mad Max quadrilogy and its tie-in video games and comics take place in Australia, but a post-apocalyptic one; a dingo-eat-dingo landscape of bloodthirsty road gangs and inhospitable dust bowls; a world fuelled by blood and guzzolene. Mad to the max.

The franchise throws up many fictional locations to populate its wasteland setting. There's the desert refuge of Bartertown, home of the notorious Thunderdome, ruled with an iron fist by Tina Turner's Aunty Entity. The most recent film, *Fury Road*, gave us the triumvirate of the Citadel, Gas Town and the Bullet Farm, as well as the titular highway connecting them.

Because much of the action takes place in featureless outback, it's very difficult to pin these locations to a real map. Needless to say, we've given it a try. The one fixed location everybody can agree on is Tomorrow-morrow Land, the mythical homeland of the Lost Tribe in the third film. Although broken and ruined, when reached at the end of the film, this mythic land is revealed to be Sydney. You can see the Harbour Bridge.

The rest of our locations are mere guesswork. Bartertown is often assumed to be near the real-world Adelaide, perhaps because most of the scenes were shot in South Australia. Fury Road is even trickier to pin down; partly because the narrative quickly veers off the titular 'last' road, partly because production was forced to relocate to Namibia when unexpected rain caused outback shooting locations to erupt with blooms of wildflowers! Ultimately, we placed the dilapidated highway and the locations it connects within striking distance of Sydney, our reasoning being thus: a Fury

GULLIVER'S ADVENTURES ROUND OZ

Where would you have placed Lilliput on the globe? We'd have plumped for somewhere mid-Atlantic. Author Jonathan Swift intended the miniature kingdom to be a parody of England, forever at loggerheads with its neighbour Blefuscu (representing France), thus it has always felt distinctly European.

Surprisingly, however, these diminutive nations are to be found in Oceania, somewhere off the coast of Australia. Swift handily provides a map – albeit a confusing one. He positions the two island-kingdoms midway between 'Diemen's Land' (Tasmania) and the Sunda Strait in Indonesia. That would place them not in the ocean but within western Australia – a puzzle, as that region was well-charted by the time of the novel. Swift's map also shows no part of Australia, other than Tasmania, thus it has been suggested that he was mocking the many false travel guides in circulation during his time, which more closely resembled works of speculative fiction than true geographies. Gulliver's account provides a latitude (30 degrees, 2 minutes S) but no longitude for the islands, and so we've taken a stab at a location to the west of the main Australian landmass.

Gulliver returns to the region in his final journey. This time, he lands on a large island south of Australia whose inhabitants include human-like beasts called Yahoos, and rational, talking horses called Houyhnhnms. The geography is a little better established this time round. The author's map includes the Australian coastline, and certain non-fictional islands, although the scales are all wrong. We can therefore plot with more confidence the home of the intelligent horses off the coast of Western Australia. Everybody needs good neighhh-bours.

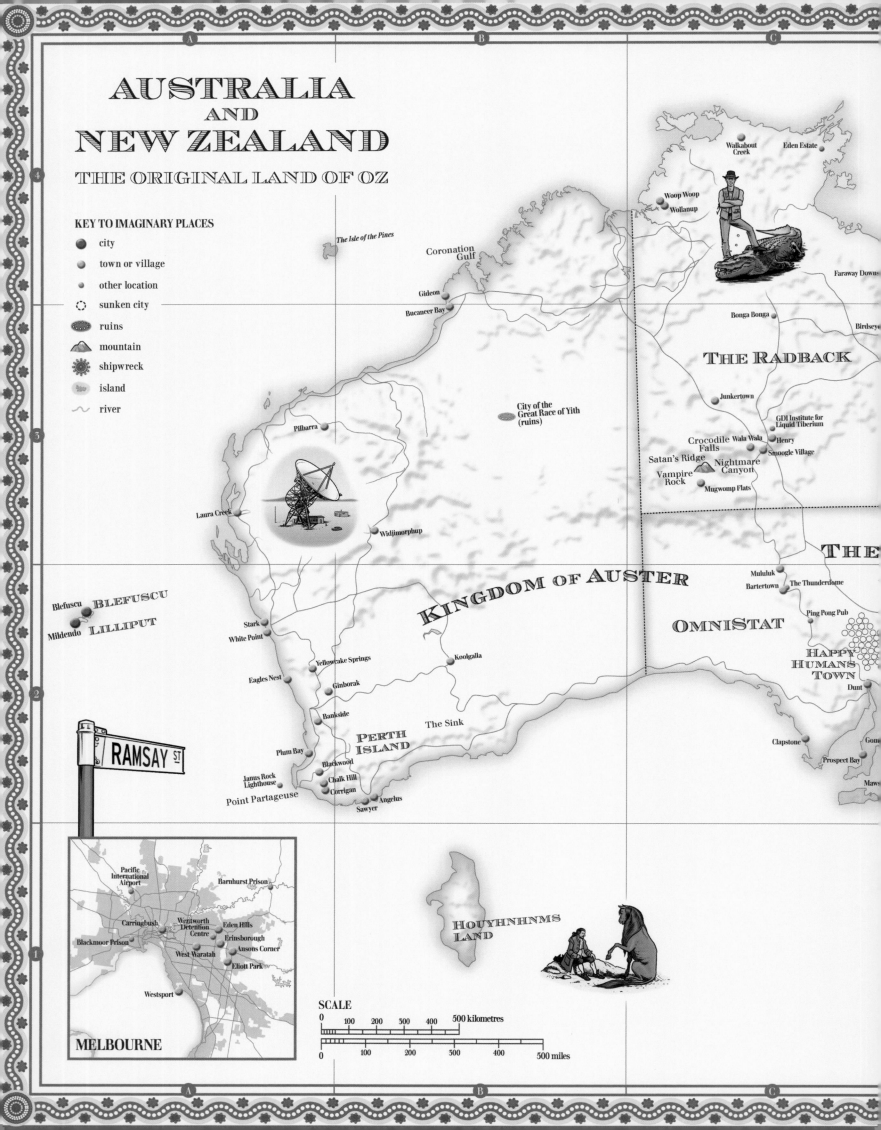

AUSTRALIA
AND
NEW ZEALAND
THE ORIGINAL LAND OF OZ

KEY TO IMAGINARY PLACES

- city
- town or village
- other location
- sunken city
- ruins
- mountain
- shipwreck
- island
- river

The Isle of the Pines

Coronation Gulf

Walkabout Creek

Eden Estate

Woop Woop
Wollanup

Faraway Downs

Gideon

Bucaneer Bay

Bonga Bonga

Birdseye

THE RADBACK

Junkertown

City of the Great Race of Yith (ruins)

GDI Institute for Liquid Tiberium

Pilbarra

Crocodile Wala Wala Falls

Henry

Smoogle Village

Satan's Ridge

Nightmare Canyon

Vampire Rock

Mugwomp Flats

Laura Creek

Widjimorphup

THE

Mululuk

Bartertown

The Thunderdome

Blefuscu **BLEFUSCU**

LILLIPUT

Mildendo

KINGDOM OF AUSTER

OMNISTAT

Ping Pong Pub

Stark

White Point

Koolgalla

HAPPY HUMANS TOWN

Yellowcake Springs

Eagles Nest

Ginborak

Dunt

Bankside

The Sink

RAMSAY ST

Plum Bay

Blackwool

PERTH ISLAND

Clapstone

Gon

Janus Rock Lighthouse

Chalk Hill

Corrigan

Prospect Bay

Maws

Point Partageuse

Sawyer

Angelus

Pacific International Airport

Barnhurst Prison

Carringbush

Wentworth Detention Centre

Eden Hills

Blackmoor Prison

Erinsborough

Ansons Corner

West Waratah

HOUYHNHNMS LAND

Eliott Park

Westport

MELBOURNE

SCALE

0   100   200   300   400   500 kilometres

0   100   200   300   400   500 miles

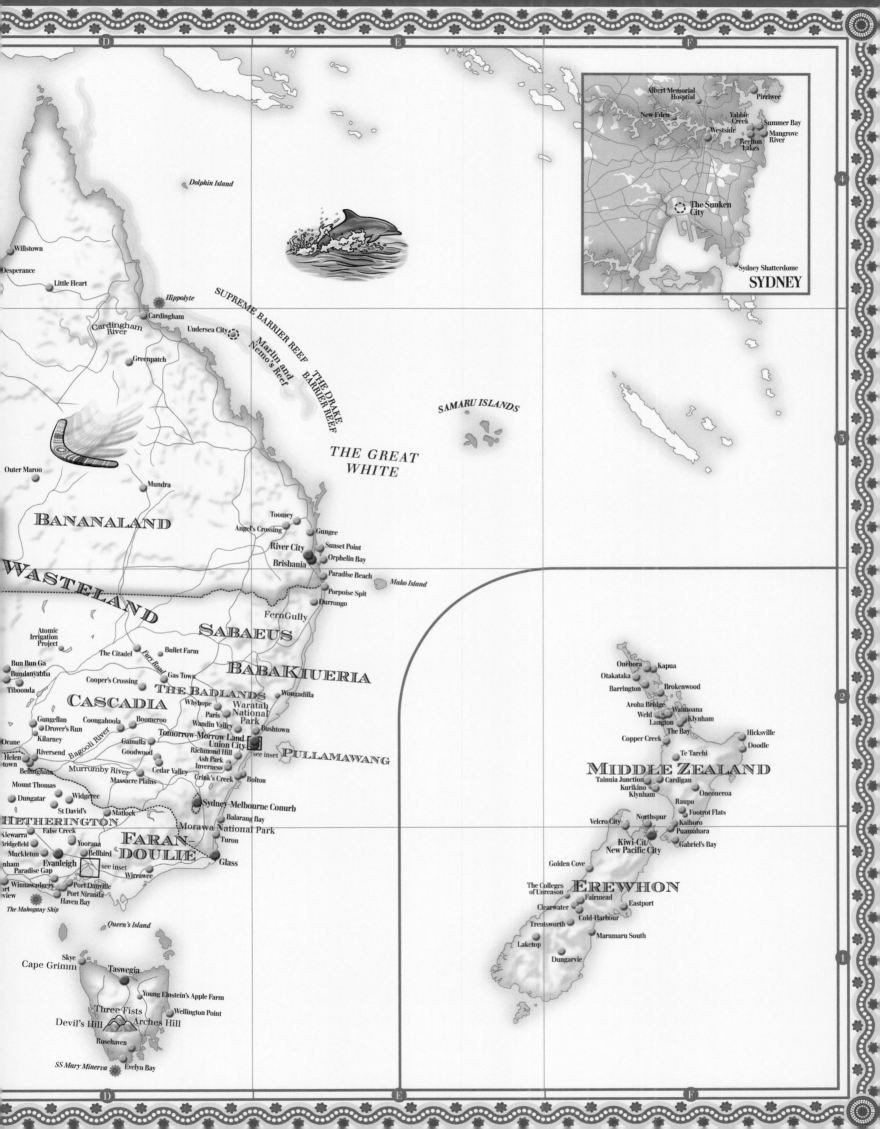

AUSTRALIA AND NEW ZEALAND

KEY LOCATIONS

For a full list of locations, see the location index on pages 130–150.

ATOMIC IRRIGATION PROJECT
Thunderbirds
NEW SOUTH WALES | TV
Produced before Three Mile Island and Chernobyl tainted the image of nuclear power, the original *Thunderbirds* TV series depicted a future where atomic reactors powered everything from construction equipment to the mighty Thunderbirds themselves. Case-in-point, this facility (from appropriately titled episode 'The Mighty Atom') employed nuclear power to pump vast amounts of seawater inland and desalinate it for use in irrigation schemes. Though a location is never specified, the plant's destruction (thanks to the actions of the villainous Hood) releases a radioactive cloud that threatens to poison Melbourne, until the wind disperses it to the south-southeast and away from the city. Based on these clues we imagine the Irrigation Project to be situated in western New South Wales.
MAP pp.108–109, D3

BARRINGTON
Material Girls **BY DEBORAH STEELE |**
NEW ZEALAND | MUSICAL
This is a fun one. Trawling the internet in search of fictional locations within New Zealand dredged up several articles from the 'Kaipara Lifestyler' (a community magazine covering events in the Kaipara District of North Island), reporting on *Material Girls*, a production by a local theatre group set in the fictional town of Barrington. We chose to include Barrington, mapping it to real-world Dargaville, where the production was staged. While obscure, it definitely brings a local touch to this atlas.
MAP pp.108–109, F2

BLEFUSCU
Gulliver's Travels
BY JONATHAN SWIFT |
INDIAN OCEAN | NOVEL
Rival island to Lilliput (see page 107). It is less well-known, but plays a significant part in the tale. Its inhabitants are on the same diminutive scale as the denizens of Lilliput. **MAP pp.108–109, A2**

CARDINGHAM
The Black Bell Buoy
BY RUPERT CHESTERTON |
QUEENSLAND | SHORT STORY
This Queensland port community faces out towards the Great Barrier Reef. The titular bell buoy is placed to warn ships away from an underwater rock just off the coast, but breaks free from its anchor and begins to drift, becoming a sinister threat to navigation. The story ends with the steamer *Hippolyte* sinking after a collision with this 'phantom' hazard, the vessel's captain confessing during the sinking that he murdered a rival and concealed his remains within the black bell buoy before it began its wayward voyage. From references in the text, Cardingham appears to lie south of Cooktown, which is where we have mapped it. **MAP pp.108–109, D3**

CITY OF THE GREAT RACE OF YITH
The Shadow Out of Time
BY H.P. LOVECRAFT |
WESTERN AUSTRALIA | NOVELLA
Ruined city of a pre-historic race of psychic time-travelling aliens, located in the Great Sandy Desert at 22 degrees, 3 minutes, 14 seconds south; 125 degrees, 0 minutes, 39 seconds east. The fictional town of Pilbarra (also shown) is described as 500 miles (805km) to the west.
MAP pp.108–109, B3

CROCODILE FALLS
The Rescuers Down Under
NORTHERN TERRITORY | FILM
One of a cluster of landmarks seen and mentioned during the film. An animated map sequence starting within running distance (for a mouse!) from Crocodile Falls shows a distress call originating in the south-central MacDonnell Ranges and a later scene conveniently maps these features out. **MAP pp.108–109, C3**

EDEN ESTATE
Return to Eden
NORTHERN TERRITORY | TV
This vast family estate was specified as Northern Territory, though filming took

place in Queensland. Other scenes were shot in Arnhem Land, which is where we've guessed. **MAP Australia, C4**

FARAWAY DOWNS
Australia
NORTHERN TERRITORY | FILM
A written prologue identifies the setting as the Northern Territory, and a map shown in the opening title places Faraway Downs close to the border with Western Australia, in the vicinity of the Keep River National Park. **MAP pp.108–109, C4**

FURY ROAD
Mad Max Fury Road
SOUTH-EAST AUSTRALIA | FILM
The titular thoroughfare is never actually called Fury Road in the movie, so we're taking a minor liberty – 'The Road' sounds too dull for such a highway.
MAP pp.108–109, D2

GABRIEL'S BAY
Gabriel's Bay **BY CATHERINE ROBERTSON | NEW ZEALAND | NOVEL**
Original Maori name: *Onemanawa*. Coastal town that could be anywhere in NZ, apparently by authorial design, since the narrative incorporates elements of various parts of the country into this one fictional town. The author is from Wellington, so we placed it near the bottom end of North Island, but other readings are equally possible.
MAP pp.108–109, F1

GUNGELLAN
McLeod's Daughters
NEW SOUTH WALES | TV
This series was filmed in Freeling, just north of Adelaide, but set in the South Australian outback on a vast expanse of bushland. We've placed it out in the bush as close as possible to this location.
MAP pp.108–109, D2

HAPPY HUMANS TOWN
Home **SOUTH AUSTRALIA | FILM**
Every human on Earth, bar one, is relocated to this sprawling metropolis by the Boov. A map in the film confirms a location north of Adelaide.
MAP pp.108–109, C2

ISLE OF THE PINES
The Isle of the Pines
BY HENRY NEVILLE | INDIAN OCEAN | NOVEL
Published in 1668, this is one of the earliest examples of a 'Robinsonade', in which people or persons are stranded on an island. In this case, the island

is somewhere close to the recently discovered (by Europeans) mass of Australia. The location is unspecified, but likely to be off the west coast.
MAP pp.108–109, A4/B4

LAURA CREEK
Marvel's Agents of S.H.I.E.L.D.
WESTERN AUSTRALIA | TV
The location of this satellite relay station is unknown, other than being somewhere in Western Australia. However, we've conflated it with the real Carnarvon Tracking Station, which played a key role in NASA's Gemini and Apollo missions.
MAP pp.108–109, A3

THE MAHOGANY SHIP **VICTORIA | MYTH**
A semi-mythical shipwreck near Armstrong Bay, said to be of Spanish or Portuguese origin and pre-dating English claims to the land. It has inspired several works of fiction, including *Wrack*, by James Bradley, which instead located the ship off New South Wales. **MAP pp.108–109, D1**

PULLAMAWANG
Micro Nation
NEW SOUTH WALES | TV
During the Federation of Australia in 1901, the tiny (and fictional) island of Pullamawang forgot to file its paperwork. By default, it became an independent micronation, free to develop its own laws and traditions. A map drawn up for promotional material (you can Google it) gives us the shape of Pullamawang, but not its size – it appears to cover a similar area to the Australian mainland, until you notice the 'not to scale' legend.
MAP pp.108–109, E2

SUPREME BARRIER REEF
Thunderbirds Are Go
QUEENSLAND | TV
Artificial replacement for the Great Barrier Reef, which no longer exists by the time in which the show is set.
MAP pp.108–109, D4/E3

SYDNEY–MELBOURNE CONURB *2000 A.D.*
SOUTH-EAST AUSTRALIA | COMICS
Mega-city sprawling from Sydney to Melbourne. It would take over the map if we showed it to its full extent, so we've settled for situating it mid-way, which coincides nicely with Canberra.
MAP pp.108–109, D2

WALKABOUT CREEK
Crocodile Dundee
NORTHERN TERRITORY | FILM
The village scenes were shot in McKinlay, Queensland (where a Walkabout Creek inn still receives tourist trade), but the location is supposed to be in the Northern Territory. We've placed it in Kakadu National Park, which was another filming location. We've also put it close to the sea, as Croc Dundee got his name from wrestling a saltwater crocodile.
MAP pp.108–109, C4

WANDIN VALLEY
A Country Practice
NEW SOUTH WALES | TV
Another long-running Australian soap that saw great success overseas, *A Country Practice* is set in the small New South Wales town of Wandin Valley somewhere, as the name implies, in the countryside. The exact location is difficult to pinpoint, though most of the outdoor filming was done north-west of Sydney. **MAP pp.108–109, D2**

WARATAH NATIONAL PARK
Skippy the Bush Kangaroo
NEW SOUTH WALES | TV
Fictionalized version of the real Waratah Park Earth Sanctuary, shot there and in the neighbouring Ku-ring-gai Chase National Park. **MAP pp.108–109, D2/E2**

WELD
800 Words
NEW ZEALAND | TV
Fictional Weld is a seaside community; so although the majority of filming for *800 Words* was done in the inland town of Warkworth, we've matched Weld to Huia and Piha, townships situated WSW of Auckland and the location where Weld's beach and surfing scenes were shot.
MAP pp.108–109, F2

ANTARCTICA

THE NIGHTMARE CONTINENT

O f all the territories in the *Atlas*, the vast lands of Antarctica are the least fictionalized. This makes sense. Few people are ever lucky enough to venture to the frigid continent. There are no towns or cities in which to tell stories. The only options for drama are in research bases, on ice ships or intrepid expeditions. Nobody has ever made an Antarctic soap opera (though there is an Antarctic anime!).

Yet the continent is not entirely bereft of storytelling. Antarctica, it seems, is a land of lost cities, rampant dinosaurs and menacing aliens. It is literally a blank page, a canvas upon which dream-weavers have projected weird fantasies and otherworldly horrors.

Maybe this has something to do with its comparatively recent discovery and the events that preceded that. The existence of a southern continent has been a subject of speculation since at least the time of Aristotle, and the search for such a landmass was a driving force during the Age of Exploration, with Antarctica being definitively sighted and landed upon in the 1820s. Thus the continent's very existence is in some part mythic, as was its discovery and exploration, which paralleled the rise of modern literature, the countless (and frequently doomed) expeditions that ventured into its harsh interior shaping a compelling and nightmarish vision of human endurance at the very limits of nature and sanity. Small wonder then that imagination has populated Antarctica with some terrifying literary nightmares alongside its mundane horrors.

Perhaps the most famous Antarctic tale originated with the 1938 novella *Who Goes There?*, by John W. Campbell Jr., the story of a US Antarctic research base menaced by a shapeshifting alien. If this sounds familiar, then you may have seen one of its various screen adaptations, most famously John Carpenter's *The Thing* (1982). Although poorly received upon release, the film has since become a cult-classic, with a recent prequel to its name and a remake in development. In both the original text and Carpenter's film, the Antarctic setting is used to its fullest effect. Though the story is couched in sci-fi concepts, the tension derives from the increasing distrust and hostility among men crowded together in confined and isolated quarters, for which Antarctica makes an ideal setting. The utter desolation and inhospitality of the surroundings not only serve to keep the men trapped, but also make the sense of deathly horror all the more profound. In this *Atlas* we've mapped the bases from both the films and the novel (US Outpost 31, Thule Station, and Big Magnet, respectively) close to one another, along with the crash site for the Thing's craft. Perhaps having neighbours will reduce the terror ...

LOST DINOSAURS AND GIANT HUMANS

It's not just film and literature that have exposited on there being something terrible lurking beneath the Antarctic ice. Indeed, the backstory of the blockbuster Japanese media franchise *Neon Genesis Evangelion* hinges on the discovery of a giant humanoid creature buried in an artificial structure beneath Mount Markham. This creature subsequently explodes following human attempts at communication, resulting in the destruction of the entire Antarctic continent. More tongue-in-cheek, the Disney Channel animated classic *Gravity Falls* informs us that a giant Time Baby is frozen in a glacier somewhere in Antarctica, which if ever freed would claim dominion over all the Earth. Thankfully, glaciers never melt, so we're sitting peachy!

Meanwhile, according to Marvel Comics, at the base of the real-world Palmer Peninsula there exists a sheltered tropical biome, shielded and heated by an encircling ring of volcanos. Here natural-born dinosaurs still walk the Earth in the Savage Land, a primeval enclave that would have done Sir Arthur Conan Doyle proud! Perhaps it was inspired by Caprona, also known as Caspak – the concealed land of dinosaurs from Edgar Rice Burroughs's *The Land That Time Forgot* (adapted into a better-known 1974 film with a screenplay by Michael Moorcock). Both are found in Antarctic waters south of the Pacific.

ANTARCTICA TORN BY MADNESS

Many other stories have picked up on this 'lost world' idea for Antarctica – not just hidden dinosaurs but also secret bases and remote civilizations. This is understandable. Even after explorers reached the South Pole, much of Antarctica's geography remained mysterious until satellite technology became available in the second half of the 20th century. Anything could have been hiding among the many ice floes and mountain chains. Lost worlds (or at least the remains of ancient biospheres) may indeed await discovery beneath the ice. The continent itself was once thought to comprise two large land masses, separated by a frozen-over channel. Such was the Antarctica of *The Narrative of Arthur Gordon Pym of Nantucket* (1838), the only complete novel by Edgar Allan Poe, and we have duly noted the islands he and subsequent authors placed within this dividing strait.

It was Poe's Pym that inspired H.P. Lovecraft to bring his own squamous, tentacular horror to the continent. His 1936 story *At the Mountains of Madness*, tells of a group of explorers led by the narrator, Dr William Dyer of Miskatonic University (based in the fictional Arkham, Massachusetts, which you'll find on the USA map). In the furthest reaches of the continent they encounter mountain ranges higher than the Himalayas, the relics of an ancient, non-human civilization (the Elder Things), the remains of prehistoric creatures, and nightmarish albino penguins, born blind and standing as tall as a man. Handily for present purposes, Lovecraft provides coordinates for the titular mountain range, allowing us to form a sketchy map. We've also included the lost city of Shub Nigruth, which although sounding eminently Lovecraftian, actually comes to us from supplementary materials to the Disney film *Atlantis: The Lost Empire*.

MARCH OF THE PENGUINS

Lovecraft's monstrous penguins aside, some of fiction's most beloved birds call this realm their home. There's the anthropomorphic town of Shiverpool from the *Surf's Up* duology, birthplace of maverick young rockhopper penguin Cody. Around the coast we can also find the home of Adélie penguin Hubie, protagonist of the Don Bluth and Gary Goldman adventure *The Pebble and the Penguin*. Both of these characters are outsiders seeking validation, and the same holds for perhaps the most famous of fictional flightless birds, Mumble. This particular emperor penguin smashed box-office returns as the tap-dancing star of *Happy Feet*, and based on evidence in the films we've confidently mapped his colony in close proximity to Hubie's home in Adélie Land. Hiya neighbour!

Finally, we come to that Antarctic anime, which is set aboard the Japanese icebreaker *Penguin Manju Go*. Entitled *A Place Further Than the Universe*, this critically acclaimed and heart-warming series tells the coming-of-age story of four schoolgirls who manage to sign themselves on to a civilian mission to Antarctica. Their journey eventually brings them to real Syowa Station on East Ongul Island. Amidst all the nightmares, it seems that dreams can be realized in Antarctica too.

Those girls just better be careful not to dig too deep, because if *Godzilla: King of the Monsters* is to be believed, Syowa is adjacent to the site where the fearsome alien dragon King Ghidorah lies in a frozen sleep, dreaming malignant dreams beneath the snowy surface. There's always something hiding beneath the ice ...

'Tekeli-li! Tekeli-li!'

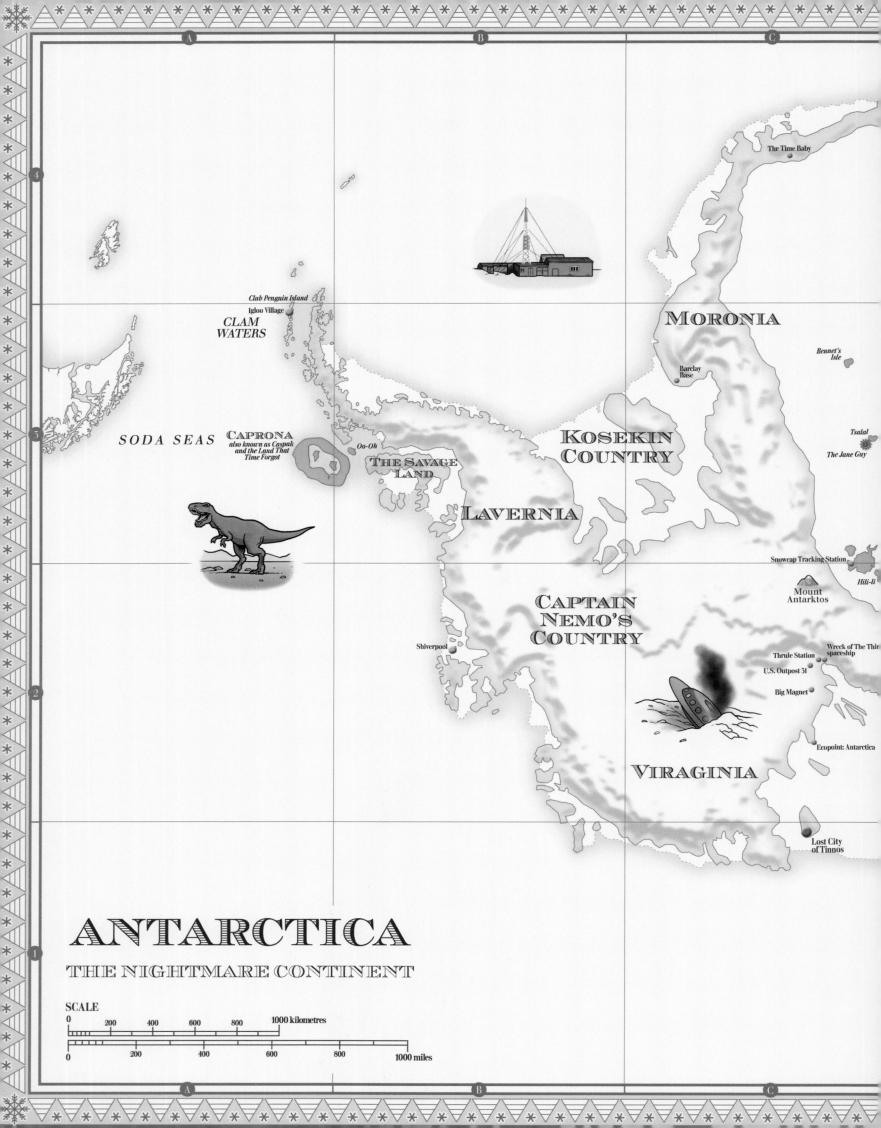

ANTARCTICA
THE NIGHTMARE CONTINENT

The Time Baby

MORONIA

Bennet's Isle

Barclay Base

KOSEKIN COUNTRY

Tsalal

The Jane Guy

Club Penguin Island
Igloo Village

CLAM WATERS

LAVERNIA

SODA SEAS

CAPRONA
also known as Caspak and the Land That Time Forgot

Oo-Oh

THE SAVAGE LAND

Snowcap Tracking Station

Hili-li

Mount Antarktos

CAPTAIN NEMO'S COUNTRY

Shiverpool

Thrule Station

Wreck of The Thir spaceship

U.S. Outpost 31

Big Magnet

Ecopoint: Antarctica

VIRAGINIA

Lost City of Tinnos

SCALE

0   200   400   600   800   1000 kilometres

0   200   400   600   800   1000 miles

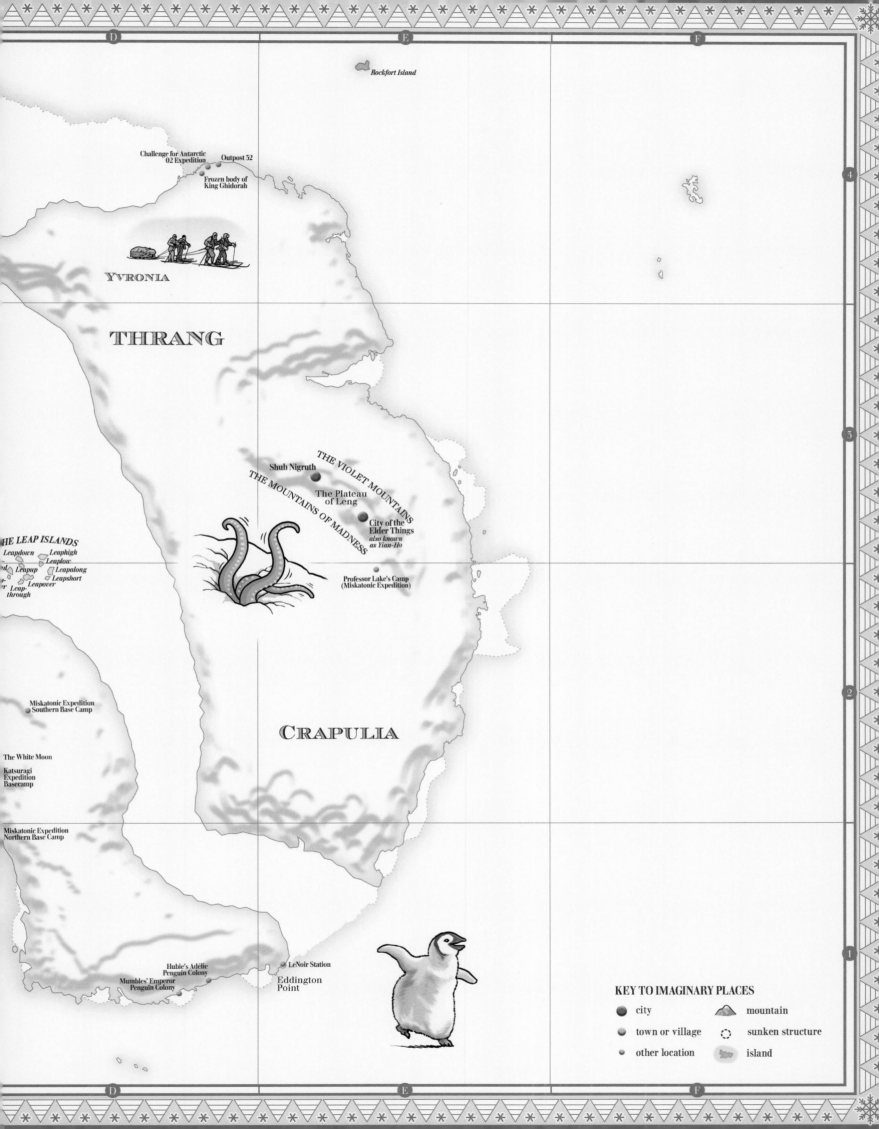

Rockfort Island

Challenge for Antarctic
02 Expedition   Outpost 32

Frozen body of
King Ghidorah

YVRONIA

THRANG

THE VIOLET MOUNTAINS

Shub Nigruth

THE MOUNTAINS OF MADNESS

The Plateau
of Leng

City of the
Elder Things
*also known
as Yian-Ho*

THE LEAP ISLANDS

Leapdown   *Leaphigh*
Leaplow
Leapup   *Leapalong*
Leapover   *Leapshort*
Leap-
through

Professor Lake's Camp
(Miskatonic Expedition)

Miskatonic Expedition
Southern Base Camp

CRAPULIA

The White Moon

Katsuragi
Expedition
Basecamp

Miskatonic Expedition
Northern Base Camp

Hubie's Adélie
Penguin Colony   LeNoir Station

Mumbles' Emperor
Penguin Colony   Eddington
Point

KEY TO IMAGINARY PLACES

- city
- town or village
- other location
- mountain
- sunken structure
- island

ANTARCTICA

KEY LOCATIONS

For a full list of locations, see the location index on pages 130–150.

CAPTAIN NEMO'S COUNTRY
20,000 Leagues Under the Sea
BY JULES VERNE | ANTARCTICA | NOVEL
Although unnamed, the entire continent of Antarctica was claimed by Captain Nemo, by placing a black flag with a golden 'N' at the South Pole. We'll encounter Nemo again, not too many degrees of latitude north, in the Pacific map. **MAP pp.114–115, B2**

CAPRONA (CASPAK)
The Land That Time Forgot
BY EDGAR RICE BURROUGHS | SOUTHERN OCEAN | NOVEL/FILMS
A lost world of dinosaurs located somewhere in the Antarctic below the South Pacific. We've placed it beside the similarly prehistoric Savage Land. **MAP pp.114–115, A3**

CRAPULIA
Mundus alter et idem
BY JOSEPH HALL | CONTINENT | NOVEL
This 400-year-old satirical novel describes, and maps, a huge mythical continent larger even than the real Antarctica would turn out to be. We've included some of the main territories, in locations that roughly translate onto the real continent. **MAP pp.114–115, E2**

ECOPOINT: ANTARCTICA
Overwatch **ANTARCTICA | VIDEO GAME**
Research facility located near the Antarctic coast. The game environment makes lots of references to 'The Thing', so a location near-ish to Outpost 31 would make sense. **MAP pp.114–115, C2**

EDDINGTON POINT
WORKS OF MADELEINE L'ENGLE | ANTARCTICA | NOVELS
L'Engle is one of those authors who pop up throughout this Atlas and she even has a well-wrapped foot in Antarctica. Eddington Point is the coastal home to the fictional LeNoir Station. Since LeNoir is a name of French origin, we've placed it within France's comparatively small Antarctic territorial claim. **MAP pp.114–115, E1**

HUBIE'S ADELIE PENGUIN COLONY/ PEBBLE BEACH
The Pebble and the Penguin
ANTARCTICA | FILM
A colony of anthropomorphic Adélie penguins from this animated film by Don Bluth. In one line of dialogue the name 'Pebble Beach' is cited, though whether this is the name of the community or just the nearby beach goes unstated. Although Adélies live all around Antarctica, we can pretty confidently place penguin protagonist Hubie's colony on the coast facing towards Australia/New Zealand – either Victoria Land or Adélie Land (from where the birds take their name)

itself. After escaping a human ship that has picked him up, Hubie washes up in French Polynesia (identified in dialogue as either Moorea or Tahiti). Three days after being captured (and right before escaping the ship), Hubie is also joined by a captured Rockhopper penguin named Rocko, and the Rockhopper distribution map shows colonies on the islands between Antarctica and Australia/New Zealand. **MAP pp.114–115, D1**

THE LEAP ISLANDS
The Monikins
BY JAMES FENIMORE COOPER | ISLAND CHAIN | NOVEL
Best known for Mohicans, Cooper also tackled Monikins (a fictional race) in this little-loved novel that is sometimes described as an American *Gulliver's Travels*. The book features an Antarctic island chain of ten independent kingdoms all with the word 'Leap' in their name, for reasons no one seems quite sure of. **MAP pp.114–115, D2/D3**

LOST CITY OF TINNOS
Tomb Raider III
ANTARCTICA | VIDEO GAME
Coastal city established by Polynesian explorers on Antarctica near the coast, but since abandoned. In real life, there's speculation that a fleet of Polynesian explorers made it to the Ross Ice Shelf, so we've placed Tinnos on the Antarctic land close by. Lara Croft reaches the lost city after passing through the fictional RX-Tech Mines. **MAP pp.114–115, C1**

THE MOUNTAINS OF MADNESS
At the Mountains of Madness
BY HP LOVECRAFT | ANTARCTICA | VARIOUS

Vast mountain range taller than the Himalayas. 'The great mountain chain was tremendously long – starting as a low range at Luitpold Land on the coast of Weddell Sea and virtually crossing the entire continent. The really high part stretched in a mighty arc from about Latitude 82°, E. Longitude 60° to Latitude 70°, E. Longitude 115°...'. The expedition which discovers these monsters later spies an even larger range, dubbed the Violet Mountains (also mapped). **MAP pp.114–115, E3**

OUTPOST 32
Godzilla: King of the Monsters
ANTARCTICA | FILM

This base for the Monarch organisation is shown on maps to lie where, in the real-world, you would find Syowa Station. This is appropriate, since Syowa is an alternate spelling of Showa – the Japanese era corresponding to the reign of Hirohito (Emperor Showa). The earliest Godzilla films date from this time, and are thus known as the 'Showa-Era' films. Outpost 32 should not be confused with US Outpost 31 (see page 112), which is a different Thing entirely. **MAP pp.114–115, D4**

SHUB NIGRUTH
Atlantis: The Lost Empire
ANTARCTICA | FILM

Though the name is clearly a nod to the Lovecraft Mythos (he invented a deity called Shub-Niggurath), this one comes to us from Disney. Bonus material on the DVD for *Atlantis: the Lost Empire* credits the discovery (and subsequent destruction) of this lost city to the movie's villain Rourke in an in-universe dossier. **MAP pp.114–115, E3**

SNOWCAP TRACKING STATION
Doctor Who **ANTARCTICA | TV**

A space tracking station and missile base somewhere near the South Pole. Though we haven't mapped all fictional locations from Doctor Who, this one is a biggy. The Tenth Planet is doubly notable for the first appearance of A-list baddies the Cybermen, as well as showing the regeneration of the Doctor for the first time (William Hartnell regenerates into Patrick Troughton). **MAP pp.114–115, C2/C3**

THRANG **CTHULHU MYTHOS | ANTARCTICA | VARIOUS**

Name which the alien species the 'Ithra (native to Belegeuse) gave to Antarctica when they established a colony there three billion years ago. This must surely be the oldest place name in the Atlas. **MAP pp.114–115, D3**

TSALAL
The Narrative of Arthur Gordon Pym of Nantucket
BY EDGAR ALLAN POE
AND *An Antarctic Mystery*
BY JULES VERNE | ISLAND | NOVELS

Poe's only complete novel was later revisited in a sequel by Jules Verne. Both stories visit the mysterious island of Tsalal, whose coordinates put it deep within the Antarctic continent, in a jet black sea. Verne's map of the continent shows the location and water channel. **MAP pp.114–115, C3**

THE WHITE MOON / KATSURAGI EXPEDITION BASECAMP
Neon Genesis Evangelion
UNDERGROUND WRECK/CAMP | MANGA/ANIME

An immense alien transport vessel 13.75km (8½ miles) in diameter (the 'twin' of the Black Moon buried underneath the Hakone mountains in Japan). The Katsuragi Expedition set out to examine the craft and its occupant – a giant inert creature dubbed 'Adam', and began by establishing a base camp on the surface before boring down into the craft. The outcome was catastrophic. 'Adam' exploded, taking the entire continent of Antarctica with it. Two billion people were killed in the mega-tsunamis, sea-level rises, earthquakes, natural disasters and wars that followed. May not be based on actual events. **MAP pp.114–115, D2**

THE PACIFIC OCEAN

ISLAND HOPPING

acific means *peaceful*. Appropriately, this vast ocean is among the quietest of maps in our atlas, being a part of the globe that lacks notable landmasses, save for the pinprick island chains that pepper its surface. But that doesn't mean there's nothing going on; when we pay attention to the individual locations, we spot all manner of features, creatures and tropical beaches.

Most bizarre of all has to be the unpromisingly named Standard Island. Its alternative name, which hints at its peculiarities, is given in the title of its source: *Propeller Island*, by Jules Verne. This 4-mile (6.4km)long platform is entirely artificial – the ultimate cruise ship on which millionaires voyage around the Pacific. We could have placed the island-ship anywhere along its known route, though we've chosen a berth in French Polynesia as a nod to the Gallic author.

Perhaps instead we might have positioned this engineering marvel in the western Pacific, alongside another artificial island drawn from sci-fi. Here, on the equator, rises the Heaven Pillar Orbital Elevator from the *Gundam* anime franchise, a means of accessing space without using rocketry. It thus supersedes the nearby Solomon Space Center (from the *Rocket Girls* novels), whose space tech is only powerful enough to send high-school astronauts aloft. Northwards of New Zealand

we've charted a pair of satellite-tracking ships unlucky enough to have made first contact with a malevolent extraterrestrial intelligence: the Chinese *Wan Xuan III* hailing from the graphic novel *Virus*; and the Russian *Akademik Vladislav Volkov* steaming in from the comic's 1999 film adaptation.

The hostile entity who inhabited these hulls would have had plenty of options in choosing an island to make port, especially if using our map as reference. Fiction has ballooned Hawaii into a horseshoe (ironic, given that no horse set hoof on Hawaii until the 1800s). The island-chain now contains such destinations as Gilligan's Island, *Joe Versus the Volcano's* Waponi Woo, and *The Tick's* Pokoponesia archipelago. Herman Melville meanwhile enriches the equator with the 30 or so islands of the Mardi archipelago, each representing a particular philosophy or allegory. We've deliberately chained together the islands of Altruria and Utopia (from the opera *Utopia, Limited*, not Thomas More's original), and even encounter parody, with August Bank Holiday Island (*The Goodies*) and the Mothering Sunday Islands (Terry Pratchett's *Nation*) directing wry nods towards Easter and Christmas Islands.

But the Pacific isn't all about islands. Some of literature's greatest characters have navigated this vast expanse. Captain Nemo, Jules Verne's Indian prince, master mariner and scientific genius, built and berthed

his legendary *Nautilus* on fictional Lincoln Island (sometimes dubbed Vulcania). That most famous of submarines was ultimately scuttled here to serve as Nemo's tomb. Ahab, a captain of equally 'grand, ungodly, god-like' stature, is also documented as meeting his fate in these waters. Driven mad with desire for revenge against Moby Dick, the master of the *Pequod* steers his ship on a course as inflexible as iron rails, bound for a fatal encounter with the great white whale just north of the equator, not far from the Marshall Islands.

Ahab's cetacean nemesis reminds us of all that is hidden beneath the Pacific's tranquil surface. Its depths teem with life, some of it deeply weird. After all, this is the ocean that gave forth the great *kaiju*, creatures such as Godzilla and his titanic brethren, plus the entire bestiary of the *Pacific Rim* films. Further east, you might be unlucky enough to bump into one of the genetically modified sharks of *Deep Blue Sea*, escaped from the Aquatica Research Station. Swimmers to the west, meanwhile, should look out for the prehistoric Megalodon said to menace the Marianas.

But there are life forms here of a less threatening nature; Bikini Bottom, located beneath the atoll of the same name, is home to an especially chipper and beloved anthropomorphic poriferan. Absorbent and yellow and porous is he. For further clarification consult the nearest five-year-old.

ALL BOUND FOR MU-MU LAND

Just as the Atlantic has its Atlantis and the Indian Ocean its Lemuria, the fictional Pacific also conceals a vanished, sunken continent. The mythical land of Mu started life in the 1890s as an alternative name for Atlantis, coined (from a mistranslated Mayan word) by antiquarian Augustus Le Plongeon, a man with a name to rival Dumas and a beard that would have made Rasputin proud. From these humble origins Mu migrated eastwards to the Indian and Pacific Oceans – the ultimate exercise in continental drift! Here it became conflated with Lemuria by the British occultist James Churchward, who described Mu as home to an advanced people called the Naacal, who in their travels founded all the great civilizations of antiquity.

Needless to say, Mu has found its way into many works of fiction over its 130 years of non-existence. H.P. Lovecraft and the inheritors of his Cthulhu Mythos have dipped their toes (and tentacles) into this ocean, beginning with the 1935 short story *Out of the Aeons*. The lost land has also appeared in Marvel Comics, where it remains connected to Lemuria. Dozens of other authors, including Thomas Pynchon and Tom Robbins, have given us unique glimpses of Mu. Its influence has even spilled over into music; British readers of a certain age might remember *The Justified Ancients of Mu Mu* (better known as the KLF), whose name was indirectly inspired by the lost continent.

Mu is not the only continent concealed beneath our fictional ocean. In 1882, spiritualist (and dentist) John Ballou Newbrough penned the bizarre *Oahspe: A New Bible*, a pseudo-religious text apparently dictated by angels, channelling their knowledge through Newbrough's pen. Among many revelations (including one of the first uses of the phrase 'star-ship'), the book details a triangular continent known as Pan, or Whaga, that once filled much of the North Pacific before sinking 24,000 years ago. We hope Newbrough's angelic host will not be too offended if we conflate Pan with Mu on our map. Likewise, a third submerged continent known as Rutas and proposed by French occultist Louis Jacolliot shares many similarities with Mu, and is included as a region of that land.

All these inundated lands are self-evidently bunkum, but the Pacific does hold at least one genuinely 'lost' continent. 'Zealandia' is a submerged mass of continental crust that was once dry land, but which vanished beneath the waves some 23 million years ago (long before humans walked the Earth). Only 6 per cent of Zealandia remains above the waves today, in the forms of New Zealand and New Caledonia. Although this lost continent is factual – and therefore not within our remit to map – we can rescue some portion of it through works of fiction.

Take the Crown Colony of Britannula (from Anthony Trollope's *The Fixed Period*), or *Crash Bandicoot*'s Wumpa Islands. On the basis of their location, both must be hewn from Zealandia's ancient rock.

Our map contains one final mysterious continent, about which little is known, not even its name! René Daumal's remarkable (and posthumous) 1952 novel *Mount Analogue* is a banquet of riddles, set on a fictional landmass south of New Zealand, almost impossible to find, and centered around a mountain (the titular Mount Analogue) of such stupendous mass that it bends light and radio signals, thus rendering the continent all but invisible. We can only guess at its coastline, though a location in the waters south of Tasmania and New Zealand is confirmed in the novel.

MOANA: WE (SORT-OF) KNOW WHERE WE ARE

One of cinema's greatest musicals is set among these seas. We're talking not about Rodgers and Hammerstein's *South Pacific* (which provides the fictional island of Bali Ha'i near Vanuatu), but of Disney's *Moana*.

This 2016 hit tells the story of the titular Moana, an adventurous Polynesian girl who yearns to see what lies beyond the horizons of Motunui, her island home. Her subsequent travels see Moana meeting the demi-god Maui, battling a giant crab beneath the isle of Lalotai, and eventually freeing the island-goddess Te Fiti. Needless to say, all of these locations are fictional, and almost impossible to pinpoint.

But where would be the fun in that?

Truthfully, Moana's home waters could be anywhere in Polynesia. The filmmakers at Disney set out to express multiple regional cultures across a single narrative. Ultimately we had to pick somewhere, and ended up geocaching the movie's islands in between Samoa and the Marquesas. Why? Well, several fan sites have plumped for Samoa as a leading inspiration, Maui's tattoos are modelled on Marquesan designs, and the name 'Te Fiti' sounds a bit like nearby Tahiti.

But even with a location picked, we needed to establish where these islands lie in relation to one another, and succeeded with the help of similar wayfinding tricks to those shown in the film. Moana's first stop is Maui's Island, a barren rock which we can assume is not too far from Motunui, as the navigational novice reaches it with little bother. Maui joins her as a reluctant companion, and the dynamic duo squabble their way to the monster-laden Lalotai, whose location is also nebulous. The pair are subsequently shown sailing directly into the sunrise, and so their final destination, Te Fiti, logically lies north-east of Lalotai, and probably Motunui, too.

As Maui himself might say 'You're welcome.' Now, bring us that horizon, and perhaps a sequel or two!

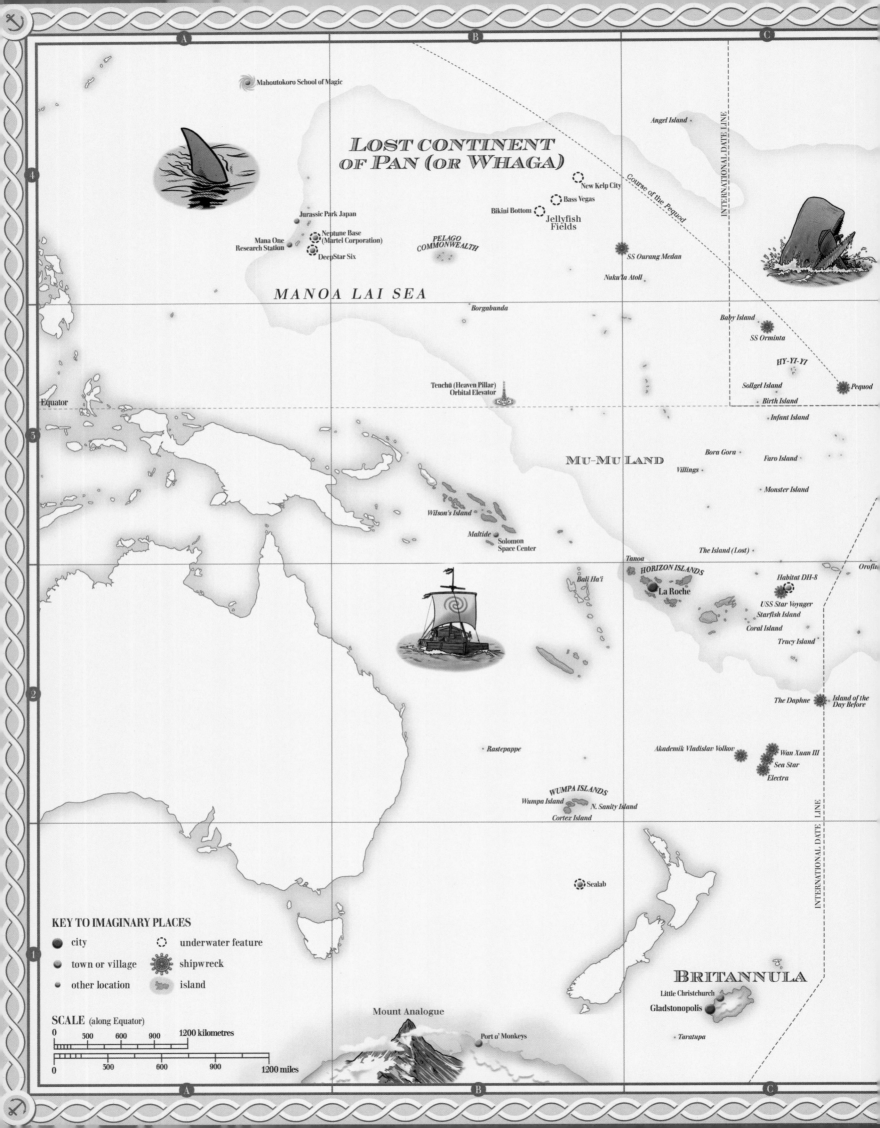

LOST CONTINENT
OF PAN (OR WHAGA)

Mahoutokoro School of Magic

Angel Island

New Kelp City
Bass Vegas
Bikini Bottom
Jellyfish
Fields

Jurassic Park Japan

Mana One
Research Station
Neptune Base
(Martel Corporation)
DeepStar Six

PELAGO
COMMONWEALTH

SS Ourang Medan

Nuku'la Atoll

MANOA LAI SEA

Borgabunda

Baby Island
SS Orminta

HY-YI-YI

Tenchū (Heaven Pillar)
Orbital Elevator

Sollgel Island
Pequod
Birth Island

Equator

Infant Island

MU-MU LAND

Bora Gora
Faro Island
Villings
Monster Island

Wilson's Island

Maltide
Solomon
Space Center

The Island (Lost)

Tanoa
HORIZON ISLANDS
Bali Ha'i
Habitat DH-8
La Roche
USS Star Voyager
Starfish Island
Coral Island
Tracy Island

Orofin

The Daphne
Island of the
Day Before

Rastepappe

Akademik Vladislav Volkov
Wan Xuan III
Sea Star
Electra

WUMPA ISLANDS
Wumpa Island
N. Sanity Island
Cortex Island

Sealab

BRITANNULA

KEY TO IMAGINARY PLACES

● city
◐ town or village
• other location
○ underwater feature
✺ shipwreck
island

Little Christchurch
Gladstonopolis

SCALE (along Equator)

0   500   600   900   1200 kilometres

0   500   600   900   1200 miles

Mount Analogue

Port o' Monkeys

Taratupa

INTERNATIONAL DATE LINE

INTERNATIONAL DATE LINE

Course of the Pequod

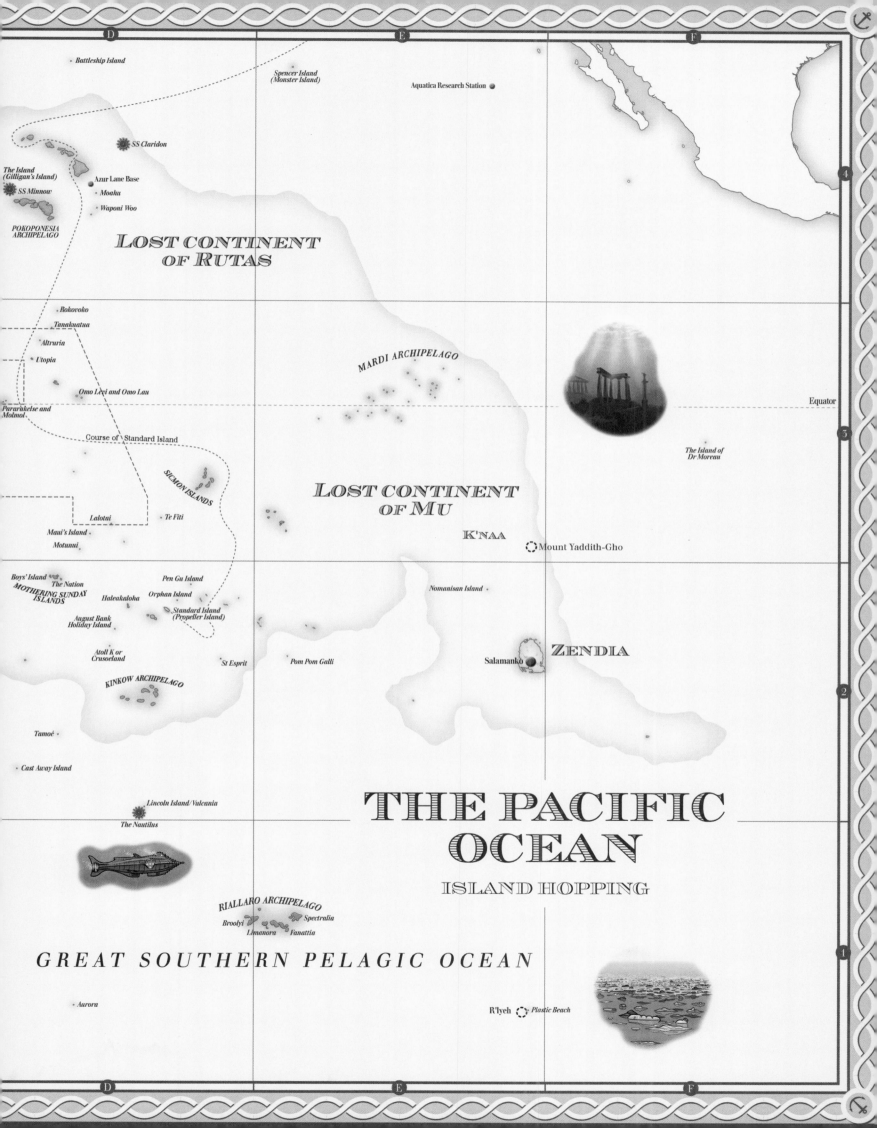

D · E · F

4

· Battleship Island

Spencer Island
(Monster Island)

Aquatica Research Station ●

SS Claridon ☀

*The Island
(Gilligan's Island)*
☀ *SS Minnow*
■ Azur Lane Base
· Moahu
· Waponi Woo

*POKOPONESIA
ARCHIPELAGO*

LOST CONTINENT
OF RUTAS

3

· Rokovoko
· Tanakuatua
· Altruria
· Utopia

· Omo Levi and Omo Lau

*Pararukelse and
Molmol*

Course of Standard Island

MARDI ARCHIPELAGO

Equator

*The Island of
Dr Moreau*

SICMON ISLANDS

LOST CONTINENT
OF MU

· Te Fiti

· Lalotai

Maui's Island ·
Motunui ·

K'NAA

◌ Mount Yaddith-Gho

Boys' Island
The Nation
*MOTHERING SUNDAY
ISLANDS*
Haleakaloha

Pen Gu Island
Orphan Island
*Standard Island
(Propeller Island)*

Nomanisan Island ·

August Bank
Holiday Island

Atoll K or
Crusoeland

· St Esprit

· Pom Pom Galli

ZENDIA
Salamanko ●

2

KINKOW ARCHIPELAGO

Tamoé ·

· Cast Away Island

Lincoln Island/Vulcania
The Nautilus

THE PACIFIC
OCEAN
ISLAND HOPPING

RIALLARO ARCHIPELAGO

Broolyi ·· Spectralia
Limanora Fanattia

1

GREAT SOUTHERN PELAGIC OCEAN

· Aurora

R'lyeh ◌ *Plastic Beach*

D · E · F

THE PACIFIC OCEAN

KEY LOCATIONS

For a full list of locations, see the location index on pages 130–150.

AUGUST BANK HOLIDAY ISLAND
The Goodies
SOUTHERN PACIFIC | TV
A Commonwealth nation, lying 'between Easter Island and Christmas Island'. We've put it near the Mothering Sunday Islands for obvious reasons.
MAP pp.120–121, D2

BALI HA'I
South Pacific
SOUTH PACIFIC | FILM
What's the first film you think of when someone says the words 'South Pacific'? *South Pacific*, of course. The much-loved musical features a mysterious island called Bali-ha'i. Its location is easily identified if we go to the film's source material, *Tales of the South Pacific*, by James Micherner. The author based Bali Ha'i on the real island of Ambae, which he'd glimpsed from far off while serving in Vanuatu during the Second World War.
MAP pp.120–121, B2

BRITANNULA
The Fixed Period
BY ANTHONY TROLLOPE |
SOUTH-WEST PACIFIC | NOVEL
The great novelist's contribution to the dystopian genre, Britannula is a moderately sized British Crown Colony, somewhere in the region of New Zealand.
MAP pp.120–121, C1

CAST AWAY ISLAND
Cast Away **SOUTH PACIFIC | FILM**
This popular Tom Hanks film was shot on the Fijian island of Monuriki (which gained additional tourists as a result). However, the in-film setting is said to be 965km (600 miles) south of the Cook Islands. **MAP pp.120–121, D2**

DEEPSTAR SIX / NEPTUNE BASE
Deepstar Six / Lords of the Deep **PACIFIC OCEAN | FILMS**
The tail end of the 1980s saw a brief boom of horror and thriller films set within submarine environments. Alongside more publicized works such as James Cameron's *The Abyss*, there were lesser-known films such as *Deepstar Six* and *Lords of the Deep*, both of which are set within research facilities located at the bottom of the Pacific. Since both were released in 1989, we decided it would be fun to map the two locations as neighbours. **MAP pp.120–121, A4**

HORIZON ISLANDS
ARMA 3
SOUTH PACIFIC | VIDEO GAME
Tropical islands inspired by Fiji. The main island is Tanoa, while the smaller islands are Tuvanaka, Balavu, Katkoula and Moddergat. **MAP pp.120–121, C2**

HY-YI-YI
Legend of the Rhinogradentia
CENTRAL PACIFIC | FAKED INFORMATION
Hi-yi-yi is one of those locations whose whereabouts are very sketchy, yet we

felt compelled to include it because the details will send you down a rabbit hole – or maybe a snouter hole. This imaginary mid-Pacific archipelago (comprising 18 named islands and many smaller ones) is home to a whole ecosystem of peculiar creatures, dominated by the muppet-nosed rhinogrades. The small mammals were dreamed up by German zoologist Gerolf Steiner and presented as though a genuine zoological treatise. Sadly, this unique fauna was wiped out by an atomic bomb test – our main clue to a possible location. Be sure to look them up.
MAP pp.120–121, C3

THE ISLAND
Gilligan's Island
PACIFIC OCEAN | TV
This tiny scrap of land, where the shipwrecked castaways of the SS *Minnow* endured the challenges offered by nature and bumbling first-mate Gilligan for 96 episodes, is officially located some 250 miles from Hawaii. Given that the *Minnow* became wrecked here while on a three-hour tour out of Honolulu, it seems incredible that it took three whole seasons before the cast were rescued!
MAP pp.120–121, D4

THE ISLAND
Lost **CENTRAL PACIFIC | TV**
A tricky one to map as the island is known to move from point-to-point on the Earth's surface. For the majority of the show, however, it exists at a location which, based on dialogue regarding the flight plan of Oceanic Flight 815, is near

to the real-world Wallis Island, north-east of Fiji. Later on in the series, the island is relocated to a location somewhere between Hawaii and Guam, based on the flight path of Ajira Airways Flight 316. MAP pp.120–121, C3

THE ISLAND OF THE DAY BEFORE
The Island of the Day Before
BY UMBERTO ECO | SOUTH PACIFIC | NOVEL
An island situated right on the International Date Line, which plays a key role in the set-up (even though the date line was not universally placed in these parts until well after the period of the novel). A sailor is stranded on the Dutch derelict *Daphne*, just west of the date line. From here, he can see the island 'of the day before', just across the date line and therefore forever a day in his past. MAP pp.120–121, C2

MOTHERING SUNDAY ISLANDS
Nation BY TERRY PRATCHETT | SOUTH PACIFIC | NOVEL
An archipelago located in the Southern Ocean. A map inside the book hints at the extent and location of the islands, at roughly the same longitude as Hawaii. MAP pp.120–121, D2

MU-MU LAND
'Justified & Ancient'
BY THE KLF | CENTRAL PACIFIC | MUSIC
This song features repeated references to Mu-Mu Land. The name is drawn from *The Illuminatus! Trilogy* by Robert Shea and Robert Anton Wilson, in which the Justified Ancients of Mummu are a secret society. Both trace inspiration back to the lost continent of Mu, and we've mapped Mu-Mu Land as one of its regions. MAP pp.120–121, B3/C3

NOMANISAN ISLAND
The Incredibles
CENTRAL PACIFIC | FILM
Can you see what they did with the name? Syndrome's island lair has the rough position of 125 degrees West, 20 degrees South, according to a GPS display glimpsed in the film. MAP pp.120–121, E2

PLASTIC BEACH
Plastic Beach BY GORILLAZ | CENTRAL PACIFIC | MUSIC
The music of Gorillaz is usually accompanied by animation and storylines. For this album, the group imagined a plastic island at 'Point Nemo', the place in the Pacific Ocean furthest from land. MAP pp.120–121, E1

R'LYEH CTHULHU MYTHOS | SOUTH PACIFIC | VARIOUS
The sunken city where great Cthulhu sleeps and dreams in the deep. Lovecraft and his friend August Derleth gave subtly different co-ordinates for R'lyeh, but as with Plastic Beach (above), both are located in proximity to Point Nemo. MAP pp.120–121, E1

RASTEPAPPE
Archibald the Koala
SOUTH PACIFIC | TV
An island populated by anthropomorphic koalas and badgers. The location is not specified, but it requires no intellectual leap to place it near Australia, given the koalas. MAP pp.120–121, B2

RIALLARO ARCHIPELAGO
Riallaro: The Archipelago of Exiles BY GODFREY SWEVEN | SOUTH PACIFIC | NOVEL
A mysterious archipelago shrouded in mist, which few have penetrated. At least 15 islands are named, of which we've labelled the most prominent. The islands also appear in *The League of Extraordinary Gentlemen* comics. MAP pp.120–121, D1/E1

ROKOVOKO
Moby Dick BY HERMAN MELVILLE | NORTHERN PACIFIC | NOVEL
Sometimes known as Kokovoko, this is the Polynesian island home of Queequeg. The precise location is never given, only described as 'an island far away to the West and South' (of New England). We've put it reasonably close to the final resting place of the Pequod, which is given with more accuracy. MAP pp.120–121, D3

SICMON ISLANDS
The Griffin and Sabine Trilogy
NORTHERN PACIFIC | NOVELS
These islands are named as Arbah, Katie, Katin, Ta Fin, Quepol and Typ (not shown on map). MAP pp.120–121, D3

SPENCER ISLAND (MONSTER ISLAND)
Godfrey Morgan
BY JULES VERNE | NORTHERN PACIFIC | NOVEL/FILM
This novel begins with the US Government auctioning off fictional Spencer Island, whose position is handily given as 32 degrees 15 minutes north, 145 degrees 18 minutes west. A film adaptation, starring Peter Cushing and Terrance Stamp, changes the name (and plot) to Monster Island. MAP pp.120–121, E4

SS CLARIDON
The Last Voyage
NORTH PACIFIC | FILM
Veteran ocean liner that sinks *en route* from San Francisco to Tokyo. Inferred to have sunk in the vicinity of Hawaii, given the ship is rescued by a ship named the *Hawaiian Fisherman*. Notable for filming aboard the actual ocean liner *Ile de France* prior to her scrapping, and demolishing most of her interiors in the process! MAP pp.120–121, D4

STARFISH ISLAND
Green Arrow
DC COMICS | SOUTH PACIFIC | COMICS
The shipwreck island of Green Arrow is identified as a Fijian island in *Green Arrow: Year One*. See also Lian Yu (page 105). MAP pp.120–121, C2

TRACY ISLAND
Thunderbirds
SOUTH PACIFIC | TV
The exact location of the Tracy brothers' tropical hideaway is a closely guarded secret, especially in the original series. However, a navigation display in the 2004 movie places it mid-Pacific, while *Thunderbirds Are Go* (2015) more specifically locates it in the vicinity of 22 degrees south, 170 degrees west. F.A.B.! MAP pp.120–121, C2

USS STAR VOYAGER
Sphere BY MICHAEL CRICHTON | SOUTH PACIFIC | NOVEL/FILM
Time-displaced spacecraft from the future, discovered crashed in the present between Samoa and Fiji in the South Pacific. Habitat DH-8 is set up beside it. MAP pp.120–121, C2

WUMPA ISLANDS
Crash Bandicoot SERIES | SOUTH PACIFIC | VIDEO GAMES
The three main islands from the *Crash Bandicoot* series are sometimes described as 'near Tasmania', though a satellite image from one game shows them to be further out towards New Zealand. We've included them on the Pacific map because they tie in with the idea of the lost continents of the Pacific (see page 119). MAP pp.120–121, B2

ZENDIA
The Zendian Problem
SOUTH PACIFIC | INTELLIGENCE EXERCISE
This fictional island was invented at the USA's National Intelligence Agency as the setting for exercises in communications intelligence. It is said to be at a similar latitude to Cuba (22 degrees), but flipped south (22 degrees). MAP pp.120–121, E2/F2

THE ATLANTIC OCEAN

LOST WORLDS OF THE WESTERN SEA

The Atlantic might be made from the same briny stuff as the Pacific, but its fictional waters hold a very different flavour. This is a sea of mythical islands and vanished continents, to which Ancient Greek philosophers, Norse traditions, Irish folklore and the Age of Discovery have all made contributions.

Sunken continents are usually regarded as myth, but many fictional Atlantic islands were once taken as fact. Thule, like legendary Atlantis hailing from the time of Plato, was once a shorthand used for any distant island beyond the regularly travelled world, the name later being applied to Iceland, Greenland, parts of the Orkneys, and eventually to entirely made-up islands. Many similar 'phantom islands'

populate our Atlantic, including the razor-shaped Antillia, an Iberian legend that graduated onto real navigational charts in the 14th and 15th centuries. St Brendan's Island, Hy-Brasil and Frisland are further examples of non-existent landmasses that have enjoyed a brief dalliance with actuality. Dozens more can be found in Edward Brooke-Hitching's *Phantom Atlas*.

Then we have those lands that come to us from popular culture. The most famous of these might be Pepperland, the music-loving subaquatic realm of The Beatles' *Yellow Submarine*, cheekily included here despite very few clues as to its location. Since the film features a stepped pyramid we've plumped for the South American coast, placing Pepperland midway between Mexico and Thomas More's Utopia, the

original island paradise. We've also tentatively mapped the seas of Time, Science, Monsters, Nothing and Holes, which all must be traversed to reach Pepperland from Liverpool.

Another surprise inclusion is the hexagonal isle of Catan, from the popular *Settlers of Catan* board game. Creator Klaus Teuber had the Azores in mind when developing this famous creation, with the titular settlers being expeditionary Norsemen. Games of the video persuasion also intrude upon these waters: Sahrani, Malden and Everon from the *ARMA* series are presented here just a short island-hop away from Catan. The proposed Jurassic Park Europe, from Michael Crichton's original novel, would have also glorified the Azores, had the Costa Rican original been a roaring success.

TUNNEL VISIONS

Our Atlantic map contains a feature noticeably absent from other maps in this atlas – undersea tunnels. The idea of a tunnel connecting Europe with America remains fanciful even today, due to insurmountable engineering and economic challenges, but the notion goes back well over a century. Michel Verne, son of Jules, proposed such a scheme as early as 1888, but the first detailed exploration is attributed to Bernhard Kellermann's 1913 novel *Der Tunnel*. This now-forgotten story, once a best-seller, described construction of a 3,000-mile (4,828km) tunnel from New Jersey to France, with portals on Bermuda, the Azores and northern Spain. Completed at immense cost, Kellermann's fictional tunnel is immediately made redundant by improvements in air travel.

This transatlantic tunnel concept was further developed in the 1914 novel *Il tunnel sottomarino* by Luigi Motta, which this time saw the tunnel driven from New York, and sadly destroyed by saboteurs on its opening day. A few passengers manage to escape in breathing apparatus, and discover a suburb of Atlantis (Atlanteja) on their way back to shore … frustratingly distant from where we've mapped Atlantis … but perhaps it's an outlying colony of the Lost Empire.

The concept of the transatlantic tunnel has been resuscitated many times since. Later works usually link together Britain and North America, including the 1935 film *Transatlantic Tunnel* (based on Kellermann's novel) and the titular engineering marvel of Harry Harrison's *Tunnel Through the Deeps* (1972). We've conflated all these schemes into one super-entity, but had to separately map the tunnel that, in the world of *Thunderbirds Are Go*, connects Great Britain with Iceland!

SLIPPERY WHEN WET: THE HUNT FOR ATLANTIS

Atlantis! Few places in this atlas are so famous, and yet so sketchily placed. We could have drawn it almost anywhere in the world, including Antarctica, the Arctic Circle or even the Pacific, and still matched up with at least one of the many interpretations of this ancient myth. It is the lost continent that can be found anywhere.

Atlantis's legend begins, so far as anyone knows, with Plato. The great philosopher conjured it into being in 375 BCE as part of *The Republic*, a treatise on statehood. Described as a vast island nation located somewhere beyond the Pillars of Hercules (usually interpreted as the Straits of Gibraltar), *The Republic* casts Atlantis as an antagonist to Athens, which represents the 'ideal' state. The island is ultimately sunk 'in a single day and night of misfortune', banished below the waves by the gods.

Atlantis only plays a bit-part in Plato's canon, but it struck a chord with other writers. The delightfully named Theopompus of Chios penned a parody version just a few years later, but his Meropis, though described as being both larger than Atlantis and even more distantly located, could never match the original's stature in the imagination, and the myth of Atlantis has grown and evolved ever since. We might list dozens, even hundreds of works of fiction (and supposed non-fiction) set in Atlantean realms, and call forth an endless parade of psychics, theosophists, cranks, pseudoscientists and conspiracy theorists who, like us, have 'rediscovered' Atlantis to suit their own book deals.

Consequently, we could place Atlantis pretty much anywhere, even within the Mediterranean; one theory links it to the volcanic island of Thera (Santorini) in the Aegean Sea. Thera erupted catastrophically c.1600 BCE, an event which caused immense damage to surrounding civilizations and possibly later inspired Plato's Atlantis via oral tradition. Others connect Atlantis's inundation to the fate of Doggerland, the land bridge that once joined Britain to continental Europe. Still more fanciful theories place it within Antarctica, a largely unexplored continent whose ice sheets may conceal any number of secrets.

But Atlantis, surely, *belongs* in the Atlantic. The name alone is reason enough to place it there, and this location also has a great deal of support from cartographers and writers over many generations. The great ocean marked the edge of the world for the Ancient Greeks, and is a logical place to locate Plato's lost continent.

Fiction has followed suit. Major recent films from DC (*Aquaman*), Disney (*Atlantis: The Lost Empire*) and Sony (*Hotel Transylvania 3*) have all plumped for an Atlantic setting, as did most of their forebears of page and screen. Of the many proposed locations, sizes and shapes, we've opted for an Atlantis that mirrors the one sketched by Athanasius Kircher in his celebrated 1669 map. Though drawn entirely from the imagination, it is one of the most carefully defined charts of the pseudo-continent, complete with rivers and mountains, proving very influential on later writers. Beyond lies the parody continent of Meropis, whose shape and size are undefined by any tradition, thus our illustrator Mike has the privilege of being the first to chart this lost continent.

One further Atlantis deserves mention here: the former ocean liner of that name, which after retirement from transatlantic service was repurposed as a cruise vessel. The ship also gained a new name, that of her mythic namesake's patron deity, Poseidon. The newly named SS *Poseidon*'s tragic maiden cruise drives the narrative of Paul Gallico's *The Poseidon Adventure*, and appropriately enough the ship sinks adjacent to the Azores, in the heart of where we have chosen to map 'our' Atlantis …

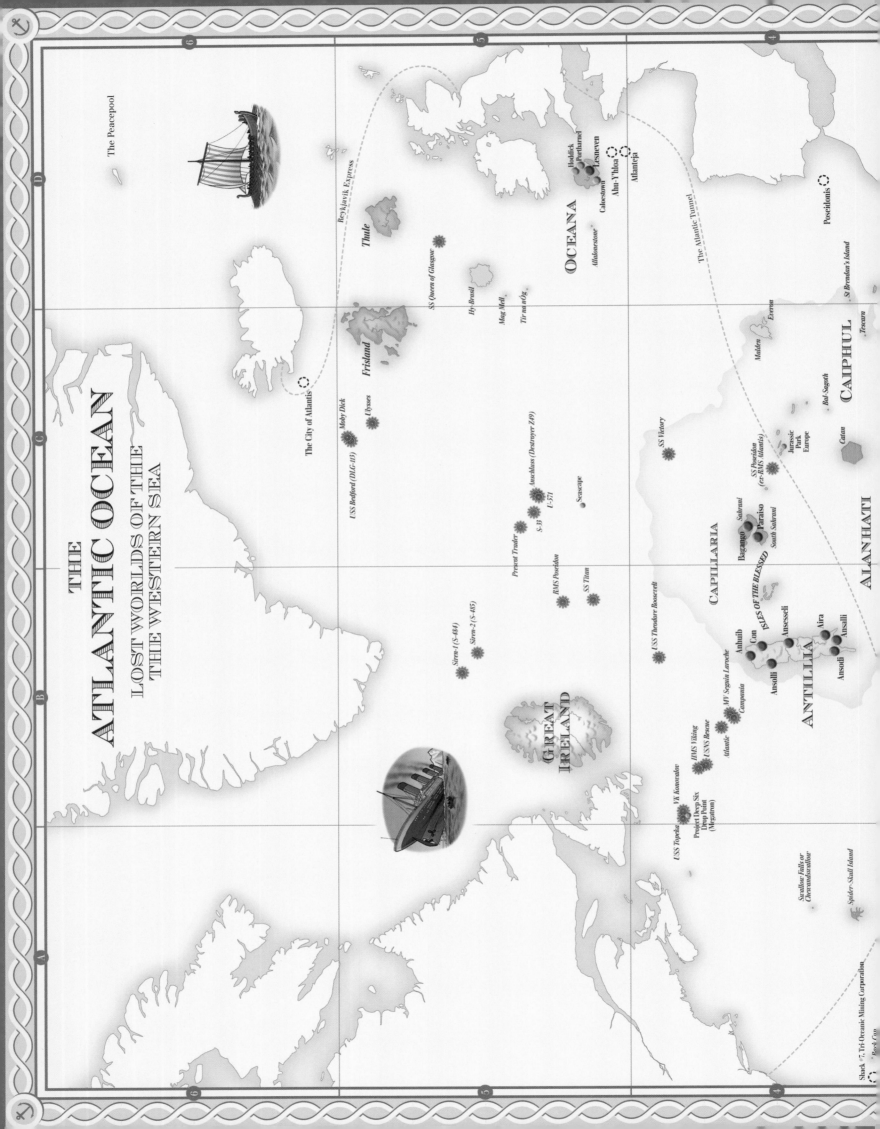

THE
ATLANTIC OCEAN

LOST WORLDS OF THE
THE WESTERN SEA

The Peacepool

The Atlantic Tunnel

The City of Atlantis

Reykjavik Express

Thule

Frisland

Hy-Brasil

Mag Mell

Tir na nÓg

SS Queen of Glasgow

Moby Dick

Ulysses

USS Bedford (DLG-113)

Anschluss (Destroyer Z49)

U-571

Seascape

Present Trader

RMS Poseidon

SS Titan

Siren-1 (S-484)

Siren-2 (S-485)

USS Theodore Roosevelt

MV Seguin Laroche

Campania

Atlantic

USNS Rescue

HMS Viking

USS Topeka

Project Deep Six
Drop Point (Megatron)

Swallow Falls or
Chewandswallow

Spider-Skull Island

OCEANA

Hoddick
Portharnel
Lesneven
Caboestown
Abu-Yhboa
Atlanteja

Alkalonestone

Poseidonis

St Brendan's Island

Everon

Tescara

Maltern

Bal-Sagoth

CAIPHUL

Catan

Jurassic
Park
Europe

SS Victory

SS Poseidon
(ex-RMS Atlantis)

Bazango
Paraiso

Sahrani

South Sahrani

CAPILLARIA

ISLES OF THE BLESSED

Anhuib

Con

Ansesseli

Afra

Ansalli

ALANHATI

ANTILLIA

Ansolli

Ansotli

GREAT
IRELAND

Shark #7, Tri-Oceanic Mining Corporation

Rock Cay

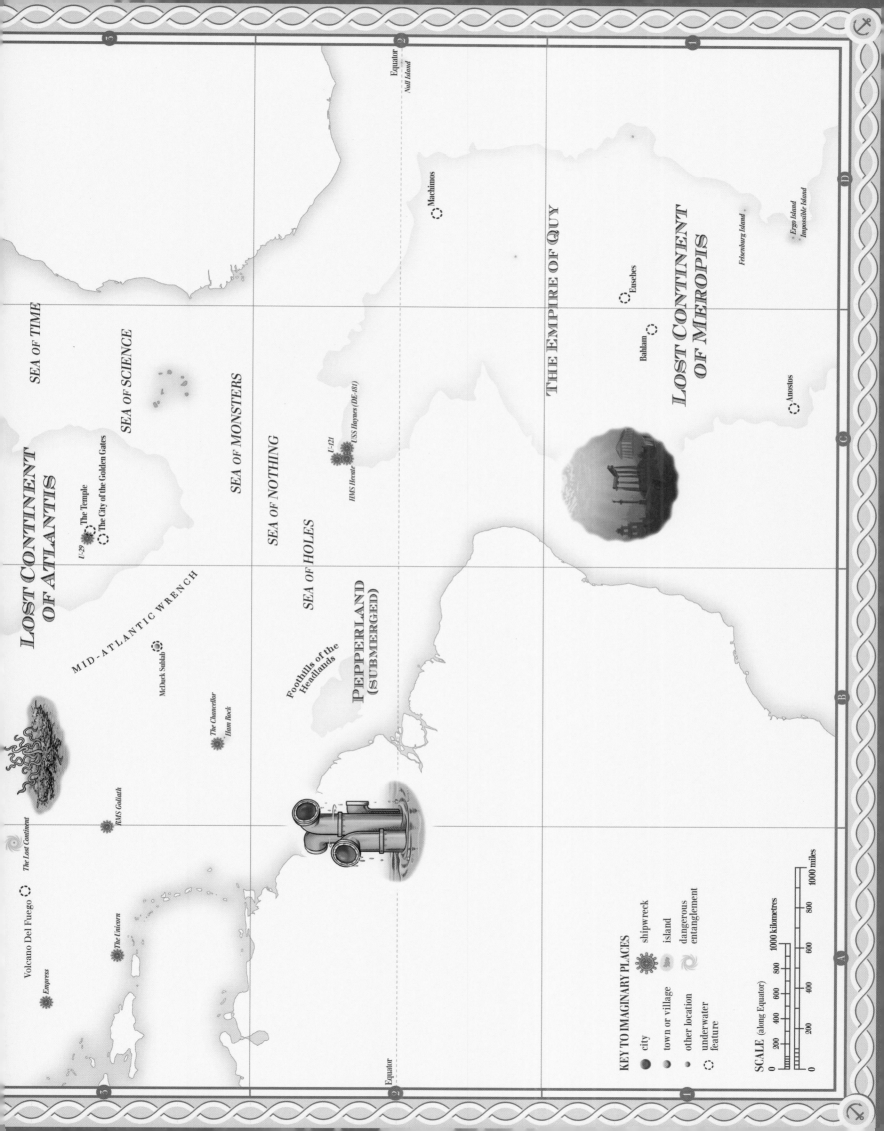

LOST CONTINENT
OF ATLANTIS

SEA OF TIME

SEA OF SCIENCE

SEA OF MONSTERS

SEA OF NOTHING

SEA OF HOLES

THE EMPIRE OF QUY

LOST CONTINENT
OF MEROPIS

MID-ATLANTIC WRENCH

PEPPERLAND
(SUBMERGED)

Foothills of the
Headlands

Equator

Null Island

Equator

Volcano Del Fuego

The Lost Continent

Empress

The Unicorn

RMS Goliath

McDuck Sublab

The Chancellor
Ham Rock

U-29 The Temple
The City of the Golden Gates

U-121

HMS Hecate *USS Haynes (DE-181)*

Machinos

Eusebes

Bahlam

Anostos

Felsenburg Island

Ergo Island
Impossible Island

KEY TO IMAGINARY PLACES

● city   ⚙ shipwreck
●● town or village   🏝 island
● other location   ∙ dangerous
◌ underwater   entanglement
   feature

SCALE (along Equator)

0   200 400 600 800 1000 kilometres

0   200   400   600   800   1000 miles

THE ATLANTIC OCEAN

KEY LOCATIONS

For a full list of locations, see the location index on pages 130–150.

ANTILLIA
NORTH ATLANTIC | LEGEND
A bizarrely shaped island that featured on many real navigational charts from the Age of Discovery. It contained seven cities, named here. **MAP pp.126–127, B4**

ATLANTIC
Atlantic **NORTH ATLANTIC | FILM**
A ship called the *Atlantic*, that sank in the Atlantic, from a 1929 film named *Atlantic*! One of the earlier talkies, that retold the *Titanic* disaster on a fictional liner named the *Atlantic*. The SOS in the film gives exact coordinates, which translate to about 64km (40 miles) west-north-west of the wreck of the actual *Titanic*. **MAP pp.126–127, B4**

ATLANTIC TUNNEL
Il Tunnel Sottomarino
BY LUIGI MOTTA AND OTHER SOURCES | ATLANTIC OCEAN | NOVEL
The idea of a transatlantic tunnel has been mooted in numerous novels and films. We've combined them into one tunnel. See main text for full details. **MAP pp.126–127, A4/B4/C4/C6/D4/D5**

BAL-SAGOTH
CTHULHU MYTHOS | NORTH ATLANTIC | VARIOUS
The last fragment of Atlantis remaining above the surface. Was landed on by Norsemen around the time of the Crusades, suggesting a North Atlantic location. We've mapped it nearby to Catan, which has its own Norse connection. **MAP pp.126–127, C4**

CAPILLARIA
Capillaria
BY FRIGYES KARINTHY | NORTH ATLANTIC | NOVEL
Vast underwater kingdom stretching between Norway and the USA, inhabited only by females. We've considered it part of Atlantis. **MAP pp.126–127, B4/C4**

GREAT IRELAND
NORTH ATLANTIC | LEGEND
A large island reputed to lie far out in the Atlantic. It features in many stories, and numerous locations have been suggested for it, including here, out near Newfoundland. **MAP pp.126–127, B5**

HY-BRASIL
NORTH ATLANTIC | LEGEND
One of several mythical islands off Ireland, though this one gained enough credibility to find its way onto actual maps. Hy-Brasil has also featured in works of fiction, such as the film *Erik the Viking* (1989). **MAP pp.126–127, D5**

ISLES OF THE BLESSED
MID-ATLANTIC | MYTHOLOGY
The Blessed Isles or Fortunate Isles were a recurring idea in ancient Greek storytelling – an earthly paradise inhabited by heroes. Their location is vague and varied, though Plutarch gives the best hint, putting them 10,000 furlongs (2,000km/1,250 miles) off Africa. This would put them further out than the Azores. **MAP pp.126–127, B4**

THE LOST CONTINENT
The Lost Continent
MID-ATLANTIC | FILM
More bizarre than usual fare from Hammer Studios. The so-called Lost Continent is a mysterious landmass that consists of some rocky islands surrounded by a vast raft of carnivorous, sargassum-like seaweed, in which countless ships have become enmeshed over the years. In reality, the exotic morass was filmed in a giant tank at Elstree Studios, on a site now covered by a supermarket. **MAP pp.126–127, A3**

MAG MELL
NORTH ATLANTIC | LEGEND
Like the Fields of Elysium in Greek mythology, Mag Mell was a place for the glorious dead. Its location varied, but was often said to be far off the coast of Ireland, presumably in the Atlantic. **MAP pp.126–127, D5**

MALDEN
ARMA: Cold War Assault
NORTH ATLANTIC | VIDEO GAME
Islands discovered and colonized by the French, but later ceded to the Russians, whose fleet uses the islands as a stop-off *en route* to the Mediterranean. Its coordinates are given on a fan wiki as 38 degrees, 48 minutes, 0 seconds north and 20 degrees, 42 minutes, 0 seconds

west. The terrain was based on a Greek island. MAP pp.126–127, C4

MEROPIS (LOST CONTINENT OF)
Meropis
BY THEOPOMPUS OF CHIOS | SOUTH ATLANTIC | BOOK

A parody of Plato's *Atlantis*, Meropis is described as larger than the more famous sunken continent. Three cities are named, Anostos, Eusebes and Machimos. It is not clear from the fragmentary manuscript whether Theopompus intended Meropis to be inundated like Atlantis; however, we've shown it as a similarly sunken continent, as it has inspired other underwater fictions, such as the Meropis of Sonic the Hedgehog. MAP pp.126–127, C1/D1/C2/D2

NULL ISLAND
MID-ATLANTIC | REAL LIFE

Non-existent 'island' located where the Greenwich Meridian meets the Equator off the coast of West Africa. See also Zero Zero Land on the Africa map (A3/B3). MAP pp.126–127, D2

PEPPERLAND
Yellow Submarine
MID-ATLANTIC | FILM

The zany geography of this Beatles film would seem unmappable. However, it is suggested that the sunken kingdom of Pepperland is somewhere off South America, due to the presence of a step pyramid. The idea was given added weight by *The League of Extraordinary Gentlemen* comics, which also place Pepperland off the continent – though further south near Argentina. MAP pp.126–127, B2

PROJECT DEEP SIX DROP POINT (MEGATRON)
Transformers: Revenge of the Fallen
NORTH ATLANTIC | FILM

After his apparent death in the first live-action *Transformers* movie, Megatron's remains were dumped in the Laurentian Abyss. MAP pp.126–127, B4

RMS GOLIATH
Goliath Awaits
MID-ATLANTIC | FILM

Not the best-known film, but one with an intriguing premise. The *Goliath* is a British ocean-liner torpedoed and sunk in 1939. It is rediscovered 40 years later with hundreds of survivors and their descendants still alive within an air-bubble contained in the hull.

According to an in-film newscast (which also includes a map) she lies 1,500 miles off the tip of Florida. MAP pp.126–127, A3/B3

SS POSEIDON
The Poseidon Adventure
BY PAUL GALLICO | MID-ATLANTIC | NOVEL

In Paul Gallico's original novel, the ship is sunk on Boxing Day *en route* from Curaçao to Lisbon. The exact co-ordinates are never given, but how's this for some reasoning? At 7am the ship is stated to be 640km (400 miles) south-west of the Azores, making about 26 knots/48kmph/30mph (her speed inferred given she is said to cover 200km/120 miles in four hours) and wallowing heavily in strange swells. At 6pm the sea conditions improve and the captain increases speed to 31 knots (about 57kmph/36mph). The ship capsizes at 9.08pm directly above the mid-Atlantic ridge when a fault-line undergoes a sudden 30m (100ft) displacement. Based on all this, we suspect the ship covered about 700km (440 miles) between 7am and 9.08pm, putting her right in the middle of the Azores when she sank, possibly between the islands of Flores and Faial. MAP pp.126–127, C4

SS QUEEN OF GLASGOW
The Twilight Zone
ATLANTIC OCEAN | TV

British cargo liner bound for New York, sunk by a German U-boat one day out of Liverpool in 1942. Based on historical practice, her course would have taken her around the north coast of Ireland and out into the Atlantic, where she quickly lost her convoy in fog and met her end. But while the *Queen of Glasgow* and her complement died but once, the Kriegsmarine captain who sank her finds himself doomed in death to forever live out the terrified final moments of his victims, eternally trapped in a personal night of judgement, within that strange neverland known as the Twilight Zone. MAP pp.126–127, D5

SS TITAN
The Wreck of the Titan: Or, Futility BY MORGAN ROBERTSON | MID-ATLANTIC | NOVELLA

This is the story that is famously claimed to have predicted the sinking of the *Titanic*. Written over a decade before the loss of that great ship, Robertson's 'practically unsinkable' *Titan* collides with an iceberg one April night, leading to catastrophic loss of life. The *Titan* herself is sailing New York to England along

the northern transatlantic route when she collides with an iceberg and sinks on her third night at sea (about halfway through a five-day voyage). This would put her some distance east and north of *Titanic*, which was two nights away from New York and following the more southerly 'winter' route. MAP pp.126–127, B5

ST BRENDAN'S ISLAND
The Water Babies BY CHARLES KINGSLEY AND LEGEND | MID-ATLANTIC | NOVEL/MYTH

St Brendan's Island was first mentioned in a 9th-century text as a supposed discovery of St Brendan three centuries earlier. Though entirely mythical, it went on to feature as a phantom island on serious maps. We include it because it became a key fictional location in *The Water Babies*. MAP pp.126–127, D4

SWALLOW FALLS/ CHEWANDSWALLOW
Cloudy With a Chance of Meatballs WEST ATLANTIC | NOVEL/FILM

Named Chewandswallow in the original book, Swallow Falls is an island community so small that on maps it is hidden under the 'A' in 'Atlantic Ocean'. Well, not on our map. MAP pp.126–127, A4

THULE
NORTH ATLANTIC | LEGEND

A mythical island, said since ancient times to lie to the far north of Europe, and a common feature on pre-Enlightenment maps. Thule has appeared in countless works of fiction, including those by Edgar Allan Poe, Jorge Luis Borges and Bernard Cornwell. It has been identified with Iceland, Greenland, parts of the British Isles, the Faroes and Scandinavia. We've placed it in between Britain and Iceland. MAP pp.126–127, D5

TÍR NA NÓG
NORTH ATLANTIC | LEGEND

Like Mag Mell, this island is considered a supernatural realm and so is impossible to place with any authority. The island is said to be three days' boat ride from Ireland, and so we place it beside Mag Mell. MAP pp.126–127, D5

LOCATION INDEX

A&E NorthernRailroad, Alaska (railway), *Runaway Train* (film), pp.18–19, B1

100 Aker Wood, England (natural feature), *Winnie the Pooh* by A.A. Milne (various), pp.64–65, D1

Abandawe, Jamaica (stone circle), *Outlander* by Diana Gabaldon (novel/TV), pp.32–33, D2

Abar Layla, Iraq (town), military training exercise, pp.72–73, C2

Abari (fictional country), works of John Hearne, pp.38–39, C5

Abbottsville, Alabama (town), *To Kill A Mockingbird* by Harper Lee (novel), pp.14–15, A2

Aber Alph, Wales (town), *Headlong Down the Years* by Amabel Williams-Ellis (novel), pp.64–65, C2

Abercorran, Wales (village), *Keeping Faith* (TV), pp.64–65, B2

Aberdarcy, Wales (town), *Only Two Can Play* (film), pp.64–65, C2

Abergarth, Wales (town), *Island of Apples* by Glyn Jones (novel), pp.64–65, C2

Abernirvana, Wales (village), *The Puddleduck Affair* by David Sheperd (novel), pp.64–65, C2

Aberowen, Wales (town), *Century Trilogy* by Ken Follett (novels), pp.64–65, C2

Aberwyvern Castle, Wales (building), *Castle* by David Macaulay (book), pp.64–65, C2

Abhirampur, Bangladesh (village), *Nojir Bibin Nojor Ali* (TV), pp.78–79, D4

Ablach Farm, Scotland (building), *Under the Skin* by Michael Faber (novel), pp.64–65, C5

Absaroka County, Wyoming (county), Walt Longmire series by Craig Johnson (novels), pp.18–19, D5

Absolution, New Mexico (town), *Cowboys and Aliens* (film), pp.18–19, D3

Abuddin (fictional country), *Tyrant* (TV), pp.72–73, B2

Abudin, Saudi Arabia (city), *Tintin: Cigars of the Pharaoh* by Hergé (novel), pp.72–73, B1/B2

Aburiria (fictional country), *Wizard of the Crow* by Ngũgĩ wa Thiong'o (novel), pp.84–85, D4

Academy City, Japan (city/state), *A Certain Magical Index* by Kazuma Kamachi and Kiyotaka Haimura (novel), pp.96–97, E1

Acélváros, Hungary (town), *Csocsó avagy éljen május eleje* (film), pp.50–51, A2

Achnaleish, Scotland (town), *The Shootings of Achnaleish* by E.F. Benson (novel), pp.64–65, B5

Achoria, Utopia (fictional region), *Utopia* by Thomas More (novel/parable), pp.38–39, C2

Achourian Kingdom, The (fictional country), *Sultan Achour 10* (TV), pp.84–85, B5

Acker's Gap, West Virginia (town), Bel Elkins series by Julia Keller (novels), pp.14–15, B4

Ackley Bridge, England (town), *Ackley Bridge* (TV), pp.64–65, C3

Acme Acres, Missouri (city), *Tiny Toon Adventures* (TV), pp.16–17, C4

Acorn, Texas (town), *The Acorn Stories* by Duane Simolke (novel), pp.16–17, A2

Acre County, Tennessee (county), law, pp.14–15, B3

Adam's Country, Indonesia (region), *Lettres de Malaise* by Paul Adam (novel), pp.90–91, C1

Adano, Italy (town), *A Bell for Adano* by John Hersey (novel), pp.44–45, D1

Addley, Pennsylvania (town), *Saving Private Ryan* (film), pp.14–15, B5

Adenville, Utah (town), *The Great Brain* by John D. Fitzgerald (novels), pp.18–19, C4

Adjikistan (fictional country), *SOCOM U.S. Navy SEALs: Combined Assault* (video game), pp.72–73, D2/E2

Admiral Benbow, The, England (building) *Treasure Island* by Robert Louis Stevenson (novel), pp.64–65, C2

Adrianopolis, Angria (city), Brontë juvenilia and later writings of Charlotte Brontë, pp.84–85, B4

Aeaea, Mediterranean Sea (island), *The Odyssey* by Homer (mythology), pp.44–45, D2

Aepyornis Island, Indian Ocean (island), *Aepyornis Island* by H.G. Wells (short story), pp.84–85, D2

Afghulistan (fictional country), Conan novels of Robert E. Howard, pp.72–73, D2/E2

African Confederation (fictional bloc), *Star Trek: The Next Generation* (TV), pp.84–85, D4

Agate Village, Arizona (town), *Pokémon* (video games), pp.18–19, C3

Agerstown, Pennsylvania (town), *The Catcher in the Rye* by J.D. Salinger (novel), pp.14–15, C5

Aghybogey, Northern Ireland (town), *Big Girl, Small Town* by Michelle Gallen (novel), pp.64–65, B3

Agloe, New York (town), real world (map), pp.14–15, D1

Agnarr and Iduna's Ship, Lands of the Northuldra (wreck), *Frozen II* (film), pp.56–57, B4

Agrabah (Al-Kal'as), Jordan (city), *Aladdin* (film), pp.72–73, B2

Agrestic, California (town), *Weeds* (TV), pp.18–19, A2

Agua Azul, Mexico (town), *Lo Que la Vida Me Robó* (TV), pp.32–33, C2

Agua Caliente, New Mexico (town), *For a Few Dollars More* (film), pp.18–19, D2

Agua Hermosa, Colombia (town), *Doña Bella* (TV), pp.38–39, A5

Agua Verde, Bolivia (lake), *Ghost Recon: Wildlands* (video game), pp.38–39, B4

Agzceazigüls (fictional country), *Les Conquerants d'indoles* by Charles Derennes (novel), pp.38–39, B3

Aihichattra, India (village), *Street Fighter II V* (video game), pp.78–79, D4

Ahtohallan, Lands of the Northuldra (island), *Frozen II* (film), pp.56–57, B4

Ahu-Y'hloa (fictional country), Cthulhu Mythos (various), pp.126–127, D5

Aidensfield, England (village), *Heartbeat* (TV), pp.64–65, D3

Aintry, Georgia (town), *Deliverance* (novel/film), pp.14–15, B3

Aira, Antillia (fictional island, legend), pp.126–127, B4

Airfowlness, Scotland (region), *The Water-Babies* by Charles Kingsley (novel), pp.64–65, A5

Akademik Vladislav Volkov, Pacific Ocean (wreck), *Virus* (comic/film), pp.120–121, C2

Akakawa, Japan (town), *Rainbirds* by Clarissa Goenawan (novel), pp.96–97, C2

Akala Island, Hawaii (island), *Pokémon* (video games), pp.18–19, D1

Akator, Brazil (city), *Indiana Jones and the Kingdom of the Crystal Skull* (film), pp.38–39, B4

Akenfield, England (town), *Akenfield* by Ronald Blythe (novel/film), pp.64–65, D2

Akiba Town, Eastal (fictional town), *Log Horizon* by Mamare Touno and Kazuhiro Hara (novels/anime), pp.96–97, E1

Al Amarja, Mediterranean Sea (island nation), *Over the Edge* (role-playing game), pp.44–45, D1

Al Hayba, Lebanon (town), *Al Hayba* (TV), pp.72–73, B2

Al Pacino, San Escobar (fictional city), internet humour (internet), pp.32–33, B2

Al Quolanudar (fictional country), *What We Do in the Shadows* (TV), pp.72–73, C2

Al-Amok, Iraq (city), *Doonesbury* (comic), pp.72–73, D3

Al-Awafi, Oman (town), *Celestial Bodies* by Jokha Alharthi (novel), pp.72–73, D1

Al-Hamra, Iraq (city), Vanderbilt University (academic exercise), pp.72–73, C3

Al-Tafar, Iraq (town), *The Yellow Birds* by Kevin Powers (novel), pp.72–73, C2/C3

Al-Wardiya (or Waddihya), Iraq (city), *Tactical Iraqi* (video game), pp.72–73, C2

Alabangor, Alabama (state), *MacTrump* by Ian Doescher and Jacopo Della Quercia (book), pp.14–15, A3

Aladeen Desert, Wadiya (fictional desert), *The Dictator* (film), pp.84–85, D4

Alamo Sea, The, San Andreas (fictional natural feature), *Grand Theft Auto* series (video game), pp.18–19, B3

Alamont Harbour, Bell Mountain, Cape Washington, Fort Providence, Johnson Island, Victoria Bay, Arctic (natural feature), *The Voyages and Adventures of Captain Hatteras* by Jules Verne (novel), pp.26–27, C4

Alanhati, Atlantis (fictional country), Cthulhu Mythos (various), pp.126–127, B4/C4

Alaskatchewan, Alaska (state), *MacTrump* by Ian Doescher and Jacopo Della Quercia (book), pp.18–19, A1/B1

Alastor's Cavern, Georgia/Southern Russia (natural feature), *Alastor, or the Spirit of Solitude* by Percy Bysshe Shelley (poem), pp.50–51, A1

Albert Memorial Hosptial, New South Wales (building), *The Young Doctors* (TV), pp.108–109, F4

Albores, Mexico (village), *Infierno Grande by Alfredo Espinosa* (novel), pp.32–33, B1

Albuquerque, Brazil (city), *Estúpido Cupido* (TV), pp.38–39, C3

Alcacia (fictional country), *Making Wolf* by Tade Thompson (novel), pp.84–85, B4

Alcanfor de las Infantas, Spain (village), *Volver* (film), pp.44–45, B2

Alcolea, Spain (town), *The Tree of Knowledge* by Pío Baroja (novel), pp.44–45, B2

Alcona (fictional country), Brontë juvenilia, pp.90–91, E4

Alconleigh, England (estate), *The Pursuit of Love* by Nancy Mitford (novel/TV), pp.64–65, C3

Aldama, Mexico (region), *The Crime of Padre Amaro (El Crimen del Padre Amaro)* (film), pp.32–33, B2

Aldastan (fictional country), *Comand and Conquer: Generals* (video game), pp.72–73, E3

Alderney City, Alderney (fictional city), *GTA IV* (video game), pp.14–15, D1

Alderney (fictional state), *Grand Theft Auto* series (video game), pp.14–15, D1

Aldovia (fictional country), *A Christmas Prince* series (film), pp.50–51, B2

Aldport, England (town), *The Secret Railway* by Elisabeth Beresford (novel), pp.64–65, C2

Alexandria Safe Zone, Virginia (village), *The Walking Dead* (TV), pp.14–15, C4

Algonquin Bay, Ontario (town), *Forty Words for Sorrow* and other novels by Giles Blunt (novels), pp.26–27, A4

Algonquin, Liberty City (fictional town), *GTA IV* (video game), pp.14–15, D5

Algren, Manitoba (town), *A Boy of Good Breeding* by Miriam Toews (novel), pp.26–27, D1

Alifbay (fictional country), *Haroun and the Sea of Stories* by Salman Rushdie (novel), pp.78–79, B5

Alkali Lake, Alberta (lake), Marvel/X-Men (films), pp.26–27, C1

Alkmeenon, Greece (building), Conan novels of Robert E. Howard, pp.44–45, E1

All Saints (fictional island), *Caribbean* by James A. Michener (novel), pp.32–33, F2

All-Muggleton, England (village), *The Pickwick Papers* by Charles Dickens (novel), pp.64–65, C3

Allalonestone, Atlantic Ocean (island), *The Water-Babies* by Charles Kingsley (novel), pp.126–127, D5

Allegheny & West Virginia Railroad, Pennsylvania (railway), *Unstoppable* (film), pp.14–15, B5

Allerdale Hall, England (building), *Crimson Peak* (film), pp.64–65, C3

Allington, England (town), *Thunderbirds* (TV), pp.64–65, D3

Almanzora, Spain (island), *Who Can Kill A Child? (¿Quién puede matar a un niño?)* (film), pp.44–45, B1

Almore, India (town), *Ishaqzaade* (film), pp.78–79, C4

Alola, Hawaii (region), *Pokémon* (video games), pp.18–19, C1/D1

Alpenstein Mountains, Switzerland/Germany (mountain range), *San Sombrèro* (book), pp.44–45, C3

Alph, China (river), *Kubla Khan* by Samuel Taylor Coleridge (poem), pp.102–103, C2

Alpha Flight Base Camp, Yukon (island), Marvel Comics, pp.26–27, B2

Alphenlicht (fictional country), the Marianne novels by Sheri S. Tepper, pp.72–73, B3

Alpine Emirates (fictional country), *The Years of Rice and Salt* by Kim Stanley Robinson (novel), pp.44–45, D3

Alsander (fictional city/state), *King of Alsander* by James Elroy Flecker (novel), pp.50–51, A1/B1

Alstadt/Glückstadt, Germany (towns), *Benjamin the Elephant* (radio/TV), pp.44–45, D4

Alt-na Shellach, Scotland (building), *The 39 Steps* by John Buchan (film), pp.64–65, B4/C4

Altamont, Catawba (fictional town), *Look Homeward, Angel* by Thomas Wolfe (novel), pp.14–15, B3

Altbrunnstedt, Germany (village), *Gonger – Das Böse vergisst nie* (film), pp.44–45, C4

Altis, Greece (island), *ARMA 3* (video game), pp.44–45, E1

Altruria (fictional island), *A Traveller From Altruria* by William Dean Howells (novel), pp.120–121, D3

Alvania, Poland (village), *The Shrine* (film), pp.50–51, A3

Alvarezopolis, Amerzone (fictional city), *Amerzone* (video game), pp.38–39, C5

Alvik, Norway (town), real world, pp.56–57, C5

Always Winter, Poland (town), *From the Fever-World* by Jehanne Dubrow (poems), pp.50–51, A4

Amanogawa High School, Japan (building), *Kamen Rider Fourze* (TV), pp.96–97, C2

Amaurot, Utopia (fictional city), *Utopia* by Thomas More (novel/parable), pp.38–39, C2

Amazonia (fictional country, ancient mythology), pp.72–73, B3

Ambarino (fictional state), *Red Dead Redemption* series (video game), pp.18–19, D4

Ambramovich Oil Platform, Russia (building), *Thunderbirds* (2004) (film), pp.102–103, F2

Ambrette Town, France (town), *Pokémon* (video games), pp.44–45, B3

Ambridge, England (village), *The Archers* (radio), pp.64–65, C2

Ambrose, Louisiana (town), *House of Wax* (film), pp.16–17, C2

Amerigo, British Virgin Islands (island), *Don't Stop the Carnival* by Herman Wouk (novel), pp.32–33, F2

Amerta, Indonesia (town), *Pretty Little Liars* (Indonesian version) (TV), pp.90–91, C1

Amerzone River, Amerzone (river), *Amerzone* (video game), pp.38–39, C5

Amerzone (fictional country), *Amerzone* (video game), pp.38–39, C4

Amigara Mountain, Japan (mountain), *The Enigma of Amigara Fault* by Junji Ito (manga), pp.96–97, B2

Amihama, Japan (town), *Way of the Samurai 4* (video game), pp.96–97, C2

Amity Island, Massachusetts (Town/island), *Jaws* by Peter Benchley (novel/film), pp.14–15, D5

Amity Park, Minnesota (city), *Danny Phantom* (TV), pp.16–17, C5/C6

Amma Beach, Maine (town), *The X-Files* (TV), pp.14–15, D6

Ampipe, Pennsylvania (town), *All the Right Moves* (film), pp.14–15, B4

Anagha, Anagha (fictional city/state), *Abhya* by Saiswaroopa Iyer (novel), pp.78–79, B4

Anandapur, Kingdom of (fictional country), Expedition Everest (theme park), pp.78–79, C4

Ananduper Township, Anandapur (fictional town), Kali River Rapids (theme park), pp.78–79, C4

Anarine, Texas (town), *The Last Picture Show* (film), pp.16–17, B2

Anatevka (formerly Boyberik), Ukraine (town), *Fiddler on the Roof* by Sholem Aleichem (various), pp.50–51, C3

Anaturia (fictional country), *The Burglar Who Thought He Was Bogart* by Bernie Rhodenbarr (novel), pp.50–51, B1

Anchorage Shatterdome, Alaska (building), *Pacific Rim* (film), pp.18–19, B1

Anchuria (fictional country), *Cabbages and Kings* by O. Henry (novel), pp.32–33, D2

Ancient Court of Eternal Ice, Eastal (fictional building), *Log Horizon* by Mamare Touno and Kazuhiro Hara (novels/anime), pp.96–97, E1

Anderby, England (town), *South Riding* by Winifred Holtby (novel), pp.64–65, D3

Anderhalden, Switzerland (village), *Albin Indergand* by Ernst Zahn (novel), pp.44–45, C3

Andoshen, Pennsylvania (town), *Andoshen, PA* by Darryl Ponicsan (novel), pp.14–15, C5

Andoulasia, Spain (region), *Suske en Wiske* by Wally Vandersteen (comics), pp.44–45, A2/B2

Angagua, Mexico (town), *Los Perros de Anagua* by Eugeni Aguirre (novel), pp.32–33, B2

Angel Grove, Oregon (town), *Power Rangers* (various), pp.18–19, A5

Angel Island, Pacific Ocean (island), *Angel Island* by Inez Haynes Irwin (novel), pp.120–121, C4

Angel Pine, San Andreas (fictional town), *Grand Theft Auto* series+D74 (video game), pp.18–19, A3

Angel's Crossing, Queensland (town), Constable Sammi Willis series by J.M. Peace (novels), pp.108–109, E3

Angel's Roost, Washington (town), *The Golden Apple* (musical), pp.18–19, A6

Angelus, Western Australia (town), *Lockie Leonard* by Tim Winton (novels/TV), pp.108–109, A2

Angelville plantation, Louisiana (building), *Preacher* (comic/TV), pp.16–17, C2

Anglebury, England (town), novels of Thomas Hardy, pp.64–65, C1

Angora (fictional country), Brontë juvenilia, pp.90–91, B4

Angria (fictional country), Brontë juvenilia and later writings of Charlotte Brontë, pp.84–85, B4

Anhuib, Antillia (fictional island, legend), pp.126–127, B4

Aniana, Symkaria (fictional city), Marvel Comics, pp.50–51, A1

Animal Farm, England (building), *Animal Farm* by George Orwell (novella), pp.64–65, C2

Anistar City, France (city), *Pokémon* (video games), pp.44–45, C3

Anjo, Japan (village), *Samurai Shodown* series (video games), pp.96–97, B2

Ankumersiel, Germany (town), *Stenkelfeld* (radio), pp.44–45, C4

Annabelle, Maine (wreck), *The Iron Giant* by Ted Hughes (novel/film), pp.14–15, D6

Annam, South Korea (city), *Asura: The City of Madness* (film), pp.102–103, E3

Annesburg, New Hanover (fictional town), *Red Dead Redemption* series (video games), pp.16–17, D3

Annexia (fictional country), *The Naked Lunch* by William S. Burroughs (novel), pp.50–51, D3

Annville, Texas (town), *Preacher* (comic/TV), pp.16–17, C2

Anostos, Meropis (fictional sunken city), *Meropis* by Theopompus of Chios (book), pp.126–127, C1

Anpinzhen, Taiwan (town), works of Li Ang, pp.96–97, D3

Ansalli, Antillia (fictional island, legend), pp.126–127, B4

Anschluss (Destroyer Z49), Atlantic Ocean (wreck), *U-571* (film), pp.126–127, C5

Ansesseli, Antillia (fictional island, legend), pp.126–127, B4

Anshan, Iranistan (fictional city), Conan novels of Robert E. Howard, pp.72–73, C2

Ansodi, Antillia (fictional island, legend), pp.123, B4

Ansolli, Antillia (fictional island, legend), pp.126–127, B4

Ansons Corner, Victoria (town/suburb), *Neighbours* (TV), pp.108–109, A1

Antegria (fictional country), *Papers, Please* (video game), pp.50–51, A5

Antillia (fictional island, legend), pp.126–127, B4

Antonio Bay, California (town), *The Fog* (film), pp.18–19, A4

Anvil, The, Colorado (building), *gen:LOCK* (web animation), pp.18–19, D4

Aolai (fictional country), *Journey to the West* by Wu Cheng'en (novel), pp.102–103, D2

Aorusoi (fictional country), *Log Horizon* by Mamare Touno and Kazuhiro Hara (novels/anime), pp.72–73, D3/E3

Apaco, Mexico (city), Marvel Comics, pp.32–33, C2

Ape Mountain, DRC (mountain), *George of the Jungle* (film), pp.84–85, C3

Ape River, DRC (river), *George of the Jungle* (film), pp.84–85, C3

Aperture Science Enrichment Centre, Michigan (building), *Portal* series (video game), pp.16–17, D6

Apocalypse's Pyramid, Egypt (building), Marvel Comics (various), pp.84–85, C5

Apodidraskiana (fictional state), *Crotchet Castle* by Thomas Love Peacock (novel), pp.14–15, B2

Appalachia (fictional state), *Pale Fire* by Vladimir Nabokov (novel), pp.14–15, B4/C4

Appaloosa, New Mexico (town), *Appaloosa* (film), pp.18–19, D3

Aqiria (fictional country), Marvel Comics (various), pp.72–73, B2/B3

Aqua Mexico (fictional country), *Steven Universe* (TV), pp.32–33, A3

Aquacorde Town, France (town), *Pokémon* (video games), pp.44–45, C3

Aquatica Research Station, Pacific Ocean (building), *Deep Blue Sea* (film), pp.120–121, E4

Aquelarre, Chile (town), *Aquelarre* (TV), pp.38–39, A3

Aquilonia, France (country/region), Conan novels of Robert E. Howard, pp.44–45, B2

Arabian Tunnel, Egypt (underground passage), *20,000 Leagues Under the Sea* by Jules Verne (novel), pp.84–85, C5

Aragane Station, Hinomoto (fictional city), *Kabaneri of the Iron Fortress* (anime), pp.96–97, B2

Aralbad, Kazakhstan (city), *Syberia* (video game), pp.102–103, D1

Arashon Desert, China (region), *Outlaw Star* (anime), pp.102–103, C3

Arcady, England (town), *Love on a Branch Line* by John Hadfield (novel), pp.64–65, D2

Archangel, Spain (town), *Shadow of a Bull* by Maia Wojciechowska (novel), pp.44–45, A2

Arches Hill, Tasmania (natural feature), *Tiger in the Bush* by Nan Chauncy (novel), pp.108–109, D1

Arctic Warrior, Alaska (wreck), *Ghost Ship* (film), pp.18–19, A1

Ardistan (fictional country), *ARMA 2* (video game), pp.50–51, A5

Ardsmuir Prison, Scotland (town), Outlander novels by Diana Gabaldon (novels/TV), pp.64–65, B5

Area 2, Holy Britannian Empire (fictional region), *Code Geass* (anime), pp.26–27, C1

Area 3, Holy Britannian Empire (region), *Code Geass* (anime), pp.32–33, B3

Area 4, Holy Britannian Empire (fictional region), *Code Geass* (anime), pp.26–27, D4

Area 5, Holy Britannian Empire (fictional region), *Code Geass* (anime), pp.26–27, E4

Area 7, Holy Britannian Empire (fictional region), *Code Geass* (anime), pp.18–19, C1

Area 8, Holy Britannian Empire (fictional region), *Code Geass* (anime), pp.38–39, B1/C1

Area 11, Japan (country), *Code Geass* (anime), pp.96–97, B3

Arendelle (fictional city/country), *Frozen* (film), pp.56–57, B4

Arenfjord, Arendelle (fictional natural feature), *Frozen* (film), pp.56–57, B4

Arepa, Mexico (island), *Maten al león* by Jorge Ibargüengoitia (novel), pp.32–33, C3

Argento, Oregon (town), *Are You Afraid of the Dark?* (TV), pp.18–19, A5

Arkangel Chemical Weapons Facility, Russia (building), *James Bond: Goldeneye* (film), pp.50–51, B6

Arkham, Massachusetts (city), Cthulhu Mythos/H.P. Lovecraft (various), pp.14–15, D5

Arklay Mountains, Missouri (mountain range), *Resident Evil* series (video games/films), pp.16–17, C3/D3

Arlen, Texas (town), *King of the Hill* (TV), pp.16–17, B2

Arklow, Pennsylvania (town), *Unstoppable* (film), pp.14–15, C5

Armação dos Anjos, Brazil (town), *Vamp* (TV), pp.38–39, D3

Armadillo, New Austin (fictional town), *Red Dead Redemption* series (video game), pp.16–17, A2

Armorel, Channel Islands (island), *Appointment with Venus* by Jerrard Tickell (novel/film), pp.64–65, A1

Arnette, Texas (town), *The Stand* by Stephen King (various), pp.16–17, C2

Aroha Bridge, New Zealand (town), *Aroha Bridge* (TV Animation), pp.108–109, F2

Aroma, Bacteria (fictional city), *The Great Dictator* (film), pp.44–45, D2

Arstotzka (fictional country), *Papers, Please* (video game), pp.72–73, C4

Artam (fictional country), *Artam: One Reich, One Race, a Tenth Leader* by Volkmar Weiss (novel), pp.44–45, D3; pp.50–51, C3/D3

Artámila, Spain (village), works of Ana María Matute, pp.44–45, B3

Arva, Romania (village), *The Piercing* by Helen McCabe (novel), pp.50–51, B2

Arwacas, Trinidad (town), *A House for Mr Biswas* by V.S. Naipaul (novel), pp.32–33, F1/F2

Aryavarta (fictional country), *Leila* by Prayaag Akbar (novel), pp.78–79, B3

Asa Branca, Brazil (town), *Roque Santeiro* (TV), pp.38–39, D4

Ascension, Washington (town), *Behemoth* (film), pp.18–19, A6

Asgard, Northern Scandinavia (region), Conan novels of Robert E. Howard, pp.56–57, C5

Ash Park, New South Wales (estate), *A Place to Call Home* (TV), pp.108–109, D2

Ashair (The Forbidden City), DRC (sunken city), *Tarzan and the Forbidden City* by Edgar Rice Burroughs (novel), pp.84–85, C4

Ashbury Estate, Scotland (estate), Margaret of Ashbury series by Judith Astria Merkle (novels), pp.64–65, C5

Asheville Forks, North Dakota (town), *Three Faces West* (film), pp.16–17, A6

Ashford Academy, Japan (building), *Code Geass* (anime), pp.96–97, E1

Ashfordly, England (town), *Heartbeat* (TV), pp.64–65, D3

Ashöjdens, Sweden (town), works of Max Lundgren, pp.56–57, B2

Ashton, Alabama (town), *Big Fish* (film), pp.14–15, A2

Ashuriyah, Iraq (village), *Youngblood* by Matt Gallagher (novel), pp.72–73, C2

Aslerfan (fictional country), *The Abominables* by Eva Ibbotson (novel), pp.72–73, C3

Asperin, Colorado (town), *Goof Troop* (TV), pp.18–19, D4

Assama, Iraq (region), *Bowl of Cherries* by Millard Kaufman (novel), pp.72–73, C2

Asselar, Mali (village), *Sahara* by Clive Cussler (novel/film), pp.84–85, C4

Asterix's Village, France (location), *Asterix the Gaul* by René Goscinny and Albert Uderzo (comic books), pp.44–45, B3

Astragard (fictional island/nation), *The Island at the Top of the World* (film), pp.26–27, C4

Astro City, Washington (city), *Astro City* (comic), pp.18–19, B6

Asunaro, Japan (city), *Puella Magi Madoka Magica* (anime/manga), pp.96–97, C3

Atabalpa, Mexico (town), *Donde las Voces se Guardan* (*The Whispering Voices of Atabalpa* in English editions) by Marco Antonio Samaniego (novel), pp.32–33, A4

Ataguitania (fictional country), *If on a Winter's Night a Traveller* by Italo Calvino (novel), pp.38–39, B3

Atlant-is, Norway (underground city), *The Brothers Dal* (TV), pp.56–57, C5

Atlantic, Atlantic Ocean (wreck), *Atlantic* (film), pp.126–127, B4

Atlantic Tunnel, Atlantic Ocean (tunnel), *Il tunnel sotomarino* by Luigi Motta and other sources (novel), pp.126–127, A4/B4/C4/C6/D4/D5

Atlantica (fictional country), *The Little Mermaid* (film), pp.56–57, A2

Atlantis (base), Sardinia (building), *James Bond: The Spy Who Loved Me* (film), pp.44–45, C2

Atlantis, Lost Continent of (fictional sunken continent), various, pp.126–127, B3/C3

Atlantis of the Sands (Ubar), Saudi Arabia (city), mythology, pp.72–73, D4

Atlas States (fictional bloc), *The Golden Compass* by Philip Pullman (novel/film), pp.84–85, A5

Atoll K or Crusoeland, Pacific Ocean (island), *Atoll K* (film), pp.120–121, D2

Atomic Irrigation Project, New South Wales (building), *Thunderbirds* (TV), pp.108–109, D2

Atreno Island, Atlantic Ocean (island), *Villanos* (TV), pp.108–109, D2

Aubrey, Missouri (town), *The X-Files* (TV), pp.16–17, C4

Auchenlochan, Scotland (town), novels of John Buchan, pp.64–65, B3

Auchenshoogle, Scotland (town), *Oor Wullie* (comic strip), pp.64–65, C4

Auchinmurn, Scotland (island), *Hollow Earth* by Carol and John Barrowman (novel), pp.64–65, B4

Auchterturra, Scotland (town), Scotland the What? (comedy troupe), pp.64–65, C5

Audiovideo, San Escobar (fictional city, internet humour), pp.32–33, A2

Audubon Bay, Calisota (fictional natural feature), *Darkwing Duck* (various), pp.18–19, A5

August Bank Holiday Island, Pacific Ocean (island), *The Goodies* (TV), pp.120–121, D2

Aurora, Pacific Ocean (island), *Ghost Recon: Breakpoint* (video game), pp.120–121, D1

Autobot City, Tennessee (city), *Transformers* (various), pp.14–15, A3

Avalon, England (estate), King Arthur stories (folklore), pp.64–65, C1

Averna (fictional country), *Sweet Danger* by Margaret Allingham (novel), pp.44–45, D2

Averoigne, France (region), works of Clark Ashton Smith (short stories), pp.44–45, C3

Avgatiganitsa (fictional country), works of Eugene Trivizas (books), pp.72–73, D2

Avocado Jungle, The, California (natural feature), *Cannibal Women in the Avocado Jungle of Death* (film), pp.18–19, B3

Avonlea, Prince Edward Island (town), *Anne of Green Gables* by Lucy Maud Montgomery (novel), pp.26–27, F1

Axa Delta, Uqbar (fictional river), *Tlön, Uqbar, Orbis Tertius* by Jorge Luis Borges (short story), pp.72–73, C3

Ayanagi City, Japan (city), *Persona* series (video games), pp.96–97, E1

Azadistan, Kingdom of (fictional country), *Gundam 00* (anime), pp.72–73, C2

Azalea Town, Japan (town), *Pokémon* (video games), pp.96–97, B1

Azanian Empire (fictional country/empire), *Black Mischief* by Evelyn Waugh (novel), pp.84–85, D4

Azkaban Prison, Scotland (unmappable building), Harry Potter novels by J.K. Rowling (novels/films), pp.64–65, D5

Azmenistan (fictional country), *The Expendables 3* and *The Onion Movie* (films), pp.72–73, D4

Azul, Spain (city), *Hurricanes* (TV), pp.44–45, B2

Azumanga High School, Japan (building), *Azumanga Daioh* by Kiyohiko Azuma (manga/anime), pp.96–97, E1

Azur Lane Base, Pacific Ocean (building), *Azur Lane* (video game/anime), pp.120–121, D4

Azure Bay, France (sea), *Pokémon* (video games), pp.44–45, B4/C4

B'Dar, Kamistan (fictional city), *24* (TV), pp.72–73, C2

Baba Yaga Castle, Brazil (location), *Soul Eater* by Atsushi Okubo (manga/anime), pp.38–39, B4

BabaKiueria, Australia (whole country), *BabaKiueria* (film), pp.108–109, D2/E2

Babiliary (fictional nation), *The New Gulliver* by Abbé Pierre François Guyot-Desfontaines (novel), pp.96–97, A1

Baby Island, Pacific Ocean (island), *Baby Island* by Carol Ryrie Brink (novel), pp.120–121, C3

Back Cup, Atlantic Ocean (island), *Facing the Flag* by Jules Verne (novel), pp.126–127, B4

Backwater, Oklahoma (town), *The Backwater Gospel* (short film), pp.16–17, D4

Baconburg, Illinois (city), Snarkout Boys books by Daniel Pinkwater, pp.16–17, D4/D5

Bacteria (fictional country), *The Great Dictator* (film), pp.44–45, D2

Bad City, Iran (town), *A Girl Walks Home Alone At Night* (film), pp.72–73, C2

Badenburg, Germany (town), 1632 series by Eric Flint (novels), pp.44–45, D3

Badenheim, Austria (town), *Badenheim 1939* by Aharon Appelfeld (novel), pp.44–45, D3

Bangalla (fictional country), *The Phantom* (comic), pp.84–85, D3

Badlands, The, New Mexico (region), *Team Fortress 2* (video game), pp.18–19, D2

Badlands, The, The Wasteland (fictional region), *Mad Max Fury Road* (film), pp.108–109, D2

Badrick, Northern Ireland (city), *Hellsing* (anime), pp.64–65, D2

Bagango, Sahrini (fictional city), *ARMA: Armed Assault* (video game), pp.126–127, C4

Bagghar/The Sultanate of Bagghar, Morocco (city/state), *The Adventures of Tintin by Hergé* (various), pp.84–85, A3

Bagong Pag-asa, Philippines (town), *May Bukas Pa* (TV), pp.90–91, C3

Bagooli River, New South Wales (river), *All Our Secrets* by Jennifer Lane (novel), pp.108–109, D2

Bahia Anasco, Costa Rica (town), *Jurassic Park* by Michael Crichton (various), pp.32–33, D1

Bahia Bay, California (town), *The Weekenders* (TV), pp.18–19, B3

Bahlam, Atlantic Ocean (sunken city), *Outbuddies* (video game), pp.126–127, C1

Baile an Chaisil, Ireland (town), *Lig Sinn i gCathú* (*Lead us into Temptation*) by Breandán Ó hEithir (novel), pp.64–65, A2

Bailey Downs, Ontario (town), *Ginger Snaps* films and *Orphan Black* (films/TV), pp.26–27, A4

Bailey, Ireland (town), *Dark Wood Dark Water* by Tina Callaghan (novel), pp.64–65, B2

Bailu Village, China (village), *Shenmue III* (video game), pp.102–103, C1

Bal-Sagoth, Atlantis (fictional island), Cthulhu Mythos (various), pp.126–127, B2

Balamory, Scotland (town), *Balamory* (TV), pp.64–65, B4

Balarang Bay, New South Wales (town), *Another Night in Mullet Town* by Steven Herick (novel), pp.108–109, D2

Balbec, France (town), *In Search of Lost Time* by Marcel Proust (novel), pp.44–45, C3

Balboa County, California (county), *Veronica Mars* (TV), pp.18–19, B3

Balemont (fictional country), *A Prince For Christmas* (film), pp.44–45, C3

Bali Ha'i, Pacific Ocean (island), *South Pacific* (film), pp.120–121, D2

Baling, China (town), *A Dictionary of Maqiao* by Han Shaogong (novel), pp.102–103, D2

Balistan (fictional country), *The Prince of Balkistan* by Allen Upward (novel), pp.50–51, B2

Ballakreen, Ireland (village), *Brass Eye* (TV), pp.64–65, A2

Ballinatoom, Ireland (town), *Asking for It* by Louise O'Neill (novel), pp.64–65, A2

Bally, Ireland (town), *Killinaskully* (TV), pp.64–65, A3

Ballybaile, Northern Ireland (town), *Every Sparrow Falling* by Shirley-Anne McMillan (novel), pp.64–65, B3

Ballybeg (Baile Beag), Ireland (town), *Crying Through the Wind: The Story of Oisin Kelly* by Iona Carroll (novel), pp.64–65, A3

Ballybeg, Ireland (town), novels of Brian Friel (novels), pp.64–65, A3

Ballybucklebo, Ireland (town), the Irish Country series by Patrick Taylor (novels), pp.64–65, A3

Ballyfeeny, Ireland (town), *Giselle* by Michael Keegan-Dolan (play), pp.64–65, B2

Ballyfin, Ireland (town), Finfarran Peninsula novels of Felicity Hayes-McCoy, pp.64–65, A2

Ballyglass, Northern Ireland (town), *Utterly Monkey* by Nick Laird (novel), pp.64–65, B3

Ballygullion, Northern Ireland (town), works of Lynn Doyle (books), pp.64–65, B3

Ballykiltara, Ireland (town), *The Summer of Serendipity* by Ali McNamara (novel), pp.64–65, A2

Ballykissangel, Ireland (village), *Ballykissangel* (TV), pp.64–65, B2

Ballylough, Ireland (village), *The Moon-Bog* by H.P. Lovecraft (short story), pp.64–65, A3

Ballyyahoo, Ireland (town), Ballyyahoo books by Grace Jolliffe (books), pp.64–65, A3

Balnibari (fictional island), *Gulliver's Travels* by Jonathan Swift (novel), pp.96–97, F3/F4

Balou Mountains, China (mountain range), works of Yan Lianke (novel), pp.102–103, D2

Baltania (fictional country), *A Royal Christmas Ball* (film), pp.50–51, B4

Baltish (fictional country), *Baltish* (TV), pp.50–51, B4

Bamfylde School, England (building), *To Serve Them All My Days* by R.F. Delderfield (novel/film), pp.64–65, D2

Bananaland (fictional region), *2000 AD* (comics), pp.108–109, D3

Banapur, Kyrat (fictional village), *Far Cry 4* (video game), pp.78–79, C4

Bandrika (fictional country), *The Lady Vanishes* (film), pp.50–51, A2

Bangalla (fictional country), *The Phantom* (comic), pp.84–85, D3

Banjo Crossing, Winnemac (fictional town), works of Sinclair Lewis, pp.14–15, A4

Bankside, Western Australia (town), *That Eye, The Sky* by Tim Winton (novel), pp.108–109, A2

Banoi (fictional island/chain), *Dead Island* (video game), pp.90–91, F1

Banville, California (town), *My Name is Khan* (film), pp.18–19, A4

Banyan Key, Florida (town), *Out of Time* (film), pp.14–15, C1

Bapetikosweti (fictional country), satires of Pieter-Dirk Uys, pp.84–85, C2

Bar Killi, Afghanistan (village), *New Home, New Life* (radio), pp.72–73, D2

Baraka, France (city), *The Years of Rice and Salt* by Kim Stanley Robinson (novel), pp.44–45, B2/B3

Barash, Sudan (village), *East of Sudan* (film), pp.84–85, C4

Barataria, Mediterranean Sea (island nation), *Don Quixote* by Cervantes (novel), pp.44–45, C2

Barbaric Archipelago, The (fictional island chain), *How to Train Your Dragon* by Cressida Cowell (novels/films), pp.56–57, C1/D1

Barbeau Observatory, Nunavut (building), *Good Morning, Midnight* by Lily Brooks-Dalton (novel) and *The Midnight Sky* (film), pp.26–27, D4

Barbituros Islands, The (fictional country/island chain), *San Sombrèro* (book), pp.32–33, F2

Barchester, England (city), novels of Anthony Trollope, pp.64–65, D2

Barclay Base (building), *Gundam Wing* (anime), pp.114–115, C3

Barclay Islands (fictional islands), *The Deceiver* by Frederick Forsyth (novel), pp.32–33, D3

Barkley Bluffs, New Jersey (town), *Extreme Ghostbusters* (TV), pp.14–15, C4

Barkley Dam, Illinois (building), *The Fugitive* (film), pp.16–17, D4

Barmet Bay, New York (natural feature), the Hardy Boys novels by various, pp.14–15, C5

Barnaby Prison, Victoria (building), *Prisoner (Cell Block H)* (TV), pp.108–109, A1

Barnstoneworth, England (town), *Ripping Yarns: Golden Gordon* (TV), pp.64–65, C3

Barntrosna, Ireland (town), *Mondo Desperado* by Patrick McCabe (book), pp.64–65, B3

Barrandale, Scotland (island), *Sweet Caress* by William Boyd (novel), pp.64–65, B4

Barrington, New Zealand (town), *Material Girls* by Deborah Steele (musical), pp.108–109, A4

Barrockstadt, Germany (city), *Syberia* (video game), pp.44–45, D3

Barrytown, Ireland (town), the Barrytown Trilogy by Roddy Doyle (novels), pp.64–65, B3

Barscheit (fictional country), *The Princess Elopes* by Harold MacGrath (novel), pp.50–51, A3/B3

Barsetshire, England (county), novels of Anthony Trollope, pp.64–65, C1

Barstock, England (town), *Pie in the Sky* (TV), pp.64–65, D2

Bartertown, The Wasteland (fictional town), *Mad Max Beyond the Thunderdome* (film), pp.108–109, C2

Bartovia (fictional country), *The Simpsons* (TV), pp.72–73, C3

Barvechos, Bolivia (town), *Ghost Recon: Wildlands* (video game), pp.38–39, B4

Barwick, England (town), *The Line of Beauty* by Alan Hollinghurst (novel), pp.64–65, D2

Bashkortostan (fictional country), *Largo Winch 2* (film), pp.50–51, C2/D2

Basin City (Sin City), California (city), *Sin City* by Frank Miller (comic/film), pp.18–19, A4

Baskerville Hall, England (building), *Sherlock Holmes: The Hound of the Baskervilles* by Arthur Conan Doyle (novel), pp.64–65, C1

Basrayatha, Iraq (city), works of Muhammad Khudayyir (short stories), pp.72–73, C2

Bass Vegas, Pacific Ocean (city), *SpongeBob SquarePants* (TV), pp.120–121, D2

Bastrona (fictional country), Marvel Comics, pp.38–39, A5/B5

Bates Motel, California (building), *Psycho* (novel/film), pp.18–19, A4

Batesville, Utah (town), Marvel Cinematic Universe (various), pp.18–19, C4

Battleship Island, Pacific Ocean (island), *Killer7* (video game), pp.120–121, D4

Baxton Creek, Maryland (town), *Tywo at Large* (web animation), pp.14–15, C4

Bay City, Illinois (city), *Another World* (TV), pp.16–17, D5

Bay City, California (city), *Farewell, My Lovely* by Raymond Chandler (novel), pp.18–19, A2

Bay Saint Lucille, Mississippi (town), *One Mississippi* (TV), pp.16–17, D2

Bay, The, New Zealand (town), *Short Poppies* (mockumentary), pp.108–109, F2

Bayou Fantom, Louisiana (natural feature), *Mafia 3* (video game), pp.16–17, D2

Bayview, California (city), *Need for Speed* (video game), pp.18–19, A2

Bazrakhistan (fictional country), *Act of War* (film), pp.72–73, D4/E4

Beach City, Delmarva (fictional town), *Steven Universe* (TV), pp.14–15, C4

Beacon Hills, California (town), *Teen Wolf* (TV), pp.18–19, A4

Beanotown, Scotland (town), *The Beano* (comics), pp.64–65, C4

Beatosu, Ohio (town, map), pp.14–15, A4/A5

Beautiful Ocean Bridge, Florida (building), *Log Horizon* by Mamare Touno (novels/anime), pp.14–15, C1

Beauxbatons Academy, France (unmappable building), Harry Potter/Wizarding World by J.K. Rowling (novel/film), pp.44–45, B2

Beaverly Hills, California (city), DC Comics, pp.18–19, A2

Bedford Falls, New York (town), *It's a Wonderful Life* (film), pp.14–15, C5

Bednaya Mountain, Russia (mountain), *Raise the Titanic* by Clive Cussler (novel/film), pp.50–51, D6

Bedrock River (river), The Flintstones Bedrock River Adventure (theme park), pp.18–19, C3

Bedrock, Arizona (city), *The Flintstones* (various), pp.18–19, A3

Beechers Corners, New York (town), ABC Soap Opera Universe (*General Hospital*), pp.14–15, B5

Beeton, California (Town), *War of the Worlds* (TV), pp.18–19, A4

Beggarlee Colliery, England (building), *Sons and Lovers* by D.H. Lawrence (novel), pp.64–65, C2

Begoy, Croatia (town), Sword of Honour trilogy by Evelyn Waugh (novels), pp.50–51, A2

Beisha, China (town), *Blood Prejudice* by A.R. Nai (novel), pp.102–103, D1

Belchester, England (town), *The Quarry Line Mystery* by A.C. Stewart (novel), pp.64–65, C3

Belesbat, Bay of Biscay (sunken city), *La Mer Mysterieuse* by Claire Kenin (novel), pp.44–45, B3

Belgistan (fictional country), *Gasaraki* (anime), pp.72–73, B3/C3

Belgravia (fictional country), *A Christmas Prince* series (film), pp.50–51, C3

Bell Mountain, Arctic (mountain), *The Voyages and Adventures of Captain Hatteras* by Jules Verne (novel), pp.26–27, C4

Bellabegwinnie, Scotland (island), *The Maggie* (film), pp.64–65, B4

Bellavista, Spain (island), *El don de Alba* (TV), pp.44–45, B2

Bellbird, Victoria (village), *Bellbird* (TV), pp.108–109, D1

Belle Reve Penitentiary, Lousiana (building), DC Comics, pp.16–17, D2

Bellefleur, Oregon (town), *The X-Files* (TV), pp.18–19, A5

Belles-Feuilles, Guadaloupe (building), *Windward Heights* (*La migration des coeurs*) by Maryse Condé (novel), pp.32–33, F2

Bellevue, Quebec (town), *Bellvue* (TV), pp.26–27, E1

Bellina, Italy (town), *The Italian Wife* by Kate Furnivall (novel), pp.44–45, D2

Bellingham, New South Wales (town), *Scrublands* by Chris Hammer (novel), pp.108–109, D2

Bellona, Kansas (city), *Dhalgren* by Samuel R. Delany (novel), pp.16–17, B4

Belmont Falls, Massachusetts (town), *Boston Legal* (TV), pp.14–15, D5

Belo Quinto, Brazil (village), *Stigmata* (film), pp.38–39, D3

Belpher, England (village), novels of P.G. Wodehouse, pp.64–65, C1

Belvedere, Ohio (town), *The Silence of the Lambs* (novel/film), pp.14–15, B4

Benengeli, Spain (town), *The Moor's Last Sigh* by Salman Rushdie (novel), pp.44–45, B2

Benimidori, Japan (village), *Red Girls* by Sakuraba Kazuki (novel), pp.96–97, B2

Beninia (fictional country), *Stand on Zanzibar* by John Brunner (novel), pp.84–85, C4

Benne Seed Island, South Carolina (island), works of Madeleine L'Engle, pp.14–15, C4

Bennett Plantation, Tennessee (building), *Django Unchained* (film), pp.14–15, B3

Bennet's Isle (island), *The Narrative of Arthur Gordon Pym of Nantucket* by Edgar Allan Poe and *An Antarctic Mystery* by Jules Verne (novels), pp.114–115, C3

Bentrock, Montana (town), *Montana 1948* by Larry Watson (novel), pp.16–17, A6

Benzheen (fictional country/emirate), *Transformers* and GI Joe (comics), pp.72–73, D1/D2

Beringland (country), *His Dark Materials* by Philip Pullman (various), pp.18–19, A2

131

Berk, the Barbaric Archipelago (fictional village), *How to Train Your Dragon* by Cressida Cowell (novels/films), pp.56–57, D1

Berlozhniki, Russia (town), *Lights All Night Long* by Lydia Fitzpatrick (novel), pp.50–51, B6

Bernt Arse, England (town), *Riddley Walker* by Russell Hoban (novel), pp.64–65, D1/D2

Berun, Germany (city), *Youjo Senki/The Saga of Tanya the Evil* by Carlo Zen and Shinobu Shinotsuki (novels/manga/anime), pp.44–45, D4

Berzerkistan (fictional country), *Doonesbury* (comic), pp.72–73, C3

Best Exotic Marigold Hotel, India (building), *Best Exotic Marigold Hotel* (film), pp.78–79, B4

Bestburg, Cobrastan (fictional city), *Papers, Please* (video game), pp.50–51, A5

Bet Hatikva, Israel (town), *The Band's Visit* (theatre), pp.72–73, B2

Bethany, Vermont (town), *The X-Files* (TV), pp.14–15, C5

Bethtown, New York (town), works of Ed McBain, pp.14–15, C5

Beyhualé, Mexico (town), *Cuentos de Beyhualé* by Joaquín Bestard Vázquez (novel), pp.32–33, A2

Bharatnagar, India (city), *Z* by Vassilis Vassilikos, and Shanghai (novel/film), pp.78–79, B3

Bhimra (fictional city/state), *Unrest* (video game), pp.78–79, B4

Bhowani, India (town), *Bhowani Junction* by John Masters (novel/film), pp.78–79, B4

Biacra (fictional region), Islandia novels and sequels by Austin Tappan Wright and Mark Saxton, pp.84–85, A2

Bialya (fictional country), DC Comics, pp.72–73, B3

Big Apple, New York (city), *Log Horizon* by Mamare Touno (novels/anime), pp.14–15, D1

Big Dipper Gold Mine, The, California (mine), *Greed* (film), pp.18–19, A4

Big Eden, Montana (town), *Big Eden* (film), pp.18–19, C6

Big Magent (building), *Who Goes There?* by John W. Campbell Jr (novel), pp.114–115, C2

Big Narrows, Nova Scotia (town), Dave and Morley stories by Stuart McLean (radio/short stories), pp.26–27, F2

Big Nothin', The, Ireland (region), *City of Bohane* by Kevin Barry (novel), pp.64–65, A3

Big Thunder Mountain, Utah/Arizona (mountain), Big Thunder Mountain Railroad (theme parks), pp.18–19, C3

Big Town, The, Hungary (city), *The Notebook* by Agota Kristóf (novel), pp.50–51, A2

Big Tuna, Texas (town), *Wild at Heart* by Barry Gifford (novel/film), pp.16–17, B3

Big Whiskey, Wyoming (town), *Unforgiven* (film), pp.16–17, A4

Bigg City Port, Maine (city), *Tugs* (TV), pp.14–15, D5/D6

Bikini Bottom, Pacific Ocean (city), *SpongeBob SquarePants* (TV), pp.120–121, B4

Billy the Mountain, California (mountain), 'Billy the Mountain' by Frank Zappa (song), pp.18–19, A3/B3

Bilya (fictional country), *Iron Eagle* (film), pp.84–85, C5

Bilyarsk Air Base (MiG-31 'Firefox' Development Facility), Russia (building), *Firefox* by Craig Thomas (novel/film), pp.50–51, D5

Bingo, Nebraska (town), *Hex* (film), pp.16–17, A4

Binhai, China (town), *Angels Wear White* (film), pp.102–103, D1

Binomo (fictional island/nation), Vladimir Kuznetsov and Alexei Stolyarov (prank), pp.90–91, C3

Birani (fictional country), *The Gods Must Be Crazy* (film), pp.84–85, B2

Birch Ridge, South Dakota (town), *Iron Will* (film), pp.16–17, B5

Birchester, England (city), Severn Valley of the Cthulhu Mythos by Ramsey Campbell (novels), pp.64–65, C2

Birdseye, Queensland (town), *Dragonfly* by Bernard Cronin (novel), pp.108–109, C3

Biringan, Philippines (city, mythology), pp.90–91, D3

Birnin Zana (The Golden City), Wakanda (fictional city), Marvel Comics (various), pp.84–85, B4

Birth Island, Pacific Ocean (island), Godzilla films, pp.120–121, D4

Bishops Wallop, England (town), *Where's the Fire* (film), pp.64–65, D2

Bitanga, Equatorial Kundu (fictional city), *The West Wing*, pp.84–85, A4

Bitterroot, Montana (town), *Day of the Outlaw* (film), pp.18–19, D6

Bitters, Wyoming (town), *Tremors* (film), pp.18–19, B4

Bixby, Texas (town), 'Billy the Mountain' by Frank Zappa (song), pp.18–19, B4

Biyoro, Japan (city), *Poppoya* (film), pp.96–97, C4

Black Atlantic, Atlantic Ocean (sea), *Judge Dredd* (comics), pp.64–65, A3

Black Hawk, Nebraska (town), *My Antonia* by Willa Cather (novel), pp.16–17, B4

Black Island, The, Scotland (island), *Tintin* by Hergé (comic books), pp.64–65, B4

Black Jungle, The, India (natural feature), *The Mystery of the Black Jungle* by Emilio Salgari (novel), pp.78–79, D4

Black Lake, Maine (lake), *Lake Placid* (film), pp.14–15, D6

Black Mesa Research Facility, New Mexico (building), *Half-Life* (video game), pp.18–19, D3

Black Sand Island, Caribbean (island), *Pirates of the Caribbean* (various), pp.32–33, F2

Black Spot Spit, Florida (natural feature), *The Pirates! Band of Misfits!* (film), pp.14–15, C2

Blackacre/Whiteacre, Tennessee (building, law), pp.14–15, B3

Blackland, Saharan West Africa (city), *The Barsac Mission* by Jules and Michel Verne (novel), pp.84–85, B4

Blackmoor Prison, Victoria (building), *Prisoner (Cell Block H)* (TV), pp.108–109, A1

Blackmore, Alberta (town), *Still Mine* by Amy Stuart (novel), pp.26–27, A1

Blackstable, England (town), *Of Human Bondage* by W. Somerset Maugham (novel), pp.64–65, D2

Blackthorn City, Japan (city), Pokémon (video games), pp.96–97, C2

Blackwater, West Elizabeth (fictional town/city), *Red Dead Redemption* series (video game), pp.16–17, C3

Blackwater, Mississippi (town), *Straw Dogs* (2011) (film), pp.16–17, D2

Blackwood Mountain, Alberta (mountain), *Until Dawn* (video game), pp.26–27, B1

Blackwood, Western Australia (town), *Wherever You Go* by Monique Mulligan (novel), pp.108–109, A3

Blaendy, Wales (village), *The Proud Valley* (film), pp.64–65, C2

Blaine County, San Andreas (fictional county), *Grand Theft Auto* series (video game), pp.18–19, B2/B3

Blaine, Missouri (town), *Waiting for Guffman* (film), pp.14–15, B4

Blair, Maryland (town), *The Blair Witch Project* (film), pp.14–15, C4

Blake Castle, Scotland (building), *Scooby Doo and the Loch Ness Monster* (TV), pp.64–65, B4

Blandings Castle, England (building), novels of P.G. Wodehouse, pp.64–65, C2

Blankshire, Scotland (county), Court of Lord Lyon (heraldry), pp.64–65, B4

Blanktown, Scotland (town), Court of Lord Lyon (heraldry), pp.64–65, B4

Blazing World, Portal to the, North Pole, *The Blazing World* by Margaret Cavendish (novel), pp.26–27, C4

Blaszka, Poland (village), *The River Midnight* by Lilian Nattel (novel), pp.50–51, B3

Bleak House, England (building), *Bleak House* by Charles Dickens (novel), pp.64–65, D2

Blefuscu (fictional island/nation), *Gulliver's Travels* by Jonathan Swift (novel), pp.108–109, A2

Blessing, North Dakota (town), Red River of the North series by Lauraine Snelling (novels), pp.16–17, B4

Blessing, Tennessee (town), *The X-Files* (TV), pp.14–15, A3

Blight, Idaho (town), stories of Patrick McManus (novels), pp.18–19, B6

Blood Island, Caribbean (island), *Monkey Island* series/*The Pirates! Band of Misfits!* (video games), pp.32–33, E3

Blood's Haven, Maryland (town), *Oyster War* (comic), pp.14–15, C4

Blooming Woods, Michigan (town), *Life in the Fat Lane* by Cherie Bennett (novel), pp.14–15, A5

Blossom, Alberta (town), *Green Grass, Running Water* by Thomas King (novel), pp.26–27, A2

Bludhaven, New Jersey (city), DC Comics, pp.14–15, C4

Blue Valley, Nebraska (city), DC Comics, pp.16–17, B4/B5

Bluebell, Alabama (town), *Hart of Dixie* (TV), pp.14–15, A2

Bluffington, Virginia (city), *Doug* (TV), pp.14–15, C4

Blush Mountain, Hawaii (mountain), Pokémon (video games), pp.18–19, D1

Bly, England (estate), *The Turn of the Screw* by Henry James (novel/TV), pp.64–65, D2

Bmzklfrpz City, Berzerkistan (fictional city), *Doonesbury* (comic), pp.72–73, C3

Boarfruit Village, Malaysia (town), *Wild Boars Cross the River* by Zhang Guixing (novel), pp.90–91, C2

Bob's Country Bunker, Indiana (building), *The Blues Brothers* (film), pp.14–15, A4

Boca Caliente (fictional island/nation), Marvel Comics (comics), pp.32–33, F2

Boca Grande (fictional country), *A Book of Common Prayer* by John Didion (novel), pp.32–33, C2

Bocamo (fictional country), *Mission Impossible* (TV), pp.84–85, A4

Bociany, Poland (town), *Bociany* by Chava Rosenfarb (novel), pp.50–51, B3

Bodoni, San Serriffe (fictional city), *The Guardian* (newspaper), pp.78–79, A2

Bogle Bay, Scotland (natural feature), *Captain Pugwash* by John Ryan (various), pp.64–65, B5

Bogshire, Scotland (county), *Captain Pugwash* by John Ryan (various), pp.64–65, B5

Bohan, Liberty State (fictional town), *GTA IV* (video game), pp.14–15, D1

Bohane, Ireland (town), *City of Bohane* by Kevin Barry (novel), pp.64–65, A3

Bok Köy, Turkey (village), *The Delights of Turkey* by Edouard Roditi (stories), pp.72–73, B3

Bokuto Police Station, Japan (building), *You're Under Arrest*, Kōsuke Fujishima (manga/anime), pp.96–97, B4

Bolingbroke, Nova Scotia (village), *Anne of Green Gables* by Lucy Maud Montgomery (novel), pp.26–27, F1/F2

Bolivar, San Lorenzo (island, city), *Cat's Cradle* by Kurt Vonnegut (novel), pp.32–33, E2

Bologa (fictional country), *Hero's Dawn* (film), pp.84–85, B4

Bolton, New South Wales (town), *Blue* by Pat Grant (graphic novel), pp.108–109, D2

Bolvangar (The Station), Finland (building), *His Dark Materials* by Philip Pullman (various), pp.56–57, D5

Bomont, Utah (town), *Footloose* (1984, film), pp.18–19, C4

Bon Temps, Louisiana (town), *True Blood* (TV), pp.16–17, C1

Bonai Province, Nibia (fictional region), *Ace Ventura: When Nature Calls* (film), pp.84–85, C3

Bondänger, Sweden (town), *Bondänger* (TV), pp.56–57, C4

Boneyard, The, California (city), *Fallout 1* (video game), pp.18–19, A3

Bonga Bonga, Northern Territory (estate), *Thunderbirds* (TV), pp.108–109, D2

Boomeroo, New South Wales (town), the Boomeroo Trilogy (Jack Radley novels) by Paul John Radley, pp.108–109, D2

Boone City, Ohio (city), *The Best Years of Our Lives* (film), pp.14–15, A4

Booty Island, Caribbean (island), *Monkey Island* series (video games), pp.32–33, E3

Bora Gora, Pacific Ocean (island/nation), *Tales of the Gold Monkey* (TV), pp.120–121, C1

Boraqua, Venezuela (town), *Parks and Recreation* (TV), pp.38–39, B5

Borchester, England (town), *The Archers* (radio), pp.64–65, C2

Border Kingdoms, The, Germany/Denmark (region), Conan novels of Robert E. Howard, pp.56–57, A1/B1/C1

Borduria (fictional country), *The Adventures of Tintin* by Hergé (various), pp.50–51, B3

Borgabunda, Pacific Ocean (island), *McHale's Navy* (TV), pp.120–121, B3/B4

Borostyria (fictional country), Arsène Lupin novels by Maurice Leblanc, pp.50–51, A2/B2

Borough, The, England (town), *The Borough* by George Crabbe (poem), pp.64–65, C2

Borrioboola-Gha, Nigeria (village), *Bleak House* by Charles Dickens (novel), pp.84–85, B4

Borsetshire, England (county), *The Archers* (radio), pp.64–65, C2

Boscombe Valley, England (natural feature), *Sherlock Holmes: The Adventure of Silver Blaze* by Arthur Conan Doyle (short story), pp.64–65, C2

Bosqueverde (fictional country), Marvel Comics (comics), pp.38–39, B5/C5

Bostone, Massachusetts (city), *The Flintstones* (various), pp.14–15, D5

Bottom Rock, Barbados (village), *Song of Night* by Glenville Lovell (novel), pp.32–33, C2

Boulder Beach, Gulf of Melange (fictional island), *Monkey Island* series (video games), pp.32–33, E3

Bowers Bank, Alaska (island chain), *Ghost Ship* (film), pp.18–19, A1

Boys' Island, Pacific Ocean (island), *Nation* by Terry Pratchett (novel), pp.120–121, D1

BrabraJunction, Northern Ireland (village), *Oh, Mr Porter!* (film), pp.64–65, A3

Braddage, England (town), *The Quarry Line Mystery* by A.C. Stewart (novel), pp.64–65, C3

Braeston, Scotland (town), *One of Us* (TV), pp.64–65, B5

Brahmpur, India (town), *A Suitable Boy* by Vikram Seth (novel), pp.78–79, C4

Brajikistan (fictional country), *Wingin' It* (TV), pp.72–73, E3

Brantford, New Hampshire (town), *Jumanji* (film), pp.14–15, C5

Brazuela (fictional country), *Totally Spies!* (TV), pp.38–39, B4

Breach, The, Pacific Ocean (dimensional portal), *Pacific Rim* (film), pp.90–91, F3

Breakheart Pass, Nevada (natural feature), *Breakheart Pass* by Alistair MacLean (novel/film), pp.18–19, B4

Brendam, England (town), *Thomas the Tank Engine* by Rev W. Audrey (books/TV), pp.64–65, C2

Brewer, Pennsylvania (town), works of John Updike, pp.14–15, C4

Brewster, Pennsylvania (town), *Unstoppable* (film), pp.14–15, C4

Brickleberry National Park, Illinois (natural feature), *Brickleberry* (TV), pp.16–17, D4/D5

Bricksville, Arkansas (town), *Adventures of Huckleberry Finn* by Mark Twain, pp.16–17, D3

Brideshead, England (building), *Brideshead Revisited* by Evelyn Waugh (novel/film), pp.64–65, C2

Bridgefield, Victoria (town), *Wildflower Creek* by Maya Linnell (novel), pp.108–109, A3

Bridgetown, South Australia (town), *First Person Shooter* by Cameron Raynes (novel), pp.108–109, A3

Bridmouth-on-Sea, England (town), novels of P.G. Wodehouse, pp.64–65, C2

Brigadoon, Scotland (unmappable village), *Brigadoon*, pp.64–65, C4

Bright Hyu City, India (city), *Jelle's Marble Runs* (web series), pp.78–79, B2/C2

Bright River, Prince Edward Island (town), *Anne of Green Gables* by Lucy Maud Montgomery (novel), pp.26–27, F1

Brighton Falls, California (town), *Transformers: Bumblebee* (film), pp.18–19, A4

Brinkley Court, England (estate), novels of P.G. Wodehouse, pp.64–65, C2

Brinquillo, Mexico (town), *Porque Parece Mentira la Verdad Nunca se Sabe* by Daniel Sada (novel), pp.32–33, A2

Brisbania, Bananaland (fictional city), *2000 AD* (comics), pp.108–109, D2

Bristo Camino, California (town), *Hostage* (film), pp.18–19, A3

Britannian Concession, Japan (region), *Code Geass* (anime), pp.96–97, E1/F1

Britannula (fictional country), *The Fixed Period* by Anthony Trollope (novel), pp.120–121, C1

British Santa Maya (fictional island/nation), *Whoops! Apocalypse* (film), pp.32–33, F2/F3

Broadchurch, England (village), *Broadchurch* (TV), pp.64–65, C1

Brobdingnag (fictional country), *Gulliver's Travels* by Jonathan Swift (novel), pp.26–27, A1

Brockton, Scotland (town), Outlander novels by Diana Gabaldon (novels/TV), pp.64–65, B4

Brodny, Hungary (town), *The Inspector General* (film), pp.50–51, B3

Brogavia (fictional country), *Commando* (comics), pp.50–51, A2

Brogodó, Brazil (town), *Cordel Encantado* (TV), pp.38–39, D4

Brokeback Mountain, Wyoming (mountain), *Brokeback Mountain* (short story/film), pp.18–19, D5

Brokenwood, New Zealand (town), *The Brokenwood Mysteries* (TV), pp.108–109, F2

Broker, Liberty State (fictional town), *GTA IV* (video game), pp.14–15, D1

Bronson, Missouri (town), *The Simpsons* (TV), pp.16–17, C1

Brookside, England (area/street), *Brookside* (TV), pp.64–65, C2

Broolyi, Pacific Ocean (island), *Riallaro, the Archipelago of Exiles* by Godfrey Sweven (novel), pp.120–121, D1

Bruddersford, England (city), *The Good Companions* by J.B. Priestley (novel), pp.64–65, C2

Brungaria (fictional country), Tom Swift novels by Edward Stratemeyer, pp.50–51, D4

Brunndorf, Austria (village), Zwölf mal Polt novels by Alfred Komarek, pp.44–45, D3

Brunswick, Iowa (town), *State Fair* by Phil Stong (novel), pp.16–17, C4

Brythunia (region), Conan novels of Robert E. Howard, pp.50–51, B4

Bucaneer Bay, Western Australia (town), *The Pearler's Wife* by Roxane Dhand (novel), pp.108–109, B2

Buckhorn, South Dakota (town), *Twin Peaks: The Return* (TV), pp.16–17, A5

Buckland, Utah (town), *The Shining* by Stephen King (various), pp.18–19, D4

Buckman, West Virginia (town), Hatfords and Malloys books by Phyllis Reynolds Naylor, pp.14–15, B4

Budgie Islands, The, Caribbean (island chain), *The Pirates! Band of Misfits!* (film), pp.32–33, D3

Budmouth, England (town), novels of Thomas Hardy, pp.64–65, C1

Buenas Peras, Chile (city), *Condorito* (comics), pp.38–39, B4

Buenaventura, Costa Perdita (fictional city), *Air America* (TV), pp.32–33, F2

Buggleskelly, Northern Ireland (village), *Oh, Mr Porter!* (film), pp.64–65, B3

Bugia Sea/Bugis Sea, Anandapur (fictional sea), Walt Disney World (theme park), pp.78–79, D3

Bukowa, Poland (village), *Poland* by James A. Michener (novel), pp.50–51, A4

Bukuvu, The, DRC (region), *George of the Jungle* (film), pp.84–85, C3

Bulashah, India (town), *Untouchable* by Mulk Raj Anand (novel), pp.78–79, B5

Bullet Farm, The Wasteland (fictional building), *Mad Max Fury Road* (film), pp.108–109, D2

Bullworth, New Hampshire (town), *Bully* (video game), pp.14–15, C5

Bultan (fictional country), *Designated Survivor* (TV), pp.90–91, B2

Bulungi (fictional country), *The Onion* (online satire), pp.84–85, A4

Bumblescum, England (town), *Family Guy* (TV), pp.14–15, A2

Bumblyburg, Maine (city), *Larry-Boy and VeggieTales* (animation), pp.14–15, D5

Bun Bun Ga, New South Wales (town), *A Girl in Australia* (film), pp.108–109, D2

Buncarragh, Ireland (town), novels of Graham Norton, pp.64–65, A3

Bund, The, Japan (city), *Dance in the Vampire Bund* by Nozomu Tamaki (manga/anime), pp.96–97, B4

Bundanyabba, New South Wales (town), *Wake in Fright* by Kenneth Cook (novel/TV), pp.108–109, D2

Bunkerton Castle, Scotland (building), *The Beano* (comic), pp.64–65, C4

Buranda (fictional country), *Yes Minister* (TV), pp.84–85, B4

Burgheim, Austria (village), Zwölf mal Polt novels by Alfred Komarek, pp.44–45, D3

Burnistoun, Scotland (town), *Burnistoun* (TV), pp.64–65, C4

Burnstow, England (town), *Oh, Whistle and I'll Come To You, My Lad* by M.R. James (short story), pp.64–65, C2

Burpelson AFB, Nebraska (building), *Dr Strangelove* (film), pp.16–17, C4

Bursley, England (town), the Five Towns novels by Arnold Bennett, pp.64–65, C2

Bushtown, New South Wales (town), *Skippy: Adventures in Bushtown* (TV), pp.108–109, E2

Busnäs, Sweden (town), works of Hans-Eric Hellberg, pp.56–57, C4

Butlershill, Ireland (town), *Married Quarters* by Shane Connaughton (novel), pp.64–65, A3

Butsumetsu, Japan (city), *Binbougami ga!* by Yoshiaki Sukeno (manga/anime), pp.96–97, B2

Butterfield, Kansas (town), Wizard of Oz books by L. Frank Baum, pp.16–17, C4

Buttersby, Indian Ocean (town), *The Illegal* by Lawrence Hill (novel), pp.78–79, B1/C1

Butua (fictional country), *Aline et Valcour* by the Marquis de Sade (novel), pp.84–85, C2

Buyan, Germany (island), Russian folklore, pp.44–45, D4

Buzzard's Peak, Spain (mountain), *San Manuel Bueno, Mártir* by Miguel de Unamuno (novel), pp.44–45, B1

Byala Cherkva, Bulgaria (town), *Under the Yoke* by Ivan Vazov (novel), pp.50–51, B2

Byköping, Sweden (town), Agaton Sax stories by Nils-Olof Franzén (novels), pp.56–57, C2

C&FW Railroad, Kentucky, *Petticoat Junction/Green Acres* (TV), pp.14–15, A3

Cabot Cove, Maine (town), *Murder She Wrote* (TV), pp.14–15, D6

abovce, Slovakia (town), *Spadla z oblakov (She Came Out of the Sky)* (TV), pp.50–51, A3/B3

Cactusville, Texas (town), *Desperate Dan* (comic), pp.16–17, B2

Cadillac Range, Arizona (mountain range), *Cars* (film), pp.18–19, C3

Caer Craig, Wales (building), *The Puddleduck Affair* by David Sheperd (novel), pp.64–65, C2

Caerflwyti, Wales (village), *Rocket to the Moon* by Jules Verne (novel), pp.64–65, C2

Cahulawassee River, Georgia (river), *Deliverance* (novel/film), pp.14–15, A2

Caiphul (fictional country), Cthulhu Mythos (various), pp.126–127, D3

Caldwell, Washington (town), *The Returned* (TV), pp.14–15, B3

Calenda, Spain (town), *Luna, el misterio de Calenda* (TV), pp.44–45, B2

Caleta del Sol, Chile (town), *Caleta del Sol* (TV), pp.38–39, B3

Calisota (fictional state), *DuckTales* (various), pp.18–19, A5

Calm's Point, New York (town), works of Ed McBain, pp.14–15, D1

Caloestown, Oceania (fictional town), *The Strong Man* by H.R.F. Keating (novel), pp.126–127, D5

Calpurnia (fictional country), *A Royal Winter* (film), pp.44–45, C2/C3

Calumet, Colorado (town), *Red Dawn* (film), pp.18–19, D3

Calusa, Florida (town), *Transformers* (comic), pp.14–15, B1

Camberwick Green, England (village), *Camberwick Green* (TV), pp.64–65, D1

Camelot, Wales (estate, folklore), pp.64–65, C2

132

Camp Belica, Croatia (building), *Wolfenstein* series (video games), pp.50–51, A2

Camp Campbell, Washington (building), *Camp Camp* (web animation), pp.18–19, B6

Camp Mowester, Washington (building), *Free Willy 2* (film), pp.18–19, A6

Camp Omega, Cuba (building), *Metal Gear Solid V* (video game), pp.32–33, E2

Camp Winnepacaca, Romania (miscellaneous), *Hotel Transylvania 2* (film), pp.50–51, B2

Campania, Atlantic Ocean (wreck), *Black Butler* (manga/anime), pp.126–127, B4

Camphrier Town, France (town), *Pokémon* (video games), pp.44–45, C3

Camptounfoot, Scotland (village), *A Bridge in Time* by Elisabeth McNeill (novel), pp.64–65, C4

Campus Colony, Nebraska (town), *The Walking Dead: World Beyond* (TV), pp.16–17, B4

Canaima, California (town), *Arachnaphobia* (film), pp.18–19, A3

Canalave City, Japan (city), *Pokémon* (video games), pp.96–97, C4

Canalview, Panama (town), *The Pirates! Band of Misfits!* (film), pp.32–33, D1

Canarie Islands, The, Caribbean (island chain), *The Pirates! Band of Misfits!* (film), pp.32–33, D3

Candleford, England (town), *Lark Rise to Candleford* by Flora Thompson (novels/TV), pp.64–65, D2

Candyland Plantation, Mississippi (building), *Django Unchained* (film), pp.16–17, B2

Cani River, India (river), *Around The World in Eighty Days* by Jules Verne (novel), pp.78–79, C4

Canley, England (town), *The Bill* (TV), pp.64–65, D2

Cannonball Cove, Cuba (natural feature), *The Pirates! Band of Misfits!* (film), pp.32–33, D3

Canonry, The, Scotland (region/county), novels of John Buchan, pp.64–65, B3

Cantaloa, Spain (town), *Gran Hotel* (TV), pp.44–45, B3

Cantre'r Gwaelod (fictional island/nation), folk tradition), pp.64–65, B2

Cap City, Oklahoma (town), *The Outsider* by Stephen King (novels), pp.16–17, C3

Capa Blanca Islands, Spain (island chain), *The Voyages of Dr Dolittle* by Hugh Lofting (novel), pp.44–45, A2

Cape Flattery, Washington (town), *Ma & Pa Kettle* (films), pp.18–19, A6

Cape Grimm, Tasmania (natural feature), *Cape Grimm* by Carmel Bird (novel), pp.108–109, D1

Cape of Good Ham, The, Caribbean (natural feature), *The Pirates! Band of Misfits!* (film), pp.32–33, F2

Cape Suzette, Hawaii (city), *TaleSpin/Duck Tales 2017* (TV), pp.18–19, D1

Cape Washington, Arctic (natural feature), *The Voyages and Adventures of Captain Hatteras* by Jules Verne (novel), pp.26–27, C4

Capeside, Massachusetts (town), *Dawson's Creek* (TV), pp.14–15, D5

Capila, Mexico (region), *Porque Parece Mentira la Verdad Nunca se Sabe* by Daniel Sada (novel), pp.32–33, B3

Capillaria, Atlantis (fictional sunken country), *Capillaria* by Frigyes Karinthy (novel), pp.126–127, B4/C4

Capital City/Capitol City, North Takoma (fictional city), *The Simpsons* (TV), pp.18–19, A6

Capital Wasteland, The, District of Columbia/Virginia/Maryland (state/region), *Fallout 3* (video game), pp.14–15, C4

Capital, The, Russia (city), *Pandemic* series (video game), pp.50–51, B4

Capitol City, District of Columbia (city), *Destroy All Humans* (video game), pp.14–15, C4

Capitol City, Colorado (city), *The Man Who Shot Liberty Valance* (film), pp.18–19, A6, pp.16–17, A4

Capitol, The, Colorado (city), *The Hunger Games* by Suzanne Collins (various), pp.18–19, D4

Capoeirão dos Tucanos, Brazil (natural feature), *Sítio do Picapau Amarelo* by Monteiro Lobato (novels), pp.38–39, C3/D3

Caprljane, Bosnia and Herzegovina (town), *Bal-Can-Can* (film), pp.50–51, A2

Caprona (also known as Caspak, island), *The Land That Time Forgot* by Edgar Rice Burroughs (novel/films), pp.114–115, A3

Caprona, Italy (city state), *The Magicians of Caprona* by Diana Wynne Jones (novel), pp.44–45, C2

Captain Nemo's Country (continent), *20,000 Leagues Under the Sea* by Jules Verne (novel), pp.114–115, B2

Carbon Creek, Pennsylvania (town), *Star Trek* (various), pp.14–15, B4

Carburetor County, Arizona (county), *Cars* (film), pp.18–19, A5

Cardale, England (town), *Peak Practice* (TV), pp.64–65, C2

Cardigan, New Zealand (town), works of Geoff Spedding, pp.108–109, F2

Cardingham River, Queensland (river), *The Black Bell Buoy* by Rupert Chesterton (short story), pp.108–109, D3

Cardingham, Queensland (town), *The Black Bell Buoy* by Rupert Chesterton (short story), pp.108–109, D3

Carfax Abbey, England (estate), *Dracula* by Bram Stoker (novel), pp.64–65, D2

Carhill, Scotland (village), *The Happy Lands* (film), pp.64–65, C4

Carlotta, Peru (island), *The Bribe/Dead Men Don't Wear Plaid* (films), pp.38–39, A4

Carmody, Prince Edward Island (town), *Anne of Green Gables* by Lucy Maud Montgomery (novel), pp.26–27, F1

Carn Zawn Head, England (natural feature), *Music Hath Charms* by L.T.C. Rolt (short story), pp.64–65, B1

Carn, Ireland (town), *Carn* by Patrick McCabe (novel), pp.64–65, B3

Carnis, Afghanistan (town), military training exercise), pp.72–73, E2

Carpathia (fictional country), *Ghostbusters II/The Prince and the Showgirl* (films), pp.50–51, B2

Carrick, Ireland (town), Finfarran Peninsula novels of Felicity Hayes-McCoy, pp.64–65, A2

Carricklea, Ireland (village), *Normal People* by Sally Rooney (novel/TV), pp.64–65, B2

Carrickstowe, England (town), Adventure Island books by Helen Moss, pp.64–65, B1

Carrigeen, Ireland (town), *The South Westerlies* (TV), pp.64–65, A2

Carrigstown, Ireland (town), *Fair City* (TV), pp.64–65, B3

Carringbush, Victoria (town), *Power Without Glory* by Frank Hardy (novella), pp.108–109, A1

Carrizalejo, Mexico (town), *Setenta Veces Siete (Seventy Times Seven)* by Ricardo Elizondo Elizondo (novel), pp.32–33, B3

Carrizales, USA (town), *Setenta Veces Siete (Seventy Times Seven)* by Ricardo Elizondo Elizondo (novel), pp.32–33, B3

Carrucan Plantation, Mississippi (building), *Django Unchained* (film), pp.16–17, B2

Carsden, Scotland (town), *The Flood* by Ian Rankin (novel), pp.64–65, C4

Carsely, England (village), *Agatha Raisin* (TV), pp.64–65, D2

Casaquemada (fictional island), *A Casual Brutality* by Neil Bissoondath (novel), pp.32–33, F2

Cascade Heights, Argentina (building), *Thursday Night Widows* by Claudia Piñeiro (novel), pp.38–39, C2

Cascadia (fictional country), *Mirror's Edge* (video games), pp.108–109, D2

Cascadiopolis, Oregon (town), *In the Forests of the Night* by Amelia Atwater-Rhodes (short stories), pp.18–19, A5

Cascara (fictional island/nation), *Water* (film), pp.32–33, E2

Caspiar (fictional island/nation), the Mind of Andy Kaufman (performance art), pp.72–73, C3

Cassidy Keep, Ireland (building), Marvel Comics, pp.64–65, A3

Cast Away Island, Pacific Ocean (island), *Cast Away* (film), pp.120–121, D2

Castelobruxo, Brazil (unmappable building), Harry Potter/Wizarding World by J.K. Rowling (various), pp.38–39, B4

Casterbridge, England (town), novels of Thomas Hardy, pp.64–65, C1

Castillo, Mexico (building), *Overwatch* (video game), pp.32–33, B3

Castle Balneath, Scotland (building), *New Captain Scarlet* (TV), pp.64–65, B4

Castle Bravo, Atlantic Ocean (based on), *Godzilla: King of the Monsters* (film), pp.126–127, A3

Castle Cinderella, Japan (building), *Log Horizon* by Mamare Touno and Kazuhiro Hara (novels/anime), pp.96–97, F1

Castle Dangerous, Scotland (building), *Castle Dangerous* by Sir Walter Scott (novel), pp.64–65, C4

Castle Dracula, Romania (building), *Dracula* (various), pp.50–51, B2

Castle Duckula, Romania (building), *Count Duckula* (TV), pp.50–51, B2

Castle Frankenstein, Switzerland (building), *Frankenstein* by Mary Shelley (various), pp.44–45, C3

Castle Gay, Scotland (building), novels of John Buchan, pp.64–65, B3

Castle Karpathenburg, Romania (building), *The Castle of the Carpathians* by Jules Verne (novel), pp.50–51, B2

Castle Kaufmann, Germany (building), Marvel Comics/Marvel Cinematic Universe (various), pp.44–45, D3

Castle Leoch, Scotland (building), *Outlander* novels by Diana Gabaldon (novels/TV), pp.64–65, B5

Castle Lubov, Transylvania (?, location), *Hotel Transylvania* (film), pp.50–51, B2

Castle McDuck, Scotland (building), *Duck Tales* (TV), pp.64–65, B5

Castle McDuff, Scotland (building), *Scooby Doo* (TV), pp.64–65, B5

Castle Mordo, Romania (building), Marvel Comics, pp.50–51, B2

Castle of Aaaarrrrrrgghhh, The, Scotland (building), *Monty Python The Holy Grail* (film), pp.64–65, B4

Castle of Pain, The, Carpathia (fictional location), *Ghostbusters II* (film), pp.50–51, B2

Castle Rock, Maine (town), *Castle Rock* by Stephen King (various), pp.14–15, D6

Castle Thane, Scotland (building), *The World is not Enough* (film), pp.64–65, B4

Castle Wolfenstein, Germany (building), *Wolfenstein* series (video games), pp.44–45, D4

Castle Wyvern, Scotland (building), *Gargoyles* (TV), pp.64–65, B4

Castleford, England (city), *Tom's Midnight Garden* by Philippa Pearce (novel), pp.64–65, D2

Castlemartin, Northern Ireland (town), works of Paul Charles, pp.64–65, B3

Castletown, Scotland (town), the Inspector Jim Carruthers series by Tana Collins (novels), pp.64–65, C4

Castringham Hall, England (building), *The Ash Tree* by M.R. James (short story), pp.64–65, D2

Catan, Azores (island), *The Settlers of Catan* (board game), pp.126–127, C4

Catawba Mountains, Catawba (fictional mountain range), *Look Homeward, Angel* by Thomas Wolfe (novel), pp.14–15, B3

Catawba (fictional state), *Look Homeward, Angel* by Thomas Woolfe (novel), pp.14–15, B3/C3

Catela, California (town), *Breathing, in Dust* by Tim Z. Hernandez (novel), pp.18–19, A4

Catfish Row, South Carolina (building), *Porgy and Bess* (musical), pp.14–15, B3/C3

Cathedral, The, Turmezistan (fictional building), *Doctor Who* (TV), pp.72–73, E4

Catmere, England (region), *Kingdom of Elfin* by Sylvia Townsend Warner (short stories), pp.64–65, C4

Cattle Corner, California (town), *Once Upon a Time in the West* (film), pp.18–19, B3

Cauldron Point, Oregon (natural feature), *The Goonies* (film), pp.18–19, A6

Causton, England (town), *Midsomer Murders* (TV), pp.64–65, C2

Cave of Caerbannog, Scotland (natural feature), *Monty Python and the Holy Grail* (film), pp.64–65, B4

Cayta, Costaguana (fictional city), *Nostromo* by Joseph Conrad (novel), pp.38–39, A4

Cayuna (fictional country), works of John Hearne, pp.32–33, D2

Cedar Cove, Washington (island/town), Cedar Cove series by Debbie Macomber (novels), pp.18–19, A6

Cedar Creek, California (town), *Outbreak* (film), pp.18–19, A5

Cedar Forest, Japan (natural feature), *Princess Mononoke* (anime), pp.96–97, B2

Cedar Valley, New South Wales (town), *Cedar Valley* by Holly Throsby (novel), pp.108–109, D2

Cedarn, Utana (fictional town), *Pale Fire* by Vladimir Nabokov (novel), pp.18–19, D5

Celadon City, Japan (city), *Pokémon* (video games), pp.96–97, E1

Celestic Town, Japan (town), *Pokémon* (video games), pp.96–97, D4

Centennial Orbital Elevator, Cuba (space elevator), *Halo: Ghosts of Onyx* by Eric S. Nylund (novel), pp.32–33, D3

Centennial, Colorado (town), *Centennial* by James A. Michener (novel), pp.16–17, A4

Centertown, Indiana (town), *The Rule of the Door and Other Fanciful Regulations* by Lloyd Biggle Jr (novel), pp.14–15, A4

Central City/Centre City, Oregon (city), *Transformers* (various), pp.18–19, A6

Central City, Missouri (town), DC Comics, pp.16–17, C2

Centralia, Wisconsin (town), *Black House* by Stephen King (novel), pp.16–17, C5

Cerromaior, Portugal (town), *Cerromaior* by Manuel de Fonseca (novel), pp.44–45, A2

Certigny, France (town), *Ils sont votre épouvante et vous êtes leur crainte* by Thierry Jonquet (novel), pp.44–45, E3

Cerulean City, Japan (city), *Pokémon* (video games), pp.96–97, C2

Chaikhosi, India (village), *The Ascent of Rum Doodle* by W.E. Bowman (novel), pp.78–79, C4

Chakkahera, India (village), *Baaz* by Anjua Chauhan (novel), pp.78–79, B5

Chako Paul City, Sweden (town, hoax), pp.56–57, C4

Chakranadi River, Anandapur (fictional), Kali River Rapids (theme park), pp.78–79, C4

Chalk Hill, Western Australia (town), the Chalk Hill series by Lily Malone (novels), pp.108–109, A2

Challenge for Antarctic O2 Expedition (location), *A Place Further than the Universe* (anime), pp.114–115, D4

Chamberlain, Maine (town), *Carrie* by Stephen King (various), pp.14–15, D6

Champaneer, India (village), *Lagaan* (film), pp.78–79, B4

Chancellor, Atlantic Ocean (wreck), *The Survivors of the Chancellor* by Jules Verne (novel), pp.126–127, B4

Chanda, India (town), *The Dāk Bungalow at Dakor* by Bithia Mary Croker (short story), pp.78–79, C4

Chandrapore, India (city), *A Passage to India* by E.M. Forster (novel/film), pp.78–79, C4

Changle, China (town), *A Dictionary of Maqiao* by Han Shaogong (novel), pp.102–103, D2

Changmian, China (village), *The Hundred Secret Senses* by Amy Tan (novel), pp.102–103, C1

Chapel Mine, North Carolina (mine), *The Descent Part 2* (film), pp.14–15, B3

Charanpur, India (village), *Swades* (film), pp.78–79, C4

Charm City, Delmarva (fictional city), *Steven Universe* (TV), pp.14–15, C4

Charming, California (town), *Sons of Anarchy* (TV), pp.18–19, A4

Charnham, England (town), *Family Affairs* (TV), pp.64–65, D2

Charybdis *see* Scylla and Charybdis

Charydos, Turkey (city), *Claudian* by Henry Herman (play), pp.72–73, B3

Château de Silling, France (building), *The 120 Days of Sodom* by the Marquis de Sade (novel), pp.44–45, D2

Château Fausseflammes, France (building), works of Clark Ashton Smith (short stories), pp.44–45, C3

Chateau Picard, France (building), *Star Trek: The Next Generation/Picard* (TV), pp.44–45, C3

Chateau Thelian, France (building), *Star Trek: Articles of the Federation* by Keith R.A. Decandido (novel), pp.44–45, C3

Chatooga National Park, North Carolina (natural feature), *The Descent* (film), pp.14–15, B3

Chatswin and East Chatswin, New York (town), *Suburgatory* (TV), pp.14–15, D1

Chatzy, Chinaland (fictional town), *Little Ninja Brothers* (video game), pp.102–103, C2

Chebachinsk, Kazakhstan (town), *A Gloom is Cast Upon the Ancient Steps* by Alexander Chudakov (novel), pp.72–73, D4

Cheli, Italy (island), *The Life of Gargantua and of Pantagruel* by Fraçois Rabelais (novel), pp.44–45, D1

Chen-li, China (town), *China Sky* by Pearl S. Buck (novel/film), pp.102–103, D2

Chencuocun, Taiwan (town), works of Li Ang, pp.102–103, D1

Cherku, Tibet (village), *Cursed Mountain* (video game), pp.102–103, B2

Chernarus (fictional country), *ARMA 2* (video game), pp.50–51, A5

Chernaya, Russia (river), *Midnight in the Century* by Victor Serge (novel), pp.50–51, B5

Chernoe, Russia (town), *Midnight in the Century* by Victor Serge (novel), pp.50–51, A5

Chernoton Research Facility, Russia (building), *Snatcher* (video game), pp.50–51, D4

Cherry Falls, Virginia (town), *Cherry Falls* (film), pp.14–15, C4

Cherry Hill Temple, Japan (building), *Sailor Moon* by Naoko Takeuchi (manga/anime), pp.96–97, E1

Cherry Town, China (village), *The Lantern Bearer* by Pingwa Jia (novel), pp.102–103, D2

Cherrygrove City, Japan (city), *Pokémon* (video games), pp.96–97, C2

Cherrywood, Republia (fictional city), *The Republia Times* (video game), pp.50–51, A4

Chesney Wold, England (estate), *Bleak House* by Charles Dickens (novel), pp.64–65, D2

Chester's Mill, Maine (town), *Under the Dome* by Stephen King (various), pp.14–15, D6

Chickentown, Minnesota (town), The Books of Abarat series by Clive Barker (novels), pp.16–17, C5

Chigley, England (village), *Chigley* (TV), pp.64–65, D1

Chillingborne, England (village), *A Canterbury Tale* (film), pp.64–65, D2

Chilly Beach, Nunavut (town), *Chilly Beach* (TV), pp.26–27, D2

Chimitaxl, Cordillera (fictional mountain), *High Citadel* by Desmond Bagley (novel), pp.38–39, B3

Chiragpur, Pakistan (village), works of Qaisra Shahraz, pp.78–79, A4

Chiriguaná, Colombia (town), *The War of Don Emmanuel's Nether Parts* by Louis de Bernières (novel), pp.38–39, A5/B5

Chiselton, Scotland (town), *Super Gran* (TV), pp.64–65, C4

Chitharpatti, India (village), *Marmadesam* (TV), pp.78–79, B2

Chongsokgol, North Korea (village), *Im Kkeok Jung* (film), pp.102–103, E3

Christmasland, Colorado (town), *NOS4A2* by Joe Hill (novel/TV), pp.16–17, A4

Christminster, England (city), novels of Thomas Hardy, pp.64–65, C2

Chuffnell Regis, England (town), novels of P.G. Wodehouse, pp.64–65, C2

Chungking, China (city), *Adrift in the Middle Kingdom* by Jan Jacob Slauerhoff (novel), pp.102–103, C2

Chupakabura Kingdom, Japan (city/state), *Sakura Quest* (anime), pp.96–97, B2

Chuparosa, Mexico (town), *Red Dead Redemption* series (video games), pp.32–33, B3

Chutneypore, India (city), *The Nautch Girl, or The Rajah of Chutneypore* (comic opera), pp.78–79, C4/D4

Cianwood City, Japan (city), *Pokémon* (video games), pp.96–97, B2

Cibola, South Dakota (city), *National Treasure: Book of Secrets* (film), pp.16–17, A5

Cicely, Alaska (town), *Northern Exposure* (TV), pp.18–19, B1

Cilly City, Chinaland (fictional city), *Little Ninja Brothers* (video game), pp.102–103, D2

Cimbria (fictional country/region), *If On a Winter's Night a Traveller* by Italo Calvino (novel), pp.56–57, C5/D5

Cimbric People's Republic (fictional country), *If On a Winter's Night a Traveller* by Italo Calvino (novel), pp.56–57, C5/D5

Cimmeria (fictional country/region), *If On a Winter's Night a Traveller* by Italo Calvino (novel), pp.56–57, C5

Cinnabar Island, Japan (island), *Pokémon* (video games), pp.96–97, C2

Cinnabar, Nevada (town), Dark Horse Comics, pp.18–19, B4

Citadel, The, The Wasteland (fictional town), *Mad Max Fury Road* (film), pp.108–109, D2

Citadel, The, Turkey (city/state), Sanctus novels of Simon Toyne, pp.72–73, B3

Citiesville, California (city), *The Powerpuff Girls* (TV), pp.18–19, B3

Citrusville, Florida (town), Marvel Comics, pp.14–15, C1

City 17, Latvia (city), *Half-Life 2* (video game), pp.50–51, B4

City by the Sea, The, Pakistan (city), *In the City by the Sea* by Kamila Shamsie (novel), pp.78–79, A4

City of Atlantis, The, Atlantis (fictional city), *Atlantis: The Lost Empire* (film), pp.126–127, C6

City of Bright Moonlight, The, China (city), *Where the Mountain Meets the Moon* by Grace Lin (novel), pp.102–103, A3

City of K–, Japan (city), *The Aosawa Murders* by Riku Onda (novel), pp.96–97, B2

City of Lucid Shadows, The, Mongolia (city), *Martin Mystère* by Alfredo Castelli and Giancarlo Alessandrini (comic), pp.102–103, B4

City of Magicians, Iran (city), *Arabian Nights: Julnar the Sea-born and Her Son Badar Basim* (Burton edition, short story), pp.72–73, C3

City of Maihama, Eastal (fictional city), *Log Horizon* by Mamare Touno and Kazuhiro Hara (novels/anime), pp.96–97, F1

City of the Apes, Island of the, Indian Ocean (island), *Sinbad the Sailor* (short story), pp.78–79, B2

City of the Caesars, Chile/Argentina (unmappable city, mythology), pp.38–39, C2

City of the Elder Things (city), *At the Mountains of Madness* by H.P. Lovecraft (novels), pp.114–115, E3

City of the Golden Gates, The, Atlantis (fictional city), Cthulhu Mythos (various), pp.126–127, C3

City of the Great Race of Yith, Western Australia (city), *The Shadow Out of Time* by H.P. Lovecraft (novella), pp.108–109, B3

City of the Immortals, Ethiopia (ruined city), *The Immortal* by Jorges Luis Borges (short story), pp.84–85, D4

City-A, Kazakhstan (town), *whiteonwhite:algorithmicnoir* (film), pp.72–73, D3

Ciudad Azul, Argentina (village), *Far South* by David Enrique Spellman (novel), pp.38–39, C2

Ciudad España (fictional city state/province), *Judge Dredd* (comics), pp.44–45, A2

Ciudad Polaca, San Escobar (fictional city, internet humour), pp.32–33, B2

Ciudad Santiago, Mexico (town), *Amor Real* (TV), pp.32–33, B2

Ciudad Trinidad, Mexico (town), *Amor Real* (TV), pp.32–33, B2

Clam Waters (sea), *Club Penguin* (video game), pp.114–115, A3

Clanton, Mississippi (city), *A Time to Kill* by John Grisham, and other novels (novel), pp.16–17, D3

133

Clapstone, South Australia (town), *Dyschronia* by Jennifer Mills (novel), pp.108–109, C2

Claridge, Maryland (town), *The Bay* (film), pp.14–15, C4

Clarkson, Indian Ocean (city), *The Illegal* by Lawrence Hill (novel), pp.78–79, C1

Clarksville, Kentucky (town), *The Clovehitch Killer* (film), pp.14–15, A4

Clatterford, England (town), *Jam and Jerusalem* (TV), pp.64–65, C1

Clear River, Nebraska (town), *The House Without a Christmas Tree* (film), pp.16–17, C4

Clearwater, Erewhon (fictional town), *Erewhon* by Samuel Butler (novel), pp.108–109, F1

Clerinel, Channel Islands (island), *We Couldn't Leave Dinah* by Mary Treadgold (novel), pp.64–65, A1

Clerkship, Italy (island), *The Life of Gargantua and of Pantagruel* by François Rabelais (novel), pp.44–45, D1/D2

Clinton Corners, Georgia (town), *Carter Country* (TV), pp.14–15, B2

Clochemerle, France (town), *Clochemerle* by Gabriel Chevallier (novel), pp.44–45, C3

Clogher, Ireland (town), *The Seething Pot* by George A. Birmingham (novel), pp.64–65, A3

Cloisterham, England (town), *The Mystery of Edwin Drood* by Charles Dickens (novel), pp.64–65, D2

Clontar, New Jersey (town), works of Sinclair Lewis, pp.14–15, C5

Clotton, England (town), Severn Valley of the Cthulhu Mythos by Ramsey Campbell (novels), pp.64–65, C2

Cloud Cuckoo Land, Greece (floating city), *The Birds* by Aristophanes (myth/legend), pp.44–45, E2

Club Penguin Island (island), *Club Penguin/Club Penguin Island* (video game), pp.114–115, A3

Clumegnig, Luggnagg (fictional town), *Gulliver's Travels* by Jonathan Swift (novel), pp.96–97, E3

CM&W Railroad, Colorado (railway), *The Man Who Shot Liberty Valance* (film), pp.16–17, A3

Coal Valley (Hope Valley), Alberta (town), *When Calls the Heart* (TV), pp.26–27, C1

Coast City, Maine (city), *Transformers: Rescue Bots* (TV), pp.14–15, D6

Cobra Island, Gulf of Mexico (island), *GI Joe* (various), pp.32–33, B3/C3

Cobrastan (fictional country), *Papers, Please* (video game), pp.50–51, A5

Cochadebajo de los Gatos, Colombia (town), *The War of Don Emmanuel's Nether Parts* by Louis de Bernières (novel), pp.38–39, A5/A6

Cockleshell Bay, England (village), *Cockleshell Bay* (TV), pp.64–65, D3

Coketown, England (city), *Hard Times* by Charles Dickens (novel), pp.64–65, C3

Col Plateau, Karain continent (fictional natural feature), Islandia novels and sequels by Austin Tappan Wright and Mark Saxton, pp.84–85, B1

Colby, Texas (town), *The Lone Ranger* (film), pp.16–17, B2

Cold Bosworth, England (town), *Sleep No More* by L.T.C. Rolt (short stories), pp.64–65, D2

Cold Harbour, England (village), *South Riding* by Winifred Holtby (novel), pp.64–65, D3

Cold Mountain Penitentiary, Louisiana (building), *The Green Mile* by Stephen King (novel/film), pp.16–17, D2

Cold-Harbour, Erewhon (fictional town), *Erewhon* by Samuel Butler (novel), pp.108–109, F1

Coliflor River, San Theodoros/Neuvo-Rico (fictional river), *The Adventures of Tintin* by Hergé (various), pp.38–39, B5/C5

Colleges of Unreason, Erewhon (fictional building), *Erewhon* by Samuel Butler (novel), pp.108–109, F1

Collinsport, Maine (village), *Dark Shadows* (TV/film), pp.14–15, D6

Colonia Elena, Argentina (town), *Koblic* (film), pp.38–39, C2

Colson, Washington (town), *The X-Files* (TV), pp.18–19, B6

Columbiana (fictional state), *Pioneer, Go Home!* by Richard Powell (novel), pp.14–15, B1/B2

Comala, Mexico (town), *Pedro Páramo* by Juan Rulfo (novel), pp.32–33, B2

Comalities, Texas (town), *From the Earth to the Moon* by Jules Verne (novel), pp.16–17, B1

Combray, France (village), *In Search of Lost Time* by Marcel Proust (novel), pp.44–45, C3

Comity, New Hampshire (town), *The X-Files* (TV), pp.14–15, D5

Con, Antillia (fictional island, legend), pp.126–127, D3

Concordia (fictional country), *Romanoff and Juliet* by Peter Ustinov (play/film), pp.50–51, A3

Connemara, Ireland (town), *Oh, Mr Porter!* (film), pp.64–65, A3

Coolsville, Ohio (town), *Scooby-Doo! Curse of the Lake Monster* (film), pp.14–15, B4

Coombe Tracey, England (town), *Sherlock Holmes: The Adventure of Silver Blaze* by Arthur Conan Doyle (novel), pp.64–65, C1

Coongahoola, New South Wales (town), *All Our Secrets* by Jennifer Lane (novel), pp.108–109, D2

Cooper's Crossing, New South Wales (town), *The Flying Doctors* (TV), pp.108–109, D2

Cooper's Dell, Texas (town), *Red State* (film), pp.16–17, B3

Copenhagen City, Jamaica (town), *A Brief History of Seven Killings* by Marlon James (novel), pp.32–33, D2

Copper Beeches, England (estate), *Sherlock Holmes: The Adventure of the Copper Beeches* by Arthur Conan Doyle (short story), pp.64–65, C1

Copper Creek, New Zealand (town), the Copper Creek series by Wendy Smith (novels), pp.108–109, F2

Copperopolis, Wales (city), *Copperopolis* (comic), pp.64–65, B1

Coproliabad, Iraq (town), *Bowl of Cherries* by Millard Kaufman (novel), pp.72–73, D2

Coradine, Scotland (country), *A Crystal Age* by W.H. Hudson (novel), pp.64–65, C5

Coral Island, The, Pacific Ocean (island), *The Coral Island* by R.M. Ballantyne (novel), pp.120–121, C2

Coral Key Park Marine Reserve, Florida (natural feature), *Flipper* (TV), pp.14–15, C1

Cordillera (fictional country), *High Citadel* by Desmond Bagley (novel), pp.38–39, B3

Cordinia (fictional country), *A Royal Christmas* (film), pp.44–45, C3

Cordovia (fictional country), *BoJack Horseman* (TV), pp.50–51, A5

Corinth, Pennsylvania (town), ABC Soap Opera Universe (*Loving*, TV), pp.14–15, B4

Cornwall Coombe, Connecticut (town), *Harvest Home* by Tom Tryon (novel), pp.14–15, D5

Coroado, Brazil (town), *Irmãos Coragem* (TV), pp.38–39, C4

Corona (fictional city/state), *Tangled/Rapunzel's Tangled Adventure* (film/TV), pp.50–51, A4/B4

Coronation Gulf, Western Australia (natural feature), *Dirt Music* by Tim Winton (novel/film), pp.108–109, B4

Coronel Vallejos, Argentina (village), *Betrayed By Rita Hayworth* by Manuel Puig (novel), pp.38–39, B2

Corpus Christi (fictional island), works of Robert Antoni, pp.32–33, F1

Corrigan, Western Australia (town), *Jasper Jones* by Craig Silvey (novel/film), pp.108–109, A3/A6

Cortex Island, Pacific Ocean (island), *Crash Bandicoot* series (video games), pp.120–121, A4

Costa Bomm, Spain (region), *Carry on Abroad!* (film), pp.44–45, C3

Costa Eldorado, Spain (region), *Eldorado* (TV), pp.44–45, C3

Costa Estrella, Caribbean (island), *Princess Protection Program* (film), pp.32–33, E2

Costa Gravas (fictional island/nation), *Chuck* (TV), pp.38–39, C3/D3

Costa Lottsa (fictional country/principality), *San Sombrèro* (book), pp.44–45, C3

Costa Luna, Caribbean (island), *Princess Protection Program* (film), pp.32–33, E2

Costa Perdita (fictional country), Marvel Comics and *Air America* (comics/unrelated TV series), pp.32–33, C2

Costa Plonka, Spain (town), *Are You Being Served?* (TV), pp.44–45, B2

Costa Verde (fictional country), Marvel Comics, pp.32–33, C2

Costaguana (fictional country), *Nostromo* by Joseph Conrad (novel), pp.38–39, A4

Coulibri, Jamaica (sugar plantation), *Wide Sargasso Sea* by Jean Rhys (novel), pp.32–33, D2

Coumarine City, France (city), *Pokémon* (video games), pp.44–45, C3

Country of the Blind, The, Ecuador (region), *The Country of the Blind* by H.G. Wells (short story), pp.38–39, A5

County Finfarran, Ireland (county), Finfarran Peninsula novels of Felicity Hayes-McCoy, pp.64–65, A2

County More West, Ireland (county), *Waking Ned* (film), pp.64–65, A2

Couriway City, France (city), *Pokémon* (video games), pp.44–45, C3

Cowpertown, South Carolina (town), works of Madeleine L'Engle, pp.14–15, C3

Crab Island, Caribbean (island), *Swallows and Amazons: Peter Duck* by Arthur Ransome (novels), pp.32–33, F2

Crab Key and Dr No's Lair, Jamaica (island), *Dr No* by Ian Fleming (novel/film), pp.32–33, D2

Crackled Axle, Saskatchewan (town), *Regina Leader-Post* (newspaper column), pp.26–27, C1

Craggy Island, Ireland (island), *Father Ted* (TV), pp.64–65, A2

Craggy Tops, England (building), *The Island of Adventure* by Enid Blyton (novel), pp.64–65, B1

Cragwich, England (town), *Lesbian Vampire Killers* (film), pp.64–65, D2

Craig, Scotland (town), *Narrow-Gauge Adventure* by P.D. Hancock (book), pp.64–65, C4

Craigcorrie, Scotland (town), noted model railway, pp.64–65, B4

Craigh na Dun, Scotland (stone circle), Outlander novels by Diana Gabaldon (novels/TV), pp.64–65, C2

Craiglang, Scotland (town), *Still Game* (TV), pp.64–65, C4

Craigshire, Scotland (county), *Narrow-Gauge Adventure* by P.D. Hancock (book), pp.64–65, C2

Craigsville, Florida (town), *Thunderbirds are Go* (1966), pp.14–15, C1

Crampton Hodnet, England (town), *Crampton Hodnet* by Barbara Pym (novel), pp.64–65, C2

Cranesmuir, Scotland (village), Outlander novels by Diana Gabaldon (novels/TV), pp.64–65, B5

Cranford, England (village), *Cranford* (TV), pp.64–65, C2

Cranmer (fictional state), *The Two Georges* by Harry Turtledove (novel), pp.16–17, B3/C3

Crapulia (region), *Mundus alter et idem* by Joseph Hall (novel), pp.114–115, E2

Crawhill Cottage, Scotland (building), *When They Lay Bare* by Andrew Greig (novel), pp.64–65, C2

Crawl Berg, Virginia (town), *ThanksKilling* (film), pp.14–15, C4

Creighton-Ward Mansion, England (building), *Thunderbirds* (TV), pp.64–65, D2

Cresap's Landing, West Virginia (town), *Night of the Hunter* by Davis Grubb (novel/film), pp.16–17, D2

Crescent City, Idaho (town), *Zorro's Black Whip* (film), pp.18–19, A6

Crescent Cove (town), *Killer Klowns From Outer Space* (film), pp.18–19, A4

Crimpton-on-Sea, England (town), *Hi-de-Hi!* (TV), pp.64–65, D2

Crink's Creek, New South Wales (town), *Blue* by Pat Grant (graphic novel), pp.108–109, D2

Crinkley Bottom, England (village), *Noel's House Party* (TV), pp.64–65, C1

Crocodile Falls, Northern Territory (natural feature), *The Rescuers Down Under* (film), pp.108–109, C3

Crocus, Saskatchewan (town), *Jake and the Kid* by W.O. Mitchell (short stories), pp.26–27, A3

Croft Manor, England (building), *Tomb Raider* (video game), pp.64–65, D2

Cromartie High School, Japan (building), *Cromartie High School* by Eiji Nonaka (manga/anime), pp.96–97, D1

Cronk, England (town), *Thomas the Tank Engine* by Rev W. Audrey (books/TV), pp.64–65, C2

Crooked Cove, Caribbean (island), *Pirates of the Caribbean* (various), pp.32–33, D2/E2

Crossarra, Ireland (village), Finfarran Peninsula novels of Felicity Hayes-McCoy, pp.64–65, A2

Crossmaheart, Northern Ireland (town), *Cycle of Violence* by Colin Bateman (novel), pp.64–65, B3

Crosspatch, Scotland (town), *The Dandy* ('The Jocks and the Geordies') (comic), pp.64–65, C4

Crossroads Motel, England (building), *Crossroads* (TV), pp.64–65, C2

Crossroads, Japan (town), *Sailor Moon* by Naoko Takeuchi (manga/anime), pp.96–97, C2

Crotalophoboi Land (fictional country), *South Wind* by Norman Douglas (novel), pp.84–85, C5

Crow Lake, Ontario (town), *Crow Lake* by Mary Lawson (novel), pp.26–27, A4

Crowley Corners, Tennessee (town), *Hannah Montana* (TV/film), pp.14–15, A3

Crown City see Elwood City

Cruives, The, Scotland (natural feature), novels of John Buchan, pp.64–65, B3

Crystal Falls, North Carolina (town), *Christmas Joy* (film), pp.14–15, B3

Crystal Lake/Camp Crystal Lake, New Jersey (Town/lake), *Friday the 13th* (films), pp.14–15, C5

Crystal Palace, The, Japan (building), *Sailor Moon* by Naoko Takeuchi (manga/anime), pp.96–97, E1

Crystal River, Utah/Arizona (town), *Maverick* (film), pp.18–19, C3

Crystal Tokyo, Japan (city), *Sailor Moon* by Naoko Takeuchi (manga/anime), pp.96–97, E1/F1

Crythin Gifford, England (village), *The Woman in Black* by Susan Hill (novel/play/film), pp.64–65, C2

CSS Texas, Mali (wreck), *Sahara* by Clive Cussler (novel/film), pp.84–85, B5

Cuesta Verde, California (town), *Poltergeist* (film), pp.18–19, A4

Culdee Fell, England (mountain), *Thomas the Tank Engine* by Rev W. Audrey (books/TV), pp.64–65, C3

Cullymore, Ireland (town), novels of Patrick McCabe, pp.64–65, B3

Cursed Springs of Jusenkyo, China (natural feature), *Ranma ½* by Rumiko Takahashi (manga/anime), pp.102–103, B2

Cutter, Washington (town), *Whale Talk* by Chris Crutcher (novel), pp.18–19, B6

Cutthroat Isle, Caribbean (island), *Pirates of the Caribbean* (various), pp.32–33, E2

Cwm-Pen-Ôl, Wales (town), *High Hopes* (TV), pp.64–65, B2

Cwmderi, Wales (town), *Pobol y Cwm* (TV), pp.64–65, B2

Cwrtmynach, Wales (village), *Pobol y Cwm* (TV), pp.64–65, B2

Cyberaya, Malaysia (city), *Agent Ali* (TV), pp.90–91, A4

Cyllage City, France (city), *Pokémon* (video games), pp.44–45, B3

Cypress Cove, California (city), *Bionic 6* (TV), pp.18–19, A5

Cypress Creek, North Takoma (fictional town), *The Simpsons* (TV), pp.18–19, B6

Cyprum, Cyprus (fictional), *MacTrump* by Ian Doescher and Jacopo Della Quercia (book), pp.44–45, F1

Dadu, China (city), *Log Horizon* by Mamare Touno and Kazuhiro Hara (novels/anime), pp.102–103, D1

Dahum (fictional country), *Solo* by William Boyd (novel), pp.84–85, B4

Daikoko, Japan (town), *Denno Coil* (anime), pp.96–97, D2

Daily Mail Island, England (island), *TV Go Home* (TV, based on website), pp.64–65, B2

Dakar, Washington (wreck), *Free Willy 2* (film), pp.18–19, A6

Dakor Bungalow, The, India (building), *The Dâk Bungalow at Dakor* by Bithia Mary Croker (short story), pp.78–79, C4

Dakota City (city), Milestone Media (various), pp.18–19, B5

Dalahtibar, Adjikistan (fictional city), *SOCOM U.S. Navy SEALs: Combined Assault* (video game), pp.72–73, D2

Dalmailing, Scotland (town), *Annals of the Parish* by John Galt (novel), pp.64–65, C3

Dalquaharter, Scotland (town), novels of John Buchan, pp.64–65, B3

Damon, Washington (town), *Short Circuit* (film), pp.18–19, A6

Dande, Ewawa (fictional city), *The Death Certificate* by Alobwed'Epie (novel), pp.84–85, D2

Dandytown, Scotland (town), *The Dandy* (comics), pp.64–65, C4

Danebury, England (town), The Detectorists (TV), pp.64–65, C2

Danielstown, Ireland (estate), *The Last September* by Elizabeth Bowen (novel/film), pp.64–65, A2

Dante's Peak, Washington (mountain), *Dante's Peak* (film), pp.18–19, B6

Danu (fictional country), *The Redundancy of Courage* by Timothy Mo (novel), pp.90–91, C2

Danvers Hill, Montana (town), *Lonely Train a' Comin'/Helltracks* by William F. Nolan (short story/novel), pp.18–19, D6

Daphne, The, Pacific Ocean (wreck), *The Island of the Day Before* by Umberto Eco (novel), pp.120–121, C2

Darfar (fictional country), Conan novels of Robert E. Howard, pp.84–85, B5

Dark Deep, the Barbaric Archipelago (fictional island), *How to Train Your Dragon* by Cressida Cowell (novels/films), pp.56–57, D2

Dark Score Lake, Maine (lake), novels of Stephen King (various), pp.14–15, D6

Dark Sea, The, the Dark Sea (fictional sea), *Frozen II* (film), pp.56–57, A4/B4

Dark Tower, The, Romania (town), *Tales from the Dark Tower* by Joseph Vargo (novel), pp.50–51, C2

Darkmoor, England (natural feature), Marvel Comics, pp.64–65, C3

Darkness Falls, Maine (town), *Darkness Falls* (film), pp.14–15, D6

Darkstones Moor, Scotland (natural feature), *Ripping Yarns: Murder at Moorstones Manor* (TV), pp.64–65, B4/C4

Darkwater Island, Massachusetts (island), *Call of Cthulhu: The Official Video Game*, novels of John Buchan (various), pp.14–15, D5

Darlington Hall, England (building), *The Remains of the Day* by Kazuo Ishiguro (novel), pp.64–65, D2

Darnley Mills, England (town), Darnley Mills novels by Phillip Turner, pp.64–65, D3

Darrowby, England (town), *It Shouldn't Happen to a Vet* by James Herriot (novel), pp.64–65, C3

Dasseborg, Sweden (city), *Doktor Mugg* (TV), pp.56–57, B2

Daughtery, Texas (town), *Django Unchained* (film), pp.18–19, D2

Dave's Secret Island, Pacific Ocean (island), *Penguins of Madagascar* (film), pp.90–91, D4

Daystrom Institute, Japan (building), *Star Trek* (various), pp.96–97, D1

Dead Man's Eye, Caribbean (island), *Pirates of the Caribbean* (various), pp.32–33, D2

Dead Man's Pond, The, Norway (lake), *The Dead Man's Pond* by André Bjerkes (novel), pp.56–57, A3

Deadrock, Nevada (town), *Crazy for You* (musical), pp.18–19, B5

Deane, New South Wales (town), *The White Girl* by Tony Birch (novel), pp.108–109, D2

Death City, Nevada (city), *Soul Eater* by Atsushi Okubo (manga/anime), pp.18–19, B4

Debra Down, Azanian Empire (fictional city), *Black Mischief* by Evelyn Waugh (novel), pp.84–85, D4

Decent, Illinois (town), *Tattletail* (video game), pp.16–17, D4

Ded Moroz Palace, Russia (building, Russian folklore), pp.50–51, B6

DeepStar Six, Pacific Ocean (submerged building), *DeepStar Six* (film), pp.120–121, A4

Deer Meadow, Washington (town), *Twin Peaks* (TV), pp.18–19, B6

Deering, Indiana (town), *Hang Time* (TV), pp.14–15, B4

Deeson County, Arkansas (county), *Smokey and the Bandit* (film), pp.16–17, C2

Deika City, Japan (city), *My Hero Academia* by Kōhei Horikoshi (manga/anime), pp.96–97, C2

Deli-Chous, Chinaland (fictional city), *Little Ninja Brothers* (video game), pp.102–103, D1

Delmarva (fictional state), *Steven Universe* (TV), pp.14–15, C4

Delos Destinations (fictional island chain), *Westworld* by Michael Crichton (novel/TV), pp.90–91, C3

Delta City, Michigan (city), *Robocop* (film), pp.14–15, A5/B5

Delta Glen, Wisconsin (town), *The X-Files* (TV), pp.16–17, D5

Delvadia (fictional country), Marvel Comics, pp.38–39, A5

Demiji, The, Karain continent (fictional natural feature), Islandia novels and sequels by Austin Tappan Wright and Mark Saxton, pp.84–85, B1

Democratic Free People's United Republic of San Sombrèro (fictional country), *San Sombrèro* (book), pp.32–33, D1

Dendemille Town, France (town), *Pokémon* (video games), pp.44–45, C3

Denley Moor, England (town), *Ripping Yarns: The Testing of Eric Olthwaite* (TV), pp.64–65, C3

Denton, Ohio (town), *The Rocky Horror Picture Show* (film), pp.14–15, B4

Denton, England (town), *A Touch of Frost* by R.D. Wingfield (novels/TV), pp.64–65, C2

Depths of Palm, The, Eastal (fictional natural feature), *Log Horizon* by Mamare Touno and Kazuhiro Hara (novels/anime), pp.96–97, C3

Deriu, Italy (town), *The Little Theatre by the Sea* by Rosanna Ley (novel), pp.44–45, C2

Derkaderkastan (fictional country), *Team America: World Police* (film), pp.72–73, C2

Derlbak, Iraq (village), *Zadig* by Voltaire (novel), pp.72–73, C2

Derry, Maine (town), *It* by Stephen King (various), pp.14–15, D6

Derwentbridge, England (town), *Meeting Lydia* by Linda MacDonald (novel), pp.64–65, C3

Deseret (fictional state), *Bring the Jubilee* by Ward Moore (novel), pp.18–19, C4

Desert Bluffs, New Mexico (town), *Welcome to Night Vale* (podcast), pp.16–17, A2

Desert of Ahm Shere, The, Ethiopia (natural feature), *The Mummy Returns* (film), pp.84–85, D4

Desperance, Queensland (town), *Carpentaria* by Alexis Wright (novel), pp.108–109, D4

Desperation, Nevada (town), *Desperation, Nevada* by Stephen King (novel), pp.18–19, B4/C4

Devil's Anvil, Caribbean (island), *Pirates of the Caribbean* (various), pp.32–33, E2

Devil's Bayou, Florida (natural feature), *The Rescuers* (film), pp.14–15, C1

Devil's Breath, The, Azerbaijan (natural feature), *James Bond: The World is Not Enough* (film), pp.72–73, C3

Devil's Cape, Louisiana (town), *Devil's Cape* by Rob Rogers (novel), pp.16–17, C2

Devil's Hill, Tasmania (natural feature), *Devil's Hill* by Nan Chauncy (novel), pp.108–109, D1

Devil's Teeth, The, Greenland (mountain chain), *La Citadelle des Glaces* by Paul Alperine (novel), pp.26–27, D4

Devil's Triangle, The, Caribbean (island), *Pirates of the Caribbean* (various), pp.32–33, F2

Dewford Town, Japan (town), *Pokémon* (video games), pp.96–97, A2

Dexter, Oklahoma (town), *The X-Files* (TV), pp.16–17, B3

Dhabar, Qurac (fictional country), DC Comics, pp.72–73, C2

Di-e-Bala, Afghanistan (village), *New Home, New Life* by radio, pp.72–73, D2

Di-e-Payan, Afghanistan (village), *New Home, New Life* by radio, pp.72–73, D2

Diamond City, Massachusetts (town), *Fallout 4* (video game), pp.14–15, D5

Dianium, Spain (town), works of Clara Sánchez, pp.44–45, B3

Dibley, England (village), *The Vicar of Dibley* (TV), pp.64–65, D2

Dickens, California (town), *The Sellout* by Paul Beatty (novel), pp.18–19, A2

Diggstown, Georgia (town), *Diggstown* (film), pp.14–15, B3

Dilipabad, Pakistan (town), *Unmarriageable* by Soniah Kamal (novel), pp.78–79, B5

Dillon, Texas (town), *Friday Night Lights* (TV), pp.16–17, A2

Dimmsdale, California (town), *The Fairly OddParents* (TV), pp.18–19, B3

Ding Village, China (village), *Dream of Ding Village* by Yan Lianke (novel), pp.102–103, D2

Dingley Dell, England (village), *The Pickwick Papers* by Charles Dickens (novel), pp.64–65, D2

Dinotopia, Indian Ocean (island), *Dinotopia* (books/TV), pp.78–79, A2

Dirt, Nevada (town), *Rango* (film), pp.18–19, B3

Discovery KSNM-3, New York (wreck), *Metal Gear Solid* series (video game), pp.14–15, D5

Disham, England (town), *Night and Day* by Virginia Woolf (novel), pp.64–65, D2

Dismal Downs, Scotland (natural feature), *DuckTales* (TV), pp.64–65, B4/C4

District 1, Utah/Montana (state), *The Hunger Games* by Suzanne Collins (various), pp.18–19, C5

District 2, New Mexico (state), *The Hunger Games* by Suzanne Collins (various), pp.18–19, D3

District 3, Indiana (state), *The Hunger Games* by Suzanne Collins (various), pp.14–15, A4

District 4, Nevada/Oregon/Washington (state), *The Hunger Games* by Suzanne Collins (various), pp.18–19, B5

District 5, Nevada/Arizona (state), *The Hunger Games* by Suzanne Collins (various), pp.18–19, B3/C3

District 6, Illinois (state), *The Hunger Games* by Suzanne Collins (various), pp.16–17, D4

District 7, Montana (state), *The Hunger Games* by Suzanne Collins (various), pp.16–17, A6

District 7, Alberta/Saskatchewan (region), *The Hunger Games* by Suzanne Collins (novels/films), pp.26–27, C1

District 8, New York (state), *The Hunger Games* by Suzanne Collins (various), pp.14–15, B5/C5

District 9, Kansas/Missouri (state), *The Hunger Games* by Suzanne Collins (various), pp.16–17, C4

District 9, South Africa (town/camp), *District 9* (film), pp.84–85, C2

District 10, Texas (state), *The Hunger Games* by Suzanne Collins (various), pp.16–17, B1/B2

District 10, Mexico (region), *The Hunger Games* by Suzanne Collins (books/films), pp.32–33, A4/B4

District 11 (state), *The Hunger Games* by Suzanne Collins (various), pp.16–17, D2

District 12, West Virginia/Pennsylvania (city/region), *The Hunger Games* by Suzanne Collins (various), pp.14–15, B4/C4

District 13, Ontario/Quebec (region), *The Hunger Games* by Suzanne Collins (novels/films), pp.26–27, E1

District of Masselton, Germany (region), *Teutdorf* (short story), pp.44–45, D4

Divide, The, Nebraska (county), *O Pioneers!* by Willa Cather (novel/film), pp.16–17, B4

Divino, Brazil (town), *Avenida Brasil* (TV), pp.38–39, D3

Dnestrograd, Ukraine (town), *Hemmingway and the Dead-Bird Rain* by Boris Zaidman (novel), pp.50–51, C2

Do It Over, England (town), *Riddley Walker* by Russell Hoban (novel), pp.64–65, D1

Doblina, Poland (town), *Scenes from the Siege of Doblina* by Michael Beirigier (novels), pp.50–51, B3

Doburoku, Croatia (city), *Porco Rosso* (anime), pp.50–51, A1/A2

Dodo's Perch, Caribbean (island), *Pirates of the Caribbean* (various), pp.32–33, D2

Dods Hill, England (town), *Jacob's Room* by Virginia Woolf (novel), pp.64–65, D3

Dofras Sund, England (sea), *Total War: Thrones of Britannia* (video game), pp.64–65, D1

Dog River and Wullerton, Saskatchewan (town), *Corner Gas* (TV), pp.26–27, C1

Doglick, West Virginia (town), *Hellblazer* (comic), pp.14–15, B4

Dogpatch, Kentucky (town), *Li'l Abner* (comic), pp.14–15, A4

Dogtown, Colorado (city), *Fallout New Vegas* (video game), pp.16–17, A4

Dogville, Colorado (town), *Dogville* (film), pp.18–19, D4

Dolphin Island, Queensland (island), *Dolphin Island* by Arthur C. Clarke (novel), pp.108–109, D4

Dolphin, Greenland/Northern Provinces (wreck), *Captain Pugwash* (TV), pp.26–27, D4

Dolwyn, England (village), *The Last Days of Dolwyn* (film), pp.64–65, C2

Dominion Creek, Yukon (town), *An Klondike* (TV), pp.26–27, B2

Dominion, Ontario (city), *George Sprott* by Seth (graphic novel and cardboard model), pp.26–27, A4

Domino City, Japan (city), *Yu-Gi-Oh* by Kazuki Takahashi (manga/anime), pp.96–97, F1

Dongmakgol, South Korea (village), *Welcome to Dongmakgol* by Jang Jin (play/film), pp.102–103, E3

Dongzhou City, China (city), *The Civil Servant's Notebook* by Wang Xiaofang (novel), pp.102–103, E4

Doodle, New Zealand (town), *Custard's World* (TV), pp.108–109, F2

Dooling, Appalachia (fictional town), *Sleeping Beauties* by Stephen King and Owen King (novel), pp.14–15, B4

Doomsday Machine, The, Russia (building), *Dr Strangelove or: How I Learned to Stop Worrying and Love the Bomb* (film), pp.102–103, D2

Doomstadt, Latveria (fictional city), Marvel Comics, pp.50–51, B2

Doone Valley, England (natural feature), *Lorna Doone* by Richard Doddridge Blackmore (novel), pp.64–65, C2

Dorado (fictional state), *I-0* (video game), pp.18–19, D3

Dorado, Mexico (city), *Overwatch* (video game), pp.32–33, B3

Dorlcote Mill, England (building), *The Mill on the Floss* by George Eliot (novel), pp.64–65, D2

Dorothy Gale's Farm, Kansas (building), *The Wizard of Oz* (novel/film), pp.16–17, C4

Dos Rios, Texas (city), DC Comics, pp.16–17, A3

Dos Rios, San Escobar (fictional city), internet humour, pp.32–33, B2

Dotandcarryonetown, Apodidraskiana (fictional town), *Crotchet Castle* by Thomas Love Peacock (novel), pp.14–15, B4

Dotheboys Hall, England (building), *Nicholas Nickleby* by Charles Dickens (novel), pp.64–65, C3

Dougal County, Georgia (county), *Squidbillies* (TV), pp.14–15, B3

Doverville, Illinois (town), *The Fugitive* (film), pp.16–17, D4

Downstaple, England (town), novels of Thomas Hardy, pp.64–65, C1

Downton Abbey (estate), *Downton Abbey* (TV), pp.64–65, C3

Drackenberg (fictional country), *The Drackenberg Adventure* by Lloyd Alexander (novel), pp.44–45, C3

Dragon Island, the Barbaric Archipelago (fictional island), *How to Train Your Dragon* by Cressida Cowell (novels/films), pp.56–57, C1

Dragonite Meteorite, The, China (natural feature), *Outlaw Star* (anime), pp.102–103, D4

Drake Barrier Reef, The, Queensland (natural feature), *DuckTales* (TV), pp.108–109, E3

Draken River, Latveria/Symkaria (fictional river), Marvel Comics, pp.50–51, B2

Drambeg, Scotland (island), *Angus Og* by Ewen Bain (comic strip), pp.64–65, B5

Drane, Ireland (town), *Fillums: A Novel* by Hugh Leonard (novel), pp.64–65, B2

Drax Enterprises Launch Facility, Brazil (building), *James Bond: Moonraker* (film), pp.38–39, E5

Draxmundham, England (town), *The Secret Railway* by Elisabeth Beresford (novel), pp.64–65, D2

Dream Kingdom (fictional country), *Die Andere Seite: Ein Phantastischer Roman* by Alfred Kubin (novel), pp.102–103, A3

Drover's Run, New South Wales (estate), *McLeod's Daughters* (TV), pp.108–109, D2

Druid's Stones, The, Wales (stone circle), *Boris Karloff's Thriller* (TV), pp.64–65, C2

Drumorty, Scotland (town), *Doorways in Drumorty* by Lorna Moon (novel), pp.64–65, C5

Druznia (fictional country), *Regular Show* (TV), pp.50–51, C5

Dryland (fictional region), *Waterworld* (film), pp.78–79, C4

Duckburg, Calisota (fictional city), *DuckTales* (various), pp.18–19, A5

Ducklovia (fictional country), Count Duckula (TV), pp.50–51, B2

Dudley, Arkansas (town), *The X-Files* (TV), pp.16–17, C3/D3

Duke's Denver, England (village), Peter Wimsey stories by Dorothy L. Sayers (novels), pp.64–65, D2

Dukes, Liberty State (fictional town), *GTA IV* (video game), pp.14–15, D1

Dukesberry, New Hampshire (town), *Eight Crazy Nights* (film), pp.14–15, D5

Dull Lake, The, Alifbay (fictional lake), *Haroun and the Sea of Stories* by Salman Rushdie (novel), pp.78–79, B5

Dumpton, England (town), News from Dumpton by 'Harbert' (newspaper column), pp.64–65, D2

Dunalistair, Scotland (town, noted model railway), pp.64–65, B4

Dunbain Castle, Scotland (building), *The Ghost of St Michael's* (film), pp.64–65, B4

Duncaster, England (town), *The 17th Hole at Duncaster* by H.R. Wakefield (short story), pp.64–65, D2

Dunton Wood, England (natural feature), *Duncton Wood* by William Horwood (novels), pp.64–65, D2

Duneen, Ireland (village), *Holding* by Graham Norton (novel), pp.64–65, A2

Dungarvie, New Zealand (town), works of Owen Marshall, pp.108–109, F1

Dungatar, Victoria (town), *The Dressmaker* by Rosalie Ham (film), pp.108–109, D2

Dunkilderry, Ireland (town), *The Simpsons* (TV), pp.64–65, A3

Dunny on the Wold, England (village), *Blackadder III* (TV), pp.64–65, C4

Dunston County, Georgia (county), *Gator* (film), pp.14–15, B2

Dunt, South Australia (town), *We Can Be Heroes* (mockumentary), pp.108–109, C2

Dunwich, Massachusetts (town), Cthulhu Mythos/H.P. Lovecraft (various), pp.14–15, C5

Durant, Wyoming (town), Walt Longmire series by Craig Johnson (novels), pp.18–19, D5

Durmstrang Institute, Russia (unmappable building), Harry Potter/Wizarding World by J.K. Rowling (various), pp.50–51, A6

Durnham, England (town), *The Secret Railway* by Elisabeth Beresford (novel), pp.64–65, D2

Durrongo, New South Wales (town), *Too Much Lip* by Melissa Lucashenko (novels), pp.108–109, E2

Dusk, Pennsylvania (town), *Dusk* (video game), pp.14–15, B4

Dynmouth, England (town), *Children of Dynmouth* by William Trevor (novel), pp.64–65, C1

Eagle Hat, Alberta (town), *The Final Sacrifice* (film), pp.26–27, C1

Eagle Rock, Iowa (town), *Cold Turkey* (film), pp.16–17, C4

Eagle State (fictional state), *Desperate Housewives* (TV), pp.14–15, A4

Eagles Nest, Australia (town), *Kill Me Three Times* (film), pp.108–109, A2

Eagleton, Indiana (town), *Parks and Recreation* (TV), pp.14–15, A4

East and West Egg, New York (towns), *The Great Gatsby* by F. Scott Fitzgerald (novel), pp.14–15, D1

East and West Hun Chiu (fictional countries), *Designated Survivor* (TV), pp.102–103, E1

East Carmine, Wales (town), *Shades of Grey* by Jasper Fforde (novels), pp.64–65, C2

East Cheam, England (town), *Hancock's Half Hour* (TV), pp.64–65, D2

East Great Falls, Michigan (town), *American Pie* films (films), pp.14–15, A5

East Proctor, England (village), *An American Werewolf in London* (film), pp.64–65, D3

East Transia, Transia (fictional city), Marvel Comics, pp.50–51, B1

East-Meg One, East-Meg One (fictional city/state), *Judge Dredd* (comics), pp.50–51, C2

East-Meg Two, East-Meg Two (fictional region/city/state), *2000 AD* (comics), pp.102–103, E1

East, South and West Gackle, Alberta (town), *What's With Andy?* (TV), pp.26–27, C1

Eastal (League of Free Cities, fictional country), *Log Horizon* by Mamare Touno and Kazuhiro Hara (novels/anime), pp.96–97, C2/C3

Eastgate, England (town), *Dad's Army* (TV), pp.64–65, D1

Eastlee, England (town), *A Mother's Son* (TV), pp.64–65, D2

Eastport, New Zealand (town), *Death in April Creek* by Helena Cooke (novel), pp.108–109, F1

Eastvale, England (town), Inspector Banks novels by Peter Robinson, pp.64–65, C3

Eastwick, Rhode Island (town), *The Witches of Eastwick* (novel/film), pp.14–15, D5

Eastwick, England (town), *Metroland* by Julian Barnes (novel), pp.64–65, D2

Eastwood Ravine (Shonash Ravine/Clayton Ravine), California (natural feature), *Back to the Future Part 3* (film), pp.18–19, A4

Eatenswill, England (village), *The Pickwick Papers* by Charles Dickens (novel), pp.64–65, D2

Eaton Gomery, Wales (town, noted model railway), pp.64–65, C2

Ebbing, Missouri (town), *Three Billboards Outside Ebbing, Missouri* (film), pp.16–17, D3

Ecopoint: Antarctica (facility), *Overwatch* (video games), pp.114–115, C2

Ecotopia (country), *Ecotopia* by Ernest Callenbach (novel), pp.18–19, A5/B5

Ecruteak City, Japan (city), *Pokémon* (video games), pp.96–97, B2

Eddington Point (natural feature), works of Madeleine L'Engle, pp.114–115, E1

Eden Estate, Northern Territory (estate), *Return to Eden* (TV), pp.108–109, C4

Eden Hills, Victoria (town/suburb), *Neighbours* (TV), pp.108–109, A1

Eden, North Dakota (building), *Logan* (film), pp.16–17, A6

Eden, Illinois (town), *Martin Chuzzlewit* by Charles Dickens (novel), pp.16–17, D3

Eden, Grenada (island), *The Colour of Forgetting* by Merle Collins (novel), pp.32–33, F2

Eden-Olympia, France (building), *Super-Cannes* by J.G. Ballard (novel), pp.44–45, C2

Edge City, New Jersey (city), *The Mask* (film), pp.14–15, C4/C5

Eel Marsh House, England (building), *The Woman in Black* by Susan Hill (novel/play/film), pp.64–65, C4

Eerie-on-Sea, England (town), *Malamander* by Thomas Taylor (novel), pp.64–65, D1

Eerie, Indiana (town), *Eerie, Indiana* (TV), pp.14–15, A4

Eichwald, Germany (village), *The White Ribbon* (film), pp.44–45, D4

Eindhoven Lion, Caribbean (wreck), *Speed 2: Cruise Control* (film), pp.32–33, F2

Ekaterina, Ukraine (town), *Ekaterina* by Romain Mader (photography), pp.50–51, C1

El Castillo del Diablo, San Andreas (fictional mountain range), *Grand Theft Auto* series (video game), pp.18–19, B3/C3

El Chapo/Grand Chapo, San Theodoros/Neuvo-Rico (fictional region), *The Adventures of Tintin* by Hergé (various), pp.38–39, C5

El Coronado (fictional country), *Coronado* (film), pp.32–33, C1

El Dorado, Peru (city), *Candide* by Voltaire (novel), pp.38–39, B3

El Edén, Chile (town), *Pecadores (Sinners)* (TV), pp.38–39, B3

El Estado Dorado, Mexico (country), *Al norte del Milenio* by Gerardo Cornejo (novel), pp.32–33, A4/B4

El Golfo Nostrum, Mexico (sea), *Al norte del Milenio* by Gerardo Cornejo (novel), pp.32–33, B2

El Gran Centro-Capital, Mexico (city), *Al norte del Milenio* by Gerardo Cornejo (novel), pp.32–33, B2

El Idilio, Ecuador (village), *The Old Man Who Read Love Stories* (*Un viejo que leía novelas de amor*) by Luis Sepulveda (novel), pp.38–39, A5

El Lugar vacio, Mexico (natural feature), *Al norte del Milenio* by Gerardo Cornejo (novel), pp.32–33, A4

El Misti, Peru (mountain), *Ripping Yarns* (TV), pp.38–39, A4

El Tanika (fictional country), *Planetes* (manga/anime), pp.38–39, B3

Elanery (The City), Islandia (fictional city), Islandia novels and sequels by Austin Tappan Wright and Mark Saxton, pp.84–85, B1

Elden, France (village), *Marianne* (TV), pp.44–45, B3

Electra, Pacific Ocean (wreck), *Virus* (comic/film), pp.120–121, C2

Elephant Graveyard, The, Tanzania (natural feature), *The Lion King* (film), pp.84–85, D2

Elfhame, Scotland (region), *Kingdom of Elfin* by Sylvia Townsend Warner (novel), pp.64–65, C3

Elfwick, Scotland (region), *Kingdom of Elfin* by Sylvia Townsend Warner (novel), pp.64–65, C3

Elite Hunting Hostel, Slovakia (building), *Hostel* series (films), pp.50–51, A3

Elizabeth Dane, California (wreck), *The Fog* (film), pp.18–19, A4

Elizabeth, South Carolina (town), *When You Find Me* by P.J. Vernon (novel), pp.14–15, C3

Elk Cove, Oregon (town), *Overboard* (film), pp.18–19, A5

Elk Grove, Michigan (town), *Ash vs The Evil Dead* (TV), pp.14–15, A5

Elliot Park, Victoria (Town/suburb), *Neighbours* (TV), pp.108–109, A1

Elmo, Alaska (town), *Men in Trees* (TV), pp.18–19, B1

Elpanda, Texas (town), *From the Earth to the Moon* by Jules Verne (novel), pp.16–17, B1

Elsa's Ice Palace, Arendelle (fictional building), *Frozen II* (film), pp.56–57, B4

Elsbels, Spain (island), *Carry on Abroad!* (film), pp.44–45, C2

Elsinby, England (town), *The Royal* (TV), pp.64–65, C3

Elwood City, Crown City, Quebec (city), *Arthur* (TV), pp.26–27, E1

Emerald Isle (fictional state), *2000 AD* (comics), pp.64–65, A3/B3/A2/B2

Emishi Village, Japan (village), *Princess Mononoke* (anime), pp.96–97, C2

Emmerdale, England (village), *Emmerdale* (TV), pp.64–65, C3

Empire Bay (city), *Mafia 2* (video game), pp.14–15, D5

Empire City, New York (city), *Steven Universe* (TV), pp.14–15, D1

Empire Falls, Maine (town), *Empire Falls* by Richard Russo (novel/TV), pp.14–15, D5

Empire of Niger, The (fictional bloc), *The Golden Compass* by Philip Pullman (novel/film), pp.84–85, B4

Empire of Quy, The (fictional sunken continent/nation), Cthulhu Mythos (various), pp.126–127, C1/D1/C2/D2

Empress, Atlantic Ocean (wreck), *Death Ship* (film), pp.126–127, B3

Encante, Brazil (city, mythology), pp.38–39, C2

Endora, Iowa (town), *What's Eating Gilbert Grape* by Peter Hedges (novel/film), pp.16–17, C2

Endostan (fictional country), *Relic Hunter* (TV), pp.72–73, E3

Engelsfors, Sweden (town), the Engelsfors series by Mats Strandberg and Sara Bergmark (novels), pp.56–57, C3

England, England (region), *England, England* by Julian Barnes (novel), pp.64–65, C1

Engle Sae, England (sea), *Total War: Thrones of Britannia* (video game), pp.64–65, D2/D3

Enkyo, Impor (fictional city), *Papers, Please* (video game), pp.50–51, A5

Ennai-Sur-Blasé, France (city), *The French Dispatch* (film), pp.44–45, C3

Ennasin, Italy (island), *The Life of Gargantua and Pantagruel* by François Rabelais (novel), pp.44–45, D1

Ennui-Sur-Blasé, France (city), *The French Dispatch* (film), pp.44–45, C3

Epic, Kansas (town), works of Max Yoho, pp.16–17, C3

Equatorial Kundu (fictional country), *The West Wing*, pp.84–85, B4

Erengel, Russia (island), *Player Unknown's Battlegrounds* (video game), pp.50–51, A4

Erewhon (fictional country), *Erewhon* by Samuel Butler (novel), pp.126–127, D1

Ergo Island, Atlantic Ocean (island), *Once, Two Islands* by Dawn Garisch (novel), pp.126–127, D1

Erie Pointe, Ohio (town), *Scooby-Doo! Curse of the Lake Monster* (film), pp.14–15, B5

Erikraudebyg, Greenland (village), *La Citadelle des Glaces* by Paul Alperine (novel), pp.26–27, D4

Erinsborough, Victoria (town/suburb), *Neighbours* (TV), pp.108–109, A1

Erlandson and Skank Shipyards, Sweden (buildings), *Life of Pi* by Yann Martel (novel), pp.56–57, B1

Eroda, Irish Sea (island), 'Adore You' by Harry Styles (music), pp.64–65, B3

Ertebat Shar, Afghanistan (village, military training exercise), pp.72–73, D2

Escalera, Mexico (town), *Red Dead Redemption* series (video games), pp.32–33, B3

Escalon, Val Verde (fictional country), *Die Hard 2* (film), pp.38–39, A5

Eschberg, Austria (village), *Schlafes Bruder* by Robert Schneider (novel), pp.44–45, D4

Eschtenburg, Razkavia (fictional city), *The Tin Princess* by Philip Pullman (novel), pp.50–51, A3

Escudero, New Mexico (town), *Ace in the Hole* (film), pp.18–19, D3

Eskibahçe, Turkey (village), *Birds Without Wings* by Louis de Bernières (novel), pp.72–73, B3

Esmeralda, Costaguana (fictional town), *Nostromo* by Joseph Conrad (novel), pp.38–39, A4

Esperanza, Spain (town), *Pandora and the Flying Dutchman* (film), pp.44–45, C2

Esplendor, Brazil (town), *Esplendor* (TV), pp.38–39, D3

Essendean, Scotland (town), *Kidnapped* by Robert Louis Stevenson (novel), pp.64–65, C4

Essex, Connecticut (town), *Miss Muriel and Other Stories* by Ann Petry (short stories), pp.14–15, C5/D5

Estrella de Mar, Spain (town), *Cocaine Nights* by J.G. Ballard (novel), pp.44–45, A1

Estrella (fictional country), Marvel Comics, pp.38–39, B4

Eterna City, Japan (city), *Pokémon* (video games), pp.96–97, C4

Euphonia, Germany (city), *Les Soirées de l'Orchestre* by Hector Berlioz (book), pp.44–45, D4

Euphoria (fictional state), *The Campus Trilogy*, David Lodge (novel), pp.18–19, A4

Eureka, Oregon (town), *Eureka* (TV), pp.18–19, A5

Euro Itchy & Scratchy Land, France (theme park), *The Simpsons* (TV), pp.44–45, E3

Euro-City (fictional city state/province), *Judge Dredd* (comics), pp.44–45, C3

Eusebes, Meropis (fictional sunken city), *Meropis* by Theopompus of Chios (book), pp.126–127, D1

Evallonia (fictional country), works of John Buchan, pp.50–51, A3/B3

Evanleigh, Victoria (city), *Blue Heelers* (TV), pp.108–109, D1

Evarchia (fictional country), *Palace Without Chairs: A Baroque Novel* by Brigid Brophy (novel), pp.50–51, C2

Evelyn Bay, Tasmania (town), *The Survivors* by Jane Harper (novel), pp.108–109, D2

Ever Grande City, Japan (city), *Pokémon* (video games), pp.96–97, C5

Evergreen Forest, The, British Columbia/Alberta (region), *The Raccoons* (TV), pp.26–27, B1/B2

135

Evergreen, Vermont (town), *Christmas in Evergreen* series (films), pp.14–15, C6

Everington, England (town), *Billy Elliot* (film), pp.64–65, C3

Everon, Atlantic Ocean (island), *ARMA: Cold War Assault* (video game), pp.126–127, C4

Evers, Mississippi (city) *Bug Jack Barron* by Norman Spinrad (novel), pp.16–17, D2

Everwood, Colorado (town), *Everwood* (TV), pp.18–19, D4

Ewawa (fictional country), *The Death Certificate* by Alobwed'Epie (novel), pp.84–85, B4

Ewe, Gulf of Melange (fictional island), *Monkey Island* series (video games), pp.32–33, F2

Ewedown, England (village), *Tamara Drewe* by Posy Simmonds (comic/film), pp.64–65, C1

Excellent, Idaho (town), *The Man Who Fell in Love With the Moon* by Tom Spanbauer (novel), pp.18–19, B5

Executive Bathroom Island, Rhode Island (island), *Family Guy* (TV), pp.14–15, D5

Exile Island, Caribbean (island), Marvel Comics, pp.32–33, E3

Exina (fictional country), Brontë juvenilia, pp.90–91, E4

Exonbury, England (city), novels of Thomas Hardy, pp.64–65, C1

Explosion City (formerly Explosion Village), China (city), *The Explosion Chronicles* by Yan Lianke (novel), pp.102–103, D2

Ezono Agricultural High School, Japan (building), *Silver Spoon* by Hiromu Arakawa (manga/anime), pp.96–97, D4

Ezzo Empire (fictional country), *Log Horizon* by Mamare Touno and Kazuhiro Hara (novels/anime), pp.96–97, D4

F-City, Japan (city), *Excel Saga* by Kōshi Rikudō (manga/anime), pp.96–97, A1

F-Prefecture, Japan (region), *Excel Saga* by Kōshi Rikudō (manga/anime), pp.96–97, A1/A2

Factory/Lyoko, The, Paris, France (building), *Code Lyoko* (TV), pp.44–45, E3

Fagan Corners, Vermont (town), Marvel Cinematic Universe (various), pp.14–15, C5

Fair Haven, Ireland (village), *Star Trek Voyager* (TV), pp.64–65, A2

Fairmead, Erewhon (fictional town), *Erewhon* by Samuel Butler (novel), pp.108–109, F1

Fairport, Scotland (town), *The Antiquary* by Sir Walter Scott (novel), pp.64–65, C4

Fairvale, California (town), *Psycho* (novel/film), pp.18–19, A4

Fairview, Eagle State (fictional town), *Desperate Housewives* (TV), pp.14–15, A4

Fal Vale, England (town), *The Ghost Train* by Arnold Ridley (play), pp.64–65, B3

Falcon Beach, Vermont (town), *Falcon Beach* (TV), pp.14–15, C5

Falcon Beach, Manitoba (town), *Falcon Beach* (TV), pp.26–27, D1

Falcon Crest, California (building), *Falcon Crest* (TV), pp.18–19, A4

Falcon Island, Alaska (island), *DuckTales* (TV), pp.18–19, A1

Falkenstein Mountains, Razkavia (fictional mountain range), *The Tin Princess* by Philip Pullman (novel), pp.50–51, A3

Fall's End, Montana (town), *Far Cry 5/Far Cry New Dawn* (video game), pp.18–19, C6

Fallarbor Town, Japan (town), *Pokémon* (video games), pp.96–97, A1

Fallatown, Scotland (town), novels of John Buchan, pp.64–65, B3

Fallen Area, Pennsylvania (region), works of Steve Berman (short stories), pp.14–15, C5

Falport, England (town), *Windbag the Sailor* (film), pp.64–65, B5

False Creek, Victoria (town), *Backtrack* (film), pp.108–109, D1

Fanaron, Greece (village) *Cavafy's Stone and Other Village Stories* by Harry Mark Petrakis (short stories), pp.44–45, A1

Fanattia, Pacific Ocean (island), *Riallaro, the Archipelago of Exiles* by Godfrey Sweven (novel), pp.120–121, E1

Fang Rock, England (island), *Doctor Who: The Horror of Fang Rock* (TV), pp.64–65, D1

Fantippo (fictional country), Doctor Dolittle stories by Hugh Lofting (novels), pp.84–85, B4

Far Harbor, Maine (town), *Fallout 4* (video game), pp.14–15, D6

Farandoulie (fictional country), *Voyages Très Extraordinaires de Saturnin Farandoul* by Albert Robida (novel), pp.108–109, D1

Faraway Downs, Northern Territory (estate), *Australia* (film), pp.108–109, C4

Farmsville, California (town), *The Powerpuff Girls* (TV), pp.18–19, B3

Faro Island, Pacific Ocean (island), *King Kong vs Godzilla* (film), pp.120–121, C3

Father's Ham, England (town), *Riddley Walker* by Russell Hoban (novel), pp.64–65, D2

Fawcett City, Wisconsin (city), DC Comics, pp.16–17, C5

Fawlty Towers, England (building), *Fawlty Towers* (TV), pp.64–65, C1

Fawlty Turrets, India (building), *Goodness Gracious Me* (TV), pp.78–79, B4

Faxian, Hong Kong (city), *Transformers: Rescue Bots* (TV), pp.102–103, D1

Felpersham, England (city), *The Archers* (radio), pp.64–65, C2

Felsenburg Island, Atlantic Ocean (island), *Insel Felsenburg* by Johann Gottfried Schnabel (novel), pp.126–127, D1

Felsham Hall, England (building), *Lovejoy* (TV), pp.64–65, D2

Fenchurch St Paul, England (town), *The Nine Tailors* by Dorothy L. Sayers (novel), pp.64–65, D2

Fengzhou, China (city), *Silent Witness* (film), pp.102–103, D3

Fer-de-Lance, Louisiana (town), *GI Joe* (various), pp.16–17, C2

Ferne Bay, England (town), *Cakes and Ale* by W. Somerset Maugham (novel), pp.64–65, D2

Ferness, Scotland (town), *Local Hero* (film), pp.64–65, B4

FernGully, New South Wales (natural feature), *FernGully: The Last Rainforest* (film), pp.108–109, E2

Fernwood, Ohio (town), *Mary Hartman, Mary Hartman* (TV), pp.14–15, B4

Ffarquhar, England (town), *Thomas the Tank Engine* by Rev W. Awdry (books/TV), pp.64–65, D2

Ffhagdiwedd, Wales (town), Walians series by Daren Bowker-Powis and Richard Finlan (novels), pp.64–65, C3

Ficóbriga, Spain (town), novels of Benito Pérez Galdós, pp.64–65, A2

Fiddler's Green, Pennsylvania (town), *Land of the Dead* (film), pp.14–15, B4

Fillmore County, Kansas (county), *Jericho* (TV), pp.16–17, A4/B4

Findlay, Pennsylvania (town), *Unstoppable* (film), pp.14–15, B5

Finfarran Peninsula, Ireland (natural feature), Finfarran Peninsula novels of Felicity Hayes-McCoy, pp.64–65, A2

Finfolkaheem, Scotland (underwater feature, Orkney folklore), pp.64–65, C6

Fingerbone, Idaho (town), *Housekeeping* by Marilynne Robinson (novel), pp.18–19, B6

Finport, Scotland (town), *Still Game* (TV), pp.64–65, B4

Fiona Bay, Scotland (natural feature), *The Maggie* (film), pp.64–65, B4

Fire River, Russia (river), works of Elizabeth Marshall Thomas, pp.102–103, E1

Fireland, Iceland (country), *His Dark Materials* by Philip Pullman (various), pp.56–57, A6

Fitton, England (town), *Cabin Pressure* (radio), pp.64–65, C1

Fitzgibbon Farm, Virginia (building), *Mrs Frisby and the Rats of NIMH/The Secret of NIMH* by Robert C O'Brien (novel/film), pp.14–15, C4

Five Mountains, The, Olancho (fictional mountain range), *Soldiers of Fortune* by Richard Harding Davis (novel), pp.38–39, D5

Fix, Oklahoma (town), *Near Dark* (film), pp.16–17, B3

Flagstaff Village, Barbados (village), *The Polished Hoe* by Austin Clarke (novel), pp.32–33, F2

Flagstone, California (town), *Once Upon a Time in the West* (film), pp.18–19, B3

Flåklypa, Norway (town), works of Kjell Aukrust, pp.56–57, B3

Flambeau, Yukon (town), *The Barrier* by Rex Beach (novel), pp.26–27, B2

Flanflasnic, Brobdingnag (fictional town), *Gulliver's Travels* by Jonathan Swift (novel), pp.26–27, A1

Flatnäs, Finland (town), *Lola uppochner* by Monika Fagerholm (novel), pp.56–57, D3

Flatrock, Nevada (town), *The Andromeda Strain* by Michael Crichton (various), pp.18–19, B5

Flavonia (fictional country), works of Violet Needham, pp.50–51, A3

Flaw Valleys, England (estate), the Lymond Chronicles by Dorothy Dunnett (novels), pp.64–65, C3

Flaxborough, England (town), the Flaxborough Chronicles by Colin Watson (novels), pp.64–65, C2

Flemingtown, Arizona (town), *The X-Files* (TV), pp.18–19, C3

Flint City, Oklahoma (town), *The Outsider* by Stephen King (novel), pp.16–17, C3

Flintonbridge, England (town), *South Riding* by Winifred Holtby (novel), pp.64–65, C3

Floaroma Town, Japan (town), *Pokémon* (video games), pp.96–97, C4

Florença, Brazil (town), *Presença de Anita* (TV), pp.38–39, C4

Florence/Olive, Oklahoma (town), *Stop the Train* by Geraldine McCaughrean (novel), pp.16–17, C3

Flotsam Island, Gulf of Melange (fictional island), *Monkey Island* series (video games), pp.32–33, F2

Flower Hill, North Korea (town), *Squirrel and Hedgehog* (TV), pp.102–103, E3

Flowertown/Dalesbrook, Iowa (town), *Flowertown* by S.G. Redling (novel), pp.16–17, C5

Flying Dustman, Caribbean (wreck), *Captain Pugwash* (various), pp.32–33, F2

Foothills of the Headlands, Pepperland (fictional natural feature), *Yellow Submarine* (film), pp.126–127, B2

Footrot Flats, New Zealand (estate), *Footrot Flats* (comic), pp.108–109, F2

Forau Island, Channel Islands (island), *Devil's Rock* (film), pp.64–65, A2

Forbidden Mountain, Anandapur (fictional mountain), Expedition Everest (theme park), pp.78–79, C4

Forbidden Mountains, Indian Ocean (mountain range), *Dinotopia* (books/TV), pp.78–79, A2

Ford County, Mississippi (county), *A Time to Kill* (and other titles) by John Grisham (novels), pp.16–17, D3

Forest of the Lost Souls, The, Portugal/Spain (natural feature), *The Forest of the Lost Souls* (film), pp.44–45, A2

Fork Stoan, England (town), *Riddley Walker* by Russell Hoban (novel), pp.64–65, D1

Forsaken City, British Columbia (abandoned city), *Celeste* (video game), pp.26–27, B1

Fort Arid, Australia (building), *Beau Hunks* (film), pp.84–85, B5

Fort Carson, San Andreas (fictional town), *Grand Theft Auto* series (video games), pp.18–19, A4/B4

Fort Chicken, Illinois (town), *Cooties* (film), pp.16–17, D4

Fort Frazzle, Yukon (building), *Klondike Kat* (TV), pp.26–27, B2

Fort Grant, Oklahoma (town), *Hang 'Em High* (film), pp.16–17, C3

Fort Humboldt, Nevada (building), *Breakheart Pass* by Alistair MacLean (novel/film), pp.18–19, B4

Fort Klugman, Wyoming (building), *Sealab 2021* (TV), pp.16–17, A4

Fort Lincoln, Idaho (town), *The Man Who Fell in Love With the Moon* by Tom Spanbauer (novel), pp.18–19, C5

Fort McGurry, Yukon (town), *White Fang* by Jack London (novel), pp.26–27, B2

Fort Pastor, Wisconsin (building), *Dawn of the Dead* (2004) (film), pp.16–17, D5

Fort Providence, Arctic (natural feature), *The Voyages and Adventures of Captain Hatteras* by Jules Verne (novel), pp.26–27, C4

Fort Repose, Florida (town), *Alas, Babylon* by Pat Frank (novel), pp.14–15, B2

Fort Royal, Saskatchewan (town), *Canada* by Richard Ford (novel), pp.26–27, C1

Fort Simmer, Northwest Territories (town), *The Lesser Blessed* by Richard Van Camp (novel), pp.26–27, C2

Fort Zinderneuf, Algeria (building), *Beau Geste* by P.C. Wren (novel), pp.84–85, B5

Fortitude, Norway (town), *Fortitude* (TV), pp.56–57, A5

Fortress of Bakhine, Borduria (fictional building), *The Adventures of Tintin* by Hergé (various), pp.50–51, B1

Fortress of Solitude, The, Nunavut (building), DC Comics (various), pp.26–27, C4

Fortress of Tooth Decay, Yukon (building), *South Park* (TV), pp.26–27, B2

Fortune Islands *see* Isles of the Blessed

Forward, The, Arctic (wreck), *The Voyages and Adventures of Captain Hatteras* by Jules Verne (novel), pp.26–27, C3/C4

Four Idiots Village, China (village), *Marrow* by Yan Lianke (novel), pp.102–103, D2

Fourland Dukedom (fictional country), *Log Horizon* by Mamare Touno and Kazuhiro Hara (novels/anime), pp.96–97, B1/C1

Fowl Manor, Ireland (estate), Artemis Fowl series by Eoin Colfer (novels), pp.64–65, B2

Fowl Star, Russia (wreck), Artemis Fowl series by Eoin Colfer (novels), pp.50–51, B6

Fox River State Penitentiary, Illinois (building), *Prison Break* (TV), pp.16–17, D4

Foxcastle, Scotland (region), *Kingdom of Elfin* by Sylvia Townsend Warner (novel), pp.64–65, C4

Fraggle Rock lighthouse, England (building), *Fraggle Rock* (TV), pp.64–65, B1

Framley, England (town), *The Framley Examiner* (website), pp.64–65, D2

Franistan (fictional country), *I Love Lucy* (TV), pp.72–73, B3

Frantic City, New Jersey (city), *The Flintstones* (various), pp.14–15, C4

Franz Kafka International Airport, Czech Republic (building), *The Onion* (web series), pp.50–51, A3

Fraser's Ridge, North Carolina (natural feature), *Outlander* (novel/TV), pp.14–15, A3

Frazier, New Hampshire (town), *Doctor Sleep* by Stephen King (novel/film), pp.14–15, D6

Free Country, USA, Nebraska (town), *Homestar Runner* (web animation), pp.16–17, B4

Freedom County, Statesota (fictional county), *Moral Orel* (TV), pp.16–17, C3

Freedom State, Indian Ocean (island/nation), *The Illegal* by Lawrence Hill (novel), pp.78–79, B1/C1

Freehold, Alberta (city), Marvel Comics, Canada, pp.26–27, C1

Freeland, Georgia (city), *Black Lightning* (comic/TV), pp.14–15, B3

Freeland (fictional country), *Freiland* by Theodor Hertzka (novel), pp.84–85, C4/D4

Fremont (fictional state), *Space* by James A. Michener (novel), pp.16–17, B4/C4

French Landing, Wisconsin (town), *Black House* by Stephen King (novel), pp.16–17, C5

Frenchy Land, Glass Town Federation (fictional country), Brontë juvenilia, pp.84–85, B3

Freshitt, England (town), *Middlemarch* by George Eliot (novel), pp.64–65, C2

Friar, New Hampshire (town), *Yellow BrickRoad* (film), pp.14–15, D6

Fringe City, Virginia (city), *Son of the Mask* (film), pp.14–15, C4

Frisland, Atlantic Ocean (island, legend), pp.126–127, D1

Frogtown Hollow, Mississippi (town), *Emmet Otter's Jug-Band Christmas* (film), pp.16–17, D3

Frontera, Texas (town), *Lone Star* (film), pp.16–17, A2

Frostbite Falls, Minnesota (town), *The Adventures of Rocky and Bullwinkle* (TV), pp.16–17, C6

Frostbottom Falls, Yukon (town), *T von of the Yukon* (film), pp.26–27, B2

Fruitless Mountain, China (mountain), *Where the Mountain Meets the Moon* by Grace Lin (novel), pp.102–103, B3

Fulchester, England (city), *Viz* (comic), pp.64–65, C3

Fuller, Pennsylvania (town), *Unstoppable* (film), pp.14–15, B5

Fullmoon Island, Japan (island), *Pokémon* (video games), pp.96–97, C4

Fulton County, South Carolina (town), *American Gothic* (TV), pp.14–15, B3

Fundindelve, England (natural feature), *The Weirdstone of Brisingamen: A Tale of Alderley* by Alan Garner (novel), pp.64–65, C2/C3

Funiu Mountain, China (mountain), *The Explosion Chronicles* by Yan Lianke (novel), pp.102–103, D2

Furfuri Nagar, India (town), *Motu Patlu* (TV), pp.78–79, B3

Furinkan, Japan (town), *Ranma ½* by Rumiko Takahashi (manga/anime), pp.96–97, E1

Fury Road, the Wasteland (fictional road), *Mad Max Fury Road* (film), pp.108–109, D2

Fuschia City, Japan (city), *Pokémon* (video games), pp.96–97, C2

Futo City, Japan (city), *Kamen Rider W* (TV), pp.96–97, F1

Future Gadget Lab, Japan (building), *Steins;Gate* (video game/anime), pp.96–97, E1

Gaaldine, Pacific Ocean (island/nation), Brontë juvenilia, pp.90–91, F3

Gabriel's Bay, New Zealand (village), *Gabriel's Bay* by Catherine Robertson (novel), pp.108–109, F1

Gaea, Portugal (island), *The Arm of the Starfish* by Madeleine L'Engle (novel), pp.44–45, A2

Gaines River, Washington (river), *Astro City* (comic), pp.18–19, B6

Gaipajama, India (region), *The Adventures of Tintin* by Hergé (comics), pp.78–79, B5

Gakuju Sharaso Castle, Japan (building), *Batman Ninja* (film), pp.96–97, E1

Galakonur, Kazakhstan (city), *Jelle's Marble Runs* (web series), pp.72–73, D3

Galanos, Arizona (town), *Night of the Lepus* (film), pp.18–19, C2

Galaxy Island, Italy (island), *Our Man Flint* (film), pp.44–45, D1

Gallanach, Scotland (town), *The Crow Road* by Iain Banks (novel), pp.64–65, B4

Gallowshield, England (town), *When the Boat Comes in* (TV), pp.64–65, C3

Galt's Gulch, Colorado (town), *Atlas Shrugged* by Ayn Rand (novel), pp.18–19, D4

Galzburg, South Africa (region), *Metal Gear* (video game), pp.84–85, C2

GAMA Private Hospital, Japan (building), *Hitman* (video game), pp.96–97, C4

Gamulla, New South Wales (town), *Razorback* by Peter Brennan (novel/film), pp.108–109, E2

Gangaridia (fictional country), *The Princess of Babylon* by Voltaire (novel), pp.78–79, A2

Gaoyi County, China (region), *The Explosion Chronicles* by Yan Lianke (novel), pp.102–103, D2

Garbadale, Scotland (town), *The Steep Approach to Garbadale* by Iain Banks (novel), pp.64–65, B5

Garden of Eden Dance Hall, Scotland (town), *Father Malachy's Miracle* by Bruce Marshall (novel), pp.64–65, C4

Gargamele, San Escobar (fictional city, internet humour), pp.32–33, B2

Garkos, Island of (fictional island nation), *The Hurricanes* (TV), pp.44–45, E1

Garmouth, England (town), *The Machine Gunners* by Robert Westall (novel), pp.64–65, C3

Garradrimna, Ireland (village), *Valley of the Squinting Windows* by Brinsley MacNamara (novel), pp.64–65, B3

Garside Fell (natural feature), England (mountain), *Sleep No More* by L.T.C. Rolt (short stories), pp.64–65, C3

Garyville, Oklahoma (town), *Tex* by S.E. Hinton (novel), pp.16–17, C3

Gas Town, the Wasteland (fictional town), *Mad Max Fury Road* (film), pp.108–109, D2

Gateway City, California (city), DC Comics, pp.18–19, A4

Gateway to Olympus, Greece (building), Marvel Comics/Marvel Cinematic Universe, pp.44–45, E2

Gatlin, South Carolina (town), *Beautiful Creatures* by Kami Garcia and Margaret Stohl (novel/film), pp.14–15, B3

Gatlin, Nebraska (town), *Children of the Corn* by Stephen King (novel/film), pp.16–17, A4

Gaultshire, England (county), novels of Henry Williamson, pp.64–65, D2

Gavon, Scotland (village), *Gavon's Eve* by E.F. Benson (short story), pp.64–65, C5

Gavrik, Sweden (town), *Dark Pines* by Will Dean (novel), pp.56–57, B3

Gavrillac, France (village), *Scaramouche* by Rafael Sabatini (novel), pp.44–45, B3

GDI Institute for Liquid Tiberium, Northern Territory (building), *Command and Conquer* series (video games), pp.108–109, C3

Geheimhaven, Aegean Sea (island), *Raiders of the Lost Ark* (film), pp.44–45, E1

Gelden Island, Indonesia (island), *Biggles: The Adventure of the Golden Shirts* by W.E. Johns (novel), pp.90–91, B1

Geneva Beach, Michigan (town), *The Big Bounce* by Elmore Leonard (novel), pp.14–15, A5

Genosha (fictional island/nation), Marvel Comics (various), pp.84–85, D3

Genovia (fictional country/principality), *The Princess Diaries* by Meg Cabot (novel/film), pp.44–45, C2

Gensokyo, Japan (natural feature), *Touhou Project* series (video games), pp.96–97, C2

Geocore Power Plant/La Mancha Fissue, Spain (building), *Railroad Tycoon II: The Second Century* (video game), pp.44–45, B2

George the Volcano, France (natural feature), Volvic adverts (advertising), pp.44–45, C3

Geosenge Town, France (town), *Pokémon* (video games), pp.44–45, C3

Germaine, Oregon (town), *The Germaine Truth* (web fiction), pp.18–19, B5

German Ocean, The (fictional sea), *His Dark Materials* by Philip Pullman (various), pp.56–57, A1

Giancaldo, Italy (town), *Cinema Paradiso* (film), pp.44–45, D1

Giant Country, Scotland (country), *The BFG* by Roald Dahl (novel), pp.64–65, B5

Gibbeah, Jamaica (town), *John Crow's Devil* by Marlon James (novel), pp.32–33, F2

Gibbsville, Pennsylvania (town), works of John O'Hara, pp.14–15, C5

Gibraltar Bridge, Spain (building, various), pp.44–45, A2

Gideon, Western Australia (town), *Mystery Road* (TV), pp.108–109, B4

Gila Claw, Arizona (town), Percy Jackson series by Rick Riordan (novels/films), pp.18–19, C3

Gilas, Uzbekistan (town), *The Railway* by Hamid Ismailov (novel), pp.72–73, D4

Gillsby, Denmark (town), works of Steen Langstrup, pp.56–57, B2

Ginborak, Western Australia (town), *Shame* (film), pp.108–109, A3

Girasol, Brazil (town), *Araguaia* (TV), pp.38–39, C4

Girrasol, Brazil (town), *Estrela de Fogo* (TV), pp.38–39, C3

Gizhinsk, Russia (town), *The Midwich Cuckoos* by John Wyndham (novel), pp.102–103, F1

Glacia, North Pole (buried city), *Nelvana of the Northern Lights* (comics), pp.26–27, C4

Gladstonopolis, Britannula (fictional city), *The Fixed Period* by Anthony Trollope (novel), pp.120–121, C3

Glanbeigh, Ireland (town), *Young Skins* by Colin Barrett (novel), pp.64–65, A3

Glanguenstald, Luggnagg (fictional town), *Gulliver's Travels* by Jonathan Swift (novel), pp.96–97, D3

Glasburgh, Scotland (village), *Scooby Doo: Large Dragon at Large* (TV), pp.64–65, C4

Glass Town Confederacy, Glass Town Confederacy (fictional bloc), Brontë juvenilia, pp.84–85, A3

Glass, New South Wales (city), *Mirror's Edge* (video games), pp.108–109, D4

Glebeshire, England (county), novels of Hugh Walpole, pp.64–65, C1

136

Gledmouth, Scotland (town), novels of John Buchan, pp.64–65, C3

Glen Carry Castle, Scotland (building), *Captain Scarlet* (TV), pp.64–65, C4

Glen Falls, Ohio (town), *Hope & Faith* (TV), pp.14–15, B5

Glenarvon, Ireland (county), *The Fox of Glenarvon* (film), pp.64–65, A3

Glenbogle, Scotland (estate), *Monarch of the Glen* (TV), pp.64–65, B4

Glenbrook, Illinois (town), *Life Goes On* (TV), pp.16–17, D5

Glenbruff, Ireland (town), *You Have to Make Your Own Fun Around Here* by Frances Macken (novel), pp.64–65, A3

Glencove, Ireland (town), *Darby O'Gill and the Little People* (film), pp.64–65, A2

Glendarroch, Scotland (town), *Take the High Road* (TV), pp.64–65, B4

Glendonan, Scotland (town), novels of John Buchan, pp.64–65, C3

Glendrummie, Scotland (village), *The Night Spinner* by Abi Elphinstone (novel), pp.64–65, C4

Glenlawn, California (town), *Gimme a Break!* (TV), pp.18–19, A4

Glenoak, California (town), *7th Heaven* (TV), pp.18–19, A3

Glenraven (fictional country), Glenraven series by Marion Zimmer Bradley (novel), pp.44–45, C2

Glenroe, Ireland (village), *Glenroe* (TV), pp.64–65, B2

Glimmerdagg, Sweden (town), the Sune series by Anders Jacobsson and Sören Olsson (books), pp.56–57, B3

Glimmerdal, Norway (town), *Tonje Glimmerdal* by Maria Parr (novel), pp.56–57, A3

Glimmerhornet (mountain), *Tonje Glimmerdal* by Maria Parr (novel), pp.56–57, A3

Glogova, Hungary (village), *Saint Peter's Umbrella* by Kálmán Mikszáth (novel), pp.50–51, B3

Gloucester Island, Massachusetts (island), *The Russians Are Coming, the Russians Are Coming* (film), pp.14–15, D5

Glubbdubdrib, Luggnagg (fictional island), *Gulliver's Travels* by Jonathan Swift (novel), pp.96–97, D2

Glupov, Russia (town), *The History of a Town* by Mikhail Saltykov-Shchedrin (novel), pp.50–51, B6

Glyn Cagny, Ireland (natural feature), *Crock of Gold* by James Stephens (novel), pp.64–65, A2

Glynmawr, Wales (village), *Border Country* by Raymond Williams (novel), pp.64–65, C2

Gnu York, New York (city), DC Comics, pp.14–15, D1

Go-A-Way Mine, The, Yukon (natural feature), *Count Duckula* (TV), pp.26–27, B2

Goatswood, England (town), Severn Valley of the Cthulhu Mythos by Ramsey Campbell, pp.64–65, C2

Goblu, Ohio (town, map), pp.14–15, A5

Godric's Hollow, England (village), Harry Potter novels by J.K. Rowling (novels/films), pp.64–65, C1

Godsend Castle, England (building), *I Capture the Castle* by Dodie Smith (novel), pp.64–65, D2

Gokul, India (town), *Dream Girl* (film), pp.78–79, B4

Golden Cove, New Zealand (town), *A Madness of Sunshine* by Nalini Singh (novel), pp.108–109, F1

Golden Mount, Yukon (mountain), *The Golden Volcano* by Jules Verne (novel), pp.26–27, B2

Golden Pyramid of Ahm Shere, The, Ethiopia (building), *The Mummy Returns* (film), pp.84–85, D4

Golden River, The, China (river), *The Vagrants* by Yiyun Li (novel), pp.102–103, E4

Goldenrod City, Japan (city), *Pokémon* (video games), pp.96–97, D2

Goldville, Yukon (town), *Count Duckula* (TV), pp.26–27, B2

Golestan, Afghanistan (village), *Under the Persimmon Tree* by Suzanne Fisher Staples (novel), pp.72–73, E2

Golfo de Pollo, Caribbean (region), *Monkey Island* series (video games), pp.32–33, E3

Gondal, Pacific Ocean (fictional country), Brontë juvenalia, pp.90–91, A2

Gonunda, South Australia (town), *Sun on the Stubble* by Colin Thiele (novel/film), pp.108–109, D2

Goodwood, New South Wales (town), *Goodwood* by Holly Throsby (novel), pp.108–109, D2

Goon Docks, Oregon (town), *The Goonies* (film), pp.18–19, A6

Gopher Prairie, Minnesota (town), *Main Street* by Sinclair Lewis (novel), pp.16–17, C5

Gort Na Cloca, Ireland (village), *Crock of Gold* by James Stephens (novel), pp.64–65, A2

Gosford Park, England (estate), *Gosford Park* (film), pp.64–65, D2

Gost, Croatia (town), *The Hired Man* by Aminatta Forna (novel), pp.50–51, A2

Gotham City, New Jersey (city), DC Comics, pp.14–15, C4

Graabølle, Denmark (town), works of Johannes V. Jensen, pp.56–57, A2

Grace Junction, Arkansas (town), *Primary Colors* by Joe Klein (novel), pp.16–17, C3

Gracehope, Greenland (city), *First Light* by Rebecca Stead (novel), pp.26–27, E3

Gracey Manor, Louisiana (building), The Haunted Mansion (theme park), pp.16–17, D2

Gradec, Croatia (town), works of Ludwig Bauer, pp.50–51, A2

Grady, South Carolina (town), *Doc Hollywood* (film), pp.16–17, B3

Gran Seco City, Olifa (fictional city), *The Courts of the Morning* by John Buchan (novel), pp.38–39, B2

Gran Seco Railway, Olifa (fictional railway), *The Courts of the Morning* by John Buchan (novel), pp.38–39, B2

Granbois, Dominica (sugar plantation), *Wide Sargasso Sea* by Jean Rhys (novel), pp.32–33, F2

Grand Budapest Hotel, The, Zubrowka (fictional building), *The Grand Budapest Hotel* (film), pp.50–51, A4

Grand Fenwick (fictional country), *The Mouse that Roared* by Leonard Wibberley (novel), pp.44–45, C2

Grand Harbor, Michigan (town), *American Pie 2* (film), pp.14–15, A5

Grand Lake, The, Mediterranean Sea (sea), *Last Exile: Fam of the Silver Wing* (anime), pp.44–45, C1

Grand Senora Desert, San Andreas (fictional desert), *Grand Theft Auto* series (video game), pp.18–19, B3

Grandview, Illinois (town), *Grandview, USA* (film), pp.16–17, D4

Grantham, Ontario (town), Benny Cooperman series by Howard Engel, pp.26–27, A4

Grantleigh, England (town), *To The Manor Born* (TV), pp.64–65, C1

Grantville, West Virginia (town), 1632/ Ring of Fire series by Eric Flint, pp.14–15, B4

Grantville, Germany (town), 1632 series by Eric Flint, pp.44–45, D3

Granville, Kansas (town), DC Comics, pp.16–17, B4

Grapeseed, San Andreas (fictional town), *Grand Theft Auto* series (video game), pp.18–19, B3

Grapplin, Ireland (town), *Flanagan's Wake* (play), pp.64–65, A3

Grass River, Canada (river), works of Elizabeth Marshall Thomas, pp.102–103, E1/F1

Graustark (fictional country), *Graustark* by G.B. McCutcheon (novel), pp.50–51, B3/C3

Gravity Falls, Oregon (town), *Gravity Falls* (TV), pp.18–19, A5

Great Barley, England (village), *Minnow on the Say* by Philippa Pearce (novel), pp.64–65, D2

Great Canyon, The, Arizona (natural feature), *Mobile Suit Gundam* (anime), pp.18–19, C3

Great Ducky Mountains, The (mountain chain), *DuckTales* (TV), pp.26–27, B1/B2

Great Ireland, Atlantic Ocean (island, legend), pp.126–127, B3

Great Rapid, United Federation (fictional city), *Papers, Please* (video game), pp.50–51, D2

Great Southern Pelagic Ocean, Pacific Ocean (sea), *Nation* by Terry Pratchett (novel), pp.120–121, D1/E1

Great Todday and Little Todday, Scotland (islands), *Whisky Galore!* by Angus MacPhail (novel/film), pp.64–65, A4/A5/B4/B5

Great White, The, Pacific Ocean (desert/sea), *Mad Max* (video game), pp.108–109, E3

Great-Fish Island, Persian Gulf (island/fish), *Sinbad* (short story), pp.72–73, D1

Greater San Miguel (fictional country), *Gomer Pyle, U.S.M.C.* (TV), pp.38–39, C3

Green Inferno, The, Brazil/Venezuela (natural feature), *Cannibal Holocaust* (film), pp.38–39, B5

Green Knowe, England (building), Green Knowe series by Lucy M. Boston, pp.64–65, D2

Green Lake, British Columbia (lake), *Oakwood* (video game), pp.26–27, B1

Green Prairie (city), *Tomorrow!* by Philip Wylie (novel), pp.16–17, C5

Green Sea (fictional sea), *ARMA 2* (video game), pp.50–51, A4

Green Town, Illinois (town), *Dandelion Wine* by Ray Bradbury (novel), pp.14–15, B4

Greenborough, England (town), DI Nikki Galena books by Joy Ellis, pp.64–65, D2

Greenbow, Alabama (town), *Forrest Gump* by Winston Groom (novel/film), pp.14–15, A2

Greendale, Colorado (town), *Community* (TV), pp.16–17, A4

Greendale (town), *Riverdale/The Chilling Adventures of Sabrina* (TV), pp.14–15, D5

Greendale, England (village), *Postman Pat* (TV), pp.64–65, C3

Greenpatch, Queensland (town), *Blinky Bill* (various), pp.108–109, D3

Greenville, Brazil (TV), *A Indomada* (TV), pp.38–39, D4

Greenvoe, Scotland (town), *Greenvoe, George Mackay Brown* (novel), pp.64–65, C3

Grestin (East and West), Arstotzka/Kolechia (fictional country), *Papers, Please* (video game), pp.72–73, C3

Greyfriars School, England (building), *Billy Bunter* (TV), pp.64–65, D2

Griffin Rock, Maine (town/island), *Transformers: Rescue Bots* (TV), pp.14–15, D6

Gritzmacher Springs, Kansas (town), works of Sinclair Lewis, pp.16–17, C4

Grizzlies, The (mountain range), *Red Dead Redemption* series (video game), pp.18–19, D4

Grizzly Gulch, Arizona (town), Big Thunder Mountain Railroad (theme parks), pp.18–19, C3

Groggy Head, Cuba (natural feature), *The Pirates! Band of Misfits!* (film), pp.32–33, D3

Grönköping, Sweden (town), *Grönköpings Veckoblad* (newspaper), pp.56–57, C3

Groosham Grange, England (building), Groosham Grange books by Anthony Horowitz (novels), pp.64–65, D2

Grover's Bend, Kansas (town), *Critters* (film), pp.16–17, C3

Grover's Corner, New Hampshire (town), *Our Town* by Thornton Wilder (play), pp.14–15, D4

Grumbley, Wales (town), *Ivor the Engine* (TV), pp.64–65, C2

Guacamole, San Escobar (fictional city, internet humour), pp.50–51, A2

Guampu, Honduras (village), *The Mosquito Coast* by Paul Theroux (novel), pp.26–27, A4

Guarma, Cuba (island), *Red Dead Redemption II* (video game), pp.32–33, E2

Gudetown, Scotland (town), *The Provost* by John Galt (novel), pp.64–65, B4

Gul Daman, Afghanistan (village), *A Thousand Splendid Suns* by Khaled Hosseini (novel), pp.72–73, D2

Gulf of Benzheen, Gulf of Oman (sea), *Transformers* and *GI Joe* (comics), pp.72–73, D2

Gulf of Melange, Caribbean (region), *Monkey Island* series (video games), pp.32–33, F2

Gulfhaven, Florida (town), *Cougar Town* (TV), pp.14–15, B1

Gulistan, Pakistan (village), works of Qaisra Shahraz, pp.78–79, A4

Gullah Gullah, South Carolina (island), *Gullah Gullah Island* (TV), pp.14–15, B2/B3

Gulmira, Afghanistan (town), Marvel Cinematic Universe (films), pp.72–73, D2

Gunflint, Minnesota (town), *Wintering* by Peter Geye (novel), pp.16–17, C6

Gungee, Queensland (town), *A Descant for Gossips* by Thea Astley (novel), pp.108–109, E3

Gungellan, New South Wales (town), *McLeod's Daughters* (TV), pp.108–109, D2

Gunnerkrigg Court, Scotland (building), *Gunnerkrigg Court* by Thomas Siddell (comic), pp.64–65, C3

Guram, Pakistan (town), *North West Frontier* (film), pp.78–79, B5

Gurat, Indian Ocean (island/city), *Gunnm/Battle Angel Alita* (manga/anime/film), pp.90–91, A2

Gurówka, Poland (town), *Poklisie/Aftermath* (film), pp.50–51, B4

Gustav Graves's Ice Palace, Iceland (building), *James Bond: Die Another Day* (film), pp.56–57, A6

Gusteau's Restaurant, Paris, France (building), *Ratatouille* (film), pp.44–45, E3

Habitat D.H.-8, Pacific Ocean (submerged building), *Sphere* by Michael Crichton (novel/film), pp.120–121, A4

Hachmannsfeld, Germany (town), *Stenkelfeld* (radio), pp.44–45, D4

Haddonfield, Illinois (town), *Halloween* (films), pp.16–17, B4

Hadleyburg, Pennsylvania (town), *The Man Who Corrupted Hadleyburg/Gung Ho* (short story/film), pp.14–15, B4

Hagel, Unaudited Arab Emirates (fictional city), *San Sombrèro* (book), pp.72–73, C1

Haggard, Ireland (town), Skulduggery Pleasant series by Derek Landry (novels), pp.64–65, B3

Haiwan, China (city), *Strangers 6* (TV), pp.102–103, D1

Hajdúbékes, Hungary (town), *Never, Again* by Endre Farkas (novel), pp.50–51, B3

Hakkebakkeskogen, Norway (town), *Climbing Mouse and the Other Animals in the Hunchback Wood* by Thorbjørn Egner, pp.56–57, A3

Hakuna Matata, Tanzania (natural feature), *The Lion King/The Lion King 1½* (film), pp.84–85, D3

Haleakaloha, Pacific Ocean (island), *Donovan's Reef* (film), pp.120–121, D2

Halimunda, Indonesia (town), *Beauty is a Wound* by Eka Kurniawan (novel), pp.90–91, B1

Hallstabro, Sweden (town), *About Stig Petré's Secret* (TV), pp.56–57, C3

Halwan (fictional country), Marvel Comics, pp.84–85, B5

Halwapur, Pakistan (town), *Burka Avenger* (TV), pp.78–79, A4

Ham Rock, Atlantic Ocean (island), *The Survivors of the Chancellor* by Jules Verne (novel), pp.126–127, B3

Ham Sandwich Islands, The, South Carolina (island chain), *The Pirates! Band of Misfits!* (film), pp.14–15, C2

Ham, England (town), *The Book of Dave* by Will Self (novel), pp.64–65, D2

Hammer Bay/Black Roma, Genosha (fictional city), Marvel Comics, pp.84–85, D3

Hammond, North Carolina (town), *The Campaign* (film), pp.14–15, A4

Hamont, Ontario (town), *Roadside Picnic* by Arkady and Boris Strugatsky (novel), pp.26–27, E1

Hampden, Newfoundland (town), *The Fortunate Brother* by Donna Morrissey (novel), pp.26–27, F2

Hamunaptra, Egypt (town), *The Mummy* (film), pp.84–85, C5

Hanamura, Japan (town), *Overwatch* (video game), pp.96–97, D4

Hanbridge, England (town), the Five Towns novels by Arnold Bennett, pp.64–65, C2

Handong Province, China (region), *In the Name of the People* (TV), pp.102–103, D2

Hankston, Idaho (town), *A Home of Our Own* (film), pp.18–19, C2

Hanover, Nebraska (town), *O Pioneers!* by Willa Cather (novel/film), pp.16–17, B4

Hanratty, Ontario (town), works of Alice Munro, pp.26–27, A4

Hantu Port, Singapore (city), *Hitman 2* (video game), pp.90–91, D3

Hanu, Hawaii (town), *Anywhere But Paradise* by Anne Bustard (novel), pp.18–19, C1

Hanuda, Japan (town), *Siren/Forbidden Siren* (video game), pp.96–97, C3

Happy Humans Town, South Australia (megacity), *Home* (film), pp.108–109, C2

Hara, India (city), *The Deptford Mice* series by Robin Jarvis (books), pp.78–79, B4

Harbor City, Taiwan (city), *Black & White* (TV), pp.102–103, D1

Harchester, England (town), *Dream Team* (TV), pp.64–65, C2

Harda's Head, England (natural feature), *South Riding* by Winifred Holtby (novel), pp.64–65, D3

Hardrascliffe, England (town), *South Riding* by Winifred Holtby (novel), pp.64–65, D3

Hargrave, Kentucky (town), works of Wendell Berry, pp.14–15, A4

Harmont Zone, The, Ontario (?, region), *Roadside Picnic* by Arkady and Boris Strugatsky (novel), pp.26–27, D1/E1

Harmonville, Montana (town), *Open Range* (film), pp.18–19, C6

Harmony, San Andreas (fictional town), *Grand Theft Auto* series (video games), pp.18–19, B3

Harmony, Maine (town), *Passions* (TV), pp.14–15, D5

Harran, Turkey (city), *Dying Light* (video game), pp.72–73, B3

Hartfield, Iowa (town), *Happy Land* (film), pp.16–17, C5

Hartley, England (town), *Juliet Bravo* (TV), pp.64–65, C2

Hartsfield's Landing, New Hampshire (town), *The West Wing* (TV), pp.14–15, D6

Harvardville (city), *Resident Evil* series (video games/films), pp.18–19, B6

Hasch El Hemm, Khemed (fictional building), *The Adventures of Tintin* by Hergé (comics), pp.72–73, D2

Haserabad, Pakistan (town), *North West Frontier* (film), pp.78–79, B5

Hasetsu, Japan (town), *Yuri!!! on Ice* (anime), pp.96–97, A1

Hassett Hills, England (natural feature), *The Archers* (radio), pp.64–65, C2

Hastinapura, India (village), *Dancing to the Flute* by Manisha Jolie Amin (novel), pp.78–79, B4

Hat Island, Atlantic Ocean (island), *Villanos* (TV), pp.32–33, B4

Hatley, England (town), *Oh Doctor Beeching!* (TV), pp.64–65, C2

Hau Phat, Vietnam (town), *Apocalypse Now* (film), pp.90–91, B4

Hau'oli City, Hawaii (city), *Pokémon* (video games), pp.18–19, C1

Haunted Island (fictional island), *A Haunted Island* by Algernon Blackwood (novel), pp.26–27, D1

Hav (fictional city/state), *Last Letters From Hav* by Jan Morris (novel), pp.72–73, B2/B3

Haven Bay, Victoria (town), *The Henderson Kids* (TV), pp.108–109, D1

Haven, Maine (town), *The Tommyknockers* by Stephen King (various), pp.14–15, D6

Haven, Taiwan (town), *The Man With the Compound Eyes* by Wu Ming-Yi (novel), pp.102–103, D1

Hawkins, Indiana (town), *Stranger Things* (TV), pp.14–15, A4

Hawley Bank (building or estate), England (village), *Sleep No More* by L.T.C. Rolt (short stories), pp.64–65, C2

Hawthorne, Nebraska (town), *Nebraska* (film), pp.16–17, B4

Hayslope, England (town), *Adam Bede* by George Eliot (novel), pp.64–65, C2

Hazzard County, Georgia (county), *The Dukes of Hazzard* (TV), pp.14–15, B3

Headlong Hall, Wales (estate), *Headlong Hall* by Thomas Love Peacock (novella), pp.64–65, C2

Heahea City, Hawaii (town), *Pokémon* (video games), pp.18–19, D1

Hearthome City, Japan (city), *Pokémon* (video games), pp.96–97, D4

Heatherfield, Connecticut (city), *W.I.T.C.H.* (TV), pp.14–15, C5

Hedeby, Sweden (island/town), the Millennium Trilogy by Stig Larsson (novels), pp.56–57, C3

Hedestad, Sweden (town), the Millennium Trilogy by Stig Larsson (novels), pp.56–57, C3

Hedonikka, Themyscira (fictional island), *Harley Quinn* (TV), pp.44–45, F1

Heer, Pakistan (town), *The Blind Man's Garden* by Nadeem Aslam (novel), pp.78–79, B5

Hegeman, New York (town), Marvel Comics, pp.14–15, C5

Heikant, Netherlands (village), Baron 1898 (theme park), pp.44–45, C4

Heimlich County, Texas (county), *King of the Hill* (TV), pp.16–17, B3

Hektary, Poland (village), *Swallowing Mercury* by Wioletta Greg (novel), pp.50–51, B3

Hell Hall, England (estate), *101 Dalmations* by Dodi Smith (novel), pp.64–65, D2

Helm, Poland (city, Jewish folklore), pp.50–51, B3

Helmajistan (fictional country), *Full Metal Panic!* (books), pp.72–73, D2

Helmsbergville, Ukraine (town), *Hershel and the Hanukkah Goblins* by Eric Kimmel (book), pp.50–51, B3

Helsingfort, Finland (city), *MacTrump* by Ian Doescher and Jacopo Della Quercia (book), pp.56–57, D3

Helstonleigh, England (city), novels of Ellen Wood, pp.64–65, C2

Helvetia (fictional country), *Sound of the Sky* (anime), pp.96–97, A1/B1

Helwater, England (estate), Outlander novels by Diana Gabaldon (novels/TV), pp.64–65, C3

Hemingford Home, Nebraska (town), *Children of the Corn* by Stephen King (novel/film), pp.16–17, A4

Henbane River, Montana (river), *Far Cry 5* (video games), pp.18–19, C6

Hengasch, Germany (town), *Mord mit Aussicht (Murder with a View)* (TV), pp.44–45, C3

Hengsha, China (city), *Deus Ex: Human Revolution* (video game), pp.102–103, D2

Henry, Northern Territory (town), *Sweet Country* (film), pp.108–109, C3

Hensonville, North Carolina (town), *Muppets from Space* (film), pp.14–15, C3

Heorot, Denmark (building), *Beowulf* (poem), pp.56–57, B1

Heringsmoor, Germany (town), *Stenkelfeld* (radio), pp.44–45, D4

Herkleston, Maryland (town), *Craig of the Creek* (TV), pp.14–15, C4

Hermaphrodite Island, Portugal (floating island), *Les Hermaphrodites* by Thomas Artus (poem), pp.44–45, A4

Heron Sea, The, Alaska (sea), *DuckTales* (TV), pp.18–19, A1

Herzoslovakia (fictional country), novels of Agatha Christie, pp.50–51, A2

Hesadi, India (village), works of Mahasweta Devi, pp.78–79, C4

Hetherington, Victoria (region), *Blue Heelers* (TV), pp.108–109, D2

Hickory, California (building), *Mobile Suit Gundam* (anime), pp.18–19, A3

Hicksville, New Zealand (town), *Hicksville* by Dylan Horrocks (comic), pp.108–109, F2

Hieno Village, Japan (village), *Shikoku* (film), pp.96–97, B1/C1

High Saffron, Wales (town), *Shades of Grey* by Jasper Fforde (novels), pp.64–65, C2

Highbee, England (town), *Sleep No More* by L.T.C. Rolt (short stories), pp.64–65, C2

Highbury, England (town), *Emma* by Jane Austen (novel), pp.64–65, D2

Highland, Texas (town), *Beavis and Butthead* (TV), pp.16–17, A3

Higuerota and the Higuerota Range, Costaguana (fictional mountain), *Nostromo* by Joseph Conrad (novel), pp.38–39, A4

Hikarizaka, Japan (city), *Clannad* (manga/anime), pp.96–97, C2

Hildaland, Scotland (unmappable land, Orkney folklore), pp.64–65, C5

Hili-Li (city/island), *A Strange Discovery* by Charles Romyn Dake (novel), pp.114–115, C2

Hill House, Massachusetts (building), *The Haunting of Hill House* by Shirley Jackson and The Haunting (various), pp.14–15, C5

137

Hill of Durcha, Scotland (natural feature, traditional fairytale), pp.64–65, B5/C5

Hill Valley, California (town), *Back to the Future* (films), pp.18–19, A4

Hilldale, Iowa (town), *The Donna Reed Show* (TV), pp.16–17, C4

Hillwood, Washington (city), *Hey Arnold!* (TV), pp.18–19, A6

Himelian Mountains, Tibet (mountain range), Conan novels of Robert E. Howard, pp.102–103, A5

Himelian Mountains, Nepal (mountain range), Conan novels of Robert E. Howard, pp.78–79, C4/C5

Hinamizawa, Japan (town), *Higurashi: When They Cry* (manga/anime), pp.96–97, E1

Hinata, Japan (town), *Love Hina* by Ken Akamatsu (manga/anime), pp.96–97, C2

Hindi Ocean, Indian Ocean (ocean), *2000 AD* (comics), pp.78–79, C2/D2

Hinkley Hills, Iowa (town), *The 'Burbs* (film), pp.16–17, C4

Hinomoto (fictional country), *Kabaneri of the Iron Fortress* (anime), pp.96–97, B2

Hippolyte, Queensland (wreck), *The Black Bell Buoy* by Rupert Chesterton (short story), pp.108–109, D4

Hirumi City, Japan (city), *Yuuyami Doori Tankentai* (video game), pp.96–97, E1

Hispanola (fictional island), *Hurricanes* (TV), pp.32–33, E2

HMHS *Fort James*/USS *Tiger Shark*, Atlantic Ocean (wrecks), *Below* (film), pp.44–45, B3

HMP Slade, England (building), *Porridge* (TV), pp.64–65, C3

HMS *Devonshire*, China (wreck), *James Bond: Tomorrow Never Dies* (film), pp.102–103, D1

HMS *Endeavour*, Caribbean (wreck), *Pirates of the Caribbean* (various), pp.32–33, F2

HMS *Hecate*, Atlantic Ocean (wreck), *The Enemy Below* by Denys Rayner (novel/film), pp.126–127, A3

HMS *Interceptor*, Caribbean (wreck), *Pirates of the Caribbean* (various), pp.32–33, F2

HMS *Scorpion*, Russia (wreck), *Ghostboat* (TV), pp.50–51, B4

HMS *Thunder Child*, England (wreck), *War of the Worlds* by H.G. Wells (novel), pp.64–65, D2

HMS *Viking*, Atlantic Ocean (wreck), *Timewreck Titanic* by Rhys B. Davies (novel), pp.126–127, B4

Hobbs End, England (town), *Quatermass and the Pit* (film), pp.64–65, D2

Hobeika (fictional country), *Day of the Falcon* (film), pp.72–73, C1

Höcklage, Germany (town), *Stenkelfeld* (radio), pp.44–45, D4

Hoddick, Oceana (fictional town), *The Strong Man* by H.R.F. Keating (novel), pp.126–127, A3

Hoenn, Japan (region), *Pokémon* (video games), pp.96–97, A1

Hofbau, Ruritania (fictional town), *The Prisoner of Zelda* by Anthony Hope (novel), pp.50–51, A4

Hogan County, Wisconsin (county), *Picket Fences* (TV), pp.16–17, C3

Hogsmeade, Scotland (unmappable village), Harry Potter novels by J.K. Rowling (novels/films), pp.64–65, C4

Hogwarts, Scotland (unmappable building), Harry Potter novels by J.K. Rowling (novels/films), pp.64–65, C4

Hohman, Indiana (town), *A Christmas Story* by Jean Shepherd (story/film), pp.14–15, A4

Hoikan, Finland (town), *Mesolat* (TV), pp.56–57, D4

Hokuto, Japan (region), *Kamen Rider Build* (TV), pp.96–97, C4

Holby, England (city), *Holby City* (TV), pp.64–65, C2

Holden County, Michigan (county), *The Big Bounce* by Elmore Leonard (novel), pp.14–15, A5

Holden, Tennessee (town), *11.22.63* (TV), pp.14–15, A5

Holdwick Park Refinery, England (building), *Look Around You* (TV), pp.64–65, C2

Holihaven, England (town), *Ringing the Changes* by Robert Aickman (short story), pp.64–65, D2

Hollyoaks, England (town), *Hollyoaks* (TV), pp.64–65, C2

Hollyrock, California (city), *The Flintstones* (various), pp.18–19, A2/A3

Holstenwall, Germany (village), *The Cabinet of Dr Caligari* (film), pp.44–45, D4

Holt, Colorado (town), works of Kent Haruf, pp.16–17, A4

Holy Empire of Westelande (fictional country), *Log Horizon* by Mamare Touno and Kazuhiro Hara (novels/anime), pp.96–97, D2

Hondo City, Japan (city), *2000 AD* (comics), pp.96–97, D3

Hong Kong Shatterdome, China (building), *Pacific Rim* (film), pp.102–103, D4

Honnō City, Japan (city/island), *Kill la Kill* (anime), pp.96–97, F1

Honnōji Academy, Japan (building), *Kill la Kill* (anime), pp.96–97, F1

Honolurock, Hawaii (city), *The Jetsons Meet the Flintstones* (film), pp.18–19, C1

Honoré, Saint Marie (fictional town), *Death in Paradise* (TV), pp.32–33, F2

Hood County, Washington (county), *Astro City* (comic), pp.18–19, B6

Hookland, England (county), *Hookland* (website), pp.64–65, D1

Hooterville, Kentucky (town), *Petticoat Junction/Green Acres* (TV), pp.14–15, A3

Hope County, Montana (county), *Far Cry 5/Far Cry New Dawn* (video game), pp.18–19, C6/D6

Hope Island, Bahamas (island), *Captain Planet and the Planeteers* (TV), pp.32–33, E3

Hope Springs, Scotland (town), *Hope Springs* (TV), pp.64–65, C4

Hope, South Dakota (town), *Hitman: Absolution* (video game), pp.16–17, A5

Hope, Washington (town), *Rambo: First Blood* (film), pp.18–19, A6

Hopeton, Nova Scotia (town), *Anne of Green Gables* by Lucy Maud Montgomery (novel), pp.26–27, F1

Horizon Islands, Pacific Ocean (island), *ARMA 3* (video game), pp.120–121, C3

Horneros, Colombia (town), *Bella Calamidades* (TV), pp.38–39, A5/B5

Horny Boy, England (wreck), *Riddley Walker* by Russell Hoban (novel), pp.64–65, D2

Horomai Line, Japan (railway), *Poppoya* (film), pp.96–97, C4

Horomai, Japan (town), *Poppoya* (film), pp.96–97, C4

Hoshio Private Girls Academy, Japan (building), *Slow Start* by Yuiko Tokumi (manga/anime), pp.96–97, E1

Hosu, Japan (city), *My Hero Academia* by Kōhei Horikoshi (manga/anime), pp.96–97, E1

Hotel Adriano, Croatia (building), *Porco Rosso* (anime), pp.50–51, A2

Hotel Transylvania, Romania (building), *Hotel Transylvania* (film), pp.50–51, B2

Hotta-Watta-Bottle, Land of the Stinkas (fictional mountain), *Captain Pugwash* (various), pp.32–33, C2

Hotten, England (town), *Emmerdale* (TV), pp.64–65, C3

Hou-Ming, China (city), *Mandate of Heaven* by Tim Murgatroyd (novel), pp.102–103, B2

Houlton, England (village), *It Shouldn't Happen to a Vet* by James Herriot (novel), pp.64–65, C3

Houria, Syria (town), *Freedom Hospital* by Hamid Sulaiman (graphic novel), pp.72–73, B2

Houston (fictional state), *Southern Victory* by Harry Turtledove (novels), pp.16–17, A3/B3

Houstone, Texas (city), *The Flintstones* (various), pp.16–17, C2

Houyhnhnms Land (fictional island/ nation), *Gulliver's Travels* by Jonathan Swift (novel), pp.108–109, B1

Howards End, England (estate), *Howards End* by E.M. Forster (novel), pp.64–65, D2

Howduyustan (fictional country), *Uncle Scrooge* (comics), pp.78–79, B5

Howlett Estate, Alberta (building), Marvel Comics, pp.26–27, C1

Howling, England (village), *Cold Comfort Farm* by Stella Gibbons (novel), pp.64–65, D1

Hsinpei, Taiwan (town), *Log Horizon* by Mamare Touno and Kazuhiro Hara (novels/anime), pp.102–103, B4

Huaishi, China (city), *Party Members* by Arthur Meursault (novel), pp.102–103, D2

Hub City, Illinois (city), DC Comics, pp.16–17, D4

Hub, The, California (city), *Fallout 1* (video game), pp.18–19, B3

Hubie's Adélie Penguin Colony/Pebble Beach (colony), *The Pebble and the Penguin* (film), pp.114–115, D1

Huddersgate, England (town), Stanley Bagshaw series by Bob Wilson (novel), pp.64–65, C3

Hudson, Alberta (town), *Heartland* (TV), pp.26–27, C2

Huella Islands, French Guiana (islands), Hardy Boys novels by Franklin W. Dixon and David L. Robbins, pp.38–39, C5

Huerta, California (town), *Love and Rockets* by Los Bros Hernandez (comic), pp.18–19, A3

Hunluen, China (city), *Jelle's Marble Runs* (web series), pp.102–103, D1

Huntercombe, England (village), *The Dark is Rising* by Susan Cooper (novels), pp.64–65, C3

Hurley's Crossing, Nevada (town), *Transformers* (comic), pp.18–19, B4

Hurramabad, Tajikistan (city), *Hurramabad: A Novel of Facets* by Andrei Volos (novel), pp.72–73, D3

Hurtfew Abbey, England (building), *Jonathan Strange and Mr Norrell* by Susanna Clarke (novel/film), pp.64–65, C3

Hy-Brasil, Atlantic Ocean (island, legend), pp.126–127, D5

Hy-yi-yi, Pacific Ocean (island chain), Legend of the Rhinogradentia (faked information), pp.120–121, C3

Hyakkaou Private Academy, Japan (building), *Kakegurui* by Homura Kawamoto and Tōru Naomura (manga/ anime), pp.96–97, E1

Hyatt County, North Carolina (county), *The Descent* (film), pp.14–15, B3

Hydra Headquarters, Austria (building), Marvel Cinematic Universe (films), pp.44–45, C3

Hynen, Chinaland (fictional island/ region/town), *Little Ninja Brothers* (video game), pp.102–103, C1/D1

Hyperborea, Russia (Arctic waste, Greek mythology), pp.102–103, F1/F2

Hyperborea, Russia (Arctic waste), Conan novels of Robert E. Howard, pp.56–57, D3

Iastrae Castle, Ireland (building), *The Whistling Room* by William Hope Hodgson (short story), pp.64–65, A3

Ibansk, Russia (city/state), *Yawning Heights* by Aleksandr Zinoviev (novel), pp.50–51, A6

Ice Station Norway, Norway (building), *Wolfenstein* series (video games), pp.56–57, A5

Ice Station Zebra, Arctic (building), *Ice Station Zebra* by Alistair MacLean (novel/film), pp.26–27, D2

Idoming (fictional state), *Pale Fire* by Vladimir Nabokov (novel), pp.18–19, D5

Igloo Village (village), *Club Penguin* (video game), pp.114–115, D2

Igrivo, Bulgaria (village), *Tony Pateto* by Anani Borisov (web comic), pp.50–51, B2

Iguedo, Nigeria (village), *Things Fall Apart* by Chinua Achebe (novel), pp.84–85, B4

Iki Town, Hawaii (town), *Pokémon* (video games), pp.18–19, C1

Ilha de Boiporã, Brazil (island/town), *Segundo Sol* (TV), pp.38–39, D4

Ilium, New York (town), works of Kurt Vonnegut, pp.14–15, C5

Ilm, Austria (village), *Vier Frauen und ein Todesfall* (Four Women and one Death) (TV), pp.44–45, D3

Ilmorog, Kenya (village), *Petals of Blood* by Ngũgĩ wa Thiong'o (novel), pp.84–85, D3

Ilvermorny School of Witchcraft and Wizardry, Massachusetts (building), Harry Potter/Wizarding World by J.K. Rowling (various), pp.14–15, C5

Imboca, Spain (village), *Dagon* (film), pp.44–45, A3

Impor (fictional country), *Papers, Please* (video game), pp.50–51, A6

Impossible Island, Atlantic Ocean (island), *Once, Two Islands* by Dawn Garisch (novel), pp.126–127, D1

Inaba, Japan (town), *Persona* series (video games), pp.96–97, C2

Inchgrundle, England (town), *The Shadow Keeper* by Eli Elphinstone (novel), pp.64–65, B4

Indian River, Ontario (town), *The Forest Rangers* (TV), pp.26–27, A4

Indianrockolis, Indiana (city), *The Flintstones* (various), pp.14–15, A4

Indocarr City, Indocarr (fictional city), *Mile 22* (film), pp.90–91, B1

Indocarr (fictional country), *Mile 22* (film), pp.90–91, B1/C1

Indocine (fictional country), *Nuclear Strike* (video game), pp.90–91, B4

Indriana, Indiana (state), *Mac Trump* by Ian Doescher and Jacopo Della Quercia (book), pp.14–15, A4

Infant Island, Pacific Ocean (island), *Godzilla* series (films), pp.120–121, A4

Inferno, The, Oregon (wreck), *The Goonies* (film), pp.18–19, A6

Infinite Fortress, The, Japan (building), *Get Backers* by Yuya Aoki and Rando Ayamine (manga/anime), pp.96–97, E1

Ingledale, England (village), *Postman Pat* (TV), pp.64–65, C3

Inisfree, Ireland (town), *The Quiet Man* (film), pp.64–65, A3

Inju, South Korea (city), *Signal* (TV), pp.102–103, B4

Inner Qwghlen, Scotland (island), *The Baroque Cycle & Cryptonomicon* by Neal Stephenson (novels), pp.64–65, A5

Innsmouth, Massachusetts (town), Cthulhu Mythos/H.P. Lovecraft (various), pp.14–15, C5

Institute for Extraterrestrial Cultures, Ontario (building), *Roadside Picnic* by Arkady and Boris Strugatsky (novel), pp.26–27, E1

Interzone, Morocco (region), *Naked Lunch* by William S. Burroughs (novel), pp.84–85, A5

Inverfinnan, Scotland (town), *Hurricanes* (TV), pp.64–65, B4

Inverkerran, Scotland (town), *The Maggie* (film), pp.64–65, B4

Inverlochan, Scotland (town, noted model railway), pp.64–65, B4

Inverness, New South Wales (town), *A Place to Call Home* (TV), pp.108–109, A4

Ipeiros Mountains, Greece (mountain range), Marvel Comics/Marvel Cinematic Universe (comics/films), pp.44–45, E1

Irakistan (fictional country), *Broforce* (video game), pp.72–73, C2

Iranistan (fictional country), Conan novels of Robert E. Howard, pp.72–73, C2

Iraya, Philippines (village), *Fish-Hair Woman* by Merlinda Bobis (novel), pp.90–91, C3

Ircania (fictional country), *If on a Winter's Night a Traveller* by Italo Calvino (novel), pp.50–51, C4

Iron Giant (remains), The (being), *The Iron Giant* (film), pp.56–57, A6

Iron Island, Japan (island), *Pokémon* (video games), pp.96–97, C4

Irontown, Japan (town), *Princess Mononoke* (anime), pp.96–97, D3

Isabels, The, Costaguana (fictional islands/lighthouse), *Nostromo* by Joseph Conrad (novel), pp.38–39, A4

Isenstadt, Germany (city), *Wolfenstein* series (video games), pp.44–45, D3

Ishmaelia (fictional country), *Scoop* by Evelyn Waugh (novel), pp.84–85, D4

Ishtar (fictional country), *Ishtar* (film), pp.84–85, A5

Isla Cangrejos, Caribbean (island), *Pirates of the Caribbean* (various), pp.32–33, E2

Isla Cruces, Caribbean (island), *Pirates of the Caribbean* (various), pp.32–33, F2

Isla de Avaricia, Caribbean (island), *Pirates of the Caribbean* (various), pp.32–33, E2

Isla de la Fortaleza, Venezuela (island), *Mercenaries 2: World in Flames* (video game), pp.38–39, B6

Isla de Los Organos, Cuba (island), *James Bond: Die Another Day* (film), pp.32–33, D3

Isla de Mara, Mexico (island), *Godzilla: King of the Monsters* (film), pp.32–33, C2

Isla de Muerta, Caribbean (island), *Pirates of the Caribbean* (various), pp.32–33, F2

Isla de Tiburon, Mexico (island), Marvel Comics, pp.32–33, C3

Isla Dorada, Mexico (town), *Corazón Indomable* (TV), pp.32–33, B2

Isla Island/Bananarama (fictional island/ nation), *American Dad* (TV), pp.32–33, D2

Isla Morazan, Costa Rica (island), *Jurassic Park* by Michael Crichton (various), pp.32–33, C1

Isla Nublar, Costa Rica (island), *Jurassic Park* by Michael Crichton (various), pp.32–33, C1

Isla Paraiso, Philippines (island), *San Simeon* (*Sims 3*) (video game), pp.90–91, D3

Isla Paraiso, Chile (island), *Isla Paraíso* (Paradise Island) (TV), pp.38–39, B2

Isla Pixol, Mexico (island), *The Lacuna* by Barbara Kingsolver (novel), pp.32–33, B2

Isla Talamanca, Costa Rica (island), *Jurassic Park* by Michael Crichton (various), pp.32–33, D1

Island, The, Pacific Ocean (island), *Gilligan's Island* (TV), pp.120–121, D4

Island, The/Oceanic Flight 815, Pacific Ocean (unmappable island/wreck), *Lost* (TV), pp.120–121, D4

Island of Blue Dolphins, California (island), *Island of Blue Dolphins* by Scott O'Dell (novel), pp.18–19, A3

Island of Cairnholme, Wales (island), *Miss Peregrine's Home for Peculiar Children* by Ransom Riggs (novel/film), pp.64–65, B2

Island of California, The, Mexico (island), *Las sergas de Esplandián* by Garci Rodríguez de Montalvo (novel), pp.32–33, A2

Island of Cannibals, Indian Ocean (island), *Sinbad the Sailor* (short story), pp.78–79, A4

Island of Dr Moreau, The, Pacific Ocean (island), *The Island of Dr Moreau* by H.G. Wells (novel), pp.120–121, F3

Island of Misfit Toys, The, Arctic Ocean (island), *Rudolph the Red-Nosed Reindeer* (TV special), pp.26–27, C4

Island of Pearls, Indian Ocean (island), *Sinbad the Sailor* (short story), pp.78–79, B3

Island of Sodor, England (island), *Thomas the Tank Engine* by Rev W. Audrey (books/TV), pp.64–65, C3

Island of the City of the Apes (island), *Sinbad the Sailor* (short story), pp.78–79, B2

Island of the Day Before, Pacific Ocean (island), *The Island of the Day Before* by Umberto Eco (novel), pp.120–121, C2

Island of the Fountain of Youth, Caribbean (island), *Pirates of the Caribbean* (various), pp.32–33, D3/E3

Island of the Hattifatteners, Sweden (island), the Moomin books by Tove Jansson (short stories), pp.56–57, D3

Island of the Living Sepulchra, Indian Ocean (island), *Sinbad the Sailor* (short story), pp.78–79, A4

Island of the Old Man of the Sea, Indian Ocean (island), *Sinbad the Sailor* (short story), pp.78–79, B2

Island of the Roc, Madagascar (island), *Sinbad the Sailor* (short story), pp.84–85, D3

Island of the Sea-Horses, Persian Gulf (island), *Sinbad the Sailor* (short story), pp.72–73, D1

Island of W, Argentina (island), *W or the Memory of Childhood* by Georges Perec (novel), pp.38–39, B1

Islandia (fictional country), *Islandia* novels and sequels by Austin Tappan Wright and Mark Saxton, pp.84–85, A1/B1

Isle Esme, Brazil (island), *Twilight: Breaking Dawn* by Stephenie Meyer (novel/film), pp.38–39, D3

Isle Hyu (fictional island/nation), *Jelle's Marble Runs* (web series), pp.78–79, C2

Isle of Drear, Scotland (unmappable island), Harry Potter novels by J.K. Rowling (novels/films), pp.64–65, C5

Isle of Gloom, England (island), *The Island of Adventure* by Enid Blyton (novel), pp.64–65, B1

Isle of Kiloran, Scotland (island), *I Know Where I'm Going!* (film), pp.64–65, B4

Isle of Kiltarra, Scotland (island), *The Maggie* (film), pp.64–65, B5

Isle of Slingers, England (island), novels of Thomas Hardy, pp.64–65, C1

Isle of Struay, Scotland (island), *Katie Morag* (novels/TV), pp.64–65, B4

Isle of the Gods, Kingdom of Karin (fictional island), *Transformers: Masterforce* (anime), pp.90–91, D2

Isle of the Pines, Indian Ocean (island), *The Isle of the Pines* by Henry Neville (novel), pp.108–109, A4/B4

Isles of the Blessed, Atlantic Ocean (island chain, ancient myth/legend), pp.126–127, B5/C4

Isola, New York (city), works of Ed McBain, pp.14–15, D1

Istanbird, Turkey (city), *DuckTales* (TV), pp.72–73, B3

Isthmus City, Republic of Isthmus (fictional city), *James Bond: Licence to Kill* (film), pp.32–33, D1

Itchy & Scratchy Land, Gulf of Mexico (island), *The Simpsons* (TV), pp.32–33, D3

Itchy Armpit, the Barbaric Archipelago (fictional island), *How to Train Your Dragon* by Cressida Cowell (novels/ films), pp.56–57, D1

Ithaquack, Greece (island), *DuckTales* (TV), pp.44–45, E1

Itomori, Japan (town), *Your Name* (film), pp.96–97, C2

Ivell, England (town), novels of Thomas Hardy, pp.64–65, C1

Ivory-Lana or Fari Lana (fictional country), *The Phantom* (comic), pp.84–85, D3

Iwaya Village, Japan (village), *Varan* (film), pp.96–97, C3

Ixania (fictional country), *The Dark Frontier* by Eric Ambler (novel), pp.50–51, B2

Izayoi Island, Japan (island), *Stitch!* (anime), pp.96–97, D1

Jaburo, Brazil (underground city), *Mobile Suit Gundam/Hellsing* (anime/manga), pp.38–39, C5

Jacksea Island, Ninetail Dominions (fictional island), *Log Horizon* by Mamare Touno and Kazuhiro Hara (novels/anime), pp.96–97, A1

Jackson City, Colorado (city), *Runaway* (film), pp.16–17, A4

Jackson Summit, Colorado (natural feature), *Atomic Train* (film), pp.18–19, D4

Jacksonville, Ishmaelia (fictional city), *Scoop* by Evelyn Waugh (novel), pp.84–85, D4

Jadac, Bosnia and Herzegovina (city), *ZOS: Zone of Seperation* (TV), pp.50–51, A2

Jade River, The, China (river), *Where the Mountain Meets the Moon* by Grace Lin (novel), pp.102–103, D2

Jaffan, Trans-Sabal (fictional city), Marvel Comics (various), pp.72–73, C1

Jakkalsdrif, South Africa (building), *The Life and Times of Michael K* by J.M. Coetzee (novel), pp.84–85, D5

Jaku, Japan (city), *My Hero Academia* by Kohei Horikoshi (manga/anime), pp.96–97, B2

Jalpur (fictional city/state), *Mira, Royal Detective* (TV), pp.78–79, B4

Jam Butty Mines, England (building), imagination of Ken Dodd (comedy routines), pp.64–65, C3

Jamarbala, Indonesia (island), *Jelle's Marble Runs* (web series), pp.90–91, B1

Jambalaya Island, Caribbean (island), *Monkey Island* series (video games), pp.32–33, E3

Jamjah, India (town), *The Adventures of Tintin* by Hergé (comics), pp.78–79, B5

Jane Guy, The (wreck), *The Narrative of Arthur Gordon Pym of Nantucket* by Edgar Allan Poe (novel), pp.114–115, C3

Janjira, Japan (city), *Godzilla* (2014, film), pp.96–97, C2

Jannati Shahr, Saudi Arabia (city), *The Flying Legion* by George Allan England (novel), pp.72–73, C2

Janov, Poland (town), *The Cassandra Crossing* (film), pp.50–51, B3

Jante, Denmark (town), *A Fugitive Crosses his Tracks* by Aksel Sandemose (novel), pp.56–57, A2

Janus Oil Rig, North Sea (oil rig), *The Devil's Tattoo* (film), pp.64–65, D5

Janus Rock Lighthouse, Western Australia (building), *The Light Between Oceans* by M.L. Stedman (novel), pp.108–109, A2

Janus Satellite Control Center, Cuba (building), *James Bond: Goldeneye* (film), pp.32–33, D2

Jarmuli, India (town), *Sleeping on Jupiter* by Anuradha Roy (novel), pp.78–79, C4

Jasper, Nevada (town), *Transformers: Prime* (TV), pp.18–19, B4

Jászkarafaszajenő, Hungary (village, real life joke), pp.50–51, B2

Jauga, Peru (town), *The Adventures of Tintin* by Hergé (various), pp.38–39, A4

Jebel Kadheih Desert/Khemed (fictional country/emirate), *The Adventures of Tintin* by Hergé (novels), pp.72–73, B2/B3

Jeerulot, India (town), *Natal Fault* by Dr Manisha Saxena (novel), pp.78–79, B4

Jefferson (fictional state), works of Harry Turtledove, pp.18–19, A5

Jefferson, Mississippi (city), works of William Faulkner, pp.16–17, D3

Jefferton, California (town), *Tom Goes to the Mayor* (TV), pp.18–19, A3

Jellyfish Fields, Bikini Bottom (fictional natural feature), *SpongeBob SquarePants* (TV), pp.120–121, B4

Jellystone Park, Wyoming (natural feature), *Yogi Bear* (TV), pp.18–19, D5

Jericho, Kansas (town), *Jericho* (TV), pp.16–17, B4

Jérimadeth, Iraq (city), *So Boaz Slept* by Victor Hugo (poem), pp.72–73, C2

Jerkbait Islands, The, Gulf of Melange (fictional island chain), *Monkey Island* series (video games), pp.32–33, F2

Jeronimo, Honduras (village), *The Mosquito Coast* by Paul Theroux (novel), pp.32–33, C2

Jeru/Zalem Space Elevator, Panama (space elevator), *Gunnm/Battle Angel Alita* (manga/anime), pp.32–33, D1

Jerusalem's Lot, Maine (town), *Salem's Lot* by Stephen King (various), pp.14–15, D6

Jhumli, India (town), *Gori Tere Pyaar Mein* (film), pp.78–79, B4

Jiangzhou, China (city), *Narrow Dwelling* (TV), pp.102–103, D2

Jingzhou, China (city), *In the Name of the People* (TV), pp.102–103, D2

Jinsy, Channel Islands (island), *This is Jinsy* (TV), pp.64–65, A1

Jintian, China (city), *The Hundred Secret Senses* by Amy Tan (novel), pp.102–103, C1

Joan Bushwell's Chimp Refuge, New Zanzibar (fictional building), *The Simpsons* (TV), pp.84–85, C3

Johlpur, India (village), *The Sleeping Dictionary* by Sujata Massey (novel), pp.78–79, C4

Johnson Island, Arctic (island), *The Voyages and Adventures of Captain Hatteras* by Jules Verne (novel), pp.26–27, C4

Johto, Japan (region), *Pokémon* (video games), pp.96–97, C4

Jōkamachi, Japan (city), *Samurai Shodown* series (video games), pp.96–97, C2

Jolliginki (fictional country), *The Story of Doctor Dolittle* by Hugh Lofting (novel), pp.84–85, D3

Jolly Rock Lighthouse, North Sea (building), *The Goodies* (TV), pp.64–65, D5

Jonesy Lake, Wyoming (lake), *Firewatch* (video game), pp.18–19, C5

Jordan, Seneca, Elkins, McKessburg, Bellport, Alaska (towns), *Runaway Train* (film), pp.18–19, B1

Josefov, Poland (village), *The Slave* by Isaac Bashevis Singer (novel), pp.50–51, B3

Josette, Louisiana (town), *Joe Dirt* (film), pp.16–17, D2

Joulupukin asuinsija, Finland (building, folklore), pp.56–57, D5

Jubilee, Ontario (town), works of Alice Munro, pp.26–27, A4

Jubilife City, Japan (city), *Pokémon* (video games), pp.96–97, C4

Judgment Day, Panama (wreck), *The Three-Body Problem* by Liu Cixin (novel), pp.32–33, D1

Julia, South Carolina (town), *Gospel Hill* (film), pp.14–15, B3

Juliet, Saskatchewan (town), *Cool Water* by Dianne Warren (novel), pp.26–27, C1

Jump City, Oregon (city), DC Comics (various), pp.18–19, A6

Junchow, China (city), *The Russian Concubine* by Kate Furnivall (novel), pp.102–103, D2

Junction City, Colorado (town), *The Man Who Shot Liberty Valance* (film), pp.16–17, A4

Juneburg, Oklahoma (town), works of Larry Mike Garmon, pp.16–17, B3

Jungle Village, China (town), *The Man with the Iron Fists* (film), pp.102–103, D4

Junitaki, Japan (town), *A Wild Sheep Chase* by Haruki Murakami (novel), pp.96–97, C4

Junkertown, Northern Territory (town), *Overwatch* (video game), pp.108–109, C3

Junktown, California (town), *Fallout 1* (video game), pp.18–19, B3

Jurassic Park Europe, Azores (building),

Jurassic Park by Michael Crichton (novel), pp.126–127, C4

Jurassic Park Japan, Pacific Ocean (theme park), *Jurassic Park* by Michael Crichton (novel), pp.120–121, A4/B4

Juroku Plant Poison Castle, Japan (building), *Batman Ninja* (film), pp.96–97, C2

Juruanā, Brazil (town), *Araguaia* (TV), pp.38–39, C4

Jusendo, China (mountain), *Ranma ½* by Rumiko Takahashi (manga/anime), pp.102–103, B2

K'naa, Mu (fictional region), Cthulhu Mythos (various), pp.120–121, E3

K'un-Lun, Tibet (mountain), Marvel Comics and mythology, pp.102–103, B2

Kadic Academy, Paris, France (building), *Code Lyoko* (TV), pp.44–45, A4

Kaha, Belgistan (fictional city), *Gasaraki* (anime), pp.72–73, C3

Kahani, Alifbay (fictional city), *Haroun and the Sea of Stories* by Salman Rushdie (novel), pp.78–79, B5

Kahndaq (fictional country), DC Comics, pp.72–73, B2

Kaigoon, Singapore (island), *Road to Singapore* (film), pp.90–91, D4

Kaihoro, New Zealand (town), *Bad Taste* (film), pp.108–109, F2

Kalabar, India (region), *Carry On Up the Khyber* (film), pp.78–79, B5

Kalapur, Pakistan (town), *North West Frontier* (film), pp.78–79, B5

Kali Rapids, Anandapur (fictional natural feature), Kali River Rapids (theme park), pp.78–79, C4/D4

Kallenger, India (town), *Around the World in Eighty Days* by Jules Verne (novel), pp.78–79, C4

Kalokairi, Greece (island), *Mamma Mia!* (film), pp.44–45, E1

Kalos, France (region), *Pokémon* (video games), pp.44–45, C3

Kalubya (fictional country), *Operation Thunderbolt* (video game), pp.84–85, B5

Kamalpur, India (town), *Motu Patlu* (TV), pp.78–79, B3

Kamanga (fictional country), *Tenth Man Down* by Chris Ryan (novel), pp.84–85, C2

Kamar-Taj, Nepal (village), *Doctor Strange* (film/comic), pp.78–79, C4

Kambezi (fictional country), *MacGyver* (TV), pp.84–85, C3

Kameno, Kenya (village), *The River Between* by Ngũgĩ wa Thiong'o (novel), pp.84–85, D4

Kamihama, Japan (city), *Puella Magi Madoka Magica* (anime/manga), pp.96–97, B2

Kamino, Japan (town), *My Hero Academia* by Kōhei Horikoshi (manga/anime), pp.96–97, C2

Kamistan, Islamic Republic of (fictional country), *24* (TV), pp.72–73, C2

Kamisu 66, Japan (town), *From the New World* (video game), pp.96–97, C2

Kamiyama, Japan (town), *Hyoka* by Honobu Yonezawa (novel), pp.96–97, C2

Kamp Krusty, North Takoma (building), *The Simpsons* (TV), pp.18–19, A6

Kampung Durian Runtuh, Malaysia (village), *Upin & Ipin* (TV), pp.90–91, C2

Kamui Kotan, Japan (village), *Samurai Shodown* series (video games), pp.96–97, C2

Kamurocho, Japan (town), *Yakuza* series (video games), pp.96–97, C2

Kagan (fictional country), *Anthills of the Savannah* by Chinua Achebe (novel), pp.84–85, C2

Kanthapura, India (town), *Kanthapura* by Raja Rao (novel), pp.78–79, B4

Kanto Power Plant, Japan (building), *Pokémon* (video games), pp.96–97, C2

Kapua, New Zealand (town), *Ngati* (film), pp.108–109, F2

Karain continent (fictional natural feature), Islandia novels and sequels by Austin Tappan Wright and Mark Saxton (novels), pp.84–85, A1/A2/B1/B2

Karain River, Sulliaba (fictional river), Islandia novels and sequels by Austin Tappan Wright and Mark Saxton, pp.84–85, A2

Karakura Town, Japan (town), *Bleach* by Tite Kubo (manga/anime), pp.96–97, E1

Karaoi, Kazakhstan (village), *The Dead Wander in the Desert* by Rollan Seisenbayev (novel), pp.72–73, D3

Karasuno, Japan (town), *Haikyu!!* by Haruichi Furudate (manga/anime), pp.96–97, C2

Kardemomme, Norway (town), *When the Robbers Came to Cardamom Town* by Thorbjørn Egner (short story), pp.56–57, D4

Karin Island, Kingdom of Karin (fictional island/nation), *Transformers: Masterforce* (anime), pp.90–91, D2

Karistan (fictional country), *Legend of the White Horse* (film), pp.50–51, A3/B3

Karrocan Emirate (fictional country/emirate), DC Comics, pp.72–73, C2

Karuthupuzha, India (town), Works of Manu Bhattathiri (novels), pp.78–79, D4

Karwassa, India (town), *The Dāk Bungalow at Dakor* by Bithia Mary Croker (short story), pp.78–79, C4

Kasrilevke, Ukraine (town), works of Sholem Aleichem (stories), pp.50–51, C3

Kasundruv Presed Bridge (The Cassandra Crossing), Poland/Czech Republic (building), *The Cassandra Crossing* (film), pp.56–57, B4

Kataev, Ukraine (city), *Ninja Gaiden Z* (video game), pp.50–51, C2/D2

Katamarunde Rocket Base, Germany (building), *Wolfenstein* series (video games), pp.44–45, D4

Katanga (fictional country), *The Dogs of War* by Frederick Forsyth (novel), pp.84–85, A4

Katorga-12, Russia (island), *Singularity* (video game), pp.102–103, F1

Kattegat, Norway (village), *Vikings* (TV), pp.56–57, B3

Kawakami City, Japan (city), *Maji de Watashi ni Koi Shinasai!* (vVisual novels/video games), pp.96–97, E1

Kazamino, Japan (city), *Puella Magi Madoka Magica* (anime/manga), pp.96–97, C2

Keelut, Alaska (town), *Hold the Dark* (film), pp.18–19, B1

Kehoe, Colorado (town), *Cold Pursuit* (film), pp.18–19, D4

Kellsthorpe, England (town), *Thomas the Tank Engine* by Rev W. Audrey (books/TV), pp.64–65, C3

Kellynch Hall, England (estate), *Persuasion* by Jane Austen (novel), pp.64–65, C1

Kembleford, England (town), Father Brown stories by G.K. Chesterton (novels/TV), pp.64–65, C2

Kennaquhair, Scotland (building), *The Monastery and the Abbot* by Walter Scott (novel), pp.64–65, C4

Kesernyés, Hungary (village), *Hukkle* (film), pp.50–51, B2

Keshan (fictional country), Conan novels of Robert E. Howard, pp.84–85, C5

Keystone City, Kansas (city), DC Comics, pp.16–17, C4

Keystone (fictional state), *Steven Universe* (TV), pp.14–15, B4/C4

Kfar Keshet, Israel (town), *Jordan and the Dreadful Golem* by Karen Goldman (novel), pp.72–73, B2

Kfaryabda, Lebanon (village), *The Rock of Tanios* by Amin Maalouf (novel), pp.72–73, B2

Khandanyang (fictional country), *Hitman* series (video games), pp.102–103, A2

Khasak, India (village), *Khasak* by O.V. Vijayan (novel), pp.78–79, B2

Khaufpur, India (city), *Animal's People* by Indra Sinha (novel), pp.78–79, B4

Khauran, Crimea (country/region), Conan novels of Robert E. Howard, pp.50–51, D2

Khemed (fictional country/emirate), *The Adventures of Tintin* by Hergé (novels), pp.72–73, B2

Khemi, Morocco (city), Conan novels of Robert E. Howard, pp.84–85, A5

Khemikhal, Khemed (fictional city), *The Adventures of Tintin* by Hergé (novels), pp.72–73, B2

Khitai, China (country), Conan novels of Robert E. Howard, pp.102–103, D4

Khokarsa, Central Africa (fictional country), novels of Philip José Farmer, pp.84–85, B4/C4

Kholby, India (town), *Around the World in Eighty Days* by Jules Verne (novel), pp.78–79, C4

Khoraja (fictional country), Conan novels of Robert E. Howard, pp.72–73, B2/C2

Khorshemish, Syria (city), Conan novels of Robert E. Howard, pp.72–73, B3

Khrustal, Belarus (town), *Crystal Swan* (film), pp.50–51, C4

Kiewarra, Victoria (town), *The Dry* by Jane Harper (novel), pp.108–109, D1/D2

Kilcody, Ireland (town), *John the Revelator* by Peter Murphy (novel), pp.64–65, A2

Kilderry, Ireland (village), *The Moon-Bog* by H.P. Lovecraft (short story), pp.64–65, A2

Killarney, New South Wales (estate), *McLeod's Daughters* (TV), pp.108–109, D2

Killin Lodge, Scotland (building), *The Water Horse* (film), pp.64–65, B4

Killinaskully, Ireland (village), *Killinaskully* (TV), pp.64–65, A2

Killmancha, Ireland (city) *Eclipsed* by Patricia Burke Brogan (play), pp.64–65, A2

Kilnalough, Ireland (town), *Troubles* by J.G. Farrell (novel), pp.64–65, B2

Kiloude City, France (city), *Pokémon* (video games), pp.44–45, C3

Kiltoch, Scotland (village), *Tintin* (video comic books), pp.64–65, B4

Klaneshtetl, Poland (town), *91:an (No. 91)* (comic strip), pp.56–57, B2

Kinakuta (fictional country), *Cryptonomicron* by Neal Stephenson (novel), pp.90–91, C2

Kindle County, Illinois (county), Kindle Country series by Scott Turow (novels), pp.16–17, D4/D5

King Ghidorah (frozen body of, being), *Godzilla: King of the Monsters* (film), pp.114–115, D4

King Julien's Kingdom of Madagascar, Madagascar (country), *Madagascar* franchise (films), pp.84–85, D2

King Moonracer's Castle, Arctic Ocean (building), *Rudolph the Red-nosed Reindeer* (TV special), pp.26–27, C4

King Runeard's Dam, Lands of the Northuldra (building), *Frozen II* (film), pp.56–57, B4

King Solomon's Mines, DRC (mine), *King Solomon's Mines* by H. Rider Haggard (novel), pp.84–85, C3

King's Bay, Madagascar (city), *Just Cause 4* (video game), pp.84–85, D2/D3

King's Deverill, England (town), novels of P.G. Wodehouse, pp.64–65, C1

Kingdom of Auster (fictional country), *The Golden Compass* (film), pp.108–109, B2/C3

Kingdom of Dunbroch (fictional country), *Brave* (film), pp.64–65, B5

Kingdom of Karin (fictional island/nation), *Transformers: Masterforce* (anime), pp.90–91, D2

Kingdom of Opona, Russia (country, Russian folklore), pp.50–51, B6

Kingdom of Prester John, Ethiopia (country, folklore), pp.84–85, D4

Kingdom of Suille (fictional country), *Gundam 00* (anime), pp.72–73, C2

Kingdom of the Bears, Sweden (island/country), *His Dark Materials* by Philip Pullman (novels/TV/film), pp.56–57, A5

Kingdom, The, Scotland (county), *The Bridge* by Iain Banks (novel), pp.64–65, C4

Kings Pyland, England (village), *Sherlock Holmes: The Adventure of Silver Blaze* by Arthur Conan Doyle (short story), pp.64–65, C1

Kingsbridge, England (town), *The Pillars of the Earth* by Ken Follett (novel), pp.64–65, C2

Kingshead, Caribbean (island), *Pirates of the Caribbean* (various), pp.32–33, F2

Kingsmarkham, England (town), Inspector Wexford stories by Ruth Rendell (novels), pp.64–65, C1

Kingsport, England (city), *South Riding* by Winifred Holtby (novel), pp.64–65, D3

Kingsport, Massachusetts (town), Cthulhu Mythos/H.P. Lovecraft (various), pp.14–15, D5

Kingston Falls, New York (town), *Gremlins* (film), pp.14–15, C5

Kingston Junction, California (town), *The Kingston Fortune* by Stephen Longstreet (novel), pp.18–19, B3

Kinjanja (fictional country), *A Good Man in Africa* by William Boyd (novel/film), pp.84–85, B4

Kinkow Archipelago, Pacific Ocean (island chain), *Pair of Kings* (TV), pp.120–121, D2

Kinloch, Scotland (town), novels of Denzil Meyrick, pp.64–65, B4

Kinraddie, Scotland (village), *Sunset Song* by Lewis Grassic Gibbon (novel), pp.64–65, C4

Kiplington, England (town), *South Riding* by Winifred Holtby (novel), pp.64–65, D3

Kirai (fictional country), DC Universe (comics), pp.72–73, C2

Kirinos, Greece (island), Marvel Comics/Marvel Cinematic Universe, pp.44–45, E1

Kirk Ronan, England (town), *Thomas the Tank Engine* by Rev W. Audrey (books/TV), pp.64–65, C3

Kirkmichael, Scotland (town), novels of John Buchan, pp.64–65, C3

Kirrary, Ireland (village), *Ryan's Daughter* (film), pp.64–65, A2

Kirrin Island, England (island), *Five on a Treasure Island* by Enid Blyton (novel), pp.64–65, C1

Kirtland County, Utah (county), *Brigham City* (film), pp.18–19, C4

Kisaragi Station, (infernal portal, mythology), pp.96–97, C2

Kitahoromai, Japan (village), *Poppoya* (film), pp.96–97, D4

Kitasanriku, Japan (town), *Amachan* (TV), pp.96–97, C2

Kitezh, Russia (underwater city, Russian folklore), pp.50–51, C2

Kittur, India (town), *Between the Assassinations* by Aravind Adiga (novel), pp.78–79, B3

Kiwi-Cit/New Pacific City, New Zealand (city), *2000 AD* (comics), pp.108–109, F1

Kizhakkemuri, India (village), *Asuravithu* by M.T. Vasudevan Nair (novel), pp.78–79, B2

Kınalı Kar, Turkey (village), *Kınalı Kar* (TV), pp.72–73, B3

Kjeldby, Denmark (town), works of Johannes V. Jensen, pp.56–57, A2

Klackamo, Sweden (town), *91:an (No. 91)* (comic strip), pp.56–57, B2

Klass County, Washington (county), *The X-Files* (TV), pp.18–19, B6

Klisura, Bulgaria (village), *Stork Mountain* by Miroslav Penkov (novel), pp.50–51, C1

Kløvstad, Norway (town), *Olsenbanden tar gull* (film), pp.56–57, A4

Klow, Syldavia (fictional city), *The Adventures of Tintin* by Hergé (various), pp.50–51, A1

Klynham, New Zealand (town), *The Scarecrow* by Ronald Hugh Morrieson (novel/film), pp.108–109, F2

Knapford, England (town), *Thomas the Tank Engine* by Rev W. Audrey (books/TV), pp.64–65, C3

Knockglen, Ireland (town), *Circle of Friends* by Maeve Binchy (novel), pp.64–65, A2

Knocknaree, Ireland (town), the Dublin Murder Squad series by Tana French (novels), pp.64–65, B3

Knohult, Sweden (village), *Åsa-Nisse* by Stig Cederholm (comic strip), pp.56–57, A3

Knots Landing, California (town), *Knots Landing* (TV), pp.18–19, A4

Knype Hill, England (town), *A Clergyman's Daughter* by George Orwell (novel), pp.64–65, D2

Knype, England (town), the Five Towns novels by Arnold Bennett, pp.64–65, C2

Kokaua Town, Hawaii (town), *Lilo and Stitch* (film/TV), pp.18–19, C4

Kokkanchira, India (village), *Aalahayude Penmakkal* by Sarah Joseph (novel), pp.78–79, B2

Kolechia (fictional country), *Papers, Please* (video game), pp.72–73, C4

Kolmograd, Russia (city), *Syberia* (video game), pp.50–51, B5

Kongoukaku, Hinomoto (fictional city), *Kabaneri of the Iron Fortress* (anime), pp.96–97, B2

Konikoni City, Hawaii (town), *Pokémon* (video games), pp.18–19, C1

Koolgalla, Western Australia (town), *The Torrents* by Oriel Gray (play), pp.108–109, A4

Kootney Landing, British Columbia (town), *Open Secret* by Deryn Collier (novel), pp.26–27, C1

Kôr, Mozambique (city), *She* by H. Rider Haggard (novel), pp.84–85, D3

Koriko, Sweden (town), *Kiki's Delivery Service* (anime), pp.56–57, A3

Kornsas City, Missouri (city), DC Comics, pp.16–17, C4

Korsbæk, Denmark (town), *Matador* (TV), pp.56–57, B3

Kos, Nigeria (city), *Beasts Made of Night* by Tochi Onyebuchi (novel), pp.84–85, B4

Kosala, India (region), Conan novels of Robert E. Howard, pp.78–79, C4

Kosekin Country (country), *A Strange Manuscript Found in a Copper Bottle* by James De Mille (novel), pp.114–115, B3

Koth, Syria (country), Conan novels of Robert E. Howard, pp.72–73, B3/C3

Krakov, Czech Republic (town), *Guardians of the Civic Good* by Petra Hulová (novel), pp.50–51, A3

Krakozhia (fictional country), *The Terminal* (film), pp.50–51, C2

Krastava (fictional country), *The Mourner* by Richard Stark (novel), pp.50–51, B3

Kratsen, China (village), *Biggles Follows On* by W.E. Johns (novel), pp.102–103, D3

Kravonia (fictional country), *Sophy of Kravonia* by Anthony Hope (novel), pp.50–51, B3

Kreplanistan (fictional country), Austin Powers films, pp.72–73, E4

Krishnapur, India (town), *The Siege of Krishnapur* by J.G. Farrell (novel), pp.78–79, C4

Kritam, India (village), *A Horse and Two Goats* by R.K. Narayan (novel), pp.78–79, C3

Kroner, Kansas (town), *The X-Files* (TV), pp.16–17, C3

Krozniev, Vorozheika (fictional city), Marvel Comics, pp.72–73, C4

Krugis, Republic of (fictional country), *Gundam 00* (anime), pp.72–73, C2

Kszemieniec, Czech Republic (town/village), *The Cassandra Crossing* (film), pp.50–51, A4

Kuala Rokat, India/China (country), *Mission Impossible: 'The Seal'* (TV), pp.78–79, D4

Kudgiwa, Cimmeria (fictional town), *If On a Winter's Night a Traveller* by Italo Calvino (novel), pp.50–51, B3

Kugelstadt, Germany (city), *Wolfenstein* series (video games), pp.44–45, D3

Kukuanaland (fictional country), *King Solomon's Mines* by H. Rider Haggard (novel), pp.84–85, C3

Kulagong (fictional country), *Paper Tiger* (film), pp.90–91, D4

Kulyenchikov, Ukraine (village), *Fools* by Neil Simon (play), pp.50–51, B3

Kumari Kandam (fictional continent), mythology, pp.78–79, C1/D1

Kunami (fictional country/emirate), *Designated Survivor* (TV), pp.72–73, C2

Kunlun, Tibet (mountain, mythology), pp.102–103, B2

Kurikino, New Zealand (town), *Pallet on the Floor* by Hugh Morrieson (novel), pp.108–109, F2

Kurôzu-cho, Japan (town), *Uzumaki* by Junji Ito (manga), pp.96–97, B2

Kurtal, Switzerland (town), *Third Man on the Mountain* (film), pp.44–45, C3

Kuruda, Japan (city), works of Mahasweta Devi (stories), pp.78–79, C4

Kush (fictional country), *The Coup* by John Updike (novel), pp.84–85, D4

Kuz Killi, Afghanistan (village), *New Home, New Life* (radio), pp.72–73, D2

Kuzcek, Kazakhstan (village), *Borat* films, pp.72–73, D4

Kuzcotopia, Peru (building), *The Emperor's New Groove* (film), pp.38–39, B4

Kwik-E-Mart Central Office, India (building), *The Simpsons* (TV), pp.78–79, C4

Kyauktada, Myanmar (town), *Burmese Days* by George Orwell (novel), pp.90–91, A4

Kyrat (fictional country), *Far Cry 4* (video game), pp.78–79, C4

Kyzyl Kum, The, Aorusoi (fictional natural feature), *Log Horizon* by Mamare Touno and Kazuhiro Hara (novels/anime), pp.72–73, D3

l'Engoulvent, Guadeloupe (building), *Windward Heights* (*La migration des coeurs*) by Maryse Condé (novel), pp.72–73, D3

La Ciénaga, Argentina (town), *La Ciénaga/The Holy Girl* (films), pp.38–39, B3

La Ciudad Blanca, Honduras (city, mythology), pp.32–33, D2

La Matosa, Mexico (town), *Hurricane Season* by Fernanda Melchor (novel), pp.32–33, B2

La Paz, Philippines (town), *On the Job* (TV), pp.90–91, D4

La Ratatouille, Paris, France (building), *Ratatouille* (film), pp.44–45, E3

La Roche, Horizon Islands (fictional city), *ARMA 3* (video game), pp.120–121, C2

La Siesta, Spain (town), *Gran Reserva* (TV), pp.44–45, B2

La Tour Orbital Elevator, Somalia (space elevator), *Gundam 00* (anime), pp.84–85, D4

Laagerfontein, Bapetikosweti (fictional city), satires of Pieter-Dirk Uys, pp.84–85, C2

Laashekoh, Afghanistan (village), *Fear of Beauty* by Susan Froetschel (novel), pp.72–73, A2

Labassecour (fictional county), *Villette* by Charlotte Brontë (novel), pp.44–45, C4

Laerg, Scotland (island), *Atlantic Fury* by Hammond Innes (novel), pp.64–65, A5

Laestrygon, Italy (country), *The Odyssey* by Homer (mythology), pp.126–127, D1

Laevatia (fictional country), *Ruined City* by Nevil Shute (novel), pp.50–51, A2

Lagado, Balnibari (fictional city), *Gulliver's Travels* by Jonathan Swift (novel), pp.96–97, F3/F4

Lago Gran Paraíso, Argentina (lake), *Far South* by David Enrique Spellman (novel), pp.38–39, B3

Lago Místico, Argentina (town), *Campanas en la Noche* (TV), pp.38–39, B2

Lago, California (town), *High Plains Drifter* (film), pp.18–19, B4

Lagras, Lemoyne (fictional town), *Red Dead Redemption* series (video games), pp.16–17, D2

Lahood, California (town), *Pale Rider* (film), pp.18–19, A4

Laiport Strait, Ezzo Empire (fictional natural feature), *Log Horizon* by Mamare Touno and Kazuhiro Hara (novels/anime), pp.96–97, C3

Lake Edna, Kentucky (lake), *Kentucky Fried Chicken* (commercial), pp.14–15, A3

Lake Enara, Finland (lake), *His Dark Materials* by Philip Pullman (various), pp.56–57, C4

Lake Glimmerglass, New York (lake), *The Leatherstocking Tales* by James Fenimore Cooper (novels), pp.14–15, C5

Lake Idaho, Idaho (lake), *A Goofy Movie* (film), pp.16–17, B5

Lake Kashwakamak, Maine (lake), novels of Stephen King (various), pp.14–15, D6

Lake Lilac, Washington (lake), *Camp Camp* (web animation), pp.18–19, B6

Lake Lubana, Latvia (lake), *His Dark Materials* by Philip Pullman (various), pp.50–51, B4

Lake Mary, Idaho (lake), *Truly, Idaho* series by Rachel Gibson (novels), pp.18–19, B3

Lake of Rage, Japan (natural feature), *Pokémon* (video games), pp.96–97, B2

Lake Ossawippi, Ontario (lake), *Sunshine Sketches of a Little Town* by Stephen Leacock (short stories), pp.26–27, A4

Lake Parime, Peru (lake), El Dorado legends (various), pp.38–39, B4

Lake Titicoocoo, Peru/Bolivia (lake), *Scrooge McDuck 'The Son of the Sun'* (comics), pp.38–39, B4

Lake Verity, Japan (natural feature), *Pokémon* (video games), pp.96–97, C4

Lake Victoria Military Academy, Tanzania (building), *Mobile Suit Gundam Wing* (anime), pp.84–85, C3

Lake Visha, Russia (lake), *His Dark Materials* by Philip Pullman (various), pp.50–51, B6

Lake Wazzapamani, Wisconsin (lake), *The Blues Brothers* (film), pp.16–17, D5

Lake Willows, Wisconsin (lake/town), *Barbie* (toy line), pp.16–17, D5

Lake Wissanotti, Ontario (lake/town), *Sunshine Sketches of a Little Town* by Stephen Leacock (short stories), pp.26–27, A4

Lake Wobegon, Minnesota (town), *A Prairie Home Companion* (radio), pp.16–17, C5

Laketop, New Zealand (town), *Top of the Lake* (TV), pp.108–109, E1

Lalgaon, India (town), *Article 15* (film), pp.78–79, C4

Lallybroch, Scotland (building), Outlander novels by Diana Gabaldon (novels/TV), pp.64–65, B4

Lalotai, Pacific Ocean (island), *Moana* (film), pp.120–121, D3

Lambton, England (town), *Pride and Prejudice* by Jane Austen (novel), pp.64–65, D3

Lampsher, England (village), *Night and Day* by Virginia Woolf (novel), pp.64–65, D2

Lamson, San Serriffe (fictional town), *The Guardian* (newspaper), pp.78–79, A2

Lan Kong Town, Taiwan (town), *VOEZ* (video game), pp.102–103, D1

Land of the Stinkas (fictional region), *Captain Pugwash* (various), pp.32–33, C2

Land of Toys, Italy (island), *Pinocchio* (various), pp.44–45, C2

Lands of the Ku, Papua New Guinea (region), *The Glass-Sided Ant's Nest* by Peter Dickinson (novel), pp.90–91, E1/F1

Lands of the Northuldra/The Enchanted Forest (country), *Frozen II* (film), pp.56–57, B4

Lanford, Illinois (town), *Roseanne* (TV), pp.16–17, D5

Langbortisan (fictional country), *Donald Duck*, Danish translation (comic), pp.72–73, E3

Langhuishan, China (village), *Shenmue II* (video game), pp.102–103, C1

Langley Falls, Virginia (town), *American Dad* (TV), pp.14–15, C4

Langton, New Zealand (town), *Lester* by Bernard Beckett (novel), pp.108–109, F2

Lannahechee River, Lemoyne (fictional river), *Red Dead Redemption* series (video game), pp.16–17, D2

Lanshiang, China (region/city), *Resident Evil 6* (video game), pp.102–103, D1

Lansing, Germany (village), *Daboam is Daboam* (TV), pp.44–45, D3

Lansquenet-sous-Tannes, France (village), *Chocolat* by Joanne Harris (novel/film), pp.44–45, B2/B3

Lantham Bathery, India (building), *Litanies of Dutch Battery* by N.S. Madhavan (novel), pp.78–79, B2

Lapak, Alaska (island), *Alaska* by James A. Michener (novel), pp.18–19, A1

Laputa, Balnibari (fictional island, floating), *Gulliver's Travels* by Jonathan Swift (novel), pp.96–97, F3/F4

Lark Rise, England (town), *Lark Rise to Candleford* by Flora Thompson (novels/TV), pp.64–65, D2

Larksoken, England (town), *Devices and Desires* by P.D. James (novel), pp.64–65, D2

Larkspur, Idaho (town), *Impact* (film), pp.18–19, C5

Larkville, Ohio (town), Marvel Cinematic Universe (various), pp.14–15, A4

Las Cinco Muertes/The Five Deaths, Costa Rica (island chain), *Jurassic Park* by Michael Crichton (various), pp.32–33, C1

Las Palmeras, New Mexico (town), *For a Few Dollars More* (film), pp.18–19, D2

Las Payasadas, San Andreas (fictional town), *Grand Theft Auto* series (video game), pp.18–19, B3

Las Rémoras, Mexico (village), *Las Rémoras* by Eloy Urroz (novel), pp.32–33, A4

Las Venturas, San Andreas (fictional city), *Grand Theft Auto* series (video game), pp.18–19, B3

Last City, Colorado (city), *Maze Runner: The Death Cure* (film), pp.16–17, A4

Latham, Massachusetts (town), *Seinfeld* (TV), pp.14–15, C5

Latveria (fictional country), Marvel Comics, pp.50–51, B2

Laughlin City, Alberta (town), *X-Men* (film), pp.26–27, A1

Laura Creek, Western Australia (town), *Marvel: Agents of Shield* (TV), pp.108–109, A3

Laurania (fictional country), *Savrola* by Winston Churchill (novel), pp.44–45, B2

Lavender Town, Japan (town), *Pokémon* (video games), pp.96–97, C2

Laverlaw, Scotland (estate), novels of John Buchan, pp.64–65, C3

Lavernia (region), *Mundus alter et idem* by Joseph Hall (novel), pp.114–115, B3

Laverre City, France (city), *Pokémon* (video games), pp.44–45, C2

Lawford, New Hampshire (town), *Affliction* by Russell Banks (novel), pp.14–15, C5

Lawndale (town), *Daria* (TV), pp.14–15, C5

Lawson, California (town), *The Majestic* (film), pp.18–19, A5

Lawton, North Dakota (town), *The Missing Place* by Sophie Littlefield (novel), pp.16–17, A6

Le Devin, France (island), *Coastliners and Holy Fools* by Joanne Harris (novel), pp.44–45, B3

Le Mistral, France (region), *Plus Belle la Vie* (TV), pp.44–45, C2

Le Tetilla del Diablo (building), *From Dusk Till Dawn* (film), pp.32–33, B3

Leame Estuary, England (natural feature), *South Riding* by Winifred Holtby (novel), pp.64–65, D3

Leap Islands, The (island chain), *The Monikins* by James Fenimore Cooper (novel), pp.114–115, D2/D3

Ledenham, England (town), novels of Susan Pleydell, pp.64–65, C3

Ledsea Buttock, England (town), *South Riding* by Winifred Holtby (novel), pp.64–65, C3

Ledshire, England (county), novels of Susan Pleydell, pp.64–65, C3

Ledwardine, England (town), *A Letter From Ledwardine* by Phil Rickman (novel), pp.64–65, C2

Lee Kee Shipyards, Hong Kong (area), *Revenge of the Pink Panther* (film), pp.102–103, D1

Leestown, Ireland (village), *The Riordans* (TV), pp.64–65, B2

Lehigh Station, Pennsylvania (town), *North and South* by John Jakes (novels/TV), pp.14–15, C4

Lei Kiang, China (river), works of Preston Schoyer, pp.102–103, D1

Lemoyne (fictional state), *Red Dead Redemption* series (video game), pp.16–17, C2

Lemuel, Kansas (town), works of Sinclair Lewis, pp.16–17, B3

Lemuria (fictional continent, mythology), pp.78–79, C1/D1

LeNoir Station (building), works of Madeleine L'Engle, pp.114–115, E1

Leon City, Singapore (city), *Log Horizon* by Mamare Touno and Kazuhiro Hara (novels/anime), pp.90–91, A6

Leopardville, Colorado (town), *Citizen Kane* (film), pp.18–19, D3

LeQuint Dickey Mine, Mississippi (building), *Django Unchained* (film), pp.16–17, D2

Lerner Field, Nevada (building), *Con Air* (film), pp.18–19, C4

Lesneven, Oceana (fictional city), *The Strong Man* by H.R.F. Keating (novel), pp.126–127, D5

Letchi Island, Japan (island), *Godzilla* films, pp.96–97, D3

Letherbridge, England (town), *Doctors* (TV), pp.64–65, C2

Letsovo, Greece (village), *Alaloum* (film), pp.44–45, E1/E2

Letterkenny, Ontario (town), *Letterkenny* (TV), pp.26–27, A4

Levenford, Scotland (town), *Hatters Castle* by A.J. Cronin (novel), pp.64–65, C3

Levenham, South Australia (town), the Levenham Love Stories series by Cathryn Hein (novels), pp.108–109, A3

Leviathan, Atlantic Ocean (wreck), *Leviathan* by... (novel), pp.126–127, A4

Leyburn Castle, England (building), novels of Susan Pleydell, pp.64–65, C3

Lhando, Tibet (city), *Cursed Mountain* (video game), pp.102–103, B2

Lian Yu, China (island), *Arrow* (TV), pp.102–103, D2/E2

Libertad, Bolivia (city), *Ghost Recon: Wildlands* (video game), pp.38–39, B4

Libertatia, Madagascar (country, folklore), pp.84–85, C2

Liberty City, Liberty State (fictional city), *Grand Theft Auto* series (video game), pp.14–15, D1

Liberty Falls, Idaho (town), *All Over Creation* by Ruth Ozeki (novel), pp.18–19, C5

Liberty State (fictional state), *Grand Theft Auto* series (video game), pp.14–15, D1

Liberty, Texas (town), *The Train Robbers* (film), pp.16–17, A2

Libertyville, Pennsylvania (town), *Christine* by Stephen King (novel), pp.14–15, B4

Lichfield, Virginia (city), *The Cream of the Jest* by James Branch Cabell (novel), pp.14–15, C4

Liggett County, Washington (county), *Rambo: First Blood* (film), pp.18–19, A6/B6

Lighthaven, England (town), *The Coroner* (TV), pp.64–65, C1

Lillian, Ohio (town), *Super 8* (film), pp.14–15, B4

Lilliput (fictional island/nation), *Gulliver's Travels* by Jonathan Swift (novel), pp.108–109, A3

Lilycove City, Japan (town), *Pokémon* (video games), pp.96–97, C2

Lima Shatterdome, Peru (military base), *Pacific Rim* (film), pp.38–39, A4

Limanora, Pacific Ocean (island), *Riallaro, the Archipelago of Exiles* by Godfrey Sweven (novel), pp.120–121, E1

Limetown, Tennessee (town), *Limetown* (podcast), pp.14–15, A3

Limmeridge House, England (estate), *The Woman in White* by Wilkie Collins (novel), pp.64–65, C3

Limoerio, Brazil (town), *Turma de Monica/ Monica's Gang* (comics), pp.38–39, C3

Lincoln Island/Vulcania, Pacific Ocean (island), *The Mysterious Island* by Jules Verne/*20,000 Leagues Under the Sea* (novel/film), pp.120–121, D2

Linear Valley, California (town), *Human Highway* (film), pp.18–19, B3

Linne Forthin, Scotland (sea), *Total War: Thrones of Britannia* (video game), pp.64–65, C4

Linne Moreb, Scotland (sea), *Total War: Thrones of Britannia* (video game), pp.64–65, C5

Linzhong County, China (region), *Heaven Above* by Lu Tianming (novel/TV), pp.102–103, E4

Liparus, Sardinia (wreck), *James Bond: The Spy Who Loved Me* (film), pp.44–45, C1/C2

Lissbeg, Ireland (town), Finfarran Peninsula novels of Felicity Hayes-McCoy, pp.64–65, A2

Little Angel Mine/Satan Mine, Colorado (building), *Raise the Titanic* by Clive Cussler and *The Titanic Secret* by Clive Cussler and Jack Du Brul (novel/film), pp.18–19, D3

Little Bazeley by the Sea, England (village), *The Avengers: Town of No Return* (TV), pp.64–65, C3

Little Big Bear, Alberta (town), *Tin Star* (TV), pp.26–27, C1

Little Boston, California (town), *There Will Be Blood* (film), pp.18–19, A3/B3

Little Christchurch, Britannula (fictional city), *The Fixed Period* by Anthony Trollope (novel), pp.120–121, C1

Little Heart, Queensland (town), *The Stockman's Secret* by Mandy Magro (novel), pp.108–109, D4

Little Purlington, England (village), *Sherlock Holmes: The Adventure of Silver Blaze* by Arthur Conan Doyle (short story), pp.64–65, D2

Little Pwagmattasquarmsettport, North Takoma (fictional town), *The Simpsons* (TV), pp.18–19, A6

Little Salem, Colorado (town), *Citizen Kane* (film), pp.18–19, D3

Little Tall Island, Maine (island), *Dolores Claiborne* by Stephen King (various), pp.14–15, D6

Little Town, The, Hungary (town), *The Notebook* by Agota Kristóf (novel), pp.50–51, A2

Little Whinging, England (town), Harry Potter novels by J.K. Rowling (novels/films), pp.64–65, D2

Little Woods, North Dakota (town), *Little Woods* (film), pp.16–17, A6

Littlebourne-on-Sea, England (village), *Dad's Army* (TV), pp.64–65, D1

Littleroot Town, Japan (town), *Pokémon* (video games), pp.96–97, A1

Littleville, Colorado (town), DC Comics, pp.18–19, D3

Litzbark, Poland (village), *None Shall Escape* (film), pp.50–51, A4

Liven, China (village), *Lenin's Kisses* by Yan Lianke (novel), pp.102–103, D2

Livonia (fictional country), *ARMA 3* (video game), pp.50–51, B4

Llanabba, Wales (town), *Decline and Fall* by Evelyn Waugh (novel), pp.64–65, C2

Llanarthur, Wales (village), *Pobol y Cwm* (TV), pp.64–65, C2

Llanbobl, Wales (town), Rhod Gilbert (comedy routines), pp.64–65, C2

Llanfairfach, Wales (town), *Doctor Who: The Green Death* (TV), pp.64–65, C2

Llanfwyddwndllwnmawr, Wales (town), *Archer* (TV), pp.64–65, C2

Llanggubbin, Wales (town), *Ivor the Engine* (TV), pp.64–65, C2

Llangyllwch, Wales (town), *Don Quixote Drowned* by James Hanley (short stories), pp.64–65, C2

Llaniog, Wales (town), *Ivor the Engine* (TV), pp.64–65, C2

Llanmad, Wales (town), *Ivor the Engine* (TV), pp.64–65, C2

Llanview, Pennsylvania (town), ABC Soap Opera Universe (*One Life to Live*) (TV), pp.14–15, C4

Llareggub, Wales (town), *Under Milk Wood* by Dylan Thomas (radio), pp.64–65, C2

Lo Dung Bridge, Vietnam (building), *Apocalypse Now* (film), pp.90–91, B3

Loamshire, England (county), novels of George Eliot (novel), pp.64–65, C2/D2

Loch Androll, Scotland (natural feature), *Asterix and the Picts* by René Goscinny (comic book), pp.64–65, B5

Loch Mora, Scotland (lake), *The Maggie* (film), pp.64–65, B4

Loch Parry, Scotland (town), *An Appointment with the Wicker Man* by Greg Hemphill (play), pp.64–65, B3

Lochdubh, Scotland (town), *Hamish Macbeth* by M.C. Beaton (novels/TV), pp.64–65, B3

Locksley, England (town), Robin Hood tales (folklore), pp.64–65, D2

Lockwood Manor, California (building), *Jurassic World: Fallen Kingdom* (film), pp.18–19, A5

Locuta, Pacific Ocean (island), *Voyage to Locuta, a Fragment by Lemuel Gulliver Junior* by Elizabeth Graham (novel), pp.96–97, E4

Lodidhapura, Cambodia (city), *Jungle Girl* by Edgar Rice Burroughs (novel), pp.90–91, B3

Loftbacken, Sweden (town), real world, pp.56–57, D4

Logan, Alberta (town), Marvel Comics, pp.26–27, C1

Lomaverde, Spain (village), *Mr Lynch's Holiday* by Catherine O'Flynn (novel), pp.44–45, A1

Long Long Island, New York (island), *Futurama* (TV), pp.14–15, D5

Longbourn, England (estate), *Pride and Prejudice* by Jane Austen (novel), pp.64–65, D2

Longhampton, England (town), *A Hundred Pieces of Me* by Lucy Dillon (novel), pp.64–65, C3

Longshaw, England (town), the Five Towns novels by Arnold Bennett, pp.64–65, C2

Loo, DRC (town), *King Solomon's Mines* by H. Rider Haggard (novel), pp.84–85, C3

Loompaland, Brazil (region), *Charlie and the Chocolate Factory* by Roald Dahl (novel/films), pp.38–39, B5

Lorbrulgrud, Brobdingnag (fictional city), *Gulliver's Travels* by Jonathan Swift (novel), pp.26–27, A1

Los Aburridos, California (town), *Wreck-it-Ralph* (film), pp.18–19, B3

Los Angeles Shatterdome, California (building), *Pacific Rim* (film), pp.18–19, A3

Los Antelopes, California (town), DC Comics, pp.18–19, B3

Los Barcos, Spain (town), *Eldorado* (TV), pp.44–45, A1

Los Barrios County, New Mexico (county), *Ace in the Hole* (film), pp.18–19, D3

Los Bogus, Nevada (city), *Transformers: Robots in Disguise* (TV), pp.18–19, B3

Los Doce Apostoles, Olifa (fictional mountain range), *The Courts of the Morning* by John Buchan (novel), pp.38–39, C4

Los Dopicos, San Theodoros (fictional city), *The Adventures of Tintin* by Hergé (various), pp.38–39, C5

Los Reyes, Mexico (town), *The Crime of Padre Amaro/El Crimen del Padre Amaro* (film), pp.32–33, B2

Los Robles, Mexico (town), *Touch of Evil* (film), pp.32–33, A4

Los Santos, San Andreas (fictional city), *Grand Theft Auto* series (video game), pp.18–19, B3

Lost, the Island, *Lost* (TV), pp.120–121, C3

Lost City of Atlanta, The, Georgia (city), *Futurama* (TV), pp.14–15, B2

Lost City of Tinnos (city), *Tomb Raider III* (video game), pp.114–115, C1

Lost City of Z, The, Brazil (city), mythology), pp.38–39, C4

Lost continent of Mu, Mu (fictional submerged continent, mythology), pp.120–121, E3

Lost continent of Pan (or Whaga), Mu (fictional submerged continent), *Oahspe: A New Bible* by John Newbrough (novel), pp.120–121, A4/B4

Lost continent of Rutas, Mu (fictional submerged continent), writings of Louis Jacolliot, pp.120–121, D3/E3/D4/E4

Lost Continent, The (fictional island), *The Lost Continent* (film), pp.126–127, A3

Lost Forest National Forest, Georgia (natural feature), *Mark Trail* by Ed Dodd (comic), pp.14–15, B3

Lost Heaven, Chicago (city), *Mafia* (video game), pp.14–15, D5

Lost Pyramid of Khamandides, Egypt (building), *Thunderbirds* (TV), pp.84–85, C5

Lost Pyramid of Toth-Ra, Egypt (building), *DuckTales* (TV), pp.84–85, C5

Lost River Lake, Texas (lake), *Piranha* (1978, film), pp.16–17, A2

Lost Wages, Nevada (city), *Leisure Suit Larry in the Land of the Lounge Lizards* (video game), pp.18–19, B3

Lost World, The (Maple White Land), *The Lost World* by Arthur Conan Doyle, pp.38–39, C5

Lovecraft Country, Massachusetts (region), Cthulhu Mythos/H.P. Lovecraft (various), pp.14–15, D5

Lovecraft/Matheson, Massachusetts (town), *Locke and Key* (comic/TV), pp.14–15, D5

Lovelace Estate, Venezuela (building), *Black Lagoon* (manga/anime), pp.38–39, B5

Lower Caisse, San Serriffe (fictional island), *The Guardian* (newspaper), pp.78–79, A1

Lower Montana River (river), *Red Dead Redemption* series (video games), pp.16–17, D2

Lower Tadfield, England (town), *Good Omens* by Terry Pratchett (novel/TV), pp.64–65, D2

Lower Wessex, England (county), novels of Thomas Hardy, pp.64–65, C1

Lowerton, Colorado (city), *Kim Possible* (TV), pp.16–17, A4

Lowlands University, England (building), *A Very Peculiar Practice* (TV), pp.64–65, D2

Loxford, England (town), *Albert Herring* by Benjamin Britten (operetta), pp.64–65, D2

Lubenia (fictional country, military training exercise), pp.50–51, B4

Lucheng, Taiwan (town), works of Li Ang, pp.102–103, D1

140

Lucifer, New Mexico (town), *Married With Children* (TV), pp.18–19, D3

Lucrania (fictional country), *Biggles: Secret Agent* by W.E. Johns (novel), pp.44–45, C3

Lucre Island, Caribbean (island), *Monkey Island* series (video games), pp.32–33, E3

Ludendorff, North Yankton (fictional town), *Grand Theft Auto* series (video game), pp.16–17, B6

Lugash (fictional country), *Return of the Pink Panther* (film), pp.84–85, B5

Luggnagg (fictional island/nation), *Gulliver's Travels* by Jonathan Swift (novel), pp.96–97, D2/E2/D3/E3

Lulu, South Sudan (town), *Life in Lulu* (radio), pp.84–85, C4

Lumiose City, France (city), *Pokémon* (video games), pp.44–45, C3

Luo Kingdom, China (region), *A Dictionary of Maqiao* by Han Shaogong (novel), pp.102–103, D2

Luo River, China (river), *A Dictionary of Maqiao* by Han Shaogong (novel), pp.102–103, D2

Luping, Malaysia (village), *The Teardrop Story Woman* by Catherine Lim (novel), pp.102–103, D1

Lupusville, New York (town), *The Real Ghostbusters* (TV), pp.14–15, C5

Lutha (fictional country), *The Mad King* by Edgar Rice Burroughs (novel), pp.50–51, A2

Luxton, England (town), *On the Buses* (TV), pp.64–65, B2

Lycurgus, New York (city), *An American Tragedy* by Theodore Dreiser (novel), pp.14–15, C5

Lynx River, Northwest Territories (town), *North of 60* (TV), pp.26–27, D2

Lyonesse (fictional island/nation, folk tradition), pp.64–65, B1

Lytton, California (town), *Police Quest* (video game), pp.18–19, A3

M. Bison's Temple/Bisonopolis, Shadaloo (fictional building/city), *Street Fighter* (film), pp.90–91, A3

Ma'an, Abuddin (fictional city), *Tyrant* (TV), pp.72–73, B2

Macaria, Utopia (fictional region), *Utopia* by Thomas More (novel/parable), pp.38–39, C3

Macaw, China (city), *Duck Tales* (TV), pp.102–103, D1

MacDuich, Scotland (village), *Duck Tales* (TV), pp.64–65, B4

Machimos, Meropis (fictional sunken city), *Meropis* by Theopompus of Chios (book), pp.126–127, D2

Macondo, Colombia (town), *One Hundred Years of Solitude* by Gabriel García Márquez (novel), pp.38–39, A5/A6

Madhupur, India (Town), works of Indira Ganesan, pp.78–79, C4

Madison, Delaware (town), *Goosebumps* by R.L. Stine (novels/film), pp.14–15, C4

Madripoor (fictional city/state), Marvel Comics, pp.90–91, B2

Maerse Sea, England (sea), *Total War: Thrones of Britannia* (video game), pp.64–65, B3/C3

Mag Mell, Atlantic Ocean (island, legend), pp.126–127, D5

Magellania (fictional country), *The Survivors of the 'Jonathan'* by Jules Verne (novel), pp.38–39, B1

Mägendorf, Switzerland (village), *The Pledge: Requiem for the Detective Novel* by Friedrich Dürrenmatt (novella), pp.44–45, A2

Magga Glen, Wales (building), *Five Get Into a Fix* by Enid Blyton (novel), pp.64–65, B2

Mágina, Spain (town), *The Polish Rider* by Antonio Muñoz Molina (novel), pp.44–45, B2

Magnerstown, Ireland (town), *Death in Magnerstown* by Anne Crosse (novel), pp.64–65, A2

Maguadora (fictional island/nation), *Whoops! Apocalypse* (film), pp.32–33, F3

Magyaristan (fictional country), *The Years of Rice and Salt* by Kim Stanley Robinson (novel), pp.50–51, A2/B2

Mahogany Ship, The, Victoria (wreck, mythology), pp.108–109, D3

Mahogany Town, Japan (town), *Pokémon* (video games), pp.96–97, B2

Mahora/Mahora Academy, Japan (city/megaschool), *Negima* by Ken Akamatsu (manga/anime), pp.96–97, E2

Mahoroba, Japan (town), *Kannazuki No Miko* by Kaishaku (manga/anime), pp.96–97, B2

Mahoutokoro School of Magic, Pacific Ocean (building), Wizarding World by J.K. Rowling (various), pp.120–121, A4/B4

Maiholzen, Germany (town), *Stopfkuchen* by Wilhelm Raabe (novel), pp.44–45, D4

Main Strike Mine, California (mine), *James Bond: A View to a Kill* (film), pp.18–19, A4

Mainen, Germany (town), *Youjo Senki/The Saga of Tanya the Evil* by Carlo Zen and Shinobu Shinotsuki (novels/manga/anime), pp.44–45, C3

Majesta, New York (town), works of Ed McBain, pp.14–15, D1

Makalolo (fictional country), *The Extraordinary Adventures of Saturnin Farandoul* by Albert Robida (novel), pp.84–85, C4

Makazan, Aqiria (fictional city), Marvel Comics (various), pp.72–73, C2

Mako Island, Queensland (island), *H₂O: Just Add Water* (TV), pp.108–109, E2

Makuyu, Kenya (village), *The River Between* by Ngũgĩ wa Thiong'o (novel), pp.84–85, D4

Malacia, Croatia (city/state), *The Malacia Tapestry* by Brian Aldiss (novel), pp.50–51, A2

Malacovia, Romania (city), *Pedali sul Mar Nero* by Amedeo Tosetti (novel), pp.50–51, C2

Malarviken, Sweden (town), *Three Kronor* (TV), pp.56–57, C3

Malbry, England (town), novels of Joanne Harris, pp.64–65, C3

Malden, Atlantic Ocean (island), *ARMA: Cold War Assault* (video game), pp.126–127, C4

Maldonada, Balnibari (fictional city), *Gulliver's Travels* by Jonathan Swift (novel), pp.96–97, F3/F4

Malebolgia (fictional state), *Doctor Who: Minuet in Hell* (audio series), pp.14–15, B3

Malgudi, India (town), works of R.K. Narayan, pp.78–79, C3

Malice, California (town), *The Venture Brothers* (TV), pp.18–19, A2

Malie City, Hawaii (city), *Pokémon* (video games), pp.18–19, D1

Malino, Hawaii (town), Secret series by Annette Mahon (novels), pp.18–19, D1

Mallepa, Taiwan (town), *Moon Child* (film), pp.102–103, D1

Mallingford, England (town), *The Titfield Thunderbolt* (film), pp.64–65, C2

Malory Towers, England (building), Malory Towers series by Enid Blyton (novels), pp.64–65, C3

Malplaquet, England (estate), *Mistress Masham's Repose* by T.H. White (novel), pp.64–65, C2

Maltide, Pacific Ocean (island), *Rocket Girls* by Hōsuke Nojiri (novels/anime), pp.120–121, B3

Mamadon River, Brazil (river), *ClassicaLoid* (anime), pp.38–39, C5

Mambu Hanua, Papua New Guinea (village), *Raun Wantaim Savemahn* (radio series), pp.90–91, F1

Mämmilä, Finland (town), *Mämmilä* by Tarmo Koivisto and Hannu Virtanen (comic strip), pp.56–57, D3

Mammoth Falls, Arkansas (city), *Primary Colors* by Joe Klein (novel), pp.16–17, C3

Mana One Research Station, Pacific Ocean (building), *The Meg* (film), pp.120–121, A3/A4/B4

Managuay (fictional country), *Buck Danny* (comics), pp.32–33, C3

Manawaka, Manitoba (town), the works of Margaret Laurence, pp.26–27, D1

Manchesterford, England (city), *Acorn Antiques* (TV), pp.64–65, C3

Manderley, England (building), *Rebecca* by Daphne du Maurier (novel), pp.64–65, B2

Mandola, India (town), *Matru Ki Bijlee Ka Mandola* (film), pp.78–79, B4

Mandoras (fictional country), *Madmen of Mandoras/They Saved Hitler's Brain* (films), pp.38–39, B3

Mandorra (fictional country), *The Brigand* (film), pp.44–45, B2

Mandragora, Scotland (city), *The Testament of Yves Gundron* by Emily Barton (novel), pp.64–65, A5

Mandrake Falls, Vermont (town), *Mr Deeds Goes to Town* (film), pp.14–15, C5

Mangold Parva, England (village), *Adrian Mole: The Prostrate Years* by Sue Townsend (novel), pp.64–65, C2

Mangrove River, New South Wales (town/suburb), *Home and Away* (TV), pp.108–109, F4

Mano Majra, India (village), *Train to Pakistan* by Khushwant Singh (novel), pp.78–79, B4

Manoa Lai Sea, Pelago Commonwealth (fictional sea), *Endless Ocean* (video games), pp.120–121, A4/B4

Manoba, Papua New Guinea (island), *The Birds of Paradise* by Paul Scott (novel), pp.90–91, F1

Manonash, Alaska (town), *Northern Exposure* (TV), pp.18–19, B1

Manoyama, Japan (town), *Sakura Quest* (anime), pp.96–97, B2

Mansfield Park, England (estate), *Mansfield Park* by Jane Austen (novel), pp.64–65, C2

Mansur, Islamic Republic of (fictional country), *The Janson Directive* by Robert Ludlum (novel), pp.72–73, C1

Maple White Land, Brazil (region), *The Lost World* by Arthur Conan Doyle (novel), pp.38–39, C4

Maqiao, China (village), *A Dictionary of Maqiao* by Han Shaogong (novel), pp.102–103, D2

Mar-Iago, Florida (building), *MacTrump* by Ian Doescher and Jacopo Della Quercia (book), pp.14–15, C1

Marabar Caves, India (natural feature), *A Passage to India* by E.M. Forster (novel/film), pp.78–79, C4

Maramores, Brazil (town), *O Beijo do Vampiro* (TV), pp.38–39, D3

Marbrise, Spain (city), *The Song of Roland* (poem), pp.44–45, B2

Marbrose, Spain (city), *The Song of Roland* (poem), pp.44–45, B2

Marchbolt, Wales (town), *Why Didn't They Ask Evans?* by Agatha Christie (novel), pp.64–65, B2

Mardi Archipelago, Pacific Ocean (island chain), *Mardi, and a Voyage Thither* by Herman Melville (novel), pp.120–121, E3

Mare Rurek Glacier, Nunavut (natural feature), *Transformers: Infestation 2* (comics), pp.26–27, D2

Margaritaville, Florida (town), 'Margaritaville' by Jimmy Buffett (song), pp.14–15, C1

Marimbá, Brazil (village), *Corpo Dourado* (TV), pp.38–39, D3

Marine Life Institute, California (building), *Finding Dory* (film), pp.18–19, A3

Marinella, Italy (village), Inspector Montalbano novels by Andrea Camilleri (novels/films), pp.44–45, D1

Mariner Bay, California (city), *Power Rangers* (TV), pp.18–19, A3

Mariposa, Ontario (town), *Sunshine Sketches of a Little Town* by Stephen Leacock (short stories), pp.26–27, A4

Market Blandings, England (town), novels of P.G. Wodehouse, pp.64–65, C2

Market Shipborough, England (town), *Kingdom* (TV), pp.64–65, D2

Market Snodsbury, England (village), novels of P.G. Wodehouse, pp.64–65, C2

Markhaven, England (town), novels of John Buchan, pp.64–65, C3

Markovburg, Markovia (fictional city), DC Comics, pp.44–45, C2

Markovia (fictional country), DC Comics, pp.44–45, C2

Marlin and Nemo's Reef, Great Barrier Reef (natural feature), *Finding Nemo* (film), pp.108–109, E3

Marlinshire, England (county), *Tintin* by Hergé (comic books), pp.64–65, D3

Marlott, England (town), novels of Thomas Hardy, pp.64–65, C1

Marparaíso, Chile (town), *Marparaíso* (TV), pp.38–39, B2

Marpesia, Oceana (fictional region), *Oceana* by James Harrington (novel), pp.38–39, C2

Marsh End, England (town), *The Secret Railway* by Elisabeth Beresford (novel), pp.64–65, D2

Marsovia (fictional country), *The Merry Widow* (operetta), pp.50–51, A1

Martingale, England (town), *Cover Her Face* by P.D. James (novel), pp.64–65, D2

Martirio, Texas (town), *Vernon God Little* by D.B.C. Pierre (novel), pp.16–17, B2

Marumaru Sound, New Zealand (town), *The Mannequin Makers* by Craig Cliff (novel), pp.108–109, F1

Marvis Bay, England (town), novels of P.G. Wodehouse, pp.64–65, B1

Marysville, Texas (town), *The Outsider* by Stephen King (novels), pp.16–17, C2

Maskattawan Dam, Quebec (building), Marvel Comics, pp.26–27, E1

Massacre Plains, New South Wales (town), *The Yield* by Tara June Winch (novel), pp.108–109, D2

Massarde Enterprises Solar Plant, Mali (building), *Sahara* by Clive Cussler (novel/film), pp.84–85, B5

Master's Lodge, The, Texas (building), *Manos: The Hands of Fate* (film), pp.18–19, A2

Matlock, Victoria (town), *Matlock Police* (TV), pp.108–109, D2

Matobo (fictional country), *The Interpreter* (film), pp.84–85, C2

Matodi, Azanian Empire (fictional town), *Black Mischief* by Evelyn Waugh (novel), pp.84–85, D4

Matrubhoomi, India (village), *Matrubhoomi: A Nation Without Women*, pp.78–79, C4

Matsu, Japan (island), *James Bond: You Only Live Twice* (film), pp.96–97, A1

Matsuhara, Japan (town), *The Story of Forest Rail* (video game), pp.96–97, D4

Matsuhara Railway, Japan (railway), *The Story of Forest Rail* (video game), pp.96–97, D4

Matul, US Virgin Islands (island), *Zombi 2* (film), pp.32–33, F2

Maui's Island, Pacific Ocean (island), *Moana* (film), pp.120–121, D3

Mauna Sol, Hawaii (mountain), *Cloud Atlas* by David Mitchell (film/novel), pp.18–19, D4

Mauville City, Japan (city), *Pokémon* (video games), pp.96–97, A1

Mawitaan, Bangalla (fictional city), *The Phantom* (comic), pp.84–85, D3

Mawson, South Australia (town), *The Ghost Writer* by John Harwood (novel), pp.108–109, C2

Mayapore, India (town), *The Raj Quartet* by Paul Scott (novels), pp.78–79, C4

Mayberry, North Carolina (town), *The Andy Griffith Show/Mayberry R.F.D.* (TV), pp.14–15, B3

Maycomb, Alabama (town), *To Kill a Mockingbird* by Harper Lee (novel), pp.14–15, A2

Maycomb County, Alabama (county), *To Kill a Mockingbird* by Harper Lee (novel), pp.14–15, A2

Mayfield, California (town), *Leave it to Beaver* (TV), pp.18–19, A4

Mazapevke, Ukraine (town), works of Sholem Aleichem (stories), pp.50–51, C3

Mazikhandar (fictional country), Marvel Comics (various), pp.72–73, B1/C1

McCastle McDuckula, Scotland (building), *Count Duckula* (TV), pp.64–65, B4

McDuck Sublab, Atlantic Ocean (building), *Duck Tales* (TV), pp.126–127, B3

McGonagall Manse, Scotland (building), Harry Potter novels by J.K. Rowling (novels/films), pp.64–65, C5

McGregor Castle, Scotland (building), *Stingray* (TV), pp.64–65, B5

McGregor Farm, England (building), *Peter Rabbit* by Beatrix Potter (various), pp.64–65, B3

McKinley, Pennsylvania (town), *Final Destination* series (films), pp.14–15, C5

McMaynerbury, Texas (town), *King of the Hill* (TV), pp.16–17, B2

McSwiggan Village, Ireland (village), *Family Guy* (TV), pp.64–65, B2

Meccania (fictional country), *Meccania: The Super-State* by Owen Gregory (novel), pp.44–45, D3

Medallion, Ohio (town), *Sula* by Toni Morrison (novel), pp.14–15, B4

Medici (fictional island/country), *Just Cause 3* (video games), pp.44–45, C2

Medicine River, Alberta (town), *Medicine River* by Thomas King (novel), pp.26–27, C1

Medina Wasi, Iraq (village, military training exercise), pp.72–73, C2

Medioka (fictional country), *Mickey Mouse* (cartoon), pp.50–51, A2

Medisuela (fictional country), Marvel Comics, pp.38–39, B3/C3

Meerkovo, Russia (village), Compare the Market adverts (advertising), pp.50–51, D4

Mega-City One, Mega-City One (city/state), *Judge Dredd* (comics), pp.14–15, C4

Mega-City Two, Mega-City Two (city/state), *Judge Dredd* (comics), pp.18–19, A4/A5

Megasaki, Japan (island), *Isle of Dogs* (film), pp.96–97, A1

Mei-tan-fu, China (village), *The Painted Veil* by W. Somerset Maugham (novel/film), pp.102–103, D2

Melchester, England (city), novels of Thomas Hardy, pp.64–65, C1

Mêlée Island, Caribbean (island), *Monkey Island* series (video games), pp.32–33, E3

Melemele Island, Hawaii (island), *Pokémon* (video games), pp.18–19, C1

Melincourt Castle, England (building), *Melincourt* by Thomas Love Peacock (novel), pp.64–65, C2

Mellacai, Malaysia (city), *Jelle's Marble Runs* (web series), pp.90–91, A3

Mellick, Ireland (city), *The Ante Room* by Kate O'Brien (play), pp.64–65, A2

Mellstock, England (town), novels of Thomas Hardy, pp.64–65, C1

Melonville, Alberta (town), *SCTV* (TV), pp.26–27, A1

Melton, Kentucky (town), *Petticoat Junction/Green Acres* (TV), pp.14–15, A3

Meltybrook, Ireland (city), *Meltybrains* (band), pp.64–65, A2

Memfish, Tennessee (city), DC Comics, pp.16–17, D2

Mena Ngai (The Great Mound), Wakanda (fictional natural feature), Marvel Comics (various), pp.84–85, D4

Mercer County, Montana (county), *Montana 1948* by Larry Watson (novel), pp.16–17, A6

Mercier, Louisiana (town), *Vampire Bats* (film), pp.16–17, D2

Mercury, Minnesota (town), *Young Adult* (film), pp.16–17, C6

Mercy, Michigan (town), *Song of Solomon* by Toni Morrison (novel), pp.14–15, A6

Mercy, Saskatchewan (town), *Little Mosque on the Prairie* (TV), pp.26–27, C1

Meridiana, Argentina (city), *Cybersix* (comics), pp.38–39, B2

Merioneth, Wales (town), *Ivor the Engine* (TV), pp.64–65, C2

Mermaid's Spit, Panama (natural feature), *The Pirates! Band of Misfits!* (film), pp.32–33, D1

Meropis, Lost Continent of (fictional sunken continent), *Meropis* by Theopompus of Chios (book), pp.126–127, C1/D1/C2/D2

Mertonford, Scotland (town), *Narrow-Gauge Adventure* by P.D. Hancock (book), pp.64–65, C4

Meru, Tibet (town), *The City of Skulls* by L. Sprague de Camp and Lin Carter (novel), pp.102–103, D2

Meruza, Argentina (region), *Aconcagua* (video games), pp.38–39, B3

Mervo (fictional country), *The Prince and Betty* by P.G. Wodehouse (novel), pp.44–45, C2

Meryton, England (town), *Pride and Prejudice* by Jane Austen (novel), pp.64–65, D2

Mesa de la Luna, Mexico (mountain), *Red Dead Redemption* series (video games), pp.32–33, B3/B4

Mesa del Sol, Mexico (mountain), *Red Dead Redemption* series (video games), pp.32–33, B3

M sto, Czech Republic (town), *The Glass Room* by Simon Mawer (novel), pp.50–51, B3

Metro City, Indonesia (city), *Garuda Superhero* (film), pp.90–91, B1

Metrofulus, Malaysia (city/state), *Cicak-Man* series (films), pp.90–91, B2

Metropolis, Delaware (city), DC Comics, pp.14–15, C4

Metropolis, Germany (city), *Metropolis* (film), pp.44–45, C4

Metropolitan Nekoma High School, Japan (building), *Haikyu!!* by Haruichi Furudate (anime), pp.96–97, E1

Metroville, Illinois (city), *The Incredibles* (film), pp.16–17, D4

Mex-City (fictional city/state), *Judge Dredd* (comics), pp.32–33, B3

Mexitlán, Mexico (country), *MacTrump* by Ian Doescher and Jacopo Della Quercia (book), pp.32–33, B3

Mhomala, Azanian Empire (fictional town), *Black Mischief* by Evelyn Waugh (novel), pp.84–85, D4

Michisota (fictional state), *Avalanche Annie: A Not So Tall Tale* by Lisa Wheeler (book), pp.16–17, C6

Michuri, South Korea (village), *Village Survival, the Eight* (TV), pp.102–103, E3

Mickewa (fictional state), *The American Senator* by Anthony Trollope (novel), pp.14–15, A5

Mid-Atlantic Wench, Atlantic Ocean (region), *The Pirates! Band of Misfits!* (film), pp.126–127, D2

Midculter, Scotland (town), Lymond Chronicles by Dorothy Dunnett (novels), pp.64–65, B5

Middle Park, Colorado (town), *South Park* (TV), pp.18–19, D4

Middle Zealand, New Zealand (country), *The Lego Movie* (film), pp.108–109, F2

Middlemarch, England (town), *Middlemarch* by George Eliot (novel), pp.64–65, C2

Middleton, Colorado (city), *Kim Possible* (TV), pp.16–17, A4

Middletown, Northern Ireland (town), *Middletown* (TV), pp.64–65, B3

Midland City, Indiana (town), *Breakfast of Champions* by Kurt Vonnegut (novel/film), pp.14–15, A4

Midlands (fictional state, law), pp.16–17, B3

Midnight, Texas (town), *Midnight, Texas* (TV), pp.16–17, A2

Midorijima, Japan (island), *DRAMAtical Murder* (video game/anime), pp.96–97, D1

Midoriyama-Shi, Japan (town), *Uzumaki* by Junji Ito (manga), pp.96–97, B2

Midsomer, England (county), *Midsomer Murders* (TV), pp.64–65, C2

Midston, Maine (town), Danny Dunn series by Raymond Abrashkin and Jay Williams (novels), pp.14–15, D6

Midway City, Michigan (city), DC Comics, pp.14–15, A6

Midwich, England (village), *The Midwich Cuckoos* by John Wyndham (novel), pp.64–65, D2

Might Tower, Japan (building), *My Hero Academia* by Kōhei Horikoshi (manga/anime), pp.96–97, E1

Milanh, Afghanistan (village), *Deployment* (film), pp.72–73, D2

Milborough, Ontario (town), *For Better or For Worse* by Lynn Johnston (comic), pp.26–27, A4

Milbury, England (village), *Children of the Stones* (TV), pp.64–65, C2

Mildendo, Lilliput (fictional city), *Gulliver's Travels* by Jonathan Swift (novel), pp.108–109, D2

Milford Haven, New Hampshire (town), *The X-Files* (TV), pp.14–15, D5

Milford, Nebraska (town), *Amerika* (TV), pp.16–17, B4

Milfort, Ireland (town), Milfort: A Fictional Irish Town (stage act), pp.64–65, A2

Miller's Bend, Colorado (natural feature), *Atomic Train* (film), pp.18–19, D4

Miller's Grove, Massachusetts (town), *The X-Files* (TV), pp.14–15, D5

Millet, Minnesota (town), *A Prairie Home Companion* (radio), pp.16–17, C5

Millikan County, Georgia (county), *The X-Files* (TV), pp.14–15, B3

Milorie, Saskatchewan (town), *A Prairie as Wide as the Sea* by Sarah Ellis (novel), pp.26–27, C1

Milosis, Zu-Vendis (fictional town), *Allan Quatermain* by H. Rider Haggard (novel), pp.84–85, D3

Milton, England (town), *North and South* by Elizabeth Gaskell (novel), pp.64–65, D2

Mina Escondida, Mexico (town), *Lo Imperdonable* (TV), pp.32–33, A3

Minami, Westlande (fictional city), *Log Horizon* by Mamare Touno and Kazuhiro Hara (novels/anime), pp.96–97, B2

Minnehaha, Minnesota (city), *D2 The Mighty Ducks* (film), pp.16–17, C6

Mirat, India (region), the Raj Quartet series by Paul Scott (novels), pp.78–79, B4

Miskatonic Expedition Northern Base Camp, *At the Mountains of Madness* by H.P. Lovecraft (novella), pp.114–115, D1

Miskatonic Expedition Southern Base Camp, *At the Mountains of Madness* by H.P. Lovecraft (novella), pp.114–115, D2

Miskatonic River, Massachusetts (river), Cthulhu Mythos/H.P. Lovecraft (various), pp.14–15, C5/D5

Miss Cackle's Academy for Witches, Wales (building), *The Worst Witch* by Jill Murphy (novels/TV), pp.64–65, C2

Miss Pentangle's Academy for Witches, Wales (building), *The Worst Witch* by Jill Murphy (novels/TV), pp.64–65, C2

Miss Peregrine's Home for Peculiar Children, Wales (building), *Miss Peregrine's Home for Peculiar Children* by Ransom Riggs (novel/film), pp.64–65, B2

Missel Moor, England (natural feature), *The Secret Garden* by Frances Hodgson Burnett (novel), pp.64–65, C3

Misselthwaite Manor, England (building), *The Secret Garden* by Frances Hodgson Burnett (novel), pp.64–65, C3

Missing Mile, North Carolina (town), *Drawing Blood* by Poppy Z Brite (novel), pp.14–15, C3

Mission City, Nevada (city), *Transformers* (film), pp.18–19, B3

Missitucky (fictional state), *Finian's Rainbow* (musical), pp.14–15, A4

Mist County, Minnesota (county), *A Prairie Home Companion* (radio), pp.16–17, C5

Misty Island, England (island), *Thomas the Tank Engine* by Rev W. Audrey (books/TV), pp.64–65, C3

Mitakihara, Japan (city), *Puella Magi Madoka Magica* (anime/manga), pp.96–97, C3

Mitsuba, Japan (town), *Servant x Service* by Karino Takatsu (manga), pp.96–97, C4

Mixo-Lydia (fictional country), works of Angela Thirkell, pp.50–51, B1/A5

Mjölhagen, Sweden (town), *Uti vår hage* by Krister Petersson (comic strip), pp.56–57, B2

Moahu, Pacific Ocean (island), *The Wine-Dark Sea* by Patrick O'Brian (novel), pp.120–121, D4

Mobono (fictional region/city), Islandia novels and sequels by Austin Tappan Wright and Mark Saxton, pp.84–85, B1

Moby Dick, Atlantic Ocean (wreck), *The Bedford Incident* by Mark Rascovich (novel/film), pp.126–127, C4

Moccasin Peak, Montana (mountain), *Lonely Train a' Comin'/Helltracks* by William F. Nolan (short story/novel), pp.18–19, D6

Modern City, India (city), *Motu Patlu* (TV), pp.78–79, B3

Modesta, Michigan (town), *Daughters of Eve* by Lois Duncan (novel), pp.14–15, A5

Moesko Island, Washington (island), *The Ring* (film), pp.18–19, A6

Mohalis, Winnemac (fictional city), novels of Sinclair Lewis, pp.14–15, A4

Mojok, Malaysia (building/estate), *Biggles: The Adventure of the Oxidized Grotto* by W.E. Johns (novel), pp.90–91, C2

Mokry-Kut, Ukraine (village), *Gates of Bronze* by Haim Hazaz (novel), pp.50–51, C3

Molasses Park, Costa Rica (island), *Walter Melon* (TV), pp.32–33, C1

Moldavia (fictional country), *Dynasty* (TV), pp.50–51, C2/C3

Moldovistan (fictional country), *The Real Adventures of Jonny Quest* (TV), pp.72–73, B3

Molmol, Kingdom of, Pacific Ocean (island), *Love Hina* by Ken Akamatsu (manga/anime), pp.120–121, D2

Molvania (fictional country), *Molvania: A Land Untouched by Modern Dentistry* (book), pp.50–51, A3/B3

Mombaka (fictional country), *Red Scorpion* (film), pp.84–85, D2

Monan's Rill, Scotland (natural feature), *The Lady of the Lake* by Sir Walter Scott (poem), pp.64–65, C4

Monimaskit, Scotland (town), *The Testament of Gideon Mack* by James Robertson (novel), pp.64–65, C4

Monkey Island, Caribbean (island), *Monkey Island* series (video games), pp.32–33, B4

Monkey's Land, Glass Town Federation (fictional country), Brontë juvenilia, pp.84–85, A3

Monkshaven, England (town), *Sylvia's Lovers* by Elizabeth Gaskell (novel), pp.64–65, C3

Monmouth, Connecticut (town), *The Narrows* by Ann Petry (novel), pp.14–15, C5

Monster Island, Pacific Ocean (island), *Godzilla* films, pp.120–121, C3

Mont Porte (fictional island), *Transformers: Masterforce* (anime), pp.44–45, D2

Mont Yuron, Quebec (city), *The Shadows* by Kaitlin Prest (audio drama), pp.26–27, E1

Monte Caprabianca, Italy (town), *Necropolis* by Geoff Spedding (novel), pp.44–45, D2

Montelusa, Italy (city), Inspector Montalbano novels by Andrea Camilleri (novels/TV), pp.44–45, D2

Montenegro (fictional country), *The Centurions*, pp.38–39, C2

Montgenoux, France (town), Hugo Duchamp Investigates series by G.N. Heatherington (novels), pp.44–45, B3

Montsaurai (fictional country), *Once Upon a Holiday* (film), pp.44–45, C3

Montsou, France (village), *Germinal* by Emile Zola (novel), pp.44–45, C3

Monument, Massachusetts (town), *The Chocolate War* by Robert Cormier (novel), pp.14–15, D5

Monument, Ireland (town), *The Sea and the Silence* by Peter Cunningham (novel), pp.64–65, B2

Moominvalley, Finland (village), the Moomin books by Tove Jansson (short stories), pp.56–57, B3

Moon-Bog, The, Ireland (natural feature), *The Moon-Bog* by H.P. Lovecraft (short story), pp.64–65, B3

Moonfleet, England (town), *Moonfleet* by J. Meade Falkner (novel), pp.64–65, C1

Moonlight Bay, California (town), *Seize the Night* by Dean Koontz (novel), pp.18–19, A3

Moonscar Island, Louisiana (island), *Scooby-Doo on Zombie Island* (film), pp.16–17, C4

Moonstone, Colorado (town), *The Song of the Lark* by Willa Cather (novel), pp.16–17, A4

Moor, Austria (town), *Morbus Kitahara* by Christoph Ransmayr (novel), pp.44–45, D3

Moorstones Manor, Scotland (building), *Ripping Yarns: Murder at Moorstones Manor* (TV), pp.64–65, B4

Moosehoof, Alberta (town), *What's With Andy?* (TV), pp.26–27, C1

Mooseport, Maine (town), *Welcome to Mooseport* (film), pp.14–15, D5

Moosylvania (fictional island), *The Adventures of Rocky and Bullwinkle* (TV), pp.16–17, C6

Mooyoung, South Korea (city), *Hero* (film), pp.102–103, E2

Moperville, Illinois (town), *El Goonish Shive* (web comic), pp.16–17, D4

Mopu, India (village), *Black Narcissus* by Rumer Godden (novel/film), pp.78–79, C4/D4

Moralia, Republic of, France (country), *Gundam 00* (anime), pp.44–45, C2

Moralton, Statesota (fictional city), *Moral Orel* (TV), pp.16–17, C3

Morawa National Park, New South Wales (town), *Another Night in Mullet Town* by Steven Herick (novel), pp.108–109, D1/D2

Moresby, Banoi (fictional city), *Dead Island* (video game), pp.90–91, F1

Morgue, California (town), *The Outer Limits* (TV), pp.18–19, B3

Morioh, Japan (city), *JoJo's Bizarre Adventure* by Hirohiko Araki (manga/anime), pp.96–97, C3

Morna, Estonia (town), *Õnne 13* (TV), pp.50–51, B5

Moronia (region), *Mundus alter et idem* by Joseph Hall (novel), pp.114–115, C3

Morphopolis, France (city), *La Cité du Sommeil* by Maurice Barrère (novel), pp.44–45, C3

Morros Verdes, Portugal (town), *Tempo de Amar* (TV), pp.44–45, A2

Moshimo, Japan (town), *Fireworks* (film), pp.96–97, C2

Mossdeep City, Japan (city), *Pokémon* (video games), pp.96–97, A1

Mossdeep Space Centre, Japan (building), *Pokémon* (video games), pp.96–97, A1

Mossy Bottom, England (village), *Shaun the Sheep* (TV/film), pp.64–65, C2

Mothering Sunday Islands, Pacific Ocean (island chain), *Nation* by Terry Pratchett (novel), pp.120–121, D2

Motunui, Pacific Ocean (island), *Moana* (film), pp.120–121, D2

Moulinsart, Belgium (village), *The Adventures of Tintin* by Hergé (comic books), pp.44–45, C3/C4

Mount Abora, Ethiopia (mountain), *Kubla Khan* by Samuel Taylor Coleridge (poem), pp.84–85, D4

Mount Analogue, Pacific Ocean (continent/mountain), *Le Mont Analogue* by René Daumal (novel), pp.120–121, A1/A4

Mount Antarktos (mountain), Cthulhu Mythos (various), pp.114–115, C2

Mount Buzhou, Tajikistan (mountain, Chinese mythology), pp.72–73, D4

Mount Chiliad, San Andreas (fictional mountain), *Grand Theft Auto* series (video game), pp.18–19, A3

Mount Gordo, San Andreas (fictional mountain), *Grand Theft Auto* series (video game), pp.18–19, A3

Mount Hatteras, Arctic (volcano), *The Voyages and Adventures of Captain Hatteras* by Jules Verne (novel), pp.26–27, C4

Mount Himalachia, Michisota (mountain), *Avalanche Annie: A Not So Tall Tale* by Lisa Wheeler (book), pp.16–17, C6

Mount Hokulani, Hawaii (mountain), *Pokémon* (video games), pp.18–19, D1

Mount Huaguo, Aolai (fictional mountain), *Journey to the West* by Wu Cheng'en (novel), pp.102–103, D2

Mount Huaze, China (mountain), *Jelle's Marble Runs* (web series), pp.102–103, C2

Mount Josiah, San Andreas (fictional mountain), *Grand Theft Auto* series (video game), pp.18–19, A3

Mount Karakal, Tibet (mountain), *Lost Horizon* by James Hilton (novel), pp.102–103, A2/A3

Mount Kirby, Washington (mountain), *Astro City* (comic), pp.18–19, B6

Mount Lanakila, Hawaii (mountain), *Pokémon* (video games), pp.18–19, D1

Mount Neverest, Nepal (mountain), *DuckTales* (TV), pp.78–79, C4

Mount Penglai, China (mountain, mythology), pp.102–103, D3

Mount Qaf, Arctic (mountain, Islamic tradition), pp.26–27, D4

Mount Rockmore, South Dakota (mountain), *Cromartie High School* (TV), pp.16–17, A5

Mount Rose, Minnesota (town), *Drop Dead Gorgeous* (film), pp.16–17, C5

Mount Saint Hilary, Oregon (mountain), *Transformers* (various), pp.18–19, A6

Mount Sapo, Italy (mountain, mythology), pp.44–45, D2

Mount Snuffleupagus, Hawaii (mountain), *Sesame Street* (TV), pp.18–19, C1

Mount Thomas, Victoria (town), *Blue Heelers* (TV), pp.108–109, D2

Mount Wundagore, Transia (fictional mountain), Marvel Comics, pp.50–51, B1

Mount Yaanek, Nunavut (mountain), *Ulalume* by Edgar Allen Poe (poem), pp.26–27, C4

Mount Yaddith-Gho, Mu (fictional mountain), Cthulhu Mythos (various), pp.120–121, E3

Mount Zstophnole, Sylvania (fictional mountain), *The Adventures of Tintin* by Hergé (various), pp.50–51, A1

Mountains of Kong (mountain range, folklore), pp.84–85, C4

Mountains of Madness, The (mountain range), *At the Mountains of Madness* by H.P. Lovecraft (novella), pp.114–115, E3

Mountains of the Moon (mountain range, folklore), pp.84–85, C4/D4

Mounty County, Yukon (county), *Droopy: Northwest Hounded Police* (TV), pp.26–27, B2

Mouse Bluffs, Manitoba (town), *A Candle to Light the Sun* by Patricia Blondal (novel), pp.26–27, C2

Mousekewitz family's village, Ukraine (village), *An American Tail* (film), pp.50–51, C3

Mouseton, Calisota (fictional city), *Mickey Mouse* (various), pp.18–19, A5

Mowgli's Jungle, India (natural feature), *The Jungle Book* by Rudyard Kipling (novel), pp.78–79, B4

Moybeg, Northern Ireland (town), *My Mother and Other Strangers* (TV), pp.64–65, B3

Mr and Mrs Claus Residence, Finland (building, tradition), pp.56–57, C5

MS Antonia Graza, Atlantic Ocean (wreck), *Ghost Ship* (film), pp.18–19, A1

Mt Chimney, Japan (mountain), *Pokémon* (video games), pp.96–97, A1

Mt Moon, Japan (mountain), *Pokémon* (video games), pp.96–97, C2

Mt Mortar, Japan (mountain), *Pokémon* (video games), pp.96–97, B2

Mt Pyre, Japan (mountain), *Pokémon* (video games), pp.96–97, A1

Mt Silver, Japan (mountain), *Pokémon* (video games), pp.96–97, C2

Mt Abraham, New York (town), *Final Destination* series (films), pp.14–15, C5

Mt Pilot, North Carolina (town), *The Andy Griffith Show* (TV), pp.14–15, B3

Mu-Mu Land, Mu (fictional region), 'Justified & Ancient' by The KLF (music), pp.120–121, B3/C3

Muckleton, Victoria (town), *Field of Poppies* by Carmel Bird (novel), pp.108–109, D2

Muddy Flat, Louisiana (town), *The Real Ghostbusters* (TV), pp.16–17, C4

Muddy River, China (town), *The Vagrants* by Yiyun Li (novel), pp.102–103, D4

Mudport, England (city), *The Mill on the Floss* by George Eliot (novel), pp.64–65, D3

Mugen Academy, Japan (building), *Sailor Moon* by Naoko Takeuchi (manga/anime), pp.96–97, E1

Mugsborough, England (town), *The Ragged-Trousered Philanthropists* by Robert Tressell (novel), pp.64–65, D1

Mugwomp Flats, Northern Territory (town), *The Rescuers Down Under* (film), pp.108–109, C2

Muir Britton, Wales/Ireland (sea), *Total War: Thrones of Britannia* (video game), pp.64–65, B2

Muir Domon, Scotland (sea), *Total War: Thrones of Britannia* (video game), pp.64–65, B5

Muir Island, Scotland (island), *X-Men* (comics), pp.64–65, A5/B5

Muir Nore, Scotland (sea), *Total War: Thrones of Britannia* (video game), pp.64–65, D3/E3

Muirinish, Ireland (town), novels of Graham Norton, pp.64–65, A2

Muji City, China (city), *Saboteur* by Ha Jin (short story), pp.102–103, E3/E4

Mujin, South Korea (city), *The Crucible* by Gong Ji-young (novel), pp.102–103, E2

Mulberry Castle, Wales (estate), *Nicholas Nickleby* by Charles Dickens (novel), pp.64–65, C2

Mullinmore, Ireland (town), novels of Graham Norton, pp.64–65, A2

Mulongwe, Kasavubu (fictional city), *Tenth Man Down* by Chris Ryan (novel), pp.84–85, C2

Mululuk, South Australia (town), *All Fall Down* by Cassandra Austin (novel), pp.108–109, C2

Mumbles' Emperor Penguin Colony, *Happy Feet* (film), pp.114–115, D2

Muncaster, England (city), *The Stones of Muncaster Cathedral* by Robert Westall (novel), pp.64–65, C2

Munchausen, Germany (city), *Hurricanes* (TV), pp.44–45, D3

Mundra, Queensland (town), *Her Sister's Eye* by Vivienne Cleven (novel), pp.108–109, D3

Municiberg, Washington (city), *The Incredibles* (film), pp.18–19, B6

Muratpa a, Turkey (village), *Dance with Death* by Barbara Nadel (novel), pp.72–73, B3

Murderhorn, the North Takoma (fictional mountain), *The Simpsons* (TV), pp.18–19, A6

Murha, India (village), works of Mahasweta Devi (stories), pp.78–79, C4

Murray, Virginia (town), *The X-Files* (TV), pp.14–15, C4

Murrumby River, New South Wales (river), *The Yield* by Tara June Winch (novel), pp.108–109, D2

Muskoka River, Illinois (river), Nancy Drew mysteries (novels/TV), pp.16–17, D4

Musselcrag, Scotland (town), *The Antiquary* by Sir Walter Scott (novel), pp.64–65, C4

Musutafu, Japan (city), *My Hero Academia* by Kōhei Horikoshi (manga/anime), pp.96–97, E1

MV *Seguin Laroche*, Atlantic Ocean (wreck), *Timewreck Titanic* by Rhys B. Davies (novel), pp.126–127, B4

Mypos, Greece (island nation), *Perfect Strangers* (TV), pp.44–45, E1

Mystery Mountain, Oregon (mountain), *Gravity Falls* (TV), pp.18–19, B5

Mystery, Alaska (town), *Mystery, Alaska* (film), pp.18–19, B4

Mystic Falls, Virginia (town), *The Vampire Diaries*, pp.14–15, B4/C4

Mythmythilia, India (city), works of Robert Antoni, pp.78–79, C4

N. Sanity Island, Pacific Ocean (island), *Crash Bandicoot* series (video games), pp.120–121, D2

Nabu Island, Pacific Ocean (island), *My Hero Academia* by Kōhei Horikoshi (manga/anime), pp.96–97, C2

Nagasaki Shatterdome, Japan (building), *Pacific Rim* (film), pp.96–97, A1

Nambia (fictional country), the mysterious brain of Donald Trump (gaffe), pp.84–85, B2/C2

Nampara, England (building), *Poldark* (TV), pp.64–65, B1

Nanahama, Japan (city), *Maji de Watashi ni Koi Shinasai!* (graphic novels/video games), pp.96–97, E1

Nanda Parbat, Pakistan (city), DC Comics, pp.78–79, B5

Nandagiri, India (town), *The Tainted* by Cauvery Madhaven (novel), pp.78–79, B3

Nanga Dalle, India (mountain), *Black Narcissus* by Rumer Godden (novel/film), pp.78–79, C4

Nania, Estonia/Russia (lake), *His Dark Materials* by Philip Pullman (various), pp.50–51, C5

Nanzhao (fictional country), IDW Comics, pp.90–91, A4

Naptonshire, England (county, home defence training situations), pp.64–65, C2

Naruba (fictional country), *Designated Survivor*, pp.84–85, B4

Naruhata, Japan (town), *My Hero Academia* by Kōhei Horikoshi (manga/anime), pp.96–97, E1

Nathan Bateman's Estate, Alaska (region), *Ex Machina* (film), pp.18–19, A4

Nation, The, Pacific Ocean (island), *Nation* by Terry Pratchett (novel), pp.120–121, D2

National Central Railway, Costaguana (fictional railway), *Nostromo* by Joseph Conrad (novel), pp.38–39, A4

National City, California (city), *Supergirl* (TV), pp.18–19, A2

National Homeland One, North Dakota (region), *The Handmaid's Tale* by Margaret Atwood (novel), pp.16–17, B6

Nautilus, Iowa (town), works of Sinclair Lewis, pp.16–17, C4

Nautilus, Pacific Ocean (wreck), *The Mysterious Island* by Jules Verne (novel), pp.120–121, D2

Navarone, Greece (island), *The Guns of Navarone* by Alistair MacLean (novel/film), pp.44–45, F1

Navidad (fictional country), works of John Hearne, pp.32–33, D3

Nayapur, Anandapur (fictional city), Walt Disney World (theme park), pp.78–79, C4

NBE Supermax, Colorado (building), *Transformers: The Last Knight* (film), pp.16–17, A4

Ndotsheni, South Africa (town), *Cry the Beloved Country* by Alan Paton (novel/film), pp.84–85, C4

Nea So Copros (fictional bloc/super-region), *Cloud Atlas* by David Mitchell (novel), pp.102–103, D3/E3

Necropolis, California (city), *Fallout 1* (video game), pp.18–19, A3

Necropolis, Colorado (city), *Gunnm/Battle Angel Alita* (various), pp.16–17, A4

Needmore, Kentucky (town), *The Natural Man* by Ed McClanahan (novel), pp.14–15, A4

Nekomi, Japan (town), *Oh My Goddess!* by Kōsuke Fujishima (manga/anime), pp.96–97, C2

Nello and Patrasche, Mamarrosa (village), *Alentejo Blue* by Monica Ali (novel), pp.44–45, A2

Nemedia, Germany (region), Conan novels of Robert E. Howard, pp.44–45, D4

Nemesis, Mexico/Guatemala/Belize (wreck, spaceship), *Transformers* (TV), pp.32–33, C2

Nemeton Monastery, Wales (building), *Koudelka* (video game), pp.64–65, C2

Neo Purgatory, Utah (building), *6 Angels* (anime), pp.18–19, C4

Neo Seoul, South Korea (city), *Cloud Atlas* by David Mitchell (novel), pp.102–103, E3

Neo Tokyo, Japan (city, various), pp.96–97, E1/F1

Nepenthe, Italy (island), *South Wind* by Norman Douglas (novel), pp.44–45, C2

Neptune Base (Martel Corporation), Pacific Ocean (submerged building), *Lords of the Deep* (film), pp.120–121, A4

Neptune, California (town), *Veronica Mars* (TV), pp.18–19, B3

NERV 2nd Branch, Nevada (building), *Neon Genesis Evangelion* (anime/films), pp.18–19, B3

Netherfield, England (estate), *Pride and Prejudice* by Jane Austen (novel), pp.64–65, D2

Neustadt, Germany (city), *Benjamin the Elephant* (radio/TV), pp.44–45, D4

Neutralia, Portugal (country), *Arrival and Departure* by Arthur Koestler (novel), pp.44–45, A2

Neuvo-Rico (fictional country), *The Adventures of Tintin* by Hergé (various), pp.38–39, B5

Never-Ending Mountain, China (mountain), *Where the Mountain Meets the Moon* by Grace Lin (novel), pp.102–103, A3

Neverland, Belize (island), *Peter Pan* by J.M. Barrie (novels/films), pp.32–33, C2

New Asgard, Norway (town), *Avengers Endgame* (film), pp.56–57, B5

New Atlantis/Bensalem, Pacific Ocean (island/nation), *New Atlantis* by Francis Bacon (novel), pp.38–39, A4

New Austin (fictional state), *Red Dead Redemption* series (video games), pp.18–19, D2

New Bark Town, Japan (town), *Pokémon* (video games), pp.96–97, C2

New Bern, Kansas (town), *Jericho* (TV), pp.16–17, B4

New Bordeaux, Louisiana (city), *Mafia 3* (video game), pp.16–17, D2

New Denmark (country), *His Dark Materials* by Philip Pullman (various), pp.14–15, B5/C5

New Eden, New South Wales (building), *Return to Eden* (TV), pp.108–109, F4

New Edwards Base, California (building), *Mobile Suit Gundam Wing* (anime), pp.18–19, B3

New France (fictional country), *His Dark Materials* by Philip Pullman (various), pp.26–27, E1/E2

New Geneva, Switzerland (city), *Thunderbirds Are Go* (TV), pp.44–45, C3

New Hanover (fictional state), *Red Dead Redemption* series (video games), pp.16–17, C3/D3

New Kelp City, Pacific Ocean (city), *SpongeBob SquarePants* (TV), pp.120–121, B4

New Kirk City, Pacific Ocean (city), *Godzilla* films, pp.96–97, F4

New Liberty, Illinois (town), *Wild Wild West* (film), pp.16–17, D3

New Mombasa space tether, Kenya (space elevator), *HALO* series (video games), pp.84–85, D3

New New York, New York (city), *Futurama*, pp.14–15, D1

New Paris, France (city), *Wolfenstein* series (video game), pp.44–45, C3

New Penzance, Rhode Island (island), *Moonrise Kingdom* (film), pp.14–15, D5

New Port City, Japan (city), *Dominion Tank Police* by Masamune Shirow (manga/anime), pp.96–97, B2

New Port City, Sanc Kingdom (fictional city), *Gundam Wing* (anime), pp.56–57, B1

New Quackmore, Calisota (fictional city), *DuckTales* (various), pp.18–19, A5

New Reno, Nevada (city), *Fallout 2* (video game), pp.18–19, B4

New Salem, Oregon (town), *Monster High* (various), pp.18–19, A5

New Switzerland, Indian Ocean (island), *Swiss Family Robinson* by Johann Wyss and *Second Fatherland* by Jules Verne (novel/film), pp.90–91, A2

New Temperence (fictional state), *Gangsters 2* (video game), pp.14–15, C5/D5

New Thai Confederacy (fictional country), *2000 AD* (comics), pp.90–91, B3

New Thermopylae, Illinois (town), *Martin Chuzlewitt* by Charles Dickens (novel), pp.16–17, D4

New Troy (fictional state), *Lois & Clark: The New Adventures of Superman* (TV), pp.14–15, C5

New Vegas, Nevada (city), *Fallout New Vegas* (video game), pp.18–19, B3

New Venice, Florida (town), DC Comics, pp.14–15, C1

New Venice, Arctic (city), *Aurorarama* by Jean Christophe-Valtat (novel), pp.26–27, C3

New Wye, Appalachia (fictional town), *Pale Fire* by Vladimir Nabokov (novel), pp.14–15, B4

New Yorktown, New York (city), *MacTrump* by Ian Doescher and Jacopo Della Quercia (book), pp.14–15, D1

New Zanzibar (fictional country), *The Simpsons* (TV), pp.84–85, D3/D3

New Zebedee, Michigan (town), *The House with a Clock in its Walls* by John Bellairs (novel), pp.14–15, B4

Newbridge, Prince Edward Island (town), *Anne of Green Gables* by Lucy Maud Montgomery (novel), pp.26–27, F1

Newburg, Pennsylvania (town), *Left 4 Dead* (video games), pp.14–15, B4

Newmoon Island, Japan (island), *Pokémon* (video games), pp.96–97, C4

Newtech City, California (city), *Power Rangers SPD* (TV), pp.18–19, A4

Newton Haven, England (town), *The World's End* (film), pp.64–65, D2

Newtown, England (town), *Z-Cars* (TV), pp.64–65, C3

Niaowu, China (town), *Shenmue III* (video game), pp.102–103, C1

Nibia (fictional country), *Ace Ventura: When Nature Calls* (film), pp.84–85, C3

Night City, California (city), *Cyberpunk 2077* (games), pp.18–19, A3

Night Vale, New Mexico (town), *Welcome to Night Vale* (podcast), pp.16–17, A2

Nightmare Abbey, England (building), *Nightmare Abbey* by Thomas Love Peacock (novella), pp.64–65, D2

Nightmare Canyon, Northern Territory (natural feature), *The Rescuers Down Under* (film), pp.108–109, C4

Niihama, Japan (city/island), *Ghost in the Shell* by Masamune Shirow (manga/anime), pp.96–97, B2

Nilbog, Utah (town), *Troll 2* (film), pp.18–19, C4

Ninetail Dominions (fictional country), *Log Horizon* by Mamare Touno and Kazuhiro Hara (novels/anime), pp.96–97, A1/A2

Nirsk, Arstotzka (fictional town), *Papers, Please* (video game), pp.72–73, C4

Nischindipur, India (village), *Pather Panchali* by Bibhutibhushan Bandyopadhyay (novel/film), pp.78–79, D4

Nisi, China (city), *Bond* (play), pp.102–103, D2

Nkongsamba, Kinjaja (fictional city), *A Good Man in Africa* by William Boyd (novel/film), pp.84–85, B4

No. 1 Ladies' Detective Agency, The, Botswana (building), *The No.1 Ladies' Detective Agency* by Alexander McCall Smith (novel), pp.84–85, C4

Nöckeln, Sweden (town), *The Bert-Diaries* by Anders Jacobsson and Soren Olssen (novels), pp.56–57, B3

Nollop, South Carolina (island), *Ella Minnow Pea* by Mark Dunn (novel), pp.14–15, C3

Nomanisan Island, Pacific Ocean (island), *The Incredibles*, pp.120–121, E2

Nomp, San Serriffe (fictional town), *The Guardian* (newspaper), pp.78–79, A2

Norchester, England (city), novels of Alan Hunter, pp.64–65, D2

Norland Park, England (estate), *Sense and Sensibility* by Jane Austen (novel), pp.64–65, D1

Norramby, England (town), *Thomas the Tank Engine* by Rev W. Audrey (books/TV), pp.64–65, C3

Norroway (fictional country), *His Dark Materials* by Philip Pullman (novels), pp.56–57, A3

North China Sea, China (sea), *Arrow* (TV), pp.102–103, D2/E2

North Dakastor, North Dakota (state), *MacTrump* by Ian Doescher and Jacopo Della Quercia (book), pp.16–17, A5/B5

North Doodle, Yogistan (fictional mountain), *The Ascent of Rum Doodle* by W.E. Bowman, pp.78–79, B5/C5

North High School, Japan (building), *The Melancholy of Haruhi Suzumiya* by Nagaru Tanigawa and Noizi Ito (novels/anime), pp.96–97, B2

North India Railway, Pakistan, *North West Frontier*, pp.78–79, B5

North Killtown, Scotland (town), *The Simpsons*, pp.64–65, C5

North Korasia, North Korea (country), *MacTrump* by Ian Doescher and Jacopo Della Quercia (book), pp.102–103, E3

North Middle Branch, Minnesota (town), *Infinity Train* (TV), pp.16–17, C5

North Mountain, China (mountain), *The Vagrants* by Yiyun Li (novel), pp.102–103, D4

North Mountain, The, Arendelle (fictional mountain), *Frozen* (film), pp.56–57, B4

North Ortiz Sea, Indian Ocean (sea), *The Illegal* by Lawrence Hill (novel), pp.78–79, B1/C1

North Park, Colorado (town), *South Park* (TV), pp.18–19, D4

North Sister Island, Michigan (island), *Transformers: Animated* (TV), pp.14–15, B5

North Star, Ukraine (village), *The North Star* (film), pp.50–51, C3

North Takoma (fictional state), *The Simpsons* (TV), pp.18–19, A6

North Yankton (fictional state), *Grand Theft Auto* series (video games), pp.16–17, B6

Northanger Abbey, England (estate), *Northanger Abbey* by Jane Austen (novel), pp.64–65, C2

Northspur, New Zealand (town), *Northspur* (film), pp.108–109, F2

Norvinsk, Russia (region), *Escape from Tarkov* (video game), pp.50–51, C5

Nottamun, England (town), 'Nottamun' (folk song), pp.64–65, C2/D2

Nova Aliança, Brazil (town), *Coração de Estudante* (TV), pp.38–39, C3

Nova Esperança, Brazil (town), *Era uma vez f* (TV), pp.38–39, C3

Nova Robotics, Washington (town), *Short Circuit* (film), pp.18–19, A6

Nova Solyma, Israel (city), *Nova Solyma* by Samuel Gott (novel), pp.72–73, B2

Novac, Nevada (town), *Fallout New Vegas* (video games), pp.18–19, B3

Noventa Cannon, The, Somalia (building), *Mobile Suit Gundam Wing* (anime), pp.84–85, B4

Novi Grad, Sokovia (fictional city), Marvel Cinematic Universe, pp.44–45, A3

Novi, Virginia (town), *The X-Files* (TV), pp.14–15, C4

Novigrad, Chernarus (fictional city), *ARMA 2* (video game), pp.50–51, A5

Nowaja Lebedzewka, Ukraine (village), *The Rainbow* by Wanda Wasilewska (novel/film), pp.50–51, D3

Nowhere, Kansas (town), *Courage the Cowardly Dog* (TV), pp.16–17, B4

Nsara, France (city), *The Years of Rice and Salt* by Kim Stanley Robinson (novel), pp.44–45, B3

NTI City, The, Caribbean (submerged city), *The Abyss* (film), pp.32–33, D2

Nu Mung Ba, Cambodia (building), *Apocalypse Now* (film), pp.90–91, B3

Nu-Bangkok, New Thai Confederacy (fictional city), *2000 AD* (comics), pp.90–91, B3

Nu-Delhi, India (city), *2000 AD* (comics), pp.78–79, B3

Nueva Esperanza, Colombia (town), *Flor Salvaje* (TV), pp.38–39, A5

Nueva Voz, Solis (fictional city), *Just Cause 4* (video game), pp.38–39, A5

Nuevo Paraiso, Mexico (country), *Red Dead Redemption* series (video games), pp.32–33, B3

Nuevo Toledo, Mexico (city), *Club de Cuervos* (TV), pp.32–33, B2

Nukehavistan (fictional country), *The Onion* (online satire), pp.72–73, D3/E3

Nuku'la Atoll, Pacific Ocean (island), *San Sombrèro* (book), pp.120–121, C4

Null Island, Atlantic Ocean (island, real life), pp.126–127, D2

Numasoko, Japan (town), *The Story of Forest Rail* (video game), pp.96–97, D4

Numbani (fictional country), *Overwatch* (video game), pp.84–85, B4

Nùng River, China (river), *Apocalypse Now* (film), pp.90–91, B3, pp.102–103, C1

Nutwood, England (village), *Rupert Bear* by Mary Tourtel (comic books/TV), pp.64–65, B2

O-Town, Wisconsin (town), *Rocko's Modern Life* (TV), pp.16–17, D5

Oakdale, Illinois (town), *As the World Turns* (TV), pp.16–17, D4

Oakwood, British Columbia (town), *Oakwood* (video game), pp.26–27, B1

Oasis, Iraq (city), *Overwatch* (video game), pp.72–73, C2

Obeah, Mexico (wreck/building), *Cruise Into Terror* (film), pp.32–33, C3

Oblivion, Nebraska (town), *Oblivion, Nebraska* by Peter Moore Smith (short story/short film), pp.16–17, B4

Obra Dinn, England (wreck), *The Return of the Obra Dinn* (video game), pp.64–65, B1

Obristan (fictional country), *Papers, Please* (video game), pp.50–51, A5

Ocean Shores, California (town), *Rocket Power* (TV), pp.18–19, B3

Oceana (fictional island/nation), *The Strong Man* by H.R.F. Keating (novel), pp.126–127, D5

Oceana (fictional island/nation), *Oceana* by James Harrington (novel), pp.38–39, C2

Oceanview, Illinois (city), *Sesame Street Presents: Follow That Bird!* (film), pp.16–17, D4

Ocelot, Iowa (town), *Kingpin* (film), pp.16–17, C4

Ochichornia (fictional state), novels of Vasily Aksyonov, pp.18–19, A2/B2

Oconee (fictional state), *Count Geiger's Blues* by Michael Bishop (novel), pp.14–15, A3

Odo Island, Japan (island), *Godzilla* (film), pp.96–97, C1/C2

Odyssey, Ohio (town), *Adventures in Odyssey* (video games), pp.14–15, B4

Oedo, Japan (city), *Cyber City Oedo 808* (anime), pp.96–97, E1/F1

Off Wessex, England (town), novels of Thomas Hardy, pp.64–65, B1

Ogden Marsh, Iowa (town), *The Crazies* (film), pp.16–17, C4

Ogygia, Greece (island), *The Odyssey* by Homer (ancient mythology), pp.44–45, D1

Ohitoyo, Japan (town), *Rail Romanesque* (video game/anime), pp.96–97, A1

Okinawa New Town, Japan (city), *Stitch!* (anime), pp.96–97, A1

Okishima, Japan (island), *Battle Royale* by Koushun Takami (novel), pp.96–97, B2

Okita Station, Hinomoto (fictional city), *Kabaneri of the Iron Fortress* (anime), pp.96–97, B2

Olancho (fictional country), *Soldiers of Fortune* by Richard Harding Davis (novel), pp.38–39, D4

Old Corona, Corona (fictional town), *Tangled/Rapunzel's Tangeled Adventure* (film/TV), pp.50–51, B4

Old Moses, Alaska (mountain), *Metal Gear Solid* series (video games), pp.18–19, A1

Old Mountain, Bulgaria (town), works of Cynthia Morrison Phoel, pp.50–51, B1/B2

Old Towers, Wales (building), *Five Get Into a Fix* by Enid Blyton (novel), pp.64–65, B2

Oldale Town, Japan (town), *Pokémon* (video games), pp.96–97, A1

Olifa City, Olifa (fictional city), *The Courts of the Morning* by John Buchan (novel), pp.38–39, B2

Olifa (fictional country), *The Courts of the Morning* by John Buchan (novel), pp.38–39, B2

Olinger, Pennsylvania (town), works of John Updike, pp.14–15, B4

Olivair County, Georgia (county), *Diggstown* (film), pp.14–15, B3

Olivine City, Japan (city), *Pokémon* (video games), pp.96–97, B2

Oliwa Asylum, Poland (building), *Wolfenstein* series (video games), pp.50–51, A4

Olympia, Greece (city), Marvel Comics/Marvel Cinematic Universe, pp.44–45, E1

Om, Cambodia (city), *Jelle's Marble Runs* (web series), pp.90–91, B3

OmniStat (fictional country), *Mirror's Edge* (video games), pp.108–109, C2

Omo Lau, Pacific Ocean (island/nation), *A Feast of Freedom* by Leonard Wibberley (novel), pp.120–121, D2

Omo Levi, Pacific Ocean (island/nation), *A Feast of Freedom* by Leonard Wibberley (novel), pp.120–121, D2

Omozan River (river), *My Hero Academia* by Kōhei Horikoshi (manga/anime), pp.38–39, C4/C5

Onehora, New Zealand (town), *Nga Tohu: Signatures* (TV), pp.108–109, F2

Oneonoroa, New Zealand (town), *B & B* (TV), pp.108–109, F2

Ongsan, South Korea (town), *When the Camellia Blooms* (film), pp.102–103, E2/E3

Onita, Japan (city), *Varan* (film), pp.96–97, E1/F1

Oo-Oh (island), *The Land That Time Forgot* by Edgar Rice Burroughs (novel/films), pp.114–115, C2

Ooralunkal, India (village), *Smarakasilakal* by Punathil Kunjabdulla (novel), pp.78–79, B2

Oou, Eastal (fictional town), *Log Horizon* by Mamare Touno and Kazuhiro Hara (novels/anime), pp.96–97, B2

Opal City, Maryland (city), DC Comics, pp.14–15, C4

Opar, Congo/DRC (city), Tarzan novels of Edgar Rice Burroughs and novels of Philip José Farmer, pp.84–85, C3

Opera Populaire, Paris, France (building), *The Phantom of the Opera* by Gaston Leroux (various), pp.44–45, E3

Ophir, Italy (region), Conan novels of Robert E. Howard (novels/TV), pp.44–45, D3

Opium, Country (country), *The House of the Scorpion* by Nancy Farmer (novel), pp.18–19, C2

Oquedal, Ataguitania (fictional village), *If On a Winter's Night a Traveller* by Italo Calvino (novel), pp.56–57, C5

Orbajosa, Spain (town), *Doña Perfecta* by Benito Pérez Galdós, pp.44–45, B2

Orca, The, Massachusetts (wreck), *Jaws* by Peter Benchley (novel/film), pp.14–15, D5

Ordköping, Sweden (town), Parken Zoo (theme park), pp.56–57, C3

Oreburgh City, Japan (city), *Pokémon* (video games), pp.96–97, C4

Oreskoga, Sweden (town), *The Bert-Diaries* by Anders Jacobsson and Soren Olssen (novels), pp.56–57, B3

Orkko, Cimmeria (fictional city), *If On a Winter's Night a Traveller* by Italo Calvino (novel), pp.56–57, C5

Ormistone, Scotland (town), *Narrow-Gauge Adventure* by P.D. Hancock (book), pp.64–65, C4

Ormston, England (town), *Born and Bred* (TV), pp.64–65, C3

Ornament Valley, Arizona (natural feature), *Cars* (films), pp.18–19, A3

Orofina, Pacific Ocean (island), *When the World Shook* by H. Rider Haggard (novel), pp.120–121, D2

Orphan Island, Pacific Ocean (island), *Orphan Island* by Rose Macaulay (novel), pp.120–121, D2

Orphelin Bay, Queensland (town), *Tidelands* (TV), pp.108–109, E3

Orre, Arizona (region/state), *Pokémon* (video games), pp.18–19, C3

Orsinia (fictional country), works of Ursula K. Le Guin, pp.50–51, B2

Orson, Indiana (town), *The Middle* (TV), pp.14–15, A4

Osia Theola, Cyprus (town), *A House Like a Lotus* by Madeleine L'Engle (novels), pp.44–45, F1

Osprey Explorer, North Sea (oil rig), *Roughnecks* (TV), pp.64–65, D5

Österköping, Sweden (town, various), pp.56–57, B3

Osterlich (fictional country), *The Great Dictator* (film), pp.44–45, D3

Osyria (fictional country), *The Ocean of Osyria* by Scott Lobdell and Lea Hernandez (comic book), pp.72–73, D2

Otakataka, New Zealand (town), *The Man Who Lost His Head* (film), pp.108–109, F2

Ottermouth, England (town), *Shadow on the Crown* by Patricia Bracewell (novel), pp.64–65, B2

Ottery St Catchpole, England (village), Harry Potter novels by J.K. Rowling (novels/films), pp.64–65, C1

Ouran Academy, Japan (building), *Ouran High School Host Club* by Bisco Hatori (manga/anime), pp.96–97, C4

Ouro Negro, Brazil (town), *Começar de Novo* (TV), pp.38–39, C3

Ouro Velho, Brazil (city), *O Amor Está no Ar* (TV), pp.38–39, D3

Ouro Verde, Brazil (town), *O Salvador da Pátria* (TV), pp.38–39, C3

Outcast Island, the Barbaric Archipelago (fictional island), *How to Train Your Dragon* by Cressida Cowell (novels/films), pp.56–57, D1

Outer Heaven, Outer Heaven (fictional city/state), *Metal Gear* (video game), pp.84–85, C2

Outer Island, Indian Ocean (island), *Dinotopia* (books/TV), pp.78–79, A2

Outer Maroo, Queensland (town), *Oyster* by Janette Turner Hospital (novel), pp.108–109, D2

Outer Qwghlim, Scotland (island), *The Baroque Cycle* and *Cryptonomicon* by Neal Stephenson (novels), pp.64–65, A5

Outer Wessex, England (town), novels of Thomas Hardy, pp.64–65, C1

Outlands, The, Tanzania (region), *The Lion King 2: Simba's Pride* (film), pp.84–85, D3

Outpost 31 (U.S. camp), *The Thing* (film), pp.114–115, C2

Outpost 32 (building), *Godzilla: King of the Monsters* (film), pp.114–115, D4

Ova Mata, San Serriffe (fictional island), *The Guardian* (newspaper), pp.78–79, A1

Overlook Hotel, Colorado (building), *The Shining* by Stephen King (various), pp.16–17, A4

Owl, North Dakota (town), *Downtown Owl* by Chuck Klosterman (novel), pp.16–17, B5/B6

Pacheco, Olifa (fictional town), *The Courts of the Morning* by John Buchan (novel), pp.38–39, B2

Pacific International Airport, Victoria (building), *Skyways* (TV), pp.108–109, A1

Pacific Ocean City, California (city), *Bojack Horseman* (TV), pp.18–19, A3

Pacifidlog Town, Japan (town), *Pokémon* (video games), pp.96–97, D1

Padachinha, India (village), *Anandamath* by Bankim Chandra Chattopadhyay (novel), pp.78–79, C4

Pagoda of Pillaji, The, India (building), *Around the World in Eighty Days* by Jules Verne (novel), pp.78–79, C4

Pais de la Canela, Ecuador (region, mythology), pp.38–39, A3

Paititi, Peru (city), *Tad: The Lost Explorer* (film), pp.38–39, B3

Pajamah Islands, The, Caribbean (island chain), *Captain Pugwash* (various), pp.32–33, F2

Pajkaszeg, Hungary (village), *A mi kis falunk (Our Little Village)* (TV), pp.50–51, A2/A3

Pal-ul-Don, Zaire (region), *Tarzan the Terrible* by Edgar Rice Burroughs (novel), pp.84–85, B3/C3

Pala, United Kingdom of Rendang and Pala (fictional island), *Island* by Aldous Huxley (novel), pp.90–91, A2

Palace Hotel, The, Wisconsin (building), *The Blues Brothers* (film), pp.16–17, D5

Palace of the Talibs, Endostan (fictional building), *Relic Hunter* (TV), pp.72–73, E3

Palanai, Banoi (fictional island), *Dead Island 2* (video game), pp.90–91, F1

Paleto Bay, San Andreas (fictional town), *Grand Theft Auto* series (video game), pp.18–19, A3

Pallet Town, Japan (town), *Pokémon* (video games), pp.96–97, C2

Palm City, Florida (city), *Need for Speed Heat* (video game), pp.14–15, C2

Palm Corners, Florida (town), *The Simpsons* (TV), pp.14–15, C1

Palombia (fictional country), *Spirou et Fantasio/Marsupilami* (comics), pp.38–39, B5

Palomino Creek, San Andreas (fictional town), *Grand Theft Auto* series (video game), pp.18–19, A3

Panaki, India (city), *Karma – Koi Aa Raha Hai Waqt Badalney* (TV), pp.78–79, B3

Panama City Shatterdome, Panama (building), *Pacific Rim* (film), pp.32–33, D1

Panau (fictional island/nation), *Just Cause 2* (video game), pp.90–91, B3

Panchaia (fictional island/nation, Greek tradition), pp.84–85, D4

Panchajana, India (building), Marvel Comics, pp.78–79, B3

Panchanagar, India (village), *The Golden Son* by Shilpi Somaya Gowda (novel), pp.78–79, B4

Pandora Tower, The, Japan (building), *Kamen Rider Build* (TV), pp.96–97, C2

Pandupur, India (town), *Growing Up in Pandupur* by Aditi Rao (stories), pp.78–79, B3

Panimpura, India (village), *Tales from Panimpura* by Deeptanshu Bhaskar (book), pp.78–79, D4

Pankot Palace, India (building), *Indiana Jones and the Temple of Doom* (film), pp.78–79, B5

Pankot Province, India (region), *Indiana Jones and the Temple of Doom* (film), pp.78–79, B4/B5

Pankot, India (town), the Raj Quartet series by Paul Scott (novels), pp.78–79, C4

Panopea, Oceana (fictional region/island), *Oceana* by James Harrington (novel), pp.38–39, C2

Panorama Spaghetti Farm, Switzerland (building), *Panorama* (TV), pp.44–45, C4

Pant-y-Girdle, Wales (town), *Good Omens* by Terry Pratchett (novel/TV), pp.64–65, C2

Papilloma (fictional country), *Kath & Kimderella* (film), pp.44–45, D2

Paracuán, Mexico (town), *The Black Minutes* by Martin Solares (novel), pp.32–33, B3

Paradigm City, New York (city), *The Big O* (anime), pp.14–15, D5

Paradise Beach, Queensland (town), *Paradise Beach* (TV), pp.108–109, E2

Paradise Falls, Venezuela (natural feature), *Up* (film), pp.38–39, B5

Paradise Gap, Victoria (town), *Come Midnight Monday* by David Burke (novel/TV), pp.108–109, D1

Paradise Swamp, Flirida (natural feature), *The Muppets* (TV), pp.14–15, D5

Paradise, California (town), *Paradise* (TV), pp.18–19, A3

Paradise, Zimbabwe (town), *We Need New Names* by NoViolet Bulawayo (novel), pp.84–85, C2

Paragon City, Rhode Island (city), *City of Heroes* (video game), pp.14–15, D5

Paraiso, South Sahrini (fictional city), *ARMA: Armed Assault* (video game), pp.126–127, C4

Paraíso, Peru (town), *Tomb Raider* series (video games), pp.38–39, B4

Parajuku, Japan (town), *PriPara* (video game/anime), pp.96–97, C1

Pararakelse, Pacific Ocean (island), *Love Hina* by Ken Akamatsu (manga/anime), pp.120–121, D3

Parascotopetl, Ecuador (mountain), *The Country of the Blind* by H.G. Wells (short story), pp.38–39, A5

Parfum Palace, France (building), *Pokémon* (video games), pp.44–45, E3

Paris, New South Wales (town), *The Cars that Ate Paris* (film), pp.108–109, D2

Paris, Frenchy's Land (fictional city), Brontë juvenilia, pp.84–85, B3

Paristan (fictional country, folklore), pp.72–73, B3/C3

Parkington, New York (town), *Lolita* by Vladimir Nobokov (novel), pp.14–15, C5

Parry's Land, Glass Town Federation (fictional region), Brontë juvenilia, pp.84–85, A4

Partreau, Saskatchewan (town), *Canada* by Richard Ford (novel), pp.26–27, C1

Parville, France (town), *In Search of Lost Time* by Marcel Proust (novel), pp.44–45, D3

Passage to the Centre of the Earth, Iceland (volcano/portal), *Journey to the Centre of the Earth* by Jules Verne (novel), pp.56–57, A6

Passaperto, Brazil (town), *Desejo Proibido* (TV), pp.38–39, D4

Pastoria City, Japan (city), *Pokémon* (video games), pp.96–97, D4

Pathos, Greece (island nation), *Perfect Strangers* (TV), pp.44–45, E1

Patusan (fictional island/nation, various), pp.90–91, B3/C4

Pau d'Alho, Brazil (town), *Cabocla* (TV), pp.38–39, D3

Pawnee, Indiana (city), *Parks and Recreation* (TV), pp.14–15, A4

Payidar, Turkey (village), *Karada lar* (TV), pp.72–73, B4

Payment Islands, The, Caribbean (island chain), *MacTrump* by Ian Doescher and Jacopo Della Quercia (book), pp.32–33, D2

Paz, Grenada (island), works of Merle Collins, pp.32–33, F2

Peacepool, The, Arctic Ocean (lake), *The Water-Babies* by Charles Kingsley (novel), pp.126–127, D6

Peacock, Nebraska (town), *Peacock* (film), pp.16–17, B4

Peaksville, Ohio (town), *The Twilight Zone* (TV), pp.14–15, B4

Pequod, Pacific Ocean (wreck), *Moby Dick* by Herman Melville (novel), pp.120–121, D2

Pedra Santa, Brazil (town), *O Outro Lado do Paraíso* (TV), pp.38–39, D4

Peel Godred, England (town), *Thomas the Tank Engine* by Rev W. Audrey (books/TV), pp.64–65, C2

Peepli, India (village), *Peepli Live* (film), pp.78–79, B4

Pelago Commonwealth (fictional island/nation), *Endless Ocean* (video games), pp.120–121, B4

Pelegosto, Caribbean (island), *Pirates of the Caribbean* (various), pp.32–33, F2

Pelotillehue, Chile (city), *Condorito* (comics), pp.38–39, B4

Pemberley, England (estate), *Pride and Prejudice* by Jane Austen (novel), pp.64–65, C2

Pen Gu Island, Pacific Ocean (island), *Surf's Up* (film), pp.120–121, D2

Peña Duro, Santa Prisca (fictional island), DC Comics, pp.32–33, F2

Pencas Mudas, Mexico (town), *Porque Parece Mentira la Verdad Nunca se Sabe* by Daniel Sada (novel), pp.32–33, B3

Pencaster, England (town), *Postman Pat* (TV), pp.64–65, C3

Pendragon, Holy Britannian Empire (fictional city), *Code Geass* (anime), pp.32–33, A4

Penglia (fictional country), A Christmas Prince series (film), pp.50–51, D2

Penguinia, Channel Islands (country), *Penguin Island* by Anatole France (novel), pp.64–65, A1

Penninnk, England (town), *The Goodies* (TV), pp.64–65, B1

Pennsyltucky (fictional state, various), pp.14–15, D5

Pennyfield, Jamaica (town), *Patsy* by Nicole Dennis-Benn (novel), pp.32–33, D2

Pepperinge Eye, England (village), *Bedknobs and Broomsticks* (film), pp.64–65, D1

Pepperland (fictional submerged country), *Yellow Submarine* (film), pp.126–127, B4

Perdition, Michigan (town), *Road to Perdition* by Max Allan Collins (comic/film), pp.14–15, A4

Perfection, Nevada (town), *Tremors* (film), pp.18–19, B4

Peri Kingdom, Iran (country), *Kingdoms of Elfin* by Sylvia Townsend Warner (short stories), pp.72–73, D2

Perla de las Dunas, Bolivia (building), *James Bond: Quantum of Solace* (film), pp.38–39, B3

Perla, Dream Kingdom (fictional country), *Die Andere Seite: Ein Phantastischer Roman* by Alfred Kubin (novel), pp.72–73, D3

Personville (Poisonville), Montana (town), *Red Harvest* by Dashiell Hammett (novel), pp.18–19, C5

Perth Island, Western Australia (region), *2000 AD* (comics), pp.108–109, B2

Perusalem (fictional country), *The Inca of Perusalem* by George Bernard Shaw (play), pp.44–45, D4

Petalburg City, Japan (city), *Pokémon* (video games), pp.96–97, A1

Petit Chauve Sourie Ville, Louisiana (town), *Scooby-Doo! Music of the Vampire* (film), pp.16–17, D2

Pětkwo, Cimmeria (fictional region), *If On a Winter's Night a Traveller* by Italo Calvino (novel), pp.56–57, C5

Petroville, Ontario (town), works of William Alexander Fraser (short story), pp.26–27, A4

Petrovo, Russia (town), *A Place for Me* by James Arnold (play), pp.26–27, C1

Pewter City, Japan (city), *Pokémon* (video games), pp.96–97, C4

Peyton Place, New Hampshire (town), *Peyton Place* by Grace Metalious (novel/TV), pp.14–15, C5

Pfennig Halbpfennig (fictional country), *The Grand Duke* by Gilbert & Sullivan (opera), pp.44–45, A2

Phaic Tăn (fictional country), *Phaic Tăn* (book), pp.90–91, C4

Phansa, India (town), works of Tabish Khair, pp.78–79, C4

Phantom Canyon, Arizona (town), Phantom Manor (theme parks), pp.18–19, C3

Phantom Manor/Ravenswood Manor, Arizona (building), Phantom Manor (theme parks), pp.18–19, C3

Phatt Island, Caribbean (island), *Monkey Island* series (video games), pp.32–33, E3

Phenac City, Arizona (city), *Pokémon* (video games), pp.18–19, C3

Philistia (fictional country), *Occupation Duty* by Harry Turtledove (short story), pp.72–73, B2

Phraxos, Greece (island), *The Magus* by John Fowles (novel), pp.44–45, E1

Pi, India (island), works of Indira Ganesan, pp.78–79, C2

Pickett, Arkansas (town), *A Face in the Crowd* (film), pp.16–17, D3

Pico Mundo, Arizona (town), *Odd Thomas* by Dean Koontz (novel/film), pp.18–19, B4

Pidsea Buttock, England (town), *South Riding* by Winifred Holtby (novel), pp.64–65, D3

Piedmont, Arizona/New Mexico/Utah (town), *The Andromeda Strain* by Michael Crichton (novel/film/TV), pp.18–19, C3

Piemburg, South Africa (town), novels of Tom Sharpe, pp.84–85, D4

Piffling, England (island), *Wooden Overcoats* (podcast), pp.64–65, C1

Pig Robinson's Island, Caribbean (island), *The Tale of Little Pig Robinson* by Beatrix Potter (short story), pp.32–33, F2

Pikesville, Arkansas (town), *Adventures of Huckleberry Finn* by Mark Twain (novel), pp.16–17, D2

Pilbarra, Western Australia (town), *The Shadow Out of Time* by H.P. Lovecraft (novella), pp.108–109, A3

Pilitz, Poland (town), *The Slave* by Isaac Bashevis Singer (novel), pp.50–51, A4

Pine County, Michigan (county), *Starvation Lake* by Bryan Gruley (novel), pp.14–15, A5

Pine Cove, California (town), works of Christopher Moore, pp.18–19, A3

Pine Tree, Vermont (town), *White Christmas* (film), pp.14–15, C6

Pine Valley, Pennsylvania (town), ABC Soap Opera Universe (*All My Children*, TV), pp.14–15, C4

Ping Pong Pub, South Australia (building), *The Adventures of Priscilla, Queen of the Desert* (film), pp.108–109, C2

Pink Palace Apartments, Oregon (building), *Coraline* (film), pp.18–19, A5

Pirate Isles, The, Venezuela (islands), *Mercenaries 2: World in Flames* (video game), pp.38–39, B6

Pirriwee, New South Wales (town), *Big Little Lies* by Liane Moriarty (novel), pp.108–109, F4

Pirtha, India (village), works of Mahasweta Devi (stories), pp.78–79, C4

Pitt, The, Pennsylvania (town), *Fallout 3* (video game), pp.14–15, B4

Pittman, Kentucky (town), works of Barbara Kingsolver, pp.14–15, A4

Pittsfield, Virginia (town), *The X-Files* (TV), pp.14–15, C4

Pixley, Kentucky (town), *Petticoat Junction/Green Acres* (TV), pp.14–15, A3

Placeres, Mexico (town), *El sol que estás Mirando* by Jesús Gardea (novel), pp.32–33, B3

Plastic Beach, Pacific Ocean (island), 'Plastic Beach' by Gorillaz (music), pp.120–121, E1

Plateau of Leng, The (city), *At the Mountains of Madness* by H.P. Lovecraft (novella), pp.114–115, E3

Playa Escondida, Mexico (town), *Mar de Amor* (TV), pp.32–33, C2

Pleasant River, West Virginia (town), Silent Hill series (various), pp.14–15, B4

Pleasantville, California (town), *Pleasantville* (film), pp.18–19, A3

Plodorodno, Bulgaria (village), *The English Neighbour* by Mikhail Veshim (novel), pp.50–51, C1

Plum Bay, Western Australia (town), *The House at Plum Bay* by Geoff Morgan (novel), pp.108–109, A2

Plum Island, Delaware (island), *Survival of the Dead* (film), pp.14–15, C4

Plumbers' Base, South Dakota (building), *Ben 10* (TV), pp.16–17, A5

Plummergen, England (village), Miss Seeton novels by Hamilton Crane, pp.64–65, D3

Plunder Island, Caribbean (island), *Monkey Island* series (video games), pp.32–33, E3

Pluto, North Dakota (town), novels of Louis Erdrich, pp.16–17, B6

Plutonia, Arctic (underground realm), *Plutonia* by Vladimir Obrutcev (novel), pp.50–51, B6

Pnom Dhek, Cambodia (city), *Jungle Girl* by Edgar Rice Burroughs (novel), pp.90–91, A4

Poço do Mundo, Portugal (city), *Tempos Difíceis* (film), pp.44–45, A2

Pohjola, Finland (country, mythology), pp.56–57, C6

Poho County, Florida (county), *Jeepers Creepers* (film), pp.14–15, B2

Poictesme (fictional country), novels of James Branch Cavell, pp.44–45, B3

Point Partageus, Western Australia (natural feature), *The Light Between Oceans* by M.L. Stedman (novel), pp.108–109, D1

Point Place, Wisconsin (town), *That 70s Show* (TV), pp.16–17, D5

Poitain, France (region), Conan novels of Robert E. Howard, pp.44–45, B3

Pokesville, Arkansas (town), *Adventures of Huckleberry Finn* by Mark Twain (novel), pp.16–17, D3

Pokey Oats County, California (county), *The Powerpuff Girls* (TV), pp.18–19, B3

Pokolistan, Czech Republic (country), DC Comics, pp.50–51, A3

Pokoponesia (fictional island/nation), *The Tick* (TV), pp.120–121, D4

Polaria, Russia (city), *Jelle's Marble Runs* (web series), pp.50–51, B5

Polchester, England (city), novels of Hugh Walpole, pp.64–65, C2

Polearn, England (town), *Negotium Perambulans* by E.F. Benson (novel), pp.64–65, D1

Polnarren, England (town), *Echo Beach* (TV), pp.64–65, D1

Polongo River, Indian Ocean (river), *Dinotopia* (books/TV), pp.78–79, D3

Polrugaria (fictional country), *The Tragic Life of a Polrugarian Minister* by Isaac Deutscher (essay), pp.50–51, A3/B3

Polylerit, Iran (region), *Utopia* by Thomas More (novel/parable), pp.72–73, D2

Pom Pom Galli, Pacific Ocean (island), *The Sea Chase* (film), pp.120–121, E2

Pondarosa Ranch, Nevada (building), *Bonanza/Pondarosa* (TV), pp.18–19, A4

Pondelayo, Sri Lanka (island), *Through Darkest Pondelayo* by Joan Lindsay (novel), pp.78–79, C3

Poni Island, Hawaii (island), *Pokémon* (video games), pp.18–19, C1

Pontal D'Areia, Brazil (city), *Mulheres de Areia* (TV), pp.38–39, D3

Ponteratto, Italy (town), Don Camillo works of Giovannino Guareschi (various), pp.44–45, D2

Pontypandy, Wales (town), *Fireman Sam* (TV), pp.64–65, C2

Ponukelete-Drelchkaff (fictional country/empire), *Impressions of Africa* by Raymond Roussel (novel), pp.84–85, B4

Poop Deck Point, Caribbean (natural feature), *The Pirates! Band of Misfits!* (film), pp.32–33, E3

Porpoise Spit, New South Wales (town), *Muriel's Wedding* (film), pp.108–109, C2

Porpoise, The, Arctic (wreck), *The Voyages and Adventures of Captain Hatteras* by Jules Verne (novel), pp.26–27, C4

Port Ainslie, Ontario (town), *Murder Among the Pines* by John Lawrence Reynolds (novel), pp.26–27, A4

Port Annie, British Columbia (town), *The Resurrection of Joseph Bourne; or, A Word or Two on Those Port Annie Miracles* by Jack Hodgins (novel), pp.26–27, B1

Port Asbestos, Ontario (town), *The Red Green Show* (TV), pp.26–27, A4

Port bin Qasim, Pakistan (city), *Noon* by Aatish Taseer (novel), pp.78–79, A4

Port Cenotaph, Nova Scotia (town), *Transformers: Infestation 2* (comics), pp.26–27, F1

Port Charles, New York (city), ABC Soap Opera Universe (*General Hospital*, TV), pp.14–15, B5

Port Clarendon, San Serriffe (fictional town), *The Guardian* (newspaper), pp.78–79, A2

Port Clovis, Louisiana (town), *Maneater* (video game), pp.16–17, D2

Port D'Angerous, Oregon (city), *New Moan (The Twishite Saga)* by Stephfordy Mayo (novel), pp.18–19, A6

Port Danville, Victoria (town), *Come Midnight Monday* by David Burke (novel), pp.108–109, D1

Port de la Senoritas, Mexico (town), *The Pirates! Band of Misfits!* (film), pp.32–33, C2

Port Dunbar, Dahum (fictional country), *Solo* by William Boyd (novel), pp.84–85, B4

Port Dundas, Ontario (town), *The Calling* by Inger Ash Wolfe (novel), pp.26–27, A4

Port Elrod, San Serriffe (fictional town), *The Guardian* (newspaper), pp.78–79, A2

Port Elwyn, Wales (town), *Jennie* by J.B. Snell (novel), pp.64–65, C2

Port Fairview, Victoria (town), *Bottlebrush Creek* by Maya Linnell (novel), pp.108–109, D1

Port Germaine, Alaska (town), *Ghost Ship* (film), pp.18–19, A1/A2

Port Niranda, Victoria (town), *Round the Twist* (TV), pp.108–109, D1

Port o' Monkeys, unnamed continent (town), *Le Mont Analogue* by René Daumal (novel), pp.120–121, D3

Port Sherman, Oregon (town), *Snow Crash* by Neal Stephenson (novel), pp.18–19, A5/A6

Port St Mary, England (town), *The Quarry Line Mystery* by A.C. Stewart (novel), pp.64–65, C3

Port Ticonderoga, Ontario (town), *The Blind Assassin* by Margaret Atwood (novel), pp.26–27, A4

Port Tortuga, Caribbean (town), *Pirates of the Caribbean* (various), pp.32–33, E2

Port William, Kentucky (town), works of Wendell Berry, pp.14–15, A4

Portage Creek/Millennium Gate, Indiana (town), *Star Trek Voyager* (various), pp.14–15, A4

Portahoy, Northern Ireland (town), *Peter* by Rutherford Mayne (play), pp.64–65, B3

Portharnel, Oceana (fictional town), *The Strong Man* by H.R.F. Keating (novel), pp.126–127, D5

Portnadroleen, Ireland (town), *Harlequin's Positions* by Jack B. Yeats (play), pp.64–65, A3

Porto Corsa, Monaco (city), *Cars 2* (film), pp.44–45, C2

Porto do Céu, Brazil (town), *Cara e Coroa* (TV), pp.38–39, D3

Porto dos Milagres, Brazil (town), *Porto dos Milagres* (TV), pp.38–39, D4

Portoway, Scotland (town), novels of John Buchan, pp.64–65, B3

Portstown, Northern Ireland (town), *McCoubrey* by Mark McCaffery (novel), pp.64–65, B3

Portwenn, England (village), *Doc Martin* (TV), pp.64–65, B3

Poseidonis, Atlantis (fictional sunken city), Cthulhu Mythos (various), pp.126–127, D4

Possum Lake, Ontario (lake), *The Red Green Show* (TV), pp.26–27, A4

Potanreyland (fictional country), *The Navy Lark* (radio), pp.78–79, B2/C2

Pottibakia (fictional country), *What Does it Matter? A Morality* by E.M. Forster (short story), pp.50–51, B1

Pottsylvania (fictional country), *Rocky and Bullwinkle* (TV), pp.50–51, B4

Pozharnov, Russia (village), *Justice League* (film), pp.50–51, C1

Prawiek, Poland (village), *Primeval and Other Times* by Olga Tokarczuk (novel), pp.50–51, A4

Presbyterian Church, Washington (town), *McCabe & Mrs Miller* (film), pp.18–19, B6

Prescot Trader, Atlantic Ocean (wreck), *U-571* (film), pp.126–127, C5

Pribrezhny, Russia (town), *Leviathan* (film), pp.50–51, B6

Prickly Pines, Wisconsin (town), *Camp Lazlo*, pp.16–17, D5

Pride Lands, The, Tanzania (region), *The Lion King* (film), pp.84–85, D3

Pride Rock, Tanzania (natural feature), *The Lion King* (film), pp.84–85, D3

Prince Pondicherry's Chocolate Palace, India (building), *Charlie and the Chocolate Factory* by Roald Dahl (novel/film), pp.78–79, C3

Prism Tower, Paris, France (building), *Pokémon* (video games), pp.44–45, E3

Proctorville, Iowa (town), *The Simpsons* (TV), pp.16–17, C5

Professor Lake's Camp (Miskatonic Expedition), *At the Mountains of Madness* by H.P. Lovecraft (novella), pp.114–115, E2

Progress City, Texas (town, scam), pp.16–17, A2

Project Deep Six Drop Point (Megatron), Atlantic Ocean, *Transformers: Revenge of the Fallen* (film), pp.126–127, B4

Propwash Junction, Minnesota (town), *Planes* (film), pp.16–17, C6

Prospect Bay, South Australia (town), works of Phillip Gwynne/*Australian Rules* (novels/film), pp.108–109, C2

Prosperity, Arizona (town), *Eight-Legged Freaks* (film), pp.18–19, B5

Prospero's island *see* Caliban's island

Providence, Quebec (town), *Providence* (TV), pp.26–27, E1

Prydain (fictional country), *The Chronicles of Prydain* by Lloyd Alexander (novels), pp.64–65, D2

Psaodung, Cambodia (village), *The Lights We Carried Home* by Kay Chronister (short story), pp.90–91, B3

Puamahara, New Zealand (town), *The Carpathians* by Janet Frame (novel), pp.108–109, F1/F2

Puckoon, Northern Ireland/Ireland (village), *Puckoon* by Spike Milligan (novel), pp.64–65, C1

Puddleby-on-the-Marsh, England (village), *Doctor Doolittle* by Hugh Lofting (novel), pp.64–65, C1

Pueblo Escondido, Colombia (town), *La Marca del Deseo* (TV), pp.38–39, A6

Pueblo Nuevo, Mexico (town), *Lo Imperdonable* (TV), pp.32–33, B3

Puente Antiguo, New Mexico (town), Marvel Cinematic Universe (various), pp.16–17, A2

Puente Viejo, Spain (town), *The Secret of Puente Viejo* (TV), pp.44–45, B2

Puerto Bravo, Colombia (town), *La Tormenta* (TV), pp.38–39, B5

Puerto Clara, San Escobar (fictional city), *Hey Arnold!* (TV), pp.32–33, C4

Puerto Cortes, Costa Rica (town), *Jurassic Park* by Michael Crichton (various), pp.32–33, D1

Puerto de Los Dragones, Venezuela (town), works of Madeleine L'Engle, pp.38–39, B6

Puerto Grande, Republic of San Marco (fictional city), *Don Quixote, USA* by Richard Powell (novel), pp.32–33, B6

Puerto Grande, Mexico (city), *TUGS* (TV), pp.32–33, C4

Puerto Pollo, Peru (island), works of Ralph Ellison and Robert Wyatt (short stories), pp.38–39, A4

Pulau Rintis, Malaysia (island), *BoBoiBoy* (TV), pp.90–91, D1

Pulau-Pulau Bompa, Sondonesia (fictional island/nation), *Tintin: Flight 714 to Sydney* by Hergé (comic book), pp.90–91, D1

Pullamawang (fictional island/nation), *Micro Nation* (TV), pp.108–109, E2

Pulpit Hill, Catawba (fictional town), *Look Homeward, Angel* by Thomas Wolfe (novel), pp.14–15, C3

Pummis, Montana (town), *Kenan & Kel* (TV), pp.18–19, C5

Pumpernickel (fictional country), works of William Makepeace Thackeray, pp.44–45, D3

Punchbowl, Pennsylvania (city), *Stubbs the Zombie* (video game), pp.14–15, B5

Punt (fictional country), Conan novels of Robert E. Howard, pp.84–85, C5/D5

Pwddldwc, Wales (town), *The Puddleduck Affair* by David Sheperd (novel), pp.64–65, C2

PX-Labs, Russia (building), *Despicable Me 2* (film), pp.50–51, B6

Pyrite Town, Arizona (town), *Pokémon* (video games), pp.18–19, C3

Q, Pakistan (town), *Shame* by Salman Rushdie (novel), pp.78–79, A5

Q.V.1, Indian Ocean (wreck), *The Pirates! Band of Misfits!* (film), pp.78–79, B2

Qanada (fictional country), *MacTrump* by Ian Doescher and Jacopo Della Quercia (book), pp.26–27, C1

Qijiatun, China (village), *The Three-Body Problem* by Liu Cixin (novel), pp.102–103, D4

Quahog, Rhode Island (city), *Family Guy* (TV), pp.14–15, D5

Quartershot, England (town), novels of Thomas Hardy, pp.64–65, D2

Quataca Mountains, Brazil (mountain range), *Thunderbirds Are Go* (TV), pp.38–39, B5

Quauhnahuac, Mexico (town), *Under the Volcano* by Malcolm Lowry (novel), pp.32–33, C2

Queen's Crawley, England (town), *Vanity Fair* by William M. Thackeray (novel), pp.64–65, D2

Queen's Island, Arctic (island), *The Voyages and Adventures of Captain Hatteras* by Jules Verne (novel), pp.26–27, C4

Queen's Island, Tasmania (island), *Brother Fish* by Bryce Courtenay (novel), pp.108–109, D1

Queen's Point, New York (town), ABC Soap Opera Universe (*The Young Marrieds*, TV), pp.14–15, B5

Queimada, Lesser Antilles (island), *Burn!* (film), pp.32–33, F2

Quequena, Peru (town), *Ripping Yarns* (TV), pp.38–39, A4

Quetzalacatenango, Guatemala (village), *The Simpsons* (cartoon), pp.32–33, C4

Quiquendone, Belgium (town), *Dr Ox's Experiment* by Jules Verne (short story), pp.44–45, C4

Quisto (fictional country), *The Centurions* (TV), pp.38–39, A4

Quiyoughcohannock River, Virginia (river), *Pocahontas* (Disney film), pp.14–15, B4/C4

Qumar (fictional country), *The West Wing* (TV), pp.72–73, C2

Qurac (fictional country), DC Comics, pp.72–73, C2

Qyah, Alaska (town), *Molly of Denali* (TV), pp.18–19, B1

R'lyeh, Pacific Ocean (submerged city), Cthulhu Mythos (various), pp.120–121, E1

Raccoon City, Missouri (city), *Resident Evil* series (video games/films), pp.16–17, C6

Rachel, Kansas (town), *The Ghost and Mr Chicken* (film), pp.16–17, C3

Radar Peak, China (mountain), *The Three-Body Problem* by Liu Cixin (novel), pp.102–103, D4

Radback, The (fictional region), *2000 AD* (comics), pp.108–109, C3

Radiator Springs, Arizona (town), *Cars* (film), pp.18–19, C3

Radlands of Ji, The, China (region), *2000 AD* (comics), pp.102–103, C3

RAF Midham, England (building), *Get Some In!* (TV), pp.64–65, C3

RAF Minton, England (building), *The Shepherd* by Frederick Forsyth (novel), pp.64–65, D2

Ragaan (fictional country), *Embassy* (TV), pp.90–91, B2

Ragnarok, Alaska (town), *Gerry Anderson's New Captain Scarlet* (TV), pp.18–19, A2

Ragz, Hungary (city), *The Secret of Wilhelm Storitz* by Jules Verne (novels), pp.50–51, A2

Rainbow Ridge, Utah (town), Big Thunder Mountain Railroad (theme parks), pp.18–19, C3

Rainbow Valley, Missitucky (fictional town), *Finian's Rainbow* (musical), pp.14–15, A2

Rajnagar, India (city), Raj Comics, pp.78–79, D4

Rajpura, India (village), *Kyunki Saas Bhi Kabhi Bahu Thi/Because It's That's What Life Is* (TV), pp.78–79, B4

Ram, The (fictional city), *Riddley Walker* by Russell Hoban (novel), pp.64–65, B2

Ramaja, Babiliary (fictional city), *The New Gulliver* by Abbé Pierre François Guyot-Desfontaines (novel), pp.96–97, A1

Rambleshack, Caribbean (island), *Pirates of the Caribbean* (various), pp.32–33, D2

Ramelle, France (town), *Saving Private Ryan* (film), pp.44–45, C4

Ramgarh, India (village), *Sholay* (film), pp.78–79, B3

Rampart Junction, Iowa (town), *The Town Where No One Got Off* by Ray Bradbury (short story), pp.16–17, C4

Rampole Island, Brazil (island), *Mr Blettsworthy on Rampole Island* by H.G. Wells (novel), pp.38–39, C2

Ramsdale, Massachusetts (town), *Lolita* by Vladimir Nabokov (novel/film), pp.14–15, C5

Ramville, Ontario (town), *Les Bleus de Ramville* (TV), pp.26–27, A4

Ranchipur, India (region), *When the Rains Came* (film), pp.78–79, A4/B4

Ranjhaar, India (town), *Ram-Leela* (film), pp.78–79, A4/B4

Rankling Glacier, Yogistan (fictional natural feature), *The Ascent of Rum Doodle* by W.E. Bowman (novel), pp.78–79, C5

Ranpur, India (city), the Raj Quartet series by Paul Scott (novels), pp.78–79, B4/C4

Rapture, Atlantic Ocean (city), *Bioshock* franchise (video games), pp.26–27, F4

Rapunzel's Tower, Corona (fictional building), *Tangled/Rapunzel's Tangled Adventure* (film/TV), pp.50–51, B4

Ras el-Hadid, Egypt (city), *Wolfenstein* series (video games), pp.84–85, C5

Rastepappe, Pacific Ocean (island), *Archibald the Koala* (TV), pp.120–121, B2

Rathcullen, Ireland (town), *Darby O'Gill and the Little People* (film), pp.64–65, A2

Rathmoye, Ireland (town), *Love and Summer* by William Trevor (novel), pp.64–65, A2

Raupo, New Zealand (town), *Footrot Flats* (comic), pp.108–109, F2

Raveloe, England (town), *Silas Marner* by George Eliot (novel), pp.64–65, C2

Rawalpur, India (city), *Water* (film), pp.78–79, C4

Rawlinson End, England (estate), *Sir Henry at Rawlinson End* (radio), pp.64–65, D2

Ray, Wyoming (town), *Did You Hear About the Morgans?* (film), pp.18–19, D5

Rayhana's village, Mauritania (village), *The Desert and the Drum* by Mbarek Ould Beyrouk (novel), pp.84–85, A5

Raythune County, West Virginia (county), the Bel Elkin mysteries by Julia Keller (novels), pp.14–15, B4

Razkavia (fictional country), *The Tin Princess* by Philip Pullman (novel), pp.50–51, A2

RCAF Mackenzie Bay, Yukon/Northwest Territories (building), *Ghost Ship* (film), pp.26–27, B2/B3

Realm of the Troll Mountain King, Norway (region), *Peer Gynt* by Henrik Ibsen (music), pp.56–57, A3

Red Coast Base, China (building), *The Three-Body Problem* by Liu Cixin (novel), pp.102–103, D4

Red Noah, Indian Ocean (island), *Nadia, the Secret of Blue Water* (anime), pp.78–79, A1

Red Rock, Wyoming (town), *The Hateful Eight* (film), pp.18–19, D4

Red Rock, Ireland (town), *Red Rock* (TV), pp.64–65, B3

Redemption, Arizona (town), *The Quick and the Dead* (film), pp.18–19, C2

Rederring, England (village), *Ruddigore* by Gilbert and Sullivan (opera), pp.64–65, B1

Redmere, England (town), *The Price of Blood* by Patricia Bracewell (novel), pp.64–65, D3

Redmond College, Nova Scotia (building), *Anne of Green Gables* by Lucy Maud Montgomery (novel), pp.26–27, F1

Redskin City, North Dakota (town), *Tintin in America* by Hergé (comic), pp.16–17, A6

Redwater, Ireland (town), *EastEnders/Redwater* (TV), pp.64–65, A3

Reefton Lakes, New South Wales (town/suburb), *Home and Away* (TV), pp.108–109, F4

Reese City/Myrtle, Nevada (town), *Breakheart Pass* by Alistair MacLean (novel), pp.18–19, B2

Reflection Cave, France (natural feature), *Pokémon* (video games), pp.44–45, B3

Regina, Angora (fictional city), Brontë juvenalia, pp.90–91, F4

Reichsburg, Artam (fictional city), *Artam: One Reich, One Race, a Tenth Leader* by Volkmar Weiss (novel), pp.50–51, A3

Remadrín, Mexico (town), *Porque Parece Mentira la Verdad Nunca se Sabe* by Daniel Sada (novel), pp.32–33, B3

Remanso, Brazil (town), *Despedida de Solteiro* (TV), pp.38–39, D3

Renada, Spain (city), *San Manuel Bueno, Mártir* by Miguel de Unamuno (novel), pp.44–45, B2

Renard Parish, Louisiana (county), *True Blood* (TV), pp.16–17, C2

Rendang, United Kingdom of Rendang and Pala (fictional island), *Island* by Aldous Huxley (novel), pp.90–91, A1

Reptarland, France (theme park), *Rugrats in Paris* (film), pp.44–45, E3

Republic of Isthmus (fictional country), *James Bond: Licence to Kill* (film), pp.32–33, D1

Republic of Sacramento (fictional island/nation), *O Senhor Embaixador/ His Excellency, the Ambassador* by Erico Verissimo (novel), pp.32–33, D1

Republic of Tariba, Guyana/Venezuela (country), *Gundam 00* (anime), pp.38–39, B5/C5

República de las Bananas, Caribbean (island/nation), *Junta* (board game), pp.32–33, D2

Republica Libra (fictional island), *Shooting Script* by Gavin Lyall (novel), pp.32–33, E2

Republia (fictional country), *Papers, Please* (video game), pp.50–51, A5

Research Bunker 4 – Black Sun Project, Bosnia and Herzegovina (building), *Outpost* trilogy (films), pp.50–51, A2

Reserve (fictional state), *True Blood* (TV), pp.14–15, A4/B4

Resolution Island, Galapagos Islands (island), *Brown on Resolution* by C.S. Forester (novel), pp.38–39, A1

Resplendor, Brazil (town), *Pedra Sobre Pedra* (TV), pp.38–39, D4

Retroville, Texas (town), *Jimmy Neutron, Boy Genius* (TV), pp.16–17, B2

Revelstoke, Alaska (town), *The Barber* (film), pp.18–19, B2

Reykjavik Express, North Sea (Tunnel), *Thunderbirds Are Go: Heist Society* (TV), pp.126–127, D5/C6

Rhelasia (fictional country), *Young Justice* (TV), pp.102–103, E3

Rhodes, Lemoyne (fictional town), *Red Dead Redemption* series (video games), pp.16–17, D2

Riacho Doce, Brazil (town), *Riacho Doce* by José Lins do Rego (novel/TV), pp.38–39, D4

Riallaro Archipelago, Pacific Ocean (island chain), *Riallaro, the Archipelago of Exiles* by Godfrey Sweven (novel), pp.120–121, D1/E1

Ribeirão do Tempo, Brazil (town), *Ribeirão do Tempo* (TV), pp.38–39, D4

Richmond Hill, New South Wales (town), *Richmond Hill* (TV), pp.108–109, D2

Richville, Indiana (town), *Richie Rich* (various), pp.14–15, A4

Riddlesdale, England (village), *Clouds of Witness* by Dorothy L. Sayers (novel), pp.64–65, C3

Rincon, Costaguana (fictional town), *Nostromo* by Joseph Conrad (novel), pp.38–39, A4

Rintenjo, Japan (town), *The Story of Forest Rail* (video game), pp.96–97, D4

Rio County, Texas (county), *Lone Star* (film), pp.16–17, A2

Rio Gordo, Mexico (river), *Setenta Veces Siete/Seventy Times Seven* by Ricardo Elizondo Elizondo, pp.32–33, B3

Rio Habana, Bolivia (river), *Ghost Recon: Wildlands* (video game), pp.38–39, B4

Rio Mojito, Rio Tequila, Rio Pina Colada, San Escobar (fictional rivers, internet humour), pp.32–33, B2

Rio Novo, Brazil (river), *Fera Radical* (TV), pp.38–39, D3

Rio Sangre, Argentina (river), *High Citadel* by Desmond Bagley (novel), pp.38–39, C2

Rio Uruqui, Bolivia (river), *Ghost Recon: Wildlands* (video game), pp.38–39, B4

Rio, England (village), *Swallows and Amazons* by Arthur Ransome (novel), pp.64–65, C3

Rioguay (fictional country), DC Comics, pp.38–39, B5

Riseholme, England (village), Lucia novels by Edward Frederic Benson, pp.64–65, C2

Rive-Reine, France (town), *The Train* (film), pp.44–45, C3

River Agenda, Yogistan (fictional river), *The Ascent of Rum Doodle* by W.E. Bowman (novel), pp.120–121, D3

River City, Iowa (town), *The Music Man* (musical/film), pp.16–17, C5

River City (city), *Tomorrow!* by Philip Wylie (novel), pp.16–17, C5

River City, Queensland (city), *Cybergirl* (TV), pp.108–109, E3

River Dhun, India (river), *Growing Up in Pandupur* by Aditi Rao (stories), pp.78–79, B3

River Floss, England (river), *The Mill on the Floss* by George Eliot (novel), pp.64–65, D3

River Gorkhon, Mongolia (river), *Pathologic* series (video game), pp.102–103, C4

River Heights, Illinois (town), Nancy Drew mysteries (novels/TV), pp.16–17, D4

River Lyle, Ireland (river), *The Sea and the Silence* by Peter Cunningham (novel), pp.64–65, B2

River Run, Ohio (town), *Homefront* (TV), pp.14–15, B5

River Run Plantation, North Carolina (building), *Outlander* (novel/TV), pp.14–15, B4

Ros Na Rún, Ireland (village), *Ros Na Rún* (TV), pp.64–65, A2

Rosehaven, Tasmania (town), *Rosehaven* (TV), pp.108–109, D1

Roseiral, Brazil (town), *Alma Gêmea* (TV), pp.38–39, C3

Rosewood, Pennsylvania (town), *Pretty Little Liars* (TV), pp.14–15, C4

Roshan Basti/Andher Basti, Pakistan (town), *3 Bahadur* (film), pp.78–79, A4

Ross's Land, Glass Town Federation (fictional region), Brontë juvenalia, pp.84–85, A4

Rothal, India (town), *Around the World in Eighty Days* by Jules Verne (novel), pp.78–79, C4

Rotherwood, England (town), *Ivanhoe* by Sir Walter Scott (novel), pp.64–65, C3

Rothswell Castle, Scotland (building), *A Darker Domain* by Val McDermid (novel), pp.64–65, D4

Rotunda of Seclusion, The Nepal (building), *The Powerpuff Girls* (TV), pp.78–79, C4

Rowcester Abbey, England (building), novels of P.G. Wodehouse, pp.64–65, D2

Roxxon Norco, Florida (wreck), Marvel Cinematic Universe (various), pp.14–15, C1

Royal Woods, Michigan (town), *The Loud House* (TV), pp.14–15, A5

Royston Vasey, England (village), *The League of Gentlemen* (TV), pp.64–65, C3

Rubovia (fictional country), *A Rubovian Legend* (TV), pp.50–51, B3

Ruby Crystal Mines of Burma, The, Myanmar (natural feature), *The Transformers* (TV), pp.90–91, B4

Ruby, Oklahoma (town), *Ruby* by Toni Morrison (novel), pp.16–17, B3

Ruby River, Wyoming (river), *Firewatch* (video game), pp.18–19, C1

Ruddy Rose and HMS Monarch, Caribbean (wreck), *Pirates of the Caribbean* (various), pp.32–33, F2

Rugged Island, Ireland (island), *Father Ted* (TV), pp.64–65, A2

Ruggsville, Texas (Town/county), *House of 1000 Corpses/The Devil's Rejects* (films), pp.16–17, C2

Ruin, Turkey (city), Sanctus novels of Simon Toyne, pp.72–73, B3

Rum Doodle, India (mountain), *The Ascent of Rum Doodle* by W.E. Bowman (novel), pp.78–79, C5

Rum-runner's Isle, Caribbean (island), *Pirates of the Caribbean* (various), pp.32–33, F2

Rummidge, England (town), novels of David Lodge, pp.64–65, C2

Rummyworld (fictional country), *Doonesbury* (comic), pp.72–73, B2

Rupes Nigra, Arctic (natural feature, tradition), pp.26–27, C4

Ruritania (fictional country), *The Prisoner of Zelda* by Anthony Hope (novel), pp.50–51, A3

Rusalka (fictional country), *Ultraman Orb* (TV), pp.50–51, C4

Russian Democratic Union, RDU (fictional bloc), *Tom Clancy's Ghost Recon* (video game), pp.50–51, A5

Rustboro City, Japan (city), *Pokémon* (video game), pp.96–97, A1

Rusty Hill, Wales (town), *Shades of Grey* by Jasper Fforde (novel), pp.64–65, C2

Rutherford, Ohio (city), *3rd Rock from the Sun* (TV), pp.14–15, B4

Rutland, New York (town), *Me, Myself and Irene* (film), pp.14–15, C5

Rutshire, England (county), novels of Jilly Cooper, pp.64–65, C2

Rydsholm, Sweden (town), works of Gösta Gustaf-Janson, pp.56–57, C3

Ryhope Wood, England (natural feature), *Mythago Wood* by Robert Holdstock (novel), pp.64–65, C2

S-33, Atlantic Ocean (wreck), *U-571* (film), pp.126–127, C5

Sabaeus (fictional country), *Mirror's Edge* (video games), pp.108–109, D2

Sacheon, South Korea (town), *Sacheon-ga* (music), pp.96–97, E2/E3

Sadchester, Massachusetts (town), *30 Rock* (TV), pp.14–15, D5

Sadiq, Iraq (village, military training exercise), pp.72–73, C2

Saffron City, Japan (city), *Pokémon* (video games), pp.96–97, E1

Sagrillas, Spain (village), *Cuéntame cómo pasó* (TV), pp.44–45, B2

Saharan Sea, Saharan countries (natural feature), *Invasion of the Sea* by Jules Verne (novel), pp.84–85, C5

Sahkra, Urzikstan (fictional city), *Call of Duty: Modern Warfare* (video game), pp.72–73, C3

Sahrani (fictional island/nation), *ARMA: Armed Assault* (video game), pp.126–127, C4

Saignac, France (town), *Magellan* (TV), pp.44–45, C4

Saint Bernardino, California (city), DC Comics, pp.18–19, B3

Saint Denis, Lemoyne (fictional city), *Red Dead Redemption* series (video game), pp.16–17, D2

Saint Georges Island, Arabian Sea (island), *Yes, Prime Minister* (TV), pp.72–73, D1

Saint Jacques, Caribbean (island), *The Violins of Saint-Jacques* by Patrick Leigh-Fermor (novel), pp.32–33, D2

Saint Lucia, Mexico (town), *La Sombra del Pasado* (TV), pp.32–33, B2

Saint Marie (fictional island), *Death in Paradise* (TV), pp.32–33, F2

Saint Nicholas (fictional island), *Club Paradise* (film), pp.32–33, D2

Saint Pierre (fictional country), works of John Hearne, pp.32–33, F2

Sainte Claire, France (village), *Star Trek: Voyager* ('The Killing Game' parts I and II) (TV), pp.44–45, C3

Sakura Empire (fictional country), *Azur Lane* (video game/anime), pp.96–97, B1/C1

Sakuragaoka High School, Japan (building), *K-ON!* by Kakifly (manga/anime), pp.96–97, B2

Sakuragaoka High School, Japan (building), *The Demon Girl Next Door* by Izumo Itō (manga/anime), pp.96–97, E1

Sakurami City, Japan (city), *Future Diary* by Sakae Esuno (manga/anime), pp.96–97, B2

Sakuyu Channel, Azanian Empire (fictional sea), *Black Mischief* by Evelyn Waugh (novel), pp.84–85, D4

Sal Tlay Ka Siti, Utah (city), *The Book of Mormon* (musical), pp.18–19, C4

Salamanko, Zendia (fictional city), *The Zendian problem* (intelligence exercise), pp.120–121, E2/F2

Salas, Argentina (town), *El Ciudadano Ilustre* (film), pp.38–39, C2

Saldeoro, Spain (town), novels of Benito Pérez Galdós, pp.44–45, B2

Salem, Illinois (town), *Days of Our Lives* (TV), pp.16–17, D4/D5

Salimiento, Mexico (town), *Porque Parece Mentira la Verdad Nunca se Sabe* by Daniel Sada (novel), pp.32–33, B3

Salmaah (fictional country), *Day of the Falcon* (film), pp.72–73, C2

Salonika, Oconee (fictional city), *Count Geiger's Blues* by Michael Bishop (novel), pp.14–15, A3

Salsiccia, Italy (village), *The Simpsons* (TV), pp.44–45, D2

Saltmarsh, England (town), Ruth Galloway books by Elly Griffiths (novel), pp.64–65, D2

Salty Creek, South Carolina (town), *Sophie and the Rising Sun* (film), pp.14–15, C4

Salvation, Texas (town), *Preacher* (comic/TV), pp.16–17, C2

Sam Dent, British Columbia (town), *The Sweet Hereafter* (film), pp.26–27, B3

Samaru Islands, Pacific Ocean (island chain), *Sea Patrol* (TV), pp.108–109, E3

Samavia (fictional country), *The Lost Prince* by Frances Hodgson Burnett (novel), pp.50–51, A4

Sams Itch, England (town), *Riddley Walker* by Russell Hoban (novel), pp.64–65, D2

San Andreas (fictional state), *Grand Theft Auto* series (video games), pp.18–19, A4/B4

San Andrés, Chile (town), *Estúpido Cupido* (TV), pp.38–39, B3

San Angel, Mexico (town), *Book of Life* (film), pp.32–33, B2

San Burro, Dorado (town), *I-0* (video game), pp.18–19, C3

San Carlos (fictional country), *Delta Force 2: The Colombian Connection* (film), pp.38–39, A5/B5

San Celeste, Italy (town), *Mafia 2* (video game), pp.44–45, D1

San Chema, Mexico (town), *Porque Parece Mentira la Verdad Nunca se Sabe* by Daniel Sada (novel), pp.32–33, B3

145

San Cristóbal Tlaxico, Mexico (town), *El Hotel de los Secretos*, pp.32–33, B2

San Cristóbal (fictional island/nation), works of George Lamming, pp.32–33, F2

San Cristobal, Argentina (city), *A Luminous Republic* by Andrés Barba (novel), pp.38–39, B3

San Croce, Argentina (city), *High Citadel* by Desmond Bagley (novel), pp.38–39, C2

San Diablo (fictional country), Marvel Comics, pp.38–39, B5

San Diego, Philippines (town), works of Dr José Rizal, pp.90–91, C3

San Escobar (fictional country, gaffe/internet humour), pp.32–33, B2/C2

San Esperito, San Escobar (fictional island/nation), *Just Cause* (video game), pp.32–33, F2

San Fiasco, Scotland (wreck), *Captain Pugwash* by John Ryan (various), pp.64–65, B5

San Fierro, San Andreas (fictional city), *Grand Theft Auto* series (video game), pp.18–19, A4

San Francisco el Alto, Mexico (town), *Un Refugio Para el Amor* (TV), pp.32–33, B3

San Fransokyo, California (city), *Big Hero 6* (film/TV), pp.18–19, A4

San Futuro, California (city), *Marshall Law* (comic), pp.18–19, A4

San Gaspar, Mexico (town), *Apuesta Por un Amor* (TV), pp.32–33, B3

San Gaspar, Mexico (town), *La Vecina* (TV), pp.32–33, B2

San Ireneo, Ataguitania (fictional town), *If On a Winter's Night a Traveller* by Italo Calvino (novel), pp.38–39, B5

San Juan Romero, Mexico (village), *San Juan Romero* by Rita María Felix da Silva (novel), pp.32–33, B3

San Lazaro, Mexico (town), *El Amor que me Juraste* by Silvia Molina (novel), pp.32–33, C2

San Lazaro, Philippines (town), *San Lazaro* (film), pp.90–91, C3

San Lorenzo (island/nation), *Cat's Cradle* by Kurt Vonnegut (novel), pp.32–33, E2

San Lorenzo, San Escobar (fictional country), *Hey Arnold!* (TV), pp.32–33, C2

San Lorenzo, Olancho (fictional village), *Soldiers of Fortune* by Richard Harding Davis (novel), pp.38–39, B3

San Luis River, various (river), *Red Dead Redemption* series (video games), pp.18–19, D3

San Luis River, Mexico (river), *Red Dead Redemption* series (video games), pp.32–33, B4

San Marco, Republic of (fictional island/nation), *Don Quixote, USA* by Richard Powell (novel/film/TV), pp.32–33, D3/E3

San Martín del Sella, Spain (town), *Doctor Mateo* (TV), pp.44–45, B3

San Miguel, Mexico (town), *A Fistful of Dollars* (film), pp.32–33, B3

San Monique (fictional island/nation), *James Bond: Live and Let Die*/James Bond 007 (film/role playing game), pp.32–33, D2

San Narciso, California (town), *The Crying of Lot 49* by Thomas Pynchon (novel), pp.18–19, C3

San Pasquale (fictional country), *Commander in Chief* (TV), pp.38–39, B4

San Pedro (fictional country), *The Tiger of San Pedro* by Arthur Conan Doyle (short story), pp.32–33, D1

San Pedro de las Peñas, Mexico (town), *Soy tu Dueña* (TV), pp.32–33, B2/B3

San Pedro del Oro, Mexico (town), *La Patrona* (TV), pp.32–33, B2

San Piedro Island, Washington (island), *Snow Falling on Cedars* by David Guterson (novel/film), pp.18–19, A6

San Pueblo, California (town), *The Partridge Family* (TV), pp.18–19, A4

San Rafael, Mexico (town), *Infierno de Todos* by Sergio Pitol (short story), pp.32–33, C2

San Sebastien (fictional island), *The Triangle* (film), pp.32–33, E3

San Senovia (fictional country), *Christmas at the Palace* (film), pp.50–51, B2

San Serriffe (fictional island/nation), *The Guardian* (newspaper), pp.78–79, A1/A2

San Simeon, Philippines (city), *San Simeon* (*Sims 3*) (video game), pp.90–91, D3

San Simon, Mexico (town), *Seis Manos* (TV), pp.32–33, A4

San Theodoros (fictional country), *The Adventures of Tintin* by Hergé (various), pp.38–39, C5

San Toledo, Spain (town), *Snatch* (TV), pp.44–45, B1

San Venganza, Texas (town), *Ghost Rider* (film), pp.16–17, A2

San Zucchini, California (city), *Attack of the Killer Tomatoes* (film), pp.18–19, B3

Sanc Kingdom (fictional country), *Gundam Wing* (anime), pp.56–57, D7

Sand Rock, Arizona (town), *It Came From Outer Space* (film), pp.18–19, C2

Sandbourne, England (town), novels of Thomas Hardy, pp.64–65, C1

Sandford, England (town), *Hot Fuzz* (film), pp.64–65, C1

Sandgem Town, Japan (town), *Pokémon* (video games), pp.96–97, C4

Sandicot, New York (town), *Billions* (TV), pp.14–15, B5

Sanditon, England (town), *Sanditon* by Jane Austen (novel), pp.64–65, D1

Sandling Island, England (island), novels of Nicci French, pp.64–65, D2

Sandy Shores, San Andreas (fictional town), *Grand Theft Auto* series (video game), pp.18–19, B3

Sanfacion, Neuvo-Rico (fictional city), *The Adventures of Tintin* by Hergé (various), pp.38–39, D5

Sangari, Afghanistan (village, military training exercise), pp.72–73, D2/E2

Sankakusu, Japan (city/island), *Sailor Moon* by Naoko Takeuchi (manga/anime), pp.96–97, F1

Sankt Nikolaus, Austria (town), *Class Reunion* (film), pp.44–45, D3

Sannikov Land, Arctic Ocean (island, Russian folklore), pp.102–103, E2/F2

Sanshu, Japan (city), *Yuki Yuna Is a Hero* (anime), pp.96–97, B2

Santa Barbara, Santa Barbara (fictional country), *The Midnight Folk* by John Masefield (novel), pp.38–39, B6

Santa Bárbara, Chile (town), *Conde Vrolok*/*Count Vrolok* (TV), pp.38–39, C3

Santa Cecilia, Mexico (town), *Coco/Cars 3* (film), pp.32–33, B2

Santa City, Santa Esperanza (fictional city), *Santa Esperanza* by Aka Morchiladze (novel), pp.50–51, C2

Santa Clara, California (town), *The Lost Boys* (film), pp.18–19, A4

Santa Costa (fictional island/nation), *Mission Impossible* (TV), pp.32–33, E2

Santa Cruz, New Mexico (town), *For a Few Dollars More* (film), pp.18–19, C3

Santa Esperanza (fictional island/nation), *Santa Esperanza* by Aka Morchiladze (novel), pp.50–51, C2

Santa Luisa, California (town), *Dan August* (TV), pp.18–19, A3

Santa María, Uruguay (town), works of Juan Carlos Onetti, pp.38–39, C2

Santa Marta (Sta. Marta), Costaguana (fictional town), *Nostromo* by Joseph Conrad (novel), pp.38–39, A4

Santa Marta (fictional island), *Island in the Sun* (film), pp.32–33, F2

Santa Mira, California (town), *Invasion of the Body Snatchers* (film), pp.18–19, A4

Santa Modesta, California (town), *Destroy All Humans* (video game), pp.18–19, A4

Santa Prisca (fictional island/nation), DC Comics, pp.32–33, F2

Santa Rita, Panama (town), *Alborada* (TV), pp.32–33, D1

Santa Rosa, Mexico (town), *Volver a Santa Rosa* by Víctor Hugo Rascón Banda (novel), pp.32–33, B3

Santa Rosalia, Galapagos Islands (island), *Galápagos* by Kurt Vonnegut (novel), pp.38–39, A1

Santa Rosita, California (city), *It's a Mad, Mad, Mad, Mad World* (film), pp.18–19, A2

Santa Teresa, California (town), works of Ross McDonald, pp.18–19, A3

Santa Teresa, Mexico (city), *2666* by Roberto Bolaño, pp.32–33, B4

Santa Ynez, Utah (town), *The Car* (film), pp.18–19, C3

Santa's Workshop, North Pole (building, tradition), pp.26–27, C4

Santalune City, France (city), *Pokémon* (video games), pp.44–45, C3

Santana de Bocaiúvas, Brazil (city), *Agora E Que São Elas* (TV), pp.38–39, D3

Santana do Agreste, Brazil (town), *Tieta do Agreste* by Jorge Amado (novel/TV), pp.38–39, D4

Santana dos Ferros, Brazil (town), *Hilda Furacão* by Roberto Drummond (novel/TV), pp.38–39, D4

Santillana, Cordillera (fictional city), *High Citadel* by Desmond Bagley (novel), pp.38–39, D3

Santo Bartolomeo, Republica Libra (fictional city), *Shooting Script* by Gavin Lyall (novel), pp.32–33, E2

Santo Bugito, Texas (town), *Santo Bugito* (TV), pp.16–17, B1

Santo Domestos, San Escobar (fictional city, internet humour), pp.32–33, B2

Santo Domingo de Araxá, Brazil (town), *Doña Beija* (TV), pp.38–39, C3

Santo Rico (fictional country), Marvel Comics, pp.32–33, B2

Santo Subito, San Escobar (fictional city, internet humour), pp.32–33, B2

São Dimas, Brazil (town), *A Lei do Amor* (TV), pp.38–39, D4

São Rico (fictional country), *The Adventures of Tintin* by Hergé (various), pp.38–39, B5

São Sebastião de Valmares, Portugal (town), *O vale da paixão* by Lidia Jorge (novel), pp.44–45, A2

São Tomás de Trás, Brazil (town), *Meu Bem Querer* (TV), pp.38–39, D5

São Tomé dos Números, Brazil (town), *Armação Ilimitada* (TV), pp.38–39, C4

Sapienza, Italy (town), *HITMAN 2* (video game), pp.44–45, D2

Saradia (fictional country), *Godzilla vs Biollante* (film), pp.72–73, B2/B3

Saramandaia (Bole-Bole), Brazil (town), *Saramandaia* (TV), pp.38–39, D4

Saranza, Russia (town), *Dreams of My Russian Summers* by Andrei Makine (novel), pp.102–103, A2

Sardovia (fictional country), *Scorpion* (TV), pp.50–51, C4

Sarkhan (fictional country), *The Ugly American* by Eugene Burdick and William Lederer (novel), pp.90–91, B3

Sárszeg, Serbia (town), works of Dezs Kosztolányi, pp.50–51, B2

Satan's Ridge, Northern Territory (mountain), *The Rescuers Down Under* (film), pp.108–109, C3

Sauropolis, Indian Ocean (city), *Dinotopia* (books/TV), pp.38–39, D3

Savage Land, The (region), Marvel Comics, pp.114–115, B3

Sawyer, Western Australia (town), *Breath* by Tim Winton (novel), pp.108–109, B2

Scabb Island, Caribbean (island), *Monkey Island* series (video games), pp.32–33, B2

Scarclaw Fell, England (natural feature), *Six Stories* by Matt Wesolowski (novel), pp.64–65, C3

Scarfolk, England (town), *Scarfolk* (website), pp.64–65, C3

Scarhead, England (town), *The Railway Phantoms* by Dennis Hamley (novel), pp.64–65, C3

Scarsdale, England (town), *Oh No, It's Selwyn Froggett!* (TV), pp.64–65, D3

Scheria, Greece (island), *The Odyssey* by Homer (ancient mythology), pp.44–45, D1/E1

Schitt's Creek, Ontario (town), *Shitt's Creek* (TV), pp.26–27, A4

Schloß Adler, Germany (building), *Where Eagles Dare* (film), pp.44–45, D3

Schloss Dreiviertelstein, Austria (country, elfin), *Kingdoms of Elfin* by Sylvia Townsend Warner (short stories), pp.44–45, D3

Schlüsselburg, Germany (town), *Wolfenstein* series (video games), pp.44–45, D4

Science City/Lincoln, South Dakota/Nebraska (city), *Transformers: Armada* (comic), pp.16–17, B5

Scotsfield, Ireland (town), *Call Me The Breeze* by Patrick McCabe (novel), pp.64–65, B5

Scrapyard (Scrap Iron City)/Zalem, Panama (city), *Gunnm*/*Battle Angel Alita* (manga/anime), pp.32–33, D1

Scurvy Beach, Caribbean (island), *Pirates of the Caribbean* (various), pp.32–33, D2

Scylla & Charybdis, Italy (monsters, Greek mythology), pp.44–45, D1

Scythia-Pannonia-Transbalkania (fictional bloc), *The Enquiries of Doctor Eszterhazy* by Avram Davidson (short stories), pp.50–51, B2/C2

Sea Bird, India (wreck), *Bhoot – Part One: The Haunted Ship* (film), pp.78–79, B3

Sea Dolphin II, Vietnam (wreck), *James Bond: Tomorrow Never Dies* (film), pp.90–91, B4

Sea of Celts, Scotland (sea), *Brave* (film), pp.64–65, A4/B4

Sea of Holes, Atlantic Ocean (sea), *Yellow Submarine* (film), pp.126–127, B2/C2

Sea of Monsters, Atlantic Ocean (sea), *Yellow Submarine* (film), pp.126–127, C3

Sea of Nothing, Atlantic Ocean (sea), *Yellow Submarine* (film), pp.126–127, B2/C2

Sea of Science, Atlantic Ocean (sea), *Yellow Submarine* (film), pp.126–127, C3/D3

Sea of Time, Atlantic Ocean (sea), *Yellow Submarine* (film), pp.126–127, C3/D3

Sea Spirit's Den, Channel Islands (island), *Pokémon* (video games), pp.64–65, C4

Sea Star, Pacific Ocean (wreck), *Virus* (comic/film), pp.120–121, C2

Seaburgh, England (town), *A Warning to the Curious* by M.R. James (short story), pp.64–65, D1

Seacouver, Washington (town), *Highlander: The Series* (TV), pp.18–19, A6

Seafolk Village, Hawaii (town), *Pokémon* (video games), pp.18–19, C1

Seahaven Island, California (town/building), *The Truman Show* (film), pp.14–15, D6

Sealab, Tasman Sea (submerged building), *Sealab 2020/Sealab 2021* (TV), pp.120–121, B4

Seale-on-Sea, England (town), novels of Elizabeth Bowen, pp.64–65, D1

Seaport, England (town), *Z-Cars* (TV), pp.64–65, C3

Seascape, Atlantic Ocean (building), *Thunderbirds* (TV), pp.126–127, C5

Seatown, England (town), novels of Hugh Walpole, pp.64–65, C2

Seito, Japan (region), *Kamen Rider Build* (TV), pp.96–97, B2

Seize, Helvetia (fictional town), *Sound of the Sky* (anime), pp.72–73, B2

Selene, Serbia (town), *La Ville Vampire* by Paul Féval (novel), pp.50–51, B2

Selgina (fictional town), *Ghidorah, the Three-Headed Monster* (film), pp.78–79, D4

Selmen, Germany (town), *Hepzibah – Sie holt dich im Schlaf* (film), pp.44–45, D3

Senderos, San Escobar (fictional city, internet humour), pp.32–33, B2

Seneca River, Alaska (river), *Runaway Train* (film), pp.18–19, B1

Sensilvânia, Brazil (town), *Armação Ilimitada* (TV), pp.38–39, C3

Sequoyah (fictional state), *Southern Victory* by Harry Turtledove (novels), pp.16–17, B3

Serdaristan (fictional country, *Battlefield: Bad Company* (video game), pp.50–51, B3

Serka Zong, Anandapur (fictional town), Expedition Everest (theme park), pp.78–79, C4

Serranias, Brazil (town), *Eterna Magia* by Elizabeth Jhin (novel/TV), pp.38–39, D4

Serro Azul, Brazil (town), *O Sétimo Guardião* (TV), pp.38–39, D3

Servela, Spain (city), *Suske en Wiske* by Wally Vandersteen (comics), pp.44–45, B2

Sesam Stasjon, Norway (building), *Sesam Stasjon* (TV), pp.56–57, B3

Setton, England (town), *Spanish City* by Sarah May (novel), pp.64–65, C3

Seva, Puerto Rico (town), *Seva* by Luis López Nieves (short story), pp.32–33, F2

Seven Bay Island, Maine (island), works of Madeleine L'Engle, pp.14–15, D6

Seven Kingdoms, The (fictional bloc), *Tangled/Rapunzel's Tangled Adventure* (film/TV), pp.50–51, A4/B4

Seventh Fall, Eastal (fictional building), *Log Horizon* by Mamare Touno and Kazuhiro Hara (novels/anime), pp.96–97, C3

Severnaya Satellite Control Centre, Russia (building), *James Bond: Goldeneye* (film), pp.102–103, E1

Severnaya, Russia (region), *James Bond: Goldeneye* (film), pp.102–103, E2

Severnford, England (town), Severn Valley of the Cthulhu Mythos by Ramsey Campbell (novels), pp.64–65, C2

Shack #7, Tri-Oceanic Mining Corporation, Atlantic Ocean (building), *Leviathan* (film), pp.126–127, A4

Shadaloo City, Shadaloo (fictional city), *Street Fighter* (film), pp.90–91, A3

Shadaloo River, China (river), *Street Fighter* (film), pp.90–91, A4, pp.102–103, C1

Shadaloo (fictional country), *Street Fighter* (film), pp.90–91, A4/B4

Shadbagh, Afghanistan (village), *And the Mountains Echoed* by Khaled Hosseini (novel), pp.72–73, D2

Shadow Moses Island, Alaska (island), *Metal Gear Solid* series (video games), pp.18–19, A1

Shady Sands, California (city), *Fallout 2* (video game), pp.18–19, B3

Shalimar, Virginia (village), *Song of Solomon* by Toni Morrison (novel), pp.14–15, B4

Shalour City, France (city), *Pokémon* (video games), pp.44–45, B3

Shambali Monastery, Nepal (building), *Overwatch* (video game), pp.78–79, C4

Shamballah, City of Skulls, Tibet (city), *The City of Skulls* by L. Sprague de Camp and Lin Carter (novel), pp.102–103, C3

Shamgorod, Ukraine (town), *The Trial of God* by Elie Wiesel (play), pp.50–51, D2

Shangdu, China (city), *Engine Empire* by Cathy Park Hong (poetry), pp.102–103, D1

Shangri-La, Tibet (natural feature/building), *Lost Horizon* by James Hilton (novel), pp.102–103, A2

Sharzhad (fictional country), Marvel Comics (various), pp.84–85, C5

Shaston, England (town), novels of Thomas Hardy, pp.64–65, C3

Shaw Mountain, Idaho (mountain), *Truly, Idaho* series by Rachel Gibson (novels), pp.18–19, B5

Shawan, Oregon (town), *The X-Files* (TV), pp.18–19, A5

Shawei, China (city), works of Preston Schoyer, pp.102–103, D1/D2

Shawshank State Prison, Maine (building), *The Shawshank Redemption* by Stephen King (short story/film), pp.14–15, D6

Sheba's Breasts, DRC (mountain range), *King Solomon's Mines* by H. Rider Haggard (novel), pp.84–85, C4

Shelby, Idaho (town), *iCarly* (TV), pp.18–19, C5

Shelbyville, North Takoma (fictional town), *The Simpsons* (TV), pp.18–19, A6

Shelmerston, England (town), Aubrey-Maturin series by Patrick O'Brian (novels), pp.64–65, C1

Shelter Mountain Inn, Washington (building), *The Ring* (film), pp.18–19, A6

Sheltered Shrubs, Connecticut (town), *As Told By Ginger* (TV), pp.14–15, D7

Shem, Israel (country), Conan novels of Robert E. Howard, pp.72–73, B2

Sherman Dam, Nevada (building), *Transformers* (various), pp.18–19, B3

Sherman Reservoir, San Andreas (fictional lake), *Grand Theft Auto* series (video game), pp.18–19, B3/C3

Shermer, Illinois (town), films of John Hughes, pp.16–17, D5

Shieldinch, Scotland (town), *River City* (TV), pp.64–65, C4

Shime, Japan (town), *Sketchbook* by Totan Kobako (manga/anime), pp.96–97, A1

Shimokage, Japan (village), *Noroi: The Curse* (film), pp.96–97, B2

Shinbone, Colorado (town), *The Man Who Shot Liberty Valance* (film), pp.16–17, A3

Shining Time, Pennsylvania (town), *Shining Time Station*/*Thomas and the Magic Railroad* (TV/film), pp.14–15, C4

Ship-Trap Island, Caribbean (island), *The Most Dangerous Game* by Richard Connell (novel), pp.32–33, F2

Shipwreck Cove, Cuba (natural feature), *The Pirates! Band of Misfits* (film), pp.32–33, D3

Shipwreck Island, Caribbean (island), *Pirates of the Caribbean* (various), pp.32–33, F2

Shiroiwa, Japan (city), *Battle Royale* by Koushun Takami (novel), pp.96–97, B2

Shishan, China (city), *The Palace of Heavenly Pleasure* by Adam Williams (novel), pp.102–103, D2

Shiverme Timbers, Alaska (town), *Yvon of the Yukon* (TV), pp.18–19, B1, pp.26–27, B2

Shiverpool (town), *Surf's Up* (film), pp.114–115, B2

Shivpalganj, India (village), *Raag Darbari* by Srilal Shukla (novel), pp.78–79, C4

Shizume, Japan (town), *K* (anime), pp.96–97, E1

Shobo-n-Po, Sulliaba (fictional city), Islandia novels and sequels by Austin Tappan Wright and Mark Saxton, pp.84–85, A2

Sholo, Nevada (town), *Harts of the West* (TV), pp.18–19, B3

Shonir Char, Bangladesh (village), *Heroes of 71* series (video games), pp.78–79, D4

Shorthills, Trinidad (town), *A House for Mr Biswas* by V.S. Naipaul (novel), pp.32–33, F2

Showne, West Keystone (fictional town), *Steven Universe* (TV), pp.14–15, B4

Shoyo, Arkansas (town), *The Stand* by Stephen King (various), pp.16–17, D3

Shuanglong, China (town), *A Dictionary of Maqiao* by Han Shaogong (novel), pp.102–103, D2

Shub Nigruth (city), *Atlantis: The Lost Empire* (film), pp.114–115, E3

Shuchi'in Academy, Japan (building), *Kaguya-sama: Love is War* by Aka Akasaki (manga/anime), pp.96–97, E1

Siak Republic (fictional country), *Ghost in the Shell* (anime), pp.90–91, B2

Siberian Omnium, The, Russia (building), *Overwatch* (video game), pp.102–103, E1

Sicmon Islands, Pacific Ocean (island chain), the Griffin and Sabine Trilogy (novels), pp.120–121, D6

Sidböle Härad, Sweden (region), 'Sidböle Härad' (song), pp.56–57, C4

Sidewinder, Colorado (town), *The Shining* by Stephen King (novel/film), pp.16–17, A4

Sierra de la Plata, Bolivia (mountain range, mythology), pp.38–39, B3

Sierra Falls, California (town), Sierra Falls series by Veronica Wolff (novels), pp.18–19, A4

Sierra Vieja, Mexico (town), *Santa María del Circo* by David Toscana (novel), pp.32–33, B3

Signal, Wyoming (town), *Brokeback Mountain* (short story/film), pp.18–19, D5

Silent Hill, West Virginia (town), *Silent Hill* (film), pp.14–15, B4

Silicon Isle, China (town), *Waste Tide* by Chen Qiufan (novel), pp.102–103, D1

Silkies' Isle, Scotland (island), Outlander novels by Diana Gabaldon (novels/TV), pp.64–65, A4

Silly Islands, The, Pacific Ocean (island chain), *The Pirates! Band of Misfits!* (film), pp.96–97, D4/E4

Silograd, Nukehavistan (fictional city), *The Onion* (online satire), pp.72–73, D3/E3

Silva's HQ, China (island), *James Bond: Skyfall* (film), pp.102–103, D1

Silver Gorge, Colorado (natural feature), *Atomic Train* (film), pp.18–19, D4

Silver Hills, Washington (city), *Power Rangers Time Force* (TV), pp.18–19, A6

Silverado, Utah (town), *Wild Wild West* (film), pp.18–19, C4/C5

Silverbridge, England (town), novels of Anthony Trollope, pp.64–65, C1

Silverton, Oklahoma (town), *Into the Storm* (film), pp.16–17, C3

Silvertown, California (town), *Joe Dirt* (film), pp.18–19, A5

Sinclair Parish, Louisiana (county), *Mafia 3* (video game), pp.16–17, D2

Sinistra Zone, The (region), *The Sinistra Zone* by Ádám Bodor (novel), pp.50–51, B2/B3

Sink, The, Western Australia (natural feature), *In the Winter Dark* by Tim Winton (novel), pp.108–109, B2

Sinnoh, Japan (region), *Pokémon* (video games), pp.96–97, C4

Sino Cit One, China (city), *2000 AD* (comics), pp.102–103, D2

Sino Cit Two, China (city), *2000 AD* (comics), pp.102–103, D1

Sinsikrou, Zanzarim (fictional city), *Solo* by William Boyd (novel), pp.84–85, B4

Sinville, Statesota (fictional town), *Moral Orel* (TV), pp.16–17, C3

Sipolje, Slovenia (village), *Radetzky March* by Joseph Roth (novel), pp.50–51, A4

Siren-1 (S-484), Atlantic Ocean (wreck), *The Rift* (film), pp.123, B5

Siren-2 (S-485), Atlantic Ocean (wreck), *The Rift* (film), pp.126–127, B5

Siroun, Turkey (town), *The Promise* (film), pp.72–73, B3

Sisika Penitentiary, Lemoyne (fictional island), *Red Dead Redemption* series (video game), pp.16–17, D2

Sitapur, India (city), *Devi* (comics), pp.78–79, C4/D4

Sítio Maldito, Brazil (natural feature), *Amazon: Guardians of Eden* (video game), pp.38–39, B5

Sittaford, England (village), *The Sittaford Mystery* by Agatha Christie (novel), pp.64–65, C1

Skal, Obristan (fictional city), *Papers, Please* (video game), pp.50–51, A5

Skandistan (country), *The Years of Rice and Salt* by Kim Stanley Robinson (novel), pp.56–57, B3

Skebawn, Ireland (village), The Irish RM novels by Somerville and Ross, pp.64–65, A4

Skeleton Key, Cuba (island), *Skeleton Key* by Anthony Horowitz (novel), pp.32–33, A7

Skelthwaite, England (town), *Where the Heart is* (TV), pp.64–65, C3

Skeptos, Greece (island nation), *Perfect Strangers* (TV), pp.44–45, E1

Skidmore, Kentucky (town), *Petticoat Junction/Green Acres* (TV), pp.14–15, A3

Skipley, England (town), *Brother in the Land* by Robert Swindells (novel), pp.64–65, C3

Skira, Alaska (island), *Operation Flashpoint: Dragon Rising* (video game), pp.18–19, A1

Skirby St Mary, England (town), *The Quarry Line Mystery* by A.C. Stewart (novel), pp.64–65, C3

Skirby, England (town), *The Quarry Line Mystery* by A.C. Stewart (novel), pp.64–65, C3

Skrull Island, England (island), Groosham Grange books by Anthony Horowitz, pp.64–65, D2

Skull Cove, Somalia (natural feature), *South Park* (TV), pp.84–85, D4

Skull Island, Indian Ocean (island), *King Kong* (and spin-offs, films), pp.90–91, A1

Sky Tower, The, Ninetail Dominions (fictional building), *Log Horizon* by Mamare Touno and Kazuhiro Hara (novels/anime), pp.96–97, A1

Skye, Tasmania (village), *Cape Grimm* by Carmel Bird (novel), pp.108–109, D1

Skyfall Lodge, Scotland (building), *James Bond: Skyfall* (film), pp.64–65, B6

Skyland Mountain, Virginia (mountain), *The X-Files* (TV), pp.14–15, B4

Slaka (fictional country), novels of Malcolm Bradbury, pp.50–51, B2/C2

Slateport City, Japan (city), *Pokémon* (video games), pp.96–97, A1

Slavo-Lydia (fictional country), works of Angela Thirkell, pp.50–51, B2/C2

Sleepy Peak Peak, Washington (mountain), *Camp Camp* (web animation), pp.18–19, B6

Sleepyside-on-Hudson, New York (town), Trixie Belden series by Julie Campbell Tatham (novels), pp.14–15, C5

Slickville, Connecticut (town), *Sam Slick in England* by Thomas Chandler Haliburton (novels), pp.14–15, D5

Slieve Geal, Ireland (mountain), *Crying Through the Wind: The Story of Oisin Kelly* by Iona Carroll (novel), pp.64–65, A3

Sligo Mission Control, Ireland (building), *Irish Astronauts* (TV), pp.64–65, A3

Sloravia (fictional country), *The Onion Movie* (film), pp.72–73, C3

Slorenia (fictional country), Marvel Comics, pp.50–51, B4

Slovetzia (fictional country), *The Beautician and the Beast* (film), pp.50–51, B3

Smallville, Kansas (town), DC Comics (various), pp.16–17, B4

Smalvik, Norway (village, real world), pp.56–57, B3

Smeerensburg, Finland (island/town), *Klaus* (film), pp.56–57, C5

Smoogle Village, Northern Territory (village), *The Smurfs* (TV), pp.108–109, C3

Snackitoba (fictional province), *Whose Line is it Anyway?* (TV), pp.26–27, C2

Snakewater, Montana (town), *Jurassic Park* (various), pp.16–17, A6

Snaydon, Scotland (town), novels of Susan Pleydell, pp.64–65, C4

Sneaky's Land, Glass Town Federation (fictional region), Brontë juvenilia, pp.84–85, B4

Snottinggrad, Russia (town), *The Government Inspector* by Nikolai Gogol (play), pp.50–51, D3

Snowbelle City, France (city), *Pokémon* (video games), pp.44–45, C3

Snowcap Tracking Station (building), *Doctor Who: The Tenth Planet* (TV), pp.114–115, C2/C3

Snowfield, England (town), *Adam Bede* by George Eliot (novel), pp.64–65, C2

Snowpoint City, Japan (city), *Pokémon* (video games), pp.96–97, C4

Snydersville, Nebraska (town), *To Wong Foo, Thanks for Everything! Julie Newmar* (film), pp.16–17, B2

Sobo Steppes, Karain continent (fictional natural feature), Islandia novels and sequels by Austin Tappan Wright and Mark Saxton, pp.84–85, B1

SOCCENT Forward Operations Base, Qatar (building), *Transformers* (film), pp.72–73, C1

Soda Seas (sea), *Club Penguin* (video game), pp.114–115, B4

Sokovia (fictional country), Marvel Cinematic Universe, pp.50–51, A3

Sola Fide Beach, Caribbean (island), *Pirates of the Caribbean* (various), pp.32–33, E3

Soldier Island, England (island), *And Then There Were None* by Agatha Christie (novel), pp.64–65, C1

Solís (fictional country), *Just Cause 4* (video game), pp.38–39, A5

Sollgel Island, Pacific Ocean (island), *Godzilla* films, pp.120–121, C3

Solomon Space Center, Pacific Ocean (building), *Rocket Girls* by Hōsuke Nojiri (novels/anime), pp.120–121, B3

Somerset, Michigan (town), *Somerset* (TV), pp.14–15, A5

Sondonesia (fictional country), *Tintin: Flight 714 to Sydney* by Hergé (comic book), pp.90–91, A1

Sootopolis City, Japan (city), *Pokémon* (video games), pp.96–97, A1

Soplaviento, Colombia (town), *Te Voy a Enseñar a Querer* (TV), pp.38–39, A5

Sottrup, Germany (town), *Stenkelfeld* (radio), pp.44–45, D4

South Angel, California (city), *Log Horizon* by Mamare Touno (novels/anime), pp.18–19, B3

South Archipelago, The, *Caribbean (island)*, *Pirates of the Caribbean* (various), pp.32–33, E3

South Dakastor, South Dakota (state), *MacTrump* by Ian Doescher and Jacopo Della Quercia (book), pp.16–17, A5/B5

South Harbour, Newfoundland (town), *Orca* (film), pp.26–27, F2

South Korasia, South Korea (country), *MacTrump* by Ian Doescher and Jacopo Della Quercia (book), pp.102–103, E2

South Ortiz Sea, Indian Ocean (sea), *The Illegal* by Lawrence Hill (novel), pp.78–79, B1/B4

South Park, Colorado (town), *South Park* (TV), pp.18–19, D4

South Riding, England (county), *South Riding* by Winifred Holtby (novel), pp.64–65, D3

South Sahrani, Sahrani (fictional island/nation), *ARMA: Armed Assault* (video game), pp.126–127, C4

Southern Island, Japan (island), *Pokémon* (video games), pp.96–97, A1

Southern Isles, The, Denmark (country), *Frozen*, pp.56–57, A2

Southfork Ranch, Texas (building), *Dallas* (TV), pp.16–17, C2

Southmoltonshire, England (county), novels of P.G. Wodehouse, pp.64–65, D2

Southtown, Louisiana (town), *The Year Without a Santa Claus* (film), pp.16–17, C2

Sovogda, Russia (city), *Alias* (TV), pp.50–51, B6

Space Force Campus, Colorado (building), *Space Force* (TV), pp.16–17, A4

Spanakos, Greece (island), *The Venture Brothers* (TV), pp.44–45, E1

Spargel, Greece (town), *Last Exile: Fam of the Silver Wing* (anime), pp.44–45, E1

Sparta, Mississippi (town), *In the Heat of the Night* (film/TV), pp.16–17, D3

Spatula, Washington (town), *New Moan (The Twishite Saga)* by Stephfordy Mayo (novel), pp.18–19, A6

Spectralia, Pacific Ocean (island), *Riallaro, the Archipelago of Exiles* by Godfrey Sweven (novel), pp.120–121, E1

Spectre, Alabama (town), *Big Fish* (film), pp.14–15, C2

Spencer Island (Monster Island), Pacific Ocean (island), *Godfrey Morgan* by Jules Verne (novel/film), pp.120–121, E4

Spensonia (fictional island/nation), works of Thomas Spence, pp.38–39, C4

Spider Canyon, Utah (natural feature), *Wild Wild West* (film), pp.18–19, C4

Spider Monkey Island, Brazil (island), *The Voyages of Doctor Dolittle* by Hugh Lofting (novel), pp.38–39, C3

Spider Web Castle, Japan (building), *Throne of Blood* (film), pp.96–97, C2

Spider-Skull Island, Sargasso Sea (island), *The Venture Brothers* (TV), pp.126–127, A4

Spinner Cay, Gulf of Melange (fictional island), *Monkey Island* series (video games), pp.32–33, F2

Spirit Mountain, China (mountain), *Lenin's Kisses* by Yan Lianke (novel), pp.102–103, D2

Spirits' Mountain, The, Spain (mountain), *The Spirits' Mountain* by Gustavo Adolfo Becquer (short story), pp.44–45, C2

Splendid, Texas (town), *Dead State* (video games), pp.16–17, B2

Spoon Island, Gulf of Melange (fictional island), *Monkey Island* series (video games), pp.32–33, F2

Spoon River, Illinois (town), *Spoon River Anthology* by Edgar Lee Masters (poetry), pp.16–17, D4

Spoonerville, Ohio (town), *Goof Troop/A Goofy Movie* (various), pp.14–15, B4

Sporks, Washington (town), *Vampires Suck* (film), pp.18–19, A6

Springdale, Japan (town), *Yokai Watch* (video game/anime), pp.96–97, B2

Springfield, North Takoma (fictional town), *The Simpsons* (TV), pp.18–19, A6

Springwood, Ohio (town), *A Nightmare on Elm Street* (films), pp.14–15, B5

Sprodj Atomic Research Centre, Syldavia (fictional building), *The Adventures of Tintin* by Hergé (various), pp.50–51, A1

Spurbury, Vermont (town), *Super Troopers* (film), pp.14–15, C6

Squamash, Pennsylvania (town), *The X-Files* (TV), pp.14–15, C5

Squaw's Ankle, Wyoming (town), *The Adventures of Rocky and Bullwinkle* (TV), pp.16–17, B4

Sri Kanda, Taprobane (fictional mountain), *The Fountains of Paradise* by Arthur C. Clarke (novel), pp.78–79, C2

SS *Cabinet Minister*, Scotland (wreck), *Whisky Galore!* by Angus MacPhail (novel/film), pp.64–65, A4/B4

SS *Claridon*, Pacific Ocean (wreck), *The Last Voyage* (film), pp.120–121, D4

SS *Mary Minerva*, Tasmania (wreck), *The Survivors* by Jane Harper (novel), pp.108–109, D1

SS *Minnow*, Pacific Ocean (wreck), *Gilligan's Island* (TV), pp.120–121, D4

SS *Orminta*, Pacific Ocean (wreck), *Baby Island* by Carol Ryrie Brink (novel), pp.120–121, D4

SS *Ourang Medan*, Pacific Ocean (wreck), *Man of Medan* and real life (video game/urban legend), pp.120–121, C4/C4

SS *Poseidon* (ex-RMS *Atlantis*), Atlantic Ocean (wreck), *The Poseidon Adventure* by Paul Gallico (novel/films), pp.126–127, C4

SS *Poseidon*, Mediterranean Sea (wreck), *The Poseidon Adventure* by Paul Gallico (novel/films), pp.44–45, C1

SS *Queen of Glasgow*, Atlantic Ocean (wreck), *The Twilight Zone* (TV), pp.126–127, D4

SS *Titan*, Atlantic Ocean (wreck), *The Wreck of the Titan: Or, Futility* by Morgan Robertson (novella), pp.126–127, B5

SS *Victory*, Atlantic Ocean (wreck), *Cthulhu Mythos* (short story), pp.126–127, C4

SS *Virginian*, England (wreck), *The Legend of 1900* (film), pp.64–65, C4

St Agnes, Arizona (town), *Mobile Suit Gundam* (anime), pp.18–19, C3

St Anthony (fictional region), Islandia novels and sequels by Austin Tappan Wright and Mark Saxton, pp.84–85, B1

St Brendan's Island, Atlantic Ocean (island), *The Water-Babies* by Charles Kingsley and legend (novel/myth), pp.126–127, B3

St Canard, Calisota (fictional city), *Darkwing Duck* (various), pp.18–19, A5

St Caro, Caribbean (island), *Finding Maubee* by Albert H.Z. Carr (novel), pp.32–33, E2/F2

St David's Field, Tennessee (battleground), *Dances with Wolves* (film), pp.14–15, D4

St David's, Victoria (town), *Blue Heelers* (TV), pp.108–109, D2

St Dorca, Scotland (island), *The New Avengers: The Eagles Nest* (TV), pp.64–65, B5

St Esprit, Pacific Ocean (island), *Rushing to Paradise* by J.G. Ballard (novel), pp.120–121, D2

St Gregory, Channel Islands (island), *Island at War* (TV), pp.64–65, A1

St Gustav, Minnesota (town), *The Golden Girls* (TV), pp.16–17, C6

St Helen, Victoria (town), works of James Aldridge, pp.108–109, D2

St Honoré (fictional island), *A Caribbean Mystery* by Agatha Christie (novel), pp.32–33, F2

St Loo, England (town), *Peril at End House* by Agatha Christie (novel), pp.64–65, C1

St Maggy, Corpus Christi (fictional city), works of Robert Antoni, pp.32–33, F2

St Marmero, Antegria (fictional city), *Papers, Please* (video game), pp.50–51, A5

St Mary Mead, England (village), novels of Agatha Christie, pp.64–65, C2

St Ogg's, England (village), *The Mill on the Floss* by George Eliot (novel), pp.64–65, D3

St Olaf, Minnesota (town), *The Golden Girls* (TV), pp.16–17, C6

St Petersburg, Missouri (town), *Adventures of Huckleberry Finn* by Mark Twain (novel), pp.16–17, D4

St Roch, Louisiana (city), DC Comics, pp.16–17, D2

St Sebastian (fictional island), *I Walked with a Zombie* (film), pp.32–33, E2

St Trinians, England (building), *St Trinians* by Ronald Searle (various), pp.64–65, D2

Stacks, The, Ohio (town), *Ready Player One* (film), pp.14–15, B4

Stackton Tressell, England (town), *Dear Ladies* (TV/radio/comedy), pp.64–65, D2

Stafford, Indiana (town), *The Fugitive* (TV), pp.14–15, A4

Stahlstadt, Oregon (city), *The Begum's Fortune* by Jules Verne (novel), pp.18–19, A5

Stalag Luft 112B, Germany (building), *Ripping Yarns* (TV), pp.44–45, D3

Standard Island, Pacific Ocean (island), *Propeller Island* by Jules Verne (novel), pp.120–121, D2

Stanton, Pennsylvania (town), *Unstoppable* (film), pp.14–15, C4

Star City, California (city), DC Comics, pp.18–19, A6

Star Harvester, The, Egypt (building), *Transformers: Revenge of the Fallen* (film), pp.84–85, C5

Starfish Island, Fiji (island), *Green Arrow* (comics), pp.120–121, D2

Starfleet Headquarters, California (building), *Star Trek* (various), pp.18–19, A4

Starfleet Shipyard 2-1A (Riverside Shipyard), Iowa (building), *Star Trek* (various), pp.16–17, A4

Stargate Command, Colorado (building), *Stargate SG-1* (TV), pp.16–17, A4

Stark, Western Australia (town), *The Windy Season* by Samuel Carmody (novel), pp.108–109, A4

Starkfield, Massachusetts (town), *Ethan Frome* by Edith Wharton (novel), pp.14–15, C5

Starr, Scotland (town), novels of John Buchan, pp.64–65, B3/C3

Stars Hollow, Connecticut (town), *Gilmore Girls* (TV), pp.14–15, C5

Starvation Lake, Michigan (town), *Starvation Lake* by Bryan Gruley (novel), pp.14–15, A5

Statesota (fictional state), *Moral Orel* (TV), pp.16–17, C3

Stay More, Arkansas (town), works of Donald Harington, pp.16–17, C3

Ste-Marie-la-Mauderne, Quebec (town), *La Grande Séduction* (film), pp.26–27, F2

Steaua de Munte, Romania (town), works of John Howard, pp.50–51, B2

Steel Harbor, Michigan (city), Dark Horse Comics, pp.14–15, A5/B5

Steelerton, Slovenia (town), *Steelerton* by Jaka Bulc (photography), pp.50–51, A2

Stenkelfeld, Germany (town), *Stenkelfeld* (radio), pp.44–45, D4

Stepford, Connecticut (town), *The Stepford Wives* (novel/film), pp.14–15, C5

Steveston, Massachusetts (town), *The X-Files* (TV), pp.14–15, C5

Stillwater, Utah (town), *Atomic Train* (film), pp.18–19, D4

Stillwater, Michigan (city), *Saints Row* (video game), pp.14–15, A5

Stitchings, Poland (town), *In Red* by Magdalena Tulli (novel), pp.50–51, A4

Stodge City, Kansas (town), *Carry on Cowboy* (film), pp.16–17, D3

Stoke Moran, England (building), *Sherlock Holmes: The Adventure of Silver Blaze* by Arthur Conan Doyle (short story), pp.64–65, D2

Stone Ville, Missouri (town), *Resident Evil* series (video games/films), pp.16–17, C3

Stonehaven Prison, Alaska (building), *Runaway Train* (film), pp.18–19, A1

Stonemouth, Scotland (town), *Stonemouth* by Iain Banks (novel), pp.64–65, C4/C5

Stones Hill, Florida (mountain), *From the Earth to the Moon* by Jules Verne (novel), pp.14–15, B1

Stonetrail Park, Arizona (natural feature), The Flintstones Bedrock River Adventure (theme park), pp.18–19, C3

Stoneybridge, Scotland (village), *Absolutely* (TV), pp.64–65, C4

Stoneybrook, Connecticut (town), The Baby-Sitter's Club series by Ann M. Martin, pp.14–15, C5

Stonyshire, England (county), *Adam Bede* by George Eliot (novel), pp.64–65, C2

Stoolbend, Virginia (town), *The Cleveland Show* (TV), pp.14–15, C4

Storybrooke, Maine (town), *Once Upon a Time* (TV), pp.14–15, D6

Strackenz, Duchy of (fictional region), *Royal Flash* by George MacDonald Fraser (novel), pp.44–45, D4

Stradhoughton, England (town), *Billy Liar* by Keith Waterhouse (novel), pp.64–65, D3

Strathbane, Scotland (town), *Hamish Macbeth* by M.C. Beaton (novels/TV), pp.64–65, B5

Stratis, Greece (island), *ARMA 3* (video game), pp.44–45, E1

Strawberry, West Elizabeth (fictional town), *Red Dead Redemption* series (video games), pp.16–17, B4

Strelsau, Ruritania (fictional city), *The Prisoner of Zelda* by Anthony Hope (novel), pp.50–51, B4

Strömsvik, Sweden (town), *Vita Lögner/White Lies* (TV), pp.56–57, B2

Strong Badia, Nebraska (village), *Homestar Runner* (web animation), pp.16–17, B4

Struan, Ontario (town), *Road Ends* by Mary Lawson (novel), pp.26–27, E1

Struchtrup, Germany (town), *Stenkelfeld* (radio), pp.44–45, D4

Stuckeyville, Ohio (town), *Ed* (TV), pp.14–15, B4

Studley Constable, England (town), *The Eagle has Landed* (film), pp.64–65, D2

Stumble Head, Wales (natural feature), *Sheep* by Simon Maginn (novel), pp.64–65, D2

Stump's Land, Glass Town Federation (fictional country), Brontë juvenilia, pp.84–85, A4

Stygia (fictional country), Conan novels of Robert E. Howard, pp.84–85, C5

Styx River, Egypt (river), Conan novels of Robert E. Howard, pp.84–85, C5

Sucupira, Brazil (town), *O Bem Amado* (TV), pp.38–39, D4

Sucupira, Chile (town), *Sucupira* (TV), pp.38–39, B4

Suddenly, Washington (town), *Suddenly* (film), pp.18–19, A6

Suddery, England (city), *Thomas the Tank Engine* by Rev W. Audrey (books/TV), pp.64–65, D2

Sugomori City, Japan (city), *Kiznaiver* (anime), pp.96–97, B2

Suicide City, Paris, France (underground city), *New Arabian Nights* by Robert Louis Stevenson (novel), pp.44–45, E3

Sulaco, Costaguana (fictional city), *Nostromo* by Joseph Conrad (novel), pp.38–39, A4

Sulliaba (fictional region/city), Islandia novels and sequels by Austin Tappan Wright and Mark Saxton, pp.84–85, A1/A2

Sumaru, Japan (city), *Persona* series (video games), pp.96–97, C2

Sumeru Iso, Tibet (lake), *The City of Skulls* by L. Sprague de Camp and Lin Carter (novel), pp.102–103, B2

Summer Bay, New South Wales (town/suburb), *Home and Away* (TV), pp.108–109, F4

Summer Memory, Colorado (town), *Digimon* (anime), pp.18–19, D4

Summerisle, Scotland (island), *The Wicker Man* (film), pp.64–65, B5

Summersisle, Washington (island), *The Wicker Man* (US remake) (film), pp.18–19, A6

Summerville, Oklahoma (town), *Ghostbusters: Afterlife* (film), pp.16–17, B3

Sunda (fictional island/nation), *State of Siege* (film), pp.90–91, A4

Sunken City, The, the Wasteland (fictional town), *Mad Max Fury Road* (film), pp.108–109, F4

Sunnydale, California (town), *Buffy the Vampire Slayer* (TV), pp.18–19, A3

Sunnysands, England (town), *Grandpa in my Pocket* (TV), pp.64–65, D2

Sunnyshore City, Japan (city), *Pokémon* (video games), pp.96–97, D4

Sunset Point, Queensland (town), *The Beach House* by Helen McKenna (novel), pp.108–109, E3

Sunshine, Barclay Islands (fictional island), *The Deceiver* by Frederick Forsyth (novel), pp.32–33, D4

Supreme Barrier Reef, Queensland (natural feature), *Thunderbirds Are Go* (TV), pp.108–109, D4/E3

Sursuri Nagar, India (town), *Motu Patlu* (TV), pp.78–79, B3

Suryam, India (city), *The Body Myth* by Rheea Mukherjee (novel), pp.78–79, B3

Susukino, Ezzo Empire (fictional city), *Log Horizon* by Mamare Touno and Kazuhiro Hara (novels/anime), pp.96–97, C4

Svardlov, Russia (island), *Raise the Titanic* by Clive Cussler (novel/film), pp.50–51, B6

Sveden (country), *His Dark Materials* by Philip Pullman (novels), pp.56–57, B3

Sveti Kotar, Croatia (city), *Saint Kotar* (video game), pp.50–51, A2

Swallow Falls or Chewandswallow, Atlantic Ocean (island), *Cloudy With a Chance of Meatballs* (film), pp.126–127, A4

Sweet Valley, California (town), *Sweet Valley High* (TV), pp.18–19, A2

Sweethaven, California (town), *Popeye* (various), pp.18–19, A3

Sweetland, Newfoundland (island), *Sweetland* by Michael Crummey (novel), pp.26–27, F2

Switchblade, Oregon (town), *Nightlight: A Parody of Twilight* by The Harvard Lampoon (novel), pp.18–19, A6

Switzerloan, Switzerland (country), *MacTrump* by Ian Doescher and Jacopo Della Quercia (book), pp.44–45, C3

Syberia, Russia (fictional), *Syberia* (video game), pp.102–103, F2

Sydney Shatterdome, New South Wales (building), *Pacific Rim* (film), pp.108–109, F4

Sydney-Melbourne Conurb (fictional city), *2000 AD* (comics), pp.108–109, D2

Syldavia (fictional country), *The Adventures of Tintin* by Hergé (various), pp.50–51, A2/B2

Symkaria (fictional country), Marvel Comics, pp.50–51, B2

Szohôd, Borduria (fictional city), *The Adventures of Tintin* by Hergé (various), pp.50–51, B1

Szybusz, Ukraine (town), *The Works of SY Agnon* (novel), pp.50–51, B3

Tabacópolis, Brazil (town), *O Fim do Mundo* (TV), pp.38–39, D4

Tacañón del Todo, Spain (town), *Un, dos, tres ¡responda otra vez*) (TV), pp.44–45, C2

Tackleford, England (city), *Scary Go Round* (web comic), pp.64–65, C3

Taean-gun, North Korea (village), *Crash Landing on You* (TV), pp.102–103, E3

Taian Mountains, Egypt (mountain range), Conan novels of Robert E. Howard, pp.84–85, C3

Taibei, Taiwan (city), *Log Horizon* by Mamare Touno and Kazuhiro Hara (novels/anime), pp.102–103, D1

Taihai, China (city), *Adrift in the Middle Kingdom* by Jan Jacob Slauerhoff (novel), pp.102–103, D2

Tailorstown, Northern Ireland (village), novels of Christina McKenna, pp.64–65, B3

Tainuia Junction, New Zealand (town), *Came a Hot Friday* by Ronald Hugh Morrieson (novel), pp.108–109, F2

Takistan (fictional country), *ARMA 2* (video game), pp.50–51, A5

Tall Oaks, (fictional town), *Resident Evil* series (video games/films), pp.14–15, C6

Tallahatchee, Florida (city), DC Comics, pp.14–15, B2

Tallstoria, Iran (region), *Utopia* by Thomas More (Paul Turner translation) (novel), pp.72–73, D2

Tama (of Many Demons), Japan (city), *The Demon Girl Next Door* by Izumo Itō (manga/anime), pp.96–97, E1

Tamarind Island, British Columbia (island), Marvel Comics, pp.26–27, B1

Tamoé, Pacific Ocean (island/nation), *Aline and Valcour* by the Marquis de Sade (novel), pp.120–121, D2

Tanakuatua, Pacific Ocean (island), *Web* by John Wyndham (novel), pp.120–121, D3

Tangará, Brazil (town), *O Salvador da Pátria* (TV), pp.38–39, C3

Tangerine, Florida (town), *Tangerine* by Edward Bloor (novel), pp.14–15, B2

Tannochbrae, Scotland (town), Dr Finley stories by A.J. Cronin (novels/TV), pp.64–65, C4

Tanoa, Horizon Islands (fictional island), *ARMA 3* (video game), pp.120–121, C2

Tanz Dance Akademie, Germany (building), *Suspiria* (film), pp.44–45, C3

Tapoli, Portugal (town), *The Exhausting Summer of São Martino* by Simon Carr (novel), pp.44–45, B1

Taprobane Space Elevator, Taprobane, *The Fountains of Paradise* by Arthur C. Clarke (novel), pp.78–79, D2

Taprobane (fictional island), *The Fountains of Paradise* by Arthur C. Clarke (novel), pp.78–79, D2

Tara Plantation, Georgia (building), Gone With the Wind by Margaret Mitchell (novel/film), pp.14–15, B3

Taratupa, Pacific Ocean (island), *McHale's Navy* (TV), pp.120–121, C1

Tarbox, Massachusetts (town), *Couples* by John Updike (novel), pp.14–15, D5

Tarkov, Russia (city), *Escape from Tarkov* (video game), pp.50–51, C5

Tarlenheim, Ruritania (fictional town), *The Prisoner of Zelda* by Anthony Hope (novel), pp.50–51, A3

Tarrant, England (town), *Howard's Way* (TV), pp.64–65, C1

Tartessos (fictional country), *Nadia, The Secret of Blue Water* (anime), pp.84–85, C3

Tarzan's birthplace, Angola (building), *Tarzan of the Apes* by Edgar Rice Burroughs (novel), pp.84–85, B3

Taswegia, Tasmania (city), *2000 AD* (comics), pp.108–109, D1

Tataviam Mountains, San Andreas (fictional mountain range), *Grand Theft Auto* series (video games), pp.18–19, B3

Tate, Oklahoma (town), *For My Daughter's Honor* (film), pp.16–17, C2

Tatsumiyajima, Japan (island), *Fafner in Azure* (film), pp.96–97, B2

Taz, Caribbean (submerged city), Doc Savage series (novels), pp.32–33, D3

Tazbekistan (fictional country), *The Ambassadors* (TV), pp.72–73, E4/F4

Tblunka, Slorenia (fictional city), Marvel Comics, pp.50–51, B1

Te Fiti, Pacific Ocean (island), *Moana* (film), pp.120–121, D3

Te Tarehi, New Zealand (town), works of Owen Marshall, pp.108–109, F2

Team America's Base, South Dakota (building), *Team America: World Police* (film), pp.16–17, A5

Tearstone Mountains, Eastal (fictional mountain range), *Log Horizon* by Mamare Touno and Kazuhiro Hara (novels/anime), pp.96–97, C3

Tecala (fictional country), *Proof of Life* (film), pp.38–39, A5

Tecan (fictional country), *A Flag for Sunrise* by Robert Stone (novel), pp.32–33, C1

Tech Duinn, Ireland (island, Irish myth), pp.64–65, A2

Teito, Japan (city), *K-20: Legend of the Mask* (film), pp.96–97, E1/F1

Tekeli, Aorusoi (fictional town), *Log Horizon* by Mamare Touno and Kazuhiro Hara (novels/anime), pp.72–73, D3

Tel Ilan, Israel (town), *Scenes from Village Life* by Amos Oz (stories), pp.72–73, B2

Temenos, Argentina (village) *Far South* by David Enrique Spellman (novel), pp.38–39, B3

Tempest, Massachusetts (town), *Misfile* by Chris Hazelton (web comic), pp.14–15, C5

Temphill, England (town), Severn Valley of the Cthulhu Mythos by Ramsey Campbell (novels), pp.64–65, C4

Temple of the Golden Cricket, Tibet (building), *Duck Tales* (TV), pp.102–103, A2

Temple of the League of Shadows, Bhutan (building), *Batman Begins* (film), pp.78–79, D4

Temple of the Sun, Peru, *The Adventures of Tintin* by Hergé (various), pp.38–39, B4

Temple Prime (Brotherhood of Nod), Bosnia and Herzegovina (building), *Command and Conquer* series (video games), pp.50–51, A2

Temple, The, Atlantis (fictional sunken city), Cthulhu Mythos (short story), pp.126–127, C3

Templestowe, England (building), *Ivanhoe* by Sir Walter Scott (novel), pp.64–65, C3

Templeton, New York (town), *The Leatherstocking Tales* by James Fenimore Cooper (novels), pp.14–15, C5

Tenchu (Heaven Pillar, orbital elevator), Pacific Ocean (island), *Gundam 00* (anime), pp.120–121, B3

Tendo Dojo, Japan (building), *Ranma ½* by Rumiko Takahashi (manga/anime), pp.96–97, E1

Terkenbury, England (city), *Cakes and Ale* by W. Somerset Maugham (novel), pp.64–65, C3

Terlawk, New Jersey (town), *Earthworm Jim* (TV), pp.14–15, D1

Terminal City, Indiana (city), *Terminal City* by Dean Motter and Michael Lark (comic), pp.14–15, A4

Terminal City, British Columbia (city), *Terminal City Ricochet* (film), pp.26–27, B1

Terminus, Georgia (building), *The Walking Dead* (TV/comic), pp.14–15, B3

Terra de Pogo (fictional country), *The Golden Compass* (film), pp.38–39, B2

Terra Verde (fictional country), Marvel Comics, pp.32–33, D3

Terrormolinos, Spain (town), *Terrormolinos* (computer game), pp.44–45, B1

Tescara, Atlantic Ocean (island), *CSI* series (TV), pp.126–127, C4

Teufort, New Mexico (town), *Team Fortress 2* (video game), pp.18–19, B3

Teutdorf, Germany (town), *Teutdorf* (short film), pp.44–45, D4

Tewyn Beach, Wales (town), *Ivor the Engine* (TV), pp.64–65, C2

Texas City, Texas (city/state), *Judge Dredd* (comics), pp.16–17, C2

Thabai, Kenya (village), *A Grain of Wheat* by Ngũgĩ wa Thiong'o (novel), pp.84–85, D3

Thachanakkara, India (village), *Manushyanu Oru Aamukham* by Subhash Chandran (novel), pp.78–79, B2

Thail River, Mississippi (river), *In the Heat of the Night* (TV), pp.16–17, D3

Thaxley, England (village), novels of Susan Pleydell, pp.64–65, C3

Thekkek, Aorusoi (fictional village), *Log Horizon* by Mamare Touno and Kazuhiro Hara (novels/anime), pp.72–73, D3

Themyscira, Themyscira (fictional island nation), *Wonder Woman* (various), pp.44–45, C3

Thermostadt, Robo-Hungarian Empire (fictional city), *Futurama* (TV), pp.44–45, C3

Thing's, The spaceship (wreck), *The Thing* (film), pp.114–115, C4

Thirsty Island, Iran (island), *Arabian Nights: Julnar the Sea-born and Her Son Badar Basim*, Burton edition (short story), pp.72–73, D2

Thirty Point, San Serriffe (fictional natural feature), *The Guardian* (newspaper), pp.78–79, A1

Thistle Mountain, China (mountain), *The Hundred Secret Senses* by Amy Tan (novel), pp.102–103, C1

Thneedville, New Jersey (town), *The Lorax* (various), pp.14–15, C5

Thoat Nhin, Sin-Cong (fictional city), Marvel Comics, pp.102–103, C1

Thorn Mountains, Thorn Mountains National Forest, Virginia and beyond (mountain range), *Mrs Frisby and the Rats of NIMH/The Secret of NIMH* by Robert C. O'Brien (novel/film), pp.14–15, B4

Thorn Valley, Virginia (valley), *Mrs Frisby and the Rats of NIMH/The Secret of NIMH* by Robert C. O'Brien (novel/film), pp.14–15, C4

Thornfield Hall, England (estate), *Jane Eyre* by Charlotte Brontë (novel), pp.64–65, C3

Thornhill, Connecticut (town), works of Madeleine L'Engle, pp.14–15, C5

Thrang (continent), Cthulhu Mythos (various), pp.114–115, D3

Three Fists, Tasmania (mountain), *Tiger in the Bush* by Nan Chauncy (novel), pp.108–109, D1

Three Pines, Quebec (town), Chief Inspector Armand Gamache series by Louise Penny (novels), pp.26–27, E1

Three Skeleton Key, French Guiana (island/building), *Three Skeleton Key* by George G Toudouze (short story), pp.38–39, C2

Thrums, Scotland (village), novels of J.M., Barrie, pp.64–65, C4

Thrush Green, England (village), Thrush Green stories by Miss Read (novels), pp.64–65, C4

Thul, India (village), *The Village by the Sea* by Anita Desai (novel), pp.78–79, B3

Thule, Atlantic Ocean (island, legend), pp.126–127, D5

Thule Station (camp), *The Thing* (film), pp.114–115, C2

Thunder Mesa, Arizona (town), Big Thunder Mountain Railroad (theme parks), pp.18–19, A2

Thunder Mountains, New Mexico (mountain range), *Team Fortress 2* (video game), pp.18–19, B3

Thunderdome, The, the Wasteland (fictional building), *Mad Max Beyond the Thunderdome* (film), pp.108–109, C2

Thurnemouth, England (town), *Boomers* (TV), pp.64–65, C2

Thuvaraiyam Pathi, Lemuria (fictional sunken region, mythology), pp.78–79, B2

Tiboonda, New South Wales (town), *Wake in Fright* by Kenneth Cook (novel/TV), pp.108–109, D2

Tickle Head, Newfoundland (town), *The Grand Seduction* (film), pp.26–27, F1

Tidmouth, England (town), *Thomas the Tank Engine* by Rev W. Audrey (books/TV), pp.64–65, B3

Tierra Caliente, Olifa (fictional region), *The Courts of the Morning* by John Buchan (novel), pp.38–39, A3

Tierra Robada, San Andreas (fictional mountain range), *Grand Theft Auto* series (video game), pp.18–19, B3

Tierra Verde (fictional country), Marvel Comics, pp.38–39, C5

TigerWorld, India (building), *Jurassic Park* by Michael Crichton (novel), pp.78–79, B5

Tilbury Town, Maine (town), works of Edwin Arlington Robinson, pp.14–15, D6

Tilliettudlem Castle, Scotland (building), *Old Mortality* by Sir Walter Scott (novel), pp.64–65, C4

Tilling, England (town), novels of Edward Frederic Benson, pp.64–65, D1

Time Baby, The (the being), *Gravity Falls* (TV), pp.114–115, C4

Tin Min, Myanmar (village), *It Ain't Half Hot Mum* (TV), pp.90–91, A4

Tinny Waters, Texas (city), *The Age of the Bicycle* by Miriam Webster (novel), pp.16–17, C2

Tinworth, England (town), Harry Potter novels by J.K. Rowling (novels/films), pp.64–65, B1

Tir na nÓg, Atlantic Ocean (island, legend), pp.126–127, D5

Tiriltoppen, Norway (town), works of Anne-Catharina Vestly, pp.56–57, B3

Tirtha, Kyrat (fictional village), *Far Cry 4* (video game), pp.78–79, C4

Tirulia (fictional country), *The Little Mermaid* (film), pp.56–57, A2

Titan Project, The, Colorado (building), *Titan A.E.* (film), pp.16–17, A4

Titfield, England (town), *The Titfield Thunderbolt* (novel), pp.64–65, C2

Titipu, Japan (town), *The Mikado* by W.S. Gilbert and Arthur Sullivan (light opera), pp.96–97, C2

Titty Twister (La Tetilla del Diablo), Mexico (building), *From Dusk Till Dawn* (film), pp.32–33, C3

Titus, The, New Switzerland (wreck), *Swiss Family Robinson* by Johann Wyss and *Second Fatherland* by Jules Verne (novel/film), pp.90–91, A2

Toad Hall, England (estate), *The Wind in the Willows* by Kenneth Grahame (novel/TV), pp.64–65, C2

Toadstool, Indiana (city), *Sesame Street Presents: Follow That Bird!* (film), pp.14–15, A4

Toarushi, Japan (village), *Crows* by Hiroshi Takahashi (manga), pp.96–97, C2

Tobiki, Japan (village), *The Teahouse of the August Moon* by John Patrick Goggan (novel), pp.96–97, A4

Tocaia Grande, Brazil (town), *Showdown* by Jorge Amado (novel), pp.38–39, D4

Tokisadame High School, Japan (building), *Nichijou* by Keiichi Arawi (manga/anime), pp.96–97, C2

Tokyo Shatterdome, Japan (building), *Pacific Rim* (film), pp.96–97, F1

Tokyo-2, Japan (city), *Neon Genesis Evangelion* (anime), pp.96–97, C2

Tokyo-3, Japan (city), *Neon Genesis Evangelion* (anime), pp.96–97, C2

Tollington, West Virginia (lake), *Silent Hill* (film), pp.14–15, B4

Toluca Lake, West Virginia (lake), *Silent Hill* (film), pp.14–15, B4

Toluca River (river), Silent Hill series (various), pp.14–15, B4

Tomainia (fictional country), The Great Dictator (film), pp.44–45, D3

Tomatán, Mexico (town), *Life of Pi* by Yann Martel (novel), pp.32–33, A4

Tomb of Mary Magdalen, Paris, France (building), *The Da Vinci Code* by Dan Brown (novel/film), pp.44–45, D2

Tomb of Qualopec, Peru (location), Tomb Raider series (video games), pp.38–39, B4

Tomb of Ramses Amun Ankh, Egypt (building), *Cruise Into Terror* (TV), pp.84–85, C5

Tomb of Rascar Capac, Peru (location), *The Adventures of Tintin* by Hergé (various), pp.38–39, B4

Tomobiki, Japan (town), *Urusei Yatsura* by Rumiko Takahashi (manga/anime), pp.96–97, E1

Tomoeda, Japan (city), *Cardcaptor Sakura* by CLAMP (manga/anime), pp.96–97, C2

Tomorrow-Morrow Land, New South Wales (city), *Mad Max 3* (film), pp.108–109, D2/C2

Tone's Grave, Aorusoi (fictional building), *Log Horizon* by Mamare Touno and Kazuhiro Hara (novels/anime), pp.72–73, D3

Tong Mountain, China (mountain), *China Sky* by Pearl S. Buck (novel/film), pp.102–103, D2

Toomey, Queensland (town), *Front Page News* by Katie Rowney (novel), pp.108–109, D2

Toontown, California (town), *Who Framed Roger Rabbit?* (film), pp.18–19, A3

Torchwood 2, Scotland (building), *Doctor Who/Torchwood* (TV), pp.64–65, C4

Torchwood 3, Wales (building), *Torchwood* (TV), pp.64–65, C2

Torland, Germany (city), *Tessa – Leben für die Liebe* (TV), pp.44–45, D4

Torminster, England (town), *The Torminster Saga* by Elizabeth Goudge (novel), pp.64–65, C2/D2

Torquilstone, England (building), *Ivanhoe* by Sir Walter Scott (novel), pp.64–65, C2/D2

Torregreca, Italy (town), *Torregreca: Life, Death and Miracles* by Ann Cornelisen (novel), pp.44–45, D2

Tortilla Flat, California (town), *Tortilla Flat* by John Steinbeck (novel), pp.18–19, A4

Torturpuram, India (town), *The Hero's Walk* by Anita Rau Badami (novel), pp.78–79, D4

Torus, The, Bhutan (object), *Epoch* (film), pp.78–79, D4

Tottington Hall, England (building), *Wallace and Gromit: Curse of the Were-rabbit* (film), pp.64–65, C3

Touto, Japan (region), *Kamen Rider Build* (TV), pp.96–97, C2

Tower of Mastery, France (building), *Pokémon* (video games), pp.44–45, B3

Town of 'Inspector Khlestakov', The, Russia (town), *The Government Inspector* by Nikolai Gogol (play), pp.50–51, D3

Townsville, California (city), *The Powerpuff Girls* (TV), pp.18–19, B3

Tracy Island, Pacific Ocean (island), *Thunderbirds* (various), pp.120–121, C2

Trafalgar, British Columbia (town), *A Cold White Sun* by Vicki Delany (novel), pp.26–27, B1

Traldragdubb, Luggnagg (fictional city), *Gulliver's Travels* by Jonathan Swift (novel), pp.96–97, C2

Tramplonia, Spain (town), *Chip 'n Dale: Rescue Rangers* (TV), pp.44–45, B1

Trangvik, Norway (town), *Trangviksposten* (newspaper), pp.56–57, A2

Tranquility, California (town), *Transformers* (film), pp.18–19, A3

Trans-Sabal (fictional country), Marvel Comics, pp.72–73, B1/C1

Transia (fictional country), Marvel Comics, pp.50–51, B1

Transverse City, Illinois/Indiana/ Michigan (city), Marvel Comics, pp.14–15, A5

Transylvania, Pennsylvania (town), *Scooby-Doo! Frankencreepy* (film), pp.14–15, B5

Transylvania (fictional country), *Young Frankenstein* (film), pp.50–51, B2

Trash Island (Isle of Dogs), Japan (island), *Isle of Dogs* (film), pp.96–97, A1

Treasure Island, British Virgin Islands (island), *Treasure Island* by Robert Louis Stevenson (novel), pp.32–33, F2

Treasure Valley, Austria (natural feature), *King of the Golden River* by John Ruskin (novel), pp.44–45, D3

Treaty Port, China (city), *China Sky* by Pearl S. Buck (novel/film), pp.102–103, D2

Trebiglie, Italy (town), Don Camillo works of Giovanni Guareschi (various), pp.44–45, C3

Trebil, Iraq (village, military training exercise), pp.72–73, C2

Tree Hill, North Carolina (town), *One Tree Hill* (TV), pp.14–15, C3

Tremannon, England (town), *Five Go Down to the Sea* by Enid Blyton (novel), pp.64–65, B1

Tremorton, Pennsylvania (town), *My Life as a Teenage Robot* (TV), pp.14–15, B5

Trentsworth, New Zealand (town), *The Trentswood Terrors* by Peter Jordan (novels), pp.108–109, F1

Trewissick, England (town), *Over Sea, Under Stone* by Susan Cooper (novel), pp.64–65, B1

Tri-Island Area, Caribbean (region/ island chain), Monkey Island series (video games), pp.32–33, E2

Trinidad, Colombia (town), *La Viuda de Blanco* (TV), pp.38–39, B6

Trinity, South Carolina (town), *American Gothic* (TV), pp.14–15, B3

Truiunion (fictional island/nation), *Daughters* by Paule Marshall (novel), pp.32–33, C5

Trojan Birdman Castle, Japan (building), *Batman Ninja* (film), pp.96–97, C2

Trollesund, Finland (town), *His Dark Materials* by Philip Pullman (various), pp.56–57, C5

Tromaville, New Jersey (town), films of Troma Entertainment, pp.14–15, C5

Tropico (fictional island/nation), *Tropico* (video game), pp.32–33, D2

Trout River (river), *Mrs Frisby and the Rats of NIMH/Rosco and the Rats of NIMH* by Robert C. O'Brien (novels), pp.14–15, C4

Trouville, France (town), *In Search of Lost Time* by Marcel Proust (novel), pp.44–45, C3

Trucial Abusmia (fictional country/ emirate), *Transformers and GI Joe* (comics), pp.72–73, D1

True Glorian, Republia (fictional city), *Papers, Please* (video game), pp.50–51, A5

Truly, Idaho (town), *Truly, Idaho* series by Rachel Gibson (novels), pp.18–19, B5

Trumpton, England (village), *Trumpton* (TV), pp.64–65, D2

Trzebiatów, Poland (town), *Wiosna Panie Sierzancie/It's Spring, Sargeant* (film), pp.50–51, A4

Tsai Fu, China (village), *The Man with the Iron Fists 2* (film), pp.102–103, C2

Tsai Khaldun, Uqbar (fictional region), *Tlön, Uqbar, Orbis Tertius* by Jorge Luis Borges (short story), pp.72–73, D3

Tsalal (island), *The Narrative of Arthur Gordon Pym of Nantucket* by Edgar Allan Poe, and *An Antarctic Mystery* by Jules Verne (novels), pp.114–115, C2

Tsimtsum, Pacific Ocean (wreck), *Life of Pi* by Yann Martel (novel/film), pp.90–91, D4

Tubiacanga, Brazil (town), *Fera Ferida* (TV), pp.38–39, D4

Tuen-Baka, DRC (mountain/volcano), *Tarzan and the Forbidden City* by Edgar Rice Burroughs (novel), pp.84–85, C4

Tula County, California (county), *War of the Worlds* (TV), pp.18–19, A4

Tulczyn, Poland (village), *Plebania* (TV), pp.50–51, B3

Tulls Point, Maine (town), *Dad's Army* (TV), pp.14–15, D5

Tully-Veolan, Scotland (village), *Waverley* by Sir Walter Scott (novel), pp.64–65, C4

Tullymore (Tulaigh Mhór), Ireland (town), *Waking Ned* (film), pp.64–65, A2

Tum Boom Island, Caribbean (island), *Pirates of the Caribbean* (various), pp.32–33, E2

Tumbleweed, Arizona (town), Big Thunder Mountain Railroad (theme parks), pp.18–19, C3

Tumdrum, Northern Ireland (town), novels of Ian Sansom, pp.64–65, B3

Tuna, Texas (town), *The Tuna Trilogy* (theatre), pp.16–17, C2

Tung Shao Pass, China (natural feature), *Mulan* (film), pp.102–103, D3

Tungan Valley, Khandanyang (fictional natural feature), *Hitman* franchise (video games), pp.102–103, E3

Tunnel to Atvatabar, North Pole (portal), *The Goddess of Atvatabar* by William R. Bradshaw (novel), pp.26–27, C4

Tuong Lai, Vietnam (village), *Water Puppets* (musical), pp.90–91, A4

Turaqistan (fictional country), *War, Inc.* (film), pp.72–73, D3

Turgistan (fictional country), *6 Underground* (film), pp.72–73, D3

Turi, Alpine Emirates (fictional city), *The Years of Rice and Salt* by Kim Stanley Robinson, pp.44–45, C3

Turmezistan (fictional country), *Doctor Who* (TV), pp.72–73, E4/F4

Turnhill, England (town), the Five Towns novels of Arnold Bennett, pp.64–65, C3

Turon, New South Wales (town), *Another Night in Mullet Town* by Steven Herrick (novel), pp.108–109, D4

Turtalia (fictional region), *Photopia* (video game), pp.72–73, D3

Turtle Cove, Colorado (city), *Power Rangers Wild Force* (TV), pp.16–17, A4

Turtle Island Bay, Ontario (town), *Northern Rescue* (TV), pp.26–27, A4

Turtle Lake, Colorado (lake), *Power Rangers Wild Force* (TV), pp.16–17, A4

Tweedy's Farm, England (building), *Chicken Run* (film), pp.64–65, C3

Twelve Sleep, Wyoming (region), *Open Season* by C.J. Box (novel), pp.18–19, D5

Twin Peaks, Washington (town), ABC Soap Opera Universe (*Twin Peaks*, TV), pp.18–19, B6

Twinleaf Town, Japan (town), *Pokémon* (video games), pp.96–97, C4

Two Forks, Wyoming (region), *Firewatch* (video game), pp.18–19, D5

Two Mills, Pennsylvania (town), *Maniac Magee* by Jerry Spinelli (novel), pp.14–15, D4

Two Rivers County, Mississippi (county), works of Tennessee Williams (plays), pp.16–17, D3

Tynsham, England (town), *The Day of the Triffids* by John Wyndham (novel), pp.64–65, C2

Tyos, Norway (town), *In Order of Disappearance* (film), pp.56–57, A3

Tyranistan (fictional country), *San Sombrèro* (book), pp.72–73, D4/E4

Tyreelin, Ireland (town), *Breakfast on Pluto* by Patrick McCabe (novel/film), pp.64–65, A3

Tyrgyzstan (fictional country), *The State Within* (TV), pp.72–73, E3

Tyrus, Turgistan (fictional city), *6 Underground* (film), pp.72–73, D3

U-121, Atlantic Ocean (wreck), *The Enemy Below* by Denys Rayner (novel/film), pp.126–127, C3

U-29, Atlantic Ocean (wreck), Cthulhu Mythos (short story), pp.126–127, C3

U-571, Atlantic Ocean (wreck), *U-571* (film), pp.126–127, C5

U.S. Outpost 31 (camp), *The Thing* (film), pp.114–115, C2

Ubangiba (fictional country), *Mrs Pollifax Pursued, Mrs Pollifax and the Lion Killer* by Dorothy Gilman (novels), pp.84–85, C4

Ubar *see* Atlantis of the Sands

Ube, Philippines (region), *Woman With Horns and Other Stories* by Cecilia Manguerra Brainard (short stories), pp.90–91, D3

Ubec City, Philippines (city), *Woman With Horns and Other Stories* by Cecilia Manguerra Brainard (short stories), pp.90–91, D3

Udana (fictional state), *Lolita* by Vladimir Nabokov (novel), pp.18–19, D1

Udon Khai (fictional country), *Batman: The Ultimate Evil* by Andrew Vachss (novel), pp.90–91, B3

Uigigistan (fictional country), *War, Inc.* (film), pp.72–73, D3

Ula'ula Island, Hawaii (island), *Pokémon* (video games), pp.18–19, D1

Ulthar, England (town), *The Ancient Magus' Bride* by Kore Yamazaki (manga), pp.64–65, C2

Ultocar, Peru (town), *Fábula del animal que no tiene paradero* by Juan Morillo Ganoza (novel), pp.38–39, A4

Ulysses, Atlantic Ocean (wreck), *Atlantis: The Lost Empire* (film), pp.126–127, C5

Umbutu, National Republic of (fictional country), *Independence Day: Resurgence* (film), pp.84–85, C2

Umoleso, Russia (lake), *His Dark Materials* by Philip Pullman (various), pp.50–51, A4

Umuofia (the nine villages), Nigeria (village), *Things Fall Apart* by Chinua Achebe (novel), pp.84–85, B4

Unato Station, Hinomoto (fictional city), *Kabaneri of the Iron Fortress* (anime), pp.96–97, C2

Unaudited Arab Emirates (fictional country/emirate), *San Sombrèro* (book), pp.72–73, C1

Underland (country), *Venture Brothers* (TV), pp.14–15, A5

Undersea City, Pacific Ocean (submerged building), *Diving Adventure* by Willard Price (novel), pp.108–109, D3

Ungeheuerhorn (The Horror-Horn), Switzerland (mountain), *The Horror-Horn* by E.F. Benson (short story), pp.44–45, C3

Unicorn, The, Atlantic Ocean (wreck), *The Adventures of Tintin: Red Rackham's Treasure* by Hergé (comic book), pp.126–127, A3

Union City, Wyoming (town), Marvel Cinematic Universe (various), pp.18–19, D4

Union City, New South Wales (city/state), *Beneath a Steel Sky* (video game), pp.108–109, E2

Union Town, Virginia (town), *Destroy All Humans* (video game), pp.14–15, C4

United Kingdom (fictional country), *Papers, Please* (video game), pp.50–51, D2

United Islamic Republic (fictional country), *Executive Orders* by Tom Clancy (novel), pp.72–73, C2

United Kingdom of Anatoray-Disith, The (fictional country), *Last Exile: Fam of the Silver Wing* (anime), pp.44–45, C2

United Kingdom of Rendang and Pala, (fictional island chain), *Island* by Aldous Huxley (novel), pp.90–91, A2

Univille (unnamed unincorporated settlement), South Dakota (town), *Warehouse 13* (TV), pp.16–17, B5

Unova, New York (region/state), *Pokémon* (video games), pp.14–15, D1

Unthank, Scotland (city), *Lanark* by Alasdair Grey (novel), pp.64–65, C4

Upper Caisse, San Serriffe (fictional island), *The Guardian* (newspaper), pp.78–79, A2

Upper Montana River (river), *Red Dead Redemption* series (video games), pp.16–17, B3/C3

Uppercross, England (town), *Persuasion* by Jane Austen (novel), pp.64–65, C1

Upperton, Colorado (city), *Kim Possible* (TV), pp.16–17, A4

Upyermukluk, Yukon (town), *Yvon of the Yukon* (TV), pp.26–27, A2

Uqbar (fictional country), *Tlön, Uqbar, Orbis Tertius* by Jorge Luis Borges (short story), pp.72–73, A4

Urbania, Ohio (town), *Little Giants* (film), pp.14–15, A4/B4

Ursula, Wyoming (town), *I Take This Woman* (film), pp.18–19, D4

Uruk (fictional country), *Descendants of the Sun* (TV), pp.50–51, B1

Urzikstan (fictional country), *Call of Duty: Modern Warfare* (video game), pp.72–73, B3/C3

USNS *Rescue*, Atlantic Ocean (wreck), *Timewreck Titanic* by Rhys B. Davies (novel), pp.126–127, C2

USS *Bedford* (*DLG-113*), Atlantic Ocean (wreck), *The Bedford Incident* by Mark Rascovich (novel/film), pp.126–127, C2

USS *Candlefish*, Pacific Ocean (wreck), *Ghostboat* by George E. Simpson and Neal R. Burger (novel), pp.96–97, D1

USS *Haynes* (*DE-181*), Atlantic Ocean (wreck), *The Enemy Below* by Denys Rayner (novel/film), pp.126–127, C2

USS *Star Voyager*, Pacific Ocean (wreck), *Sphere* by Michael Crichton (novel/film), pp.120–121, C2

USS *Theodore Roosevelt*, Atlantic Ocean (wreck), *Transformers: Revenge of the Fallen* (film), pp.126–127, B4

USS *Topeka*, Atlantic Ocean (wreck), *Transformers: Revenge of the Fallen* (film), pp.126–127, B4

Ust-Chilim, Russia (city), Buerak (band), pp.102–103, E1

Utana (fictional state), *Pale Fire* by Vladimir Nabokov (novel), pp.18–19, C5/D5

Utkarsh, Kyrat (fictional village), *Far Cry 4* (video game), pp.78–79, A4

Utopaea, India (city), *Overwatch* (video game), pp.78–79, B3

Utopia (fictional island/nation), *Utopia* by Thomas More (novel/parable), pp.38–39, B1

Utopia, Pacific Ocean (island/nation), *Utopia, Ltd* (opera), pp.120–121, D3

Utrøst, Norway (island, real world), pp.56–57, B5

Uttara Kuru, Pakistan (region), *Conan the Avenger* by Björn Nyberg (novels), pp.78–79, B5

Utterley, England (town), *Brass* (TV), pp.64–65, C3

Utti, Finland (town), *The Colournauts* by Mona Paalanen and Anni Pöyhönen (books), pp.56–57, D4

Vachau, Channel Islands (island), *The Divine and the Decay* by Bill Hopkins (novel), pp.64–65, A1

Val Verde (fictional country), various (films), pp.38–39, A5

Valadiléne, France (village), *Syberia* (video game), pp.44–45, C2/C3

Vale Abraão, Portugal (natural feature), *Vale Abraão* by Agustina Bessa-Luís (novel), pp.44–45, A4

Vale do Café, Brazil (natural feature), *Orgulho e Paixão*/*Pride and Passion* (TV), pp.38–39, D3

Valencia, Olancho (fictional city), *Soldiers of Fortune* by Richard Harding Davis (novel), pp.38–39, D5

Valentine Bluffs, Nova Scotia (town), *My Bloody Valentine* (film), pp.26–27, F2

Valentine, New Hanover (fictional town), *Red Dead Redemption* series (video games), pp.16–17, C3

Valerie Sinatra's Mile-High Travel Pod, England (building), *The Day Today* (TV), pp.64–65, C3

Valkenvania, New Jersey (town), *Nothing But Trouble* (film), pp.14–15, C4/C5

Valley Fields, England (town), novels of P.G. Wodehouse, pp.64–65, D2

Valley of Ashes, The, New York (town), *The Great Gatsby* by F. Scott Fitzgerald (novel), pp.14–15, D1

Valley of Snakes, Kenya (natural feature), *Sinbad* (short story), pp.84–85, D3

Valley of the Tartars, Iraq (natural feature), *Biggles: Foreign Legionnaire* by W.E. Johns (novel), pp.72–73, C2

Valverde de Lucerna, Spain (village), *San Manuel Bueno, Mártir* by Miguel de Unamuno (novel), pp.44–45, B1/B2

Vampire Rock, Northern Territory (natural feature), *Scooby-Doo! and the Legend of the Vampire* (film), pp.108–109, C3

Van Horn Trading Post, New Hanover (fictional town), *Red Dead Redemption* series (video games), pp.16–17, D3

Van Husen, Indonesia (wreck), Biggles: The Adventure of the Golden Shirts by W.E. Johns (novel), pp.90–91, B1

Van Tieren's Land (fictional country), *His Dark Materials* by Philip Pullman (various), pp.26–27, C3

Vane, Channel Islands (island), *The Lie Tree* by Frances Hardinge (novel), pp.64–65, A1

Vaniville Town, France (town), *Pokémon* (video games), pp.44–45, C3

Villamojada and the mines of Socartes, Spain (town), *Marianela* by Benito Pérez Galdós (novel), pp.44–45, B2

Vardeting, Glimmerhornet, Nakken and Storesnuten, Norway (mountains), *Tonje Glimmerdal* by Maria Parr (novel), pp.56–57, A3

Varf Mandra, Romania (town), Marvel Comics, pp.50–51, B2

Varg, Norway (town), *Heimebane* (TV), pp.56–57, A3

Vasaria, Romania (town), *Tales from the Dark Tower* by Joseph Vargo (novel), pp.50–51, B2/C2

Vasco, India (town), *Josh* (film), pp.78–79, B3

Vault 13, California (building), *Fallout 1* (video game), pp.18–19, B3

Vault 15, California (building), *Fallout 1* (video game), pp.18–19, B3

Vedmediv, Ukraine (town), *Carbide* by Andriy Lyubka (novel), pp.50–51, B3

Veilstone City, Japan (city), *Pokémon* (video games), pp.96–97, D4

Velcro City, New Zealand (theatre), pp.108–109, F1/F2

Veld, France (village), *Wonder Woman* (film), pp.44–45, C4

Vendhya, India (country), Conan novels of Robert E. Howard, pp.78–79, B4/C4

Ventura, Brazil (town), *Chocolate com Pimenta* (TV), pp.38–39, C3

Venusberg, Estonia (city), *Venusberg* by Anthony Powell (novel), pp.50–51, B4

Verano, Philippines (region), *Sa Ngalan ng Ina* (TV), pp.90–91, A3

Verdanturf Town, Japan (town), *Pokémon* (video games), pp.96–97, A1

Verdopolis, Glass Town Federation (fictional city), Brontë juvenalia, pp.84–85, B4

Vermilion City, Japan (city), *Pokémon* (video games), pp.96–97, C4

Vermillion Sands, California (town), *Vermillion Sands* by J.G. Ballard (short stories), pp.18–19, B3

Vermillion, England (town), *Shades of Grey* by Jasper Fforde (novels), pp.64–65, C2

Verona Beach, Florida (city), *Romeo + Juliet* (film), pp.14–15, C1

Vesbaria (fictional country, military training exercise), pp.50–51, B4

Vespugia (fictional country), works of Madeleine L'Engle, pp.38–39, B1

Vetusta, Spain (city), *La Regenta* by Leopoldo Alas Clarín (novel), pp.44–45, A4

Veyshnoria (fictional country, military training exercise), pp.50–51, B4/C4

Vicarstown, England (town), *Thomas the Tank Engine* by Rev W. Audrey (books/TV), pp.64–65, C2

Vice City, Florida (city), *Grand Theft Auto* series (video games), pp.14–15, C4

Viceroy, South Carolina (city), DC Comics, pp.14–15, B4

Victoria Bay, Arctic (natural feature), *The Voyages and Adventures of Captain Hatteras* by Jules Verne (novel), pp.26–27, C4

Victory/Decepticon HQ, Oregon (wreck), *Transformers* (various), pp.18–19, A5

Vigàta, Italy (town), Inspector Montalbano novels by Andrea Camilleri (novels/TV), pp.44–45, D1

Vila Abobrinha, Brazil (village), *Turma do Chico Bento*/*Chuck, Billy 'n' Folks* (comics), pp.38–39, C2

Vila da Mata, Brazil (town), *Cabocla* (TV), pp.38–39, D3

Vila de Sant'Anna, Brazil (town), *Força de um Desejo* (TV), pp.38–39, C3

Vila dos Ventos, Brazil (town), *Flor do Caribe* (TV), pp.38–39, D4

Vila Feliz, Brazil (town), *Felicidade* (TV), pp.38–39, D3

Vila Xuripita, Brazil (town), Disney cartoons (TV), pp.38–39, D3

Vilamaninhos, Portugal (town), *O Dia dos Prodígios* by Lídia Jorge (novel), pp.44–45, A2

Vilayet Sea, Caspian Sea (sea), Conan novels of Robert E. Howard, pp.72–73, C3

Vilena (fictional island/nation), *The Expendables* (film), pp.32–33, C3

Villa Éco, Ireland (building), Artemis Fowl series by Eoin Colfer (novel), pp.64–65, B2

Villa Fuerte, Colombia (town), *Las Hermanitas Calle* (TV), pp.38–39, A5

Villa Pica, San Serriffe (fictional town), *The Guardian* (newspaper), pp.78–79, A1

Villa Ruiseñor, Chile (town), *Perdona Nuestros Pecados*/*Pardon our Sins* (TV), pp.38–39, B4

Vila Nueve, Bolivia (city), *Ghost Recon: Wildlands* (video game), pp.38–39, B4

Village of B—, The, Lithuania (village), *A Lithuanian Village* by Leon Kobri (book), pp.50–51, B4

Village of Fruitless Mountain, The, China (village), *Where the Mountain Meets the Moon* by Grace Lin (novel), pp.102–103, B3

Village of Moon Rain, The, China (village), *Where the Mountain Meets the Moon* by Grace Lin (novel), pp.102–103, A3

Village of the Bat Clan, Japan (village), *Batman Ninja* (film), pp.96–97, B2

Village, The, Wales (unmappable village), *The Prisoner* (TV), pp.64–65, C2

Ville-France, Oregon (city), *The Begum's Fortune* by Jules Verne (novel), pp.18–19, A5

Villefranche, France (town), *Black Spot* (TV), pp.44–45, C2

Villette, Labassecour (fictional city), *Villette* by Charlotte Brontë (novel), pp.44–45, C4

Villings, Pacific Ocean (island), *La invención de Morel* by Adolfo Bioy Casares (novel), pp.120–121, C3

Villings, Indonesia (island), *The Invention of Morel* by Adolfo Bioy Casares (novel), pp.90–91, F1

Vin Din Drop/Charlie's Point, Vietnam (village), *Apocalypse Now* (film), pp.90–91, A4

Vindsele, Sweden (town), *The Twin Detectives* by Sivar Ahlrud (novels), pp.56–57, A4

Vinkelboda, Sweden (village), *Kronblom* by Elov Persson (comic strip), pp.56–57, B3

Violet City, Japan (city), *Pokémon* (video games), pp.96–97, B2

Violet Mountains, The (mountain range), *At the Mountains of Madness* by H.P. Lovecraft (novella), pp.114–115, E3

Viraginia (region), *Mundus alter et idem* by Joseph Hall (novel), pp.114–115, C2

Virgil, Texas (town), *True Stories* (film), pp.16–17, C2

Viridian City, Japan (city), *Pokémon* (video games), pp.96–97, C4

Viscas Island, Kingdom of Karin (fictional island), *Transformers: Masterforce* (anime), pp.90–91, D1

Viscayin Mountains, Latveria/Symkaria (fictional mountain range), Marvel Comics, pp.50–51, C2

VK Konovalov, Atlantic Ocean (wreck), *The Hunt for Red October* by Tom Clancy (novel/film), pp.126–127, B4

Vladivostok Shatterdome, Russia (building), *Pacific Rim* (film), pp.102–103, E3

Vlyvalle, New Jersey (town), *Fierce People* by Dirk Wittenborn (novel/film), pp.14–15, C5

Volcano Del Fuego, Atlantic Ocean (natural feature), *Hotel Transylvania 3* (film), pp.126–127, C3

Vömmeldalen, Norway (town), music of Vømmøl Spellmannslag, pp.56–57, B4

Vondervotteimittiss, Netherlands (village), *The Devil in the Belfry* by Edgar Allan Poe (short stories), pp.44–45, C4

Vorotolivke, Ukraine (town), works of Sholem Aleichem (stories), pp.50–51, C3

Vorozheika (fictional country), Marvel Comics, pp.72–73, C2

Vulgaria (fictional country), *Chitty Chitty Bang Bang* by Ian Fleming (novel/film), pp.44–45, B2

Vyones, France (city), works of Clark Ashton Smith (short stories), pp.44–45, C3

Wachati Village, Nibia (fictional village), *Ace Ventura: When Nature Calls* (film), pp.84–85, C2

Wachootoo Village, Nibia (fictional village), *Ace Ventura: When Nature Calls* (film), pp.84–85, C2

Wachau, Channel Islands (island), *The Divine and the Decay* by Bill Hopkins (novel), pp.64–65, A1

Wacketshire, New York (town), *Night Probe* by Clive Cussler (novel), pp.14–15, C5

Wadesbah, Khemed (fictional city), *The Adventures of Tintin* by Hergé (novels), pp.72–73, B1/B2

Wadi al-Sahara, Iraq (town, military training exercise), pp.72–73, C2

Wadiya (fictional country), *The Dictator* (film), pp.84–85, D4

Wadkoping, Sweden (town), works of Hjalmar Bergman, pp.56–57, B3/C3

Wahdeh, Lebanon (village), *The Myrtle Tree* by Jad el-Hage (novel), pp.72–73, B2

Wahlheim, Germany (village), *The Sorrows of Young Werther* by Wolfgang von Goethe (novel), pp.44–45, C3

Waimoana, New Zealand (city), *This is Not My Life* (TV), pp.108–109, F2

Wakanda (fictional country), Marvel Comics (various), pp.84–85, D4

Wake Wood, Northern Ireland (town), *Wake Wood* (film), pp.64–65, A3

Wala Wala, Northern Territory (village), *Dead Heart* (film), pp.108–109, C3

Waldberghoff-trarbk-dikdorff, Germany (town), *Candide* by Voltaire (novel), pp.44–45, C4

Walford, England (town), *EastEnders* (TV), pp.64–65, D2

Walkabout Creek, Northern Territory (village), *Crocodile Dundee* (film), pp.108–109, A4

Walkerville, Illinois (town), *The Magic School Bus* (TV), pp.16–17, D5

Wallaceville, Belize (village), *On the Nervous Edge of an Impossible Paradise* by Kenneth Little (short stories), pp.32–33, C2

Walley, Ontario (town), works of Alice Munro, pp.26–27, A4

Walmington on Sea, England (village), *Dad's Army* (TV), pp.64–65, D1

Walter Scott, Missouri (wreck), *Adventures of Huckleberry Finn* by Mark Twain (novel), pp.16–17, D4

Walton's Mountain, Virginia (town), *The Waltons* (TV), pp.14–15, C4

Wamapoke County, Indiana (county), *Parks and Recreation* (TV), pp.14–15, A4

Wan Xuan III, Pacific Ocean (wreck), *Virus* (comic/film), pp.120–121, C2

Wandernburg, Germany (town), *Traveler of the Century* by Andrés Neuma (novel), pp.44–45, D3

Wandin Valley, New South Wales (town), *A Country Practice* (TV), pp.108–109, D2

Waponi Woo, Pacific Ocean (island), *Joe Versus the Volcano* (film), pp.120–121, D4

Waratah National Park, New South Wales (natural feature), *Skippy the Bush Kangaroo* (TV), pp.108–109, D2/E2

Warehouse 13, South Dakota (building), *Warehouse 13* (TV), pp.16–17, B5

Warhedna, Nukehavistan (fictional city), *The Onion* (online satire), pp.72–73, D3/E3

Warp Five Complex, Montana (building), *Star Trek* (various), pp.18–19, C5

Wasaychigan Hill Indian Reserve, Ontario (region), plays of Tomson Highway (theatre), pp.26–27, A4

Washagon (fictional state), *Book: A Novel* by Robert Grudin (novel), pp.18–19, B6

Washington, BC, District of Columbia (city), *The Flintstones* (various), pp.14–15, C4

Washington Lodge, Alberta (building), *Until Dawn* (video game), pp.26–27, B1

Wassamotta University, Minnesota (building), *The Adventures of Rocky and Bullwinkle* (TV), pp.16–17, C5

Wasteland, The (fictional country/desert), *Mad Max* films (films), pp.108–109, C2/D2

Wataribashi, Japan (city), *Samurai Shodown* series (video games), pp.96–97, A1

Watermouth, England (city), *The History Man* by Malcolm Bradbury (novel), pp.64–65, D1

Waterside, England (town), *Meeting Lydia* by Linda MacDonald (novel), pp.64–65, C3

Waterville, British Columbia (town), novels of Jack Hodgins, pp.26–27, B1

Waubanakee, Illinois (town), works of Sinclair Lewis, pp.16–17, D4

Wayne Island, New Jersey (island), *Lego Batman Movie* (film), pp.14–15, C4

Wayward Island, Maine (island), *Transformers: Rescue Bots* (TV), pp.14–15, D6

Wayward Pines, Idaho (town), *Wayward Pines* (TV), pp.18–19, C6

Wazoo, Alabama (town), *My Cousin Vinny* (film), pp.14–15, A3

Weapon X Facility, Alberta (building), Marvel Comics, pp.26–27, C1

Weatherfield, England (town), *Coronation Street* (TV), pp.64–65, C2

Web, The, Indonesia (natural feature), *2000 AD* (comics), pp.90–91, B3/C1

Wedinburgh, Scotland (city), *Little Witch Academia* (anime), pp.64–65, C4

Weisbachtal, Austria (natural feature), Zwölf mal Polt novels by Alfred Komarek, pp.44–45, D3

Weld, New Zealand (town), *800 Words* (TV), pp.108–109, F2

Wellenbeck, West Virginia (town), *The Hateful Eight* (film), pp.14–15, B4

Wellington Point, Tasmania (town), *Secrets of the Sea* by Nicholas Shakespeare (novel), pp.108–109, D1

Wellington's Land, Glass Town Federation (fictional region), Brontë juvenalia, pp.84–85, A4

Wells, South Carolina (town), *In the Heat of the Night* by John Ball (novel), pp.14–15, C4

Weng, Austria (village), *Frost* by Thomas Bernhard (novel), pp.44–45, D3

Wentworth Detention Centre, Victoria (building), *Prisoner (Cell Block H)* (TV), pp.108–109, A1

Wentworth Prison, Scotland (building), Outlander novels by Diana Gabaldon (novels/TV), pp.64–65, C4

Werst, Romania (village), *The Carpathian Castle* by Jules Verne (novels), pp.50–51, B2

West African Union (fictional bloc), *Seafighter* by James H. Cobb (novel), pp.84–85, A4

West Canaan, Texas (town), *Varsity Blues* (film), pp.16–17, B2

West Durndell, Texas (town), *King of the Hill* (TV), pp.16–17, B2

West Elizabeth (fictional state), *Red Dead Redemption* series (video game), pp.16–17, C3

West Keystone (fictional state), *Steven Universe* (TV), pp.14–15, B4

West River, New York (river), *Grand Theft Auto* series (video game), pp.14–15, C5

West Waratah, Victoria (town/suburb), *Neighbours* (TV), pp.108–109, A1

Westbridge, Massachusetts (town), *Sabrina the Teenage Witch* (TV), pp.14–15, D5

Wesernesse (fictional country, folklore), pp.64–65, B3

Westfield, England (town), *The Rose Garden* by M.R. James (short story), pp.64–65, D2

Westover Hall, Maine (building), Percy Jackson series by Rick Riordan (novels/films), pp.14–15, D6

Westport, Victoria (town), *The Henderson Kids II* (TV), pp.108–109, A1

Westrail, Utah/Colorado (railway), *Atomic Train* (film), pp.18–19, D4

Westside, New South Wales (town/suburb), *E-Street* (TV), pp.108–109, F4

Westview, USA (town), *WandaVision* (TV), pp14–15, C5

Westworld, Delos Destinations (fictional island), *Westworld* by Michael Crichton (novel/TV), pp.90–91, C4

Wet Moon, Florida (town), *Wet Moon* by Sophie Campbell (comic), pp.14–15, B2

Wham, Texas (town), *Destry Rides Again* by Max Brand (novel), pp.18–19, D2

Whatchacallit, Maine (town), *Non Sequitur* (comic), pp.14–15, D5

Wheaton, New Jersey (town), Marvel Cinematic Universe (various), pp.14–15, C4

Wheatsylvania, North Dakota (town), works of Sinclair Lewis, pp.16–17, B6

Whipstaff Manor, Maine (building), *Casper* (film), pp.14–15, D6

Whispering Island, England (island), *Five Have a Mystery to Solve* by Enid Blyton (novel), pp.64–65, C1

Whistle Stop, Alabama (town), *Fried Green Tomatoes at the Whistle Stop Café* by Fannie Flagg (novel/film), pp.14–15, A3

Whiteacre *see* Blackacre

White Agony Creek, Yukon (river), *DuckTales* (various), pp.26–27, B2

White City, The, Iran (city), *Arabian Nights: Julnar the Sea-born and Her Son Badar Basim* Burton edition (short story), pp.72–73, C2

White Moon/Katsuragi Expedition Basecamp, The (underground wreck/camp), *Neon Genesis Evangelion* (manga/anime), pp.114–115, D2

White Mountain, China (mountain), *The Vagrants* by Yiyun Li (novel), pp.102–103, D4

White Point, Western Australia (town), *Dirt Music* by Tim Winton (novel/film), pp.108–109, A2

White Rocks, New Mexico (town), *For a Few Dollars More* (film), pp.18–19, D4

White Sands, Prince Edward Island (town), *Anne of Green Gables* by Lucy Maud Montgomery (novel), pp.26–27, F1

Whizztown, Scotland (town), *The Beano* (comics), pp.64–65, C4

Whyhope, New South Wales (town), *The Heart Guy* (TV), pp.108–109, D2

Whylah Falls, Nova Scotia (town), *Whylah Falls* by George Elliott Clarke (novel), pp.26–27, F1

WICKED Maze, California (building), *The Maze Runner* by James Dashner (novel/film), pp.18–19, A4

Widdershins, England (town), *Widdershins* by Kate Ashwin (web comic), pp.64–65, C3

Widgeree, Victoria (town), *Blue Heelers* (TV), pp.108–109, D2

Widjimorphup, Western Australia (town), works of Leon Pericles (artworks), pp.108–109, B3

Wilbur County, Oregon (county), *The Germaine Truth* (web fiction), pp.18–19, B5

Wildenberg River, Washington (river), *Astro City* (comic), pp.18–19, B6

Wildfell Hall, England (estate), *The Tenant of Wildfell Hall* by Anne Brontë (novel), pp.64–65, C3

Wildfire, Nevada (building), *The Andromeda Strain* by Michael Crichton (various), pp.18–19, B5

Willow, Maine (town), *Rainy Season* by Stephen King (short story), pp.14–15, D6

Willowbutton, Dorado (town), *I-0* (video game), pp.18–19, D3

Willows, Wisconsin (town), Barbie (toy line), pp.16–17, D5

Willstown, Queensland (village), *A Town Like Alice* by Nevil Shute (novel/Film/TV), pp.108–109, D4

Wilmingmore, Delmarva (fictional city), *Steven Universe* (TV), pp.14–15, C4

Wilson's Island, Pacific Ocean (island), *Commandos 2: Men of Courage* (video game), pp.120–121, B3

Wilvercombe, England (town), *Have His Carcase* by Dorothy L Sayers (novel), pp.64–65, C2

Wind Gap, Missouri (town), *Sharp Objects* by Gillian Flynn (novel/TV), pp.16–17, D3

Winden, Germany (town), *Dark* (TV), pp.44–45, C3

Winesburg, Ohio (town), *Winesburg, Ohio* by Sherwood Anderson (short stories), pp.14–15, B4

Winnawadgery, Victoria (town), *Come Midnight Monday* by David Burke (novel/TV), pp.108–109, D1

Winnemac (fictional state), novels of Sinclair Lewis (novel), pp.14–15, A5

Winshire (fictional country), *Crown For Christmas* (film), pp.44–45, C3

Winter River, Connecticut (town), *Beetlejuice* (film), pp.14–15, C5

Winterstoke, England (town), *Winterstoke* by L.T.C. Rolt (novel), pp.64–65, C2

Wirrawee, Victoria (town), the Tomorrow series by John Marsden (novels), pp.108–109, D1

Wisborg, Germany (town), *Nosferatu* (film), pp.44–45, D4

Witch Mountain (mountain), *Escape to Witch Mountain* (novel/films), pp.14–15, B3

Witney Scrotum, England (town), *Tales from Witney Scrotum* by Peter Tinniswood (novel), pp.64–65, D1

Wokenwell, England (town), *Wokenwell* (TV), pp.64–65, C3

Wolf City, Wyoming (town), *Cat Ballou* (film), pp.18–19, D5

Wolfjaw, Montana (town), *War of the Worlds* (TV), pp.18–19, C6

Wollanup, Northern Territory (town), *The Dead Heart* by Douglas Kennedy (novel), pp.108–109, C4

Wolyna, Poland (village), *Like a Tear in the Ocean* by Manes Sperber (novel), pp.50–51, B3

Woman Lake, Russia (lake), works of Elizabeth Marshall Thomas, pp.102–103, E1

Wongadilla, New South Wales (estate), *The Nargun and the Stars* by Patricia Wrightson (novel), pp.108–109, E2

Wongnaileum (fictional country), *The Bodyguard 2* (film), pp.90–91, B4

Woodcrest, Maryland (city), *The Boondocks* (TV), pp.14–15, C4

Woodpine Park, British Columbia (natural feature), *Oakwood* (video game), pp.26–27, B1

Woodsboro, California (town), *Scream* films, pp.18–19, A4

Woodston, England (estate), *Northanger Abbey* by Jane Austen (novel), pp.64–65, C2

Woop Woop, Northern Territory (town), *Welcome to Woop Woop* (film), pp.108–109, C4

Worford, England (town), *Blott on the Landscape* by Tom Sharpe (novel/TV), pp.64–65, C2

World's End Inn, Wales (building), *Sleep No More* by L.T.C. Rolt (short story), pp.64–65, B2

Wragby Hall, England (building), *Lady Chatterley's Lover* by D.H. Lawrence (novel), pp.64–65, C2

Wreck of The Thing's spaceship (wreck), *The Thing* (film), pp.114–115, D2

Wrigley, Pennsylvania (town), *Agents of SHIELD* (TV), pp.14–15, C5

Wu Chi Temple, China (building), *The Man with the Iron Fists 2* (film), pp.102–103, B2

Wulfsee, Germany (lake), *Wolfenstein* series (video games), pp.44–45, D3

Wumpa Island, Pacific Ocean (island), *Crash Bandicoot* series (video games), pp.120–121, B2

Wumpa Islands, Pacific Ocean (island chain), *Crash Bandicoot* series (video games), pp.120–121, B2

Wuthering Heights, England (building), *Wuthering Heights* by Emily Brontë (novel), pp.64–65, C3

Wyvern, England (county), *Holby City* (TV), pp.64–65, C3

Xanadu, Florida (building), *Citizen Kane* (film), pp.14–15, C5

Xavier Institute (Xavier School for Gifted Youngsters), X-Men (town), *X-Men* (various), pp.14–15, C5

Xijing, China (city), works of Jia Pingua, pp.102–103, C2

Xijing (fictional city/state), *Xijing Men* (various), pp.102–103, C2

Ximes, France (town), works of Clark Ashton Smith (short stories), pp.44–45, C3

Xinchun, China (village), *Further News of Defeat* by Michael X. Wang (short story), pp.102–103, D3

Xuji, Tanzania (city), *Tarzan the Untamed* by Edgar Rice Burroughs (novel), pp.84–85, C3

Y'ha-nthlei, Massachusetts (underwater city), Cthulhu Mythos/H.P. Lovecraft (short story), pp.14–15, D5

Yaad Sheher, India (town), *Yadoon Ka Idiotbox* (radio show), pp.78–79, C5

Yabba-Dabba, Bulungi (fictional city), *The Onion* (online satire), pp.84–85, A4

Yabbie Creek, New South Wales (town/suburb), *Home and Away* (TV), pp.108–109, F4

Yakkagala, Ruins of, Taprobane (fictional building), *The Fountains of Paradise* by Arthur C. Clarke (novel), pp.78–79, C2

Yamacraw Island, South Carolina (island), *Conrack* (film), pp.14–15, B2

Yamaku Academy, Japan (building), *Katawa Shoujo* (video game), pp.96–97, C3

Yaman (fictional country), *Recorded by Arizal* (web series), pp.90–91, D2

Yamatai Island, Japan (island), *Tomb Raider* (video games), pp.96–97, B1/C1

Yamatai, Japan (country), later Conan novels inspired by Robert E. Howard, pp.96–97, C2

Yandu, China (city), *Log Horizon* by Mamare Touno and Kazuhiro Hara (novels/anime), pp.102–103, D3

Yangdon (fictional country), *Princess and I* (film), pp.78–79, D4

Yangdu, China (city), *Log Horizon* by Mamare Touno and Kazuhiro Hara (novels/anime), pp.102–103, D1

Yankerville, Nevada (town), *Crank Yankers* (TV), pp.18–19, B3

Yarrold, England (town), *South Riding* by Winifred Holtby (novel), pp.64–65, D3

Yashiro Station, Hinomoto (fictional city), *Kabaneri of the Iron Fortress* (anime), pp.96–97, B2

Yaughton, England (town), *Everybody's Gone to the Rapture* (video game), pp.64–65, C2

Yehupetz, Ukraine (city), works of Sholem Aleichem (stories), pp.50–51, C3

Yekaterina Bridge, Russia (building), *Snowpiercer* (film), pp.50–51, B6

Yellow Belt, The, Hobeika/Salmaah (fictional natural feature), *Day of the Falcon* (film), pp.72–73, C1

Yellowcake Springs, Western Australia (town), *Yellowcake Springs* by Guy Salvidge (novel), pp.108–109, A2

Yewaire (fictional country), *Operation Red Sea* (film), pp.72–73, C1

Yogistan (fictional country), *The Ascent of Rum Doodle* by W.E. Bowman (novel), pp.78–79, B5/C5

Yoknapatawpha County, Mississippi (county), works of William Faulkner, pp.16–17, D3

Yongan, China (city), *The Hundred Secret Senses* by Amy Tan (novel), pp.102–103, C1

Yonville-l'Abbaye, France (village), *Madame Bovary* by Gustave Flaubert (novel), pp.44–45, C3

Yoorana, Victoria (town), *Glitch* (TV), pp.108–109, D1

Young Einstein's Apple Farm, Tasmania (building), *Young Einstein* (film), pp.108–109, D1

Ys, France (sunken city, French folklore), pp.44–45, B3

Yuanmaotun, China (village), *The Hurricane* by Zhou Libo (novel), pp.102–103, E3

Yuba City, California (town), *Pale Rider* (film), pp.18–19, A4

Yul, South Korea (island/nation), *Hong Gildon Jeon* (novel), pp.102–103, E2

Yunosagi Onsen, Japan (town), *Hanasaku Iroha* (anime), pp.96–97, B2

Yurko City, Kolechia (fictional city), *Papers, Please* (video game), pp.72–73, C4

Yvronia (region), *Mundus alter et idem* by Joseph Hall (novel), pp.114–115, D4

Z, Spain (town), *The Skating Rink* by Roberto Bolaño (novel), pp.44–45, C2

Zacatillo, Mexico (town), *Zacatillo, un Lugar en tu Corazón* (TV), pp.32–33, B2

Zafarra, Zekistan (fictional city), *Full Spectrum Warrior* (video game), pp.72–73, E2

Zahrain (fictional country/emirate), *Escape from Zahrain* (film), pp.72–73, C1/C2

Zamana, Pakistan (town), *The Golden Legend* by Nadeem Aslam (novel), pp.78–79, B5

Zaminej, Iran (village), *Missing Soluch* by Mahmoud Dowlatabadi (novel), pp.72–73, D2

Zamunda (fictional country), *Coming to America* (film), pp.84–85, B3/C3

Zangaro (fictional country), *The Dogs of War* by Frederick Forsyth (novel), pp.84–85, B4

Zantleaf Peninsula, Eastal (fictional region), *Log Horizon* by Mamare Touno and Kazuhiro Hara (novels/anime), pp.96–97, C2

Zantoroland, Indian Ocean (island/nation), *The Illegal* by Lawrence Hill (novel), pp.78–79, B1/C1

Zanza River, Zanzarim/Dahum (fictional river), *Solo* by William Boyd (novel), pp.84–85, A4/B4

Zanzarim, Nigeria (country), *Solo* by William Boyd (novel), pp.84–85, B4

Zanzibar, England (wreck), *The Wreck of the Zanzibar* by Michael Morpurgo (novel), pp.64–65, B1

Zanzibar, Zanzibarland (fictional city), *Metal Gear Solid 2* (video game), pp.72–73, E2

Zanzibarland (fictional country), *Metal Gear Solid 2* (video game), pp.72–73, E2

Zarakal (fictional country), *No Enemy But Time* by Michael Bishop (novel), pp.84–85, D4

Zarkheba River (river), Conan novels of Robert E. Howard, pp.84–85, C4

Zaronza, France (town), *The Corsican Widow* by Vanessa Couchman (novel), pp.44–45, C2

Zawame, Japan (city), *Kamen Rider Gaim* (TV), pp.96–97, B2/C2

Zebwa (fictional country), *Hardy Boys* (comic), pp.84–85, C3

Zekistan (fictional country), *Full Spectrum Warrior* (video game), pp.72–73, E3

Zembabwei (fictional country), Conan novels of Robert E. Howard, pp.84–85, D4

Zembala (fictional country), *The Wild Geese* (film), pp.84–85, C2

Zemenia (fictional country), *Monk* (TV), pp.50–51, A2

Zenda, Ruritania (fictional town), *The Prisoner of Zelda* by Anthony Hope (novel), pp.50–51, A4

Zendia, Pacific Ocean (island), The Zendian Problem (intelligence exercise), pp.120–121, E2/F2

Zenith, Winnemac (fictional city), novels of Sinclair Lewis (novel), pp.14–15, A5

Zero Zero Island, Atlantic Ocean (region), *Colonel Bleep* (TV), pp.84–85, A3/B3

Zero-One (The Machine City), Iraq (city/state), *The Matrix* films, pp.72–73, C2

Zerzura, Egypt (city, folklore), pp.84–85, C5

Zevo Toys, Idaho (building), *Toys* (film), pp.18–19, B6

Zhangjia, China (city), *A Dictionary of Maqiao* by Han Shaogong (novel), pp.102–103, D2

Zhangtai City, China (city), *Heaven Above* by Lu Tianming (novel/TV), pp.102–103, E4

Zig/Gurat Space Elevator, Indian Ocean, *Gunnm/Battle Angel Alita* (manga/anime/film), pp.90–91, A2

Zinctown, New Mexico (town), *Salt of the Earth* (film), pp.18–19, D2

Zingara, Spain/Portugal (region), Conan novels of Robert E. Howard, pp.44–45, A2/B2

Zinj (The Lost City of Zinj), DRC (city/state), *Congo* by Michael Crichton (novel), pp.84–85, C3

Zivatar, Hungary (village), *Valeria's Last Stand* by Marc Fitten (novel), pp.50–51, B2

Zloda, Belarus (town), *Marvel: Agents of SHIELD* (TV), pp.50–51, C4

Zlotshev, Ukraine (town), *Kiddush Ha-Shem: An Epic of 1648* by Sholem Asch (novel), pp.50–51, C3

Zokof, Poland (village), *A Day of Small Beginnings* by Lisa Pearl Rosenbaum (novel), pp.50–51, B4

Zokov Islands, The, Russia (island chain), *Dr Strangelove or: How I Learned to Stop Worrying and Love the Bomb* (film), pp.102–103, F2

Zonama River, Brazil (river), *Himouto! Umaru-chan* (anime), pp.38–39, B5

Zu-Vendis (fictional country), *Allan Quatermain* by H. Rider Haggard (novel), pp.84–85, D3

Zubrowka (fictional country), *The Grand Budapest Hotel* (film), pp.50–51, A3

Zulabwe (fictional country), *The A-Team* (TV), pp.84–85, C2

Zymylpathian Mountains, Syldavia (fictional mountain range), *The Adventures of Tintin* by Hergé (various), pp.50–51, B2

101 Dalmations by Dodi Smith (novel), Hell Hall, England (estate), pp.64–65, D2

11.22.63 (TV), Holden, Tennessee (town), pp.14–15, A3

1632 series by Eric Flint (novels)
Badenburg, Germany (town), pp.44–45, D3
Grantville, Germany (town), pp.44–45, D3

1632/Ring of Fire series by Eric Flint (novels), Grantville, West Virginia (town), pp.14–15, B4

20,000 Leagues Under the Sea by Jules Verne (novel)
Arabian Tunnel, Egypt (underground passage), pp.84–85, C5
Captain Nemo's Country (continent), pp.114–115, B2

2000 AD (comics)
Bananaland (fictional region), pp.108–109, D3
Brisbania, Bananaland (fictional city), pp.108–109, B3
East-Meg Two (fictional region/city/ state), pp.102–103, E1
Emerald Isle (fictional country), pp.64–65, A3/B3/A2/B2
Hindi Ocean, Indian Ocean (ocean), pp.78–79, C2/D2
Hondo City, Japan (city), pp.96–97, B3/ C3
Kiwi-Cit/New Pacific City, New Zealand (city), pp.108–109, F1
New Thai Confederacy (fictional country), pp.90–91, B3
Nu-Bangkok, New Thai Confederacy (fictional city), pp.90–91, B3
Nu-Delhi, India (city), pp.78–79, B3
Perth Island, Western Australia (region), pp.108–109, B3
The Radback (fictional region), pp.108–109, D3
The Radlands of Ji, China (region), pp.102–103, C3
Sino Cit One, China (city), pp.102–103, D2
Sino Cit Two, China (city), pp.102–103, D1
Sydney-Melbourne Conurb (fictional city), pp.108–109, D2
Taswegia, Tasmania (city), pp.108–109, D1
The Web, Indonesia (natural feature), pp.90–91, B1/C1

24 (TV)
B'Dar, Kamistan (fictional city), pp.72–73, C2
Kamistan (Islamic Republic of), Kamistan (fictional country), pp.72–73, C2

2666 by Roberto Bolaño (novel), Santa Teresa, Mexico (city), pp.32–33, B4

3 Bahadur (film), Roshan Basti/Andher Basti, Pakistan (town), pp.78–79, A4

30 Rock (TV), Sadchester, Massachusetts (town), pp.14–15, B4

3rd Rock from the Sun (TV), Rutherford, Ohio (city), pp.14–15, B4

6 Angels (anime), Neo Purgatory, Utah (building), pp.18–19, C4

6 Underground (film)
Turgistan (fictional country), pp.72–73, D3
Tyrus, Turgistan (fictional city), pp.72–73, C3

7th Heaven (TV), Glenoak, California (town), pp.18–19, B4

800 Words (TV), Weld, New Zealand (town), pp.108–109, F2

91:an/No. 91 (comic strip), Klackamo, Sweden (town), pp.56–57, B3

A Bell for Adano by John Hersey (novel), Adano, Italy (town), pp.44–45, D1

A Book of Common Prayer by John Didion (novel), Boca Grande (fictional country), pp.32–33, C2

A Boy of Good Breeding by Miriam Toews (novel), Algren, Manitoba (town), pp.26–27, D1

A Bridge in Time by Elisabeth McNeill (novel), Camptounfoot, Scotland (town), pp.64–65, C4

A Brief History of Seven Killings by Marlon James (novel), Copenhagen City, Jamaica (town), pp.32–33, D2

A Candle to Light the Sun by Patricia Blondal (novel), Mouse Bluffs, Manitoba (town), pp.26–27, C1

A Canterbury Tale (film), Chillingborne, England (village), pp.64–65, D2

A Caribbean Mystery by Agatha Christie (novel), St Honoré (fictional island), pp.32–33, F2

A Casual Brutality by Neil Bissoondath (novel), Casaquemada (fictional island), pp.32–33, F2

A Certain Magical Index by Kazuma Kamachi and Kiyotaka Haimura (novel), Academy City, Japan (city/state), pp.96–97, E1

A Christmas Story by Jean Shepherd (story/ film), Hohman, Indiana (town), pp.14–15, A4

A Clergyman's Daughter by George Orwell (novel), Knype Hill, England (town), pp.64–65, D2

A Cold White Sun by Vicki Delany (novel), Trafalgar, British Columbia (town), pp.26–27, B1

A Country Practice (TV), Wandin Valley, New South Wales (town), pp.108–109, D2

A Crystal Age by W.H. Hudson (novel), Coradine, Scotland (country), pp.64–65, C5

A Darker Domain by Val McDermid (novel), Rothswell Castle, Scotland (building), pp.64–65, C4

A Descent for Gossips by Thea Astley (novel), Gungee, Queensland (town), pp.108–109, E3

A Dictionary of Maqiao by Han Shaogong (novel)
Baling, China (town), pp.102–103, D2
Changle, China (town), pp.102–103, D2
Luo Kingdom, China (region), pp.102–103, D2
Luo River, China (river), pp.102–103, D2
Maqiao, China (village), pp.102–103, D2
Shuanglong, China (town), pp.102–103, D2
Zhangjia, China (city), pp.102–103, C2

A Face in the Crowd (film), Pickett, Arkansas (town), pp.16–17, D3

A Feast of Freedom by Leonard Wibberley (novel)
Omo Lau, Pacific Ocean (island/nation), pp.120–121, D3
Omo Levi, Pacific Ocean (island/nation), pp.120–121, D3

A Fistful of Dollars (film), San Miguel, Mexico (town), pp.32–33, C4

A Flag for Sunrise by Robert Stone (novel), Tecan (fictional country), pp.32–33, C1

A Fugitive Crosses His Tracks by Aksel Sandemose (novel), Jante, Denmark (town), pp.56–57, A3

A Girl in Australia (film), Bun Bun Ga, New South Wales (town), pp.108–109, D2

A Girl Walks Home Alone At Night (film), Bad City, Iran (town), pp.72–73, B2

A Gloom is Cast Upon the Ancient Steps by Alexander Chudakov (novel), Chebachinsk, Kazakhstan (town), pp.72–73, D4

A Good Man in Africa by William Boyd (novel/film), Kinjaja (fictional country), pp.84–85, B4

A Good Man in Africa by William Boyd (novel/film), Nkongsamba, Kinjaja (fictional city), pp.84–85, B4

A Goofy Movie (film), Lake Idaho, Idaho (lake), pp.16–17, B5

A Grain of Wheat by Ngũgĩ wa Thiong'o (novel), Thabai, Kenya (village), pp.84–85, D3

A Haunted Island by Algernon Blackwood (novel), Haunted Island, Ontario (island), pp.26–27, A4

A Home of Our Own (film), Hankston, Idaho (town), pp.18–19, C5

A Horse and Two Goats by R.K. Narayan (novel), Kritam, India (village), pp.78–79, C3

A House for Mr Biswas by V.S. Naipaul (novel)
Arwacas, Trinidad (town), pp.32–33, F2
Shorthills, Tinidad (town), pp.32–33, F1/F2

A House Like a Lotus by Madeleine L'Engle (novels), Osia Theola, Cyprus (town), pp.44–45, F1

A Hundred Pieces of Me by Lucy Dillon (novel), Longhampton, England (town), pp.64–65, C2

A Indomada (TV), Greenville, Brazil (town), pp.38–39, D4

A Lei do Amor (TV), São Dimas, Brazil (town), pp.38–39, D1

A Letter From Ledwardine by Phil Rickman (novel), Ledwardine, England (town), pp.64–65, C2

A Luminous Republic by Andrés Barba (novel), San Cristobal, Argentina (city), pp.38–39, B3

A Madness of Sunshine by Nalini Singh (novel), Golden Cove, New Zealand (town), pp.108–109, F1

A Mind Forever Voyaging (video game), Rockvil, South Dakota (town), pp.16–17, A5

A Mother's Son (TV), Eastlee, England (town), pp.64–65, D2

A Nightmare on Elm Street (films), Springwood, Ohio (town), pp.14–15, B5

A Passage to India by E.M. Forster (novel/ film)
Chandrapore, India (city), pp.78–79, C4
Marabar Caves, India (natural feature), pp.78–79, C4

A Place Further Than the Universe (anime), Challenge for Antarctic 02 Expedition (location), pp.114–115, D4

A Place to Call Home (TV)
Ash Park, New South Wales (estate), pp.108–109, D2
Inverness, New South Wales (town), pp.108–109, D2

A Prairie as Wide as the Sea by Sarah Ellis (novel), Milorie, Saskatchewan (town), pp.26–27, C1

A Prairie Home Companion (radio)
Lake Wobegon, Minnesota (town), pp.16–17, C5
Millet, Minnesota (town), pp.16–17, C5
Mist County, Minnesota (county), pp.16–17, C5

A Prince For Christmas (film), Balemont (fictional country), pp.44–45, C3

A Royal Christmas (film), Cordinia (fictional country), pp.44–45, C3

A Royal Winter (film), Calpurnia (fictional country), pp.44–45, C2/C3

A Stange Manuscript Found in a Copper Bottle by James De Mille (novel), Kosekin Country (country), pp.114–115, B3

A Strange Discovery by Charles Romyn Dake (novel), Hili-Li (city/island), pp.114–115, C2

A Suitable Boy by Vikram Seth (novel), Brahmpur, India (town), pp.78–79, C4

A Thousand Splendid Suns by Khaled Hosseini (novel), Gul Daman, Afghanistan (village), pp.72–73, D2

A Time to Kill (and other novels) by John Grisham (novel)
Clanton, Mississippi (city), pp.16–17, D3
Ford County, Mississippi (county), pp.16–17, D3

A Touch of Frost by R.D. Wingfield (novels/ TV), Denton, England (town), pp.64–65, C2

A Town Like Alice by Nevil Shute (novel/ Film/TV), Willstown, Queensland (village), pp.108–109, D4

A Traveller From Altruria by William Dean Howells (novel), Altruria (fictional island), pp.120–121, C1

A Very Peculiar Practice (TV), Lowlands University, England (building), pp.64–65, D2

A Warning to the Curious by M.R. James (short story), Seaburgh, England (town), pp.64–65, D2

A Wild Sheep Chase by Haruki Murakami (novel), Junitaki, Japan (town), pp.96–97, C4

Aalabayude Penmakkal by Sarah Joseph (novel), Kokkanchira, India (village), pp.78–79, B2

ABC Soap Opera Universe, *All My Children* (TV), Pine Valley, Pennsylvania (town), pp.14–15, C4

ABC Soap Opera Universe, *General Hospital* (TV)
Beechers Corners, New York (town), pp.14–15, B5
Port Charles, New York (city), pp.14–15, B5

ABC Soap Opera Universe, *Loving* (TV), Corinth, Pennsylvania (town), pp.14–15, B4

ABC Soap Opera Universe, *One Life to Live* (TV), Llanview, Pennsylvania (town), pp.14–15, C4

ABC Soap Opera Universe, *The Young Marrieds* (TV), Queen's Point, New York (town), pp.14–15, B5

ABC Soap Opera Universe, *Twin Peaks* (TV), Twin Peaks, Washington (town), pp.18–19, B6

Abhya by Saiswaroopa Iyer (novel), Anagha (fictional city/state), pp.78–79, B4

About Stig Petrè's Secret (TV), Hallstabro, Sweden (town), pp.56–57, C3

Absolutely (TV), Stoneybridge, Scotland (village), pp.64–65, C4

Ace in the Hole (film)
Escudero, New Mexico (town), pp.18–19, D3
Los Barrios County, New Mexico (county), pp.18–19, D3

Ace Ventura: When Nature Calls (film)
Bonai Province, Nibia (fictional region), pp.84–85, C3
Nibia (fictional country), pp.84–85, C3
Wachati Village, Nibia (fictional village), pp.84–85, C3
Wachootoo Village, Nibia (fictional village), pp.84–85, C3

Ackley Bridge (TV), Ackley Bridge, England (town), pp.64–65, C3

Aconagua (video game), Meruza, Argentina (region), pp.38–39, B3

Acorn Antiques (TV), Manchesterford, England (city), pp.64–65, C3

Act of War (film), Bazrakhistan (fictional country), pp.72–73, D4/E4

Adam Bede by George Eliot (novel)
Hayslope, England (town), pp.64–65, C2
Snowfield, England (town), pp.64–65, C2
Stonyshire, England (county), pp.64–65, C2

'Adore You' by Harry Styles (music), Eroda, Irish Sea (island), pp.64–65, B3

Adrian Mole: The Prostrate Years by Sue Townsend (novel), Mangold Parva, England (village), pp.64–65, C2

Adrift in the Middle Kingdom by Jan Jacob Slauerhoff (novel)
Chungking, China (city), pp.102–103, C2
Taihai, China (city), pp.102–103, C2

Adventure Island books by Helen Moss (novels), Carrickstowe, England (town), pp.64–65, B1

Adventures in Odyssey (video games), Odyssey, Ohio (town), pp.14–15, B4

Adventures of Huckleberry Finn by Mark Twain (novel), Bricksville, Arkansas (town), pp.16–17, D3

Adventures of Huckleberry Finn by Mark Twain (novel)
Pikesville, Arkansas (town), pp.16–17, D2
Pokesville, Arkansas (town), pp.16–17, D3
St Petersburg, Missouri (town), pp.16–17, D3
Walter Scott, Missouri (wreck), pp.16–17, D4

Aepyornis Island by H.G. Wells (short story), Aepyornis Island, Indian Ocean (island), pp.84–85, D2

Affliction by Russell Banks (novel), Lawford, New Hampshire (town), pp.14–15, C5

Agatha Raisin (TV), Carsely, England (village), pp.64–65, C2

Agaton Sax stories by Nils-Olof Franzén (novels), Byköping, Sweden (town), pp.56–57, C2

Agent Ali (TV), Cyberaya, Malaysia (city), pp.90–91, B2

Agents of SHIELD (TV)
Laura Creek, Western Australia (town), pp.108–109, A3
Wrigley, Pennsylvania (town), pp.14–15, C5

Agora É Que São Elas (TV), Santana de Bocaiúvas, Brazil (city), pp.38–39, D4

Air America (TV), Buenaventura, Costa Perdita (fictional city), pp.32–33, C2

Akenfield by Ronald Blythe (novel/film), Akenfield, England (town), pp.64–65, D2

Al Hayba (TV), Al Hayba, Lebanon (town), pp.72–73, B2

Al norte del Milenio by Gerardo Cornejo (novel)
El Estado Dorado, Mexico (country), pp.32–33, A4/B4
El Golfo Nostrum, Mexico (sea), pp.32–33, D1
El Gran Centro-Capital, Mexico (city), pp.32–33, B2
El Lugar vacío, Mexico (natural feature), pp.32–33, A4

Aladdin (film), Agrabah (Al-Kal'as), Jordan (city), pp.72–73, B2

Alaloum (film), Letsovo, Greece (village), pp.44–45, E1/E2

Alas, Babylon by Pat Frank (novel), Fort Repose, Florida (town), pp.14–15, B2

Alaska by James A. Michener (novel), Lapak, Alaska (island), pp.18–19, A1

Albert Herring by Benjamin Britten (operetta), Loxford, England (town), pp.64–65, D2

Albin Indergand by Ernst Zahn (novel), Anderhalden, Switzerland (village), pp.44–45, C3

Alborada (TV), Santa Rita, Panama (town), pp.32–33, D1

Alentejo Blue by Monica Ali (novel), Nello and Patrasche, Mamarrosa (village), pp.44–45, A3

Aline et Valcour by the Marquis de Sade (novel)
Butua (fictional country), pp.84–85, C2
Tamoé, Pacific Ocean (island/nation), pp.120–121, D3

All Fall Down by Cassandra Austin (novel), Mululuk, South Australia (town), pp.108–109, C2

All Our Secrets by Jennifer Lane (novel)
Bagooli River, New South Wales (river), pp.108–109, D2
Coongahoola, New South Wales (town), pp.108–109, D2

All Over Creation by Ruth Ozeki (novel), Liberty Falls, Idaho (town), pp.18–19, C5

All the Right Moves (film), Ampipe, Pennsylvania (town), pp.14–15, B4

Allan Quatermain by H. Rider Haggard (novel)
Milosis, Zu-Vendis (fictional town), pp.84–85, D3
Zu-Vendis (fictional country), pp.84–85, D3

Alma Gêmea (TV), Roseiral, Brazil (town), pp.38–39, C3

Amachan (TV), Kitasanriku, Japan (town), pp.96–97, C3

Amazon: Guardians of Eden (video game), Sitio Maldito, Brazil (natural feature), pp.38–39, B5

American Dad (TV)
Isla Island/Bananarama (fictional island/ nation), pp.32–33, D2
Langley Falls, Virginia (town), pp.14–15, C4

American Gothic (TV)
Fulton County, South Carolina (town), pp.14–15, B3
Trinity, South Carolina (town), pp.14–15, B3

American Pie films, East Great Falls, Michigan (town), pp.14–15, A5

American Pie 2 (film), Grand Harbor, Michigan (town), pp.14–15, A5

Amerika (TV), Milford, Nebraska (town), pp.16–17, B4

Amerzone (video game)
Alvarezopolis, Amerzone (fictional city), pp.38–39, C5
Amerzone (fictional country), pp.38–39, C4
Amerzone River, Amerzone (fictional river), pp.38–39, C5

Amor Real (TV)
Ciudad Santiago, Mexico (town), pp.32–33, B2
Ciudad Trinidad, Mexico (town), pp.32–33, B2/B3

An American Tragedy by Theodore Dreiser (novel), Lycurgus, New York (city), pp.14–15, C5

An American Werewolf in London (film), East Proctor, England (village), pp.64–65, D3

An Appointment with the Wicker Man by Greg Hemphill (play), Loch Parry, Scotland (town), pp.64–65, B5

An Klondike (TV), Dominion Creek, Yukon (town), pp.26–27, B2

Anandamath by Bankim Chandra Chattopadhyay (novel), Padachinha, India (village), pp.78–79, C4

And the Mountains Echoed by Khaled Hosseini (novel), Shadbagh, Afghanistan (village), pp.72–73, D2

And Then There Were None by Agatha Christie (novel), Soldier Island, England (island), pp.64–65, C1

Andoshen, PA by Darryl Ponicsan (novel), Andoshen, Pennsylvania, pp.14–15, C5

Angel Island by Inez Haynes Irwin (novel), Angel Island, Pacific Ocean (island), pp.120–121, C4

Angels Wear White (film), Binhai, China (town), pp.102–103, D1

Angus Og by Ewen Bain (comic strip), Drambeg, Scotland (island), pp.64–65, B5

Animal Farm by George Orwell (novella), Animal Farm, England (building), pp.64–65, D2

Animal's People by Indra Sinha (novel), Khaufpur, India (city), pp.78–79, B4

Anita and Me by Meera Syal (novel), Tollington, England (town), pp.64–65, C2

Annals of the Parish by John Galt (novel), Dalmailing, Scotland (town), pp.64–65, C4

Anne of Green Gables by Lucy Maud Montgomery (novel)
Avonlea, Prince Edward Island (town), pp.26–27, F1
Bolingbroke, Nova Scotia (village), pp.26–27, F1/F2
Bright River, Prince Edward Island (town), pp.26–27, F1
Carmody, Prince Edward Island (town), pp.26–27, F1
Hopeton, Nova Scotia (town), pp.26–27, F1
Newbridge, Prince Edward Island (town), pp.26–27, F1
Redmond College, Nova Scotia (building), pp.26–27, F1
White Sands, Prince Edward Island (town), pp.26–27, F1

Another Night in Mullet Town by Steven Herick (novel)
Balarang Bay, New South Wales (town), pp.108–109, D2
Morawa National Park, New South Wales (town), pp.108–109, D1/D2
Turon, New South Wales (town), pp.108–109, D1

Another World (TV), Bay City, Illinois (city), pp.16–17, D5

Anthills of the Savannah by Chinua Achebe (novel), Kagan (fictional country), pp.84–85, B4

Anywhere But Paradise by Anne Bustard (novel), Hanu, Hawaii (town), pp.18–19, C1

Apocalypse Now (film)
Hau Phat, Vietnam (town), pp.90–91, B3
Lo Dung Bridge, Vietnam (building), pp.90–91, B3
Nu Mung Ba, Cambodia (building), pp.90–91, B3
Nùng River, China (river), pp.90–91, B3, pp.102–103, C2
Vin Din Drop/Charlie's Point, Vietnam (village), pp.90–91, B3

Appaloosa (film), Appaloosa, New Mexico (town), pp.18–19, D3

Appointment with Venus by Jerrard Tickell (novel/film), Armorel, Channel Islands (island), pp.64–65, A1

Apuesta Por un Amor (TV), San Gaspar, Mexico (town), pp.32–33, C2

Aquelarre (TV), Aquelarre, Chile (town), pp.38–39, B3

Arabian Nights: Julnar the Sea-born and Her Son Badar Basim, Burton edition (short story)
City of Magicians, Iran (city), pp.72–73, C3
Thirsty Island, Iran (island), pp.72–73, C3
White City, The, Iran (city), pp.72–73, C2

Arachnaphobia (film), Canaima, California (town), pp.18–19, A3

Araguaia (TV), Girassol, Brazil (town), pp.38–39, C4

Araguaia (TV), Juruanã, Brazil (town), pp.38–39, C4

Archer (TV), Llanflwnyddwndllwnmawr, Wales (town), pp.64–65, C2

Archibald the Koala (TV), Rastepappe, Pacific Ocean (island), pp.120–121, B2

Are You Afraid of the Dark? (TV), Argento, Oregon (town), pp.18–19, A5

Are You Being Served? (film), Costa Plonka, Spain (town), pp.44–45, B2

ARMA 3 (video game)
Altis, Greece (island), pp.44–45, E1
Horizon Islands, Pacific Ocean (island), pp.120–121, B2
La Roche, Horizon Islands (fictional city), pp.120–121, B2
Stratis, Greece (island), pp.44–45, E1
Tanoa, Horizon Islands (fictional island), pp.120–121, B2

ARMA: Armed Assault (video game)
Bagango, Sahrini (fictional city), pp.126–127, C4
Paraiso, South Sahrini (fictional city), pp.126–127, C4
Sahrani (fictional island/nation), pp.126–127, C4
South Sahrani, Sahrani (fictional island/nation), pp.126–127, C4

ARMA: Cold War Assault (video game)
Everon, Atlantic Ocean (island), pp.126–127, C4
Malden, Atlantic Ocean (island), pp.126–127, C4

Armação Ilimitada (TV)
São Tomé dos Números, Brazil (town), pp.38–39, C4
Sensilvânia, Brazil (town), pp.38–39, C3

Aroba Bridge (TV Animation), Aroha Bridge, New Zealand (town), pp.108–109, F2

Around the World in Eighty Days by Jules Verne (novel)
Cani River, India (river), pp.78–79, C4
Kallenger, India (town), pp.78–79, C4
Kholby, India (town), pp.78–79, C4
Pagoda of Pillaji, The, India (building), pp.78–79, C4
Rothal, India (town), pp.78–79, C4

Arrival and Departure by Arthur Koestler (novel), Neutralia, Portugal (country), pp.44–45, A2

Arrow (TV)
Lian Yu, China (island), pp.102–103, D2/E2
North China Sea, China (sea), pp.102–103, D2/E2

Artam: One Reich, One Race, a Tenth Leader by Volkmar Weiss (novel), Artam (fictional country), pp.44–45, D3

Artemis Fowl series by Eoin Colfer (novels)
Fowl Manor, Ireland (estate), pp.64–65, B2
Villa Éco, Ireland (building), pp.64–65, B2

Arthur (TV), Elwood City, Crown City, Quebec (city), pp.26–27, E1

Article 15 (film), Lalgaon, India (town), pp.78–79, C4

As the World Turns (TV), Oakdale, Illinois (city), pp.16–17, D4

As Told By Ginger (TV), Sheltered Shrubs, Connecticut (town), pp.14–15, C5

Asa-Nisse by Stig Cederholm (comic strip), Knohult, Sweden (village), pp.56–57, B2

Ash vs The Evil Dead (TV), Elk Grove, Michigan (town), pp.14–15, A5

Asking for It by Louise O'Neill (novel), Ballinatoom, Ireland (town), pp.64–65, A2

Asterix and the Picts by René Goscinny (comic book), Loch Androll, Scotland (natural feature), pp.64–65, B5

Asterix the Gaul by René Goscinny and Albert Uderzo (comic books), Asterix's Village, France (village), pp.44–45, B3

Astro City (comic)
Astro City, Washington (city), pp.18–19, B6
Gaines River, Washington (river), pp.18–19, B6
Hood County, Washington (county), pp.18–19, B6
Mount Kirby, Washington (mountain), pp.18–19, B6
Wildenberg River, Washington (river), pp.18–19, B6

Asura: the City of Madness (film), Annam, South Korea (city), pp.102–103, E3

Asuravithu by M.T. Vasudevan Nair (novel), Kizhakkemuri, India (village), pp.78–79, B2

At the Mountains of Madness by H.P. Lovecraft (novella)
City of the Elder Things (city), pp.114–115, E3
Miskatonic Expedition Southern Base Camp (camp), pp.114–115, D2
Miskatonic Expedition Northern Base Camp (camp), pp.114–115, E1
Mountains of Madness, The (mountain range), pp.114–115, E3
Plateau of Leng, The (city), pp.114–115, E3
Professor Lake's Camp (Miskatonic Expedition, camp), pp.114–115, E2
Violet Mountains, The (mountain range), pp.114–115, E3

Atlantic (film), Atlantic, Atlantic Ocean (wreck), pp.126–127, B4

Atlantic Fury by Hammond Innes (novel), Laerg, Scotland (island), pp.64–65, A5

Atlantis: The Lost Empire (film)
City of Atlantis, The, Atlantis (fictional city), pp.126–127, C6
Shub Nigruth (city), pp.114–115, E3
Ulysses, Atlantic Ocean (wreck), pp.126–127, C5

Atlas Shrugged by Ayn Rand (novel), Galt's Gulch, Colorado (town), pp.18–19, D4

Atoll K (film), Atoll K or Crusoeland, Pacific Ocean (island), pp.120–121, D2

Atomic Train (film)
Jackson Summit, Colorado (natural feature), pp.18–19, D4
Miller's Bend, Colorado (natural feature), pp.18–19, D4
Silver Gorge, Colorado (natural feature), pp.18–19, D4
Stillwater, Utah (town), pp.18–19, D4
Westrail, Utah/Colorado (railway), pp.18–19, D4

Attack of the Killer Tomatoes (film), San Zucchini, California (city), pp.18–19, B3

Aubrey-Maturin series by Patrick O'Brian (novels), Shelmerston, England (town), pp.64–65, C1

Aurorarama by Jean Christophe-Valtat (novel), New Venice, Arctic (city), pp.26–27, C2

Austin Powers films (films), Kreplachistan (fictional country), pp.72–73, E4

Australia (film), Faraway Downs, Northern Territory (estate), pp.108–109, C4

Avalanche Annie: A Not So Tall Tale by Lisa Wheeler (book)
Michisota (fictional state), pp.16–17, C6
Mount Himalachia, Michisota (mountain), pp.16–17, C6

Avengers Endgame (film), New Asgard, Norway (town), pp.56–57, B5

Avenida Brasil (TV), Divino, Brazil (town), pp.38–39, D3

Azumanga Daioh by Kiyohiko Azuma (manga/anime), Azumanga High School, Japan (building), pp.96–97, E1

Azur Lane (video game/anime)
Azur Lane Base, Pacific Ocean (building), pp.120–121, B4
Sakura Empire (fictional country), pp.96–97, B1/C1

B & B (TV), Oneonroa, New Zealand (town), pp.108–109, F2

Baaz by Anjua Chauhan (novel), Chakkahera, India (village), pp.78–79, B5

BabaKiueria (film), BabaKiueria (whole) (country), pp.108–109, D2/E2

Baby Island by Carol Ryrie Brink (novel)
Baby Island, Pacific Ocean (island), pp.120–121, C3
SS *Orminta*, Pacific Ocean (wreck), pp.120–121, C3

Back to the Future films, Hill Valley, California (town), pp.18–19, A4

Back to the Future Part 3 (film), Eastwood Ravine (Shonash Ravine/Clayton Ravine), California (natural feature), pp.18–19, A4

Backtrack (film), False Creek, Victoria (town), pp.108–109, D1

Bad Taste (film), Kaihoro, New Zealand (town), pp.108–109, F2

Badenheim 1939 by Aharon Appelfeld (novel), Badenheim, Austria (town), pp.44–45, D3

Balamory (TV), Balamory, Scotland (town), pp.64–65, B4

Ballykissangel (TV), Ballykissangel, Ireland (village), pp.64–65, B2

Ballyyahoo books by Grace Jolliffe (books), Ballyyahoo, Ireland (town), pp.64–65, A3

Barbie (toy line)
Lake Willows, Wisconsin (lake/town), pp.16–17, D5
Willows, Wisconsin (town), pp.16–17, D5

Baron 1898 (theme park), Heikant, Netherlands (village), pp.44–45, C4

Batman Begins (film), Temple of the League of Shadows, Bhutan (building), pp.78–79, D4

Batman Ninja (film)
Gakuju Sharaso Castle, Japan (building), pp.96–97, C3
Juroku Plant Poison Castle, Japan (building), pp.96–97, C2
Trojan Birdman Castle, Japan (building), pp.96–97, C2
Village of the Bat Clan, Japan (village), pp.96–97, B2/C2

Batman: The Ultimate Evil by Andrew Vachss (novel), Udon Khai (fictional country), pp.90–91, B3

Battle Royale by Koushun Takami (novel)
Okishima, Japan (island), pp.96–97, B2
Shiroiwa, Japan (city), pp.96–97, B2

Beasts Made of Night by Tochi Onyebuchi (novel), Kos, Nigeria (city), pp.84–85, B4

Beau Geste by P.C. Wren (novel), Fort Zinderneuf, Algeria (building), pp.84–85, B5

Beau Hunks (film), Fort Arid, Algeria (building), pp.84–85, B5

Beautiful Creatures by Kami Garcia and Margaret Stohl (novel/film), Gatlin, South Carolina (town), pp.14–15, B3

Beauty is a Wound by Eka Kurniawan (novel), Halimunda, Indonesia (town), pp.90–91, B1

Beavis and Butthead (TV), Highland, Texas (town), pp.16–17, A3

Bedknobs and Broomsticks (film), Pepperinge Eye, England (village), pp.64–65, D1

Beetlejuice (film), Winter River, Connecticut (town), pp.14–15, C5

Behemoth (film), Ascension, Washington (town), pp.18–19, A6

Bella Calamidades (TV), Horneros, Colombia (town), pp.38–39, A5/B5

Bellbird (TV), Bellbird, Victoria (village), pp.108–109, D1

Bellevue (film), Bellevue, Quebec (town), pp.26–27, E1

Below (film), HMHS *Fort James*/USS *Tiger Shark*, Atlantic Ocean (wrecks), pp.44–45, B3

Ben 10 (TV), Plumbers' Base, South Dakota (building), pp.16–17, A5

Beneath a Steel Sky (video game), Union City, New South Wales (city/state), pp.108–109, E2

Benjamin the Elephant (radio/TV)
Alstadt/Glückstadt, Germany (towns), pp.44–45, D4
Neustadt, Germany (city), pp.44–45, D4

Benny Cooperman series by Howard Engel (novels), Grantham, Ontario (town), pp.26–27, C2

Beowulf (poem), Heorot, Denmark (building), pp.56–57, B1

Best Exotic Marigold Hotel (film), Best Exotic Marigold Hotel, India (building), pp.78–79, B4

Betrayed By Rita Hayworth by Manuel Puig (novel), Coronel Vallejos, Argentina (village), pp.38–39, B2

Between the Assassinations by Aravind Adiga (novel), Kittur, India (town), pp.78–79, B3

Bhoot – Part One: The Haunted Ship (film), *Sea Bird*, India (wreck), pp.78–79, B3

Bhowani Junction by John Masters (novel/film), Bhowani, India (town), pp.78–79, B4

Bienvenido Mr Marshall (film), Villar del Rio, Spain (town), pp.44–45, B2

Big Eden (film), Big Eden, Montana (town), pp.18–19, C6

Big Fish (film)
Ashton, Alabama (town), pp.14–15, A2
Spectre, Alabama (town), pp.14–15, A2

Big Girl, Small Town by Michelle Gallen (novel), Aghybogey, Northern Ireland (town), pp.64–65, B3

Big Hero 6 (film/TV), San Fransokyo, California (city), pp.18–19, A4

Big Little Lies by Liane Moriarty (novel), Pirriwee, New South Wales (town), pp.108–109, F4

Big Thunder Mountain Railroad (theme parks)
Big Thunder Mountain, Utah/Arizona (mountain), pp.18–19, C3
Grizzly Gulch, Arizona (town), pp.18–19, C3
Rainbow Ridge, Utah (town), pp.18–19, C3
Thunder Mesa, Arizona (town), pp.18–19, C3
Tumbleweed, Arizona (town), pp.18–19, C3

Biggles: Secret Agent by W.E. Johns (novel), Lucrania (fictional country), pp.44–45, C3

Biggles Follows On by W.E. Johns (novel), Kratsen, China (village), pp.102–103, D3

Biggles Foreign Legionnaire by W.E. Johns (novel), Valley of the Tartars, Iraq (natural feature), pp.72–73, C3

Biggles: The Adventure of the Golden Shirts by W.E. Johns (novel)
Gelden Island, Indonesia (island), pp.90–91, B1
Van Husen, Indonesia (wreck), pp.90–91, B1

Biggles: The Adventure of the Oxidized Grotto by W.E. Johns (novel), Mojok, Malaysia (building/estate), pp.90–91, B2

Billions (TV), Sandicot, New York (town), pp.14–15, B5

Billy Bunter (TV), Greyfriars School, England (building), pp.64–65, D2

Billy Elliot (film), Everington, England (town), pp.64–65, D2

Billy Liar by Keith Waterhouse (novel), Stradhoughton, England (town), pp.64–65, C3

'Billy the Mountain' by Frank Zappa (song), Billy the Mountain, California (mountain), pp.18–19, A3/B3

Binbougami ga! by Yoshiaki Sukeno (manga/anime), Butsumetsu, Japan (city), pp.96–97, C2

Bionic 6 (TV), Cypress Cove, California (city), pp.18–19, A5

Bioshock franchise (video games), Rapture, Atlantic Ocean (city), pp.26–27, F4

Birds Without Wings by Louis de Bernières (novel), Eskibahçe, Turkey (village), pp.72–73, B3

Black & White (TV), Harbor City, Taiwan (city), pp.102–103, D1

Black Butler (manga/anime), *Campania*, Atlantic Ocean (wreck), pp.126–127, B4

Black House by Stephen King (novel)
Centralia, Wisconsin (town), pp.16–17, C5
French Landing, Wisconsin (town), pp.16–17, C5

Black Lagoon by Rei Hiroe (manga/anime), Lovelace Estate, Venezuela (building), pp.38–39, B5
Roanapur, Thailand (city), pp.90–91, B3

Black Lightning (comic/TV), Freeland, Georgia (city), pp.14–15, B3

Black Mischief by Evelyn Waugh (novel)
Azanian Empire (fictional country/empire), pp.84–85, D4
Debra Down, Azanian Empire (fictional city), pp.84–85, D4
Matodi, Azanian Empire (fictional town), pp.84–85, D4
Mhomala, Azanian Empire (fictional town), pp.84–85, D4
Sakuyu Channel, Azanian Empire (fictional sea), pp.84–85, D4

Black Narcissus by Rumer Godden (novel/film)
Mopu, India (village), pp.78–79, C4/D4
Nanga Dalle, India (mountain), pp.78–79, C4/D4

Black Spot (TV), Villefranche, France (town), pp.44–45, C3

Blackadder III (TV), Dunny on the Wold, England (village), pp.64–65, D2

Blazing Saddles (film), Rock Ridge, Unknown (town), pp.18–19, B3

Bleach by Tite Kubo (manga/anime), Karakura Town, Japan (town), pp.96–97, E1

Bleak House by Charles Dickens (novel)
Bleak House, England (building), pp.64–65, D1
Borrioboola-Gha, Nigeria (village), pp.84–85, B4
Chesney Wold, England (estate), pp.64–65, D3

Blinky Bill (various), Greenpatch, Queensland (town), pp.108–109, D3

Blood Prejudice by A.R. Nai (novel), Beisha, China (town), pp.102–103, D1

Blott on the Landscape by Tom Sharpe (novel/TV), Worford, England (town), pp.64–65, C2

Blue by Pat Grant (graphic novel)
Bolton, New South Wales (town), pp.108–109, D2
Crink's Creek, New South Wales (town), pp.108–109, D2

Blue Heelers (TV)
Evanleigh, Victoria (city), pp.108–109, D1
Hetherington, Victoria (region), pp.108–109, D2
Mount Thomas, Victoria (town), pp.108–109, D2
St David's, Victoria (town), pp.108–109, D2
Widgeree, Victoria (town), pp.108–109, D2

BoBoiBoy (TV), Pulau Rintis, Malaysia (island), pp.90–91, B2

Bojack Horesem (TV), Pacific Ocean City, California (city), pp.18–19, A3

Bonanza / Ponderosa (TV), Pondarosa Ranch, Nevada (building), pp.18–19, C3

Bond (play), Nisi, China (city), pp.102–103, D2

Bondänger (TV), Bondånger, Sweden (town), pp.56–57, F1

Book of Life (film), San Angel, Mexico (town), pp.32–33, D2

Book: A Novel by Robert Grudin (novel), Washagon (fictional state), pp.18–19, B6

Boomers (TV), Thurnemouth, England (town), pp.64–65, D2

Borat (film), Kuzcek, Kazakhstan (village), pp.72–73, D4

Border Country by Raymond Williams (novel), Glynmawr, Wales (village), pp.64–65, C2

Boris Karloff's Thriller (TV), Druid's Stones, The, Wales (stone circle), pp.64–65, C2

Born and Bred (TV), Ormston, England (town), pp.64–65, C3

Boston Legal (TV), Belmont Falls, Massachusetts (town), pp.14–15, C5

Bottlebrush Creek by Maya Linnell (novel), Port Fairview, Victoria (town), pp.108–109, D2

Bowl of Cherries by Millard Kaufman (novel)
Assama, Iraq (region), pp.72–73, C2
Coproliabad, Iraq (town), pp.72–73, C2

Brass (TV), Utterley, England (town), pp.64–65, C3

Brass Eye (TV), Ballakreen, Ireland (village), pp.64–65, A2

Brave (film)
Kingdom of Dunbroch, Dunbroch (fictional country), pp.64–65, B5
Sea of Celts, Scotland (sea), pp.64–65, A4/B4

Breakfast of Champions by Kurt Vonnegut (novel/film), Midland City, Indiana (town), pp.14–15, A4

Breakfast on Pluto by Patrick McCabe (novel/film), Tyreelin, Ireland (town), pp.64–65, A3

Breakheart Pass by Alistair MacLean (novel/film)
Breakheart Pass, Nevada (natural feature), pp.18–19, B4
Fort Humboldt, Nevada (building), pp.18–19, B4
Reese City/Myrtle, Nevada (town), pp.18–19, C4

Breath by Tim Winton (novel), Sawyer, Western Australia (town), pp.108–109, B2

Breathing in Dust by Tim Z. Hernandez (novel), Catela, California (town), pp.18–19, A3

Brickleberry (TV), Brickleberry National Park, Illinois (natural feature), pp.16–17, D4/D5

Brideshead Revisited by Evelyn Waugh (novel/film), Brideshead, England (estate), pp.64–65, C2

Black Mischief...

Brigadoon (film), Brigadoon, Scotland (unmappable village), pp.64–65, C4

Brigham City (film), Kirtland County, Utah (town), pp.18–19, C4

Bring the Jubilee by Ward Moore (novel), Deseret (fictional state), pp.18–19, C4

Broadchurch (TV), Broadchurch, England (village), pp.64–65, C2

Broforce (video game), Irakistan (fictional country), pp.72–73, C2

Brokeback Mountain (short story/film)
Brokeback Mountain, Wyoming (mountain), pp.18–19, D5
Signal, Wyoming (town), pp.18–19, D5

Brontë juvenalia and later writings of Charlotte Brontë
Adrianopolis, Angria (city), pp.84–85, B4
Angria, Angria (country), pp.84–85, B4

Brontë juvenalia
Alcona (fictional country), pp.90–91, E4
Angora (fictional country), pp.90–91, E4
Exina (fictional country), pp.90–91, E4
Frenchy Land, Glass Town Federation (fictional country), pp.84–85, B3
Gaaldine, Pacific Ocean (island/nation), pp.90–91, F3
Glass Town Confederacy (fictional bloc), pp.84–85, A3
Gondal, Pacific Ocean (fictional country), pp.90–91, F4
Monkey's Land, Glass Town Federation (fictional country), pp.84–85, A3
Paris, Frenchy's Land (fictional city), pp.84–85, B3
Parry's Land, Glass Town Federation (fictional region), pp.84–85, A4
Regina, Angora (fictional city), pp.90–91, F4
Ross's Land, Glass Town Federation (fictional region), pp.84–85, A4
Sneaky's Land, Glass Town Federation (fictional region), pp.84–85, B4
Stump's Land, Glass Town Federation (fictional country), pp.84–85, A4
Verdopolis, Glass Town Federation (fictional city), pp.84–85, B4
Wellington's Land, Glass Town Federation (fictional region), pp.84–85, A4

Brookside (TV), Brookside, England (Area/Street), pp.64–65, C3

Brother Fish by Bryce Courtenay (novel), Queen's Island, Tasmania (island), pp.108–109, D1

Brother in the Land by Robert Swindells (novel), Skipley, England (town), pp.64–65, C3

Brown on Resolution by C.S. Forester (novel), Resolution Island, Galapagos Islands (island), pp.38–39, A1

Buck Danny (comics), Managuay (fictional country), pp.32–33, D2

Buerak (band), Ust-Chilim, Russia (city), pp.102–103, E1

Buffy the Vampire Slayer (TV), Sunnydale, California (town), pp.18–19, A3

Bug Jack Barron by Norman Spinrad (novel), Evers, Mississippi (city), pp.16–17, D2

Bully (video game), Bullworth, New Hampshire (town), pp.14–15, D5

Burka Avenger (TV), Halwapur, Pakistan (town), pp.78–79, B5

Burmese Days by George Orwell (novel), Kyauktada, Myanmar (town), pp.90–91, A4

Burn! (film), Queimada, Lesser Antilles (island), pp.32–33, F2

Burnistoun (TV), Burnistoun, Scotland (town), pp.64–65, C4

Cabbages and Kings by O. Henry (novel), Anchuria (fictional country), pp.32–33, D2

Cabin Pressure (radio), Fitton, England (town), pp.64–65, D3

Cabocla (TV), Pau d'Alho, Brazil (town), pp.38–39, D3
Vila da Mata, Brazil (town), pp.38–39, D3

Cakes and Ale by W. Somerset Maugham (novel)
Ferne Bay, England (town), pp.64–65, D2
Terkenbury, England (city), pp.64–65, D2

Caleta del Sol (TV), Caleta del Sol, Chile (town), pp.38–39, B3

Call Me the Breeze by Patrick McCabe (novel), Scotsfield, Ireland (town), pp.64–65, A3

Call of Cthulhu: The Official Video Game (video game), Darkwater Island, Massachusetts (island), pp.14–15, D5

Call of Duty: Modern Warfare (video game)
Sahkra, Urzikstan (fictional city), pp.72–73, C3
Urzikstan (fictional country), pp.72–73, B3/C3

Camberwick Green (TV), Camberwick Green, England (village), pp.64–65, D1

Came a Hot Friday by Ronald Hugh Morrieson (novel), Tainuia Junction, New Zealand (town), pp.108–109, F2

Camp Camp (web animation)
Camp Campbell, Washington (building), pp.18–19, B6
Lake Lilac, Washington (lake), pp.18–19, B6
Sleepy Peak Peak, Washington (mountain), pp.18–19, B6

Camp Lazlo (TV), Prickly Pines, Wisconsin (town), pp.16–17, D5

Campanas en la Noche (TV), Lago Místico, Argentina (town), pp.38–39, B2

Campus Trilogy, David Lodge (novel)
Euphoria (fictional state), pp.18–19, A4
Plotinus, Euphoria (fictional city), pp.18–19, A4
Canada by Richard Ford (novel)
Fort Royal, Saskatchewan (town), pp.26–27, C1
Partreau, Saskatchewan (town), pp.26–27, C1
Candide by Voltaire (novel)
El Dorado, Peru (city), pp.38–39, B4
Waldberghoff-trarbk-dikdorff, Germany (town), pp.44–45, C4
Cannibal Holocaust (film), Green Inferno, The, Brazil/Venezuela (natural feature), pp.38–39, B5
Cannibal Women in the Avocado Jungle of Death (film), Avocado Jungle, The, California (natural feature), pp.18–19, B4
Cape Grimm by Carmel Bird (novel)
Cape Grimm, Tasmania (natural feature), pp.108–109, D1
Skye, Tasmania (village), pp.108–109, D1
Capillaria by Frigyes Karinthy (novel), Capillaria, Atlantis (fictional sunken country), pp.126–127, B4/C4
Captain Planet and the Planeteers (TV), Hope Island, Bahamas (island), pp.32–33, E3
Captain Pugwash by John Ryan (various)
Bogle Bay, Scotland (natural feature), pp.64–65, B5
Bogshire, Scotland (county), pp.64–65, B5
Dolphin, Greenland/Northern Provinces (wreck), pp.26–27, D4
Flying Dustman, Caribbean (wreck), pp.32–33, F2
Hotta-Watta-Bottle, Land of the Stinkas (fictional mountain) pp.32–33, C2
Land of the Stinkas (fictional region), pp.32–33, C2
Pajamah Islands, The, Caribbean (island chain), pp.32–33, F2
San Fiasco, Scotland (wreck), pp.64–65, B5
Captain Scarlet (TV), Glen Carry Castle, Scotland (building), pp.64–65, C4
Cara e Coroa (TV), Porto do Céu, Brazil (town), pp.38–39, D3
Cardcaptor Sakura by CLAMP (manga/anime), Tomoeda, Japan (city), pp.96–97, D3
Caribbean by James A. Michener (novel), All Saints (fictional island), pp.32–33, F2
Carn by Patrick McCabe (novel), Carn, Ireland (town), pp.64–65, B3
Carpentaria by Alexis Wright (novel), Desperance, Queensland (town), pp.108–109, D4
Carrie by Stephen King (various), Chamberlain, Maine (town), pp.14–15, D6
Carry on Abroad! (film)
Costa Bomm, Spain (region), pp.44–45, C2
Elsbels, Spain (island), pp.44–45, C2
Carry on Cowboy (film), Stodge City, Kansas (town), pp.16–17, B4
Carry On Up the Khyber (film), Kalabar, India (region), pp.78–79, B5
Cars (film)
Cadillac Range, Arizona (mountain range), pp.18–19, C3
Carburetor County, Arizona (county), pp.18–19, C3
Radiator Springs, Arizona (town), pp.18–19, C3
Ornament Valley, Arizona (natural feature), pp.18–19, C3
Cars 2 (film), *Porto Corsa*, Monaco (city), pp.44–45, C2
Carter Country (TV), Clinton Corners, Georgia (town), pp.14–15, B2
Casper (film), Whipstaff Manor, Maine (building), pp.14–15, C6
Cast Away (film), Cast Away Island, Pacific Ocean (island), pp.120–121, D2
Castle by David Macaulay (book), Aberwyvern Castle, Wales (building), pp.64–65, C4
Castle Dangerous by Sir Walter Scott (novel), Castle Dangerous, Scotland (building), pp.64–65, C4
Castle Rock by Stephen King (various), Castle Rock, Maine (town), pp.14–15, D6
Cat Ballou (film), *Wolf City, Wyoming* (town), pp.18–19, D5
Cat's Cradle by Kurt Vonnegut (novel)
Bolivar, San Lorenzo (island) (city), pp.32–33, E2
San Lorenzo, San Lorenzo (island) (island/nation), pp.32–33, E2
Cavafy's Stone and Other Village Stories by Harry Mark Petrakis (short stories), Fanaron, Greece (village), pp.44–45, E1
Cedar Cove by Debbie Macomber (novels), Cedar Cove, Washington (island/town), pp.18–19, A6
Cedar Valley by Holly Throsby (novel), Cedar Valley, New South Wales (town), pp.108–109, D2
Celeste (video game), Forsaken City, British Columbia (abandoned town), pp.26–27, B1
Celestial Bodies by Jokha Alharthi (novel), Al-Awafi, Oman (town), pp.72–73, D1
Centennial by James A. Michener (novel), Centennial, Colorado (town), pp.16–17, A4
Century Trilogy by Ken Follett (novels), Aberowen, Wales (town), pp.64–65, C2
Cerromaior by Manuel de Fonseca (novel), Cerromaior, Portugal (town), pp.44–45, A2

Charlie and the Chocolate Factory by Roald Dahl (novel/film)
Prince Pondicherry's Chocolate Palace, India (building), pp.78–79, C3
Loompaland, Brazil (region), pp.38–39, B5
Cherry Falls (film), Cherry Falls, Virginia (town), pp.14–15, C5
Chicken Run (film), Tweedy's Farm, England (building), pp.64–65, C3
Chief Inspector Armand Gamache series by Louise Penny (novels), Three Pines, Quebec (town), pp.26–27, E1
Chigley (TV), Chigley, England (village), pp.64–65, D1
Children of Dynmouth by William Trevor (novel), Dynmouth, England (town), pp.64–65, C1
Children of the Corn by Stephen King (novel/film)
Gatlin, Nebraska (town), pp.16–17, A4
Hemingford Home, Nebraska (town), pp.16–17, A4
Children of the Stones (TV), Milbury, England (village), pp.64–65, C2
Chilly Beach (TV), Chilly Beach, Nunavut (town), pp.26–27, D4
China Sky by Pearl S. Buck (novel/film)
Chen-li, China (town), pp.102–103, D3
Tong Mountain, China (mountain), pp.102–103, D2
Treaty Port, China (city), pp.102–103, D2
Chip 'n' Dale: Rescue Rangers (TV), Tramplonia, Spain (town), pp.44–45, B2
Chitty Chitty Bang Bang by Ian Fleming (novel/film), Vulgaria (fictional country), pp.44–45, D3
Chocolat by Joanne Harris (novel/film), Lansquenet-sous-Tannes, France (village), pp.44–45, B2/B3
Chocolate com Pimenta (TV), Ventura, Brazil (town), pp.38–39, C3
Christine by Stephen King (novel/film)
Libertyville, Pennsylvania (town), pp.14–15, B4
Rockbridge, California (town), pp.18–19, A3
Christmas in Evergreen series (films), Evergreen, Vermont (town), pp.14–15, C6
Christmas Joy (film), Crystal Falls, North Carolina (town), pp.14–15, B3
Chuck (TV), Costa Gravas (fictional island/nation), pp.38–39, D3/D3
Churyō Manroku (literature/folklore), Rokurokubi Village, Japan (village), pp.96–97, B2
Cicak-Man series (films), Metrofulus, Malaysia (city/state), pp.90–91, B2
Cinema Paradiso (film), Giancaldo, Italy (town), pp.44–45, D1
Circle of Friends by Maeve Binchy (novel), Knockglen, Ireland (town), pp.64–65, B2
Citizen Kane (film)
Little Salem, Colorado (town), pp.18–19, D3
Xanadu, Florida (building), pp.14–15, B2
City of Bohane by Kevin Barry (novel)
Big Nothin', The, Ireland (region), pp.64–65, A3
Bohane, Ireland (city), pp.64–65, A3
City of Heroes (video game), Paragon City, Rhode Island (city), pp.14–15, C5
Clannad (manga/anime), Hikarizaka, Japan (city), pp.96–97, D2
Class Reunion (film), Sankt Nikolaus, Austria (town), pp.44–45, D3
ClassicaLoid (anime), Mamadon River, Brazil (river), pp.38–39, C5
Claudian by Henry Herman (play), Charydos, Turkey (city), pp.72–73, B3
Climbing Mouse and the Other Animals in the Hunchback Wood (TV), Hakkebakkeskogen, Norway (town), pp.56–57, A2
Clochermerle by Gabriel Chevallier (novel), Clochemerle, France (village), pp.44–45, C3
Cloud Atlas by David Mitchell (film)
Neo Seoul, South Korea (city), pp.102–103, E3
Mauna Sol, Hawaii (mountain), pp.18–19, D1
Ne So Copros (fictional bloc/super-region), pp.102–103, D3/E3
Clouds of Witness by Dorothy L. Sayers (novel), Riddlesdale, England (village), pp.64–65, C3
Cloudy With a Chance of Meatballs (film), Swallow Falls or Chewandswallow, Atlantic Ocean (island), pp.126–127, A4
Club de Cuervos (TV), Nuevo Toledo, Mexico (city), pp.32–33, B2
Club Paradise (film), Saint Nicholas, pp.32–33, D2
Club Penguin (video game)
Clam Waters (sea), pp.114–115, A3
Igloo Village (village), pp.114–115, A3
Soda Seas (sea), pp.114–115, A3
Club Penguin Island (village), pp.114–115, A3
Coastliners and Holy Fools by Joanne Harris (novel), Le Devin, France (island), pp.44–45, A3
Cocaine Nights by J.G. Ballard (novel), Estrella de Mar, Spain (town), pp.44–45, A1
Cockleshell Bay (TV), Cockleshell Bay, England (village), pp.64–65, D1
Coco/Cars 3 (film), Santa Cecilia, Mexico (town), pp.32–33, B2
Code Geass (anime)
Area 2, Holy Britannian Empire (fictional region), pp.26–27, C1

Area 3, Holy Britannian Empire (fictional region), pp.32–33, B3
Area 4, Holy Britannian Empire (fictional region), pp.26–27, D4
Area 5, Holy Britannian Empire (fictional region), pp.26–27, E4
Area 7, Holy Britannian Empire (fictional region), pp.18–19, D3
Area 8, Holy Britannian Empire (fictional region), pp.38–39, B1/C1
Area 11, Japan (country), pp.96–97, B3
Ashford Academy, Japan (building), pp.96–97, E1
Britannian Concession, Japan (region), pp.96–97, E1/F1
Pendragon, Holy Britannian Empire (fictional city), pp.32–33, A4
Code Lyoko (TV)
Factory/Lyoko, The, Paris, France (building), pp.44–45, E3
Kadic Academy, Paris, France (building), pp.44–45, E3
Cold Comfort Farm by Stella Gibbons (novel), Howling, England (village), pp.64–65, C2
Cold Pursuit (film), Kehoe, Colorado (town), pp.18–19, D4
Cold Turkey (film), Eagle Rock, Iowa (town), pp.16–17, C4
Colonel Bleep (TV), Zero Zero Island (land), Atlantic Ocean (land), pp.84–85, A3/B3
Come Midnight Monday by David Burke (novel/TV)
Paradise Gap, Victoria (town), pp.108–109, D1
Port Danville, Victoria (town), pp.108–109, D1
Winnawadgery, Victoria (town), pp.108–109, D1
Começar de Novo (TV), Ouro Negro, Brazil (town), pp.38–39, C4
Coming to America (film), Zamunda (fictional country), pp.84–85, B3/C3
Command and Conquer: Generals (video game), Aldastan (fictional country), pp.72–73, D2
Command and Conquer series (video games), GDI Institute for Liquid Tiberium, Northern Territory (building), pp.108–109, C4
Commander in Chief (TV), San Pasquale (fictional country), pp.38–39, D4
Commandos 2: Men of Courage (video game), Wilson's Island, Pacific Ocean (island), pp.120–121, B3
Community (TV), Greendale, Colorado (town), pp.16–17, A4
Con Air (film), Lerner Field, Nevada (building), pp.18–19, B4
Conan books of Robert E. Howard (novels)
Alkmeeon, Greece (building), pp.44–45, E1
Afghulistan, Afghanistan (country), pp.72–73, D2/E2
Anshan, Iranistan (fictional city), pp.72–73, D2
Aquilonia, France (country/region), pp.44–45, B3
Asgard, Northern Scandinavia (region), pp.56–57, A1
Border Kingdoms, The, Germany/Denmark (region), pp.56–57, A1/B1/C1
Darfar (fictional country), pp.84–85, B3
Himelian Mountains, Nepal (mountain range), pp.78–79, C4/C5
Himelian Mountains, Tibet (mountain range), pp.102–103, E3
Hyperborea, Finland (region), pp.56–57, D3
Iranistan (fictional country), pp.72–73, D2
Kesham (fictional country), pp.72–73, D2
Khemi, Morocco (city), pp.84–85, A5
Khitai, China (country), pp.102–103, D4
Khoraja (fictional country), pp.72–73, B2/C2
Khorshemish, Syria (city), pp.72–73, D3
Kosala, India (region), pp.78–79, C4
Koth, Syria (country), pp.72–73, B3/C3
Nemedia, Germany (region), pp.44–45, D4
Ophir, Italy (region), pp.44–45, B3
Poitain, France (region), pp.44–45, B3
Punt (fictional country), pp.84–85, C5/D5
Shem, Israel (country), pp.72–73, A4
Stygia (fictional country), pp.84–85, C5
Styx River, Egypt (river), pp.84–85, C5
Taian Mountains, Egypt (mountain range), pp.84–85, C5
Vendhya, India (country), pp.78–79, B4/C4
Vilayet Sea, Caspian Sea (sea), pp.72–73, C3
Yamatai, Japan (country) later Conan novels inspired by Robert E. Howard, pp.96–97, C2
Zarkheba River, various (river), pp.84–85, C4
Zembabwei (fictional country), pp.84–85, D4
Zingara, Spain/Portugal (region), pp.44–45, A2/B2
Conan the Avenger by Björn Nyberg (novels), Uttara Kuru, Pakistan (region), pp.78–79, B5
Conde Vrolok/Count Vrolok (TV), Santa Bárbara, Chile (town), pp.38–39, B4
Condorito (comics)
Buenas Peras, Chile (town), pp.38–39, B2
Pelotillehue, Chile (city), pp.38–39, B2
Congo by Michael Crichton (novel), Zinj (The Lost City of Zinj), DRC (city/state), pp.84–85, C3

Conrack (film), Yamacraw Island, South Carolina (island), pp.14–15, B2
Cool Water by Dianne Warren (novel), Juliet, Saskatchewan (town), pp.26–27, C1
Cooties (film), Fort Chicken, Illinois (town), pp.16–17, D4
Copperopolis (comic), Copperopolis, Wales (city), pp.64–65, C3
Coração de Estudante (TV), Nova Aliança, Brazil (town), pp.38–39, D3
Coraline (film), Pink Palace Apartments, Oregon (building), pp.18–19, A5
Corazón Indomable (TV), Isla Dorada, Mexico (town), pp.32–33, B2
Cordel Encantado (TV), Brogodó, Brazil (town), pp.38–39, D4
Corner Gas (TV), Dog River and Wullerton, Saskatchewan (town), pp.26–27, C1
Coronado (film), El Coronado (fictional country), pp.32–33, D1
Coronation Street (TV), Weatherfield, England (town), pp.64–65, C2
Corpo Dourado (TV), Marimbá, Brazil (village), pp.38–39, D3
Cougar Town (TV), Gulfhaven, Florida (town), pp.14–15, B1
Count Duckula
Go-A-Way Mine, The, Yukon (natural feature), pp.26–27, B2
Goldville, Yukon (town), pp.26–27, B2
McCastle McDuckula, Scotland (building), pp.64–65, B4
Count Geiger's Blues by Michael Bishop (novel)
Oconee (fictional state), pp.14–15, A3
Salonika, Oconee (fictional city), pp.14–15, A3
Couples by John Updike (novel), Tarbox, Massachusetts (town), pp.14–15, D5
Courage the Cowardly Dog (TV), Nowhere, Kansas (town), pp.16–17, B4
Court of Lord Lyon (heraldry)
Blankshire, Scotland (county), pp.64–65, B4
Blanktown, Scotland (town), pp.64–65, B4
Cover Her Face by P.D. James (novel), Martingale, England (building), pp.64–65, D2
Cowboys and Aliens (film), Absolution, New Mexico (town), pp.18–19, B3
Craig of the Creek (TV), Herkleston, Maryland (town), pp.14–15, C4
Crampton Hodnet by Barbara Pym (novel), Crampton Hodnet, England (town), pp.64–65, C2
Cranford (TV), Cranford, England (village), pp.64–65, C2
Crank Yankers (TV), Yankerville, Nevada (town), pp.18–19, B3
Crash Bandicoot series (video games)
Cortex Island, Pacific Ocean (island), pp.120–121, D2
N. Sanity Island, Pacific Ocean (island), pp.120–121, B2
Wumpa Islands, Pacific Ocean (island chain), pp.120–121, B3
Crash Landing on You (TV), Taean-gun, North Korea (village), pp.102–103, E3
Crazy for You (musical), Deadrock, Nevada (town), pp.18–19, B5
Crimson Peak (film), Allerdale Hall, England (building), pp.64–65, C3
Critters (film), Grover's Bend, Kansas (town), pp.16–17, C3
Crock of Gold by James Stephens (novel)
Glyn Cagny, Ireland (natural feature), pp.64–65, A2
Gort Na Cloca, Ireland (village), pp.64–65, A2
Crocodile Dundee (film), Walkabout Creek, Northern Territory (village), pp.108–109, C4
Cromartie High School (TV), Mount Rockmore, South Dakota (mountain), pp.16–17, A5
Cromartie High School by Eiji Nonaka (manga/anime), Cromartie High School, Japan (building), pp.96–97, D2
Crossroads (TV), Crossroads Motel, England (building), pp.64–65, C2
Crotchet Castle by Thomas Love Peacock (novel)
Apodidraskiana (fictional state), pp.14–15, B2
Dotandcarryonetown, Apodidraskiana (fictional town), pp.14–15, B2
Crow Lake by Mary Lawson (novel), Crow Lake, Ontario (town), pp.26–27, A4
Crown For Christmas (film), Winshire (fictional country), pp.44–45, C3
Crows by Hiroshi Takahashi (manga), Toarushi, Japan (city), pp.96–97, C2
Cruise Into Terror (film)
Obeah, Mexico (wreck/building), pp.32–33, C3
Tomb of Ramses Amun Ankh, Egypt (building), pp.84–85, C5
Cry the Beloved Country by Alan Paton (novel/film), Ndotsheni, South Africa (town), pp.84–85, C2
Crying Through the Wind: The Story of Oisin Kelly by Iona Carroll (novel)
Ballybeg (Baile Beag), Ireland (town), pp.64–65, A3
Slieve Geal, Ireland (mountain), pp.64–65, A3
Cryptonomicron by Neal Stephenson (novel), Kinakuta (fictional country), pp.90–91, C2
CSI series (TV), Tescara, Atlantic Ocean (island), pp.126–127, C4

Cthulhu (film), Rivermouth, Oregon (town), pp.18–19, A6
Cthulhu Mythos/H.P. Lovecraft (various)
Ahu-Y'hloa (fictional country), pp.126–127, D5
Alanhati, Atlantis (fictional country), pp.126–127, B4/C4
Arkham, Massachusetts (city), pp.14–15, D5
Bal-Sagoth, Atlantis (fictional island), pp.126–127, C4
Caiphul (fictional country), pp.126–127, D5
City of the Golden Gates, The, Atlantis (fictional city), pp.126–127, C3
Dunwich, Massachusetts (town), pp.14–15, D5
Empire of Quy, The, Quy (fictional sunken continent/nation), pp.126–127, C1/D1/C2/D2
Innsmouth, Massachusetts (town), pp.14–15, D5
K'naa, Mu (fictional region), pp.120–121, E3
Kingsport, Massachusetts (town), pp.14–15, D5
Lovecraft Country, Massachusetts (region), pp.14–15, D5
Miskatonic River, Massachusetts (river), pp.14–15, C5/D5
Mount Antarktos (mountain), pp.114–115, D5
Mount Yaddith-Gho, Mu (fictional mountain), pp.120–121, E3
Poseidonis, Atlantis (fictional sunken city), pp.126–127, C4
R'lyeh, Pacific Ocean (submerged city), pp.120–121, E1
SS *Victory*, Atlantic Ocean (wreck), pp.126–127, C4
Temple, The, Atlantis (fictional sunken City), pp.126–127, C3
Thrang (continent), pp.114–115, D3
U-29, Atlantic Ocean (wreck), pp.126–127, C3
Y'ha-nthlei, Massachusetts (underwater city), pp.14–15, D5
Cuéntame cómo pasó (TV), Sagrillas, Spain (village), pp.44–45, B2
Cuentos de Beyhualé by Joaquín Bestard Vázquez (novel), Beyhualé, Mexico (town), pp.32–33, C2
Cursed Mountain (video game)
Cherku, Tibet (village), pp.102–103, B2
Lhando, Tibet (city), pp.102–103, B2
Custard's World (TV), Doodle, New Zealand (town), pp.108–109, F2
Cyber City Oedo 808 (anime), Oedo, Japan (city), pp.96–97, E1/F1
Cybergirl (TV), River City, Queensland (city), pp.108–109, E3
Cyberpunk 2077 (games), Night City, California (city), pp.18–19, A3
Cybersix (comics), Meridiana, Argentina (city), pp.38–39, B4

D2 The Mighty Ducks (film), Minnehaha, Minnesota (city), pp.16–17, C6
Dad's Army (TV)
Eastgate, England (town), pp.64–65, D1
Littlebourne-on-Sea, England (village), pp.64–65, D1
Tulls Point, Maine (town), pp.14–15, D5
Walmington on Sea, England (village), pp.64–65, D1
Dagon (film), Imboca, Spain (village), pp.44–45, A3
Dahoam is Dahoam (TV), Lansing, Germany (village), pp.44–45, D1
Dallas (TV), Southfork Ranch, Texas (building), pp.16–17, C4
Dan August (TV), Santa Luisa, California (town), pp.18–19, A3
Dance in the Vampire Bund by Nozomu Tamaki (manga/anime), Bund, The, Japan (city), pp.96–97, F1
Dance with Death by Barbara Nadel (novel), Muratpaşa, Turkey (village), pp.72–73, B3
Dances with Wolves (film), St David's Field, Tennessee (battleground), pp.14–15, A3
Dancing to the Flute by Manisha Jolie Amin (novel), Hastinapore, India (village), pp.78–79, B4
Dandelion Wine by Ray Bradbury (novel), Green Town, Illinois (town), pp.16–17, D5
Danny Dunn series by Raymond Abrashkin and Jay Williams (novels), Midston, Maine (town), pp.14–15, D6
Danny Phantom (TV), Amity Park, Minnesota (city), pp.16–17, C5/C6
Dante's Peak (film), Dante's Peak, Washington (mountain), pp.18–19, B6
Darby O'Gill and the Little People (film)
Glencove, Ireland (town), pp.64–65, A2
Rathcullen, Ireland (town), pp.64–65, A2
Daria (TV), Lawndale, Unknown (town), pp.14–15, C5
Dark (TV), Winden, Germany (town), pp.44–45, C3
Dark Horse Comics
Cinnabar, Nevada (town), pp.18–19, A6
Steel Harbor, Michigan (city), pp.14–15, A5/B5
Dark Pines by Will Dean (novel), Gavrik, Sweden (town), pp.56–57, B3
Dark Shadows (TV/film), Collinsport, Maine (village), pp.14–15, D6
Dark Wood Dark Water by Tina Callaghan (novel), Bailey, Ireland (town), pp.64–65, B2

153

Darkness Falls (film), Darkness Falls, Maine (town), pp.14–15, D6

Darkwing Duck (various)
Audubon Bay, Calisota (fictional natural feature), pp.18–19, A5
St Canard, Calisota (fictional city), pp.18–19, A5

Darnley Mills novels by Phillip Turner (novels), Darnley Mills, England (town), pp.64–65, D3

Daughters by Paule Marshall (novel), Truiunion (fictional island/nation), pp.32–33, E2

Daughters of Eve by Lois Duncan (novel), Modesta, Michigan (town), pp.14–15, A5

Dave and Morley stories by Stuart McLean (radio/short stories), Big Narrows, Nova Scotia (town), pp.26–27, F2

Dawn of the Dead (2004 film), Fort Pastor, Wisconsin (building), pp.16–17, D5

Dawson's Creek (TV), Capeside, Massachusetts (town), pp.14–15, D5

Day of the Falcon (film)
Hobeika (fictional country), pp.72–73, C1
Salmaah (fictional country), pp.72–73, C2
Yellow Belt, The, Hobeika/Salmaah (fictional natural feature), pp.72–73, C1/C2

Day of the Outlaw (film), Bitters, Wyoming (town), pp.18–19, D5

Days of Our Lives (TV), Salem, Illinois (town), pp.16–17, D4/D5

DC Comics/Universe
Beaverly Hills, California (city), pp.18–19, A2
Belle Reve Penitentiary, Lousiana (building), pp.16–17, D2
Bialya (fictional country), pp.72–73, B3
Bludhaven, New Jersey (city), pp.14–15, C4
Blue Valley, Nebraska (city), pp.16–17, B4/B5
Central City, Missouri (city), pp.16–17, C4
Dhabar, Qurac (fictional country), pp.72–73, C2
Dos Rios, Texas (city), pp.16–17, A3
Fawcett City, Wisconsin (city), pp.16–17, C5
Fortress of Solitude, The, Nunavut (building), pp.26–27, C4
Gateway City, California (city), pp.18–19, A4
Gnu York, New York (city), pp.14–15, D1
Gotham City, New Jersey (city), pp.14–15, C4
Granville, Kansas (town), pp.16–17, B4
Hub City, Illinois (city), pp.16–17, D4
Jump City, Oregon (city), pp.18–19, A6
Kahndaq (fictional country), pp.72–73, B2
Karrocan Emirate, Karrocan Emirate (fictional country/emirate), pp.72–73, C2
Keystone City, Kansas (city), pp.16–17, C4
Kirai (fictional country), pp.72–73, C2
Kornsas City, Missouri (city), pp.16–17, C4
Littleville, Colorado (town), pp.18–19, D3
Los Antelopes, California (town), pp.18–19, B3
Markovburg, Markovia (fictional city), pp.44–45, C3
Markovia (fictional country), pp.44–45, C3
Memfish, Tennessee (city), pp.16–17, D4
Metropolis, Delaware (city), pp.14–15, C4
Midway City, Michigan (city), pp.14–15, A6
Nanda Parbat, Pakistan (city), pp.78–79, B5
New Venice, Florida (town), pp.14–15, C1
Opal City, Maryland (city), pp.14–15, C4
Peña Duro, Santa Prisca (fictional island), pp.32–33, F2
Qurac (fictional country), pp.72–73, C2
Rioguay (fictional country), pp.38–39, B5
Saint Bernardino, California (city), pp.18–19, B3
Santa Prisca (fictional island/nation), pp.32–33, F2
Smallville, Kansas (town), pp.16–17, B4
St Roch, Louisiana (city), pp.16–17, D2
Star City, California (city), pp.18–19, A4
Tallahatchee, Florida (city), pp.14–15, B2
Viceroy, South Carolina (city), pp.14–15, B3

Dead Heart (film), Wala Wala, Northern Territory (village), pp.108–109, C3

Dead Island (video game)
Banoi (fictional island/chain), pp.90–91, F1
Moresby, Banoi (fictional city), pp.90–91, pp.108–109, F1

Dead Island 2 (video game), Palanai, Banoi (fictional island), pp.90–91, F1

Dead State (video games), Splendid, Texas (town), pp.16–17, B2

Dear Ladies (TV/radio/comedy), Stackton Tressell, England (town), pp.64–65, D2

Death in April Creek by Helena Cooke (novel), Eastport, New Zealand (town), pp.108–109, F1

Death in Magnerstown by Anne Crosse (novel), Magnerstown, Ireland (town), pp.64–65, A2

Death in Paradise (TV)
Honoré, Saint Marie (fictional town), pp.32–33, F2
Saint Marie (fictional island), pp.32–33, F2

Death Ship (film), *Empress*, Atlantic Ocean (wreck), pp.126–127, A3

Decline and Fall by Evelyn Waugh (novel), Llanabba, Wales (town), pp.64–65, C2

Deep Blue Sea (film), Aquatica Research Station, Pacific Ocean (building), pp.120–121, E4

DeepStar Six (film), DeepStar Six, Pacific Ocean (submerged building), pp.120–121, A4

Deliverance (novel/film)
Aintry, Georgia (town), pp.14–15, B3
Cahulawassee River, Georgia (river), pp.14–15, A2/A3

Delta Force 2: The Colombian Connection (film), San Carlos (fictional country), pp.38–39, A4/B5

Denno Coil (anime), Daikoko, Japan (town), pp.96–97, B2

Deployment (film), Milanh, Afghanistan (village), pp.72–73, D2

Desejo Proibido (TV), Passaperto, Brazil (town), pp.38–39, D4

Designated Survivor (TV)
Bultan (fictional country), pp.90–91, B2
East and West Hun Chiu, East and West Hun Chiu (fictional Countries), pp.102–103, E3
Kunami (fictional country/emirate), pp.72–73, C2
Naruba (fictional country), pp.84–85, B4

Despedida de Solteiro (TV), Remanso, Brazil (town), pp.38–39, D3

Desperate Dan (comic), Cactusville, Texas (town), pp.16–17, B2

Desperate Housewives (TV)
Eagle State (fictional state), pp.14–15, A4
Fairview, Eagle State (fictional town), pp.14–15, A4

Desperation, Nevada by Stephen King (novel), Desperation, Nevada (town), pp.18–19, B4/C4

Destroy All Humans (video game)
Capitol City, District of Columbia (city), pp.14–15, C4
Rockwell, New Mexico (town), pp.16–17, A2
Santa Modesta, California (town), pp.18–19, A2
Union Town, Virginia (town), pp.14–15, C4

Destry Rides Again by Max Brand (novel), Wham, Texas (town), pp.18–19, D2

Deus Ex: Human Revolution (video game), Hengsha, China (city), pp.102–103, D2

Devi (comics), Sitapur, India (city), pp.78–79, C4/D4

Devices and Desires by P.D. James (novel), Larksoken, England (town), pp.64–65, D2

Devil's Cape by Rob Rogers (novel), Devil's Cape, Louisiana (town), pp.16–17, D2

Devil's Hill by Nan Chauncy (novel), Devil's Hill, Tasmania (natural feature), pp.108–109, D1

Devil's Rock (film), Forau Island, Channel Islands (island), pp.64–65, B4

Dhalgren by Samuel R. Delany (novel), Bellona, Kansas (city), pp.16–17, B4

DI Nikki Galena books by Joy Ellis (novels), Greenboroough, England (town), pp.64–65, D2

Did You Hear About the Morgans? (film), Ray, Wyoming (town), pp.18–19, D5

Die Andere Seite: Ein Phantastischer Roman by Alfred Kubin (novel)
Dream Kingdom, The (fictional country), pp.72–73, E3, pp.102–103, A3
Perla, Dream Kingdom (fictional country), pp.72–73, D3

Die Hard 2 (film), Escalon, Val Verde (fictional city), pp.38–39, A5

Diggstown (film)
Diggstown, Georgia (town), pp.14–15, B3
Olivair County, Georgia (county), pp.14–15, B3

Digimon (anime), Summer Memory, Colorado (town), pp.18–19, D4

Dinotopia (books/TV)
Dinotopia, Indian Ocean (island), pp.78–79, A2
Forbidden Mountains, Indian Ocean (mountain range), pp.78–79, A2
Outer Island, Indian Ocean (island), pp.78–79, A2
Polongo River, Indian Ocean (river), pp.78–79, A2
Sauropolis, Indian Ocean (city), pp.78–79, A2

Dirt Music by Tim Winton (novel/film)
Coronation Gulf, Western Australia (natural feature), pp.108–109, B4
White Point, Western Australia (town), pp.108–109, A2

Disney cartoons (TV), Vila Xuripita, Brazil (town), pp.38–39, D3

District 9 (film), District 9, South Africa (town/camp), pp.84–85, C2

Diving Adventure by Willard Price (novel), Undersea City, Pacific Ocean (submerged building), pp.108–109, D3

Django Unchained (film)
Bennet Plantation, Tennessee (building), pp.14–15, B3
Candyland Plantation, Mississippi (building), pp.16–17, D3
Carrucan Plantation, Mississippi (building), pp.16–17, D2
Daughtery, Texas (town), pp.18–19, D2
LeQuint Dickey Mine, Mississippi (building), pp.16–17, D2

Doc Hollywood (film), Grady, South Carolina (town), pp.14–15, B3

Doc Martin (TV), Portwenn, England (village), pp.64–65, B1

Doc Savage series (novels), Taz, Caribbean (submerged city), pp.32–33, D1

Doctor Dolittle stories by Hugh Lofting (novels)
Fantippo (fictional country), pp.84–85, B4
Puddleby-on-the-Marsh, England (village), pp.64–65, C1

Doctor Mateo (TV), San Martín del Sella, Spain (town), pp.44–45, B3

Doctor Sleep by Stephen King (novel/film), Frazier, New Hampshire (town), pp.14–15, D6

Doctor Strange (film/comic), Kamar-Taj, Nepal (village), pp.78–79, C4

Doctor Who (TV)
Cathedral, The, Turmezistan (fictional building), pp.72–73, E4
Turmezistan (fictional country), pp.72–73, E4/F4

Doctor Who: Minuet In Hell (audio series), Malebolgia (fictional state), pp.14–15, B3

Doctor Who: The Green Death (TV), Llanfairfach, Wales (town), pp.64–65, C2

Doctor Who: The Horror of Fang Rock (TV), Fang Rock, England (natural feature), pp.64–65, D1

Doctor Who: The Tenth Planet (TV), Snowcap Tracking Station (building), pp.114–115, C2/C3

Doctor Who/Torchwood (TV), Torchwood 3, Scotland (building), pp.64–65, C4

Doctors (TV), Letherbridge, England (town), pp.64–65, C2

Dodd, Ken (comedy routines), Jam Butty Mines, England (building), pp.64–65, C3

Dogville (film), Dogville, Colorado (town), pp.18–19, D4

Doktor Mugg (TV), Dasseborg, Sweden (city), pp.56–57, B2

Dolores Claiborne by Stephen King (various), Little Tall Island, Maine (island), pp.14–15, D6

Dolphin Island by Arthur C. Clarke (novel), Dolphin Island, Queensland (island), pp.108–109, D4

Dominion Tank Police (manga/anime), New Port City, Japan (city), pp.96–97, B2

Don Camillo works of Giovannino Guareschi (various)
Ponteratto, Italy (town), pp.44–45, D2
Trebiglie, Italy (town), pp.44–45, C3

Don Quixote by Cervantes (novel), Barataria, Mediterranean Sea (island nation), pp.44–45, C2

Don Quixote Drowned by James Hanley (short stories), Llangyllwch, Wales (town), pp.64–65, B4

Don Quixote, USA by Richard Powell (novel)
Puerto Grande, Republic of San Marco (fictional city), pp.32–33, E3
Republic of San Marco (fictional island/nation), pp.32–33, D3/E3

Don't Stop the Carnival by Herman Wouk (novel), Amerigo, British Virgin Islands (island), pp.32–33, F2

Doña Beija (TV), Santo Domingo de Araxá, Brazil (town), pp.38–39, C3

Doña Bella (TV), Agua Hermosa, Colombia (town), pp.38–39, A5

Doña Perfecta by Benito Pérez Galdós (novel), Orbajosa, Spain (town), pp.44–45, A2

Donald Duck, Danish translation (comic), Langbortisan (fictional country), pp.72–73, E3

Donde las Voces se Guardan (*The Whispering Voices of Atabalpa* in English editions) by Marco Antonio Samaniego (novel), Atabalpa, Mexico (town), pp.32–33, A4

Donovan's Reef (film), Haleakaloha, Pacific Ocean (island), pp.120–121, D2

Doonesbury (comic)
Al-Amok, Iraq (city), pp.72–73, B2
Berzerkistan (fictional country), pp.72–73, C3
Bmzklfrpz City, Berzerkistan (fictional city), pp.72–73, C3
Rummyworld (fictional country), pp.72–73, B2

Doorways in Drumorty by Lorna Moon (novel), Drumorty, Scotland (town), pp.64–65, C5

Doug (TV), Bluffington, Virginia (city), pp.14–15, C4

Downton Abbey (TV), Downton Abbey, England (estate), pp.64–65, C3

Downtown Owl by Chuck Klosterman (novel), Owl, North Dakota (town), pp.16–17, B5/B6

Dr Finlay stories by A.J. Cronin (novels/TV), Tannochbrae, Scotland (town), pp.64–65, C4

Dr No by Ian Fleming (novel/film), Crab Key and Dr No's Lair, Jamaica (island), pp.32–33, D2

Dr Ox's Experiment by Jules Verne (short story), Quiquendone, Belgium (town), pp.44–45, C4

Dr Strangelove or: How I Learned to Stop Worrying and Love the Bomb (film)
Burpelson AFB, Nebraska (building), pp.16–17, B2
Doomsday Machine, The, Russia (building), pp.102–103, F2
Zokov Islands, The, Russia (island chain), pp.102–103, F2

Dracula by Bram Stoker (novel), Carfax Abbey, England (estate), pp.64–65, D2

Dragonfly by Bernard Cronin (novel), Birdseye, Queensland (town), pp.108–109, C3

DRAMAtical Murder (video game/anime), Midorijima, Japan (island), pp.96–97, D1

Drawing Blood by Poppy Z. Brite (novel), Missing Mile, North Carolina (town), pp.14–15, C3

Dream Girl (film), Gokul, India (town), pp.78–79, B4

Dream of Ding Village by Yan Lianke (novel), Ding Village, China (village), pp.102–103, D2

Dream Team (TV), Harchester, England (town), pp.64–65, C2

Dreams of My Russian Summers by Andrei Makine (novel), Saranza, Russia (town), pp.102–103, E1

Droopy: Northwest Hounded Police (TV), Mounty County, Yukon (county), pp.26–27, A2

Drop Dead Gorgeous (film), Mount Rose, Minnesota (town), pp.16–17, C5

DuckTales (various)
Calisota (fictional state), pp.18–19, A5
Castle McDuck, Scotland (building), pp.64–65, B4/C4
Dismal Downs, Scotland (natural feature), pp.64–65, B4/C4
Drake Barrier Reef, The, Queensland (natural feature), pp.108–109, E3
Duckburg, Calisota (fictional city), pp.18–19, A5
Falcon Island, Alaska (island), pp.18–19, A1
Great Ducky Mountains, The, various (mountain chain), pp.26–27, B1/B2
Heron Sea, The, Alaska (sea), pp.18–19, A1
Istanbird, Turkey (city), pp.72–73, B3
Ithaquack, Greece (island), pp.44–45, E1
Lost Pyramid of Toth-Ra, Egypt (building), pp.84–85, D1
Macaw, China (city), pp.102–103, E1
MacDuich, Scotland (village), pp.64–65, B4
McDuck Sublab, Atlantic Ocean (building), pp.126–127, B3
Mount Neverest, Nepal (mountain), pp.78–79, C4
New Quackmore, Calisota (fictional city), pp.18–19, A5
Temple of the Golden Cricket, Tibet (building), pp.78–79, C4
White Agony Creek, Yukon (river), pp.26–27, B2

Duncton Wood by William Horwood (novels), Duncton Wood, England (natural feature), pp.64–65, D2

Dusk (video game), Dusk, Pennsylvania (town), pp.14–15, B4

Dying Light (video game), Harran, Turkey (city), pp.72–73, B3

Dyschronia by Jennifer Mills (novel), Clapstone, South Australia (town), pp.108–109, C2

E-Street (TV), Westside, New South Wales (town/suburb), pp.108–109, F4

Earthworm Jim (TV), Terlawk, New Jersey (town), pp.14–15, D1

East of Sudan (film), Barash, Sudan (village), pp.84–85, C4

EastEnders (TV)
Walford, England (town), pp.64–65, D2

EastEnders/Redwater (TV), Redwater, Ireland (town), pp.64–65, A3

Echo Beach (TV), Polnarren, England (town), pp.64–65, B1

Eclipsed by Patricia Burke Brogan (play), Killmancha, Ireland (city), pp.64–65, A2

Ecotopia by Ernest Callenbach (novel), Ecotopia, Country (country), pp.18–19, A5/B5

Ed (TV), Stuckeyville, Ohio (town), pp.14–15, B4

Eerie, Indiana (TV), Eerie, Indiana (town), pp.14–15, A4

Eight Crazy Nights (film), Dukesberry, New Hampshire (town), pp.14–15, D5

Eight-Legged Freaks (film), Prosperity, Arizona (town), pp.18–19, C4

El Amor que me Juraste by Silvia Molina (novel), San Lazaro, Mexico (town), pp.32–33, C2

El Ciudadano Ilustre (film), Salas, Argentina (town), pp.38–39, C2

El don de Alba (TV), Bellavista, Spain (town), pp.44–45, B2

El Dorado legends (various), Lake Parime, Peru (lake), pp.38–39, B4

El Goonish Shive (web comic), Moperville, Illinois (town), pp.16–17, D4

El Hotel de los Secretos (TV), San Cristóbal Tlaxico, Mexico (town), pp.32–33, C2

El sol que estás Mirando by Jesús Gardea (novel), Placeres, Mexico (town), pp.32–33, A4

Eldorado (TV)
Costa Eldorado, Spain (region), pp.44–45, A1
Los Barcos, Spain (town), pp.44–45, A1

Ella Minnow Pea by Mark Dunn (novel), Nollop, South Carolina (island), pp.14–15, C3

Embassy (TV), Ragaan (fictional country), pp.90–91, B2

Emma by Jane Austen (novel), Highbury & Hartfield, England (town), pp.64–65, D2

Emmerdale (TV)
Emmerdale, England (village), pp.64–65, C3
Hotten, England (town), pp.64–65, C3

Emmet Otter's Jug-Band Christmas (film), Frogtown Hollow, Mississippi (town), pp.16–17, D3

Empire Falls by Richard Russo (novel/TV), Empire Falls, Maine (town), pp.14–15, D5

Endless Ocean (video games)
Manoa Lai Sea, Pelago Commonwealth (fictional sea), pp.120–121, A4/B4
Pelago Commonwealth (fictional island/nation), pp.120–121, B4

Engine Empire by Cathy Park Hong (poetry), Shangdu, China (city), pp.102–103, D1

England, England by Julian Barnes (novel), England, England (town), pp.64–65, C1

Epoch (film), Torus, The, Bhutan (object), pp.78–79, D4

Era uma vez/I (TV), Nova Esperança, Brazil (town), pp.38–39, C3

Erewhon by Samuel Butler (novel)
Clearwater, Erewhon (fictional town), pp.108–109, F1
Cold-Harbour, Erewhon (fictional town), pp.108–109, F1
Colleges of Unreason, Erewhon (fictional Building), pp.108–109, F1
Erewhon (fictional country), pp.108–109, F1
Fairmead, Erewhon (fictional town), pp.108–109, F1

Escape from Zahrain (film), Zahrain (fictional country/emirate), pp.72–73, C1/C2

Escape to Witch Mountain (novel/films), Witch Mountain, various (mountain), pp.14–15, B3

Esplendor (TV), Esplendor, Brazil (town), pp.38–39, C3

Estrela de Fogo (TV), Girrasol, Brazil (town), pp.38–39, C3

Estúpido Cupido (TV)
Albuquerque, Brazil (city), pp.38–39, B3
San Andrés, Chile (town), pp.38–39, B3

Eterna Magia by Elizabeth Jhin (novel/TV), Serranias, Brazil (town), pp.38–39, D4

Ethan Frome by Edith Wharton (novel), Starkfield, Massachusetts (town), pp.14–15, C5

Eureka (TV), Eureka, Oregon (town), pp.18–19, A5

Everwood (TV), Everwood, Colorado (town), pp.18–19, D4

Every Sparrow Falling by Shirley-Anne McMillan (novel), Ballybaile, Northern Ireland (town), pp.64–65, B3

Everybody's Gone to the Rapture (video game), Yaughton, England (town), pp.64–65, C2

Ex Machina (film), Nathan Bateman's Estate, Alaska (region), pp.18–19, A1

Excel Saga by Kōshi Rikudō (manga/anime)
F-City, Japan (city), pp.96–97, A1
F-Prefecture, Japan (region), pp.96–97, A1/A2

Executive Orders by Tom Clancy (novel), United Islamic Republic, United Islamic Republic (fictional country), pp.72–73, C2

Expedition Everest (theme park)
Anandapur, Kingdom of (fictional country), pp.78–79, C4
Forbidden Mountain, Anandapur (fictional mountain), pp.78–79, C4
Serka Zong, Anandapur (fictional town), pp.78–79, C4

Extreme Ghostbusters (TV), Barkley Bluffs, New Jersey (town), pp.14–15, C4

Fábula del animal que no tiene paradero by Juan Morillo Ganoza (novel), Ultocar, Peru (town), pp.38–39, B4

Facing the Flag by Jules Verne (novel), Back Cup, Atlantic Ocean (island), pp.126–127, A4

Fafner in Azure (film), Tatsumiyajima, Japan (island), pp.96–97, B4

Fair City (TV), Carrigstown, Ireland (town), pp.64–65, B3

Fairy Liquid/Villarriba y Villabajo (TV), Villarriba and Villabajo, Spain (village), pp.44–45, B2

Falcon Beach (TV)
Falcon Beach, Manitoba (town), pp.26–27, D1
Falcon Beach, Vermont (town), pp.14–15, D1

Falcon Crest (TV), Falcon Crest, California (building), pp.18–19, A4

Fallout 1 (video game)
Boneyard, The, California (city), pp.18–19, A3
Hub, The, California (city), pp.18–19, B3
Junktown, California (town), pp.18–19, B3
Necropolis, California (city), pp.18–19, A3
Vault 13, California (building), pp.18–19, B3
Vault 15, California (building), pp.18–19, B3

Fallout 2 (video game)
New Reno, Nevada (city), pp.18–19, B4
Shady Sands, California (city), pp.18–19, B3

Fallout 3 (video game)
Capital Wasteland, The, District of Columbia/Virginia/Maryland (state/region), pp.14–15, C4
Pitt, The, Pennsylvania (city), pp.14–15, B4

Fallout 4 (video game)
Diamond City, Massachusetts (town), pp.14–15, D5
Far Harbor, Maine (town), pp.14–15, D6

Fallout New Vegas (video game)
Dogtown, California (city), pp.16–17, A4
New Vegas, Nevada (city), pp.18–19, B3
Novac, Nevada (town), pp.18–19, B3

Family Affairs (TV) Charnham, England (town), pp.64–65, D2

Family Guy (TV)
Bumblescum, Alabama (town), pp.14–15, A2
Executive Bathroom Island, Rhode Island (island), pp.14–15, D5
McSwiggan Village, Ireland (village), pp.64–65, B2
Quahog, Rhode Island (city), pp.14–15, D5
Fanhunter by Cels Piñol (various), Barnacity, Spain (city), pp.44–45, B2
Far Cry 3 (video game), Rook Islands, Indonesia (islands), pp.90–91, C1
Far Cry 4 (video game)
Banapur, Kyrat (fictional village), pp.78–79, C4
Kyrat (fictional country), pp.78–79, C4
Tirtha, Kyrat (fictional village), pp.78–79, C4
Utkarsh, Kyrat (fictional village), pp.78–79, C4
Far Cry 5/*Far Cry New Dawn* (video game)
Fall's End, Montana (town), pp.18–19, C6
Henbane River, Montana (river), pp.18–19, C6
Hope County, Montana (county), pp.18–19, C6/D6
Far South by David Enrique Spellman (novel)
Ciudud Azul, Argentina (village), pp.38–39, B3
Lago Gran Paraíso, Argentina (lake), pp.38–39, B3
Temenos, Argentina (village), pp.38–39, B3
Farewell, My Lovely by Raymond Chandler (novel), Bay City, California (city), pp.18–19, A3
Father Brown stories by G.K. Chesterton (novels/TV), Kembleford, England (town), pp.64–65, C2
Father Malachy's Miracle by Bruce Marshall (novel), Garden of Eden Dance Hall, Scotland (town), pp.64–65, C4
Father Ted (TV)
Craggy Island, Ireland (island), pp.64–65, A2
Rugged Island, Ireland (island), pp.64–65, A2
Fawlty Towers (TV), Fawlty Towers, England (building), pp.64–65, C1
Fear of Beauty by Susan Froetschel (novel), Laashekoh, Afghanistan (village), pp.72–73, A3
Felicidade (TV), Vila Feliz, Brazil (town), pp.38–39, D3
Fera Ferida (TV), Tubiacanga, Brazil (town), pp.38–39, D4
Fera Radical (TV), Rio Novo, Brazil (town), pp.38–39, D3
FernGully: The Last Rainforest (film), FernGully, New South Wales (natural feature), pp.108–109, E2
Field of Poppies by Carmel Bird (novel), Muckleton, Victoria (town), pp.108–109, D1
Fierce People by Dirk Wittenborn (novel/film), Vlyvalle, New Jersey (town), pp.14–15, C5
Fillums: A Novel by Hugh Leonard (novel), Drane, Ireland (town), pp.64–65, B2
Films of John Hughes, Shermer, Illinois (town), pp.16–17, D5
Films of Troma Entertainment, Tromaville, New Jersey (town), pp.14–15, C5
Final Destination series (films)
McKinley, Pennsylvania (town), pp.14–15, C5
Mt. Abraham, New York (town), pp.14–15, C5
Finding Dory (film), Marine Life Institute, California (building), pp.18–19, A3
Finding Maubee by Albert HZ Carr (novel), St Caro, Caribbean (island), pp.32–33, E2/F2
Finding Nemo (film), Marlin and Nemo's Neef, Great Barrier Reef (natural feature), pp.108–109, E3
Finfarran Peninsula novels of Felicity Hayes-McCoy (novels)
Ballyfin, Ireland (town), pp.64–65, A2
Carrick, Ireland (town), pp.64–65, A2
County Finfarran, Ireland (county), pp.64–65, A2
Crossarra, Ireland (village), pp.64–65, A2
Finfarran Peninsula, Ireland (natural feature), pp.64–65, A2
Lissbeg, Ireland (town), pp.64–65, A2
Finian's Rainbow (musical)
Missitucky (fictional state), pp.14–15, A4
Rainbow Valley, Missitucky (fictional town), pp.14–15, A4
Fireman Sam (TV), Pontypandy, Wales (town), pp.64–65, C2
Firewatch (video game)
Jonesy Lake, Wyoming (lake), pp.18–19, C5
Ruby River, Wyoming (river), pp.18–19, C5
Two Forks, Wyoming (region), pp.18–19, D5
Fireworks (film), Moshimo, Japan (town), pp.96–97, C2
First Light by Rebecca Stead (novel), Gracehope, Greenland (city), pp.26–27, E3
First Person Shooter by Cameron Raynes (novel), Bridgeton, South Australia (town), pp.108–109, D2
Fish-Hair Woman by Merlinda Bobis (novel), Iraya, Philippines (village), pp.90–91, C3

Five Get Into a Fix by Enid Blyton (novel)
Magga Glen, Wales (building), pp.64–65, B2
Old Towers, Wales (building), pp.64–65, B2
Five Go Down to the Sea by Enid Blyton (novel), Tremannon, England (town), pp.64–65, B1
Five Have a Mystery to Solve by Enid Blyton (novel), Whispering Island, England (island), pp.64–65, C1
Five on a Treasure Island by Enid Blyton (novel), Kirrin Island, England (island), pp.64–65, C1
Five Towns novels by Arnold Bennett
Bursley, England (town), pp.64–65, C2
Hanbridge, England (town), pp.64–65, C2
Knype, England (town), pp.64–65, C2
Longshaw, England (town), pp.64–65, C2
Turnhill, England (town), pp.64–65, C2
Flanagan's Wake (play), Grapplin, Ireland (town), pp.64–65, A3
Flipper (TV), Coral Key Park Marine Reserve, Florida (natural feature), pp.14–15, C1
Flor do Caribe (TV), Vila dos Ventos, Brazil (town), pp.38–39, D4
Flor Salvaje (TV), Nueva Esperanza, Colombia (town), pp.38–39, A5
Flowertown by S.G. Redling (novel), Flowertown/Dalesbrook, Iowa (town), pp.16–17, C5
Footloose (1984 film), Bomont, Utah (town), pp.18–19, C4
Footrot Flats (comic)
Footrot Flats, New Zealand (estate), pp.108–109, F2
Raupo, New Zealand (town), pp.108–109, F2
For a Few Dollars More (film)
Agua Caliente, New Mexico (town), pp.18–19, D2
Las Palmeras, New Mexico (town), pp.18–19, D2
Santa Cruz, New Mexico (town), pp.18–19, D2
White Rocks, New Mexico (town), pp.18–19, D2
For Better or For Worse by Lynn Johnston (comic), Milborough, Ontario (town), pp.26–27, A4
For My Daughter's Honor (film), Tate, Oklahoma (town), pp.16–17, B3
Força de um Desejo (TV), Vila de Sant'Anna, Brazil (town), pp.38–39, D4
Forrest Gump by Winston Groom (novel/film), Greenbow, Alabama (town), pp.14–15, A2
Fortitude (TV), Fortitude, Norway (town/island), pp.56–57, A5
Forty Words for Sorrow and other novels by Giles Blunt, Algonquin Bay, Ontario (town), pp.26–27, A4
Fraggle Rock (TV), Fraggle Rock lighthouse, England (building), pp.64–65, B1
Frankenstein by Mary Shelley (various), Castle Frankenstein, Switzerland (building), pp.44–45, C3
Free Willy 2 (film)
Camp Mowester, Washington (building), pp.18–19, A6
Dakar, Washington (wreck), pp.18–19, A6
Freedom Road by Hamid Sulaiman (graphic novel), Houria, Syria (town), pp.72–73, A3
Freiland by Theodor Hertzka (novel), Freeland (fictional country), pp.84–85, C4/D4
French folklore, Ys, France (sunken city), pp.44–45, B3
Friday Night Lights (TV), Dillon, Texas (town), pp.16–17, A2
Friday the 13th series (films), Crystal Lake/Camp Crystal Lake, New Jersey (town/lake), pp.14–15, C5
Fried Green Tomatoes at the Whistle Stop Café by Fannie Flagg (novel/film), Whistle Stop, Alabama (town), pp.14–15, A3
From Dusk Till Dawn (film), Titty Twister (La Tetilla del Diablo), Mexico (building), pp.32–33, B3
From the Earth to the Moon by Jules Verne (novel)
Comalities, Texas (town), pp.16–17, B1
Elpanda, Texas (town), pp.16–17, B1
Stones Hill, Florida (mountain), pp.14–15, B1
From the New World (video game), Kamisu 66, Japan (town), pp.96–97, C2
Front Page News by Katie Rowney (novel), Toomey, Queensland (town), pp.108–109, E3
Frost by Thomas Bernhard (novel), Weng, Austria (village), pp.44–45, D3
Frozen (film)
Arendelle (fictional city/country), pp.56–57, B4
Arenfjord, Arendelle (fictional natural feature), pp.56–57, A4/B4
North Mountain, The, Arendelle (fictional mountain), pp.56–57, B4
Southern Isles, The, Denmark (country), pp.56–57, A2
Frozen II (film)
Agnarr and Iduna's Ship, Lands of the Northuldra (wreck), pp.56–57, B4
Ahtohallan, Lands of the Northuldra (island), pp.56–57, B4
Dark Sea, The (fictional sea), pp.56–57, A4/B4

Elsa's Ice Palace, Arendelle (fictional building), pp.56–57, B4
King Runeard's Dam, Lands of the Northuldra (building), pp.56–57, B4
Lands of the Northuldra/The Enchanted Forest (country), pp.56–57, B4
Full Metal Panic! (books), Helmajistan, Helmajistan (fictional country), pp.72–73, D2
Full Spectrum Warrior (video game)
Zafarra, Zekistan (fictional city), pp.72–73, E2
Zekistan (fictional country), pp.72–73, E3
Further News of Defeat by Michael X. Wang (short story), Xinchun, China (village), pp.102–103, D3
Futurama (TV)
Long Long Island, New York (island), pp.14–15, D5
Lost City of Atlanta, The, Georgia (city), pp.14–15, D1
New New York, New York (city), pp.14–15, D1
Robo-Hungarian Empire (fictional country/empire), pp.44–45, D3
Thermostadt, Robo-Hungarian Empire (fictional country), pp.44–45, D3
Future Diary by Sakae Esuno (manga/anime), Sakurami City, Japan (city), pp.96–97, C2
Gabriel's Bay by Catherine Robertson (novel), Gabriel's Bay, New Zealand (town), pp.108–109, F1
Gaffe, San Escobar (fictional country), pp.32–33, B2/C2
Galápagos by Kurt Vonnegut (novel), Santa Rosalia, Galapagos Islands (island), pp.38–39, A1
Gangsters 2 (video game), New Temperence (fictional state), pp.14–15, C5/D5
Gargoyles (TV), Castle Wyvern, Scotland (building), pp.64–65, B4
Garuda Superhero (film), Metro City, Indonesia (fictional city), pp.90–91, B1
Gasaraki (anime)
Belgistan (fictional country), pp.72–73, B3/C3
Kaha, Belgistan (fictional city), pp.72–73, C3
Gator (film), Dunston County, Georgia (county), pp.14–15, B2
Gavon's Eve by E.F. Benson (short story), Gavon, Scotland (village), pp.64–65, C4
gen:LOCK (web animation), Anvil, The, Colorado (building), pp.18–19, D4
George of the Jungle (film)
Ape Mountain, DRC (mountain), pp.84–85, C3
Ape River, DRC (river), pp.84–85, C3
Bukuvu, The, DRC (region), pp.84–85, C3
George Sprott by Seth (graphic novel and cardboard model.), Dominion, Ontario (city), pp.26–27, A4
Germinal by Emile Zola (novel), Montsou, France (village), pp.44–45, C3
Gerry Anderson's New Captain Scarlet (TV), Ragnarok, Alaska (town), pp.18–19, A2
Get Some In! (TV), RAF Midham, England (building), pp.64–65, C2
GetBackers by Yuya Aoki and Rando Ayamine (manga/anime), Infinite Fortress, The, Japan (building), pp.96–97, E1
Ghidorah, The Three-Headed Monster (film), Selgina, Selgine (fictional country), pp.78–79, D4
Ghost in the Shell (manga/anime)
Niihama, Japan (city/island), pp.96–97, B2
Siak Republic (fictional country), pp.90–91, B4
Ghost Recon: Breakpoint (video game), Aurora, Pacific Ocean (island), pp.120–121, D1
Ghost Recon: Wildlands (video game)
Agua Verde, Bolivia (lake), pp.38–39, B4
Barvechos, Bolivia (city), pp.38–39, B4
Libertad, Bolivia (city), pp.38–39, B4
Rio Habana, Bolivia (river), pp.38–39, B4
Rio Uruqui, Bolivia (river), pp.38–39, B4
Villa Verde, Bolivia (city), pp.38–39, B4
Ghost Rider (film), San Venganza, Texas (town), pp.16–17, A2
Ghost Ship (film)
Arctic Warrior, Alaska (wreck), pp.18–19, A1
Bowers Bank, Alaska (island chain), pp.18–19, A1
MS Antonia Graza, Alaska (wreck), pp.18–19, A1
Port Germaine, Alaska (town), pp.18–19, A1/A2
RCAF Mackenzie Bay, Yukon/Northwest Territories (building), pp.26–27, B2/B3
Ghostboat by George E. Simpson and Neal R. Burger (novel), USS Candlefish, Pacific Ocean (wreck), pp.96–97, D1
Ghostbusters: Afterlife (film), Summerville, Oklahoma (town), pp.16–17, B3
GI Joe (various)
Cobra Island, Gulf of Mexico (island), pp.32–33, B3/C3
Fer-de-Lance, Louisiana (town), pp.16–17, C5
Gilbert, Rhod (comedy routines), Llanbobl, Wales (town), pp.64–65, C2
Gilligan's Island (TV), Island, The, Pacific Ocean (island), pp.120–121, D4
SS Minnow, Pacific Ocean (wreck), pp.120–121, D4
Gilmore Girls (TV), Stars Hollow, Connecticut (town), pp.14–15, C5

Gimme a Break! (TV), Glenlawn, California (town), pp.18–19, A4
Ginger Snaps and *Orphan Black* (films, TV), Bailey Downs, Ontario (town), pp.26–27, A4
Giselle by Michael Keegan-Dolan (play), Ballyfeeny, Ireland (town), pp.64–65, A3
Glenraven series by Marion Zimmer Bradley (novel), Glenraven (fictional country), pp.44–45, C2
Glenroe (TV), Glenroe, Ireland (village), pp.64–65, B2
Glitch (TV), Yoorana, Victoria (town), pp.108–109, D1
Godfrey Morgan by Jules Verne (novel/film), Spencer Island (Monster Island), Pacific Ocean (island), pp.120–121, E4
Godzilla (2014) (film), Janjira, Japan (city), pp.96–97, C2
Godzilla films
Birth Island, Pacific Ocean (island), pp.120–121, C3
Infant Island, Pacific Ocean (island), pp.120–121, C3
Letchi Island, Japan (island), pp.96–97, D3
Monster Island, Pacific Ocean (island), pp.120–121, C3
New Kirk City, Pacific Ocean (city), pp.96–97, F4
Odo Island, Japan (island), pp.96–97, C1/C2
Rolisica, Pacific Ocean (island/nation), pp.96–97, F4
Sollgel Island, Pacific Ocean (island), pp.120–121, C3
Godzilla vs Biollante (film), Saradia (fictional country), pp.72–73, B2/B3
Godzilla: King of the Monsters (film)
Castle Bravo, Atlantic Ocean (building), pp.126–127, A3/B3
Isla de Mara, Mexico (island), pp.32–33, C2
King Ghidorah, frozen body of (being), pp.114–115, D4
Outpost 32 (building), pp.114–115, D4
Goliath Awaits (film), RMS Goliath, Atlantic Ocean (wreck), pp.126–127, A3/B3
Gomer Pyle, U.S.M.C. (TV), Greater San Miguel (fictional country), pp.38–39, C4
Gone With the Wind by Margaret Mitchell (novel/film), Tara Plantation, Georgia (building), pp.14–15, D2
Gonger – Das Böse vergisst nie (film), Altbrunnstedt, Germany (village), pp.44–45, C3
Good Morning, Midnight by Lily Brooks-Dalton (novel), Barbeau Observatory, Nunavut (building), pp.26–27, D4
Good Omens by Terry Pratchett (novel/TV)
Lower Tadfield, England (town), pp.64–65, D2
Pant-y-Girdle, Wales (town), pp.64–65, C2
Goodness Gracious Me (TV), Fawlty Turrets, India (building), pp.78–79, B4
Goodwood by Holly Throsby (novel), Goodwood, New South Wales (town), pp.108–109, D2
Goof Troop/*A Goofy Movie* (various)
Asperin, Colorado (town), pp.18–19, D4
Spoonerville, Ohio (town), pp.14–15, D4
Goosebumps novels by R.L. Stine (novels/film), Madison, Delaware (town), pp.14–15, C4
Gori Tere Pyaar Mein (film), Jhumli, India (town), pp.78–79, B4
Gosford Park (film), Gosford Park, England (estate), pp.64–65, C2
Gospel Hill (film), Julia, South Carolina (town), pp.14–15, C2
Gran Hotel (TV), Cantaloa, Spain (town), pp.44–45, B3
Gran Reserva (TV), La Siesta, Spain (town), pp.44–45, B2
Grand Theft Auto series (video game)
Alamo Sea, The, San Andreas (fictional natural feature), pp.18–19, B3
Alderney (fictional state), pp.14–15, D1
Alderney City, Alderney (fictional city), pp.14–15, D1
Algonquin, Liberty City (fictional city), pp.14–15, D1
Angel Pine, San Andreas (fictional town), pp.18–19, A3
Blaine County, San Andreas (fictional county), pp.18–19, B2/B3
Bohan, Liberty State (fictional town), pp.14–15, D1
Broker, Liberty State (fictional town), pp.14–15, D1
Dukes, Liberty State (fictional town), pp.14–15, D1
El Castillo del Diablo, San Andreas (fictional mountain range), pp.18–19, B3/C3
Fort Carson, San Andreas (fictional town), pp.18–19, A4/B4
Grand Senora Desert, San Andreas (fictional desert), pp.18–19, B3
Grapeseed, San Andreas (fictional town), pp.18–19, B3
Harmony, San Andreas (fictional town), pp.18–19, B3
Las Payasadas, San Andreas (fictional town), pp.18–19, B3
Las Venturas, San Andreas (fictional city), pp.18–19, B3
Liberty City, Liberty State (fictional city), pp.14–15, D1
Liberty State (fictional state), pp.14–15, D1

Los Santos, San Andreas (fictional city), pp.18–19, B3
Ludendorff, North Yankton (fictional town), pp.16–17, B6
Mount Chiliad, San Andreas (fictional mountain), pp.18–19, A3
Mount Gordo, San Andreas (fictional mountain), pp.18–19, A3
Mount Josiah, San Andreas (fictional mountain), pp.18–19, A3
North Yankton, North Yankton (fictional state), pp.16–17, B6
Paleto Bay, San Andreas (town), pp.18–19, A3
Palomino Creek, San Andreas (fictional town), pp.18–19, A3
San Andreas (fictional state), pp.18–19, A4/B4
San Fierro, San Andreas (fictional city), pp.18–19, A3
Sandy Shores, San Andreas (fictional town), pp.18–19, B3
Sherman Reservoir, San Andreas (fictional lake), pp.18–19, B3/C3
Tataviam Mountains, San Andreas (fictional mountain range), pp.18–19, B3
Tierra Robada, San Andreas (fictional mountain range), pp.18–19, B3
Vice City, Florida (city), pp.14–15, C1
West River, New York (river), pp.14–15, C5
Grandpa in my Pocket (TV), Sunnysands, England (town), pp.64–65, D2
Grandview, USA (film), Grandview, Illinois (town), pp.16–17, D4
Gravity Falls (TV)
Gravity Falls, Oregon (town), pp.18–19, A5
Mystery Mountain, Oregon (mountain), pp.18–19, B5
Roadkill County, Oregon (county), pp.18–19, A5
Time Baby, The (being), pp.114–115, C4
Greed (film), The Big Dipper Gold Mine California (mine), pp.18–19, A3
Green Arrow (DC Comics), Starfish Island, Fiji (island), pp.120–121, C4
Green Grass, Running Water by Thomas King (novel), Blossom, Alberta (town), pp.26–27, C1
Green Knowe novels by Lucy M. Boston (novels), Green Knowe, England (building), pp.64–65, D2
Greenvoe, George Mackay Brown (novel), Greenvoe, Scotland (town), pp.64–65, C5
Gremlins (film), Kingston Falls, New York (town), pp.14–15, C5
Grönköpings Veckoblad (newspaper), Grönköping, Sweden (town), pp.56–57, B2
Groosham Grange books by Anthony Horowitz (novels)
Groosham Grange, England (building), pp.64–65, D2
Skrull Island, England (island), pp.64–65, D2
Growing Up in Pandupur by Aditi Rao (stories)
Pandupur, India (town), pp.78–79, B3
River Dhun, India (river), pp.78–79, B3
Guardian newspaper (newspaper), Bodoni, San Serriffe (fictional city), pp.78–79, A2
Guardian newspaper (newspaper), Lamson, San Serriffe (fictional town), pp.78–79, A2
Guardian newspaper (newspaper), Lower Caisse, San Serriffe (fictional island), pp.78–79, A1
The Guardian (newspaper)
Nomp, San Serriffe (fictional town), pp.78–79, A2
Ova Mata, San Serriffe (fictional island), pp.78–79, A1
Port Clarendon, San Serriffe (fictional town), pp.78–79, A2
Port Elrod, San Serriffe (fictional town), pp.78–79, A2
San Serriffe (fictional island/nation), pp.78–79, A1/A2
Thirty Point, San Serriffe (fictional natural feature), pp.78–79, A1
Upper Caisse, San Serriffe (fictional island), pp.78–79, A1
Villa Pica, San Serriffe (fictional town), pp.78–79, A2
Gullah Gullah Island (TV), Gullah Gullah, South Carolina (island), pp.14–15, B2/B3
Gulliver's Travels by Jonathan Swift (novel)
Balnibari (fictional island), pp.96–97, F3/F4
Blefuscu (fictional island/nation), pp.108–109, A2
Brobdingnag (fictional country), pp.26–27, A1
Clumegnig, Luggnagg (fictional town), pp.96–97, E3
Flanflasnic, Brobdingnag (fictional town), pp.26–27, A1
Glanguenstald, Luggnagg (fictional town), pp.96–97, E3
Glubbdubdrib, Luggnagg (fictional island), pp.96–97, D2/E2
Houyhnhnms Land (fictional island/nation), pp.108–109, B1
Lagado, Balnibari (fictional island/nation), pp.96–97, F3/F4
Laputa, Balnibari (floating fictional island), pp.96–97, E4/F4
Lilliput (fictional island/nation), pp.108–109, A2
Lorbrulgrud, Brobdingnag (fictional city), pp.26–27, A1
Luggnagg (fictional island/nation), pp.96–97, D2/E2/D3/E3

Maldonada, Balnibari (fictional city), pp.96–97, F3/F4

Mildendo, Lilliput (fictional city), pp.108–109, A2

Traldragdubb, Luggnagg (fictional city), pp.96–97, E2

Gundam 00 (anime)
Kingdom of Azadistan (fictional county), pp.72–73, C2
Kingdom of Suille (fictional country), pp.72–73, C2
La Tour Orbital Elevator, Somalia (space elevator), pp.84–85, D4
Moralia (Republic of), France (country), pp.44–45, C2
Republic of Krugis (fictional country), pp.72–73, C2
Republic of Tariba, Guyana/Venezuela (country), pp.38–39, B5/C4
Tenchu (Heaven Pillar) Orbital Elevator, Pacific Ocean (island), pp.120–121, B3

Gundam Wing (anime)
Barclay Base (building), pp.114–115, A2
New Port City, Sanc Kingdom (fictional city), pp.56–57, B1
Sanc Kingdom (fictional country), pp.56–57, B1

Gunnerkrigg Court by Thomas Siddell (comic), Gunnerkrigg Court, Scotland (building), pp.64–65, C3

Gunnm/Battle Angel Alita (various)
Gurat, Indian Ocean (island/city), pp.90–91, A2
Jeru/Zalem Space Elevator, Panama (space elevator), pp.32–33, D1
Necropolis, Colorado (city), pp.16–17, A4
Scrapyard /Scrap Iron City/Zalem, Panama (city), pp.32–33, D1
Zig/Gurat Space Elevator, Indian Ocean (space elevator), pp.90–91, A2

Guns of the South by Harry Turtledove (novel), Rivington, North Carolina (town), pp.14–15, C3

H₂O: Just Add Water (TV), Mako Island, Queensland (island), pp.108–109, E2

Haikyu!! by Haruichi Furudate (manga/anime)
Metropolitan Nekoma High School, Japan (building), pp.96–97, E1
Karasuno, Japan (town), pp.96–97, C3

Half-Life (video game), Black Mesa Research Facility, New Mexico (building), pp.18–19, D3

Halloween (films), Haddonfield, Illinois (town), pp.16–17, D4

HALO series (video games) New Mombasa space tether, Kenya (space elevator), pp.84–85, D3

Halo: Ghosts of Onyx by Eric S. Nylund (novel), Centennial Orbital Elevator, Cuba (space elevator), pp.32–33, D1

Hamish Macbeth by M.C. Beaton (novels/TV)
Lochdubh, Scotland (town), pp.64–65, B5
Strathbane, Scotland (town), pp.64–65, B5

Hanasaku Iroha (anime), Yunosagi Onsen, Japan (town), pp.96–97, B2

Hancock's Half Hour (TV), East Cheam, England (town), pp.64–65, D2

Hang 'Em High (film), Fort Grant, Oklahoma (town), pp.16–17, C3

Hang Time (TV), Deering, Indiana (town), pp.14–15, A4

Hannah Montana (TV/film), Crowley Corners, Tennessee (town), pp.14–15, A3

Happy Feet (film), Mumbles' Emperor Penguin Colony (colony), pp.114–115, D1

Happy Land (film), Hartfield, Iowa (town), pp.16–17, C5

Hard Times by Charles Dickens (novel), Coketown, England (city), pp.64–65, C3

Hardy Boys (comic), Zebwa (fictional country), pp.84–85, C3

Hardy Boys novels (novels), Huella Islands, French Guiana (islands), pp.38–39, C5

Harlequin's Positions by Jack B. Yeats (play), Portnadroleen, Ireland (town), pp.64–65, A3

Harley Quinn (TV), Hedonikka, Themyscira (fictional city), pp.44–45, F1

Haroun and the Sea of Stories by Salman Rushdie (novel)
Alifbay (fictional country), pp.78–79, B5
Dull Lake, The, Alifbay (fictional lake), pp.78–79, B5
Kahani, Alifbay (fictional city), pp.78–79, B5

Harry Potter novels/Wizarding World by J.K. Rowling (novels/films)
Azkaban Prison, Scotland (unmappable building), pp.64–65, D5
Beauxbatons Academy, France (unmappable building), pp.44–45, B2
Castelobruxo, Brazil (unmappable building), pp.38–39, B4
Godric's Hollow, England (village), pp.64–65, C1
Hogsmeade, Scotland (unmappable village), pp.64–65, C4
Hogwarts, Scotland (unmappable building), pp.64–65, C4
Ilvermorny School of Witchcraft and Wizardry, Massachusetts (building), pp.14–15, C5
Isle of Drear, Scotland (unmappable island), pp.64–65, C5
Little Whinging, England (town), pp.64–65, D2
McGonagall Manse, Scotland (building), pp.64–65, C5
Mahoutokoro School of Magic,

Pacific Ocean (building), pp.120–121, A4/B4

Ottery St Catchpole, England (village), pp.64–65, C1

Tinworth, England (town), pp.64–65, B1

Hart of Dixie (TV), Bluebell, Alabama (town), pp.14–15, A2

Harts of the West (TV), Sholo, Nevada (town), pp.18–19, B3

Harvest Home by Tom Tryon (novel), Cornwall Coombe, Connecticut (town), pp.14–15, D5

Hatfords and Malloys books by Phyllis Reynolds Naylor (novels), Buckman, West Virginia (town), pp.14–15, B4

Hatters Castle by A.J. Cronin (novel), Levenford, Scotland (town), pp.64–65, B4

Have His Carcase by Dorothy L Sayers (novel), Wilvercombe, England (town), pp.64–65, C2

Headlong Down the Years by Amabel Williams-Ellis (novel), Aber Alph, Wales (town), pp.64–65, C2

Headlong Hall by Thomas Love Peacock (novella), Headlong Hall, Wales (estate), pp.64–65, C2

Heartbeat (TV)
Aidensfield, England (village), pp.64–65, D3
Ashfordly, England (town), pp.64–65, D3

Heartland (TV), Hudson, Alberta (town), pp.26–27, C1

Heaven Above by Lu Tianming (novel/TV)
Linzhong County, China (region), pp.102–103, E4
Zhangtai City, China (city), pp.102–103, E4

Heimebane (TV), Varg, Norway (town), pp.56–57, A3

Hellblazer (comic), Doglick, West Virginia (town), pp.14–15, B4

Hellsing (anime), Badrick, Northern Ireland (city), pp.64–65, B3

Hepzibah - Sie holt dich im Schlaf (film), Selmen, Germany (town), pp.44–45, D3

Her Sister's Eye by Vivienne Clevens (novel), Mundra, Queensland (town), pp.108–109, D3

Hero (film), Mooyoung, South Korea (city), pp.102–103, E1

Hero's Dawn (film), Bologa (fictional country), pp.84–85, B4

Heroes of 71 series (video games), Shonir Char, Bangladesh (village), pp.78–79, D4

Hex (film), Bingo, Nebraska (town), pp.16–17, A4

Hey Arnold! (TV)
Hillwood, Washington (city), pp.18–19, A6
Puerto Clara, San Escobar (fictional city), pp.32–33, C2
San Lorenzo, San Escobar (fictional country), pp.32–33, C2

Hi-de-Hi! (TV), Crimpton-on-Sea, England (town), pp.64–65, D2

Hicksville by Dylan Horrocks (comic), Hicksville, New Zealand (town), pp.108–109, F2

High Citadel by Desmond Bagley (novel)
Chimitaxl, Cordillera (fictional mountain), pp.38–39, B3
Cordillera (fictional country), pp.38–39, B3
Rio Sangre, Argentina (river), pp.38–39, C2
San Croce, Argentina (city), pp.38–39, C2
Santillana, Cordillera (fictional city), pp.38–39, B3

High Hopes (TV), Cwm-Pen-Ôl, Wales (town), pp.64–65, C2

High Plains Drifter (film), Lago, California (town), pp.18–19, B4

Highlander: The, series (TV), Seacouver, Washington (town), pp.18–19, A6

Highway Tomson plays (theatre), Wasaychigan Hill Indian Reserve, Ontario (region), pp.26–27, A4

Higurashi: When They Cry (manga/anime), Hinamizawa, Japan (town), pp.96–97, B2

Hilda Furacão by Roberto Drummond (novel/film), Santana dos Ferros, Brazil (town), pp.38–39, D4

Himouto! Umaru-chan (anime), Zonama River, Brazil (river), pp.38–39, D4

His Dark Materials by Philip Pullman (various)
Beringland, Country (country), pp.18–19, A2
Bolvangar (The Station), Finland (building), pp.56–57, D5
Fireland, Country (country), pp.56–57, A6
German Ocean, The (fictional sea), pp.56–57, A1
Kingdom of the Bears, Sweden (island/country), pp.56–57, A5
Lake Enara, Finland (lake), pp.56–57, C6
New Denmark, Country (country), pp.14–15, B5/C5
New France (fictional country), pp.26–27, E1/E2
Norroway (fictional country), pp.56–57, A3
Sveden (fictional country), pp.56–57, B3
Trollesund, Finland (town), pp.56–57, C5
Van Tieren's Land (fictional country), pp.26–27, C3

I-o (video game)
Dorado (fictional state), pp.18–19, D3
San Burro, Dorado (town), pp.18–19, D3
Willowbutton, Dorado (town), pp.18–19, D3

iCarly (TV), Shelby, Idaho (town), pp.18–19, C5

Ice Station Zebra by Alistair MacLean (novel/film), Ice Station Zebra, Arctic (building), pp.26–27, D4

Sapienza, Italy (town), pp.44–45, D2

Tungan Valley, Khandanyang (fictional natural feature), pp.102–103, D5

Hoax, Chako Paul City, Sweden (town), pp.56–57, C5

Holby City (TV)
Holby, England (city), pp.64–65, C2
Wyvern, England (town), pp.64–65, C2

Hold the Dark (film), Keelut, Alaska (town), pp.18–19, B1

Holding by Graham Norton (novel), Duneen, Ireland (village), pp.64–65, A2

Hollow Earth by Carol and John Barrowman (novel), Auchinmurn, Scotland (island), pp.64–65, B4

Hollyoaks (TV), Hollyoaks, England (town), pp.64–65, C2

Home (film), Happy Humans Town, South Australia (megacity), pp.108–109, C2

Home and Away (TV)
Mangrove River, New South Wales (town/suburb), pp.108–109, F4
Reefton Lakes, New South Wales (town/suburb), pp.108–109, F4
Summer Bay, New South Wales (town/suburb), pp.108–109, F4
Yabbie Creek, New South Wales (town/suburb), pp.108–109, F4

Home Defence training situations (military code), Naptonshire, England (county), pp.64–65, D2

Homefront (TV), River Run, Ohio (town), pp.14–15, B5

Homestar Runner (web animation)
Free Country, USA, Nebraska (town), pp.16–17, B4
Strong Badia, Nebraska (village), pp.16–17, B4

Hong Gildon Jeon by unknown (novel), Yul, South Korea (island/nation), pp.102–103, E2

Hookland (website), Hookland, England (county), pp.64–65, D1

Hope & Faith (TV), Glen Falls, Ohio (town), pp.14–15, B5

Hope Springs (TV), Hope Springs, Scotland (town), pp.64–65, C4

Hostage (film), Bristo Camino, California (town), pp.18–19, A3

Hot Fuzz (film), Sandford, England (town), pp.64–65, C2

Hotel Transylvania 3 (film), Volcano Del Fuego, Atlantic Ocean (natural feature), pp.126–127, A3

House of 1000 Corpses/The Devil's Rejects (films), Ruggsville, Texas (town/county), pp.16–17, C2

House of Wax (film), Ambrose, Louisiana (town), pp.16–17, C2

Housekeeping by Marilynne Robinson (novel), Fingerbone, Idaho (town), pp.18–19, B6

How to Train Your Dragon by Cressida Cowell (novels/films)
Barbaric Archipelago, The (fictional island chain), pp.56–57, C1/D1
Berk, The Barbaric Archipelago (fictional village), pp.56–57, D1
Dark Deep, The Barbaric Archipelago (fictional island), pp.56–57, D1
Dragon Island, The Barbaric Archipelago (fictional island), pp.56–57, D1
Itchy Armpit, The Barbaric Archipelago (fictional island), pp.56–57, D1
Outcast Island, The Barbaric Archipelago (fictional island), pp.56–57, D1

Howard's Way (TV), Tarrant, England (town), pp.64–65, C1

Howards End by E.M. Forster (novel), Howards End, England (estate), pp.64–65, D2

Hugo Duchamp Investigates series by G.N. Heatherington (novels), Montgenoux, France (town), pp.44–45, B3

Human Highway (film), Linear Valley, California (town), pp.18–19, B3

Hurramabad: A Novel of Facets by Andrei Volos (novel), Hurramabad, Tajikistan (city), pp.72–73, D3

Hurricane Season by Fernanda Melchor (novel), La Matosa, Mexico (town), pp.32–33, B2

Hurricanes (TV)
Azul, Spain (city), pp.44–45, B2
Hispanola (fictional island), pp.32–33, E2
Inverfinnan, Scotland (town), pp.64–65, B4
Munchhausen, Germany (city), pp.44–45, C2

Hyoka by Honobu Yonezawa (novel), Kamiyama, Japan (town), pp.96–97, C2

I Capture the Castle by Dodie Smith (novel), Godsend Castle, England (building), pp.64–65, D2

I Know Where I'm Going! (film), Isle of Kiloran, Scotland (island), pp.64–65, B4

I Love Lucy (TV), Franistan (fictional country), pp.72–73, B3

I Take This Woman (film), Ursula, Wyoming (town), pp.18–19, D4

I Walked with a Zombie (film), St Sebastian (fictional island), pp.32–33, E2

IDW Comics, Nanzhao (fictional country), pp.90–91, A4

If On a Winter's Night a Traveller by Italo Calvino (novel)
Ataguitania (fictional country), pp.38–39, B5
Cimbria (fictional country/region), pp.56–57, C5/D5
Cimbric People's Republic (fictional country), pp.56–57, C5/D5
Cimmeria (fictional country/region), pp.56–57, C5/D5
Kudgiwa, Cimmeria (fictional town), pp.56–57, C5
Oquedal, Ataguitania (fictional village), pp.38–39, B5
Orkko, Cimmeria (fictional city), pp.56–57, C5
Petkwo, Cimmeria (fictional region), pp.56–57, C5
San Ireneo, Ataguitania (fictional town), pp.38–39, B5

Il tunnel sotomarino by Luigi Motta
Atlantic Tunnel, Atlantic Ocean (tunnel), pp.126–127, A4/B4/C4/C6/D4/D5
Atlanteja, Atlantis (fictional sunken city), pp.126–127, D4/D5

Ils sont votre épouvante et vous êtes leur crainte by Thierry Jonquet (novel), Certigny, France (town), pp.44–45, E3

Im Kkeok Jung (film), Chongsokgol, North Korea (village), pp.102–103, E3

Impact (film), Larkspur, Idaho (town), pp.18–19, C5

Impressions of Africa by Raymond Roussel (novel), Ponukele-Drelchkaff (fictional country/empire), pp.84–85, B4

In Order of Disappearance (film), Tyos, Norway (town), pp.56–57, C3

In Search of Lost Time by Marcel Proust (novel)
Balbec, France (town), pp.44–45, C3
Combray, France (village), pp.44–45, C3
Parville, France (town), pp.44–45, C3
Trouville, France (town), pp.44–45, C3

In the City by the Sea by Kamila Shamsie (novel), City by the Sea, The, Pakistan (city), pp.78–79, A4

In the Flesh (TV), Roarton, England (town), pp.64–65, C2

In the Forests of the Night by Amelia Atwater-Rhodes (short story), Cascadiopolis, Oregon (town), pp.18–19, A5

In the Heat of the Night (film/TV)
Sparta, Mississippi (town), pp.16–17, D3
Thail River, Mississippi (river), pp.16–17, D3

In the Heat of the Night by John Ball (novel), Wells, Carolina (town), pp.14–15, B3

In the Name of the People by Marilynne Robinson (novel)
Handong Province, China (region), pp.102–103, D2
Jingzhou, China (city), pp.102–103, D2

In the Winter Dark by Tim Winton (novel), Sink, The, Western Australia (natural feature), pp.108–109, B2

Independence Day: Resurgence (film), National Republic of Umbutu (fictional country), pp.84–85, C3

Indiana Jones and the Kingdom of the Crystal Skull (film), Akator, Brazil (city), pp.38–39, B4

Indiana Jones and the Temple of Doom (film)
Pankot Palace, India (building), pp.78–79, B5
Pankot Province, India (region), pp.78–79, B4/B5

Infierno de Todos by Sergio Pitol (short story), San Rafael, Mexico (town), pp.32–33, C2

Infierno Grande by Alfredo Espinosa (novel), Albores, Mexico (village), pp.32–33, B3

Infinity Train (TV), North Middle Branch, Minnesota (town), pp.16–17, C5

Insel Felsenburg by Johann Gottfried Schnabel (novel), Felsenburg Island, Atlantic Ocean (island), pp.126–127, D1

Inspector Banks novels by Peter Robinson (novels), Eastvale, England (town), pp.64–65, C4

Inspector Montalbano novels by Andrea Camilleri (novels/TV)
Marinella, Italy (village), pp.44–45, D1
Montelusa, Italy (city), pp.44–45, D1
Vigàta, Italy (town), pp.44–45, D1

Inspector Wexford stories by Ruth Rendell (novels), Kingsmarkham, England (town), pp.64–65, D1

Internet humour
Al Pacino, San Escobar (fictional city), pp.32–33, B2
Audiovideo, San Escobar (fictional city), pp.32–33, B2
Ciudad Polaca, San Escobar (fictional city), pp.32–33, B2
Dos Rios, San Escobar (fictional city), pp.32–33, B2
Gargamele, San Escobar (fictional city), pp.32–33, B2
Guacamole, San Escobar (fictional city), pp.32–33, B2
Rio Mojito, Rio Tequila, Rio Pina Colada, San Escobar (fictional river), pp.32–33, B2
Santo Domestos, San Escobar (fictional city), pp.32–33, B2
San Escobar (fictional country), pp.32–33, B2/C2
Santo Subito, San Escobar (fictional city), pp.32–33, B2
Senderos, San Escobar (fictional city), pp.32–33, B2

Into the Storm (film), Silverton, Oklahoma (town), pp.16–17, A2

Invasion of the Body Snatchers (film), Santa Mira, California (town), pp.18–19, A4

Invasion of the Sea by Jules Verne (novel), Saharan Sea, Saharan countries (natural feature), pp.84–85, C3

Irish Astronauts (TV), Sligo Mission Control, Ireland (building), pp.64–65, A3

Irmãos Coragem (TV), Coroado, Brazil (town), pp.38–39, C4

Iron Eagle (film), Bilya (fictional country), pp.84–85, A5

Iron Will (film), Birch Ridge, South Dakota (town), pp.16–17, B5

Isbaqzaade (film), Almore, India (town), pp.78–79, A4

Ishtar (film), Ishtar (fictional country), pp.84–85, A5

Isla Paraíso/Paradise Island (TV), Isla Paraíso, Chile (island), pp.38–39, B2

Islamic tradition, Mount Qaf, Arctic (mountain), pp.26–27, D4

Island at War (TV), St Gregory, Channel Islands (island), pp.64–65, C5

Island by Aldous Huxley (novel)
Greater Rendang, Indonesia (bloc), pp.90–91, A2
Pala, United Kingdom of Rendang and Pala (fictional island), pp.90–91, A2
Rendang, United Kingdom of Rendang and Pala (fictional island), pp.90–91, A2
United Kingdom of Rendang and Pala (fictional island chain), pp.90–91, A2

Island in the Sun (film), Santa Marta (fictional island), pp.32–33, E2

Island of Apples by Glyn Jones (novel), Abergarth, Wales (town), pp.64–65, C2

Island of Blue Dolphins by Scott O'Dell (novel), Island of Blue Dolphins, California (island), pp.18–19, A3

Islandia novels and sequels by Austin Tappan Wright and Mark Saxton
Biacra (fictional region), pp.84–85, A2
Col Plateau, Karain continent (fictional natural feature), pp.84–85, B1
Demiji, The, Karain continent (fictional natural feature), pp.84–85, B1
Elanery (The City), Islandia (fictional city), pp.84–85, B1
Islandia (fictional country), pp.84–85, A1/B1
Karain River, Sulliaba (fictional river), pp.84–85, A2
Lake M'Pulo, Karain continent (fictional natural feature), pp.84–85, A1
Mobono (fictional region/city), pp.84–85, B1
Shobo-n-Po, Sulliaba (fictional city), pp.84–85, B1
Sobo Steppes, Karain continent (fictional natural feature), pp.84–85, B1
St Anthony, Islandia (fictional region/city), pp.84–85, B1
Sulliaba (fictional region/city), pp.84–85, A1/A2

Isle of Dogs (film)
Megasaki, Japan (island), pp.96–97, A1
Trash Island (Isle of Dogs), Japan (island), pp.96–97, A1

It Ain't Half Hot Mum (TV), Tin Min, Myanmar (village), pp.90–91, A4

It by Stephen King (various), Derry, Maine (town), pp.14–15, D6

It Came From Outer Space (film), Sand Rock, Arizona (town), pp.18–19, C2

It Shouldn't Happen to a Vet by James Herriot (novel)
Darrowby, England (town), pp.64–65, C3
Houlton, England (village), pp.64–65, C3

It's a Mad, Mad, Mad, Mad World (film), Santa Rosita, California (town), pp.18–19, A2

It's a Wonderful Life (film), Bedford Falls, New York (town), pp.14–15, C5

Ivanhoe by Sir Walter Scott (novel)
Rotherwood, England (town), pp.64–65, C3
Templestowe, England (building), pp.64–65, C3
Torquilstone, England (building), pp.64–65, C2/D2

Ivor the Engine (TV)
Grumbley, Wales (town), pp.64–65, C2
Llanggubbin, Wales (town), pp.64–65, C2
Llaniog, Wales (town), pp.64–65, C2
Llanmad, Wales (town), pp.64–65, C2
Merioneth, Wales (town), pp.64–65, C2
Tewyn Beach, Wales (town), pp.64–65, C2

Jacob's Room by Virginia Woolf (novel), Dods Hill, England (town), pp.64–65, D2

Jake and the Kid by W.O. Mitchell (short stories), Crocus, Saskatchewan (town), pp.26–27, C1

Jam and Jerusalem (TV), Clatterford, England (town), pp.64–65, C1

James Bond: A View to a Kill (film), Main Strike Mine, California (mine), pp.18–19, A4

James Bond: Die Another Day (film)
Gustav Graves's Ice Palace, Iceland (building), pp.56–57, A6
Isla de Los Organos, Cuba (island), pp.32–33, D3

James Bond: Goldeneye (film)
Janus Satellite Control Center, Cuba (building), pp.32–33, D3
Severnaya, Russia (region), pp.102–103, E2
Severnaya Satellite Control Centre, Russia (building), pp.102–103, E1

James Bond: Licence to Kill (film)

Isthmus City, Republic of Isthmus (fictional city), pp.32–33, D1
Republic of Isthmus (fictional country), pp.32–33, D1
James Bond: Live and Let Die/James Bond 007 (film/role playing game), San Monique (fictional island/nation), pp.32–33, D2
James Bond: Moonraker (film), Drax Enterprises Launch Facility, Brazil (building), pp.38–39, B5
James Bond: Quantum of Solace (film), Perla de las Dunas, Bolivia (building), pp.38–39, B3
James Bond: Skyfall (film), Silva's HQ, China (island), pp.102–103, B5
James Bond: The Spy Who Loved Me (film) Atlantis (base), Sardinia (building), pp.44–45, C1
Liparus, Sardinia (wreck), pp.44–45, C1/C2
James Bond: The World is Not Enough (film), Devil's Breath, The, Azerbaijan (natural feature), pp.72–73, C3
James Bond: Tomorrow Never Dies (film) HMS *Devonshire*, China (wreck), pp.102–103, D1
Sea Dolphin II, Vietnam (wreck), pp.90–91, B4
James Bond: You Only Live Twice (film), Matsu, Japan (island), pp.96–97, A1
Jane Eyre by Charlotte Brontë (novel), Thornfield Hall, England (estate), pp.64–65, C3
Jasper Jones by Craig Silvey (novel/film), Corrigan, Western Australia (town), pp.108–109, A2
Jaws by Peter Benchley (novel/film) Amity Island, Massachusetts (town/island), pp.14–15, D5
Orca, The, Massachusetts (wreck), pp.14–15, D5
Jeepers Creepers (film), Poho County, Florida (county), pp.14–15, A6
Jelle's Marble Runs (web series) Bright Hyu City, India (city), pp.78–79, B2/B2
Galakonur, Kazakhstan (city), pp.72–73, D3
Hunluen, China (city), pp.102–103, D1
Isle Hyu (fictional island/nation), pp.78–79, C2
Jamarbala, Indonesia (city), pp.90–91, B1
Mellacai, Malaysia (city), pp.90–91, B2
Mount Huaze, China (mountain), pp.102–103, C2
Om, Cambodia (city), pp.90–91, B3
Polaria, Russia (city), pp.50–51, B5
Jennie by J.B. Snell (novel), Port Elwyn, Wales (town), pp.64–65, C3
Jericho (TV) Fillmore County, Kansas (county), pp.16–17, A4/B4
Jericho, Kansas (town), pp.16–17, B4
New Bern, Kansas (town), pp.16–17, B4
Jimmy Neutron, Boy Genius (TV), Retroville, Texas (city), pp.16–17, B4
Joe Dirt (film) Josette, Louisiana (town), pp.16–17, D2
Silvertown, California (town), pp.18–19, A5
Joe Versus the Volcano (film), Waponi Woo, Pacific Ocean (island), pp.120–121, D4
John Crow's Devil by Marlon James (novel), Gibbeah, Jamaica (town), pp.32–33, D2
John the Revelator by Peter Murphy (novel), Kilcody, Ireland (town), pp.64–65, B2
Jojo's Bizarre Adventure by Hirohiko Araki (manga/anime), Morioh, Japan (city), pp.96–97, C3
Jonathan Strange and Mr Norrell by Susanna Clarke (novel/TV), Hurtfew Abbey, England (building), pp.64–65, C3
Jordan and the Dreadful Golem by Karen Goldman (novel), Kfar Keshet, Israel (town), pp.72–73, B4
Josh (film), Vasco, India (town), pp.78–79, B3
Journey to the Centre of the Earth by Jules Verne (novel), Passage to the Centre of the Earth, Iceland (volcano/portal), pp.56–57, A6
Journey to the West by Wu Cheng'en (novel) Aolai (fictional country), pp.102–103, D2
Mount Huaguo, Aolai (fictional mountain), pp.102–103, D2
Judge Dredd (comics) Black Atlantic, Atlantic Ocean (sea), pp.64–65, A3
Ciudad España (fictional city state/ province), pp.44–45, A4
Euro-City (fictional city state/province), pp.44–45, C3
Mega-City One (city/state), pp.14–15, C4
Mega-City Two (city/state), pp.18–19, A4/A5
Mex-City (fictional city/state), pp.32–33, B2
Texas City, Texas (city/state), pp.16–17, C4
Juliet Bravo (TV), Hartley, England (town), pp.64–65, C3
Jumanji (film), Brantford, New Hampshire (town), pp.14–15, C5
Jungle Girl by Edgar Rice Burroughs (novel) Lodidhapura, Cambodia (city), pp.90–91, B3
Pnom Dhek, Cambodia (city), pp.90–91, B3
Junta (board game), República de las Bananas, Caribbean (island/nation), pp.32–33, D2
Jurassic Park by Michael Crichton (various)

Isla Morazan, Costa Rica (island), pp.32–33, C1
Isla Nublar, Costa Rica (island), pp.32–33, C1
Isla Talamanca, Costa Rica (island), pp.32–33, D1
Jurassic Park Europe, Azores (building), pp.126–127, C4
Jurassic Park Japan, Pacific Ocean (theme park), pp.120–121, A4/B4
Las Cinco Muertes/The Five Deaths, Costa Rica (island chain), pp.32–33, C1
Puerto Cortes, Costa Rica (town), pp.32–33, D1
Rojas, Costa Rica (region), pp.32–33, D1
Snakewater, Montana (town), pp.16–17, A6
TigerWorld, India (building), pp.78–79, B5
Bahia Anasco, Costa Rica (town), pp.32–33, D1
Jurassic World: Fallen Kingdom (film), Lockwood Manor, California (building), pp.18–19, A5
Just Cause series (video game) King's Bay, Madagascar (city), pp.84–85, D2/D3
Medici (fictional island nation), pp.44–45, C2
Nueva Voz, Solís (fictional city), pp.38–39, A5
Panau (fictional island/nation), pp.90–91, B2
San Esperito, San Escobar (fictional island/nation), pp.32–33, F2
Solís (fictional country), pp.38–39, A5
'Justified & Ancient' by The KLF (music), Mu-Mu Land, Mu (fictional region), pp.120–121, B3/C3
K (anime), Shizume, Japan (town), pp.96–97, E1
K-20: Legend of the Mask (film), Teito, Japan (city), pp.96–97, E1/F1
K-ON! by Kakifly (manga/anime), Sakuragaoka High School, Japan (building), pp.96–97, B2
Kabaneri of the Iron Fortress (anime) Aragane Station, Hinomoto (fictional city), pp.96–97, B2
Hinomoto (fictional country), pp.96–97, B2
Kongoukaku, Hinomoto (fictional city), pp.96–97, B2
Okita Station, Hinomoto (fictional city), pp.96–97, B2
Unato Station, Hinomoto (fictional city), pp.96–97, C2
Yashiro Station, Hinomoto (fictional city), pp.96–97, C2
Kaguya-sama: Love is War by Aka Akasaka (manga/anime), Shuchi'in Academy, Japan (building), pp.96–97, E1
Khasak by O.V. Vijayan (novel), Khasak, India (village), pp.78–79, B4
Kakegurui by Homura Kawamoto and Toru Naomura (manga/anime), Hyakkaou Private Academy, Japan (building), pp.96–97, E1
Kali River Rapids (theme park) Anandupur Township, Anandupur (fictional town), pp.78–79, C4
Chakranadi River, Anandapur (fictional river), pp.78–79, C4
Kali Rapids, Anandapur (fictional natural feature), pp.78–79, C4/D4
Kamen Rider Build (TV) Hokuto, Japan (region), pp.96–97, C4
Pandora Tower, The, Japan (building), pp.96–97, B2
Seito, Japan (region), pp.96–97, B2
outo, Japan (region), pp.96–97, C2
Kamen Rider Fourze (TV), Amanogawa High School, Japan (building), pp.96–97, C2
Kamen Rider Gaim (TV), Zawame, Japan (city), pp.96–97, B2/C2
Kamen Rider W (TV), Futo City, Japan (city), pp.96–97, F1
Kannazuki No Miko by Kaishaku (manga/ anime), Mahoroba, Japan (town), pp.96–97, B2
Kanthapura by Raja Rao (novel), Kanthapura, India (town), pp.78–79, B4
Karada lar (TV), Payidar, Turkey (village), pp.72–73, B3
Karma – Koi Aa Raha Hai Waqt Badalney (TV), Panaki, India (town), pp.78–79, B3
Katawa Shoujo (video game), Yamaku Academy, Japan (building), pp.96–97, C3
Kath & Kimderella (film), Papilloma (fictional country), pp.44–45, D2
Katie Morag (novels/TV), Isle of Struay, Scotland (island), pp.64–65, B4
Kaufman, Andy, and the mind of (performance art), Caspiar (fictional island/nation), pp.72–73, C2
Keeping Faith (TV), Abercorran, Wales (village), pp.64–65, B2
Kenan & Kel (TV), Pummis, Montana (town), pp.18–19, D5
Kentucky Fried Chicken (advertising), Lake Edna, Kentucky (town), pp.14–15, A3
Kidnapped by Robert Louis Stevenson (novel), Essendean, Scotland (town), pp.64–65, C4
Kiki's Delivery Service (anime), Koriko, Sweden (town), pp.56–57, C3
Kill la Kill (anime) Honnō City, Japan (city/island), pp.96–97, F1
Honnōji Academy, Japan (building), pp.96–97, F1

Kill Me Three Times (film), Eagles Nest, Western Australia (town), pp.108–109, A2
Killer Klowns From Outer Space (film), Crescent Cove, California (town), pp.18–19, A4
Killer7 (video game), Battleship Island, Pacific Ocean (island), pp.120–121, D4
Killinaskully (TV) Bally, Ireland (town), pp.64–65, A2
Killinaskully, Ireland (village), pp.64–65, A2
Kim Possible (TV) Lowerton, Colorado (city), pp.16–17, A4
Middleton, Colorado (city), pp.16–17, A4
Upperton, Colorado (city), pp.16–17, A4
Kindle Country series by Scott Turow (novels), Kindle County, Illinois (county), pp.16–17, D4/D5
King Arthur stories (folklore), Avalon, England (estate), pp.64–65, C1
King Kong and spin-offs (films) Skull Island, Indian Ocean (island), pp.90–91, A4
Faro Island, Pacific Ocean (island), pp.120–121, C3
King of the Golden River by John Ruskin (novel), Treasure Valley, Austria (natural feature), pp.44–45, D3
King of the Hill (TV) Arlen, Texas (town), pp.16–17, B2
Heimlich County, Texas (county), pp.16–17, B2
McMaynerbury, Texas (town), pp.16–17, B2
West Durndell, Texas (town), pp.16–17, B2
King Solomon's Mines by H. Rider Haggard (novel) Acre County, Tennessee (county), pp.14–15, B3
Blackacre/Whiteacre, Tennessee (building), pp.14–15, B3
Reserve (fictional state), pp.14–15, A4/B4
King Solomon's Mines, DRC (mine), pp.84–85, C3
Kukuanaland (fictional country), pp.84–85, C3
Loo, DRC (town), pp.84–85, C3
Sheba's Breasts, DRC (mountain range), pp.84–85, C3
Kingdom (TV), Market Shipborough, England (town), pp.64–65, B1
Kingdom of Elfin by Sylvia Townsend Warner (novel/short stories) Catmere, England (region), pp.64–65, C4
Elfhame, Scotland (region), pp.64–65, C3
Elfwick, Scotland (region), pp.64–65, C3
Foxcastle, Scotland (region), pp.64–65, C4
Peri Kingdom, Iran (country), pp.72–73, D2
Schloss Dreiviertelstein, Austria (country), pp.44–45, D3
Kingpin (film), Ocelot, Iowa (town), pp.16–17, C4
Kiznaiver (anime), Sugomori City, Japan (city), pp.96–97, B2
Kınalı Kar (TV), Kınalı Kar, Turkey (village), pp.72–73, B3
Klaus (film), Smeerensburg, Finland (island/ town), pp.56–57, B4
Klondike Kat (TV), Fort Frazzle, Yukon (building), pp.26–27, B2
Knots Landing (TV), Knots Landing, California (town), pp.18–19, A2
Koblic (film), Colonia Elena, Argentina (town), pp.38–39, B3
Koudelka (video game), Nemeton Monastery, Wales (building), pp.64–65, C2
Kronblom by Elov Persson (comic strip), Vinkelboda, Sweden (village), pp.56–57, B3
Kubla Khan by Samuel Taylor Coleridge (poem) Alph, China (river), pp.102–103, D3
Mount Abora, Ethiopia (mountain), pp.84–85, D4
Kuznetsov, Vladimir and Alexei Stolyarov (prank), Binomo (fictional island/nation), pp.90–91, A4
Kyunki fi Jeena Isi Ka Naam Hai/Because … That's What Life Is) (TV), Rajpura, India (village), pp.78–79, B4
La Ciénaga and *The Holy Girl* (films), La Ciénaga, Argentina (town), pp.38–39, B3
La Citadelle des Glaces by Paul Alperine (novel) Devil's Teeth, The, Greenland (mountain chain), pp.26–27, D4
Erikraudebyg, Greenland (village), pp.26–27, D4
La Citié du Sommeil by Maurice Barrère (novel), Morphopolis, France (city), pp.44–45, C3
La Grande Séduction (film), Ste-Marie-la-Mauderne, Quebec (town), pp.26–27, F2
La invención de Morel by Adolfo Bioy Casares (novel), Villings, Pacific Ocean (island), pp.120–121, C3
La Marca del Deseo (TV), Pueblo Escondido, Colombia (town), pp.38–39, A6
La Mer Mysterieuse by Claire Kenin (novel), Belesbat, Bay of Biscay (sunken city), pp.44–45, C2
La Patrona (TV), San Pedro del Oro, Mexico (town), pp.32–33, A2
La que se avecina (TV), Villazarcillo, Spain (town), pp.44–45, C4
La Regenta by Leopoldo Alas Clarín (novel), Vetusta, Spain (city), pp.44–45, B3
La Sombra del Pasado (TV), Saint Lucia, Mexico (town), pp.32–33, B2
La Tormenta (TV), Puerto Bravo, Colombia (town), pp.38–39, B5

La Vecina (TV), San Gaspar, Mexico (town), pp.32–33, B2
La Viuda de Blanco (TV), Trinidad, Colombia (town), pp.38–39, B6
Lady Chatterley's Lover by D.H. Lawrence (novel), Wragby Hall, England (building), pp.64–65, C2
Lagaan (film), Champaneer, India (village), pp.78–79, B4
Lake Placid (film), Black Lake, Maine (lake), pp.14–15, D6
Lanark by Alasdair Grey (novel), Unthank, Scotland (city), pp.64–65, C4
Land of the Dead (film), Fiddler's Green, Pennsylvania (town), pp.14–15, B4
Lark Rise to Candleford by Flora Thompson (novels/TV) Candleford, England (town), pp.64–65, D2
Lark Rise, England (town), pp.64–65, D2
Larry-Boy and Veggie Tales (Animation), Bumblyburg, Maine (town), pp.14–15, D5
Las Hermanitas Calle (TV), Villa Fuerte, Colombia (town), pp.38–39, A5
Las Rémoras by Eloy Urroz (novel), Las Rémoras, Mexico (village), pp.32–33, A3
Las sergas de Esplandián by Garci Rodríguez de Montalvo (novel), Island of California, The, Mexico (island), pp.32–33, A1
Last Exile: Fam of the Silver Wing (anime) Grand Lake, The, Mediterranean Sea (sea), pp.44–45, E1
Spargel, Greece (town), pp.44–45, E1
United Kingdom of Anatoray-Disith (fictional country), pp.44–45, C2
Last Letters From Hav by Jan Morris (novel), Hav (fictional city/state), pp.72–73, B2/B3
Law Acre County, Tennessee (county), pp.14–15, B3
Blackacre/Whiteacre, Tennessee (building), pp.14–15, B3
Reserve (fictional state), pp.14–15, A4/B4
Le Mont Analogue by René Daumal (novel) Mount Analogue, Pacific Ocean (continent/mountain), pp.120–121, A1/B1
Port o' Monkeys, Unnamed continent (town), pp.120–121, B1
Leave it to Beaver (TV), Mayfield, California (town), pp.18–19, A4
Left 4 Dead (video game), Newburg, Pennsylvania (town), pp.14–15, B4
Legend of the Rhinogradentia (faked information), Hy-yi-yi, Pacific Ocean (island chain), pp.120–121, D4
Lego Batman Movie (film), Wayne Island, New Jersey (island), pp.14–15, C4
Leila by Prayaag Akbar (novel), Aryavarta (fictional country), pp.78–79, B3
Leisure Suit Larry in the Land of the Lounge Lizards (video game), Lost Wages, Nevada (city), pp.18–19, B3
Lenin's Kisses by Yan Lianke (novel) Liven, China (village), pp.102–103, D2
Spirit Mountain, China (mountain), pp.102–103, D2
Les Bleus de Ramville (TV), Ramville, Ontario (town), pp.26–27, A4
Les Conquerants d'indoles by Charles Derennes (novel), Agzceaziguls (fictional country), pp.38–39, B3
Les Hermaphrodites by Thomas Artus (novel), Hermaphrodite Island, Portugal (floating island), pp.44–45, A3
Les Soirées de l'Orchestre by Hector Berlioz (book), Euphonia, Germany (city), pp.44–45, D4
Lesbian Vampire Killers (film), Cragwich, England (town), pp.64–65, C3
Lester by Bernard Beckett (novel), Langton, New Zealand (town), pp.108–109, F2
Letterkenny (TV), Letterkenny, Ontario (town), pp.26–27, A4
Lettres de Malaise by Paul Adam (novel), Adam's Country, Indonesia (region), pp.90–91, C2
Leviathan (film) Leviathan, Atlantic Ocean (wreck), pp.126–127, A4
Shack #7, Tri-Oceanic Mining Corporation, Atlantic Ocean (building), pp.126–127, A4
Li'l Abner (comic), Dogpatch, Kentucky (town), pp.14–15, B3
Life Goes On (TV), Glenbrook, Illinois (town), pp.16–17, D5
Life in Lulu (radio), Lulu, South Sudan (town), pp.84–85, C4
Life in the Fat Lane by Cherie Bennett (novel), Blooming Woods, Michigan (town), pp.14–15, A5
Life of Pi by Yann Martel (novel) Erlandson and Skank Shipyards, Sweden (building), pp.56–57, B4
Tomatán, Mexico (town), pp.32–33, A4
Tsimtsum, Pacific Ocean (wreck), pp.90–91, D4
Lig Sinn i gCathú/Lead us into Temptation by Breandán Ó hEithir (novel), Baile an Chaisil, Ireland (town), pp.64–65, A2
Lilo and Stitch (film/TV), Kokaua Town, Hawaii (town), pp.18–19, C1
Limetown (podcast), Limetown, Tennessee (town), pp.14–15, A3
Litanies of Dutch Battery by N.S. Madhavan (novel), Lantham Bathery, India (island), pp.78–79, B4
Little Giants (film), Urbania, Ohio (town), pp.14–15, A4/B4
Little Mosque on the Prairie (TV), Mercy, Saskatchewan (town), pp.26–27, C1
Little Ninja Brothers (video game)

Chatzy, Chinaland (fictional town), pp.102–103, C2
Cilly City, Chinaland (fictional city), pp.102–103, C2
Deli-Chous, Chinaland (fictional city), pp.102–103, C2
Hynen, Chinaland (fictional city), pp.102–103, C2
Little Witch Academia (anime), Wedinburgh, Scotland (city), pp.64–65, C4
Little Woods (film), Little Woods, North Dakota (town), pp.16–17, A6
Lo Imperdonable (TV) Mina Escondida, Mexico (town), pp.32–33, B3
Pueblo Nuevo, Mexico (town), pp.32–33, B3
Lo Que la Vida Me Robó (TV), Agua Azul, Mexico (town), pp.32–33, C2
Local Hero (film), Ferness, Scotland (town), pp.64–65, B4
Locke and Key (comic/TV), Lovecraft/ Matheson, Massachusetts (town), pp.14–15, D5
Lockie Leonard by Tim Winton (novels/ TV), Angelus, Western Australia (town), pp.108–109, B2
Log Horizon by Mamare Touno and Kazuhiro Hara (novels/anime) Ancient Court of Eternal Ice, Eastal (fictional building), pp.96–97, E1
Aorusoi (fictional country), pp.72–73, D3/E3
Beautiful Ocean Bridge, Florida (building), pp.14–15, C1
Big Apple, New York (city), pp.14–15, D1
Castle Cinderella, Japan (building), pp.96–97, F1
Dadu, China (city), pp.102–103, D2
Depths of Palm, The, Eastal (fictional natural feature), pp.96–97, C3
Eastal (League of Free Cities) (fictional country), pp.96–97, C2/C3
Ezzo Empire (fictional country), pp.96–97, D4
Fourland Dukedom, Fourland Dukedoms (fictional country), pp.96–97, B1/C1
Holy Empire of Westelande, Westlande (fictional country), pp.96–97, B2
Hsinpei, Taiwan (city), pp.102–103, D1
Jacksea Island, Ninetail Dominions (fictional island), pp.96–97, A1
Kyzyl Kum, The, Aorusoi (fictional natural feature), pp.72–73, D3
Laiport Strait, Ezzo Empire (fictional natural feature), pp.96–97, C3
Leon City, Singapore (city), pp.90–91, B2
Maihama, City of, Eastal (fictional city), pp.96–97, F1
Minami, Westlande (fictional city), pp.96–97, B2
Ninetail Dominions (fictional country), pp.96–97, A1/A2
Oou, Eastal (fictional town), pp.96–97, C3
Seventh Fall, Eastal (fictional building), pp.96–97, C3
Sky Tower, The, Ninetail Dominions (fictional building), pp.96–97, A1
South Angel, California (city), pp.18–19, B3
Akiba Town, Eastal (fictional city), pp.96–97, C3
Susukino, Ezzo Empire (fictional city), pp.96–97, C3
Taibei, Taiwan (city), pp.102–103, D1
Tearstone Mountains, Eastal (fictional mountain range), pp.96–97, C3
Tekeli, Aorusoi (fictional town), pp.72–73, D3
Thekkek, Aorusoi (fictional village), pp.72–73, D3
Tone's Grave, Aorusoi (fictional building), pp.72–73, D3
Yandu, China (city), pp.102–103, D3
Yangdu, China (city), pp.102–103, D1
Zantleaf Peninsula, Eastal (fictional region), pp.96–97, C2
Logan (film), Eden, North Dakota (building), pp.16–17, A6
Lois & Clark: The New Adventures of Superman (TV), New Troy (fictional state), pp.14–15, C5
Lola uppochner by Monika Fagerholm (novel), Flatnäs, Finland (town), pp.56–57, D2
Lolita by Vladimir Nabokov (novel/film) Parkington, New York (town), pp.14–15, C5
Ramsdale, Massachusetts (town), pp.14–15, C5
Udana (fictional state), pp.18–19, C5
Lone Star (TV) Frontera, Texas (town), pp.16–17, A2
Rio County, Texas (county), pp.16–17, A2
Lonely Train a' Comin'/Helltrain by William F. Nolan (short story/novel) Bitterroot, Montana (town), pp.18–19, D6
Danvers Hill, Montana (town), pp.18–19, D6
Moccasin Peak, Montana (mountain), pp.18–19, D6
Look Around You (TV), Holdwick Park Refinery, England (building), pp.64–65, C2
Look Homeward, Angel by Thomas Wolfe (novel) Altamont, Catawba (fictional town), pp.14–15, B3
Catawba Mountains, Catawba (fictional mountain range), pp.14–15, B3

157

Pulpit Hill, Catawba (fictional town), pp.14–15, C3

Catawba (fictional state), pp.14–15, B3/C3

Lords of the Deep (film), Neptune Base (Martel Corporation), Pacific Ocean (submerged building), pp.120–121, A4

Lorna Doone by Richard Doddridge Blackmore (novel), Doone Valley, England (natural feature), pp.64–65, A2

Los Perros de Anagua by Eugeni Aguirre (novel), Angagua, Mexico (town), pp.32–33, B2

Lost (TV), Island, The /Oceanic Flight 815, Pacific Ocean (unmappable island/wreck), pp.120–121, C2

Lost Horizon by James Hilton (novel)
Mount Karakal, Tibet (mountain), pp.102–103, A2/A3
Shangri-La, Tibet (natural feature/building), pp.102–103, A2

Love and Rockets by Los Bros Hernandez (comic), Huerta, California (town), pp.18–19, A3

Love and Summer by William Trevor (novel), Rathmoye, Ireland (town), pp.64–65, A2

Love Hina by Ken Akamatsu (manga/anime)
Hinata, Japan (town), pp.96–97, E1
Molmol, Kingdom of, Pacific Ocean (island), pp.120–121, D3
Pararakelse, Pacific Ocean (island), pp.120–121, D3

Love on a Branch Line by John Hadfield (novel), Arcady, England (town), pp.64–65, D2

Lovejoy (TV), Felsham Hall, England (building), pp.64–65, D2

Lucia novels by Edward Frederic Benson (novels), Riseholme, England (village), pp.64–65, D2

Luna, el misterio de Calenda (TV), Calenda, Spain (town), pp.44–45, B2

Lymond Chronicles by Dorothy Dunnett (novels)
Flaw Valleys, England (estate), pp.64–65, C3
Midculter, Scotland (town), pp.64–65, C4

Ma & Pa Kettle films, Cape Flattery, Washington (town), pp.18–19, A6

MacGyver (TV), Kambezi (fictional country), pp.84–85, C3

Mac Trump by Ian Doescher and Jacopo Della Quercia (book)
Alabangor, Alabama (state), pp.14–15, A3
Alaskatchewan, Alaska (state), pp.18–19, A1/B1
Cyprum, Cyprus (island), pp.44–45, F1
Helsingfort, Finland (city), pp.56–57, D3
Indriana, Indiana (state), pp.14–15, A4
Mar-Iago, Florida (building), pp.14–15, C1
Mexitlán, Mexico (country), pp.32–33, B3
New Yorktown, New York (city), pp.14–15, D1
North Dakastor, North Dakota (state), pp.16–17, A5/B5
North Korasia, North Korea (country), pp.102–103, E3
Payment Islands, The, Caribbean (island chain), pp.32–33, D2
Qanada (fictional country), pp.26–27, C
South Dakastor, South Dakota (state), pp.16–17, A5/B5
South Korasia, South Korea (country), pp.102–103, E2
Switzerloan, Switzerland (country), pp.44–45, C3

Mad Max (video game) (video Game), Great White, The, Pacific Ocean (desert/sea), pp.108–109, E3

Mad Max 3 (film), Tomorrow-Morrow Land, New South Wales (city), pp.108–109, D2/C2
Mad Max films, Wasteland, The (fictional country/desert), pp.108–109, C2/D2

Mad Max Beyond the Thunderdome (film)
Bartertown, The Wasteland (fictional town), pp.108–109, C2
The Thunderdome, The Wasteland (fictional building), pp.108–109, C2

Mad Max Fury Road (film)
Badlands, The, The Wasteland (fictional region), pp.108–109, D2
Bullet Farm, The Wasteland (fictional building), pp.108–109, D2
Citadel, The, The Wasteland (fictional town), pp.108–109, D2
Fury Road, The Wasteland (fictional Road, pp.108–109, D2
Gas Town, The Wasteland (fictional town), pp.108–109, D2
Sunken City, The, The Wasteland (fictional town), pp.108–109, D2

Madagascar franchise (films), King Julien's Kingdom of Madagascar, Madagascar (country), pp.84–85, D2

Madame Bovary by Gustave Flaubert (novel), Yonville-l'Abbaye, France (village), pp.44–45, C3

Madmen of Mandoras/They Saved Hitler's Brain (films), Mandoras (fictional country), pp.38–39, B3

Mafia (video game), Lost Heaven, Unknown (city), pp.14–15, D5

Mafia 2 (video game)
Empire Bay (city), pp.14–15, D5
San Celeste, Italy (town), pp.44–45, D1

Mafia 3 (video game)
Bayou Fantom, Louisiana (natural feature), pp.16–17, D2
New Bordeaux, Louisiana (city), pp.16–17, D2
Sinclair Parish, Louisiana (county), pp.16–17, D2

Magellan (TV), Saignac, France (town), pp.44–45, C4

Magnum PI (TV), Robin's Nest, Hawaii (building), pp.18–19, C1

Main Street by Sinclair Lewis (novel), Gopher Prairie, Minnesota (town), pp.16–17, C5

Maji de Watashi ni Koi Shinasai! (visual novels/video games), Kawakami City, Japan (city), pp.96–97, E1
Nanahama, Japan (city), pp.96–97, E1

Making Wolf by Tade Thompson (novel), Alcacia (fictional country), pp.84–85, A2

Malamander by Thomas Taylor (novel), Eerie-on-Sea, England (town), pp.64–65, C3

Malory Towers series by Enid Blyton (novels), Malory Towers, England (building), pp.64–65, B1

Mamma Mia! (film), Kalokairi, Greece (island), pp.44–45, E1

Mämmilä by Tarmo Koivisto and Hannu Virtanen (comic strip), Mämmilä, Finland (town), pp.56–57, D3

Man of Medan and real life (video game/urban legend), SS *Ourang Medan*, Pacific Ocean (wreck), pp.120–121, B4/C4

Mandate of Heaven by Tim Murgatroyd (novel), Hou-Ming, China (city), pp.102–103, C2

Maneater (video game), Port Clovis, Louisiana (town), pp.14–15, C1

Maniac Magee by Jerry Spinelli (novel), Two Mills, Pennsylvania (town), pp.14–15, C4

Manos: The Hands of Fate (film), Master's Lodge, The, Texas (building), pp.18–19, D2

Mansfield Park by Jane Austen (novel), Mansfield Park, England (estate), pp.64–65, D2

Manushyanu Oru Aamukham by Subhash Chandran (novel), Thachanakkara, India (village), pp.78–79, B2

Mar de Amor (TV), playa Escondida, Mexico (town), pp.32–33, C2

Mardi, and A Voyage Thither by Herman Melville (novel), Mardi Archipelago, Pacific Ocean (island chain), pp.120–121, E3

Margaret of Ashbury series by Judith Astria Merkle (novels), Ashbury Estate, Scotland (estate), pp.64–65, C5

'Margaritaville' by Jimmy Buffett (song), Margaritaville, Florida (town), pp.14–15, C1

Marianela by Benito Pérez Galdós (novel), Villamojada and the mines of Socartes, Spain (town), pp.44–45, B2

Marianne (TV), Elden, France (village), pp.44–45, B3

Mark Trail by Ed Dodd (comic), Lost Forest National Forest, Georgia (natural feature), pp.14–15, B3

Marmadesam (TV), Chitharpatti, India (village), pp.78–79, B2

Marparaíso (TV), Marparaíso, Chile (town), pp.38–39, B3

Married Quarters by Shane Connaughton (novel), Butlershill, Ireland (town), pp.64–65, A3

Married With Children (TV), Lucifer, New Mexico (town), pp.18–19, D3

Marrow by Yan Lianke (novel), Four Idiots Village, China (village), pp.102–103, D2

Marshall Law (comic), San Futuro, California (city), pp.18–19, A4

Martin Chuzzlewit by Charles Dickens (novel)
Eden, Illinois (town), pp.16–17, D3
New Thermopylae, Illinois (town), pp.16–17, D4

Martin Mystère by Alfredo Castelli and Giancarlo Alessandrini (comic), City of Lucid Shadows, The, Mongolia (city), pp.102–103, B4

Marvel Cinematic Universe (various)
Batesville, Utah (town), pp.18–19, C4
Fagan Corners, Vermont (town), pp.14–15, C5
Gulmira, Afghanistan (town), pp.72–73, D2
Hydra Headquarters, Austria (building), pp.44–45, C3
Larkville, Ohio (town), pp.14–15, A4
Puente Antiguo, New Mexico (town), pp.16–17, A2
River's End, New York (town), pp.14–15, C4
Roxxon Norco, Florida (wreck), pp.14–15, C1
Union City, Wyoming (town), pp.18–19, D4
Wheaton, New Jersey (town), pp.14–15, C4

Marvel Comics/Marvel Cinematic Universe
Alpha Flight Base Camp, Yukon (island), pp.26–27, B2
Apaco, Mexico (city), pp.32–33, C2
Apocalypse's Pyramid, Egypt (building), pp.84–85, C5
Aqiria (fictional country), pp.72–73, B2/B3
Bastrona (fictional country), pp.38–39, A5/B5
Birnin Zana (The Golden City), Wakanda (fictional city), pp.84–85, D4
Boca Caliente (fictional island/nation), pp.32–33, F2
Bosqueverde (fictional country), pp.38–39, B5/C5

Cassidy Keep, Ireland (building), pp.64–65, A3

Castle Kaufmann, Germany (building), pp.44–45, D3

Citrusville, Florida (town), pp.14–15, C1

Costa Perdita (fictional country), pp.32–33, C2

Costa Verde (fictional country), pp.32–33, C2

Darkmoor, England (natural feature), pp.64–65, B2

Delvadia (fictional country), pp.38–39, A5

Estrella (fictional country), pp.38–39, B4

Exile Island, Caribbean (island), pp.32–33, E3

Freehold, Alberta (city), pp.26–27, C1

Gateway to Olympus, Greece (building), pp.44–45, E2

Genosha (fictional island/nation), pp.84–85, D3

Halwan (fictional country), pp.84–85, B5

Hammer Bay/Black Roma, Genosha (fictional city), pp.84–85, D3

Hegeman, New York (town), pp.14–15, C5

Howlett Estate, Alberta (building), pp.26–27, C1

Ipeiros Mountains, Greece (mountain range), pp.44–45, E2

Isla de Tiburon, Mexico (island), pp.32–33, A3

Jaffan, Trans-Sabal (fictional city), pp.72–73, B2

K'un-Lun, Tibet (mountain), pp.102–103, C1

Kirinos, Greece (island), pp.44–45, E1

Krozniev, Vorozheika (fictional city), pp.72–73, C4

Logan, Alberta (town), pp.26–27, C1

Madripoor (fictional city/state), pp.90–91, B2

Makazan (fictional country), pp.72–73, C2

Maskattawan Dam, Quebec (building), pp.26–27, E1

Mazikhandar (fictional country), pp.72–73, B1/C1

Medisuela (fictional country), pp.38–39, B3/C3

Mena Ngai (The Great Mound), Wakanda (fictional natural feature), pp.84–85, D4

Olympia, Greece (city), pp.44–45, E1

Panchajana, India (building), pp.78–79, B3

Roanoke, Alberta (town), pp.26–27, C1

San Diablo (fictional country), pp.38–39, B5

Santo Rico (fictional country), pp.32–33, C2

Savage Land, The (region), pp.114–115, B3

Sharzhad (fictional country), pp.84–85, C5

Sin-Cong (fictional country), pp.102–103, C1

Tamarind Island, British Columbia (island), pp.26–27, B1

Terra Verde (fictional country), pp.32–33, C2

Thoat Nhin, Sin-Cong (fictional city), pp.102–103, C1

Tierra Verde (fictional country), pp.38–39, C5

Trans-Sabal (fictional country), pp.72–73, B1/C1

Transverse City, Illinois/Indiana/Michigan (city), pp.14–15, A5

Vorozheika (fictional country), pp.72–73, C4

Wakanda (fictional County), pp.84–85, D4

Weapon X Facility, Alberta (building), pp.26–27, D4

Marvel/X-Men (films)
Alkali Lake, Alberta (lake), pp.26–27, C1
Laughlin City, Alberta (town), pp.26–27, C1

Mary Hartman, Mary Hartman (TV), Fernwood, Ohio (town), pp.14–15, B4

Matador (TV), Korsbæk, Denmark (town), pp.56–57, B1

Maten al león by Jorge Ibargüengoitia (novel), Arepa, Mexico (island), pp.32–33, C3

Material Girls by Deborah Steele (musical), Barrington, New Zealand (town), pp.108–109, F2

Matlock Police (TV), Matlock, Victoria (town), pp.108–109, E2

Matru Ki Bijlee Ka Mandola (film), Mandola, India (town), pp.78–79, B4

Matrubhoomi: A Nation Without Women (film), Matrubhoomi, India (village), pp.78–79, C4

Maverick (film), Crystal River, Utah/Arizona (town), pp.18–19, C3

May Bukas Pa (TV), Bagong Pag-asa, Philippines (town), pp.90–91, C3

Maze Runner: The Death Cure (film), Last City, Colorado (city), pp.16–17, A4

McCabe & Mrs Miller (film), Presbyterian Church, Washington (town), pp.18–19, B6

McCoubrey by Mark McCaffery (novel), Portstown, Northern Ireland (town), pp.64–65, A3

McHale's Navy (TV)
Borgabunda, Pacific Ocean (island), pp.120–121, B3/B4
Taratupa, Pacific Ocean (island), pp.120–121, C1

McLeod's Daughters (TV)
Drover's Run, New South Wales (estate), pp.108–109, D2

Gungellan, New South Wales (town), pp.108–109, D2

Killarney, New South Wales (estate), pp.108–109, D2

Me, Myself and Irene (film), Rutland, New York (town), pp.14–15, C5

Meccania: The Super-State by Owen Gregory (novel), Meccania (fictional country), pp.44–45, D3

Medicine River by Thomas King (novel), Medicine River, Alberta (town), pp.26–27, C1

Meeting Lydia by Linda MacDonald (novel)
Derwentbridge, England (town), pp.64–65, C3
Waterside, England (town), pp.64–65, C3

Melincourt by Thomas Love Peacock (novel), Melincourt Castle, England (building), pp.64–65, C3

Meltybrains (band), Meltybrook, Ireland (city), pp.64–65, B3

Men in Trees (TV), Elmo, Alaska (town), pp.18–19, B1

Mercenaries 2: World in Flames (video game)
Isla de la Fortelaza, Venezuela (island), pp.38–39, B6
Pirate Isles, The, Venezuela (islands), pp.38–39, B6

Meropis by Theopompus of Chios (book)
Anostos, Meropis (fictional sunken city), pp.126–127, C1
Meropis (fictional sunken city), pp.126–127, D1
Machimos, Meropis (fictional sunken city), pp.126–127, D2
Lost Continent of Meropis (fictional sunken continent), pp.126–127, C1/D1/C2/D2

Mesolar (TV), Hoikan, Finland (town), pp.56–57, D4

Metal Gear (video game)
Galzburg, South Africa (region), pp.84–85, C2
Outer Heaven (fictional city/state), pp.84–85, C2

Metal Gear Solid series (video game)
Camp Omega, Cuba (building), pp.32–33, E2
Discovery KSNM-3, New York (wreck), pp.14–15, D5
Old Moses, Alaska (mountain), pp.18–19, A1
Shadow Moses Island, Alaska (island), pp.18–19, A1
Zanzibar, Zanzibarland (fictional city), pp.72–73, E2
Zanzibarland (fictional country), pp.72–73, E2

Metroland by Julian Barnes (novel), Eastwick, England (town), pp.64–65, D2

Metropolis (film), Metropolis, Germany (city), pp.44–45, C4

Meu Bem Querer (TV), São Tomás de Trás, Brazil (town), pp.38–39, D5

Mickey Mouse (various), Mouseton, Calisota (fictional city), pp.18–19, A5

Micro Nation (TV), Pullamawang (fictional island/nation), pp.108–109, E2

Middlemarch by George Eliot (novel)
Freshitt, England (town), pp.64–65, C2
Middlemarch, England (town), pp.64–65, C2

Middletown, Northern Ireland (town), pp.64–65, B3

Midnight, Texas (TV), Midnight, Texas (town), pp.16–17, A2

Midsomer Murders (TV)
Causton, England (town), pp.64–65, C2
Midsomer, England (county), pp.64–65, C2

Mile 22 (film)
Indocarr City, Indocarr (fictional city), pp.90–91, B1
Indocarr (fictional country), pp.90–91, B1/C1

Milestone Media (various), Dakota City, pp.16–17, B5

Milford: A Fictional Irish Town (stage act), Milford, Ireland (town), pp.64–65, A2

Military training exercise
Abar Layla, Iraq (town), pp.72–73, C2
Carnis, Afghanistan (village), pp.72–73, E2
Ertebat Shar, Afghanistan (village), pp.72–73, D2
Medina Wasi, Iraq (village), pp.72–73, C2
Sadiq, Iraq (village), pp.72–73, C2
Sangari, Afghanistan (village), pp.72–73, D2/E2
Trebil, Iraq (village), pp.72–73, C2
Wadi al-Sahara, Iraq (town), pp.72–73, C2

Minnow on the Say by Philippa Pearce (novel), Great Barley, England (village), pp.64–65, C2

Mira, Royal Detective (TV), Jalpur (fictional city/state), pp.78–79, B4

Mirror's Edge (video games)
Cascadia (fictional country), pp.108–109, D2
Glass, New South Wales (city), pp.108–109, D1
OmniStat (fictional country), pp.108–109, C2
Sabaeus (fictional country), pp.108–109, D2

Misfile by Chris Hazelton (web comic), Tempest, Massachusetts (town), pp.14–15, C5

Miss Muriel and Other Stories by Ann Petry (short stories), Essex, Connecticut (town), pp.14–15, C5/D5

Miss Peregrine's Home for Peculiar Children by

Ransom Riggs (novel/film)
sland of Cairnholme, Wales (island), pp.64–65, B2
Miss Peregrine's Home for Peculiar Children, Wales (building), pp.64–65, B2
RMS *Augusta*, Wales (wreck), pp.64–65, B2

Miss Seeton novels by Hamilton Crane (novels), Plummergen, England (village), pp.64–65, D1

Missing Soluch by Mahmoud Dowlatabadi (novel), Zaminej, Iran (village), pp.72–73, E4

Mission Impossible (TV)
Bocamo (fictional country), pp.84–85, A4
Santa Costa (fictional island/nation), pp.32–33, E2

Mission Impossible: 'The Seal' (TV), Kuala Rokat, India/China (country), pp.78–79, D4

Mistress Masham's Repose by T.H. White (novel), Malplaquet, England (estate), pp.64–65, C2

Moana (film)
Lalotai, Pacific Ocean (island), pp.120–121, D3
Maui's Island, Pacific Ocean (island), pp.120–121, D3
Motunui, Pacific Ocean (island), pp.120–121, D3
Te Fiti, Pacific Ocean (island), pp.120–121, D3

Mobile Suit Gundam (anime)
Great Canyon, The, Arizona (natural feature), pp.18–19, C3
Hickory, California (building), pp.18–19, A3
St Agnes, Arizona (town), pp.18–19, C3

Mobile Suit Gundam Wing (anime)
Lake Victoria Military Academy, Tanzania (building), pp.84–85, C3
New Edwards Base, California (building), pp.18–19, B3
Noventa Cannon, The, Somalia (building), pp.84–85, D4

Mobile Suit Gundam/Hellsing (anime/manga), Jaburo, Brazil (underground city), pp.38–39, C5

Moby Dick by Herman Melville (novel)
Pequod, Pacific Ocean (wreck), pp.120–121, C3
Rokovoko, Pacific Ocean (island), pp.120–121, D3

Molly of Denali (TV), Qyah, Alaska (town), pp.18–19, B1

Monarch of the Glen (TV), Glenbogle, Scotland (estate), pp.64–65, B4

Mondo Desperado by Patrick McCabe (book), Barntrosna, Ireland (town), pp.64–65, B3

Monkey Island series (video games)
Booty Island, Caribbean (island), pp.32–33, F2
Boulder Beach, Gulf of Melange (fictional island), pp.32–33, F2
Ewe, Gulf of Melange (fictional island), pp.32–33, F2
Flotsam Island, Gulf of Melange (fictional island), pp.32–33, F2
Golfo de Pollo, Caribbean (region), pp.32–33, E3
Gulf of Melange, Caribbean (region), pp.32–33, F2
Jambalaya Island, Caribbean (island), pp.32–33, E3
Jerkbait Islands, The, Gulf of Melange (fictional island chain), pp.32–33, F2
Lucre Island, Caribbean (island), pp.32–33, E3
Mêlée Island, Caribbean (island), pp.32–33, E3
Monkey Island, Caribbean (island), pp.32–33, E3
Phatt Island, Caribbean (island), pp.32–33, E3
Plunder Island, Caribbean (island), pp.32–33, E3
Rock of Gelato, Gulf of Melange (fictional island), pp.32–33, F2
Roe Island, Gulf of Melange (fictional island), pp.32–33, F2
Scabb Island, Caribbean (island), pp.32–33, E3
Spinner Cay, Gulf of Melange (fictional island), pp.32–33, F2
Spoon Island, Gulf of Melange (fictional island), pp.32–33, F2
Tri-Island Area, Caribbean (region/island chain), pp.32–33, E3

Monkey Island series/*The Pirates' Band of Misfits!* (video games), Blood Island, Caribbean (island), pp.32–33, E3

Monster High (various), New Salem, Oregon (town), pp.18–19, A5

Montana 1948 by Larry Watson (novel)
Bentrock, Montana (town), pp.16–17, A6
Mercer County, Montana (county), pp.16–17, A6

Monty Python and the Holy Grail (film)
Castle of Aaaaarrrrrrggghhh, The, Scotland (building), pp.64–65, C1
Cave of Caerbannog, Scotland (natural feature), pp.64–65, B4

Moon Child (film), Mallepa, Taiwan (town), pp.102–103, D3

Moonfleet by J. Meade Falkner (novel), Moonfleet, England (town), pp.64–65, C1

Moonrise Kingdom (film), New Penzance, Rhode Island (island), pp.14–15, D5

Moral Orel (TV)
Freedom County, Statesota (fictional County), pp.16–17, C3

Vale do Café, Brazil (natural feature), pp.38–39, C3

Orphan Island by Rose Macaulay (novel), Orphan Island, Pacific Ocean (island), pp.120–121, D2

Our Man Flint (film), Galaxy Island, Italy (island), pp.44–45, D1

Our Town by Thornton Wilder (play), Grover's Corner, New Hampshire (town), pp.14–15, C1

Ouran High School Host Club by Bisco Hatori (manga/anime), Ouran Academy, Japan (building), pp.96–97, E1

Out of Time (film), Banyan Key, Florida (town), pp.18–19, C1

Outbreak (film), Cedar Creek, California (town), pp.18–19, A5

Outbuddies (video game), Bahlam, Atlantic Ocean (sunken city), pp.126–127, C1

Outlander (novel/TV)
Abandawe, Jamaica (stone circle), pp.32–33, D2
Fraser's Ridge, North Carolina (natural feature), pp.14–15, B3
River Run Plantation, North Carolina (building), pp.14–15, B3

Outlander novels by Diana Gabaldon (novels/TV)
Ardsmuir Prison, Scotland (town), pp.64–65, B5
Brockton, Scotland (town), pp.64–65, B4
Castle Leoch, Scotland (building), pp.64–65, B5
Craigh na Dun, Scotland (stone circle), pp.64–65, C5
Cranesmuir, Scotland (village), pp.64–65, B5
Helwater, England (estate), pp.64–65, C3
Lallybroch, Scotland (building), pp.64–65, B4
Silkies' Isle, Scotland (island), pp.64–65, B5
Wentworth Prison, Scotland (building), pp.64–65, C4

Outlaw Star (anime)
Arashon Desert, China (region), pp.102–103, C3
Dragonite Meteorite, The, China (natural feature), pp.102–103, C3

Over Sea, Under Stone by Susan Cooper (novel), Trewissick, England (town), pp.64–65, B1

Over the Edge (role playing game), Al Amarja, Mediterranean Sea (island nation), pp.44–45, D1

Overboard (film), Elk Cove, Oregon (town), pp.18–19, A5

Overwatch (video game)
Castillo, Mexico (building), pp.32–33, B3
Dorado, Mexico (city), pp.32–33, B3
Ecopoint: Antarctica (facility), pp.114–115, C2
Hanamura, Japan (town), pp.96–97, C2
Junkertown, Northern Territory (town), pp.108–109, D3
Numbani (fictional city/state), pp.84–85, B4
Oasis, Iraq (city), pp.72–73, C2
Shambali Monastery, Nepal (building), pp.78–79, C4
Siberian Omnium, The, Russia (building), pp.102–103, E1
Utopaea, India (city), pp.78–79, B3

Oyster by Janette Turner Hospital (novel), Outer Maroo, Queensland (town), pp.108–109, D3

Oyster War (comic), Blood's Haven, Maryland (town), pp.14–15, C4

Pacific Rim (film), Anchorage Shatterdome, Alaska (building), pp.18–19, B1
Breach, The, Pacific Ocean (dimensional portal), pp.90–91, F3
Hong Kong Shatterdome, China (building), pp.102–103, D1
Lima Shatterdome, Peru (military base), pp.38–39, A4
Los Angeles Shatterdome, California (building), pp.18–19, A3
Nagasaki Shatterdome, Japan (building), pp.96–97, A1
Panama City Shatterdome, Panama (building), pp.32–33, D1
Sydney Shatterdome, New South Wales (building), pp.108–109, F4
Tokyo Shatterdome, Japan (building), pp.96–97, F1
Vladivostok Shatterdome, Russia (building), pp.102–103, E3

Pair of Kings (TV), Kinkow Archipelago, Pacific Ocean (island chain), pp.120–121, D2

Pale Fire by Vladimir Nabokov (novel)
Appalachia (fictional state), pp.14–15, B4/C4
Cedarn, Utana (fictional town), pp.18–19, D5
Idoming (fictional state), pp.18–19, D5
New Wye, Appalachia (town), pp.14–15, B4
Utana (fictional state), pp.18–19, C5/D5

Pale Rider (film)
Lahood, California (town), pp.18–19, A4
Yuba City, California (town), pp.18–19, A4

Pallet on the Floor by Hugh Morrieson (novel), Kurikino, New Zealand (town), pp.108–109, F2

Pandora and the Flying Dutchman (film), Esperanza, Spain (town), pp.44–45, C2

Panorama (TV), Panorama Spaghetti Farm, Switzerland (building), pp.44–45, C2

Paper Tiger (film), Kulagong (fictional country), pp.90–91, C2

Papers, Please (video game)
Arstotzka (fictional country), pp.72–73, C4
Grestin (East and West), Arstotzka/Kolechia (fictional city), pp.72–73, C4
Kolechia (fictional country), pp.72–73, C4
Nirsk, Arstotzka (fictional town), pp.72–73, C4
Yurko City, Kolechia (fictional city), pp.72–73, C4

Paradise (TV), Paradise, California (town), pp.18–19, A3

Paradise Beach (TV), Paradise Beach, Queensland (town), pp.108–109, E2

Parken Zoo (theme park), Ordköping, Sweden (town), pp.56–57, C3

Parks and Recreation (TV)
Boraqua, Venezuela (city), pp.38–39, B5
Eagleton, Indiana (town), pp.14–15, A4
Pawnee, Indiana (city), pp.14–15, A4
Wamapoke County, Indiana (county), pp.14–15, A4

Party Members by Arthur Meursault (novel), Huaishi, China (city), pp.102–103, D2

Passions (TV), Harmony, Maine (town), pp.14–15, D5

Pather Panchali by Bibhutibhushan Bandyopadhyay (novel/film), Nischindipur, India (village), pp.78–79, D4

Pathologic series (video game), River Gorkhon, Mongolia (river), pp.102–103, C4

Patsy by Nicole Dennis-Benn (novel), Pennyfield, Jamaica (town), pp.32–33, D2

Peacock (film), Peacock, Nebraska (town), pp.16–17, B4

Peak Practice (TV), Cardale, England (town), pp.64–65, C2

Pecadores/Sinners (TV), El Edén, Chile (town), pp.38–39, B3

Pedra Sobre Pedra (TV), Resplendor, Brazil (town), pp.38–39, D4

Pedro Páramo by Juan Rulfo (novel), Comala, Mexico (town), pp.32–33, B2

Peepli Live (film), Peepli, India (village), pp.78–79, B4

Peer Gynt by Henrik Ibsen (music), Realm of the Troll Mountain King, Norway (region), pp.56–57, A4

Penguin Island by Anatole France (novel), Penguinia, Channel Islands (country), pp.64–65, A1

Penguins of Madagascar (film), Dave's Secret Island, Pacific Ocean (island), pp.90–91, D4

Percy Jackson series by Rick Riordan (novels/films)
Gila Claw, Arizona (town), pp.18–19, C3
Westover Hall, Maine (building), pp.14–15, D6

Perdona Nuestros Pecados/Pardon our Sins (TV), Villa Ruiseñor, Chile (town), pp.38–39, B2

Perfect Strangers (TV)
Mypos, Greece (island nation), pp.44–45, E1
Pathos, Greece (island nation), pp.44–45, E1
Skeptos, Greece (island nation), pp.44–45, E1

Peril at End House by Agatha Christie (novel), St Loo, England (town), pp.64–65, C1

Persona series (video games)
Ayanagi City, Japan (city), pp.96–97, C2
Inaba, Japan (town), pp.96–97, C2
Sumaru, Japan (city), pp.96–97, C2

Persuasion by Jane Austen (novel)
Kellynch Hall, England (estate), pp.64–65, C1
Uppercross, England (town), pp.64–65, C1

Petals of Blood by Ngũgĩ wa Thiong'o (novel), Ilmorog, Kenya (village), pp.84–85, D3

Peter by Rutherford Mayne (play), Portahoy, Northern Ireland (town), pp.64–65, B3

Peter Pan by J.M. Barrie (novels/films), Neverland, Belize (island), pp.32–33, C2

Peter Rabbit by Beatrix Potter (various), McGregor Farm, England (building), pp.64–65, C3

Peter Wimsey stories by Dorothy L. Sayers (novels), Duke's Denver, England (village), pp.64–65, D2

Petticoat Junction/Green Acres (TV), Hooterville, Pixley, Skidmore, Melton, C&FW Railroad, Kentucky (town), pp.14–15, A3

Peyton Place by Grace Metalious (novel/TV), Peyton Place, New Hampshire (town), pp.14–15, C5

Phaic Tăn (book), Phaic Tăn (fictional country), pp.90–91, B3

Phantom Manor (theme parks)
Phantom Canyon, Arizona (town), pp.18–19, C3
Phantom Manor/Ravenswood Manor, Arizona (building), pp.18–19, C3

Photopia (video game), Turtalia (fictional region), pp.26–27, B1

Picket Fences (TV)
Hogan County, Wisconsin (county), pp.16–17, D5
Rome, Wisconsin (town), pp.16–17, D5

Pie in the Sky (TV), Barstock, England (town), pp.64–65, D2

Pinocchio (various), Land of Toys, Italy (island), pp.44–45, C2

Pioneer, Go Home! by Richard Powell (novel), Columbiana (fictional state), pp.14–15, B1/B2

Piranha (1978 film), Lost River Lake, Texas (lake), pp.16–17, B2

Pirates of the Caribbean (various)
Black Sand Island, Caribbean (island), pp.32–33, C4
Crooked Cove, Caribbean (island), pp.32–33, D2/E2
Cutthroat Isle, Caribbean (island), pp.32–33, C4
Dead Man's Eye, Caribbean (island), pp.32–33, C4
Devil's Anvil, Caribbean (island), pp.32–33, F2
Devil's Triangle, The, Caribbean (island), pp.32–33, F2
Dodo's Perch, Caribbean (island), pp.32–33, D2
HMS *Endeavour*, Caribbean (wreck), pp.32–33, F2
HMS *Interceptor*, Caribbean (wreck), pp.32–33, F2
Île d'Etable de Porc, Caribbean (island), pp.32–33, F2
Isla Cangrejos, Caribbean (island), pp.32–33, F2
Isla Cruces, Caribbean (island), pp.32–33, F2
Isla de la Avaricia, Caribbean (island), pp.32–33, F2
Isla de Muerta, Caribbean (island), pp.32–33, F2
Island of the Fountain of Youth, Caribbean (island), pp.32–33, D3/E3
Kingshead, Caribbean (town), pp.32–33, F2
Pelegosto, Caribbean (island), pp.32–33, F2
Port Tortuga, Caribbean (town), pp.32–33, E2
Rambleshack, Caribbean (island), pp.32–33, D2
Ruddy Rose and HMS *Monarch*, Caribbean (wreck), pp.32–33, F2
Rum-runner's Isle, Caribbean (island), pp.32–33, F2
Scurvy Beach, Caribbean (island), pp.32–33, D2
Shipwreck Island, Caribbean (island), pp.32–33, F2
Sola Fide Beach, Caribbean (island), pp.32–33, F2
South Archipelago, The, Caribbean (island), pp.32–33, F2
Tum Boom Island, Caribbean (island), pp.32–33, C3

Planes (film), Propwash Junction, Minnesota (town), pp.16–17, C6

Planetes (manga/anime), El Tanika (fictional country), pp.38–39, B3

'Plastic Beach' by Gorillaz (music), Plastic Beach, Pacific Ocean (island), pp.120–121, E1

Pleasantville (film), Pleasantville, California (town), pp.18–19, A3

Plus Belle la Vie (TV), Le Mistral, France (region), pp.44–45, C3

Pobol y Cwm (TV)
Cwmderi, Wales (town), pp.64–65, C2
Cwrtmynach, Wales (village), pp.64–65, C2
Llanarthur, Wales (village), pp.64–65, C2

Pocahontas (Disney film), Quiyoughcohannock River, Virginia (river), pp.14–15, B4/C4

Pokémon (video games)
Agate Village, Arizona (town), pp.18–19, C3
Akala Island, Hawaii (island), pp.18–19, D1
Alola, Hawaii (region/state), pp.18–19, C1/D1
Ambrette Town, France (town), pp.44–45, B3
Anistar City, France (city), pp.44–45, C3
Aquacorde Town, France (town), pp.44–45, C3
Azalea Town, Japan (town), pp.96–97, B1
Azure Bay, France (sea), pp.44–45, B4/C4
Blackthorn City, Japan (city), pp.96–97, C2
Blush Mountain, Hawaii (mountain), pp.18–19, D1
Camphrier Town, France (town), pp.44–45, C3
Canalave City, Japan (city), pp.96–97, C4
Celadon City, Japan (city), pp.96–97, E1
Celestic Town, Japan (city), pp.96–97, D4
Cerulean City, Japan (city), pp.96–97, C2
Cherrygrove City, Japan (city), pp.96–97, C2
Cianwood City, Japan (city), pp.96–97, B2
Cinnabar Island, Japan (island), pp.96–97, C
Coumarine City, France (city), pp.44–45, C3
Couriway Town, France (city), pp.44–45, C3
Cyllage City, France (city), pp.44–45, C3
Dendemille Town, France (town), pp.44–45, C3
Dewford Town, Japan (city), pp.96–97, A2
Ecruteak City, Japan (city), pp.96–97, B2
Eterna City, Japan (city), pp.96–97, C4
Ever Grande City, Japan (city), pp.96–97, D1
Fallarbor Town, Japan (town), pp.96–97, A1
Floaroma Town, Japan (town), pp.96–97, C4

Fullmoon Island, Japan (island), pp.96–97, C4
Fuschia City, Japan (city), pp.96–97, C2
Geosenge Town, France (town), pp.44–45, B3
Goldenrod City, Japan (city), pp.96–97, B2
Hau'oli City, Hawaii (city), pp.18–19, C1
Heahea City, Hawaii (town), pp.18–19, D1
Hearthome City, Japan (city), pp.96–97, D4
Hoenn, Japan (region), pp.96–97, A1
Iki Town, Hawaii (village), pp.18–19, C1
Iron Island, Japan (island), pp.96–97, C4
Johto, Japan (region), pp.96–97, B2
Jubilife City, Japan (city), pp.96–97, C4
Kalos, France (region), pp.44–45, C3
Kanto Power Plant, Japan (building), pp.96–97, C2
Kiloude City, France (city), pp.44–45, C3
Konikoni City, Hawaii (town), pp.18–19, C1
Lake of Rage, Japan (natural feature), pp.96–97, B2
Lake Verity, Japan (natural feature), pp.96–97, C4
Lavender Town, Japan (town), pp.96–97, C2
Laverre City, France (city), pp.44–45, C3
Lilycove City, Japan (city), pp.96–97, A1
Littleroot Town, Japan (town), pp.96–97, A1
Lumiose City, France (city), pp.44–45, C3
Mahogany Town, Japan (town), pp.96–97, B2
Malie City, Hawaii (city), pp.18–19, D1
Mauville City, Japan (city), pp.96–97, A1
Melemele Island, Hawaii (island), pp.18–19, C1
Mossdeep City, Japan (city), pp.96–97, A1
Mossdeep Space Centre, Japan (building), pp.96–97, A1
Mt Chimney, Japan (mountain), pp.96–97, A1
Mt Hokulani, Hawaii (mountain), pp.18–19, D1
Mt Lanakila, Hawaii (mountain), pp.18–19, D1
Mt Moon, Japan (mountain), pp.96–97, C2
Mt Mortar, Japan (mountain), pp.96–97, B2
Mt Pyre, Japan (mountain), pp.96–97, A1
Mt Silver, Japan (mountain), pp.96–97, C2
New Bark Town, Japan (town), pp.96–97, C2
Newmoon Island, Japan (island), pp.96–97, C4
Oldale Town, Japan (town), pp.96–97, A1
Olivine City, Japan (city), pp.96–97, B2
Oreburgh City, Japan (city), pp.96–97, C4
Orre, Arizona (region/state), pp.18–19, C3
Pacifidlog Town, Japan (town), pp.96–97, D1
Pallet Town, Japan (town), pp.96–97, C2
Parfum Palace, France (building), pp.44–45, E3
Pastoria City, Japan (city), pp.96–97, D4
Petalburg City, Japan (city), pp.96–97, A1
Pewter City, Japan (city), pp.96–97, C2
Phenac City, Arizona (city), pp.18–19, C3
Poni Island, Hawaii (island), pp.18–19, C1
Prism Tower, Paris, France (building), pp.44–45, E3
Pyrite Town, Arizona (town), pp.18–19, C3
Reflection Cave, France (natural feature), pp.44–45, B3
Rustboro City, Japan (city), pp.96–97, A1
Saffron City, Japan (city), pp.96–97, E1
Sandgem Town, Japan (town), pp.96–97, C4
Santalune City, France (city), pp.44–45, C3
Sea Spirit's Den, Channel Islands (island), pp.64–65, A1
Seafolk Village, Hawaii (town), pp.18–19, C1
Shalour City, France (city), pp.44–45, B3
Sinnoh, Japan (region), pp.96–97, C4
Slateport City, Japan (city), pp.96–97, A1
Snowbelle City, France (city), pp.44–45, C3
Snowpoint City, Japan (city), pp.96–97, C4
Sootopolis City, Japan (city), pp.96–97, A1
Southern Island, Japan (island), pp.96–97, A1
Sunnyshore City, Japan (city), pp.96–97, D4
Tower of Mastery, France (building), pp.44–45, B3
Twinleaf Town, Japan (town), pp.96–97, C4
Ula'ula Island, Hawaii (island), pp.18–19, C1
Unova, New York (region/state), pp.14–15, D1
Vaniville Town, France (town), pp.44–45, C3
Veilstone City, Japan (city), pp.96–97, D4
Verdanturf Town, Japan (town), pp.96–97, A1
Vermilion City, Japan (city), pp.96–97, C2
Violet City, Japan (city), pp.96–97, B2
Viridian City, Japan (city), pp.96–97, C2

Poldark (TV), Nampara, England (building), pp.64–65, B1

Police Quest (video game), Lytton, California (town), pp.18–19, A3

Poltergeist (film), Cuesta Verde, California (town), pp.18–19, A3

Popeye (various), Sweethaven, California (town), pp.18–19, A3

Poppoya (film)
Biyoro, Japan (city), pp.96–97, C4
Horomai, Japan (town), pp.96–97, C4
Horomai Line, Japan (railway), pp.96–97, C4
Kitahoromai, Japan (village), pp.96–97, C4

Porgy and Bess (musical), Catfish Row, South Carolina (building), pp.14–15, B3/C3

Porque Parece Mentira la Verdad Nunca se Sabe by Daniel Sada (novel)
Brinquillo, Mexico (town), pp.32–33, B3
Capila, Mexico (region), pp.32–33, B3
Pencas Mudas, Mexico (town), pp.32–33, B3
Remadrín, Mexico (town), pp.32–33, B3
Salimiento, Mexico (town), pp.32–33, B3
San Chema, Mexico (town), pp.32–33, B3

Porridge (TV), HMP Slade, England (building), pp.64–65, C3

Portal series (video game), Aperture Science Enrichment Centre, Michigan (building), pp.16–17, D6

Porto dos Milagres (TV), Porto dos Milagres, Brazil (town), pp.38–39, D4

Poseidon (film), RMS *Poseidon*, Atlantic Ocean (wreck), pp.126–127, B5

Postman Pat (TV)
Greendale, England (village), pp.64–65, C3
Ingledale, England (village), pp.64–65, C3
Pencaster, England (town), pp.64–65, C3

Power Rangers (various)
Angel Grove, Oregon (town), pp.18–19, A5
Mariner Bay, California (city), pp.18–19, A3

Power Rangers SPD (TV), Newtech City, California (city), pp.18–19, A4

Power Ranges Time Force (TV), Silver Hills, Washington (city), pp.18–19, A6

Power Rangers Wild Force (TV)
Turtle Cove, Colorado (city), pp.16–17, A4
Turtle Lake, Colorado (lake), pp.16–17, A4

Power Without Glory by Frank Hardy (novella), Carringbush, Victoria (town), pp.108–109, A4

Preacher (comic/TV)
Angelville plantation, Louisiana (building), pp.16–17, C2
Annville, Texas (town), pp.16–17, C2
Salvation, Texas (town), pp.16–17, C2

Presença de Anita (TV), Florença, Brazil (town), pp.38–39, C3

Pretty Little Liars (Indonesian version) (TV), Amerta, Indonesia (town), pp.90–91, C1

Pretty Little Liars (TV), Rosewood, Pensylvania (town), pp.14–15, C4

Pride and Prejudice by Jane Austen (novel)
Lambton, England (town), pp.64–65, C2
Longbourn, England (estate), pp.64–65, D2
Meryton, England (town), pp.64–65, D2
Netherfield, England (estate), pp.64–65, D2
Pemberley, England (estate), pp.64–65, C2

Primary Colors by Joe Klein (novel)
Grace Junction, Arkansas (town), pp.16–17, C3
Mammoth Falls, Arkansas (city), pp.16–17, C3

Princess and I (film), Yangdon (fictional country), pp.78–79, D4

Princess Mononoke (anime)
Cedar Forest, Japan (natural feature), pp.96–97, B2
Emishi Village, Japan (village), pp.96–97, C2
Irontown, Japan (town), pp.96–97, B2

Princess Protection Program (film)
Costa Estrella, Caribbean (island), pp.32–33, E2
Costa Luna, Caribbean (island), pp.32–33, E2

PriPara (video game/anime), Parajuku, Japan (town), pp.96–97, E1

Prison Break (TV), Fox River State Penitentiary, Illinois (building), pp.16–17, D4

Prisoner (Cell Block H) (TV)
Barnhurst Prison, Victoria (building), pp.108–109, A1
Blackmoor Prison, Victoria (building), pp.108–109, A1
Wentworth Detention Centre, Victoria (building), pp.108–109, A1

Proof of Life (film), Tecala (fictional country), pp.38–39, A5

Propeller Island by Jules Verne (novel), Standard Island, Pacific Ocean (island), pp.120–121, D2

Providence (TV), Providence, Quebec (city), pp.26–27, E1

Psycho (novel/film)
Bates Motel, California (town), pp.18–19, A4
Fairvale, California (town), pp.18–19, A4

Puckoon by Spike Milligan (novel), Puckoon, Northern Ireland/Ireland (village), pp.64–65, A3

Puella Magi Madoka Magica (anime/manga)
Asunaro, Japan (city), pp.96–97, C3
Kamihama, Japan (city), pp.96–97, B2
Kazamino, Japan (city), pp.96–97, C3
Mitakihara, Japan (city), pp.96–97, C3

160

Quatermass and the Pit (film), Hobbs End, England (town), pp.64–65, D2

Raag Darbari by Srilal Shukla (novel), Shivpalganj, India (village), pp.78–79, C4

Raiders of the Lost Ark (film), Aegean Sea (island), pp.44–45, E1

Rail Romanesque (video game/anime), Ohitoyo, Japan (town), pp.96–97, A1

Railroad Tycoon II: The Second Century (video game), Geocore Power Plant/La Mancha Fissue, Spain (building), pp.44–45, B2

Rainbirds by Clarissa Goenawan (novel), Akakawa, Japan (town), pp.96–97, C2

Rainy Season by Stephen King (short story), Willow, Maine (town), pp.14–15, D6

Raise the Titanic by Clive Cussler and *The Titanic Secret* by Clive Cussler and Jack Du Brul (novel/film), Little Angel Mine/Satan Mine, Colorado (building), pp.18–19, D4

Raj Comics, Rajnagar, India (city), pp.78–79, D4

Ram-Leela (film), Ranjhaar, India (town), pp.78–79, A4/B4

Rambo: First Blood (film)
Hope, Washington (town), pp.18–19, A6
Liggett County, Washington (county), pp.18–19, A6/B6

Rango (film), Dirt, Nevada (town), pp.18–19, B3

Ranma ½ by Rumiko Takahashi (manga/anime)
Cursed Springs of Jusenkyo, China (natural feature), pp.102–103, B2
Furinkan, Japan (town), pp.96–97, E1
Jusendo, China (mountain), pp.102–103, B2
Tendo Dojo, Japan (building), pp.96–97, E1

Ratatouille (film)
Gusteau's Restaurant, Paris, France (building), pp.44–45, E3
La Ratatouille, Paris, France (building), pp.44–45, E3

Raun Wantaim Savemahn (radio series), Mambu Hanua, Papua New Guinea (village), pp.90–91, A1

Razorback by Peter Brennan (novel/film), Gamulla, New South Wales (town), pp.108–109, D2

Ready Player One (film), Stacks, The, Ohio (town), pp.14–15, B4

Real world
Agloe, New York (town), pp.14–15, C5
Alvik, Norway (town), pp.56–57, B3
Loftbacken, Sweden (town), pp.56–57, B4
Null Island, Atlantic Ocean (island), pp.126–127, D2
Smalvik, Norway (village), pp.56–57, B5
Utrøst, Norway (island), pp.56–57, B5

Rebecca by Daphne du Maurier (novel), Manderley, England (building), pp.64–65, B1

Recorded by Arizal (web series), Yaman (fictional country), pp.90–91, D2

Red Dawn (film), Calumet, Colorado (town), pp.18–19, D3

Red Dead Redemption series (video game)
Ambarino (fictional state), pp.18–19, D4
Annesburg, New Hanover (fictional town), pp.16–17, A2
Armadillo, New Austin (fictional town), pp.16–17, A2
Blackwater, West Elizabeth (fictional town/city), pp.16–17, C3
Chuparosa, Mexico (town), pp.32–33, B3
Escalera, Mexico (town), pp.32–33, B3
Grizzlies, The (mountain range), pp.18–19, D4
Lagras, Lemoyne (fictional town), pp.16–17, D2
Lannahechee River, Lemoyne (fictional river), pp.16–17, D2
Lemoyne (fictional state), pp.16–17, C2
Lower Montana River, various (river), pp.16–17, C2
Mesa de la Luna, Mexico (mountain), pp.32–33, B3/B4
Mesa del Sol, Mexico (mountain), pp.32–33, B3
New Austin (fictional state), pp.18–19, D2
New Hanover (fictional state), pp.16–17, C3/D3
Nuevo Paraiso, Mexico (country), pp.32–33, B3
Rhodes, Lemoyne (fictional town), pp.16–17, D2
Saint Denis, Lemoyne (fictional city), pp.16–17, D2
San Luis River, Mexico and various (river), pp.18–19, D3, pp.32–33, B4
Sisika Penitentiary, Lemoyne (fictional island), pp.16–17, D2
Strawberry, West Elizabeth (fictional town), pp.16–17, C3
Upper Montana River, various (river), pp.16–17, B3/C3
Valentine, New Hanover (fictional town), pp.16–17, C2
Van Horn Trading Post, New Hanover (fictional town), pp.16–17, D3
West Elizabeth (fictional state), pp.16–17, C3

Red Girls by Sakuraba Kazuki (novel), Benimidori, Japan (village), pp.96–97, B2

Red Harvest by Dashiell Hammett (novel), Personville (Poisonville), Montana (town), pp.18–19, D4

Red River of the North series by Lauraine Snelling (novels), Blessing, North Dakota (town), pp.16–17, B6

Red Rock (TV), Red Rock, Ireland (town), pp.64–65, B3

Red Scorpion (film), Mombaka (fictional country), pp.84–85, C3

Red State (film), Cooper's Dell, Texas (town), pp.16–17, B3

Regina Leader-Post (newspaper column), Crackled Axle, Saskatchewan (town), pp.26–27, C1

Relic Hunter (TV)
Endostan (fictional country), pp.72–73, E3
Palace of the Talibs, Endostan (fictional building), pp.72–73, E3

Resident Evil series (video games/films)
Arklay Mountains, Missouri (mountain range), pp.16–17, C3/D
Harvardville (city), pp.18–19, B6
Lanshiang, China (region/city), pp.102–103, D1
Raccoon City, Missouri (city), pp.16–17, C3
Rockfort Island (island), pp.114–115, E4
Stone Ville, Missouri (town), pp.16–17, C3
Tall Oaks, Unknown (city), pp.14–15, C6

Return of the Pink Panther (film), Lugash (fictional country), pp.84–85, B5

Return to Eden (TV)
Eden Estate, Northern Territory (estate), pp.108–109, C4
New Eden, New South Wales (building), pp.108–109, F4

Revenge of the Pink Panther (film), Lee Kee Shipyards, Hong Kong (Area), pp.102–103, D1

Riacho Doce by José Lins do Rego (novel/TV), Riacho Doce, Brazil (town), pp.38–39, D4

Riallaro, the Archipelago of Exiles by Godfrey Sweven (novel)
Broolyi, Pacific Ocean (island), pp.120–121, D1
Fanattia, Pacific Ocean (island), pp.120–121, E1
Limanora, Pacific Ocean (island), pp.120–121, E1
Riallaro Archipelago, Pacific Ocean (island chain), pp.120–121, D1/E1
Spectralia, Pacific Ocean (island), pp.120–121, E1

Ribeirão do Tempo (TV), Ribeirão do Tempo, Brazil (town), pp.38–39, D4

Richie Rich (various), Richville, Indiana (town), pp.14–15, A4

Richmond Hill (TV), Richmond Hill, New South Wales (town), pp.108–109, D2

Riddley Walker by Russell Hoban (novel)
Bernt Arse, England (town), pp.64–65, D1/D2
Do It Over, England (town), pp.64–65, D1
Father's Ham, England (town), pp.64–65, D2
Fork Stoan, England (town), pp.64–65, D1
Horny Boy, England (town), pp.64–65, D2
Ram, The, England (town), pp.64–65, D2
Sams Itch, England (town), pp.64–65, D2

Ringing the Changes by Robert Aickman (short story), Holihaven, England (town), pp.64–65, D2

Ripping Yarns (TV)
El Misti, Peru (mountain), pp.38–39, A4
Quequenã, Peru (town), pp.38–39, A4
Stalag Luft 112B, Germany (building), pp.44–45, D3

Ripping Yarns: Golden Gordon (TV)
Barnstoneworth, England (town), pp.64–65, C3

Ripping Yarns: Murder at Moorstones Manor (TV)
Darkstones Moor, Scotland (natural feature), pp.64–65, B4/C4
Moorstones Manor, Scotland (building), pp.64–65, B4

Ripping Yarns: The Testing of Eric Olthwaite (TV), Denley Moor, England (town), pp.64–65, C3

River City (TV), Shieldinch, Scotland (town), pp.64–65, C4

Riverdale/The Chilling Adventures of Sabrina (TV)
Greendale (town), pp.14–15, D5
Riverdale (town), pp.14–15, C6

Road Ends by Mary Lawson (novel), Struan, Ontario (town), pp.26–27, E1

Road to Perdition, Max Allan Collins (comic/film), Perdition, Michigan (town), pp.14–15, A5

Road to Singapore (film), Kaigoon, Singapore (island), pp.90–91, B2

Roadside Picnic by Arkady and Boris Strugatsky (novel)
Hamont, Ontario (town), pp.26–27, E1
Harmont Zone, The, Ontario (?) (region), pp.26–27, D1/E1
Institute for Extraterrestrial Cultures, Ontario (building), pp.26–27, E1

Robin Hood tales (folklore), Locksley, England (town), pp.64–65, D2

Robinson Crusoe by Daniel Defoe (novel), Robinson Crusoe's Island, Caribbean (island), pp.32–33, F2

Robocop (film), Delta City, Michigan (city), pp.14–15, A5/B5

Rocket Girls by Hōsuke Nojiri (novels/anime)
Maltide, Pacific Ocean (island), pp.120–121, B3
Solomon Space Center, Pacific Ocean (building), pp.120–121, B3

Rocket Power (TV), Ocean Shores, California (town), pp.18–19, D3

Rocket to the Moon by Jules Verne (novel), Caerflwyti, Wales (village), pp.64–65, C2

Rocko's Modern Life (TV), O-Town, Wisconsin (town), pp.16–17, D5

Romeo + Juliet (film), Verona Beach, Florida (city), pp.14–15, C1

Roque Santeiro (TV), Asa Branca, Brazil (town), pp.38–39, D4

Ros Na Rún (TV), Ros Na Rún, Ireland (village), pp.64–65, A2

Roseanne (TV), Lanford, Illinois (town), pp.16–17, D5

Rosehaven (TV), Rosehaven, Tasmania (town), pp.108–109, D1

Roughnecks (TV), Osprey Explorer, North Sea (oil rig), pp.64–65, D5

Round the Twist (TV), Port Niranda, Victoria (town), pp.108–109, D1

Royal Flash by George MacDonald Fraser (novel), Duchy of Strackenz, Strackenz (fictional region), pp.44–45, D4

Ruby by Toni Morrison (novel), Ruby, Oklahoma (town), pp.16–17, B3

Ruddigore by Gilbert and Sullivan (opera), Rederring, England (village), pp.64–65, B1

Rudolph the Red-Nosed Reindeer (TV special)
Island of Misfit Toys, The, Arctic Ocean (island), pp.26–27, C4
King Moonracer's Castle, Arctic Ocean (building), pp.26–27, C4

Rugrats in Paris (film), Reptarland, France (theme park), pp.44–45, E3

Runaway (film), Jackson City, Colorado (city), pp.16–17, A4

Runaway Train (film), Jordan, Seneca, Elkins, McKessburg, Bellport (towns), Seneca River (river), Stonehaven Prison (building) and A&E NorthernRailroad (railway), Alaska, pp.18–19, B1

Rupert Bear by Mary Tourtel (comic books/TV), Nutwood, England (village), pp.64–65, D2

Rushing to Paradise by J.G. Ballard (novel), St Esprit, Pacific Ocean (island), pp.120–121, D2

Russian folklore
Buyan, Germany (island), pp.44–45, D4
Sannikov Land, Arctic Ocean (island), pp.102–103, E2/F2

Ruth Galloway books of Elly Griffiths (novel), Saltmarsh, England (town), pp.64–65, D2

Ryan's Daughter (film), Kirrary, Ireland (village), pp.64–65, B5

Sa Ngalan ng Ina (TV), Verano, Philippines (region), pp.90–91, D2

Saboteur by Ha Jin (short story), Muji City, China (city), pp.102–103, E3/E4

Sabrina the Teenage Witch (TV), Westbridge, Massachusetts (town), pp.14–15, D5

'Sacheon-ga' (music), Sacheon, South Korea (town), pp.102–103, E2/E3

Sahara by Clive Cussler (novel/film)
Asselar, Mali (town), pp.84–85, B4
CSS *Texas*, Mali (wreck), pp.84–85, B5
Massarde Enterprises Solar Plant, Mali (building), pp.84–85, B5

Sailor Moon by Naoko Takeuchi (manga/anime)
Cherry Hill Temple, Japan (building), pp.96–97, E1
Crossroads, Japan (town), pp.96–97, E1
Crystal Palace, The, Japan (building), pp.96–97, E1
Crystal Tokyo, Japan (city), pp.96–97, E1/F1
Mugen Academy, Japan (building), pp.96–97, E1
Sankakusu, Japan (city/island), pp.96–97, F1

Saints Row (video game), Stillwater, Michigan (city), pp.14–15, A5

Sakura Quest (anime)
Chupakabura Kingdom, Japan (city/state), pp.96–97, B2
Manoyama, Japan (town), pp.96–97, B2

Salem's Lot by Stephen King (various), Jerusalem's Lot, Maine (town), pp.14–15, D6

Salt of the Earth (film), Zinctown, New Mexico (town), pp.18–19, D4

Sam Slick in England by Thomas Chandler Haliburton (novel), Slickville, Connecticut (town), pp.14–15, D5

Samurai Shodown series (video games)
Anjo, Japan (village), pp.96–97, B2
Jōkamachi, Japan (city), pp.96–97, C2
Wataribashi, Japan (city), pp.96–97, A1

San Juan Romero by Rita Maria Felix da Silva (novel), San Juan Romero, Mexico (village), pp.32–33, B3

San Lazaro (film), San Lazaro, Philippines (town), pp.90–91, D3

San Manuel Bueno, Mártir by Miguel de Unamuno (novel)
Buzzard's Peak, Spain (mountain), pp.44–45, B4
Renada, Spain (city), pp.44–45, B2
Valverde de Lucerna, Spain (town), pp.44–45, B2
Valverde de Lucerna, Spain (village), pp.44–45, B4

San Simeon (Sims 3) (video game)
Isla Paraiso, Philippines (island), pp.90–91, D3
San Simeon, Philippines (city), pp.90–91, D3

San Sombrèro (book)
Alpenstein Mountains, Switzerland/Germany (mountain range), pp.44–45, C3
Barbituros Islands, The (fictional country/island chain), pp.32–33, F2
Costa Lottsa (fictional country/principality), pp.32–33, F2
Democratic Free People's United Republic of San Sombrèro (fictional country), pp.32–33, D1
Hagel, Unaudited Arab Emirates (fictional country), pp.72–73, C1
Nuku'la Atoll, Pacific Ocean (island), pp.120–121, C4
Tyranistan (fictional country), pp.72–73, D4/E4
Unaudited Arab Emirates (fictional country/emirate), pp.72–73, C1

Sanctus novels of Simon Toyne (novels)
Citadel, The, Turkey (city/state), pp.72–73, B3
Ruin, Turkey (city), pp.72–73, B3

Sanditon by Jane Austen (novel), Sanditon, England (town), pp.64–65, D1

Santa María del Circo by David Toscana (novel), Sierra Vieja, Mexico (town), pp.32–33, B3

Santo Bugito (TV), Santo Bugito, Texas (city), pp.16–17, B1

Saramandia by Lins do Rego, Saramandaia (Bole-Bole), Brazil (town), pp.38–39, D4

Saving Private Ryan (film)
Addley, Pennsylvania (town), pp.14–15, B5
Ramelle, France (town), pp.44–45, B3

Savrola by Winston Churchill (novel), Laurania (fictional country), pp.44–45, B2

Scaramouche by Rafael Sabatini (novel), Gavrillac, France (village), pp.44–45, B3

Scarfolk (website), Scarfolk, England (town), pp.64–65, D2

Scary Go Round (web comic), Tackleford, England (town), pp.64–65, C3

Scenes from Village Life by Amos Oz (stories), Tel Ilan, Israel (town), pp.72–73, A2

Schlafes Bruder by Robert Schneider (novel), Eschberg, Austria (village), pp.44–45, C3

Scoop by Evelyn Waugh (novel)
Ishmaelia (fictional country), pp.84–85, D4
Jacksonville, Ishmaelia (fictional city), pp.84–85, D4

Scotland the What? comedy troupe (live comedy), Auchterturra, Scotland (town), pp.64–65, C5

Scream (films), Woodsboro, California (town), pp.18–19, A4

Scrooge McDuck 'The Son of the Sun' (comics), Lake Titicoocoo, Peru/Bolivia (lake), pp.38–39, B4

Scrublands by Chris Hammer (novel)
Bellington, New South Wales (town), pp.108–109, D2
Riversend, New South Wales (town), pp.108–109, D2

SCTV (TV), Melonville, Alberta (town), pp.26–27, C1

Sea Patrol (TV), Samaru Islands, Pacific Ocean (island), pp.108–109, E3

Seafighter by James H. Cobb (novel), West African Union (fictional bloc), pp.84–85, A4

Sealab 2020/Sealab 2021 (TV), Sealab, Tasman Sea (submerged building), pp.120–121, B3

Sealab 2021 (TV), Fort Klugman, Wyoming (building), pp.16–17, A4

Secret series by Annette Mahon (novels), Malino, Hawaii (town), pp.18–19, D1

Secrets of the Sea by Nicholas Shakespeare (novel), Wellington Point, Tasmania (town), pp.108–109, D1

Segundo Sol (TV), Ilha de Boiporã, Brazil (island/town), pp.38–39, D4

Seinfeld (TV), Latham, Massachusetts (town), pp.14–15, C5

Seis Manos (TV), San Simon, Mexcio (town), pp.32–33, A4

Seize the Night by Dean Koontz (novel), Moonlight Bay, California (town), pp.18–19, A4

Sense and Sensibility by Jane Austen (novel), Norland Park, England (estate), pp.64–65, D1

Servant of Service by Karino Takatsu (manga), Mitsuba, Japan (town), pp.96–97, C4

Sesam Stasjon (TV), Sesam Stasjon, Norway (building), pp.56–57, B3

Sesame Street, Mount Snuffleupagus, Hawaii (mountain), pp.18–19, C1

Sesame Street Presents: Follow That Bird! (film)
Oceanview, Illinois (city), pp.16–17, D
Toadstool, Indiana (city), pp.14–15, A4

Setenta Veces Siete/Seventy Times Seven by Ricardo Elizondo Elizondo (novel)
Carrizalejo, Mexico (town), pp.32–33, B3
Carrizales, USA (town), pp.32–33, B3
Rio Gordo, Mexico (river), pp.32–33, B3

Seva by Luis López Nieves (short story), Seva, Puerto Rico (town), pp.32–33, F2

Severn Valley of the Cthulhu Mythos by Ramsey Campbell (novels)
Birchester, England (city), pp.64–65, C2
Clotton, England (town), pp.64–65, C2
Goatswood, England (town), pp.64–65, C2
Severnford, England (town), pp.64–65, C2
Temphill, England (town), pp.64–65, C2

Shades of Grey by Jasper Fforde (novels/TV)
East Carmine, Wales (town), pp.64–65, C2
High Saffron, Wales (town), pp.64–65, C2
Rusty Hill, Wales (town), pp.64–65, C2
Vermillion, England (town), pp.64–65, C2

Shadow of a Bull by Maia Wojciechowska (novel), Archangel, Spain (town), pp.44–45, A2

Shadow on the Crown by Patricia Bracewell (novel), Ottermouth, England (town), pp.64–65, C2

Shame (film), Ginborak, Western Australia (town), pp.108–109, A2

Shame by Salman Rushdie (novel), Q, Pakistan (town), pp.78–79, A5

Sharp Objects by Gillian Flynn (novel/TV), Wind Gap, Missouri (town), pp.16–17, D3

Shaun the Sheep (TV/film), Mossy Bottom, England (village), pp.64–65, C2

She by H. Rider Haggard (novel), Kôr, Mozambique (city), pp.84–85, C3

Sheep by Simon Maginn (novel), Stumble Head (natural feature), pp.64–65, B2

Shenmue II (video game), Langhuishan, China (village), pp.102–103, C1

Shenmue III (video game)
Bailu Village, China (village), pp.102–103, C1
Niaowu, China (town), pp.102–103, C1

Sherlock Holmes: The Hound of the Baskervilles by Arthur Conan Doyle (novel)
Baskerville Hall, England (building), pp.64–65, C1
Boscombe Valley, England (natural feature), pp.64–65, C1
Coombe Tracey, England (town), pp.64–65, C1
Kings Pyland, England (village), pp.64–65, C1
Little Purlington, England (village), pp.64–65, C1
Stoke Moran, England (building), pp.64–65, C1

Sherlock Holmes: The Adventure of the Copper Beeches by Arthur Conan Doyle (short story), Copper Beeches, England (estate), pp.64–65, C1

Shikoku (film), Hieno Village, Japan (village), pp.96–97, B1/C1

Shining Time Station/Thomas and the Magic Railroad (TV/film), Shining Time, Pennsylvania (town), pp.14–15, C4

Shitt's Creek (TV), Schitt's Creek, Ontario (?) (town), pp.26–27, A4

Sholay (film), Ramgarh, India (village), pp.78–79, B3

Shooting Script by Gavin Lyall (novel), Republica Libra (fictional island), pp.32–33, E2
Santo Bartolomeo, Republica Libra (fictional town), pp.32–33, E2

Short Circuit (film)
Damon, Washington (town), pp.18–19, A6
Nova Robotics, Washington (town), pp.18–19, A6

Short Poppies (mockumentary), Bay, The, New Zealand (town), pp.108–109, F2

Showdown by Jorge Amado (novel), Tocaia Grande, Brazil (town), pp.38–39, D4

'Sidböle Härad' (song), Sidböle Härad, Sweden (region), pp.56–57, C4

Sierra Falls series by Veronica Wolff (novel), Sierra Falls, California (town), pp.18–19, A4

Signal (TV), Inju, South Korea (city), pp.102–103, E2

Silas Marner by George Eliot (novel), Raveloe, England (town), pp.64–65, C2

Silent Hill (film)
Silent Hill, West Virginia (town), pp.14–15, B4
Toluca Lake, West Virginia (lake), pp.14–15, B4

Silent Hill series (various)
Pleasant River, West Virginia (town), pp.14–15, B4
Toluca River, various (river), pp.14–15, B4

Silent Witness (film), Fengzhou, China (city), pp.102–103, D3

Silver Spoon, Hiromu Arakawa (manga/anime), Ezono Agricultural High School, Japan (building), pp.96–97, D4

Sin City by Frank Miller (comic/film)
Basin City (Sin City), California (city), pp.18–19, A4

Sinbad the Sailor (short story)
City of the Apes, Island of the, Indian Ocean (island), pp.78–79, D1
Great-Fish Island, Persian Gulf (island/fish), pp.72–73, D1
Island of Cannibals, Indian Ocean (island), pp.78–79, A4
Island of Pearls, Indian Ocean (island), pp.78–79, B3
Island of the Living Sepulchra, Indian Ocean (island), pp.78–79, A4
Island of the Old Man of the Sea, Indian Ocean (island), pp.78–79, B2
Island of the Roc, Madagascar (island), pp.84–85, D3
Island of the Sea-Horses, Persian Gulf (island), pp.72–73, D1
Valley of Snakes, Kenya (natural feature), pp.84–85, D3
Singularity (video game), Katorga-12, Russia (island), pp.102–103, F1
Sir Henry at Rawlinson End (radio), Rawlinson End, England (estate), pp.64–65, D2
Siren/Forbidden Siren (video game), Hanuda, Japan (town), pp.96–97, C3
Sítio do Picapau Amarelo by Monteiro Lobato (novels), Capoeirão dos Tucanos, Brazil (natural feature), pp.38–39, C3/D3
Six Stories by Matt Wesolowski (novel), Scarclaw Fell, England (natural feature), pp.64–65, D3
Skeleton Key by Anthony Horowitz (novel), Skeleton Key, Cuba (island), pp.32–33, D2
Sketchbook by Totan Kobako (manga/anime), Shime, Japan (town), pp.96–97, A1
Skippy the Bush Kangaroo (TV), Waratah National Park, New South Wales (natural feature), pp.108–109, D2/E2
Skippy: Adventures in Bushtown (TV), Bushtown, New South Wales (town), pp.108–109, E2
Skulduggery Pleasant series by Derek Landry (novels)
Haggard, Ireland (town), pp.64–65, B3
Roarhaven, Ireland (city), pp.64–65, A3
Skyfall (film), Skyfall Lodge, Scotland (building), pp.64–65, B4
Skyways (TV), Pacific International Airport, Victoria (building), pp.108–109, A1
Sleep No More by L.T.C. Rolt (short stories)
Cold Bosworth, England (town), pp.64–65, D2
Garside Fell (natural feature), England (mountain), pp.64–65, C3
Hawley Bank (building or estate), England (village), pp.64–65, C2
Highbeck, England (town), pp.64–65, C3
World's End Inn, Wales (building), pp.64–65, B4
Sleeping Beauties by Stephen King and Owen King (novel), Dooling, Appalachia (fictional town), pp.14–15, B4
Sleeping on Jupiter by Anuradha Roy (novel), Jarmuli, India (town), pp.78–79, D3
Slow Start by Yuiko Tokumi (manga/anime), Hoshio Private Girls Academy, Japan (building), pp.96–97, C2
Smarakasilakal by Punathil Kunjabdulla (novel), Ooralunkal, India (village), pp.78–79, D3
Smokey and the Bandit (film), Deeson County, Arkansas (county), pp.16–17, C2
Snarkout Boys books by Daniel Pinkwater (novels), Baconburg, Illinois (city), pp.16–17, D4/D5
Snatch (film), San Toledo, Spain (town), pp.44–45, B1
Snow Crash by Neal Stephenson (novel), Port Sherman, Oregon (town), pp.18–19, A5/A6
Snow Falling on Cedars by David Guterson (novel/film), San Piedro Island, Washington (island), pp.18–19, A6
Snowpiercer (film), Yekaterina Bridge, Russia (building), pp.50–51, B6
So Boaz Slept by Victor Hugo (poem), Jérimadeth, Iraq (city), pp.72–73, C2
SOCOM U.S. Navy SEALs: Combined Assault (video game)
Adjikistan (fictional country), pp.72–73, D2/E2
Dalahtibar, Adjikistan (fictional city), pp.72–73, D2
Soldiers of Fortune by Richard Harding Davis (novel)
Five Mountains, The, Olancho (fictional mountain range), pp.38–39, D5
Olancho (fictional country), pp.38–39, D4
San Lorenzo, Olancho (fictional village), pp.38–39, D5
Valencia, Olancho (fictional city), pp.38–39, D5
Solo by William Boyd (novel)
Dahum (fictional country), pp.84–85, B4
Port Dunbar, Dahum (fictional city), pp.84–85, B4
Sinsikrou, Zanzarim (fictional city), pp.84–85, B4
Zanza River, Zanzarim/Dahum (fictional river), pp.84–85, A4/B4
Zanzarim, Nigeria (country), pp.84–85, B4
Somerset (TV), Somerset, Michigan (town), pp.14–15, A5
Son of the Mask (film), Fringe City, Virginia (city), pp.14–15, C4
Song of Night by Glenville Lovell (novel/film), Bottom Rock, Barbados (village), pp.32–33, A2
Song of Solomon by Toni Morrison (novel)
Mercy, Michigan (town), pp.14–15, A6
Shalimar, Virginia (village), pp.14–15, B4

Sons and Lovers by D.H. Lawrence (novel), Beggarlee Colliery, England (building), pp.64–65, C3
Sons of Anarchy (TV), Charming, California (town), pp.18–19, A4
Sophie and the Rising Sun (film), Salty Creek, South Carolina (town), pp.14–15, C3
Soul Eater by Atsushi Okubo (manga/anime)
Baba Yaga Castle, Brazil (location), pp.38–39, B4
Death City, Nevada (city), pp.18–19, B4
Sound of the Sky (anime)
Helvetia (fictional country), pp.96–97, A1/B1
Rome (fictional country), pp.96–97, C3
Seize, Helvetia (fictional town), pp.96–97, C2
South Pacific (film), Bali Ha'i, Pacific Ocean (island), pp.120–121, B2
South Park (TV)
Fortress of Tooth Decay, Yukon (building), pp.26–27, B2
Middle Park, Colorado (town), pp.18–19, D4
North Park, Colorado (town), pp.18–19, D4
Skull Cove, Somalia (natural feature), pp.84–85, D4
South Park, Colorado (town), pp.18–19, D4
South Riding by Winifred Holtby (novel)
Anderby, England (town), pp.64–65, D3
Cold Harbour, England (village), pp.64–65, D3
Flintonbridge, England (town), pp.64–65, D3
Harda's Head, England (natural feature), pp.64–65, D3
Hardrascliffe, England (town), pp.64–65, D3
Kingsport, England (city), pp.64–65, D3
Kiplington, England (town), pp.64–65, D3
Leame Estuary, England (natural feature), pp.64–65, D3
Ledsea Buttock, England (town), pp.64–65, D3
Pidsea Buttock, England (town), pp.64–65, D3
South Riding, England (county), pp.64–65, D3
Yarrold, England (town), pp.64–65, D3
South Wind by Norman Douglas (novel)
Crotalophoboi Land, Crotolophoboi (fictional country), pp.84–85, C5
Nepenthe, Italy (island), pp.44–45, C2
Southern Victory by Harry Turtledove (novels)
Houston (fictional state), pp.16–17, A3/B3
Sequoyah (fictional state), pp.16–17, B3
Soy tu Dueña (TV), San Pedro de las Peñas, Mexico (town), pp.32–33, B2/B3
Space by James A. Michener (novel), Fremont (fictional state), pp.16–17, B4/C4
Space Force (TV), Space Force Campus, Colorado (building), pp.16–17, A4
Spanish City by Sarah May (novel), Setton, England (town), pp.64–65, C4
Speed 2: Cruise Control (film), Eindhoven Lion, Caribbean (wreck), pp.32–33, F2
Sphere by Michael Crichton (novel/film)
Habitat DH-8, Pacific Ocean (submerged building), pp.120–121, B4
USS *Star Voyager*, Pacific Ocean (wreck), pp.120–121, B4
Spirou et Fantasio/Marsupilami (comics), Palombia (fictional country), pp.38–39, B5
SpongeBob SquarePants (TV)
Bass Vegas, Pacific Ocean (city), pp.120–121, B4
Bikini Bottom, Pacific Ocean (city), pp.120–121, B4
Jellyfish Fields, Bikini Bottom (fictional natural feature), pp.120–121, B4
New Kelp City, Pacific Ocean (city), pp.120–121, B4
Spoon River Anthology by Edgar Lee Masters (poetry), Spoon River, Illinois (town), pp.16–17, D4
Squidbillies (TV), Dougal County, Georgia (county), pp.14–15, B3
Squirrel and Hedgehog (TV), Flower Hill, North Korea (town), pp.102–103, E3
St Trinians series by Ronald Searle (various), St Trinians, England (building), pp.64–65, C2
Stacey Stone (TV), Rockferry, Scotland (town), pp.64–65, B4
Stand on Zanzibar by John Brunner (novel)
Beninia (fictional country), pp.84–85, B4
Yatakang (fictional country), pp.90–91, C2
Stanley Bagshaw series by Bob Wilson (novel), Huddersgate, England (town), pp.64–65, C3
Star Trek (various)
Carbon Creek, Pennsylvania (town), pp.14–15, B4
Daystrom Institute, Japan (building), pp.96–97, D1
Starfleet Headquarters, California (building), pp.18–19, A4
Starfleet Shipyard 2-1A (riverside Shipyard), Iowa (building), pp.16–17, C4
Warp Five Complex, Montana (building), pp.18–19, C4
Star Trek: Voyager (TV)
Fair Haven, Ireland (village), pp.64–65, A2
Portage Creek/Millennium Gate, Indiana (town), pp.14–15, A4

Star Trek: Voyager 'The Killing Game I & II' (TV), Sainte Claire, France (village), pp.44–45, C3
Star Trek: Articles of the Federation by Keith R.A. Decandido (novel), Château Thelian, France (building), pp.44–45, C3
Star Trek: The Next Generation/Picard (TV)
African Confederation (fictional bloc), pp.84–85, D4
Chateau Picard, France (building), pp.44–45, C2
Stargate SG-1 (TV), Stargate Command, Colorado (building), pp.16–17, A4
Starvation Lake by Bryan Gruley (novel)
Pine County, Michigan (county), pp.14–15, A5
Starvation Lake, Michigan (town), pp.14–15, A5
State Fair by Phil Stong (novel), Brunswick, Iowa (town), pp.16–17, C1
State of Siege (film), Sunda (fictional island/nation), pp.90–91, B1
Steins;Gate (video game/anime), Future Gadget Lab, Japan (building), pp.96–97, E1
Stenkelfeld (radio)
Ankumersiel, Germany (town), pp.44–45, C4
Hachmannsfeld, Germany (town), pp.44–45, D4
Heringsmoor, Germany (town), pp.44–45, D4
Höcklage, Germany (town), pp.44–45, D4
Sottrup, Germany (town), pp.44–45, D
Stenkelfeld, Germany (city), pp.44–45, D4
Struchtrup, Germany (town), pp.44–45, D4
Steven Universe (TV)
Aqua Mexico, Aqua Mexico (fictional country), pp.32–33, A3
Beach City, Delmarva (fictional town), pp.14–15, C4
Charm City, Delmarva (fictional city), pp.14–15, C4
Delmarva (fictional state), pp.14–15, C4
Empire City, New York (city), pp.14–15, D1
Keystone (fictional state), pp.14–15, B4/C4
Showne, West Keystone (fictional town), pp.14–15, B4
West Keystone (fictional state), pp.14–15, B4
Wilmingmore, Delmarva (fictional city), pp.14–15, C4
Stigmata (film), Belo Quinto, Brazil (town), pp.38–39, D3
Still Game (TV)
Craiglang, Scotland (town), pp.64–65, C4
Finport, Scotland (town), pp.64–65, B4
Still Mine by Amy Stuart (novel), Blackmore, Alberta (town), pp.26–27, C1
Stingray (TV), McGregor Castle, Scotland (building), pp.64–65, B5
Stitch! (anime)
Izayoi Island, Japan (island), pp.96–97, A1
Okinawa New Town, Japan (city), pp.96–97, A1
Stonemouth by Iain Banks (novel), Stonemouth, Scotland (town), pp.64–65, C4/C5
Stop the Train by Geraldine McCaughrean (novel), Florence/Olive, Oklahoma (town), pp.16–17, B3
Stopfkuchen by Wilhelm Raabe (novel), Maiholzen, Germany (town), pp.44–45, D4
Stranger Things (TV)
Hawkins, Indiana (town), pp.14–15, A4
Roane County, Indiana (county), pp.14–15, A4
Strangers 6 (TV), Haiwan, China (city), pp.102–103, D1
Straw Dogs (2011) (film), Blackwater, Mississippi (town), pp.16–17, D2
Street Fighter (film)
M. Bison's Temple/Bisonopolis, Shadaloo (fictional building/city), pp.90–91, A3
Shadaloo City, Shadaloo (fictional city), pp.90–91, A3
Shadaloo River, China and various (river), pp.90–91, A4, pp.102–103, C1
Shadaloo (fictional country), pp.90–91, A4/B4
Street Fighter II V (video game), Ahichattra, India (village), pp.78–79, D4
Stubbs the Zombie (video game), Punchbowl, Pennsylvania (city), pp.14–15, B5
Suburgatory (TV), Chatswin and East Chatswin, New York (city), pp.14–15, D1
Sucupira (TV), Sucupira, Chile (town), pp.38–39, B3
Suddenly (film), Suddenly, Washington (town), pp.18–19, A6
Sula by Toni Morrison (novel), Medallion, Ohio (town), pp.14–15, B4
Sultan Achbour 10 (TV), The Achourian Kingdom (fictional country), pp.84–85, B5
Sun on the Stubble by Colin Thiele (novel/film), Gonunda, South Australia (town), pp.108–109, C2
Sunset Song by Lewis Grassic Gibbon (novel), Kinraddie, Scotland (village), pp.64–65, C4
Sunshine Sketches of a Little Town by Stephen Leacock (short stories)
Lake Ossawippi, Ontario (lake), pp.26–27, A4

Lake Wissanotti, Ontario (lake), pp.26–27, A4
Mariposa, Ontario (town), pp.26–27, A4
Super 8 (film), Lillian, Ohio (town), pp.14–15, A4
Super-Cannes by JG Ballard (novel), Eden-Olympia, France (building), pp.44–45, C2
Super Chinese series (video game), Chinaland (fictional country), pp.102–103, D1/D2
Super Gran (TV), Chiselton, Scotland (town), pp.64–65, B4
Super Troopers (film), Spurbury, Vermont (town), pp.14–15, C4
Supergirl (TV), National City, California (city), pp.18–19, A4
Surf's Up (film), Pen Gu Island, Pacific Ocean (island), pp.120–121, D2
Survival of the Dead (film), Plum Island, Delaware (island), pp.14–15, C4
Suske en Wiske by Wally Vandersteen (comics)
Andoulasia, Spain (region), pp.44–45, A2/B2
Servela, Spain (city), pp.44–45, A2
Suspiria (film), Tanz Dance Akademie, Germany (building), pp.44–45, C3
Swades (film), Charanpur, India (village), pp.78–79, C4
Swallows and Amazons by Arthur Ransome (novel), Rio, England (village), pp.64–65, C3
Swallows and Amazons: Peter Duck by Arthur Ransome (novels), Crab Island, Caribbean (island), pp.32–33, F2
Sweet Caress by William Boyd (novel), Barrandale, Scotland (island), pp.64–65, B4
Sweet Country (film), Henry, Northern Territory (town), pp.108–109, D2/D3
Sweet Danger by Margaret Allingham (novel), Averna (fictional country), pp.44–45, C2
Sweet Valley High (TV), Sweet Valley, California (town), pp.18–19, A4
Sweetland by Michael Crummey (novel), Sweetland, Newfoundland (island), pp.26–27, F2
Swiss Family Robinson by Johann Wyss; and *Second Fatherland* by Jules Verne (novel/film)
New Switzerland, Indian Ocean (island), pp.90–91, A2
Titus, the, New Switzerland (fictional shipwreck), pp.90–91, A2
Syberia (video game)
Aralbad, Kazakhstan (city), pp.72–73, D3
Barrockstadt, Germany (city), pp.44–45, D3
Syberia, Russia (island), pp.102–103, F2
Valadilène, France (village), pp.44–45, C2/C3
Syberia II (video game), Romansburg, Russia (city), pp.102–103, E1
Sylvia's Lovers by Elizabeth Gaskell (novel), Monkshaven, England (town), pp.64–65, D3
Tactical Iraqi (video game), Al-Wardiya (or Waddihya), Iraq (city), pp.72–73, C4
Tad: The Lost Explorer (film), Paititi, Peru (city), pp.38–39, B5
Take the High Road (TV), Glendarroch, Scotland (town), pp.64–65, B4
Tales from Panimpura by Deeptanshu Bhaskar (book), Panimpura, India (village), pp.78–79, D4
Tales from Witney Scrotum by Peter Tinniswood (novel), Witney Scrotum, England (town), pp.64–65, D1
Tales of the Gold Monkey (TV), Bora Gora, Pacific Ocean (island/nation), pp.120–121, A4
Strangers 6 → *Tale Spin/Duck Tales 2017* (TV), Cape Suzette, Hawaii (city), pp.18–19, D1
Tamara Drewe by Posy Simmonds (comic/film), Ewedown, England (village), pp.64–65, C1
Tangerine by Edward Bloor (novel), Tangerine, Florida (town), pp.14–15, B2
Tarzan and the Forbidden City by Edgar Rice Burroughs (novel)
Ashair (The Forbidden City), DRC (sunken city), pp.84–85, C3
Tuen-Baka, DRC (mountain/volcano), pp.84–85, C3
Tarzan novels of Edgar Rice Burroughs and novels of Philip José Farmer (novels), Opar, Congo/DRC (city), pp.84–85, C3
Tarzan of the Apes by Edgar Rice Burroughs (novel), Tarzan's birthplace, Angola (building), pp.84–85, A5
Tarzan the Terrible by Edgar Rice Burroughs (novel), Pal-ul-Don, Zaire (region), pp.84–85, B3/C3
Tarzan the Untamed by Edgar Rice Burroughs (novel), Xuji, Tanzania (city), pp.84–85, C3
Tattletail (video game), Decent, Illinois (town), pp.16–17, D4
Te Voy a Enseñar a Querer (TV), Soplaviento, Colombia (town), pp.38–39, A2
Team America: World Police (film)
Derkaderkastan (fictional country), pp.72–73, B4
Team America's Base, South Dakota (building), pp.16–17, A5
Team Fortress 2 (video game), Badlands, The, New Mexico (region), pp.18–19, D3
Team Fortress 2 (video game), Teufort, New Mexico (town), pp.18–19, D3

Team Fortress 2 (video game), Thunder Mountains, New Mexico (mountain range), pp.18–19, D3
Teen Wolf (TV), Beacon Hills, California (town), pp.18–19, A4
Tempo de Amar (TV), Morros Verdes, Portugal (town), pp.44–45, A2
Tempos Difíceis (film), Poço do Mundo, Portugal (city), pp.44–45, A2
Tenth Man Down by Chris Ryan (novel)
Kamanga (fictional country), pp.84–85, C2
Mulongwe, Kamanga (fictional city), pp.84–85, C2
Terminal City by Dean Motter and Michael Lark (comic), Terminal City, Indiana (city), pp.14–15, A4
Terminal City Ricochet (film), Terminal City, British Columbia (city), pp.26–27, B1
Terrormolinos (computer game), Terrormolinos, Spain (town), pp.44–45, B1
Tessa – Leben für die Liebe (TV), Torland, Germany (city), pp.44–45, D4
Teutdorf (short film)
District of Masseltow, Germany (region), pp.44–45, D4
Teutdorf, Germany (town), pp.44–45, D4
Tex by S.E. Hinton (novel), Garyville, Oklahoma (town), pp.16–17, C3
ThanksKilling (film), Crawl Berg, Virginia (town), pp.14–15, C4
That 70s Show (TV), Point Place, Wisconsin (town), pp.16–17, D5
That Eye, The Sky by Tim Winton (novel), Bankside, Western Australia (town), pp.108–109, A2
The 'Burbs (film), Hinkley Hills, Iowa (town), pp.16–17, C4
The 120 Days of Sodom by the Marquis de Sade (novel), Château de Silling, France (building), pp.44–45, C2
The 17th Hole at Duncaster by H.R. Wakefield (short story), Duncaster, England (town), pp.64–65, D2
The 39 Steps by John Buchan (film), Alt-na Shellach, Scotland (building), pp.64–65, B4/C4
The A-Team (TV), Zulabwe (fictional country), pp.84–85, C2
The Abominables by Eva Ibbotson (novel), Aslerfan (fictional country), pp.72–73, C3
The Abyss (film), The NTI Caribbean (submerged city), pp.32–33, D2
The Acorn Stories by Duane Simolke (novel), Acorn, Texas (town), pp.16–17, A4
The Adventures of Priscilla, Queen of the Desert (film), Ping Pong Pub, South Australia (building), pp.108–109, C2
The Adventures of Rocky and Bullwinkle (TV)
Frostbite Falls, Minnesota (town), pp.16–17, C6
Moosylvania (fictional island), pp.16–17, C6
Squaw's Ankle, Wyoming (town), pp.16–17, A5
Wassamotta University, Minnesota (building), pp.16–17, C5
The Adventures of Tintin: Red Rackham's Treasure by Hergé (comic book), Unicorn, The, Atlantic Ocean (wreck), pp.126–127, A3
The Adventures of Tintin by Hergé (various)
Bagghar/The Sultanate of Bagghar, Morocco (city/state), pp.84–85, A5
Black Island, The, Scotland (island), pp.64–65, B4
Coliflor River, San Theodoros/Neuvo-Rico (fictional river), pp.38–39, B5/C5
El Chapo/Grand Chapo, San Theodoros/Neuvo-Rico (fictional region), pp.38–39, C5
Gaipajama, India (region), pp.78–79, B5
Hasch El Hemm, Khemed (fictional building), pp.72–73, B1
Jamjah, India (town), pp.78–79, B5
Jauga, Peru (town), pp.38–39, A4
Jebel Kadheih Desert, The, Khemed (fictional country/emirate), pp.72–73, B2/B3
Khemed (fictional country/emirate), pp.72–73, B2
Khemikhal, Khemed (fictional city), pp.72–73, B
Kiltoch, Scotland (village), pp.64–65, B4
Los Dopicos, San Theodoros (fictional city), pp.38–39, C5
Marlinshire, England (county), pp.64–65, D3
Moulinsart, Belgium (village), pp.44–45, C3/C4
Neuvo-Rico (fictional country), pp.38–39, B5
San Theodoros (fictional country), pp.38–39, C5
Sanfacion, Neuvo-Rico (fictional city), pp.38–39, B5
São Paulo (fictional country), pp.38–39, B1
Temple of the Sun, Peru (location), pp.38–39, B4
Tomb of Rascar Capac, Peru (location), pp.38–39, B4
Wadesdah, Khemed (fictional city), pp.72–73, B1/B2
The Age of the Bicycle by Miriam Webster (novel), Tinny Waters, Texas (city), pp.16–17, B2
The Ambassadors (TV), Tazbekistan (fictional country), pp.72–73, E4/F4
The American Senator by Anthony Trollope (novel), Mickewa (fictional state), pp.14–15, A5

The Ancient Magus' Bride by Kore Yamazaki (manga), Ulthar, England (town), pp.64–65, B3

The Andromeda Strain by Michael Critchton (various)
Flatrock, Nevada (town), pp.18–19, B5
Piedmont, Arizona/New Mexico/Utah (town), pp.18–19, C3
Wildfire, Nevada (building) pp.18–19, B5

The Andy Griffith Show (TV), Mt. Pilot, North Carolina (town), pp.14–15, B3

The Andy Griffith Show/Mayberry R.F.D. (TV), Mayberry, North Carolina (town), pp.14–15, B3

The Ante Room by Kate O'Brien (play), Mellick, Ireland (city), pp.64–65, A2

The Antiquary by Sir Walter Scott (novel)
Fairport, Scotland (town), pp.64–65, C4
Musselcrag, Scotland (town), pp.64–65, C4

The Aosawa Murders by Riku Onda (novel), City of K–, Japan (city), pp.96–97, B3

The Archers (radio)
Ambridge, England (village), pp.64–65, C2
Borchester, England (town), pp.64–65, C2
Borsetshire, England (county), pp.64–65, C2
Felpersham, England (city), pp.64–65, C2
Hassett Hills, England (natural feature), pp.64–65, C2

The Arm of the Starfish by Madeleine L'Engle (novel), Gaea, Portugal (island), pp.44–45, A2

The Ascent of Rum Doodle by W.E. Bowman (novel)
Chaikhosi, India (town), pp.78–79, C4
North Doodle, Yogistan (fictional mountain), pp.78–79, B5/C5
Rankling Glacier, Yogistan (fictional natural feature), pp.78–79, C5
River Agenda, Yogistan (fictional river), pp.78–79, B5/C5
Rum Doodle, India (mountain), pp.78–79, C5
Yogistan (fictional country), pp.78–79, B5/C5

The Ash Tree by M.R. James (novel), Castringham Hall, England (building), pp.64–65, D2

The Avengers: Town of No Return (TV), Little Bazeley by the Sea, England (village), pp.64–65, D2

The Baby-Sitter's Club series by Ann M. Martin (novels), Stoneybrook, Connecticut (town), pp.14–15, C5

The Backwater Gospel (short film), Backwater, Oklahoma (town), pp.16–17, B3

The Band's Visit (theatre), Bet Hatikva, Israel (town), pp.72–73, B2

The Barber (film), Revelstoke, Alaska (town), pp.18–19, B2

The Baroque Cycle and *Cryptonomicon* by Neal Stephenson (novels)
Inner Qwghlm, Scotland (island), pp.64–65, A5
Outer Qwghlm, Scotland (island), pp.64–65, A5

The Barrier by Rex Beach (novel), Flambeau, Yukon (town), pp.26–27, B2

The Barrytown Trilogy by Roddy Doyle (novels), Barrytown, Ireland (town), pp.64–65, B3

The Barsac Mission by Jules and Michel Verne (novel), Blackland, Saharan West Africa (city), pp.84–85, B4

The Bay (film), Claridge, Maryland (town), pp.14–15, C4

The Beach House by Helen McKenna (novel), Sunset Point, Queensland (town), pp.108–109, E3

The Beano (comics)
Beanotown, Scotland (town), pp.64–65, C4
Bunkerton Castle, Scotland (building), pp.64–65, C4
Whizztown, Scotland (town), pp.64–65, C4

The Bedford Incident by Mark Rascovich (novel/film)
Moby Dick, Atlantic Ocean (wreck), pp.126–127, C2
USS *Bedford* (DLG-113), Atlantic Ocean (wreck), pp.126–127, C2

The Begum's Fortune by Jules Verne (novel)
Stahlstadt, Oregon (city), pp.18–19, A5
Ville-France, Oregon (city), pp.18–19, A5

The Bert-Diaries by Anders Jacobsson and Sören Olsson (novels)
Nöckeln, Sweden (town), pp.56–57, B3
Öreskoga, Sweden (town), pp.56–57, B3

The Best Years of Our Lives (film), Boone City, Ohio (city), pp.14–15, A4

The BFG by Roald Dahl (novel), Giant Country, Scotland (country), pp.64–65, B5

The Big Bounce by Elmore Leonard (novel)
Geneva Beach, Michigan (town), pp.14–15, A5
Holden County, Michigan (county), pp.14–15, A5

The Big O (anime), Paradigm City, New York (city), pp.14–15, D1

The Bill (TV), Canley, England (town), pp.64–65, D2

The Birds by Aristophanes (myth/legend), Cloud Cuckoo Land, Greece (floating city), pp.44–45, E2

The Birds of Paradise by Paul Scott (novel), Manoba, Papua New Guinea (island), pp.90–91, F1

The Black Bell Buoy by Rupert Chesterton (short story)
Cardingham, Queensland (town), pp.108–109, D3
Cardingham River, Queensland (river), pp.108–109, D3
Hippolyte, Queensland (wreck), pp.108–109, D4

The Black Minutes by Martin Solares (novel), Paracuán, Mexico (town), pp.32–33, B3

The Blair Witch Project (film), Blair, Maryland (town), pp.14–15, C4

The Blazing World by Margaret Cavendish (novel), Portal to the Blazing World, North Pole (portal), pp.26–27, C4

The Blind Assassin by Margaret Atwood (novel), Port Ticonderoga, Ontario (town), pp.26–27, A4

The Blind Man's Garden by Nadeem Aslam (novel), Heer, Pakistan (town), pp.78–79, B5

The Blues Brothers (film)
Bob's Country Bunker, Indiana (building), pp.14–15, A4
Lake Wazzapamani, Wisconsin (lake), pp.16–17, D5
Palace Hotel, The, Wisconsin (building), pp.16–17, D5

The Body Myth by Rheea Mukherjee (novel), Suryam, India (city), pp.78–79, B3

The Bodyguard 2 (film), Wongnaileum (fictional country), pp.90–91, B4

The Book of Dave by Will Self (novel), Ham, England (town), pp.64–65, D2

The Book of Mormon (musical), Sal Tlay Ka Siti, Utah (city), pp.18–19, C4

The Books of Abarat by Clive Barker (novels), Chickentown, Minnesota (town), pp.16–17, C5

The Boomeroo Trilogy by Paul John Radley Jack Radley (novels), Boomeroo, New South Wales (town), pp.108–109, D2

The Boondocks (TV), Woodcrest, Maryland (city), pp.14–15, C4

The Borough by George Crabbe (poem), Borough, The, England (town), pp.64–65, D2

The Bribe, and *Dead Men Don't Wear Plaid* (films), Carlotta, Peru (island), pp.38–39, A4

The Bridge by Iain Banks (novel), Kingdom, The, Scotland (county), pp.64–65, C4

The Brigand (film), Mandorra (fictional country), pp.44–45, B2

The Brokenwood Mysteries (TV), Brokenwood, New Zealand (town), pp.108–109, F2

The Brothers Dal (TV), Atlant-is, Norway (underground city), pp.56–57, C5

The Cabinet of Dr Caligari (film), Holstenwall, Germany (village), pp.44–45, D4

The Calling by Inger Ash Wolfe (novel), Port Dundas, Ontario (town), pp.26–27, A4

The Campaign (film), Hammond, North Carolina (town), pp.14–15, B3

The Car (film), Santa Ynez, Utah (town), pp.18–19, C3

The Carpathians by Janet Frame (novel), Puamahara, New Zealand (town), pp.108–109, F1/F2

The Cars that Ate Paris (film), Paris, New South Wales (town), pp.108–109, D2

The Catcher in the Rye by J.D. Salinger (novel), Agerstown, Pennsylvania (town), pp.14–15, C5

The Centurions (TV)
Montenego (fictional country), pp.38–39, C2
Quisto (fictional country), pp.38–39, B2

The Chalk Hill series by Lily Malone (novels), Chalk Hill, Western Australia (town), pp.108–109, A2

The Chocolate War by Robert Cormier (novel), Monument, Massachusetts (town), pp.14–15, D5

The Chronicles of Prydain by Lloyd Alexander (novels), Prydain (fictional country), pp.64–65, C2

The City of Skulls by L. Sprague de Camp and Lin Carter (novel)
Meru, Tibet (city), pp.102–103, B2
Shamballah, City of Skulls, Tibet (city), pp.102–103, B2
Sumeru Tso, Tibet (lake), pp.102–103, B2

The Civil Servant's Notebook by Wang Xiaofang (novel), Dongzhou City, China (city), pp.102–103, E4

The Cleveland Show (TV), Stoolbend, Virginia (town), pp.14–15, C4

The Clovebitch Killer (film), Clarksville, Kentucky (town), pp.14–15, B3

The Colour of Forgetting by Merle Collins (novel), Eden (island), pp.32–33, F2

The Colournauts by Mona Paalanen and Anni Pöyhönen (books), Utti, Finland (town), pp.56–57, D4

The Constable Sammi Willis series by J.M. Peace (novels), Angel's Crossing, Queensland (town), pp.108–109, E3

The Copper Creek series by Wendy Smith (novels), Copper Creek, New Zealand (town), pp.108–109, F1

The Coral Island by R.M. Ballantyne (novel), Coral Island, The, Pacific Ocean (island), pp.120–121, A3

The Coroner (TV), Lighthaven, England (town), pp.64–65, C1

The Corsican Widow by Vanessa Couchman (novel), Zaronza, France (town), pp.44–45, C2

The Country of the Blind by H.G. Wells (short story)
Country of the Blind, The, Ecuador (region), pp.38–39, A5
Parascotopetl, Ecuador (mountain), pp.38–39, A5

The Coup by John Updike (novel), Kush (fictional country), pp.84–85, D4

The Courts of the Morning by John Buchan (novel)
Gran Seco City, Olifa (fictional city), pp.38–39, B2
Gran Seco Railway, Olifa (fictional railway), pp.38–39, B2
Los Doce Apostoles, Olifa (fictional mountain range), pp.38–39, B2
Olifa (fictional country), pp.38–39, B2
Olifa City, Olifa (fictional city), pp.38–39, B2
Pacheco, Olifa (fictional town), pp.38–39, B2
Tierra Caliente, Olifa (fictional region), pp.38–39, B2

The Crazies (film), Ogden Marsh, Iowa (town), pp.16–17, C4

The Cream of the Jest by James Branch Cabell (novel), Lichfield, Virginia (city), pp.14–15, C4

The Crime of Padre Amaro/El Crimen del Padre Amaro (film)
Aldama, Mexico (region), pp.32–33, B2
Los Reyes, Mexico (town), pp.32–33, B2

The Crow Road by Iain Banks (novel), Gallanach, Scotland (town), pp.64–65, B4

The Crucible by Gong Ji-young (novel), Mujin, South Korea (city), pp.102–103, E2

The Crying of Lot 49 by Thomas Pynchon (novel), San Narciso, California (town), pp.18–19, A2

The Da Vinci Code by Dan Brown (novel/film), Tomb of Mary Magdalen, Paris, France (building), pp.44–45, C3

The Dâk Bungalow at Dakor by Bithia Mary Croker (short story)
Chanda, India (town), pp.78–79, C4
Dakor Bungalow, The, India (building), pp.78–79, C4
Karwassa, India (town), pp.78–79, C4

The Dandy (comics), Dandytown, Scotland (town), pp.64–65, C4

The Dandy ('The Jocks and the Geordies') (comic), Crosspatch, Scotland (town), pp.64–65, C4

The Dark is Rising by Susan Cooper (novels), Huntercombe, England (village), pp.64–65, D2

The Day of the Triffids by John Wyndham (novel), Tynsham, England (town), pp.64–65, C2

The Day Today (TV), Valerie Sinatra's Mile-High Travel Pod, England (building), pp.64–65, C3

The Dead Heart by Douglas Kennedy (novel), Wollanup, Northern Territory (town), pp.108–109, C4

The Dead Man's Pond by André Bjerkes (novel), Dead Man's Pond, The, Norway (lake), pp.56–57, A3

The Dead Wander in the Desert by Rollan Seisenbayev (novel), Karaoi, Kazakhstan (village), pp.72–73, A3

The Death Certificate by Alobwed'Epie (novel)
Dande, Ewawa (fictional city), pp.84–85, B4
Ewawa (fictional country), pp.84–85, B4

The Deceiver by Frederick Forsyth (novel)
Barclay Islands (fictional islands), pp.32–33, D3
Sunshine, Barclay Islands (fictional island), pp.32–33, D3

The Delights of Turkey by Edouard Roditi (stories), Bok Köy, Turkey (village), pp.72–73, C2

The Demon Girl Next Door by Izumo Itō (manga/anime)
Sakuragaoka High School, Japan (building), pp.96–97, E1
Tama (of Many Demons), Japan (city), pp.96–97, E1

The Deptford Mice series by Robin Jarvis (books), Hara, India (city), pp.78–79, B5

The Descent (film)
Chatooga National Park, North Carolina (natural feature), pp.14–15, C3
Hyatt County, North Carolina (county), pp.14–15, B3

The Descent Part 2 (film), Chapel Mine, North Carolina (mine), pp.14–15, B3

The Desert and the Drum by Mbarek Ould Beyrouk (novel), Rayhana's village, Mauritania (village), pp.84–85, A3

The Detectorists (TV), Danebury, England (town), pp.64–65, D2

The Devil in the Belfry by Edgar Allan Poe (short story), Vondervotteimittiss, Netherlands (village), pp.44–45, D4

The Devil's Tattoo (film), Janus Oil Rig, North Sea (oil rig), pp.64–65, D5

The Dictator (film)
Aladeen Desert, Wadiya (fictional desert), pp.84–85, D4
Wadiya (fictional country), pp.84–85, D4

The Divine and the Decay by Bill Hopkins (novel), Vachau, Channel Islands (island), pp.64–65, A1

The Dogs of War by Frederick Forsyth (novel)
Katanga (fictional country), pp.84–85, A4
Zangaro (fictional country), pp.84–85, B4

The Donna Reed Show (TV), Hilldale, Iowa (town), pp.16–17, C4

The Drackenberg Adventure by Lloyd Alexander (novel), Drackenberg (fictional country), pp.44–45, C3

The Dressmaker by Rosalie Ham (film), Dungatar, Victoria (town), pp.108–109, D2

The Dry by Jane Harper (novel), Kiewarra, Victoria (town), pp.108–109, D1/D2

The Dublin Murder Squad series by Tana French (novel), Knocknaree, Ireland (town), pp.64–65, B3

The Dukes of Hazzard (TV), Hazzard County, Georgia (county), pp.14–15, B3

The Eagle has Landed (film), Studley Constable, England (town), pp.64–65, D2

The Emperor's New Groove (film), Kuzcotopia, Peru (building), pp.38–39, B4

The Enemy Below by Denys Rayner (novel/film)
HMS *Hecate*, Atlantic Ocean (wreck), pp.126–127, C3
U-121, Atlantic Ocean (wreck), pp.126–127, C2
USS *Haynes* (DE-181), Atlantic Ocean (wreck), pp.126–127, C3

The Engelsfors series by Mats Strandberg and Sara Bergmark (novels), Engelsfors, Sweden (town), pp.56–57, C3

The Englishman who Went Up a Hill But Came Down a Mountain (film), Fynnon Garw, Wales (village), pp.64–65, C2

The Enigma of Amigara Fault by Junji Ito (manga), Amigara Mountain, Japan (mountain), pp.96–97, C4

The Exhausting Summer of São Martino by Simon Carr (novel), Tapoli, Portugal (town), pp.44–45, A2

The Expendables (film), Vilena (fictional island/nation), pp.32–33, C2

The Expendables 3 and *The Onion Movie* (films), Azmenistan (fictional country), pp.72–73, D4

The Explosion Chronicles by Yan Lianke (novel), Explosion City (formerly Explosion Village), China (city), pp.102–103, D2

The Explosion Chronicles by Yan Lianke (novel)
Funiu Mountain, China (mountain), pp.102–103, D2
Gaoyi County, China (region), pp.102–103, D2

The Extraordinary Adventures of Saturnin Farandoul by Albert Robida (novel), Makaloló (fictional country), pp.84–85, C4

The Fairly OddParents (TV), Dimmsdale, California (town), pp.18–19, B3

The Final Sacrifice (film), Eagle Hat, Alberta (town), pp.26–27, C1

The Fixed Period by Anthony Trollope (novel)
Britannula (fictional island), pp.120–121, C1
Gladstonopolis, Britannula (fictional city), pp.120–121, C1
Little Christchurch, Britannula (fictional town), pp.120–121, C1

The Flaxborough Chronicles by Colin Watson (novels), Flaxborough, England (town), pp.64–65, D2

The Flintstones (various), Bedrock Arizona (city), pp.18–19, C3
Bostone, Massachusetts (city), pp.14–15, D5
Frantic City, New Jersey (city), pp.14–15, C4
Hollyrock, California (city), pp.18–19, A2/A3
Houstone, Texas (city), pp.16–17, C
Indianrockolis, Indiana (city), pp.14–15, A4
Rock Vegas, Nevada (city), pp.18–19, B3
Rockadelphia, Pennsylvania (city), pp.14–15, C4
Washingstone, B.C., District of Columbia (city), pp.14–15, C4

The Flintstones Bedrock River Adventure (theme park)
Bedrock River, various (river), pp.18–19, C3
Stonetrail Park, Arizona (natural feature), pp.18–19, C3

The Flood by Ian Rankin (novel), Carsden, Scotland (town), pp.64–65, C4

The Flying Doctors (TV), Cooper's Crossing, New South Wales (town), pp.108–109, D2

The Flying Legion by George Allan England (novel), Jannati Shahr, Saudi Arabia (city), pp.72–73, C1

The Fog (film)
Antonio Bay, California (town), pp.18–19, A4
Elizabeth Dane, California (wreck), pp.18–19, A4

The Forest of the Lost Souls (film), Forest of the Lost Souls, The, Portugal/Spain (natural feature), pp.44–45, A2

The Forest Rangers (TV), Indian River, Ontario (town), pp.26–27, A4

The Fortunate Brother by Donna Morrissey (novel), Hampden, Newfoundland (town), pp.26–27, F2

The Fountains of Paradise by Arthur C. Clarke (novel)
Sri Kanda, Taprobane (fictional mountain), pp.78–79, C2
Taprobane Space Elevator, Taprobane (fictional space elevator), pp.78–79, C2

Taprobane (fictional island), pp.78–79, C2
Yakkagala, Ruins of, Taprobane (fictional building), pp.78–79, C2

The Fox of Glenarvon (film), Glenarvon, Ireland (town), pp.64–65, A3

The Framley Examiner (website), Framley, England (town), pp.64–65, D2

The French Dispatch (film), Ennui-Sur-Blasé, France (city), pp.44–45, C3

The Fugitive (film)
Barkley Dam, Illinois (building), pp.16–17, D4
Doverville, Illinois (town), pp.16–17, D4

The Fugitive (TV), Stafford, Indiana (town), pp.14–15, A4

The General (Buster Keaton) (film), Rock River Bridge, Georgia (building), pp.14–15, B3

The Germaine Truth (web fiction)
Germaine, Oregon (town), pp.18–19, B5
Wilbur County, Oregon (county), pp.18–19, B5

The Ghost and Mr Chicken (film), Rachel, Kansas (town), pp.16–17, C3

The Ghost of St Michael's (film), Dunbain Castle, Scotland (building), pp.64–65, B4

The Ghost Train by Arnold Ridley (play), Fal Vale, England (town), pp.64–65, B1

The Ghost Writer by John Harwood (novel), Mawson, South Australia (town), pp.108–109, C4

The Glass-Sided Ant's Nest by Peter Dickinson (novel), Lands of the Ku, Papua New Guinea (region), pp.90–91, E1/F1

The Goddess of Atvatabar by William R. Bradshaw (novel), Tunnel to Atvatabar, North Pole (portal), pp.26–27, C4

The Gods Must Be Crazy (film), Birani (fictional country), pp.84–85, C4

The Golden Apple (musical), Angel's Roost, Washington (town), pp.18–19, A6

The Golden Compass (novel/film)
Atlas States (fictional bloc), pp.84–85, A5
Empire of Niger, The (fictional bloc), pp.84–85, D5
Kingdom of Auster (fictional country), pp.108–109, B2/C3
Terra de Pogo (fictional country), pp.38–39, D2

The Golden Girls (TV)
St Gustav, Minnesota (town), pp.16–17, C6
St Olaf, Minnesota (town), pp.16–17, C6

The Golden Legend by Nadeem Aslam (novel), Zamana, Pakistan (town), pp.78–79, B5

The Golden Son by Shilpi Somaya Gowda (novel), Panchanagar, India (village), pp.78–79, B4

The Golden Volano by Jules Verne (novel), Golden Mount, Yukon (mountain), pp.26–27, B2

The Good Companions by J.B. Priestley (novel), Bruddersford, England (city), pp.64–65, D2

The Goodies (TV)
August Bank Holiday Island, Pacific Ocean (island), pp.120–121, B2
Jolly Rock Lighthouse, North Sea (building), pp.64–65, D5
Pennenink, England (town), pp.64–65, B1

The Goonies (film)
Cauldron Point, Oregon (natural feature), pp.18–19, A6
Goon Docks, Oregon (village), pp.18–19, A6
Inferno, The, Oregon (wreck), pp.18–19, A6

The Grand Duke by W.S. Gilbert and Arthur Sullivan (light opera), Pfennig Halbpfennig (fictional country), pp.44–45, D3

The Grand Seduction (film), Tickle Head, Newfoundland (town), pp.26–27, F2

The Great Brain by John D. Fitzgerald (novels), Adenville, Utah (town), pp.18–19, C4

The Great Dictator (film)
Aroma, Bacteria (fictional city), pp.44–45, D2
Bacteria (fictional country), pp.44–45, D2
Osterlich (fictional country), pp.44–45, D3
Tomainia (fictional country), pp.44–45, D3

The Great Gatsby by F. Scott Fitzgerald (novel)
East and West Egg, New York (town), pp.14–15, D1
Valley of Ashes, The, New York (town), pp.14–15, D1

The Green Child by Herbert Read (novel), Roncador (fictional country), pp.38–39, C3

The Green Mile by Stephen King (novel/film), Cold Mountain Penitentiary, Louisiana (building), pp.16–17, D2

The Griffin and Sabine Trilogy (novels), Sicmon Islands, Pacific Ocean (island chain), pp.120–121, D4

The Guns of Navarone by Alistair MacLean (novel/film), Navarone, Greece (island), pp.44–45, E4

The Handmaid's Tale by Margaret Atwood (novel), National Homeland One, North Dakota (region), pp.16–17, B6

The Happy Lands (film), Carhill, Scotland (village), pp.64–65, C4

The Hardy Boys novels by various (novels), Barmet Bay, New York (natural feature), pp.14–15, C5

The Hateful Eight (film)

163

Red Rock, Wyoming (town), pp.18–19, D4

Wellenbeck, West Virginia (town), pp.14–15, B4

The Haunted Mansion (theme park), Gracey Manor, Louisiana (building), pp.16–17, D2

The Haunting of Hill House by Shirley Jackson and The Haunting (various), Hill House, Massachusetts (building), pp.14–15, C5

The Heart Guy (TV), Whyhope, New South Wales (town), pp.108–109, D2

The Henderson Kids (TV)
Haven Bay, Victoria (town), pp.108–109, D1
Westport, Victoria (town), pp.108–109, A1

The Hero's Walk by Anita Rau Badami (novel), Torturpuram, India (town), pp.78–79, C3

The History Man by Malcolm Bradbury (novel), Watermouth, England (city), pp.64–65, D1

The Horror-Horn by E.F. Benson (short story), Ungeheuerhorn (The Horror-Horn), Switzerland (mountain), pp.44–45, D4

The House at Plum Bay by Geoff Morgan (novel), Plum Bay, Western Australia (town), pp.108–109, A1

The House of the Scorpion by Nancy Farmer (novel), Opium, Country (country), pp.18–19, C2

The House with a Clock in its Walls by John Bellairs (novel), New Zebedee, Michigan (town), pp.14–15, A5

The House Without A Christmas Tree (film), Clear River, Nebraska (town), pp.16–17, C4

The Hundred Secret Senses by Amy Tan (novel)
Changmian, China (village), pp.102–103, C1
Jintian, China (city), pp.102–103, C1
Thistle Mountain, China (mountain), pp.102–103, C1
Yongan, China (city), pp.102–103, C1

The Hunger Games by Suzanne Collins (various)
Capitol, The, Colorado (city), pp.18–19, D4
District 1, Utah/Montana (state), pp.18–19, C5
District 2, New Mexico (state), pp.18–19, D3
District 3, Indiana (state), pp.14–15, A4
District 4, Nevada/Oregon/Washington (state), pp.18–19, B5
District 5, Nevada/Arizona (state), pp.18–19, B3/C3
District 6, Illinois (state), pp.16–17, D4
District 7, Alberta/Saskatchewan (region), pp.26–27, C1
District 7, Montana (state), pp.16–17, A6
District 8, New York (state), pp.14–15, B5
District 9, Kansas/Missouri (state), pp.16–17, C4
District 10, Mexico (region), pp.32–33, A4/A6
District 10, Texas (state), pp.16–17, B1/B2
District 11 (state), pp.16–17, D2
District 12, West Virginia/Pennsylvania (city/region), pp.14–15, B4/C4 District 13, Ontario/Quebec (region), pp.26–27, E1

The Hunt for Red October by Tom Clancy (novel/film), *VK Konovalov*, Atlantic Ocean (wreck), pp.126–127, D4

The Hurricane by Zhou Libo (novel), Yuanmaotun, China (village), pp.102–103, E3

The Hurricanes (TV), Garkos (fictional island nation), pp.44–45, E1

The Illegal by Lawrence Hill (novel)
Buttersby, Indian Ocean (town), pp.78–79, B1/C1
Clarkson, Indian Ocean (city), pp.78–79, C1
Freedom State, Indian Ocean (island/ nation), pp.78–79, B1/C1
North Ortiz Sea, Indian Ocean (sea), pp.78–79, B1/C1
South Ortiz Sea, Indian Ocean (sea), pp.78–79, B1/C1
Zantoroland, Indian Ocean (island/ nation), pp.78–79, B1/C1

The Immortal by Jorges Luis Borges (short story), City of the Immortals, Ethiopia (ruined city), pp.84–85, D4

The Inca of Perusalem by George Bernard Shaw (play), Perusalem (fictional country), pp.44–45, D4

The Incredibles (film)
Metroville, Illinois (city), pp.16–17, D4
Municiberg, Washington (city), pp.18–19, A6
Nomanisan Island, Pacific Ocean (island), pp.120–121, E2

The Inspector Jim Carruthers series by Tana Collins (novels), Castletown, Scotland (town), pp.64–65, C4

The Interpreter (film), Matobo (fictional country), pp.84–85, C3

The Invention of Morel by Adolfo Bioy Casares (novel), Villings, Indonesia (island), pp.90–91, A4

The Irish Country series by Patrick Taylor (novels), Ballybucklebo, Ireland (town), pp.64–65, B3

The Irish R.M. novels by Somerville and Ross (novels), Skebawn, Ireland (village), pp.64–65, A2

The Iron Giant by Ted Hughes (novel/film)
Annabelle, Maine (wreck), pp.14–15, D6
Rockwell, Maine (town), pp.14–15, D6

The Iron Giant (film), The Iron Giant (remains), Iceland (being), pp.56–57, A6

The Island at the Top of the World (film), Astragard (fictional island/nation), pp.26–27, C4

The Island of Adventure by Enid Blyton (novel)
Craggy Tops, England (building), pp.64–65, B1
Isle of Gloom, England (island), pp.64–65, B1

The Island of Dr Moreau by H.G. Wells(novel), Island of Dr Moreau, The, Pacific Ocean (island), pp.120–121, C2

The Island of the Day Before by Umberto Eco (novel)
Island of the Day Before, Pacific Ocean (island), pp.120–121, C2
The Daphne, Pacific Ocean (wreck), pp.120–121, C2

The Isle of the Pines by Henry Neville (novel), Isle of the Pines, Indian Ocean (island), pp.108–109, A4/B4

The Italian Wife by Kate Furnivall (novel), Bellina, Italy (town), pp.44–45, D2

The Janson Directive by Robert Ludlum (novel), Islamic Republic of Mansur (fictional country), pp.72–73, C1

The Jetsons Meet the Flintstones (film), Honolurock, Hawaii (city), pp.18–19, C1

The Jungle Book by Rudyard Kipling (novel), Mowgli's Jungle, India (natural feature), pp.78–79, B4/C4

The Kingston Fortune by Stephen Longstreet (novel), Kingston Junction, California (town), pp.18–19, B3

The Lacuna by Barbara Kingsolver (novel), Isla Pixol, Mexico (island), pp.32–33, A3

The Lady of the Lake by Sir Walter Scott (poem), Monan's Rill, Scotland (natural feature), pp.64–65, C4

The Land That Time Forgot by Edgar Rice Burroughs (novel)
Caprona (also known as Caspak), island), pp.114–115, A3
Oo-Oh (island), pp.114–115, B3

The Lantern Bearer by Pingwa Jia (novel), Cherry Town, China (village), pp.102–103, D2

The Last Days of Dolwyn (film), Dolwyn, England (village), pp.64–65, C2

The Last Picture Show (film), Anarine, Texas (town), pp.16–17, C2

The Last September by Elizabeth Bowen (novel/film), Danielstown, Ireland (estate), pp.64–65, A2

The Last Voyage (film), SS *Claridon*, Pacific Ocean (wreck), pp.120–121, D4

The League of Gentlemen (TV), Royston Vasey, England (village), pp.64–65, C3

The Leatherstocking Tales by James Fenimore Cooper (novels)
Lake Glimmerglass, New York (lake), pp.14–15, C5
Templeton, New York (town), pp.14–15, C5

The Legend of 1900 (film), SS *Virginian*, England (wreck), pp.64–65, C1

The Lego Movie (film), Middle Zealand, New Zealand (country), pp.108–109, F2

The Lesser Blessed by Richard Van Camp (novel), Fort Simmer, Northwest Territories (town), pp.26–27, C2

The Levenham Love Stories series by Cathryn Hein (novels), Levenham, South Australia (town), pp.108–109, D1

The Lie Tree by Frances Hardinge (novel), Vane, Channel Islands (island), pp.64–65, A1

The Life and Times of Michael K. by J.M. Coetzee (novel), Jakkalsdrif, South Africa (building), pp.84–85, C2

The Life of Gargantua and Pantagruel by François Rabelais (novel)
Cheli, Italy (island), pp.44–45, D1
Clerkship, Italy (island), pp.44–45, D1/ D2
Ennasin, Italy (island), pp.44–45, D1

The Light Between Oceans by M.L. Stedman (novel)
Janus Rock Lighthouse, Western Australia (building), pp.108–109, A2
Point Partageus, Western Australia (natural feature), pp.108–109, A2

The Lights We Carried Home by Kay Chronister (short story), Psaodung, Cambodia (village), pp.90–91, B3

The Line of Beauty by Alan Hollinghurst (novel), Barwick, England (town), pp.64–65, D2

The Lion King (film)
Elephant Graveyard, The, Tanzania (natural feature), pp.84–85, D3
Pride Lands, The, Tanzania (region), pp.84–85, D3
Pride Rock, Tanzania (natural feature), pp.84–85, D3

The Lion King 2: Simba's Pride (film), Outlands, The, Tanzania (region), pp.84–85, D3

The Lion King/The Lion King 1 ½ (film), Hakuna Matata, Tanzania (natural feature), pp.84–85, D3

The Little Mermaid (film)
Atlantica (fictional country), pp.56–57, A2
Tirulia (fictional country), pp.56–57, A2

The Little Theatre by the Sea by Rosanna Ley (novel), Deriu, Italy (town), pp.44–45, C2

The Lone Ranger (film), Colby, Texas (town), pp.16–17, B2

The Lorax (various), Thneedville, New Jersey (town), pp.14–15, C5

The Lost Boys (film), Santa Clara, California (town), pp.18–19, A4

The Lost Continent (film), The Lost Continent (fictional island), pp.126–127, A3

The Lost World by Arthur Conan Doyle (novel), Maple White Land, Brazil (region), pp.38–39, C3

The Loud House (TV), Royal Woods, Michigan (town), pp.14–15, A5

The Machine Gunners by Robert Westall (novel), Garmouth, England (town), pp.44–45, B2

The Maggie (film)
Bellabegwinnie, Scotland (island), pp.64–65, B4
Fiona Bay, Scotland (natural feature), pp.64–65, B4
Inverkerran, Scotland (town), pp.64–65, B4
Isle of Kiltarra, Scotland (island), pp.64–65, B5
Loch Mora, Scotland (town), pp.64–65, B4

The Magic School Bus (TV), Walkerville, Illinois (town), pp.16–17, D5

The Magicians of Caprona by Diana Wynne Jones (novel), Caprona, Italy (city state), pp.44–45, C2

The Magus by John Fowles (novel), Phraxos, Greece (island), pp.44–45, E1

The Majestic (film), Lawson, California (town), pp.18–19, A4

The Man Who Corrupted Hadleyburg/Gung Ho (short story/film), Hadleyburg, Pennsylvania (town), pp.14–15, B4

The Man Who Fell in Love With the Moon by Tom Spanbauer (novel)
Excellent, Idaho (town), pp.18–19, B5
Fort Lincoln, Idaho (town), pp.18–19, C5

The Man Who Lost His Head (film), Otakataka, New Zealand (town), pp.108–109, B4

The Man Who Shot Liberty Valance (film)
Capitol City, Colorado (city), pp.18–19, A6, pp.16–17, A4
CM&W Railroad, Colorado (railway), pp.16–17, A3
Junction City, Colorado (town), pp.16–17, A4
Shinbone, Colorado (town), pp.16–17, A3

The Man With the Compound Eyes by Wu Ming-Yi (novel), Haven, Taiwan (town), pp.102–103, D4

The Man with the Iron Fists (film), Jungle Village, China (village), pp.102–103, D4

The Man with the Iron Fists 2 (film)
Tsai Fu, China (village), pp.102–103, D2
Wu Chi Temple, China (building), pp.102–103, D2

The Mannequin Makers by Craig Cliff (novel), Marumaru South, New Zealand (town), pp.108–109, F1

The Marianne novels by Sheri S. Tepper (novels), Alphenlicht (fictional country), pp.72–73, B3

The Mask (film), Edge City, New Jersey (city), pp.14–15, C5/C6

The Matrix series (films), Zero-One (The Machine City), Iraq (city/state), pp.72–73, C2

The Maze Runner by James Dashner (novel/ film), WICKED Maze, California (building), pp.18–19, A4

The Meg (film), Mana One Research Station, Pacific Ocean (building), pp.120–121, A4/B4

The Melancholy of Haruhi Suzumiya by Nagaru Tanigawa and Noizi Ito (novels/ anime), North High School, Japan (building), pp.96–97, B4

The Middle (TV), Orson, Indiana (town), pp.14–15, A4

The Midnight Folk by John Masefield (novel), Santa Barbara (fictional country), pp.38–39, B6

The Midnight Sky (film), Barbeau Observatory, Nunavut (building), pp.26–27, D4

The Midwich Cuckoos by John Wyndham (novel)
Gizhinsk, Russia (town), pp.102–103, F1
Midwich, England (village), pp.64–65, D2

The Mikado by W.S. Gilbert and Arthur Sullivan (light opera), Titipu, Japan (town), pp.96–97, C2

The Mill on the Floss by George Eliot (novel)
Dorlcote Mill, England (building), pp.64–65, D3
Mudport, England (city), pp.64–65, D3
River Floss, England (river), pp.64–65, D3
St Ogg's, England (village), pp.64–65, D3

The Millennium Trilogy by Stig Larsson (novels)
Hedeby, Sweden (island/town), pp.56–57, C3
Hedestad, Sweden (town), pp.56–57, C3

The Missing Place by Sophie Littlefield (novel), Lawton, North Dakota (town), pp.16–17, A6

The Monastery and the Abbot by Walter Scott (novel), Kennaquhair, Scotland (building), pp.64–65, C4

The Monikins by James Fenimore Cooper (novel), The Leap Islands (island chain), pp.114–115, D2/D3

The Moomin books by Tove Jansson (short stories)
Island of the Hattifatteners, Sweden (island), pp.56–57, D3
Moominvalley, Finland (village), pp.56–57, D3

The Moon-Bog by H.P. Lovecraft (short story)
Ballylough, Ireland (village), pp.64–65, B3
Kilderry, Ireland (village), pp.64–65, B3
Moon-Bog, The, Ireland (natural feature), pp.64–65, B3

The Moor's Last Sigh by Salman Rushdie (novel), Benengeli, Spain (town), pp.44–45, B2

The Mosquito Coast by Paul Theroux (novel)
Guampu, Honduras (village), pp.32–33, D2
Jeronimo, Honduras (village), pp.32–33, C2

The Most Dangerous Game by Richard Connell (novel), Ship-Trap Island, Caribbean (island), pp.32–33, F2

The Mouse that Roared by Leonard Wibberley (novel), Grand Fenwick (fictional country), pp.44–45, C2

The Mummy (film), Hamunaptra, Egypt (city), pp.84–85, C5

The Mummy Returns (film)
Desert of Ahm Shere, The, Ethiopia (natural feature), pp.84–85, D4
Golden Pyramid of Ahm Shere, Ethiopia (building), pp.84–85, D4

The Muppets (TV), Paradise Swamp, Flordia (natural feature), pp.14–15, C2

The Music Man (musical/film), River City, Iowa (town), pp.16–17, C3

The Myrtle Tree by Jad el-Hage (novel), Wahdeh, Lebanon (village), pp.72–73, B2

The Mysterious Island by Jules Verne (novel), *Nautilus*, The, Pacific Ocean (wreck), pp.120–121, C2

The Mysterious Island by Jules Verne/*20,000 Leagues Under the Sea* (novel/film), Lincoln Island/Vulcania, Pacific Ocean (island), pp.120–121, C2

The Mystery of Edwin Drood by Charles Dickens (novel), Cloisterham, England (town), pp.64–65, D2

The Mystery of the Black Jungle by Emilio Salgari (novel), Black Jungle, The, India (natural feature), pp.78–79, D4

The Mystery series by Julia Keller (novel)
Acker's Gap, West Virginia (town), pp.14–15, B4
Raythune County, West Virginia (county), pp.14–15, B4

The Nargun and the Stars by Patricia Wrightson (novel), Wongadilla, New South Wales (estate), pp.108–109, E2

The Narrative of Arthur Gordon Pym of Nantucket by Edgar Allan Poe (novel) *Jane Guy*, The (wreck), pp.114–115, C3

The Narrative of Arthur Gordon Pym of Nantucket by Edgar Allan Poe and *An Antarctic Mystery* by Jules Verne (novels)
Bennet's Isle (island), pp.114–115, C3
Tsalal (island), pp.114–115, C3

The Narrows by Ann Petry (novel), Monmouth, Connecticut (town), pp.14–15, C5

The Natural Man by Ed McClanahan (novel), Needmore, Kentucky (town), pp.14–15, A4

The Nautch Girl, or The Rajah of Chutneypore (comic opera), Chutneypore, India (city), pp.78–79, C4/D4

The Navy Lark (radio), Potarneyland (fictional country), pp.78–79, B2/C2

The New Avengers: The Eagles Nest (TV), St Dorca, Scotland (island), pp.64–65, B5

The New Gulliver by Abbé Pierre François Guyot-Desfontaines (novel)
Babiliary (fictional island/nation), pp.96–97, A1
Ramaja, Babiliary (fictional city), pp.96–97, A1

The Night Spinner by Abi Elphinstone (novel), Glendrummie, Scotland (village), pp.64–65, C4

The Nine Tailors by Dorothy L Sayers (novel), Fenchurch St Paul, England (village), pp.64–65, D2

The No.1 Ladies' Detective Agency by Alexander McCall Smith (novel), No. 1 Ladies' Detective Agency, The, Botswana (building), pp.84–85, C2

The Ocean of Osyria by Scott Lobdell and Lea Hernandez (comic book), Osyria (fictional country), pp.72–73, D2

The Odyssey by Homer (mythology)
Aeaea, Mediterranean Sea (island), pp.44–45, D2
Laestrygon, Italy (country), pp.44–45, D1
Ogygia, Greece (island), pp.44–45, D1
Scheria, Greece (island), pp.44–45, D1/ E1

The Old Man Who Read Love Stories/Un viejo que leía novelas de amor by Luis Sepulveda (novel), El Idilio, Ecuador (village), pp.38–39, A5

The Onion (online satire)
Bulungi (fictional country), pp.84–85, A4
Nukehavistan (fictional country), pp.72–73, D3/E3
Silograd, Nukehavistan (fictional city), pp.72–73, D3/E3
Warhednya, Nukehavistan (fictional city), pp.72–73, D3/E3
Yabba-Dabba, Bulungi (fictional city), pp.84–85, A4

The Onion Movie (film), Sloravia (fictional country), pp.72–73, C3

The Outer Limits (TV), Morgue, California (town), pp.18–19, B3

The Outsider by Stephen King (novels)
Cap City, Oklahoma (town), pp.16–17, C3
Flint City, Oklahoma (town), pp.16–17, C3
Marysville, Texas (town), pp.16–17, C2

The Painted Veil by W. Somerset Maugham (novel/film), Mei-tan-fu, China (village), pp.102–103, D1

The Palace of Heavenly Pleasure by Adam Williams (novel), Shishan, China (city), pp.102–103, D3

The Partridge Family (TV), San Pueblo, California (town), pp.18–19, A4

The Pearler's Wife by Roxane Dhand (novel), Bucaneer Bay, Western Australia (town), pp.108–109, B3

The Pebble and the Penguin (film), Hubie's Adélie Penguin Colony/Pebble Beach (colony), pp.114–115, D1

The Phantom (comic)
Bangalla (fictional country), pp.84–85, D3
Ivory-Lana or Fari Lana, Ivory-Lana (fictional country), pp.84–85, D3
Mawitaan, Bangalla (fictional city), pp.84–85, D3

The Phantom of the Opera by Gaston Leroux (various), Opera Populaire, Paris, France (building), pp.44–45, E3

The Pickwick Papers by Charles Dickens (novel)
All-Muggleton, England (village), pp.64–65, D2
Dingley Dell, England (village), pp.64–65, D2
Eatenswill, England (village), pp.64–65, D2

The Pillars of the Earth by Ken Follett (novel), Kingsbridge, England (town), pp.64–65, D2

The Pirates! Band of Misfits! (film)
Black Spot Spit, Florida (natural feature), pp.14–15, C2
Budgie Islands, The, Caribbean (island chain), pp.32–33, D3
Canalview, Panama (town), pp.32–33, D1
Canarie Islands, The, Caribbean (island chain), pp.32–33, D3
Cannonball Cove, Cuba (natural feature), pp.32–33, D3
Cape of Good Ham, The, Caribbean (natural feature), pp.32–33, F2
Groggy Head, Cuba (natural feature), pp.32–33, D3
Ham Sandwich Islands, The, South Carolina (island chain), pp.14–15, C3
Mermaid's Spit, Panama (natural feature), pp.32–33, D1
Mid Atlantic Wench, Atlantic Ocean (region), pp.126–127, B3
Poop Deck Point, Caribbean (natural feature), pp.32–33, D3
Port de la Senoritas, Mexico (town), pp.32–33, D1
Q.V.1, Indian Ocean (wreck), pp.78–79, B2
Shipwreck Cove, Cuba (natural feature), pp.32–33, D3
Silly Islands, The, Pacific Ocean (island chain), pp.96–97, D4/E4

The Pledge: Requiem for the Detective Novel by Friedrich Dürrenmatt (novella), Mägendorf, Switzerland (village), pp.44–45, C3

The Polish Rider by Antonio Muñoz Molina (novel), Mágina, Spain (town), pp.44–45, B2

The Polished Hoe by Austin Clarke (novel), Flagstaff Village, Barbados (village), pp.32–33, F2

The Poseidon Adventure by Paul Gallico (novel)
SS Poseidon, Mediterranean Sea (wreck), pp.44–45, C1
SS Poseidon (ex-RMS *Atlantis*), Atlantic Ocean (wreck), pp.126–127, C4

The Powerpuff Girls (TV)
Citiesville, California (city), pp.18–19, B3
Farmsville, California (town), pp.18–19, B3
Pokey Oats County, California (county), pp.18–19, B3
Rotunda of Seclusion, The, Nepal (building), pp.78–79, C4
Townsville, California (city), pp.18–19, B3

The Price of Blood by Patricia Bracewell (novel), Redmere, England (town), pp.64–65, D3

The Prince and Betty by P.G. Wodehouse (novel), Mervo (fictional island), pp.44–45, C2

The Princess Diaries by Meg Cabot (novel/ film), Genovia (fictional country/ principality), pp.44–45, C2

The Princess of Babylon by Voltaire (novel), Gangaridia (fictional country), pp.78–79, D4

The Prisoner (TV), Village, The, Wales (village), pp.64–65, C2

The Promise (film), Siroun, Turkey (village), pp.72–73, B3

The Proud Valley (film), Blaendy, Wales (unmappable, village), pp.64–65, C2

The Provost by John Galt (novel), Gudetown, Scotland (town), pp.64–65, B4

The Puddleduck Affair by David Sheperd (novel)
Abernirvana, Wales (village), pp.64–65, C2
Caer Craig, Wales (building), pp.64–65, C2
Pwddldwc, Wales (town), pp.64–65, C2

The Pursuit of Love by Nancy Mitford (novel/TV), Alconleigh, England (estate), pp.64–65, C2

The Quarry Line Mystery by A.C. Stewart (novel)
Belchester, England (town), pp.64–65, C3
Braddage, England (town), pp.64–65, C3
Port St Mary, England (town), pp.64–65, C3
Skirby, England (town), pp.64–65, C3
Skirby St Mary, England (town), pp.64–65, C3

The Quick and the Dead (film), Redemption, Arizona (town), pp.18–19, C2

The Quiet Man (film), Inisfree, Ireland (town), pp.64–65, A3

The Raccoons (TV), Evergreen Forest, The, British Columbia/Alberta (region), pp.26–27, B1/B2

The Ragged-Trousered Philanthropists by Robert Tressell (novel), Mugsborough, England (town), pp.64–65, D1

The Railway by Hamid Ismailov (novel), Gilas, Uzbekistan (town), pp.72–73, D3

The Railway Phantoms by Dennis Hamley (novel), Scarhead, England (town), pp.64–65, C4

The Raj Quartet series by Paul Scott (novels)
Mayapore, India (town), pp.78–79, C4
Mirat, India (region), pp.78–79, B4
Pankot, India (town), pp.78–79, C4
Ranpur, India (city), pp.78–79, B4/C4

The Real Adventures of Jonny Quest (TV), Moldovistan (fictional country), pp.72–73, D3

The Real Ghostbusters (TV)
Lupusville, New York (town), pp.14–15, C5
Muddy Flat, Louisiana (town), pp.16–17, D2

The Red Green Show (TV)
Port Asbestos, Ontario (town), pp.26–27, A4
Possum Lake, Ontario (lake), pp.26–27, A4

The Redundancy of Courage by Timothy Mo (novel), Danu (fictional country), pp.90–91, D1

The Remains of the Day by Kazuo Ishiguro (novel), Darlington Hall, England (building), pp.64–65, D2

The Rescuers (film), Devil's Bayou, Florida (natural feature), pp.14–15, C1

The Rescuers Down Under (film)
Crocodile Falls, Northern Territory (natural feature), pp.108–109, C3
Mugwomp Flats, Northern Territory (town), pp.108–109, C3
Nightmare Canyon, Northern Territory (natural feature), pp.108–109, C3
Satan's Ridge, Northern Territory (mountain), pp.108–109, C3

The Resurrection of Joseph Bourne, or, A Word or Two on Those Port Annie Miracles by Jack Hodgins (novel), Port Annie, British Columbia (town), pp.26–27, B1

The Return of the Obra Dinn (video game), Obra Dinn, England (wreck), pp.64–65, B1

The Returned (TV), Caldwell, Washington (town), pp.18–19, B6

The Rift (film)
Siren-1 (S-484), Atlantic Ocean (wreck), pp.126–127, B5
Siren-2 (S-485), Atlantic Ocean (wreck), pp.126–127, B5

The Ring (film)
Moesko Island, Washington (island), pp.18–19, A6
Shelter Mountain Inn, Washington (building), pp.18–19, A6

The Riordans (TV), Leestown, Ireland (village), pp.64–65, B2

The River Between by Ngũgĩ wa Thiong'o (novel)
Kameno, Kenya (village), pp.84–85, D4
Makuyu, Kenya (village), pp.84–85, D4

The Rock of Tanios by Amin Maalouf (novel), Kfaryabda, Lebanon (village), pp.72–73, B2

The Rocky Horror Picture Show (film), Denton, Ohio (town), pp.14–15, B4

The Rose Garden by M.R. James (short story), Westfield, England (town), pp.64–65, D2

The Royal (TV), Elsinby, England (town), pp.64–65, D3

The Rule of the Door and Other Fanciful Regulations by Lloyd Biggle Jr (novel), Centertown, Indiana (town), pp.14–15, A4

The Russian Concubine by Kate Furnivall (novel), Junchow, China (city), pp.102–103, D3

The Russians Are Coming, the Russians Are Coming (film), Gloucester Island, Massachusetts (island), pp.14–15, D5

The Scarecrow by Ronald Hugh Morrieson (novel/film), Klynham, New Zealand (town), pp.108–109, C2

The Sea and the Silence by Peter Cunningham (novel)
Monument, Ireland (town), pp.64–65, B2
River Lyle, Ireland (river), pp.64–65, B2

The Sea Change (film), Pom Pom Galli, Pacific Ocean (island), pp.120–121, E2

The Secret Garden by Frances Hodgson Burnett (novel)
Missel Moor, England (natural feature), pp.64–65, C3
Misselthwaite Manor, England (building), pp.64–65, C3

The Secret of Puente Viejo (TV), Puente Viejo, Spain (town), pp.44–45, B2

The Secret Railway by Elisabeth Beresford (novel)
Aldport, England (town), pp.64–65, D2
Draxmundham, England (town), pp.64–65, D2
Durnham, England (town), pp.64–65, D2
Marsh End, England (town), pp.64–65, D2

The Seething Pot by George A. Birmingham (novel), Clogher, Ireland (town), pp.64–65, A3

The Sellout by Paul Beatty (novel), Dickens, California (town), pp.18–19, A2

The Settlers of Catan (board game), Catan, Azores (island), pp.126–127, C4

The Shadow Keeper by Eli Elphinstone (novel), Inchgrundle, England (town), pp.64–65, B1

The Shadow Out of Time by H.P. Lovecraft (novella)
City of the Great Race of Yith, Western Australia (city), pp.108–109, B3
Pilbarra, Western Australia (town), pp.108–109, A3

The Shadows by Kaitlin Prest (Audio drama), Mont Yuron, Quebec (city), pp.26–27, E1

The Shawshank Redemption by Stephen King (short story/film), Shawshank State Prison, Maine (building), pp.14–15, D6

The Shepherd by Frederick Forsyth (novel), RAF Minton, England (building), pp.64–65, D2

The Shining by Stephen King (various)
Buckland, Utah (town), pp.18–19, D4
Overlook Hotel, Colorado (building), pp.16–17, A4
Sidewinder, Colorado (town), pp.16–17, A4

The Shootings of Achnaleish by E.F. Benson (novel), Achnaleish, Scotland (town), pp.64–65, B5

The Siege of Krishnapur by J.G. Farrell (novel), Krishnapur, India (town), pp.78–79, C4

The Silence of the Lambs (novel/film), Belvedere, Ohio (town), pp.14–15, B4

The Simpsons
Bartovia (fictional country), pp.72–73, C3
Bronson, Missouri (town), pp.16–17, C3
Capital City/Capitol City, North Takoma (fictional city), pp.18–19, A6
Cypress Creek, North Takoma (fictional town), pp.18–19, B6
Dunkilderry, Ireland (town), pp.64–65, A3
Euro Itchy & Scratchy Land, France (theme park), pp.44–45, E3
Itchy & Scratchy Land, Gulf of Mexico (island), pp.32–33, D3
Joan Bushwell's Chimp Refuge, New Zanzibar (fictional building), pp.84–85, D3
Kamp Krusty, North Takoma (building), pp.18–19, A6
Kwik-E-Mart Central Office, India (building), pp.78–79, C4
Little Pwagmattasquarmsettport, North Takoma (fictional town), pp.18–19, A6
Murderhorn, The, North Takoma (fictional mountain), pp.18–19, A6
New Zanzibar, New Zanzibar (fictional country), pp.84–85, C3/D3
North Kilttown, Scotland (town), pp.64–65, C5
North Takoma, North Takoma (fictional state), pp.18–19, A6
Palm Corners, Florida (town), pp.14–15, C1
Proctorville, Iowa (town), pp.16–17, C5
Quetzalacatenango, Guatemala (village), pp.32–33, D1
Salsiccia, Italy (village), pp.44–45, D2
Shelbyville, North Takoma (fictional town), pp.18–19, A6
Springfield, North Takoma (fictional town), pp.18–19, A6

The Sittaford Mystery by Agatha Christie (novel), Sittaford, England (village), pp.64–65, C1

The Skating Rink by Roberto Bolaño (novel), Z, Spain (town), pp.44–45, C2

The Sleeping Dictionary by Sujata Massey (novel), Johlpur, India (town), pp.78–79, C4

The Smurfs (TV), Smoogle Village, Northern Territory (village), pp.108–109, C3

The Song of Roland (poem)
Marbrise, Spain (city), pp.44–45, B2
Marbrose, Spain (city), pp.44–45, B2

The Song of the Lark by Willa Cather (novel), Moonstone, Colorado (town), pp.16–17, A4

The Sorrows of Young Werther by Wolfgang von Goethe (novel), Wahlheim, Germany (village), pp.44–45, C3

The South Westerlies (TV), Carrigeen, Ireland (town), pp.64–65, A2

The Spirits' Mountain by Gustavo Adolfo Becquer (short story), Spirits' Mountain, The, Spain (mountain), pp.44–45, B2

The Stand by Stephen King (novel)
Arnette, Texas (town), pp.16–17, C2
Shoyo, Arkansas (town), pp.16–17, D3

The State Within (TV), Tyrgyzstan (fictional country), pp.72–73, E2

The Steep Approach to Garbadale by Iain Banks (novel), Garbadale, Scotland (town), pp.64–65, B5

The Stepford Wives (novel/film), Stepford, Connecticut (town), pp.14–15, C5

The Stockman's Secret by Mandy Magro (novel), Little Heart, Queensland (town), pp.108–109, F1

The Stones of Muncaster Cathedral by Robert Westall (novel), Muncaster, England (city), pp.64–65, C2

The Story of Doctor Dolittle by Hugh Lofting (novel), Jolliginki (fictional country), pp.84–85, D3

The Story of Forest Rail (video game)
Matsuhara, Japan (town), pp.96–97, D4
Matsuhara Railway, Japan (railway), pp.96–97, D4
Numasoko, Japan (town), pp.96–97, D4
Rintenjo, Japan (town), pp.96–97, D4

The Strong Man by H.R.F. Keating (novel)
Caloeswon, Oceana (fictional town), pp.126–127, D5
Hoddick, Oceana (fictional town), pp.126–127, D5
Lesneven, Oceana (fictional city), pp.126–127, D5
Oceana (fictional island/nation), pp.126–127, D5
Portharnel, Oceana (fictional town), pp.126–127, D5

The Summer of Serendipity by Ali McNamara (novel), Ballykiltara, Ireland (town), pp.64–65, A2

The Sune series by Anders Jacobsson and Sören Olsson (books), Glimmerdagg, Sweden (town), pp.56–57, B3

The Survivors by Jane Harper (novel)
Evelyn Bay, Tasmania (town), pp.108–109, D1
SS *Mary Minerva*, Tasmania (wreck), pp.108–109, D1

The Survivors of the 'Jonathan' by Jules Verne (novel), Magellania (fictional country), pp.38–39, B1

The Survivors of The Chancellor by Jules Verne (novel)
Chancellor, The, Atlantic Ocean (wreck), pp.126–127, B3
Ham Rock, Atlantic Ocean (island), pp.126–127, B3

The Sweet Hereafter (film), Sam Dent, British Columbia (town), pp.26–27, A1

The Tainted by Cauvery Madhaven (novel), Nandagiri, India (town), pp.78–79, B3

The Tale of Little Pig Robinson by Beatrix Potter (short story), Pig Robinson's Island, England (island), pp.32–33, F2

The Teahouse of the August Moon by John Patrick Goggan (novel), Tobiki, Japan (village), pp.96–97, D1

The Teardrop Story Woman by Catherine Lim (novel), Luping, Malaysia (village), pp.90–91, B2

The Tempest by William Shakespeare (play), Caliban's Island, Mediterranean Sea (island), pp.44–45, D1

The Tenant of Wildfell Hall by Anne Brontë (novel), Wildfell Hall, England (estate), pp.64–65, C2

The Testament of Gideon Mack by James Robertson (novel), Monimaskit, Scotland (town), pp.64–65, C4

The Testament of Yves Gundron by Emily Barton (novel), Mandragora, Scotland (island), pp.64–65, A5

The Thing (film)
Thule Station (camp), pp.114–115, C2
U.S. Outpost 31 (camp), pp.114–115, C2
Wreck of The Thing's spaceship, pp.114–115, C2

The Three Investigators series by Robert Arthur Jr. (novels), Rocky Beach, California (town), pp.18–19, A2

The Three-Body Problem by Liu Cixin (novel)
Judgment Day, Panama (wreck), pp.32–33, D1
Qijiatun, China (village), pp.102–103, D4
Radar Peak, China (mountain), pp.102–103, D4
Red Coast Base, China (building), pp.102–103, D4

The Tick (TV), Pokoponesia (fictional island/nation), pp.120–121, D4

The Tiger of San Pedro by Arthur Conan Doyle (short story), San Pedro (fictional country), pp.32–33, D4

The Titfield Thunderbolt (film)
Mallingford, England (town), pp.64–65, C2
Titfield, England (town), pp.64–65, C2

The Tommyknockers by Stephen King (various), Haven, Maine (town), pp.14–15, D6

The Tomorrow series by John Marsden (novels), Wirrawee, Victoria (town), pp.108–109, D1

The Torminster Saga by Elizabeth Goudge (novel), Torminster, England (town), pp.64–65, C2

The Torrents by Oriel Gray (play), Koolgalla, Western Australia (town), pp.108–109, B2

The Town Where No One Got Off by Ray Bradbury (short story), Rampart Junction, Iowa (town), pp.16–17, C4

The Train (film), Rive-Reine, France (town), pp.44–45, C3

The Train Robbers (film), Liberty, Texas (town), pp.16–17, A2

The Transformers (various)
Autobot City, Tennessee (city), pp.14–15, A3
Ruby Crystal Mines of Burma, The, Myanmar (natural feature), pp.90–91, A4

The Tree of Knowledge by Pío Baroja (novel), Alcolea, Spain (town), pp.44–45, B2

The Trentswood Terrors by Peter Jordan (novels), Trentsworth, New Zealand (town), pp.108–109, F1

The Triangle (film), RMS Queen of Scots, Caribbean (wreck), pp.32–33, E3

The Triangle (film), San Sebastien (fictional island), pp.32–33, E3

The Truman Show (film), Seahaven Island, California (town/building), pp.18–19, A2/A3

The Tuna Trilogy (theatre), Tuna, Texas (town), pp.16–17, B3

The Turn of the Screw by Henry James (novel/TV), Bly, England (estate), pp.64–65, D2

The Twilight Zone (TV)
Peaksville, Ohio (town), pp.14–15, B4
SS Queen of Glasgow, Atlantic Ocean (wreck), pp.126–127, D5

The Twin Detectives by Sivar Ahlrud (novel), Vindsele, Sweden (town), pp.56–57, C4

The Two Georges by Harry Turtledove (novel), Cranmer (fictional state), pp.16–17, B3/C3

The Ugly American by Eugene Burdick and William Lederer (novel), Sarkhan (fictional country), pp.90–91, B3

The Vagrants by Yiyun Li (novel)
Golden River, The, China (river), pp.102–103, E4
Muddy River, China (town), pp.102–103, D4
North Mountain, China (mountain), pp.102–103, D4
White Mountain, China (mountain), pp.102–103, D4

The Vampire Diaries (TV), Mystic Falls, Virginia (town), pp.14–15, B4/C4

The Venture Brothers (TV)
Malice, California (town), pp.18–19, A2
Spanakos, Greece (island), pp.44–45, E1
Spider-Skull Island, Sargasso Sea (island), pp.126–127, A4

The Vicar of Dibley (TV), Dibley, England (village), pp.64–65, D2

The Village by the Sea by Anita Desai (novel), Thul, India (village), pp.78–79, B3

The Violins of Saint-Jacques by Patrick Leigh-Fermor (novel), Saint Jacques, Caribbean (island), pp.32–33, F2

The Voyages and Adventures of Captain Hatteras by Jules Verne (novel)
Alamont Harbour, Arctic (natural feature), pp.26–27, C4
Bell Mountain, Arctic (mountain), pp.26–27, C4
Cape Washington, Arctic (natural feature), pp.26–27, C4
Fort Providence, Arctic (natural feature), pp.26–27, C4
Forward, The, Arctic (wreck), pp.26–27, C3/C4
Johnson Island, Arctic (island), pp.26–27, C4
New America, Greenland (country/region), pp.26–27, C4
Porpoise, The, Arctic (wreck), pp.26–27, C4
Queen's Island, Arctic (island), pp.26–27, C4
Victoria Bay, Arctic (natural feature), pp.26–27, C4

The Voyages of Doctor Dolittle by Hugh Lofting (novel)
Capa Blanca Islands, Spain (island chain), pp.44–45, A2
Spider Monkey Island, Brazil (island), pp.38–39, C3

The Walking Dead (TV/comic)
Alexandria Safe Zone, Virginia (village), pp.14–15, C4
Terminus, Georgia (building), pp.14–15, B3

The Walking Dead: World Beyond (TV), Campus Colony, Nebraska (town), pp.16–17, B4

The Waltons (TV), Walton's Mountain, Virginia (town), pp.14–15, C4

The War of Don Emmanuel's Nether Parts by Louis de Bernières (novel)
Chiriguaná, Colombia (town), pp.38–39, A5/B5
Cochadebajo de los Gatos, Colombia (town), pp.38–39, A5/A6

The Water Horse (film), Killin Lodge, Scotland (building), pp.64–65, B4

The Water-Babies by Charles Kingsley (novel)
Airfowlness, Scotland (region), pp.64–65, A5
Allalonestone, Atlantic Ocean (island), pp.126–127, D5
Peacepool, The, Arctic Ocean (lake), pp.126–127, D6
St Brendan's Island, Atlantic Ocean (island), pp.126–127, D4

The Wedding Promise by Emma Hannigan (novel), Rondilla, Spain (town), pp.44–45, A1

The Weekenders (TV), Bahia Bay, California (town), pp.18–19, A3

The Weirdstone of Brisingamen: A Tale of Alderley by Alan Garner (novel), Fundindelve, England (natural feature), pp.64–65, C2/C3

The West Wing (TV)
Bitanga, Equatorial Kundu (fictional city), pp.84–85, B4
Equatorial Kundu (fictional country), pp.84–85, B4

Hartsfield's Landing, New Hampshire (town), pp.14–15, D6
Qumar (fictional country), pp.72–73, D2

The Whistling Room by William Hope Hodgson (short story), Iastrae Castle, Ireland (building), pp.64–65, A3

The White Girl by Tony Birch (novel), Deane, New South Wales (town), pp.108–109, D2

The White Ribbon (film), Eichwald, Germany (village), pp.44–45, D4

The Wicker Man (film), Summerisle, Scotland (island), pp.64–65, B5

The Wicker Man (US remake) (film), Summersisle, Washington (island), pp.18–19, A6

The Wild Geese (film), Zembala (fictional country), pp.84–85, C4

The Wind in the Willows by Kenneth Grahame (novel/TV), Toad Hall, England (estate), pp.64–65, D2

The Windy Season by Samuel Carmody (novel), Stark, Western Australia (town), pp.108–109, A2

The Wine-Dark Sea by Patrick O'Brian (novel), Moahu, Pacific Ocean (island), pp.120–121, C4

The Witches of Eastwick (novel/film), Eastwick, Rhode Island (town), pp.14–15, D5

The Wizard of Oz (novel/film), Dorothy Gale's Farm, Kansas (building), pp.16–17, C4

The Wizard of Oz series by L. Frank Baum (novels), Butterfield, Kansas (town), pp.16–17, C4

The Woman in Black by Susan Hill (novel/play/film), Crythin Gifford, England (village), pp.64–65, C4
Eel Marsh House, England (building), pp.64–65, C4

The Woman in White by Wilkie Collins (novel), Limmeridge House, England (estate), pp.64–65, C3

The World is Not Enough (film), Castle Thane, Scotland (building), pp.64–65, B4

The World's End (film), Newton Haven, England (town), pp.64–65, D2

The Worst Witch by Jill Murphy (novels/TV)
Miss Cackle's Academy for Witches, Wales (building), pp.64–65, C4
Miss Pentangle's Academy for Witches, Wales (building), pp.64–65, C4

The Wreck of the Titan: Or, Futility by Morgan Robertson (novella), SS *Titan*, Atlantic Ocean (wreck), pp.126–127, B5

The Wreck of the Zanzibar by Michael Morpurgo (novel), Zanzibar, England (wreck), pp.64–65, B1

The X-Files (TV)
Amma Beach, Maine (town), pp.14–15, D6
Aubrey, Missouri (town), pp.16–17, C4
Bellefleur, Oregon (town), pp.18–19, A5
Bethany, Vermont (town), pp.14–15, C5
Blessing, Tennessee (town), pp.14–15, A3
Chaney, Texas (town), pp.16–17, B2
Colson, Washington (town), pp.18–19, B6
Comity, New Hampshire (town), pp.14–15, C5
Delta Glen, Wisconsin (town), pp.16–17, D5
Dexter, Oklahoma (town), pp.16–17, C4
Dudley, Arkansas (town), pp.16–17, C3/D3
Flemingtown, Arizona (town), pp.18–19, C3
Klass County, Washington (county), pp.18–19, B6
Kroner, Kansas (town), UYSA C, C3
Milford Haven, New Hampshire (town), pp.14–15, D5
Miller's Grove, Massachusetts (town), pp.14–15, C5
Millikan County, Georgia (county), pp.14–15, B3
Murray, Virginia (town), pp.14–15, C4
Novi, Virginia (town), pp.14–15, C4
Pittsfield, Virginia (town), pp.14–15, C4
Shawan, Oregon (town), pp.18–19, A5
Skyland Mountain, Virginia (mountain), pp.14–15, B4
Squamash, Pennsylvania (town), pp.14–15, C5
Steveston, Massachusetts (town), pp.14–15, C5

The Year Without a Santa Claus (film), Southtown, Louisiana (town), pp.16–17, C2

The Years of Rice and Salt by Kim Stanley Robinson (novel)
Alpine Emirates (fictional country), pp.44–45, D3
Baraka, France (city), pp.44–45, B2/B3
Nsara, France (city), pp.44–45, B3
Skandistan (fictional country), pp.56–57, B3
Turi, Alpine Emirates (fictional city), pp.44–45, D3

The Yellow Birds by Kevin Powers (novel), Al-Tafar, Iraq (town), pp.72–73, C2/C3

The Yield by Tara June Winch (novel)
Massacre Plains, New South Wales (town), pp.108–109, D2
Murrumby River, New South Wales (river), pp.108–109, D2

The Young Doctors (TV), Albert Memorial Hospital, New South Wales (building), pp.108–109, F4

The Zendian problem (intelligence exercise)
Salamanko, Zendia (fictional city),
pp.120–121, E2/F2
Zendia, Pacific Ocean (island),
pp.120–121, E2/F2
There Will Be Blood (film), Little Boston,
California (town), pp.18–19, A3/B3
Things Fall Apart by Chinua Achebe (novel),
Iguedo, Nigeria (village), pp.84–85, B4
Things Fall Apart by Chinua Achebe (novel),
Umuofia (the nine villages), Nigeria
(village), pp.84–85, B4
Third Man on the Mountain (film), Kurtal,
Switzerland (town), pp.44–45, C3
This is Jinsy (TV), Jinsy, Channel Islands
(island), pp.64–65, A1
This is Not My Life (TV), Waimoana, New
Zealand (town), pp.108–109, F2
Thomas the Tank Engine by Rev W. Audrey
(books/TV)
Brendam, England (town), pp.64–65, C3
Cronk, England (town), pp.64–65, C3
Culdee Fell, England (mountain),
pp.64–65, C3
Ffarquhar, England (town), pp.64–65, C3
Island of Sodor, England (island),
pp.64–65, C3
Kellsthorpe, England (town), pp.64–65,
C3
Kirk Ronan, England (town), pp.64–65,
C3
Knapford, England (town), pp.64–65,
C3
Misty Island, England (island), pp.64–65,
C3
Norramby, England (town), pp.64–65, C3
Peel Godred, England (town), pp.64–65,
C3
Suddery, England (city), pp.64–65, C3
Tidmouth, England (town), pp.64–65, B3
Vicarstown, England (town), pp.64–65,
C3
Three Billboards Outside Ebbing, Missouri
(film), Ebbing, Missouri (town), pp.16–17,
D3
Three Faces West (film), Asheville Forks,
North Dakota (town), pp.16–17, A6
Three Kronor (TV), Mälarviken, Sweden
(town), pp.56–57, C3
Three Skeleton Key by George G Toudouze
(short story), Three Skeleton Key, French
Guiana (island/building), pp.38–39, E4
Throne of Blood (film), Spider Web Castle,
Japan (building), pp.96–97, C3
Through Darkest Pondelayo by Joan Lindsay
(novel), Pondelayo, Sri Lanka (island),
pp.78–79, C3
Thrush Green series by Miss Read (novels),
Thrush Green, England (village),
pp.64–65, C2
Thunderbirds (2004 film), Ambramovich Oil
Platform, Russia (building), pp.102–103,
F2
Thunderbirds (TV)
Allington, England (town), pp.64–65, D3
Atomic Irrigation Project, New South
Wales (building), pp.108–109, D2
Bonga Bonga, Northern Territory (estate),
pp.108–109, C3
Creighton-Ward Mansion, England
(building), pp.64–65, D2
Lost Pyramid of Khamandides, Egypt (?)
(building), pp.84–85, C5
Seascape, Atlantic Ocean (building),
pp.126–127, C5
Tracy Island, Pacific Ocean (island),
pp.120–121, D3
Thunderbirds Are Go (1966 film), Craigsville,
Florida (town), pp.14–15, C1
Thunderbirds Are Go (TV)
Quataca Mountains, Brazil (mountain
range), pp.38–39, B5
New Geneva, Switzerland (city),
pp.44–45, C3
Supreme Barrier Reef, Queensland
(natural feature), pp.108–109, D4/E3
Thunderbirds Are Go: Heist Society (TV),
Reykjavik Express, North Sea (tunnel),
pp.126–127, D5/C6
Thursday Night Widows by Claudia Piñeiro
(novel), Cascade Heights, Argentina
(building), pp.38–39, C4
Tidelands (TV), Orphelin Bay, Queensland
(town), pp.108–109, E3
Tieta do Agreste by Jorge Amado (novel/
TV), Santana do Agreste, Brazil (town),
pp.38–39, D4
Tiger in the Bush by Nan Chauncy (novel)
Arches Hill, Tasmania (natural feature),
pp.108–109, D1
Three Fists, Tasmania (mountain),
pp.108–109, D1
Timewreck Titanic by Rhys B. Davies (novel)
HMS *Viking*, Atlantic Ocean (wreck),
pp.126–127, B4
MV *Seguin Laroche*, Atlantic Ocean
(wreck), pp.126–127, B4
USNS *Rescue*, Atlantic Ocean (wreck),
pp.126–127, B4
Tin Star (TV), Little Big Bear, Alberta
(town), pp.26–27, C1
Tintin in America by Hergé (comic book),
Redskin City, North Dakota (town),
pp.16–17, A6
Tintin: Cigars of the Pharaoh by Hergé (comic
book), Abudin, Saudi Arabia (city),
pp.72–73, B1/B2
Tintin: Flight 714 to Sydney by Hergé (comic
book)
Pulau-Pulau Bompa, Sondonesia
(fictional island/nation), pp.90–91, D1
Sondonesia (fictional country), pp.90–91,
D1

Tiny Toon Adventures (TV), Acme Acres,
Missouri (city), pp.16–17, C4
Titan A.E. (film), Titan Project, The,
Colorado (building), pp.16–17, A4
Tlön, Uqbar, Orbis Tertius by Jorge Luis
Borges (short story)
Axa Delta, Uqbar (fictional river),
pp.72–73, C3
Tsai Khaldun, Uqbar (fictional region),
pp.72–73, C3
Uqbar (fictional country), pp.72–73, C3
To Kill a Mockingbird by Harper Lee (novel)
Abbottsville, Alabama (town), pp.14–15,
A2
Maycomb, Alabama (town), pp.14–15, A2
Maycomb County, Alabama (county),
pp.14–15, A2
To Serve Them All My Days by R.F.
Delderfield (novel/film), Bamfylde
School, England (building), pp.64–65, C2
To the Manor Born (TV), Grantleigh,
England (town), pp.64–65, C3
*To Wong Foo, Thanks for Everything! Julie
Newmar* (film), Snydersville, Nebraska
(town), pp.16–17, A3
Tom Goes to the Mayor (TV), Jefferton,
California (town), pp.16–17, B4
Tom's Midnight Garden by Philippa Pearce
(novel), Castleford, England (city),
pp.64–65, D2
Tomb Raider (video game)
Croft Manor, England (building),
pp.64–65, D2
Yamatai Island, Japan (island), pp.96–97,
B1/C1
Tomb Raider III (video game), Lost City of
Tinnos (city), pp.114–115, C1
Tomb Raider series (video games)
Paraíso, Peru (town), pp.38–39, B4
Tomb of Qualopec, Peru (location),
pp.38–39, B4
Tomorrow! by Philip Wylie (novel)
Green Prairie, Unknown (city), pp.16–17,
C5
River City, Unknown (city), pp.16–17, C5
Tonje Glimmerdal by Maria Parr (novel)
Glimmerdal, Norway (town), pp.56–57,
A3
Vardeting, Glimmerhornet, Nakken
and Storesnuten, Norway (mountains),
pp.56–57, A3
Too Much Lip by Melissa Lucashenko
(novels), Durrongo, New South Wales
(town), pp.108–109, E2
Top of the Lake (TV), Laketop, New Zealand
(town), pp.108–109, E1
Torchwood (TV), Torchwood 3, Wales
(building), pp.64–65, C3
Torregreca: Life, Death and Miracles by Ann
Cornelisen (novel), Torregreca, Italy
(town), pp.44–45, D2
Tortilla Flat by John Steinbeck (novel),
Tortilla Flat, California (town), pp.18–19,
A4
Total War: Thrones of Britannia (video game)
Dofras Sund, England (sea), pp.64–65,
D1
Engle Sae, England (sea), pp.64–65,
D2/D3
Linne Forthin, Scotland (sea), pp.64–65,
C4
Linne Moreb, Scotland (sea), pp.64–65,
C4
Maerse Sea, England (sea), pp.64–65,
B3/C3
Muir Britton, Wales/Ireland (sea),
pp.64–65, B3
Muir Domon, Scotland (sea), pp.64–65,
B5
Muir Nore, Scotland (sea), pp.64–65, C5
Totally Spies! (TV), pp.38–39, B4
Touch of Evil (film), Los Robles, Mexico
(town), pp.32–33, A4
Touhou Project series (video games),
Gensokyo, Japan (natural feature),
pp.96–97, C2
Toys (film), Zevo Toys, Idaho (building),
pp.18–19, B6
Train to Pakistan by Khushwant Singh
(novel), Mano Majra, India (village),
pp.78–79, D2
Trangviksposten (newspaper), Trangvik,
Norway (town), pp.56–57, A2
Transformers (various)
Calusa, Florida (city), pp.14–15, B1
Central City/Centre City, Oregon (city),
pp.18–19, A6
Hurley's Crossing, Nevada (town),
pp.18–19, B4
Mission City, Nevada (city), pp.18–19, B3
Mount Saint Hilary, Oregon (mountain),
pp.18–19, A6
Nemesis, Mexico/Guatemala/Belize
(wreck, spaceship), pp.32–33, C2
Sherman Dam, Nevada (building),
pp.18–19, B4
SOCCENT Forward Operations Base,
Qatar (building), pp.72–73, C1
Tranquility, California (town), pp.18–19,
A3
Victory/Decepticon HQ, Oregon (wreck),
pp.18–19, A5
Transformers and GI Joe (comics),
Benzheen (fictional country/emirate),
pp.72–73, D1/D2
Gulf of Benzheen, Gulf of Oman (sea),
pp.72–73, D1
Trucial Abusmia (fictional country/
emirate), pp.72–73, D1
Transformers: Animated (TV), North Sister
Island, Michigan (island), pp.14–15, B5

Transformers: Armada (comic), Science City/
Lincoln, South Dakota/Nebraska (city),
pp.16–17, B5
Transformers: Bumblebee (film), Brighton
Falls, California (town), pp.18–19, A4
Transformers: Cybertron (TV), Rockville,
Colorado (town), pp.18–19, D4
Transformers: Infestation 2 (comics)
Mare Rurek Glacier, Nunavut (natural
feature), pp.26–27, D2
Port Cenotaph, Nova Scotia (town),
pp.26–27, F1
Transformers: Masterforce (anime)
Isle of the Gods, Kingdom of Karin
(fictional island), pp.90–91, D2
Karin Island, Kingdom of Karin (fictional
island/nation), pp.90–91, D2
Kingdom of Karin (fictional island/
nation), pp.90–91, D2
Mont Porte (fictional island), pp.44–45,
D2
Viscas Island, Kingdom of Karin (fictional
island), pp.90–91, D2
Transformers: Prime (TV), Jasper, Nevada
(town), pp.18–19, B4
Transformers: Rescue Bots (TV)
Coast City, Maine (city), pp.14–15, D6
Faxian, Hong Kong (city), pp.102–103, D1
Griffin Rock, Maine (town/island),
pp.14–15, D6
Wayward Island, Maine (island),
pp.14–15, D6
Transformers: Revenge of the Fallen (film)
Project Deep Six Drop Point (Megatron),
Atlantic Ocean (location), pp.126–127, B4
Star Harvester, The, Egypt (building),
pp.84–85, C5
USS *Theodore Roosevelt*, Atlantic Ocean
(wreck), pp.126–127, B4
USS *Topeka*, Atlantic Ocean (wreck),
pp.126–127, B4
Transformers: Robots in Disguise (TV), Los
Bogus, Nevada (city), pp.18–19, B3
Transformers: The Last Knight (film), NBE
Supermax, Colorado (building), pp.16–17,
A4
Traveler of the Century by Andrés Neuma
(novel), Wandernburg, Germany (town),
pp.44–45, D3
Treasure Island by Robert Louis Stevenson
Admiral Benbow, The, England
(building), pp.64–65, C2
Treasure Island, British Virgin Islands
(island), pp.32–33, C4
Tremors (film)
Bixby, Nevada (town), pp.18–19, B4
Perfection, Nevada (town), pp.18–19, B4
Trixie Belden series by Julie Campbell
Tatham (novels), Sleepyside-on-Hudson,
New York (town), pp.14–15, C5
Troll 2 (film), Nilbog, Utah (town),
pp.18–19, C4
Tropico (video game), Tropico (fictional
island/nation), pp.32–33, D2
Troubles by J.G. Farrell (novel), Kilnalough,
Ireland (town), pp.64–65, B2
True Blood (TV)
Bon Temps, Louisiana (town), pp.16–17,
C2
Renard Parish, Louisiana (county),
pp.16–17, C2
True Stories (film), Virgil, Texas (town),
pp.16–17, C2
Truly, Idaho series by Rachel Gibson
(novels)
Lake Mary, Idaho (lake), pp.18–19, B5
Shaw Mountain, Idaho (mountain),
pp.18–19, B5
Truly, Idaho (town), pp.18–19, B5
Trump, Donald, The mysterious brain
of (gaffe), Nambia (fictional country),
pp.84–85, B2/C2
Trumpton (TV), Trumpton, England
(village), pp.64–65, D1
TUGS (TV)
Bigg City Port, Maine (city), pp.14–15,
D5/D6
Puerto Grande, Mexico (city), pp.32–33,
A3
Turma de Monica/Monica's Gang (comics),
Limoeiro, Brazil (village), pp.38–39, D2
Turma do Chico Bento/Chuck, Billy 'n' Folks
(comics), Vila Abobrinha, Brazil (village),
pp.38–39, C3
TV Go Home (TV, based on website), Daily
Mail Island, England (island), pp.64–65,
B2
Twilight: Breaking Dawn by Stephenie
Meyer (novel/film), Isle Esme, Brazil
(island), pp.38–39, D3
Twin Peaks (TV), Deer Meadow,
Washington (town), pp.18–19, B6
Twin Peaks: The Return (TV), Buckhorn,
South Dakota (town), pp.16–17, A5
Two Thousand Acres of Sky (TV), Ronansay,
Scotland (town), pp.64–65, B4
Two Years' Vacation by Jules Verne (novel),
Chairman Island, Chile (island),
pp.38–39, B1
Tyrant (TV)
Abuddin (fictional country), pp.72–73, D2
Ma'an, Abuddin (fictional city), pp.72–73,
D2
Tywo at Large (web animation), Baxton
Creek, Maryland (town), pp.14–15, C4
U-571 (film)
Anschluss (Destroyer Z49), Atlantic Ocean
(wreck), pp.126–127, C5
Prescot Trader, Atlantic Ocean (wreck),
pp.126–127, C5
S-33, Atlantic Ocean (wreck), pp.126–127,
C5

U-571, Atlantic Ocean (wreck),
pp.126–127, C5
Ulalume by Edgar Allen Poe (poem),
Mount Yaanek, Nunavut (mountain),
pp.26–27, C4
Umineko no Naku Koro ni (video games),
Rokkenjima, Japan (island), pp.96–97, C2
Un Refugio Para el Amor (TV), San Francisco
el Alto, Mexico, pp.32–33, B3
Un, dos, tres! responda otra vez (TV), Tacañón
del Todo, Spain (town), pp.44–45, C4
Uncle Scrooge (comics), Howduyustan
(fictional country), pp.78–79, B5
Under Milk Wood by Dylan Thomas (radio),
Llareggub, Wales (town), pp.64–65, B2
Under the Dome by Stephen King (various),
Chester's Mill, Maine (town), pp.14–15, D6
Under the Persimmon Tree by Suzanne Fisher
Staples (novel), Golestan, Afghanistan
(village), pp.72–73, E2
Under the Skin by Michael Faber (novel),
Ablach Farm, Scotland (building),
pp.64–65, C2
Under the Volcano by Malcolm Lowry
(novel), Quaunahuac, Mexico (town),
pp.32–33, C2
Unforgiven (film), Big Whiskey, Wyoming
(town), pp.16–17, A4
Unmarriageable by Soniah Kamal (novel),
Dilipabad, Pakistan (town), pp.78–79, D2
Unrest (video game), Bhimra (fictional city/
state), pp.78–79, B4
Unstoppable (film)
Allegheny & West Virginia Railroad
(railway), Findlay (town), Fuller (town),
Pennsylvania, pp.14–15, B5
Arklow, Pennsylvania (town), pp.14–15,
C5
Brewston (town), Stanton (town),
Pennsylvania, pp.14–15, C4
Until Dawn (video game)
Blackwood Mountain, Alberta
(mountain), pp.26–27, B1
Washington Lodge, Alberta (building),
pp.26–27, B1
Untouchable by Mulk Raj An omic strip),
Mjolhagen, Sweden (town), pp.56–57, B2
Utopia by Thomas More (novel/parable)
Achoria, Utopia (fictional region),
pp.38–39, C2
Amaurot, Utopia (fictional city),
pp.38–39, C2
Macaria, Utopia (fictional region),
pp.38–39, C2
Polylerit, Iran (region), pp.72–73, D2
Utopia (fictional island/nation), pp.38–39,
C2
Utopia by Thomas More (Paul Turner
translation, novel), Tallstoria, Iran
(region), pp.72–73, D2
Utopia, Ltd (opera), Utopia, Pacific Ocean
(island/nation), pp.120–121, D3
Utterly Monkey by Nick Laird (novel),
Ballyglass, Northern Ireland (town),
pp.64–65, B3
Uys, Pieter-Dirk (satire)
Bapetikosweti (fictional country),
pp.84–85, C2
Laagerfontein, Bapetikosweti (fictional
city), pp.84–85, C2
Uzumaki by Junji Ito (manga)
Kurôzu-cho, Japan (town), pp.96–97, B2
Midoriyama-Shi, Japan (town), pp.96–97,
B2
Vale Abraão by Agustina Bessa-Luís (novel),
Vale Abraão, Portugal (natural feature),
pp.44–45, A2
Valley of the Squinting Windows by Brinsley
MacNamara (novel), Garradrimna,
Ireland (village), pp.64–65, B3
Vamp (TV), Armação dos Anjos, Brazil
(town), pp.38–39, D4
Vampire Bats (film), Mercier, Louisiana
(city), pp.16–17, D2
Vampires Suck (film), Sporks, Washington
(town), pp.18–19, A6
Vanderbilt University (academic exercise),
Al-Hamra, Iraq (city), pp.72–73, C3
Vanity Fair by William M. Thackeray
(novel), Queen's Crawley, England (town),
pp.64–65, D2
Varan (film)
Iwaya Village, Japan (village), pp.96–97,
C2
Onita, Japan (city), pp.96–97, E1/F1
Varsity Blues (film), West Canaan, Texas
(town), pp.16–17, C2
Velcro City (theatre), Velcro City, New
Zealand (town), pp.108–109, F1/F2
Venture Brothers (TV), Underland, Country
(country), pp.14–15, C4
Vermillion Sands by J.G. Ballard (short
stories), Vermillion Sands, California
(town), pp.18–19, B3
Vernon God Little by D.B.C. Pierre (novel),
Martirio, Texas (town), pp.16–17, B2
Veronica Mars (TV)
Balboa County, California (county),
pp.18–19, B3
Neptune, California (town), pp.18–19, B3
Vier Frauen und ein Todesfall (Four Women
and one Death) (TV), Ilm, Austria
(village), pp.44–45, D3
Vikings (TV), Kattegat, Norway (village),
pp.56–57, B3
Village Survival, The Eight (TV), Michuri,
South Korea (village), pp.102–103, E3
Villanos (TV)
Atreno Island, Atlantic Ocean (island),
pp.32–33, E3
Hat Island, Atlantic Ocean (island),
pp.32–33, E3

Villaviciosa de al Lado (film), Villaviciosa de
al Lado, Spain (town), pp.44–45, B2
Villette by Charlotte Brontë (novel)
Labassecour (fictional county), pp.44–45,
C4
Villette, Labassecour (fictional city),
pp.44–45, C4
Virus (comic/film)
Akademik Vladislav Volkov, Pacific Ocean
(wreck), pp.120–121, C2
Electra, Pacific Ocean (wreck), pp.120–121,
C2
Sea Star, Pacific Ocean (wreck),
pp.120–121, C2
Wan Xuan III, Pacific Ocean (wreck),
pp.120–121, C2
Vita Lögner/White Lies (TV), Strömsvik,
Sweden (town), pp.56–57, B2
Viz (comic), Fulchester, England (city),
pp.64–65, C3
VOEZ (video game), Lan Kong Town,
Taiwan (town), pp.102–103, D1
Volver (film), Alcanfor de las Infantas, Spain
(village), pp.44–45, C3
Volver a Santa Rosa by Víctor Hugo Rascón
Banda (novel), Santa Rosa, Mexico
(town), pp.32–33, A3
Volvic adverts (advertising), George
the Volcano, France (natural feature),
pp.44–45, C3
Voyage to Locuta, a Fragment by Lemuel
Gulliver Junior by Elizabeth Graham
(novel), Locuta, Pacific Ocean (island),
pp.120–121, E4
*Voyages Très Extraordinaires de Saturnin
Farandoul* by Albert Robida (novel),
Farandoulie (fictional country),
pp.108–109, D1
W, or the Memory of Childhood by Georges
Perec (novel), Island of W, Argentina
(island), pp.38–39, C2
W.I.T.C.H. (TV), Heatherfield, Connecticut
(city), pp.14–15, C5
Waiting for Guffman (film), Blaine, Missouri
(town), pp.16–17, C4
Wake in Fright by Kenneth Cook (novel/TV)
Bundanyabba, New South Wales (town),
pp.108–109, D2
Tiboonda, New South Wales (town),
pp.108–109, D2
Wake Wood (film), Wake Wood, Northern
Ireland (village), pp.64–65, A3
Waking Ned (film)
County More West, Ireland (county),
pp.64–65, A2
Tullymore (Tulaigh Mhór), Ireland
(town), pp.64–65, A2
Walians series by Daren Bowker-Powis and
Richard Finlan (novels), Ffhagdiwedd,
Wales (town), pp.64–65, C2
Wallace and Gromit: Curse of the Wererabbit
(film), Tottington Hall, England
(building), pp.64–65, C3
Walt Disney World (theme park)
Bugia Sea/Bugis Sea, Anandapur
(fictional sea), pp.78–79, D3
Nayapur, Anandapur (fictional city),
pp.78–79, D3
Walt Longmire series by Craig Johnson
(novels), Absaroka County, Wyoming
(county), pp.18–19, D5
Walt Longmire series by Craig Johnson
(novels), Durant, Wyoming (town),
pp.18–19, D5
Walter Melon (TV), Molasses Park, Costa
Rica (island), pp.32–33, C1
WandaVision (TV), Westview, New Jersey
(town), pp.14–15, C5
War of the Worlds (TV)
Beeton, California (town), pp.18–19, A4
Tula County, California (county),
pp.18–19, A4
Wolfjaw, Montana (town), pp.18–19, C6
HMS *Thunder Child*, England (wreck),
pp.64–65, D2
War, Inc. (film)
Turaqistan (fictional country), pp.72–73,
D3
Ugigistan (fictional country), pp.72–73,
D3
Warehouse 13 (TV)
Univille (unnamed unincorporated
settlement), South Dakota (town),
pp.16–17, B5
Warehouse 13, South Dakota (building),
pp.16–17, B5
Waste Tide by Chen Qiufan (novel),
Silicon Isle, China (town), pp.102–103,
D1
Water (film)
Cascara (fictional island/nation),
pp.32–33, E2
Rawalpur, India (city), pp.78–79, C4
Water Puppets (musical), Tuong Lai, Vietnam
(village), pp.90–91, B3
Waterworld (film), Dryland, Dryland
(fictional region), pp.78–79, C4
Waverley by Sir Walter Scott (novel),
Tully-Veolan, Scotland (village),
pp.64–65, C4
Way of the Samurai 4 (video game),
Amihama, Japan (town), pp.96–97, C2
Wayward Pines (TV), Wayward Pines, Idaho
(town), pp.18–19, C6
We Can Be Heroes (mockumentary), Dunt,
South Australia (town), pp.108–109, C2
We Couldn't Leave Dinah by Mary Treadgold
(novel), Clerinel, Channel Islands (island),
pp.64–65, A1
We Need New Names by NoViolet Bulawayo
(novel), Paradise, Zimbabwe (town),
pp.84–85, C2

166

Web by John Wyndham (novel), Tanakuatua, Pacific Ocean (island), pp.120–121, D3

Weeds (TV), Agrestic, California (town), pp.18–19, A4

Welcome to Dongmakgol by Jang Jin (play/film), Dongmakgol, South Korea (village), pp.102–103, E3

Welcome to Mooseport (film), Mooseport, Maine (town), pp.14–15, D5

Welcome to Night Vale (podcast) Desert Bluffs, New Mexico (town), pp.16–17, A2
Night Vale, New Mexico (town), pp.16–17, A2

Welcome to Woop Woop (film), Woop Woop, Northern Territory (town), pp.108–109, C4

Westworld by Michael Crichton (novel/TV) Delos Destinations (fictional island chain), pp.90–91, C3
Westworld, Delos Destinations (fictional island), pp.90–91, C3

Wet Moon by Sophie Campbell (comic), Wet Moon, Florida (town), pp.14–15, B2

Whale Talk by Chris Crutcher (novel), Cutter, Washington (town), pp.18–19, B6

What We Do in the Shadows (TV), Al Quolanudar (fictional country), pp.72–73, C2

What's Eating Gilbert Grape by Peter Hedges (novel/film), Endora, Iowa (town), pp.16–17, C4

What's With Andy? (TV) East, South and West Gackle, Alberta (town), pp.26–27, C1
Mooseehoof, Alberta (town), pp.26–27, C1

When Calls the Heart (TV), Coal Valley (Hope Valley), Alberta (town), pp.26–27, C1

When the Boat Comes in (TV), Gallowshield, England (town), pp.64–65, C4

When the Camellia Blooms (film), Ongsan, South Korea (town), pp.102–103, E2/E3

When the Rains Came (film), Ranchipur, India (region), pp.78–79, A4/B4

When the Robbers Came to Cardamom Town by Thorbjørn Egner (short story), Kardemomme, Norway (town), pp.56–57, A2

When the World Shook by H. Rider Haggard (novel), Orofina, Pacific Ocean (island), pp.120–121, C2

When They Lay Bare by Andrew Greig (novel), Crawhill Cottage, Scotland (building), pp.64–65, C4

When You Find Me by P.J. Vernon (novel), Elizabeth, South Carolina (town), pp.14–15, C3

Where Eagles Dare (film), Schloß Adler, Germany (building), pp.44–45, D3

Where the Heart is (TV), Skelthwaite, England (town), pp.64–65, C4

Where the Mountain Meets the Moon by Grace Lin (novel) City of Bright Moonlight, The, China (city), pp.102–103, A3
Fruitless Mountain, China (mountain), pp.102–103, B3
Jade River, The, China (river), pp.102–103, A3
Never-Ending Mountain, China (mountain), pp.102–103, A3
Village of Fruitless Mountain, The, China (village), pp.102–103, B3
Village of Moon Rain, The, China (village), pp.102–103, A3

Where's the Fire (film), Bishops Wallop, England (town), pp.64–65, D2

Wherever You Go by Monique Mulligan (novel), Blackwood, Western Australia (town), pp.108–109, A2

Whisky Galore! by Angus MacPhail (novel/film) Great Todday & Little Todday, Scotland (islands), pp.64–65, A4/A5/B4/B5
SS Cabinet Minister, Scotland (wreck), pp.64–65, A4/B4

White Christmas (film), Pine Tree, Vermont (town), pp.14–15, C6

White Fang by Jack London (novel), Fort McGurry, Yukon (town), pp.26–27, B2

whiteonwhite:algorithmicnoir (film), City-A, Kazakhstan (city), pp.72–73, D3

Who Can Kill a Child?/¿Quién puede matar a un niño? (film), Almanzora, Spain (island), pp.44–45, B1

Who Framed Roger Rabbit (film), Toontown, California (town), pp.18–19, A3

Who Goes There? by John W. Campbell Jr (novel), Big Magent (building), pp.114–115, F1

Whoops! Apocalypse (film) British Santa Maya (fictional island/nation), pp.32–33, F2/F3
Maguadora (fictional island/nation), pp.32–33, F3

Whose Line is it Anyway? (TV), Snackitoba (fictional Province), pp.26–27, F1

Why Didn't They Ask Evans? by Agatha Christie (novel), Marchbolt, Wales (town), pp.64–65, B2

Whylah Falls by George Elliott Clarke (novel), Whylah Falls, Nova Scotia (town), pp.26–27, F1

Widdershins by Kate Ashwin (web comic), Widdrshins, England (town), pp.64–65, C3

Wide Sargasso Sea by Jean Rhys (novel) Coulibri, Jamaica (sugar plantation), pp.32–33, D3
Granbois, Dominica (sugar plantation), pp.32–33, F2

Wild at Heart by Barry Gifford (novel/film), Big Tuna, Texas (town), pp.16–17, B3

Wild Boars Cross the River by Zhang Guixing (novel), Boarfruit Village, Malaysia (village), pp.90–91, C2

Wild Wild West (film) New Liberty, Illinois (town), pp.16–17, D4
Silverado, Utah (town), pp.18–19, C4/C5
Spider Canyon, Utah (natural feature), pp.18–19, C4

Wildflower Creek by Maya Linnell (novel), Bridgefield, Victoria (town), pp.108–109, D1

Windbag the Sailor (film), Falport, England (town), pp.64–65, B1

Windward Heights/La migration des coeurs by Maryse Condé (novel) Belles-Feuilles, Guadaloupe (building), pp.32–33, F2
l'Engoulvent, Guadaloupe (building), pp.32–33, F2

Winesburg, Ohio by Sherwood Anderson (short stories), Winesburg, Ohio (town), pp.14–15, B4

Wingin' It (TV), Brakistan (fictional country), pp.72–73, E3

Winnie the Pooh by A.A. Milne (various), 100 Aker Wood, England (natural feature), pp.64–65, D1

Wintering by Peter Geye (novel), Gunflint, Minnesota (town), pp.16–17, C6

Winterstoke by L.T.C. Rolt (novel), Winterstoke, England (town), pp.64–65, C2

Wizard of the Crow by Ngũgĩ wa Thiong'o (novel), Aburiria (fictional country), pp.84–85, D4

Wokenwell (TV), Wokenwell, England (town), pp.64–65, C3

Wolfenstein series (video games) Castle Wolfenstein, Germany (building), pp.44–45, D4
Ice Station Norway, Norway (building), pp.56–57, B5
Isenstadt, Germany (city), pp.44–45, D3
Katamarunde Rocket Base, Germany (building), pp.44–45, D4
Kugelstadt, Germany (city), pp.44–45, D3
New Paris, France (city), pp.44–45, C3
Ras el-Hadid, Egypt (city), pp.84–85, C5
Schlüsselburg, Germany (town), pp.44–45, D4
Wulfsee, Germany (lake), pp.44–45, D3

Woman With Horns and Other Stories by Cecilia Manguerra Brainard (short stories) Ubec, Philippines (region), pp.90–91, D3
Ubec City, Philippines (city), pp.90–91, D3

Wonder Woman (film), Veld, France (village), pp.44–45, C4

Wonder Woman (various), Themyscira (fictional island nation), pp.44–45, F1

Wooden Overcoats (podcast), Piffling, England (island), pp.64–65, C1

Works of Alice Munro (novels) Hanratty, Ontario (town), pp.26–27, A4
Jubilee, Ontario (town), pp.26–27, A4
Walley, Ontario (town), pp.26–27, A4

Works of Ana María Matute (novels), Artámila, Spain (village), pp.44–45, B2

Works of Anne-Catharina Vestly (novels), Tiriltoppen, Norway (town), pp.56–57, B3

Works of Barbara Kingsolver (novels), Pittman, Kentucky (town), pp.14–15, A4

Works of Christopher Moore (novels), Pine Cove, California (town), pp.18–19, A3

Works of Clara Sánchez (novels), Dianium, Spain (town), pp.44–45, B2

Works of Clark Ashton Smith (short stories) Averoigne, France (region), pp.44–45, C3
Château Faussesflammes, France (building), pp.44–45, C3
Vyones, France (city), pp.44–45, C3
Ximes, France (city), pp.44–45, C3

Works of Donald Harington (novels), Stay More, Arkansas (town), pp.16–17, C3

Works of Dr José Rizal (novels), San Diego, Philippines (town), pp.90–91, C3

Works of Ed McBain (novels) Bethtown, New York (town), pp.14–15, D1
Calm's Point, New York (town), pp.14–15, D1
Isola, New York (town), pp.14–15, D1
Majesta, New York (town), pp.14–15, D1
Riverhead, New York (town), pp.14–15, D1

Works of Edwin Arlington Robinson (novels), Tilbury Town, Maine (town), pp.14–15, D6

Works of Elizabeth Marshall Thomas (novels) Char River, Russia (river), pp.102–103, E1/F1
Fire River, Russia (river), pp.102–103, E1
Grass River, Russia (river), pp.102–103, E1/F1
Woman Lake, Russia (lake), pp.102–103, E1

Works of Eugene Trivizas (books), Avgatiganistan (fictional country), pp.72–73, D2

Works of Geoff Spedding (novels), Cardigan, New Zealand (town), pp.108–109, F2

Works of George Lamming (novels), San Cristobal (fictional island/nation), pp.32–33, F2

Works of Gösta Gustaf-Janson (novels), Rydsholm, Sweden (town), pp.56–57, C3

Works of Ross McDonald (novels), Santa Teresa, California (town), pp.18–19, A3

Works of Hans-Eric Hellberg (novels), Busnäs, Sweden (town), pp.56–57, B3

Works of Harry Turtledove (novels), Jefferson (fictional state), pp.18–19, A5

Works of Hjalmar Bergman (novels), Wadköping, Sweden (town), pp.56–57, B3/C3

Works of Indira Ganesan (novels) Madhupur, India (town), pp.78–79, C2
Pi, India (island), pp.78–79, C2

Works of James Aldridge (novels), St Helen, Victoria (town), pp.108–109, D2

Works of Jia Pingua (novels), Xijing, China (city), pp.102–103, C2

Works of Johannes V. Jensen (novels) Graabølle, Denmark (town), pp.56–57, A2
Kjeldby, Denmark (town), pp.56–57, A2

Works of John Hearne (novels) Abari (fictional country), pp.38–39, C2
Cayuna (fictional country), pp.32–33, D2
Navidad (fictional country), pp.32–33, D3
Saint Pierre (fictional country), pp.32–33, E2

Works of John O'Hara (novels), Gibbsville, Pennsylvania (town), pp.14–15, C5

Works of John Updike (novels) Brewer, Pennsylvania (town), pp.14–15, C4
Olinger, Pennsylvania (town), pp.14–15, C4

Works of Juan Carlos Onetti (novels), Santa María, Uruguay (town), pp.38–39, C2

Works of Kent Haruf (novels), Holt, Colorado (town), pp.16–17, A4

Works of Kjell Aukrust (novels), Flåklypa, Norway (town), pp.56–57, B3

Works of Kurt Vonnegut (novels), Ilium, New York (town), pp.14–15, C5

Works of Larry Mike Garmon (novels), Juneburg, Oklahoma (town), pp.16–17, B3

Works of Leon Pericles (Artworks), Widjimorphup, Western Australia (town), pp.108–109, B3

Works of Li Ang (novels) Anpingzhen, Taiwan (town), pp.102–103, D1
Chencuocun, Taiwan (town), pp.102–103, D1
Lucheng, Taiwan (town), pp.102–103, D1

Works of Louis Jacolliot (books), Lost Continent of Rutas, Mu (fictional submerged continent), pp.120–121, D3/E3/D4/E4

Works of Lynn Doyle (books), Ballygullion, Northern Ireland (town), pp.64–65, B3

Works of Madeleine L'Engle (novels) Benne Seed Island, South Carolina (island), pp.14–15, C3
Cowpertown, South Carolina (town), pp.14–15, C3
Eddington Point (natural feature), pp.114–115, E1
LeNoir Station (building), pp.114–115, E1
Puerto de Los Dragones, Venezuela (town), pp.38–39, B6
Seven Bay Island, Maine (island), pp.14–15, D6
Thornhill, Connecticut (town), pp.14–15, C5
Vespugia (fictional country), pp.38–39, B1

Works of Mahasweta Devi (stories) Hesadi, India (village), pp.78–79, C4
Karuthupuzha, India (town), pp.78–79, B2
Kuruda, India (village), pp.78–79, C4
Murha, India (village), pp.78–79, C4
Pirtha, India (village), pp.78–79, C4

Works of Margaret Laurence (novels), Manawaka, Manitoba (town), pp.26–27, D1

Works of Max Lundgren (novels), Åshöjdens, Sweden (town), pp.56–57, B2

Works of Max Yoho (novels), Epic, Kansas (town), pp.16–17, B4

Works of Merle Collins (novels), Paz, Grenada (town), pp.32–33, F2

Works of Muhammad Khudayyir (short stories), Basrayatha, Iraq (city), pp.72–73, C2

Works of Owen Marshall (novels) Dungarvie, New Zealand (town), pp.108–109, F1
Te Tarehi, New Zealand (town), pp.108–109, F2

Works of Paul Charles (novels), Castlemartin, Northern Ireland (town), pp.64–65, B3

Works of Phillip Gwynne/Australian Rules (novels/film), Prospect Bay, South Australia (town), pp.108–109, C2

Works of Preston Schoyer (novels) Lei Kiang, China (river), pp.102–103, D1
Shawei, China (city), pp.102–103, D1/D2

Works of Qaisra Shahraz (novels) Chiragpur, Pakistan (village), pp.78–79, A4
Gulistan, Pakistan (village), pp.78–79, A4

Works of Ralph Ellison and Robert Wyatt (short stories), Puerto Pollo, Peru (island), pp.38–39, A4

Works of R.K. Narayan (novels), Malgudi, India (town), pp.78–79, C3

Works of Robert Antoni (novels) Corpus Christi (fictional island), pp.32–33, F1
Mythmythilia, India (city), pp.78–79, C4
St Maggy, Corpus Christi (fictional city), pp.32–33, F2

Works of Sinclair Lewis (novels) Banjo Crossing, Winnemac (fictional city), pp.14–15, A4
Clontar, New Jersey (town), pp.14–15, C5
Gritzmacher Springs, Kansas (town), pp.16–17, C4
Lemuel, Kansas (town), pp.16–17, B3
Nautilus, Iowa (town), pp.16–17, C4
Waubanakee, Illinois (town), pp.16–17, D4
Wheatsylvania, North Dakota (town), pp.16–17, B6

Works of Steen Langstrup (novels), Gillsby, Denmark (town), pp.56–57, B2

Works of Steve Berman (short stories), Fallen Area, Pennsylvania (region), pp.14–15, C5

Works of Tabish Khair (novels), Phansa, India (town), pp.78–79, C4

Works of Tennessee Williams (plays), Two Rivers County, Mississippi (county), pp.16–17, D3

Works of Thomas Spence (novel), Spensonia (fictional island/nation), pp.38–39, C2

Works of Wendell Berry (novels) Hargrave, Kentucky (town), pp.14–15, A4
Port William, Kentucky (town), pp.14–15, A4

Works of William Alexander Fraser (short stories), Petroville, Ontario (town), pp.26–27, A4

Works of William Faulkner (novels) Jefferson, Mississippi (town), pp.16–17, D3
Yoknapatawpha County, Mississippi (county), pp.16–17, D3

Works of William Makepeace Thackeray (novels), Pumpernickel (fictional country), pp.44–45, D3

Works of Yan Lianke (novel), Balou Mountains, China (mountain range), pp.102–103, D2

World's Scariest Model Train Wrecks (web video), Rollingstock, Kentucky (town), pp.14–15, B4

Wreck-it-Ralph (film), Los Aburridos, California (town), pp.18–19, B3

Wuthering Heights by Emily Brontë (novel), Wuthering Heights, England (building), pp.64–65, C3

X-Men (comics) Muir Island, Scotland (island), pp.64–65, A5/B5

X-Men (various) Xavier Institute (Xavier School for Gifted Youngsters), New York (town), pp.14–15, C5

Xijing Men (various), Xijing (fictional city/state), pp.102–103, C2

Yadoon Ka Idiotbox (radio show), Yaad Sheher, India (town), pp.78–79, C5

Yakuza series (video games), Kamurocho, Japan (city), pp.96–97, E1

Yellow Submarine (film) Foothills of the Headlands, Pepperland (fictional natural feature), pp.126–127, B2
Pepperland (fictional submerged country), pp.126–127, B2
Sea of Holes, Atlantic Ocean (sea), pp.126–127, B2/B3
Sea of Monsters, Atlantic Ocean (sea), pp.126–127, C3
Sea of Nothing, Atlantic Ocean (sea), pp.126–127, B2
Sea of Science, Atlantic Ocean (sea), pp.126–127, C3/D3
Sea of Time, Atlantic Ocean (sea), pp.126–127, C3/D3

Yellow Brick Road (film), Friar, New Hampshire (town), pp.14–15, D6

Yellowcake Springs by Guy Salvidge (novel), Yellowcake Springs, Western Australia (town), pp.108–109, A2

Yes Minister (TV), Buranda (fictional country), pp.84–85, B4

Yes, Prime Minister (TV), Saint Georges Island, Arabian Sea (island), pp.72–73, D1

Yogi Bear (TV), Jellystone Park, Wyoming (natural feature), pp.18–19, D5

Yokai Watch (video game/anime), Springdale, Japan (town), pp.96–97, F2

You Have to Make Your Own Fun Around Here by Frances Macken (novel), Glenbruff, Ireland (town), pp.64–65, A3

You Know They Got a Hell of a Band by Stephen King (short story), Rock and Roll Heaven, Oregon (town), pp.18–19, A5

You're Under Arrest, Kōsuke Fujishima (manga/anime), Bokuto Police Station, Japan (building), pp.96–97, E1

Youjo Senki/The Saga of Tanya the Evil by Carlo Zen and Shinobu Shinotsuki (novels/manga/anime) Berun, Germany (city), pp.44–45, D4
Mainen, Germany (town), pp.44–45, C3

Young Adult (film), Mercury, Minnesota (town), pp.16–17, C6

Young Einstein (film), Young Einstein's Apple Farm, Tasmania (building), pp.108–109, D1

Young Justice (TV), Rhelasia (fictional country), pp.102–103, E3

Young Skins by Colin Barrett (novel), Glanbeigh, Ireland (town), pp.64–65, A3

Youngblood by Matt Gallagher (novel), Ashuriyah, Iraq (village), pp.72–73, C4

Your Name (film), Itomori, Japan (town), pp.96–97, C2

Yu-Gi-Oh by Kazuki Takahashi (manga/anime), Domino City, Japan (city), pp.96–97, F1

Yuki Yuna is a Hero (anime), Sanshu, Japan (city), pp.96–97, B2

Yuri!!! on Ice (anime), Hasetsu, Japan (town), pp.96–97, A1

Yuuyami Doori Tankentai (video game), Hirumi City, Japan (city), pp.96–97, E1

Yvon of the Yukon (TV) Frostbottom Falls, Yukon (town), pp.26–27, B2
Shiverme Timbers, Alaska (town), pp.18–19, B1
Shivermetimbers, Yukon (town), pp.26–27, B2
Upyermukluk, Yukon (town), pp.26–27, B2

Z by Vassilis Vassilikos, and Shanghai (novel/film), Bharatnagar, India (city), pp.78–79, B3

Z-Cars (TV), Newtown, England (town), pp.64–65, C3
Seaport, England (town), pp.64–65, C3

Zacatillo, un Lugar en tu Corazón (TV), Zacatillo, Mexico (town), pp.32–33, B2

Zadig by Voltaire (novel), Derlbak, Iraq (village), pp.72–73, C2

Zombi 2 (film), Matul, US Virgin Islands (island), pp.32–33, F2

Zorro's Black Whip (film), Crescent City, Idaho (town), pp.18–19, B5

Zwölf mal Polt novels by Alfred Komarek (novels) Brunndorf, Austria (village), pp.44–45, D3
Burgheim, Austria (village), pp.44–45, D3
Weisbachtal, Austria (natural feature), pp.44–45, D3

ACKNOWLEDGEMENTS

We'd first and foremost like to thank all the authors, filmmakers, artists, animators, illustrators, mangaka, screenwriters, software developers, military wargamers and hapless politicians who created all these fictional locations in the first place. This atlas stands as a celebration of your work, and (we hope) an enticing gateway for readers to discover stories they would not have otherwise found.

Both authors would like to thank their families for support during the compilation of this atlas. A big thank you, also, to everyone at the publisher (Batsford) for their friendly and professional handling of the project during the uncertainties of 2020, particularly Tina Persaud, Kristy Richardson and Gemma Doyle. We'd also like to thank Katie Hewett for copyediting a complex manuscript and her heroic efforts with the indexes.

Hundreds of people have contributed ideas and information to this atlas. First among them all is David Riffkin who, from the earliest days of the Londonist 'Fake Britain' map, has contributed key placenames toward the maps. Thank you sir! Rhys would also like to personally thank the staff and volunteers of the National Library of Wales, and his old English teacher, Hugh Griffiths, who encouraged him to take up writing. Others who have been particularly helpful include Rhodri Davies, Henry Gee, Nicola Jones, Peter Kidd, Maria Fernanda Flores Luna, David Somerlinck, Stuart Vandal and Douglas Walters.

ABOUT THE AUTHORS

Matt Brown is an absolute map geek who once, on a very drawn-out whim, read every single Charles Dickens novel and mapped all the locations. He then did the same for Virginia Woolf, Jane Austen and the stories of Sherlock Holmes. Matt is the author of 10 books, all with Batsford, including the popular *Everything You Know ... is Wrong*' series (books that tackle popular myths). He is co-author and map contributor of *Londonist Mapped* (AA Publishing), a cartographic guide to London that won Stanford's Illustrated Travel Book of the Year award in 2018. He also drew the maps for three of Patricia Bracewell's historical novels about Emma of Normandy, beginning with *Shadow on the Crown* (2014). He serves as Editor-at-Large (formerly Editor) of Londonist.com.

Rhys B. Davies was born in 1986, and hails from West Wales. Growing up as a child of the 1990s, he was reared on an eclectic mix of Saturday-morning cartoons, blockbuster films and all manner of literature, from Enid Blyton and Roald Dahl to the airport bookstore staples of Crichton, Clancy and Cussler. These influences coalesced into a deep love of fiction and the worlds that imagination can build – definitely useful when trying to map those worlds out! His first novel '*Timewreck Titanic*' was independently published in 2012, and has since been reissued by Sealion Press. As of writing, he physically resides in Aberystwyth, while his mind roams the webways of the internet.

Mike Hall is a freelance illustrator and obsessive mapmaker based in Valencia, Spain. He has been fascinated by maps and architecture for as long as he can remember, spending endless days of his childhood drawing buildings in his hometown of Harlow and maps of places both real and imaginary. Since graduating from the University of Westminster, London, in 2008 he has developed a specialism in map illustration and architectural drawings for a broad range of clients, including Butlins, HarperCollins, Penguin and the Royal Horticultural Society. He is represented by the international agency IllustrationX.

CONTACT THE AUTHORS

We fully appreciate that many of the locations in this atlas are open to interpretation, and readers will undoubtedly have different opinions on where certain places should be located. That's all to the good! We'd love to hear from you with any corrections, additions or further evidence concerning a location. Please contact Matt Brown on i.am. mattbrown@gmail.com with any constructive thoughts, and we'll consider them for any future edition.